D1519665

BETWEEN COMMUNICATION
AND INFORMATION

Information and Behavior
Volume 4

Editorial Board

BETWEEN COMMUNICATION AND INFORMATION

Edited by
Jorge R. Schement
Brent D. Ruben

Information and Behavior
Volume 4

Transaction Publishers
New Brunswick (U.S.A.) and London (U.K.)

Contents

Introduction

The Information and Behavior Series

When the idea for the *Information and Behavior* series was developed in 1983, one could be only partially aware of the significance of relationship between the concepts of information and behavior would come to have today. The emerging popularity of the term "information" and phrases like "The Information Age," and "The information society" were, of course, hard to miss. But it was the view of the series editor and members of the editorial board that beyond what even then seemed in part a faddish preoccupation with the newspeak of "information age," there were important issues of substance for scholars from a wide range of fields.

It was noted in the introduction to *Information and Behavior: Volume 1* that the relationship between information and behavior was, indeed, a very fundamental one (Ruben, 1985a): Information and information processing is one of two primary means through which living organisms adapt to their physical and social environments. Both play an indispensable role in physiological self-regulation, mating, reproduction, parent-offspring relations and socialization, navigation and the establishment and maintenance of territory. Moreover, information and information processes are essential to higher-level processes including perception, cognition, personality development, and other forms of complex individual behavior.

It was indicated also that information and information processes were of fundamental importance at the interpersonal, group, and societal level of analysis and were basic to the establishment and maintenance of relationships, groups, organizations and societies, and to the cultures, and normative realities, rules, and roles of each.

Finally, it was observed that the central role of concepts of information in generic theories such as system theory, cybernetics, information theories, and in disciplines such as communication, media studies, information science, computer science and cognitive psychology pointed in the direction of heightening interdisciplinary interest and significance for the information concept.

But it was difficult to envision then precisely how broadly-based the preoccupation with "information" was to become, and to fully appreciate the potential for emerging concepts of information to link and further scholarship in a variety fields. In many ways we have only begun to realize this later challenge, and continue to search for the best ways for this forum to assist in the quest.

Relationships Between Communication and Information

Studies of communication and information as distinct entities date back to the early decades of the century. Most notably, studies of the social role of the mass media, conducted in the 1930s and 1940s, gave impetus to the growth of the modern field of communication; while, at about the same time, studies of information theory and cybernetics established information science. For most of the following decades, each field developed separately with its own theories and literatures. However, in recent years, the attention of researchers has begun to converge on the relationship between communication and information. Across the social sciences, scholars are fitting basic concepts of communication into their theories of culture, animal behavior, social psychology, folklore, personal relationships, literature, group process, international diplomacy, and consumer behavior. In these pursuits, they are recognizing the power of information as an explanatory variable when constructing theoretical perspectives. So, where formerly each set of phenomena was studied in isolation, now, growing numbers of scholars are reformulating their research agendas to integrate the two (Beniger, 1988; Borgman & Schement, 1988; Borgman & Schement, 1990; Ehrenhaus, 1988; Kim, 1985; Paisley, 1986; Ruben, 1979, 1985b, 1989, 1992; Ruben & Lievrouw, 1989; Schement & Ruben, 1991). While the definitional boundaries have yet to emerge, discussions at recent meetings of the International Communication Association and the American Society for Information Service reveal a growing ferment.

At Rutgers, the formation of the School of Communication, Information and Library Studies, brought together the departments of Communication, Library and Information Studies, Journalism and Mass Media, and Speech and Hearing Science. Faculty previously spread across several campuses found themselves in new proximity with predictable results. Simple expedients, such as combining faculty from different departments in doctoral and masters classes, fostered discussions at the boundaries between the fields; although intended to strengthen our instructional offerings, team teaching also enriched our thinking. When, at the inception of the school, Ruben was appointed Director of the Ph.D. program, he convened a Colloquium series which has consistently offered a forum for trying out new ideas. In addition, the students, lacking the disciplinary biases of their professors, formed doctoral committees by drawing on faculty from different departments, and, in so doing, created informal settings for exchanging views.

Against this background, informal faculty seminars convened to explore the relationship between communication and information. In 1987, Tefko Saracevic formed the Information Indicators Group to explore the quantitative measurement of structures of information and patterns of communication in large social units. The following year, Schement initiated the Communication and Information Research Committee [CIRCE] with the specific intent of establishing a research front at the intersection of the fields of communication and information studies. The papers written for that seminar led to the idea for this issue.

Scholarly ideas rarely emerge in a vacuum. Beyond the university, the coming of the information society, with its dramatically changing technologies, markets, organizations, and public relationships, has brought a public need to understand the nature and consequences of these changes. In fact, almost anyone old enough to remember manual typewriters and colorless television pictures, understands something of the wave of changes that have overtaken daily life. Cable television, satellite dishes, video cassette players, compact discs, radar detectors, automatic teller machines, answering machines, copy machines, fax machines, multi-use telephones, and personal computers, populate the topography of nearly every American's familiar terrain. When they pay attention to the news, Americans routinely receive stories attesting to the fact that the U.S. economy now exchanges information as its primary commodity. Furthermore, most adult's work in occupations where the manipulation of information constitutes the main activity of their work (Debons, King, Mansfield, & Shirey, 1981; Machlup & Kronwinkler, 1975; Mills, 1951/1956; Porat, 1977; Schement, 1990; Schement & Lievrouw, 1984; U.S. Department of Commerce, 1985). It is, therefore, not surprising that this transformation has captured the popular imagination as the dawn of a new era; and, as always, the concerns of the larger society have found their way onto the agenda of the academic community. As such, these popular images have further sensitized social scientists, making them aware of the mutually supporting interplay between communication and information.

Our purpose in the fourth volume of *Information and Behavior,* is to map out a research front addressing the relationships between communication and information. The contributors, themselves, come from numerous fields with diverse outlooks. Some present new perspectives on either communication or information. Others explore the connection between communication and information, as each is traditionally studied. Still others, synthesize interdisciplinary findings, while a few apply their perspectives in specific settings. Accordingly, the volume presents theoretical perspectives, empirical research, and essays, which, taken together, advance our understanding of integrative communication/information frameworks and present a rich sweep of interdisciplinary research. Finally, though of equal importance, mapping out the research front, led us to identify this group of likeminded scholars for the first time. (For most, their previous research had been pursued in isolation or in contact with one or two others sharing the same interest.)

The organization of the issue reflects currently established lines of research, as well as the weight of interest in those lines. In Part I, the contributors explore the junction between communication and information from various theoretical perspectives; their explorations delve into the multi-layered relationship between the two phenomena. Two cross-disciplinary approaches are presented in Part II; Schement applies an etymological framework, while Rice and Crawford conduct a citation analysis. Part III groups together case studies which examine the interaction between communication and information at the levels of the individual and the group. Part IV focuses on the level of society, in which the interactions between communication and information affect the evolution of institutions and culture.

Social scientists are beginning to question the relationship between communication and information as they become more sensitive to the presence of communication and information-oriented variables within their theories. Over the next decade, new theory construction is certain to mirror this recognition, and other disciplines will enter the conceptual territory which we are now exploring. We present the following articles in the hopes of extending and challenging the thinking of our fellow scholars, and those who also seek to better understand human behavior.

References

Beniger, J. R. (1988). Information and communication. *Communication Research, 15*(2), 198–218.

Borgman, C. L., & Schement, J. R. (1988). Communication research and information science: Models of convergence. *International Communication Association, New Orleans, LA.*

Borgman, C. L., & Schement, J. R. (1990). Information science and communication research. In J. M. Pemberton & A. E. Prentice (Eds.), *Information science: The interdisciplinary context* (pp. 42–59). New York: Neal-Schuman.

Debons, A., King, D. W., Mansfield, U., & Shirey, D. L. (1981). *The information professional: Survey of an emerging field.* New York: Marcel Dekker, Inc.

Ehrenhaus, P. (1988). Attributing intention to communication: Information as the interpretation of interaction. In B. D. Ruben (Eds.), *Information and Behavior* (pp. 248–271). New Brunswick, NJ: Transaction.

Kim, Y. Y. (1985). Communication, information, and adaptation. In B. D. Ruben

(Eds.), *Information and Behavior* (pp. 324–340). New Brunswick, NJ: Transaction.

Machlup, F., & Kronwinkler, T. (1975). Workers who produce knowledge: a steady increase, 1900 to 1970. *Weltwirtschaftliches Archiv., 111*(4), 752–59.

Mills, C. W. (1951/1956). *White collar.* Oxford, UK: Oxford University Press.

Paisley, W. J. (1986). The convergence of communication and information science. In H. Edelman (Eds.), *Libraries and information science in the electronic age* Philadelphia, PA: ISI Press.

Porat, M. U. (1977). *The information economy: Definition and measurement* No. OT Special Publication 77-12 (1). Washington DC: Department of Commerce/ Office of Telecommunications.

Ruben, B. D. (1985a). The coming of the information age: Information, technology and the study of human behavior. In B. D. Ruben (Ed.), *Information and behavior, Volume 1,* (pp. 3–26). New Brunswick, NJ: Transaction.

Ruben, B. D. (1985b). Introduction. In B. D. Ruben (Ed.), *Information and behavior, Volume 1,* (pp. xxi–xxiv). New Brunswick, NJ: Transaction.

Ruben, B. D. (1989). Redefining the boundaries of graduate education in communication, information and library studies: Theoretical and practical considerations. In J. M. Pemberton & A. Prentice (Eds.), *Information science in its interdisciplinary context.* New York: Neal-Schuman.

Ruben, B. D. (1992). The communication-information relationship in system-theoretic perspective. *Journal of the American Society for Information Science, 43*(1), 14–27.

Ruben, B. D., & Lievrouw, L. A. (1989). *Information and Behavior, Volume 3. Mediation, Information and Communication.* New Brunswick, NJ: Transaction.

Schement, J. R. (1990). Porat, bell, and the information society reconsidered: The growth of information work in the early twentieth century. *Information Processing and Management, 26*(4), 449–65.

Schement, J. R., & Lievrouw, L. A. (1984). A behavioural measure of information work. *Telecommunications Policy, 8*(4), 321–334.

U.S. Department of Commerce (1985). *Automation of America's Offices, 1985–2000* No. PB-185055). Office of Technology Assessment, Congress of the United States, National Technical Information Service.

PART I

THEORIES

1

Communication and Information

Jorge Reina Schement

*In the rhetoric of the Information Age, communication and infor-
mation are converging toward synonymous meanings.* Consider
organizational structures like information systems/communication
systems, *which executives speak of managing without differentiation.* Or, information technology/communication technology, *typically used interchangeably by engineers. Indeed, managerial professionals speak of* communication flows *as functionally equivalent to*
information flows, *all the while disregarding the semantic differences. Similarly, in the technical press, one reads of* global informa-
tion/world communication, *and* communications flows/information
flows, *where journalists freely exchange information and communication; and, in the world of international politics, United Nations
diplomats have long debated the relationship between the capitalist
West and the less developed countries, as part of a* New World
Communication Order, *or* New World Information Order.

*On the streets, Americans implicitly assume some connection
between the two concepts when engaging in ordinary discourse. The
questions, "Did you receive the message sent to you?" and, "Do
you understand what I said?" both require an understanding of
communication and information, as concepts, in order to make sense
of them. Similarly, the statements, "He will give a lecture" and
"Say that again" have meaning only if the receiver understands
some connection between communication and information. As for
more technical usages, phrases such as* information retrieval, data
transmission, signal interference, *and* electronic media, *assume an
explicit-to-implicit relationship between the two concepts; and,* ac-

3

cess, interface, compatibility, *and* fidelity, *terms used commonly in technical jargon, combine the two concepts within their meanings. (Ruben, 1992b)*

The purpose of this article is to explore the links between conceptualizations of information and conceptualizations of communication, and propose some research directions which may advance our understanding of these closely related phenomena.

Previous Adaptations and Investigations

As words, communication and information took on meanings which approximate mordern use in the eighteenth century. By the end of the nineteenth century, common meanings of the two words were indistinguishable from some current usages. However, in the early decades of the twentieth century, scientists and engineers writing in technical journals began to adapt the two words to new technological developments in electronics. The sense of communication as a transmission of electronic signals, and information as a quantity, derive from this period. (See Schement, J.R., "An Etymological Exploration of the Links Between Information and Communication" in this volume.) Furthermore, as American society shifted to one heavily dependent on the production, distribution, and consumption of information, individuals found themselves compelled to adapt these old words to new meanings. In the face of novel circumstances, Americans invented the terms illustrated at the beginning of this article.

At the same time, scientists and scholars began to grapple with diverse phenomena and label them communication and/or information. For example, in 1949, Claude Shannon published his mathematical theory of communication, in which he sought to explain the transmission of an electrical signal from one point to another. Shannon proposed that the measure of information is the logarithmic function which expresses the choice of one message (pattern of signals) from the set of all possible messages (Shannon & Weaver, 1949, p. 32). At about the same time, Norbert Wiener visualized information as part of the process of any system's adjustment to the outer world. He posited that, in a system, information counters entropy, and postulated that a system decays when it can no longer process information from the environment or communicate information within the system (Wiener, 1950; Wiener, 1961, pp. 26–27, 31). In the 1950s, Robert M. Hayes, a founder of information studies, saw a hierarchical connection between information and data, and suggested that information resulted from processed data (Hayes, 1969). In effect, Shannon, Wiener, Hayes, and their contemporaries, considered information and communication as general concepts applicable to diverse situations, even though their definitions did not always harmonize, so that by the second half of the twentieth century, other scholars had also begun to adapt conceptualizations of communication and information, either explicitly or implicitly (Bertalanffy, 1968, p. 111; Boulding, 1956, p. 14; Dewey, 1926, p. 332; Hoskovsky, 1968, p. 331; Machlup, 1958, p. 187; Machlup, 1962, p. 53; Mackay, 1952, p. 54; Mayo, 1933, p. 190; McLuhan, 1964, p. 59; Mumford, 1934/1962, p. 299; Miller, 1965, p. 872; Pierce, 1961, p. 72; Price, 1963, p. 200; Rapoport, 1966, p. 77; Ruben, 1972, p. 82; Smith, 1966, p. 323). Thus, economists like John Hirshleifer, Donald Lamberton, Meheroo Jussawalla, and Fritz Machlup, successfully brought information into economics, defining it there as consisting of those events which reduce uncertainty in making a decision, thus, adapting its meaning to conform with traditional economic perspectives (Hirshleifer, 1973; Jussawalla, 1988; Lamberton, 1971; Machlup, 1962; Machlup & Mansfield, 1983c). Machlup further argued for a view of information encompassing both the telling of something and the something that is told (significantly, Machlup's view of information does not distinguish it from communication) (Machlup & Mansfield, 1983b).

Today, in the social sciences, the resulting literatures cross the boundaries of communication, computer science, economics, information studies, sociology, and psychology (Anderson, 1959; Artandi, 1973; Ashby, 1964; Borgman & Schement, 1990; Boulding, 1984; Farradane, 1976; Fox, 1983; Krippendorff, 1977; Lancaster & Gillespie, 1970; Mackay, 1952; Nitecki, 1985; Otten, 1975; Pierce, 1961; Pratt, 1977; Rapoport, 1966; Repo, 1989; Ruben, 1992b; Ruben & Kim, 1975; Schroder, Driver, & Streufert, 1967; Shannon & Weaver, 1949; Yovitz, 1975). Consequently, certain interpretations dominate in some social sciences, while the associated definitions do not necessarily conform to usages in other disciplines. Farther afield, in the laboratory, unanimity is equally elusive. Cellular biologists describe DNA as a "library" containing information (Dawkins, 1976; Machlup & Mansfield, 1983a), while a few physicists contend that the fundamental elements of the universe consist of binary bits of information (Campbell, 1982; Fredkin & Toffoli, 1982; Simon, 1969; Wright, 1989). So, clearly, information and communication contain utility for researchers as concepts. But, though the concepts fascinate many social, biological, and physical scientists, no interdisciplinary agreement on basic premises has emerged, and no unified theory appears imminent.

A Catalog of Observations Toward a Theory of Communication and Information

In this section, definitions of information and communication that are important in the fields of information studies, and communication studies are reviewed. I further examine the possible connections between the two sets of definitions, in order to determine if a possible overlap exists between them. Thus, although, most scholars do not consciously apply one definition over another to their work, the particular characteristics they assume influence the conduct of their research. Moreover, since communication researchers and information scientists tend to define communication and information as distinct phenomena, each field has focused on one phenomenon to the relative neglect of the other. Therefore, the analysis of definitions offers insights into the characteristics of the basic phenomena studied in each field, and to the possibility for commonalities.

Definitions of information

As twentieth century scholars have become sensitive to the significance of information as a concept valuable for the construction of their theories (see Schement, J. R., "An Etymological Exploration . . ."), they have sometimes approached information more as an enigma than as a concept open to systematic investigation. For example, Norbert Wiener, the founder of cybernetics, responded with a puzzle: "Information is information, not matter or energy. No materialism which does not admit this can survive at the present day," and further speculated, "The fact that one finds so many different meanings for the word 'information' has led some to suggest that it is an irreducible term." (Wiener, 1961, p. 5, 7) The Marxist physicist, Peter Paul Kirschenmann took Wiener one step further: " 'Information' has a definite meaning only in a determined systematic way. We must, therefore, describe the contexts" (Kirschenmann, 1970, p. 17). He went on to state that information receives different meanings according to whether it results from ordinary language, linguistic processes, information theory, or signal theory. He then placed the question of information squarely athwart the whole tradition of Western logic. "The assumption of only two components of reality—materiality and spirituality—is based on a simplification since there is always a remnant which cannot be assigned to either and which cybernetics designates with the word 'information.' The very foundations of our thought—classical, two-valued logic as corresponding to a metaphysical dualism—are shaken. We must turn to a logic with at least three values" (Kirschenmann, 1970, p. 7). In other words, like energy, information challenges the two ontic elements of Aristotle's forms. This may explain why some scientists equate information with energy (Fredkin & Toffoli, 1982); but if one follows Wiener's and Kirschenmann's supposition, to understand information requires a profound reorientation of our intellectual perspectives and traditions.

In the wake of such daunting challenges, other scholars have set more limited goals (see appendix 1.1). From their efforts, we can distinguish fundamental themes which outline current thinking on the nature of information. The foremost is one which runs strongly through the literature and is sometimes termed information-as-thing. First of all, to imagine information, which is cognitive and ephemeral, as a thing facilitates discussion, whether expressed literally, as in Diener's unequivical description:

> Information is an entity; but a thing that exists without mass or energy. . . . Information exists primarily in the societal universe: the domain of human, and societal, interaction. . . . Some of the properties of information that make it unique, and so difficult to understand, are: (a) as mentioned, it is an intangible entity not made of matter or energy; (b) by corollary, it can be reproduced and shared without loss and may even be enhanced through use; (c) it has veracity or at least a relative truth value; (d) it has a lifecycle and is ephemeral; (e) it must be processed to exist, for members of a society to totally cease to remember an item of information spells its permanent loss; and (f) it exists in two states: subjective [in the mind as "image"] and objective [in society in "language"]. (Diener, 1989, p. 17)

or metaphorically, as in Ruben's definition.

> Information is a coherent collection of data, messages, or cues organized in a particular way that has meaning or use for a particular human system. (Ruben, 1988, p. 19)

(Metaphorically, that is, because, in so far as data and messages constitute "things" as part of a linguistic category, they are not material things.) Nevertheless, it is clear that information can be encoded in material objects like books, disks, letters, and clay tablets. Consequently, some scholars take this fact as their point of departure (Diener, 1989; Fox, 1983; Hayes, 1969; Langefors & Samuelson, 1976; Ruben, 1988; Schramm, 1971). In addition, the development of technologies for storing, retrieving, and manipulating data encourage a perspective that configures information as a thing (Buckland, 1991). Yet when scholars discuss information as though it were a thing, they must contend with the social reality of information; that is, the information most scholars concern themselves with is that which is shared and transmitted in society. However, things don't transmit themselves; for if information is to exist in the domain of the human and societal, the act of transmission must take place. This act of transmission relates closely to what many scholars refer to as communication. Thus, to the extent that scholars make that assumption of information-as-thing, there is a case to be made for the necessary assumption of communication-as-transmission.

But though information is often thought of as a thing, it can also be a process, in the sense that information is part of the act of becoming informed, or, as Belkin, and Robertson put it (see also Belkin, 1975),

> Information is that which is capable of transforming structures. (Belkin & Robertson, 1976, p. 198)

This theme is echoed in economics and associated with the reduction of uncertainty. In this regard, the association with process is much stronger than in Information Studies. Notes Hirshliefer on information as an economic concept,

> Uncertainty is summarized by the dispersion of individuals' subjective probability [or belief] distributions over possible states of the world. Information, for our purposes, consists of events tending to change these probability distributions. . . . But it is changes in belief distributions—a process, not a condition—that constitute here the essence of information. Note that the economics of information is active where the economics of uncertainty is passive. (Hirshleifer, 1973, p. 31)

The reduction of uncertainty represents an important subtheme, especially among computer scientists and economists. In this context, uncertainty may refer to the measure of the amount of choice involved in the selection of an event from a known set of probabilities, as derived from Shannon's theory (Shannon & Weaver, 1949, p. 49), or, it may refer to that information which assists an individual in making a choice from a set of possibilities, as in Hirshleifer's explanation. Machlup tried to move beyond the uncertainty dimension, and, although accepting the view that information can be a thing, "something that is told" (p. 644), also incorporates the view of information-as-process, "the telling of something" (p. 644, 645). He then proposes the conjunction of the two phrases as a definition (Machlup & Mansfield, 1983c). But if information can be thought of as "the telling of something," then so too can communication; and, if the emphasis in the process view is on the phenomenon of informing or altering (Belkin, 1978; Belkin & Robertson, 1976; Hayes, 1969; Hoskovsky & Massey, 1968; Machlup & Mansfield, 1983c), then that comes close to the process or action notion associated with communication. Indeed, for those who subscribe to the view of information-as-process, an assumption of communication would seem necessary.

Closely accompanying information-as-process, is the perspective that combines information with the concept of manipulation, as in the definitions by Fox, and Hayes:

> Assuming that information is an entity communicated among two or more individuals, he [Fox] defines information as a proposition: the information carried by a sentence S is a proposition appropriately associated with S. (Fox, 1983, p. 389)

> "Information" is data produced as a result of a process upon data. That process may be one of transmission . . . it may be one of selection; it may simply be one of organization; it may be one of analysis. (Hayes, 1969)

Fox's and Hayes' connection of information to a manipulation is similar to the notion of information-as-process, but not the same. In the above examples, information is discussed as though it were a thing, but a thing that must be manipulated, in order to exist. Again, communication must be closely associated for the definitions to work, especially in Fox's notion of the information conveyed in a sentence and in Hayes' statement that information may be transmitted. But Hayes also mentions other forms of processing that do not necessarily coincide with communication. For example, the selection or organization of information is not usually thought of as part of the act of communicating. So, while the process view implicitly connects information and communication, it also points to dimensions of information that occur beyond the communication act.

Taken together, the themes of information-as-thing, as-process, and, as-product-of-manipulation, demonstrate a dependence on some conceptualization of communication, in order to succeed. In this regard, it seems that information scientists and other scholars have incorporated this assumption into their definitions; thereby, implying an elemental connection to the phenomenon of communication. Should communication scholars also introduce implicit or explicit notions of information into their definitions of communication, a significant symmetry would exist and require explanation.

Definitions of Communication

A sampling of definitions of communication drawn from major articles and textbooks reveals three central themes.

The most commonly understood theme, perhaps because of the success of Shannon and Weavers' *Mathematical Theory of Communication* (Shannon & Weaver, 1949), revolves around the concept of communication-as-transmission. But ironically, since most communication researchers cite Shannon as a contributor to the early impetus of the field, it is Weaver's definition that holds the higher influence, because Weaver defined communication in a context adaptable to the social sciences:

> The word *communication* will be used here in a very broad sense to include all procedures by which one mind may affect another. This, of course, involves not only written and oral speech, but also music, the pictorial arts, the theater, the ballet, and in fact all human behavior. (P. 3)

For his part, Shannon addressed the question as one of linear transmission, within the engineering variables of noise and fidelity.

> The fundamental problem of communication is that of reproducing at one point either exactly or approximately a message selected at another point. (P. 31)

In the view derived from Weaver, the communication process consists of the transmission of something, as in Hoben's (Hoben, 1954) two-way definition, "Communication is the verbal interchange of thought or idea." Sometimes, the act of transmission is characterized as elemental and behavioristic, as in Cherry's explication from the 1950s:

> Communication is an act through which a first [stimulus] sign calls up a second [response] sign which depends upon a particular recipient, according to the habits he has acquired from his past communicative experiences. (Cherry, 1957, p. 265)

Moreover, while some scholars explicitly stressed the two-way nature of this transmission (Avery, 1959; Cherry, 1957; Ellsworth & Ludwig, 1972; Wilson, 1975), others (Ayer, 1955; Bennet, 1972; Berelson & Steiner, 1964; Cathcart, 1966; Cherry, 1957; Emery, Ault, & Agee, 1963; Miller, 1951; Miller, 1966; Newcomb, 1966) left it implicit by calling attention to the act of sending—for example:

> Communication must be two-way, for the response is part of the process. (Avery, 1959, p. 5)

> Communication among human beings is the art of transmitting information, ideas and attitudes from one person to another (Emery et al., 1963, p. 3)

Of those scholars visualizing communication as an act of transmission, only Cherry (Cherry, 1957) seems to emphasize both dimensions.

But if communication consists of transmissions, then what is transmitted? On this point, there is loosely defined agreement. With the exception of those, like Ayer (Ayer, 1955), who resist committing themselves to a position ("The connecting thread appears to be the idea of something's being transferred from one thing, or person, to another" [pp. 12–13]), most scholars taking the transmission view suggest that the content of the transmission is an information-related variable (Bennet, 1972; Berelson & Steiner, 1964; Cathcart, 1966; Cherry, 1957; Cherry, 1966; Ellsworth & Ludwig, 1972; Emery et al., 1963; Hoben, 1954; Miller, 1951; Miller, 1966; Newcomb, 1966), as the following examples illustrate:

> Communication: the transmission of information, ideas, emotion, skills, etc., by the use of symbols—words, pictures, figures, graphs, etc. It is the act or process of transmission that is usually called communication. (Berelson & Steiner, 1964, p. 527)

> In the main, communication has as its central interest those behavioral situations in which a source transmits a message to a receiver[s] with conscious intent to affect the latter's behaviors. (Miller, 1966, p. 89)

> Communication means that information is passed from one place to another. (Miller, 1951, p. 6)

> Every communication act is viewed as a transmission of information, consisting of a discriminative stimuli, from a source to a recipient. (Newcomb, 1966, p. 66)

By connecting communication and information, the communication-as-transmission view establishes the basic relationship. Scholars in this group suggest that communication is a process of movement, and that information is what's moved. These definitions fit well into the engineering perspective articulated by Shannon via Weaver. Moreover, because the fit between communication and information is so obvious in this view, there is a tendency to oversimplify the variations of human behavior.

The second view counters the tendency to oversimplify by explicating the communication process as a sharing process. Its inspiration stems from the linguistic roots of the word communication. In Latin, *communicare* means to share, or to make common. For example, Caesar, in his Gallic commentaries, uses *communicare* to relate the sharing of food [Book VI ¶ 23, line 9]; of money [VII 37, 2]; and, the matching of a dowry [VI 19, 1]; but also to pass on information [VII 36, 3]; and, to tell [IV 13, 4] (Caesar, 50 B.C./1980; Caesaris, 50 B.C./1927; Meusel, 1893). While, to be sure, *communicare* is not a popular word in Caesar's vocabulary (he uses it just eleven times), our word communication comes from these Latin meanings, nevertheless. Indeed, though the last two meanings, in particular, come closest to current usage, the root *communis* forms the genesis of definitions that revolve around sharing. As Gover puts it,

In the discussion that follows, "to communicate" shall mean "to make common" [to share] experience, regardless of the nature of the experiential event, or the method of its transmission or projection. "Communication" is therefore that particular event which culminates in some degree of shared experience. (Gover, 1970)

Gover clearly connects with the Latin meanings and maintains the concept of communication-as-sharing across all of the original Latin expressions.

Yet the most widely known of the definitions which stress sharing is probably Schramm's, of which the following is one of many he proposed during his long career.

Today we might define communication simply by saying that it is the sharing of an orientation toward a set of informational signs. . . . Communication is therefore based on a relationship. (Schramm, 1971, p. 13)

What is interesting here is that information appears as an ambiguous modifer, but not as an active ingredient; the sharing approximates that of a mutual state, as, for example, when a group of individuals shares knowledge of a common language. His pioneering role in communication studies, and his influential, *The Process and Effects of Mass Communication* (Schramm & Roberts, 1971), introduced an entire generation of communication scholars to the idea of communication as a process of sharing. Though initially attracted by Shannon's linear thinking, Schramm eventually came around to the concept of "field of experience" as the essential condition determining the communication act. As a result, the connection between sharing and communication is a rich one; and opens up the possibility that communication may take place across all senses and through many media simultaneously, so that nonverbal gestures and tactile exchanges can also be considered part of the communication act. Consequently, within the context of communication-as-sharing, the communication environment appears rich and multileveled. So, if communication researchers who devoted their energies to mapping out the patterns in this environment tended to neglect the question of information, their omission is understandable given the complexity introduced by the idea of communication-as-sharing. However, the assumption of information continued to surface in communication studies.

For about the time that Schramm was deviating from Shannon and Weaver's transmission centered views, other scholars were drawn to system's theory, whose focus stresses a view of phenomena with interactive parts and capabilities greater than the sum of the parts (Buckley, 1967; Checkland, 1981; Krippendorff, 1977; Miller, 1965; Ruben, 1972; Thayer, 1968). Given the growing sense that the communication act was really a process, the systems approach offered insights into this complex event with greater attention to specific patterns than the more ambiguous concept of sharing. Ruben's most recent definition exemplifies this line of reasoning.

> Human communication is the process through which individuals in relationships, groups, organizations and societies create, transmit, and use information to relate to the environment and one another. (Ruben, 1992a, p. 18)

The influence of systems thinking is apparent. In Ruben's definition, the communication process is described in terms of components, boundaries, and interactions. Though not all definitions centering on interaction, do so with the explicitness of systems theory, the theme of communication-as-interactiveness distinguishes this approach, as the following examples illustrate.

> It is communication: the establishment of cooperation in an activity in which there are partners and in which the activity of each is modified and regulated by partnership. (Dewey, 1926, p. 179)
>
> Communication is social interaction through symbols and message systems. (Gerbner, 1966, p. 102)
>
> Communication can be understood as that indispensible function of people and organizations through which the organization of the organism relates itself to its environment, and relates its parts and its internal processes to one another. (Thayer, 1968, p. 17)

In turn, these examples raise a question less explicitly addressed in the communication-as-sharing definitions: Of what is the stuff of interaction? Taken as a group, communication scholars provide many answers, symbols, ideas, skills, words, pictures, figures, graphs, signs, messages, gestures, and information.

To be sure, though there is no easily identified pattern, information does appear quite often in definitions of communication, but not so as to obviously dominate. Yet of the above possibilities, information captures the rest by serving as an umbrella category. Thus, as some communication scholars have suspected all along, it appears that, in order to define communication, some conceptualization of information is necessary; and, given the similar position taken by scholars studying information, it is reasonable to suggest a strong link between the two phenomena; yet explicating these links is not so easy.

Linking Information and Communication

Any effort to understand information faces incongruities with the world of material things that seem to have nothing to do with communication. To start with, information is infinitely reproducible, and, to the extent that accuracy is maintained, the organization of symbols in the nth copy perfectly reflects the original; as a result, the Declaration of Independence when recorded on a compact disk contains the same information as the copy preserved in the National Archives (albeit, a reader of the original Declaration of Independence may derive extra meaning from experiencing the words as written on 200 year old paper; but such an experience goes beyond the documentary information per se). It follows, therefore, that the consumption of information does not eliminate it, that is, unlike the world of material things where the consumption of a thing like an apple cancels its existence, in the world of information, students who hear a lecture do not empty that information from the head of the instructor (Yang, 1990). Also, because the symbolic essence of information means that it is interpreted subjectively, the outcome of its exchange cannot be determined precisely; in other words, no one can predict what meanings will be derived by two separate readers of, say, the Iliad (Artandi, 1973; Bates, 1990; Buckland, 1991; Kirschenmann, 1970; Lamberton, 1971; Rapoport, 1966).

These characteristics of information pose problems when applied to the phenomena studied by the social sciences. For example, in economics, where scholars focus on the exchange of goods and services, the market value of information has long been recognized, mostly because information, though ephemeral, can be fixed as a commodity. Yet an individual's unwillingness to purchase yesterday's copy of the Los Angeles Times or to purchase software written onto an incompatible disk illustrates the volatility of time, package, and value, in the marketplace; that is, to the reader in this instance, yesterday's copy of the Los Angeles Times has low value because the information is no longer timely, while software written onto an incompatible disk has low value because the information has been encoded in an inaccessible package. In addition, because information can be easily reproduced, it is difficult to control over time, thus threatening its commodity value. As all producers of software for profit know, information leaks. In fact, it is so easy for commoditized information to leak, that a complex legal structure has been erected to protect the exchange of information in the marketplace. So, all capitalist countries enact copyright and patent laws to protect against the reproduction of information outside of the legitimized marketplace (Chamberlin & Singleton, 1987).

However, fear of unauthorized reproducibility, the bogeyman of information entrepreneurs, may actually be fear of communication. For when a software user makes an illegal copy of a program and then passes the illegal copy on to a friend, the conditions for some definitions of communication have been met; and, in so doing, defeated efforts to limit the exchange of that software in the marketplace. Similarly, the reader who gives the used copy of the *Los Angeles Times* to a friend at work is transmitting information; and, therefore, participating in the communication act, while depriving the publishers of the *Los Angeles Times* of some income. Therefore, it would seem that, as with the the *Los Angeles Times* and the illegal software, in every similar instance of information being leaked or stolen, the communication process must come into play. Moreover, while these examples are relevant to the interpersonal level where individuals meet individuals, the same can be said for the level of telecommunications. Beginning with the diffusion of the telegraph in the nineteenth century, a proliferation of communications technologies has emerged that facilitate communication at a distance and the establishment of new markets for information commodities. However, the ability to push back the physical limits of communication also threatens property controls in the marketplace by increasing the ease with which information can be transmitted by unauthorized users. What's more, these technologies challenge the exchange of information in the marketplace by increasing the numbers of people who may be included as part of the communication act. Thus, in the case of economics, the inherent characteristics of information allow it to be converted into a commodity, although its exchange in the marketplace falls within some definitions of the process of communication. At the same time, the inherent characteristics of information, specifically its ephemeral state, allow it to be reproduced so that it may be stolen without the owner's awareness, nevertheless, to pass it on requires communication.

So, although economics represents one field where the special problem of information and communication is encountered; and, because the links described above are in the nature of information and communication, rather than of economics, they apply to other fields as well. In the social sciences, the attempts of scholars to adapt a conceptualization of information to their distinct fields exhibits aspects of this special problem. For example, economists, information scientists, and computer scientists treat information as a material commodity that is constructed, bought, sold, stored, retrieved, and packaged; they pay little attention to the dimension of communication, as though information commodities move exactly like material goods. Librarians, some information scientists and some economists, discuss information as if it is a public resource to be husbanded, made accessible, distributed, broadcast, channeled, and allowed to flow freely, implying that it has been unnaturally forced into the constraints of the marketplace; they must assume the presence of communication, in order to articulate their model. In communication studies, marketing, and journalism, the communication process attracts the focus of scholars, while information, per se, is largely treated as the content of the process. Sometimes, the special problem finds voice in controversies. In library studies, the "fee or free" controversy involves disagreement over whether the public welfare is better served when information is provided within or without the marketplace. In economics, ambiguities involving the nature of information are reflected in the "private good/public good" debate. Across the social sciences, the links between information and communication appear as special problems within each field, and, in nearly every case, the tendency is to focus on one side of the link or the other.

Moreover, the link between information and communication is so complex, that identifying it in the context of human actions presents a challenge. The two following examples depict the intricacies involved; the first describes the intertwining of communication in and out of the marketplace, while the second involves the ownership of information as ideas.

In the first example, a book publisher contracts with an author to publish the author's manuscript. In their contract, they each assert rights and obligations. The author, as creator of the information, maintains ownership rights of the information presented in the book, and agrees not to sell that information through any other publisher. The publisher agrees to place the author's information in a book (ie. the package) for sale, and agrees to share profits from the sale of the book by paying the author royalties. The publisher then offers the book for sale as the sole vendor of that information. However, upon entering the marketplace with the book, author and publisher encounter difficulties that diminish their control over the information in the book, and, consequently, their profits. Some individuals photocopy all or portions of the manuscript without reimbursing the author or publisher. In addition, book lovers on limited incomes purchase used copies of the book, while others borrow it from the library, thus further depriving the author and publisher of revenues. At the same time, in countries that have not signed international copyright agreements, the book is published and sold without paying royalties. So, the author communicates with her audience, but because some of the information is also communicated beyond her control, the author, and publisher, experience financial frustration.

In the second example, a young naval lieutenant receives an assignment to write a report on naval operations in the Persian Gulf. His superiors forbid him to communicate with unauthorized personnel while he is writing the report. Implicitly, the lieutenant understands that, from the moment of his assignment, the information he creates does not belong to him, but is property of the Department of Defense. Moreover, because he agreed to subordinate his claim to the information in the report, he cannot express ownership of the original ideas he contributes to the report. Yet while loyal to his mandate, the lieutenant experiences ego frustration as senior officers take ideas from his report and repeat them in lectures as if they were their own. Inevitably, some information leaks to the press, who attribute the information to anonymous sources. Also, offical interpretations of the report appear in military journals under the names of the lieutenant's superiors. References to it appear in congressional documents, and even in some popular newspapers and magazines. The lieutenant communicates with a diverse audience; but, though the originator of the ideas in the report, he receives no public re gnition for his intellectual contribution. In a sense, the ideas, which he still possesses, ceased belonging to him the moment he committed them to paper.

The point of these two examples is that information and communication are ever present and connected, that is, to attempt a description of human behavior attendant to one requires recognition of the other. So, as the above examples indicate, individuals may try to control information for their own purposes, yet their goals are always partially frustrated since no information package is completely proof against communication. Even so, neat distinctions between information and communication are difficult to pin down in these examples. At this point, it seems fair to say that for information to exist the potential for communication must be present; and, in most cases, the communication process must take place. But beyond the observation that an intricate link exists between information and communication, we know little of the dynamics of the relationship. Nevertheless, based on that observation, the following propositions open avenues for further research.

1. *Information and communication are social constructions.* Not only does language betray the assumption of a connection, as discussed in the beginning of this article, but the two words are often used interchangeably, almost as synonyms. This indicates the possibility that native uses of the two terms reflect an underlying connection which is acted out in behavior. While this is not to say that information and communication lack properties as distinct phenomena, it draws attention to their social dimensions. In this sense, the popular uses of the two concepts may be explored as social constructions; that is, the presence of the idea of information and the idea of communication suggest analysis as cultural values that facilitate or inhibit forces in society, in much the way that the idea of progress or the idea of democracy shaped modern society; and, in so far as these ideas contributed to the formation of society, they also have histories, something that most scholars of information and communication have, heretofore, overlooked.

2. *The study of information and communication share concepts in*

common. Terms that emerge from a review of the definitions display concepts that both scholars of information, and communication, employ in their respective areas of inquiry. Indeed, aside from the presence of information and communication as concepts in both fields, the following concepts can also be found as commonly shared foci: symbol, cognition, content, structure, process, feedback, interaction, technology, and system. That, for example, communication researchers and information scientists both study content suggests two possibilities: (a) a commonly held conceptualization; or (b) a single term operationalized differently. Studying the role played by this concept in each field may shed light on the link between information and communication. Thus, for all of the concepts listed above, what lies in common, and what does not, should be of significance to the primary question. So, while direct analysis of the link between information and communication presents significant obstacles, indirect inquiry through analysis of these attendant concepts may offer rewarding insights.

3. *Information and communication form dual aspects of a broader phenomenon.* For most Americans, it is a transparent assumption that information has the properties of a thing and that communication has the properties of movement or transmission. Moreover, these assumptions are deeply ingrained because they facilitate perceptions. For example, the growth of information markets and commodities dating back to the middle of the nineteenth century is predicated on the assumption of information-as-thing; while the establishment of the nation's telecommunications infrastructure and the development of institutionalized communication channels as the basis for modern corporate bureaucracies rests on the assumption of communication-as-transmission. Yet as we have seen, each of these assumptions depends on the other for its success. Observations such as these raise the possibility that the special problem of information and communication reflects a duality embraced by some larger phenomenon for which there is no name at present.

Consideration of this proposition leads to the inference that uncertainty will be encountered when measuring information structures or tracing communication flows. In other words, measuring the amount of information present in a certain situation may present difficulties because communication acts to prevent complete measurement; for example, it is impossible to know with certainty how many copies of a software application exist because of the possibility that someone may be communicating it, and, therefore increasing the total. Furthermore, the corollary can be established for communication. Information is present in so many different forms, that it is impossible to know with certainty that no communication is taking place; thus, to place a person in isolation prevents direct communication, but generates the information that this person is in isolation, and that may be transmitted, so that some communication still occurs.

So, it would seem that each phenomenon pulls on the other. As the definitions demonstrate, to focus on either information or communication requires the assumption of the other, most often as a simple construction. Therefore, it may be that the nature of information and communication is such that the act of concentrating attention on one obscures the other. If so, then communication and information may be inextricably tied, but in such a way as to thwart direct observation. Admittedly, to suggest the possibility that information and communication constitute dual aspects of an x phenomenon seems like a leap of faith. Yet the consistency with which scholars have assumed either information or communication in their definitions indicates an interaction. In the absence of more definite evidence, the possibility of a duality bears consideration.

In conclusion, can one reasonably suggest the formation of a research front, in the absence of firmer evidence? For one thing, no consensual definitions of information or communication exist as yet. Without them, scholars may easily become bogged down in fundamental research, where each reigns as expert over his or her own narrowly defined focus with little integration into a larger body of theory. Such conditions amount to wandering in the wilderness, with no promise that any organizing theory will emerge. Still, as the review of definitions demonstrates, a general focus exists; and, although agreement is loose, the beginnings of a common discussion can be discerned. Furthermore, the importance of concepts related to information and communication across the physical, biological, and social sciences indicates the value of the enterprise. For while physicists, biologists, computer scientists, and economists may well be masking diverse phenomena within the same terminology, the possibility that some are tapping into a commonly held framework implies the potential for a theory capable of integration across disciplines. Indeed, if the relationship between information and communication can be explained within any of the social sciences, then the explanation must hold for the others as well. Here, then, is the opportunity for an interdiciplinary approach to the problem. Whereas, within each of the social sciences descriptions of information and communication are subordinated to the demands of the paradigms which define the disciplines [as in economics where the logic of individual choice in the marketplace encourages a conception of information as the reduction of uncertainty], an approach open to scholars from different disciplines may transcend the constraints of disciplinary paradigms. So, though each discipline incorporates a characteristic view of human behavior, a theory explaining the relationship between communication and information might provide a common denominator across disciplines.

That so many have gone before, with so little concluded, testifies to the promise and the challenge.

The author wishes to thank the members of the Circe Group, Professors Carl Botan, Leah Lievrouw, Hartmut B. Mokros, and Brent Ruben, along with student members, Inhee Lee, Maureen McCreadie, Kyung Shim, and Jane Wallace, as well as Nicholas J. Belkin, for contributing to the discussions that led to this paper.

Appendix 1.1 Selected Definitions of Information

1. Langefors, B. and Samuelson, K. (1976). *Information and data systems*. Petrocelli/Charter.

   Information—(1) any knowledge or message useful for decision or action (2) a computer idea or meaning derived from the data.

2. Ahituv, N. and Neumann, S. (1983). *Principles of information systems for management*. W. C. Brown.

   [Information] is data that have been processed and are meaningful to a user.

3. Checkland, P. (1981). *Systems thinking, systems practice*. Wiley.

   The word "information" is best used to denote a combination of fact plus a meaning an observer attributes to it.

4. McCosh, M. and Scott-Morton, M. (1978). *Management decision support systems*. Macmillan.

   Information is all material pieces of knowledge which may be used rationally in making a choice among alternatives by a decision maker who has the responsibility and authority to make that choice.

5. Tully, C. J. (1985). Information, human activity, and the nature of relevant theories, *The Computer Journal*, 28(3), pp. 206–10.

   INFORMATION—That which is constructed from symbols, using language, to convey meaning (p. 207).

6. Hoskovsky, A. G. and Massey, R. J. (1968). Information science: Its end, means and operations. In *Information Transfer*. Proc. ASIS, 5. New York.

   Information . . . is a process which occurs within the human mind when a problem and data useful for its solution are brought into productive union.

7. Hayes, R. M. (1969). Education in information science. *American Documentation*, 20, 362–65.
"Information" is data produced as a result of a process upon data. That process may be one of transmission . . . it may be one of selection; it may simply be one of organization; it may be one of analysis.

8. Montgomery, E. G. (1968). *Four "new" sciences.* AGARD.
We would define information as the position of all the atoms and molecules in the universe and of all sets and combinations of those atoms and molecules at any time.

9. Koszyk, K. and Prugs, K. H. (1969). *dtv-Wörterbuch zur Publizistik.* München.
. . . whereby information . . . is defined as symbols being produced by a communicator to realize his communication intent.

10. Fritz Machlup. (1983). Semantic Quirks in Studies of Information. In Fritz Machlup and Una Mansfield eds., *The study of information: Interdisciplinary messages,* John Wiley & Sons, pp. 641–71.
Information refers to telling something, or the something that is being told.

To sum up, information in the sense of telling and being told is always different from knowledge in the sense of knowing: the former is a process, the latter is a state.

Information in the sense of that which is being told may be the same as knowledge in the sense of that which is known, but need not be the same (p. 644).

Information takes at least two persons: one who tells [by speaking, writing, imprinting, pointing, signalling] and one who listens, reads, watches (p. 645).

11. Nicholas J. Belkin and Stephen E. Robertson. (1976). Information Science and the Phenomenon of Information, *Journal of the American Society for Information Science,* July–August, pp. 197–204.
Information is that which is capable of transforming structure (p. 198).

12. Richard L. Derr. (1985). The Concept of Information in Ordinary Discourse, *Information Processing & Management*, 21, 6, pp. 489–99.

12a. As we have seen, information as it is conceptualized in everyday experience, is an objective phenomenon. It exists independently of whether it produces an effect on a receiver. This holds no matter what representational form it is given (p. 495).

12b. Information, in the ordinary sense, is the product of a cognitive act in which an individual or individuals has resolved an uncertainty as to what is the case in regard to certain objects (p. 495).

16. J. Hirshleifer. (1973). Economics of Information: Where Are We in the Theory of Information? *American Economic Association*, 63, 2, May 1973, pp. 31–39.

Uncertainty is summarized by the dispersion of individuals' subjective probability [or belief] distributions over possible states of the world. Information, for our purposes, consists of events tending to change these probability distributions. A rather different concept of "information" is employed in communications and statistical theory, according to which a dispersed probability distribution is called less "informative" than a concentrated one [for certain applications see H. Theil]. This latter concept uses the term "information" merely as a negative measure of uncertainty. But it is changes in belief distributions—a process, not a condition—that constitute here the essence of information. Note that the economics of information is active where the economics of uncertainty is passive (p. 31).

17. Joseph Z. Nitecki. (1985). The Concept of Information-Knowledge Continuum: Implications for Librarianship, *The Journal of Library History*, 20, 4, Fall, pp. 387–407.

Information is considered here as a popular term for a cluster of perceptions brought to our attention, but not yet fully assimilated. Knowledge is perceived as a state, at any particular time, of relations known that are expressed in a system of knowing that has been already acquired by an individual (p. 388).

18. From J. Koblitz. (1969). Librarianship and Documentation/Information: Distinctive Features and Common Aspects. In *On Theoretical Problems in Informatics, All-Union Institute for Scientific and Technical Information*, Moscow, pp. 120–42.

Koblitz distinguishes among three kinds of semantic definitions of information: as a message, as a process, and as a documental, facto-graphic information [i.e., information containing new facts or statements] (p. 388–89).

19. From Christopher John Fox. (1983). *Information and misinformation: An Investigation of the Notions of Information, Misinformation, informing, and misinforming*, Greenwood Press, 1983.

. . . who concentrates on 'the ordinary notion of information.' Assuming that information is an entity communicated among two or more individuals, he [Fox] defines information as a proposition: 'the information carried by a sentence S is a proposition appropriately associated with S (p. 389).

20. Schramm, W. (1972). The nature of communication between humans. In *The process and effects of mass communication*, Schramm, E. and Roberts D. F. (Eds.), Urbana, IL: University of Illinois Press.

Information, in this sense, we must define very broadly. Obviously it is not limited to news or "facts" or what is taught in the classroom or contained in reference books. It is any content that reduces uncertainty or the number of alternative possibilities in a situation. It may include emotions. It may include facts or opinion or guidance or persuasion. It does not have to be in words, or even explicitly stated: the latent meanings "the silent language" are important information. It does not have to be precisely identical in both sender and receiver— we doubt that it ever is, and we are unlikely to be able to measure that correspondence very completely anyway. The ancient idea of transferring a box of facts from one mind to another is no longer a very satisfactory way of thinking about human communication. It is more helpful to think of one or more people or other entities coming to a given piece of information, each with his own needs and intentions, each comprehending and using the information in his own way (p. 13).

21. Ruben, B. (1988). *Communication and human behavior*. New York: Macmillan, pp. 18–19.

Human communication is the process through which individuals in relationships, groups, organizations and societies create, transmit and use information to relate to the environment and one another.

Information is a coherent collection of data, messages, or cues organized in a particular way that has meaning or use for a particular human system.

22. Diener, R. A. V. (1989). Information science: What is it? . . . what

should it be? *Bulletin of the American Society for Information Science,* 15[5] June/July, p. 17.

1. Information is an entity; but a thing that exists without mass or energy.

2. Information, per se, is not a component of the physical universe of matter and energy. It is not constrained by the law of conservation of matter and energy. It is intangible and can be reproduced without loss of content or meaning. To seek to understand information using the mindset, theories, research, methodologies, hypotheses, and/or data analysis techniques of the physical sciences, is, therefore, fundamentally flawed.

3. Information exists primarily in the societal universe; the domain of human, and societal, interaction. Given the general weakness of sociological research methodologies, however, I do not suggest that they should form the basis of research in the science of information. Because information is so fundamental to sociality [it is ubiquitous to all human and societal interaction], we need to develop our own general and specific theories, hypotheses, research methodologies and units of measure.

4. Some of the properties of information that make it unique, and so difficult to understand, are: a) as mentioned, it is an intangible entity not made of matter or energy; b) by corollary, it can be reproduced and shared without loss and may even be enhanced through use; c) it has veracity or at least a relative truth value; d) it has a life cycle and is ephemeral; and e) it must be processed to exist, for the members of a society to totally cease to remember an item of information spells its permanent loss; and f) it exists in two states: subjective [in the mind as "image"] and objective [in society in "language"].

Appendix 1.2: Selected Definitions of Communication

1. Anderson, M. P. (1959). What is communication. *The Journal of Communication,* 9:5.
   Communication is the process by which we understand others and in turn endeavor to be understood by them. It is dynamic, constantly changing and shifting in response to the total situation.

2. Ayer, A. J. (1955). What is communication? In *Studies in communication.* A. J. Ayer et al. (Eds.). London: Secker and Warburg, pp. 11–28.
   The connecting thread appears to be the idea of something's being

transferred from one thing, or person, to another. We use the word "communication" sometimes to refer to what is so transferred, sometimes to the means by which it is transferred, sometimes to the whole process. In many cases, what is transferred in this way continues to be shared; if I convey information to another person, it does not leave my own possession through coming into his. Accordingly, the word "communication" acquires also the sense of participation. It is in this sense, for example, that religious worshipers are said to communicate.

3. Berelson, B. and Steiner, G. A. (1964). *Human behavior: An inventory of scientific findings.* New York: Harcourt Brace Jovanovich.

Communication: the transmission of information, idea, emotion, skills, etc., by the use of symbols—words, pictures, figures, graphs, etc. it is the act or process of transmission that is usually called communication.

4. Cartier, F. A. and Harwood, K. A. (1953). On definition of communication. *The Journal of Communication,* 3:71–75, p. 73.

Communication is the process of conducting the attention of another person for the purpose of replicating memories.

5. Cushman, D. and Whiting, G. C. (1972). An approach to communication theory: toward consensus on rules. *The Journal of Communication,* 22 [3], 217–38, p. 217.

Communication is an activity which gains meaning and significance from consensually shared rules. What is transmitted in communication is structure or information, but not all experiences from which we extract information are communication experiences. Communication requires in addition that at least two individuals attempt to take one another into account by developing and utilizing communication rules to guide and constitute the significance of their communicative acts. These rules guide choices made in decoding and encoding messages. The rules' components are indications (1) of where they apply and (2) of what action or choice they stipulate. The rules are social, human creations subject to change and recreation.

6. Gerbner, G. (1966). On defining communication: still another view. *The Journal of Communication,* June (2), p. 102.

Communication is social interaction through symbols and message systems.

7. Gode, A. (1959). What is communication. *The Journal of Communication*, 9:5.

It [communication] is a process that makes common to two or several what was the monopoly of one or some.

8. Goyer, R. S. (1970). Communication, communicative process, meaning: toward a unified theory. *The Journal of Communication*, 20 (2), 4–16, p. 6.

In the discussion that follows, "to communicate" shall mean "to make common" [to share] experience, regardless of the nature of the experiential event, or the method of its transmission or projection. "Communication" is therefore that particular event which culminates in some degree of shared experience.

9. Hoben, J. B. (1954). English communication at Colgate re-examined. *The Journal of Communication*, 4:76–86, p. 77.

Communication is the verbal interchange of thought or idea.

10. Lundberg, G. A. (1939). *Foundations of sociology*. New York: Macmillan, p. 253.

We shall use the word communication, then, to designate interaction by means of signs and symbols. The symbols may be gestural, pictorial, plastic, verbal, or any other which operate as stimuli to behavior which would not be invoked by the symbol itself in the absence of the special conditioning of the person who responds.

11. Miller, G. A. (1951). Language and communication. New York: McGraw-Hill, p. 6.

Communication means that information is passed from one place to another.

12. Miller, G. R. (1966). On defining communication: Another stab. *The Journal of Communication*, June, 16 [2], 88–98.

In the main, communication has as its central interest those behavioral situations in which a source transmits a message to a receiver[s] *with conscious intent to affect the latter's behaviors* (p. 89).

13. Newcomb, T. M. (1966). An approach to the study of the communicative acts. In *Communication and culture*, A. G. Smith (Ed.). New York: Holt, Rinehart and Winston, 66–79.

Every communication act is viewed as a transmission of information, consisting of a discriminative stimuli, from a source to a recipient (p. 66).

14. Newman, E. B. (1948). Hearing. In *Foundations of psychology*, E. G. Boring, H. S. Langfeld, and H. P. Weld (Eds.). New York: Wiley, p. 346.
Communication is the process by which an aggregation of men is changed into a functioning group. Moreover, the basic mode of communication is speech.

15. Nwankwo, R. L. (1973). Communication as symbolic interaction: a synthesis. *The Journal of Communication*, 23 [3], pp. 195–215.
. . . an interaction between a minimum of two symbolic systems . . .

16. Platt, J. H. (1955). What do we mean—"communication"?. *The Journal of Communication*, 5 (1), 21–26.
On the basis of what has been said thus far, let us define communication as being that process through which individuals observe stimuli and react in varying degrees to their perceptions of those stimuli through the drawing of inferences with or without observable concomitant physical responses.

17. Ruben, B. (1992). *Communication and human behavior*. New York: Prentice Hall, pp. 18–19.
Human communication is the process through which individuals in relationships, groups, organizations and societies create, transmit and use information to relate to the environment and one another.
Information is a coherent collection of data, messages, or cues organized in a particular way that has meaning or use for a particular human system.

18. Ruesch, J., and Bateson, G. (1951). *Communication: The social matrix of psychology*. New York: Norton, pp. 5–6.
Communication does not refer to verbal, explicit, and intentional transmission of messages alone. . . . The concept of communication would include all those processes by which people influence one another. . . . This definition is based upon the premise that all actions and events have communicative aspects, as soon as they are perceived by a human being; it implies, furthermore, that such perception changes the information which an individual possesses and therefore influences him.

19. Ruesch, J. (1957). Technology and social communication. In *Commu-*

nication Theory and Research, L. Thayer [Ed.]. Springfield, IL: Charles C. Thomas, pp. 452–481.
Communication is the process that links discontinuous parts of the living world to one another (p. 462).

20. Schacter, S. (1951). Deviation, rejection, and communication. *Journal of Abnormal and Social Psychology,* 46:190–207.
Communication is the mechanism by which power is exerted (p. 191).

21. Schramm, W. (1972). The nature of communication between humans. In *The Process and Effects of Mass Communication,* Schramm, E. and Roberts D. F. [Eds.], Urbana, IL: University of Illinois Press, p. 13.
Today we might define communication simply by saying that it is the sharing of an orientation toward a set of informational signs. . . . Communication is therefore based on a *relationship.*

22. Shannon, C. and Weaver, W. (1949). The mathematical theory of communication. Urbana IL: University of Illinois Press.
Weaver: The word *communication* will be used here in a very broad sense to include all procedures by which one mind may affect another. This, of course, involves not only written and oral speech, but also music, the pictorial arts, the theater, the ballet, and in fact all human behavior (p. 3).

Shannon: The fundamental problem of communication is that of reproducing at one point either exactly or approximately a message selected at another point (p. 31).

23. Sondel, B. (1956). Toward a field theory of communication. *The Journal of Communication,* 6:147–153.
The communication process is one of transition from one structured situation-as-a-whole to another, in preferred design (p. 148).

24. Stevens, S. S. (1950). A definition of communication. *The Journal of the Acoustical Society of America,* 22 [6], pp. 689–90.
Communication is the discriminatory response of an organism to a stimulus.

25. Thayer, L. (1968). Communication and communication systems. In *Organization, Management, and Interpersonal Relations.* Homewood, IL: Irwin, p. 17.
Thus, communication can be looked upon as one of two basic proc-

esses of all living systems—one, the transformation of food into energy; the other, the transformation of event-data into information. All living systems—people and organizations alike—exist only in and through these two basic processes.

Communication may thus be conceived of as the dynamic process underlying the existence, growth, change, the behavior of all living systems—individual or organization. Communication can be understood as that indispensable function of people and organizations through which the organization of the organism relates itself to its environment, and relates its parts and its internal processes to one another.

26. Wilson, E. O. (1975). Sociobiology. Cambridge, MA: Belknap/Harvard University Press, p. 176.

Biological communication is the action on the part of one organism [or cell] that alters the probability pattern of behavior in another organism [or cell] in a fashion adaptive to either one or both of the participants.

J. B. S. Haldane once said that a general property of communication is the pronounced energetic efficiency of signalling: a small effort put into the signal typically elicits an energetically greater response.

Appendix 1.3: Information in Relation to Communication

Information	Communication
Information can be objectively measured	Because individual interpretations are subjective, the perception of the message by the sender does not equal its perception by the receiver.
Information can have value.	The value of information is partially determined by the ability to communicate it.
Information can confer power.	The power of information is largely influenced by the power to limit communication.
Information can be consumed without destroying it.	Communication requires the expenditure of energy and takes place in a material environment.

Information can be treated as a thing, a single unit, and can be owned.	Information is so easily communicated, that one may transmit it without affecting the original.
Information can be sold as a commodity.	To purchase information, price and its potential value must be communication to the consumer.
Information can be packaged discretely and sold at varying prices.	The cost of distributing information depends mostly on the cost of communication.
Laws and other controls on access may limit distribution of information in and beyond the marketplace.	To limit access requires the prevention of communication.
Those who control information can deny it to those who do not have it.	Information can only be controlled when communication is controlled.

References

Anderson, M. P. (1959). What is communication. *The Journal of Communication, 9*(1), 5.

Artandi, S. (1973). Information concepts and their utility. *Journal of the American Society for Information Science, 24*(4), 242–45.

Ashby, W. R. (1964). *An introduction to cybernetics.* London, UK: Chapman and Hall.

Avery, C. (1959). What is communication? *Journal of Communication, 9*(1), 5.

Ayer, A. J. (1955). *What is communication?* London: Secker and Warburg.

Bates, B. J. (1990). Information as an economic good: A reevaluation of theoretical approaches. In B. D. Ruben & L. A. Lievrouw (Eds.), *Information and behavior* (pp. 379–94). New Brunswick, NJ: Transaction.

Belkin, N. J. (1975). Towards a definition of information for informatics. In V. Hornsell (Ed.), *Informatics 2* (pp. 50–56). London: ASLIB.

Belkin, N. J. (1978). Progress in documentation: Information concepts for information science. *Journal of Documentation, 34*(1), 58.

Belkin, N. J., & Robertson, S. E. (1976). Information science and the phenomenon of information. *Journal of the American Society for Information Science, 27*(4), 197–204.

Bennet, W. H. (1972). The role of debate in speech communication. *The Speech Teacher, 21,* 4 (November), 285 (footnote 19).

Berelson, B., & Steiner, G. (1964). *Human behavior: An Inventory of scientific findings.* New York: Harcourt Brace Jovanovich.

Borgman, C. L., & Schement, J. R. (1990). Information science and communication research. In J. M. Pemberton & A. E. Prentice (Eds.), *Information science. The interdisciplinary context* (pp. 42–59). New York: Neal-Schuman.

Boulding, K. (1984). Forword: A note on information, knowledge, and production.

In M. Jussawalla & H. Ebenfield (Eds.), *Communication and information economics: New perspectives* (pp. vii–ix). Elsevier Science Publishers.

Buckland, M. K. (1991). Information as thing. *Journal of the American Society for Information Science, 42*(5), 351–60.

Buckley, W. (1967). *Sociology and modern systems theory*. Englewood Cliffs, NJ: Prentice Hall.

Caesar, J. (50 B.C./1980). *The battle for gaul* (Wiseman, Anne & Wiseman, Peter, Trans.). Boston, MA: David R. Godine.

Caesaris, C. I. (50 B.C./1927). *Commentarii*. Lipsiae in Aedibus: B. G. Teubneri.

Campbell, J. (1982). *Grammatical man*. New York: Touchstone.

Cathcart, R. S. (1966). *Post-communication*. Indianapolis: Bobbs-Merrill.

Chamberlin, B. F., & Singleton, L. A. (1987). The law in an information society. In J. R. Schement & L. Lievrouw (Eds.), *Competing visions, complex realities: Social aspects of the information society* (pp. 121–39). Norwood, NJ: Ablex.

Checkland, P. (1981). *Systems thinking, systems practice*. New York: John Wiley & Sons.

Cherry, C. (1957). *On human communication* (1st ed.). New York: Wiley.

Cherry, C. (1966). *The communication of information*. New York: Holt, Rinehart, and Winston.

Dawkins, R. (1976). *The selfish gene*. New York: Oxford University Press.

Dewey, J. (1926). *Experience and nature*. New York: Norton.

Diener, R. A. V. (1989). Information science. What is it? . . . what should it be? *Bulletin of the American Society for Information Science, 15,* 5 (June/July), 17.

Ellsworth, P., & Ludwig, L. M. (1972). Visual behavior in social interaction. *Journal of Communication, 22*(4), 376.

Emery, E., Ault, P. H., & Agee, W. K. (1963). *Introduction to mass communication*. New York: Dodd, Mead.

Farradane, J. (1976). Towards a true information science. *Information Scientist, 10,* 91–101.

Fox, C. J. (1983). *Information and misinformation: An investigation of the notions of information, misinformation, informing, and misinforming*. Greenwood Press.

Fredkin, E., & Toffoli, T. (1982). Conservative logic. *International Journal of Theoretical Physics, 21*(3/4).

Gerbner, G. (1966). On defining communication: still another view. *Journal of Communication, 16,* 2 (June), 102.

Gover, R. S. (1970). Communication, communicative process, meaning: toward a unified theory. *Journal of Communication, 20*(2), 4–16.

Hayes, R. M. (1969). Education in information science. *American Documentation, 20,* 362–365.

Hirshleifer, J. (1973). Economics of information: Where are we in the theory of information? *American Economic Association, 63,* 2 (May), 31–39.

Hoben, J. B. (1954). English communication at Colgate re-examined. *Journal of Communication, 4,* 76–86.

Hoskovsky, A. G., & Massey, R. J. (1968). *Information science: Its end, means, and operations*. New York: ASIS.

Jussawalla, M. et al. (1988). *The cost of thinking: Information economics of ten pacific countries*. Norwood, NJ: Ablex.

Kirschenmann, P. P. (1970). *Information and Reflection: On some problems of*

cybernetics and how contemporary dialectical materialism copes with them.
New York: Humanities Press.

Krippendorff, K. (1977). Information systems theory and research. In B. D. Ruben (Ed.), *Communication Yearbook 1* (pp. 149–171). New Brunswick, NJ: Transaction-International Communication Association.

Lamberton, D. M. (ed.). (1971). *Economics of information and knowledge.* Harmondsworth, UK: Penguin.

Lancaster, F. W., & Gillespie, C. J. (1970). Design and evaluation of information systems. In C. Cuadra (Ed.), *Annual review of information science and technology: Volume 5* (pp. 33–70). Chicago, Il: Encyclopaedia Britannica.

Langefors, B., & Samuelson, K. (1976). *Information and data systems.* New York: Petrocelli/Charter.

Machlup, F. (1962). *The production and distribution of knowledge in the United States.* Princeton, NJ: Princeton University Press.

Machlup, F., & Mansfield, U. (1983a). Cultural diversity in studies of information. In F. Machlup & U. Mansfield (Eds.), *The study of information: Interdisciplinary messages* (pp. 3–59). New York: John Wiley & Sons.

Machlup, F., & Mansfield, U. (1983b). Semantic quirks in studies of information. In F. Machlup & U. Mansfield (Eds.), *The study of information: Interdisciplinary messages* (pp. 3–59). New York: John Wiley & Sons.

Machlup, F., & Mansfield, U. (Ed.). (1983c). *The study of information: Interdisciplinary messages.* New York: John Wiley & Sons.

Mackay, D. M. (1952). The nomenclature of information theory. In H. Von Foerster (Eds.), *Cybernetics: Transactions of the Eighth Congress* New York: Macy Foundation.

Meusel, H. (1893). *Lexicon caesarianum.* Berlin, Ger.: W. Weber.

Miller, G. A. (1951). *Language and communication.* New York: McGraw-Hill.

Miller, G. R. (1966). On defining communication: another stab. *Journal of Communication, 16,* 2 (June), 88–98.

Miller, J. G. (1965). Living systems. *Behavioral Science, 10,* 193–237.

Newcomb, T. M. (1966). *An approach to the study of the communicative acts.* New York: Holt, Rinehart, and Winston.

Nitecki, J. Z. (1985). The concept of information-knowledge continuum: Implications for librarianship. *Journal of Library History, 20,* 4 (Fall), 387–407.

Otten, K. W. (1975). Information and communication: A conceptual model as framework for the development of theories of information. In A. Debons & W. Cameron (Eds.), *Perspectives in information science* (pp. 127–48). Leyden: Noordhof.

Pierce, J. R. (1961). *Symbols, signals, and noise.* New York: Harper and Row.

Pratt, A. D. (1977). The information of the image. *Libri, 27,* 204–20.

Rapoport, A. (1966). What is information? In A. G. Smith (Ed.), *Communication and Culture* (pp. 41–55). New York: Holt, Rinehart and Winston.

Repo, A. J. (1989). The value of information: Approaches in economics, accounting, and management. *Journal of the American society for information science, 40*(2), 68–85.

Ruben, B. D. (1972). General systems theory: An approach to human communication. In R. W. Budd & B. D. Ruben (Eds.), *Approaches to human communication* (pp. 120–144). New York: Spartan.

Ruben, B. D. (1992). *Communication and human behavior* (3rd ed.). New York: Prentice Hall.

Ruben, B. D. (1992a). *Communication and Human Behavior*. New York:

Ruben, B. D. (1992b). The communication-information relationship in system-theoretic perspective. *Journal of the American Society for Information Science, [in press]*.

Ruben, B. D., & Kim, J. Y. (Eds.) (1975). *General systems theory and human communication*. Rochelle Park, NJ: Hayden.

Schramm, W. (1971). The nature of communication between humans. In W. Schramm & D. F. Roberts (Eds.), *The process and effects of mass communication* (pp. 3–53). Urbana, IL: University of Illinois Press.

Schramm, W., & Roberts D. F. (Eds.) (1971). *The process and effects of mass communication*. Urbana, IL: University of Illinois Press.

Schroder, H. M., Driver, M. J., & Streufert, S. (1967). *Human information processing*. New York: Holt, Rinehart and Winston.

Shannon, C. E., & Weaver, W. (1949). *The mathematical theory of communication*. Urbana, IL: University of Illinois press.

Simon, H. A. (1969). *The sciences of the artificial*. Cambridge, MA: MIT Press.

Thayer, L. (1968). *Communication and communication systems: In organization, management, and interpersonal relations*. Homewood, IL: Irwin.

Wiener, N. (1950). *The human use of human beings: Cybernetics and society*. New York: Avon Books.

Wiener, N. (1961). *Cybernetics, or control and communication in the animal and the machine* (2nd ed.). Cambridge, MA: MIT Press.

Wilson, E. D. (1975). *Sociobiology*. Cambridge, MA.: Belknap/Harvard University Press.

Wright, R. (1989). *Three scientists and their gods: Looking for meaning in an age of information*. New York: Harper & Row.

Yang, Q. Q. (1990). The law of information inconservation. Journal of the American Society for Information Science, *41*(6), 418.

Yovitz, M. C. (1975). A theoretical framework for the development of information science. In *Problems of information science* Moscow, USSR: VINITI.

2

A History of Information Theory in Communication Research

Everett M. Rogers and Thomas W. Valente

The present essay investigates the historical development of information theory, and traces its intellectual impact on the academic field of communication. Claude E. Shannon's information theory shaped the directions taken by the field of human communication, defined many of its concepts, and contributed to the intellectual integration of this field that arose from diverse multidisciplinary roots.

The present discussion centers on how communication scholars used Claude E. Shannon's information theory. The concept of information, while central to communication research, has been poorly constructed by communication scholars. This misconstruction and less-than-full appropriation of Shannon's information theory illuminates the relationship between communication and information in a historical light.

> "Rarely does it happen in mathematics that a new discipline achieves the character of a mature and developed scientific theory in the first investigation devoted to it. . . . So it was with information theory after the work of Shannon."
> —A. I. Khintchin

The purpose of the present essay is to investigate the historical development of information theory and to trace its intellectual impact on the academic field of communication. Claude Shannon's information theory, first published as two articles in the *Bell System Technical Journal* in 1948, is central to communication theory and research today, having shaped the directions taken by the field of human communication, defined many of its concepts, and contributed to the intellectual integration of this field that arose from diverse multidisciplinary roots.

The present discussion centers on how communication scholars used Claude Shannon's information theory. We conclude that the concept of information, while central to communication research has been poorly constructed by communication scholars. This misconstruction and less-than-full approporiation of Shannon's information theory helps us understand the relationship between communication and information in a historical light. We suggest directions for improving our understanding of the information/communication relationship.

Shannon's Information Theory

One of the most important turning points in the historical development of communication theory and research occurred when Claude E. Shannon proposed the concept of information in his two 1948 articles, which were republished in a book with Warren Weaver, *A Mathematical Theory of Communication* (Shannon & Weaver, 1949). As John R. Pierce (1973), the eminent Bell Labs communication engineer, said, "It is hard to picture the world before Shannon as it seemed to those who lived in it." Mark Kae (in his forward to McEliece, 1977, p. viii) stated, "We owe the genius of Claude Shannon the recognition that a large class of problems related to encoding, transmitting, and decoding information can be approached in a systematic and disciplined way: His classic paper of 1948 marks the birth of a new chapter on mathematics."

Information is patterned matter-energy that affects the probability of choosing a particular alternative in a decision-making situation (this definition is drawn from Rogers [1986], but based on Shannon's conceptualization). Shannon specified information as negative entropy, where entropy is the amount of uncertainty in a choice situation. Shannon developed an equation for information which is:

$$-\sum_{i=1}^{n} p_i \, log_2 \, p_i$$

where n is the number of possible alternatives and p_i is the probability of each alternative being chosen. Shannon realized that this equation is the negative of the equation for entropy. Entropy is the amount of uncertainty in a situation and is the centerpiece of the Second Law of Thermodynamics that physicists had been working with for decades.

The information of a source is computed with the above equation by determining the number of alternatives, and p, the probability of each alternative. For example, suppose there are sixteen boxes on a table, one of which contains a prize. If we are told that the prize sits in one of the eight boxes on the right, we have received one "bit" of information, since the information received reduces by one half the number of possible alternatives. Four "bits" of information are required to identify the location of the prize. The first "bit" reduces the number of possible boxes to eight, the second reduces it to four, the third reduces it to two and the fourth to one. Thus, the system is characterized by four bits of information. The equation above also yields four bits of information, with n equal to 16, and p equal to $\frac{1}{16}$, the information of the system is given as:

$$ -\sum_{i=1}^{16} .0625 \left(\log_2 (.0625) \right) = 4 $$

Shannon also provided (1) a universal measure of the concept of information, the binary digit or bit;[1] (2) a model of a linear communication process;[2] and (3) a series of twenty-three mathematical propositions about channel capacity. This composite intellectual contribution of Claude Shannon's is commonly referred to as "information theory," although Shannon (1949) mainly referred to it as "the mathematical theory of communication."[3]

Communication was defined by Weaver as "the process through which one mind influences another" (Weaver, 1949b, p. 3). So communication was viewed as intentional. A linear model of the components (source, message, transmitter, signal, noise, received signal, receiver and destination) of the communication process (see figure 2.1) was provided identically by Claude Shannon (1949, p. 34) and by Warren Weaver (1949b, p. 7).

How the several pieces of Shannon's composite intellectual contribution came together is important for understanding the ensuing impacts of information theory on the communication field in later decades.

Historical Background

Claude Shannon earned two bachelors' degrees at the University of Michigan, one in electrical engineering and one in mathematics. When he arrived for graduate work at MIT in 1936, the twenty-one-year-old Shannon worked as a research assistant to Vannever Bush, operating his differential analyzer machine (a kind of mechanical computer). Bush suggested to Shannon that he study the logical design of the machine for his masters' thesis. Shannon argued that electrical circuits could be laid

FIGURE 2.1
The Shannon Model of Communication

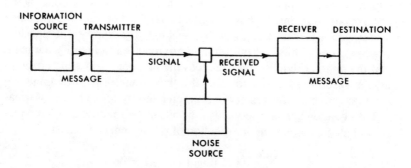

The components of this model are defined as (Shannon, 1948, p. 34): "The *information source* selects a desired *message* out of a set of possible messages . . . The *transmitter* changes the *message* into the *signal* which is actually sent over the *communication channel* from the transmitter to the *receiver* . . . The *receiver* is a sort of inverse transmitter, changing the transmitted signal back into a message, and handing this message on to the destination . . . In the process of being transmitted, it is unfortunately characteristic that certain things are added to the signal which were not intended by the information source . . . All of these changes in the transmitted signal are called *noise*."

Source: Claude E. Shannon and Warren Weaver (Eds.) (1949), *The Mathematical Theory of Communication* Urbana, University of Illinois Press, p. 7 and p. 34. Copyright 1949 by the Board of Trustees of the University of Illinois. Used by permission.

out according to Boolean principles in order to streamline the design of circuits and computers. Shannon's Masters' thesis was published in 1938, with immediate effects on the design of telephone systems. By 1939, Shannon was beginning to think about information in a statistical sense, and in measuring information in yes/no binary choices.

Shannon earned his Ph.D. degree in Mathematics at MIT in 1939, and then spent a year (1939–1940) as a National Research Fellow at the Institute for Advanced Study, Princeton University, studying mathematics and Boolean algebra with Hermann Weyl. During his year at the Institute for Advanced Study, Shannon was working on his information theory (Pierce, 1973), and he had the general idea of information theory in mind at MIT when he applied for the postdoctoral fellowship.[4] In 1940, Claude Shannon joined Bell Labs, where he worked on cryptography research.

The seeds of Shannon's information theory appeared first in a Bell Labs classified memorandum dated 1 September 1945, "A Mathematical Theory of Cryptography." It was declassified and published in a revised form after World War II as "Communication Theory of Secrecy Systems," in the *Bell System Technical Journal* (Shannon, 1949).

In 1948, in response to considerable urging from his supervisor and his colleagues,[5] Shannon published a two-part article in the *Bell System Technical Journal*. The articles appeared in the July and October, 1948 issues of the *BSTJ*, the in-house technical journal at Bell Labs, and represented the first publication of information theory (except for the 1945 classified memorandum mentioned previously).

A year later, in July 1949, Warren Weaver, an engineer and mathematician serving as a research administrator at the Rockefeller Foundation, published an article, "The Mathematics of Communication," in the magazine, *Scientific American*. Wilbur Schramm, the pioneering communication scholar then at the University of Illinois, learned of Shannon's important two-part series in the *Bell System Technical Journal* from Louis Ridenour, a physicist at the RadLab (Radiation Laboratory) at MIT during World War II and who in 1948 was dean of the graduate school at Illinois. Schramm was editor of the University of Illinois Press and he published an expanded version of the Weaver *Scientific American* article as a twenty-eight-page Part I, together with the two Shannon articles from the *Bell System Technical Journal* as a ninety-four-page Part II, in a composite book called *The Mathematical Theory of Communication* by Claude E. Shannon and Warren Weaver (1949). Part II is a word-for-word duplicate of the two *BSTJ* articles by Shannon, except for the correction of minor errata and the addition of some references. Also, the title of Shannon's Part II, and of the entire book, was changed from "*A* Mathematical Theory of Communication," to "*The* Mathematical Theory of Communication," a more ambitious title.

Weaver's Part I, "Recent Contributions to the Mathematical Theory of Communications," based on his 1949 *Scientific American* article, is primarily a discussion of how a human communication theory might be developed out of Shannon's mathematical theorems about engineering communication. Because of the very fundamental differences in content between the Weaver versus the Shannon parts of *The Mathematical Theory of Communication*, scholars should cite either Weaver or Shannon, unless referring to the entire book (Rogers, 1986, p. 86).[6] Weaver's contribution to the book was originally Part II, while Shannon's contribution was Part I. However, when the book was issued in paperback in 1964 the order was reversed, presumably to make the work more accessible to readers who found it more difficult to understand Shannon's highly mathematical style

(Stockanes, 11 December 1990). Accordingly, when the Shannon and Weaver book is cited by communication scholars, they usually are referencing ideas from Weaver's Part I rather than Shannon's Part II.[7]

Technical Communication Versus Human Communication

Claude Shannon was careful in limiting the applicability of his communication theory (Shannon, 1949):

> The fundamental problem of communication is that of reproducing at one point either exactly or approximately a message related at another point. Frequently the messages have meaning; that is they refer to, or are correlated according to, some system with certain physical or conceptual entities. These semiotic aspects of communication are irrelevant to the engineering problem. (P. 31)

So from the beginning Shannon did not claim that his model applied to human communication, the type of information-exchange in which an individual interprets the meaning of a message. Shannon said that his model was limited to "engineering" (or technical) communication, presumably to communication by such electronic channels as the telephone, telegraph, and radio. The process of human subjective interpretation obviously is also involved in engineering communication, but the mathematically inclined Shannon defined the meaning aspects of human communication as beyond the scope of his 1948/1949 conceptualization.

The engineering model of communication did not deal with emotions or attitudes, but just with strictly cognitive effects in which the receiver decoded a signal in a similar way to that in which it had been encoded by the source. Weaver, in his interpretation of the Shannon model, stressed that Shannon had limited his conceptualization to "engineering communication" (Weaver, 1949b):

> The word *information* in this [Shannon's] theory is used in a special sense that must not be confused with its ordinary usage. In particular, information must not be confused with meaning. In fact, two messages, one of which is heavily loaded with meaning and the other of which is pure nonsense, can be exactly equivalent, from the present viewpoints, as regards information. It is this, undoubtedly, that Shannon means when he says that 'The semiotic aspects of communication are irrelevant to the engineering aspects.' But this does not mean that the engineering aspects are necessarily irrelevant to the semiotic aspects. (P. 8)

Weaver (1949b, p. 4), in his introductory Part I of the Shannon and Weaver book, identified three levels of communication problems:

Level A: How accurately can the symbols of communication be transmitted? (the technical problem).
Level B: How precisely do the transmitted symbols convey the desired meaning? (the semantic problem).
Level C: How effectively does the received meaning affect conduct in the desired way? (the effectiveness or behavioral problem).

Shannon claimed that his mathematical theory of communication dealt only with Level A, which he called "engineering communication" or technical communication. Weaver, however, went far beyond Shannon's claims to suggest that "The mathematical theory of communication . . . particularly the more definitely engineering theory treated by Shannon, although ostensibly applicable only to Level A problems, actually is helpful and suggestive for the Level B and C problems" (Weaver, 1949b, p. 24). At another point in his essay, Weaver (1949b, p. 6) concluded, "The analysis at Level A discloses that this level overlaps the other levels more than one could possibly naively suspect. Thus the theory of Level A is, at least to a significant degree, also a theory of Levels B and C."

Warren Weaver thus invited the wide application of Shannon's information theory to all types of intentional communication. Weaver did not add much to the core conceptualizations of information theory, other than his optimistic broadening of its applicability. So it is appropriate to refer to *Shannon's* information theory, rather than to *Shannon and Weaver's* information theory.

Writing eight years after publication of his two articles on information theory, Claude Shannon (1956) in an article titled "The Bandwagon" stated:

> Information theory has, in the past few years, become something of a scientific bandwagon. . . . Applications are being made to biology, psychology, linguistics, fundamental physics, economics, the theory of organizations, and many other areas. In short, information is currently partaking of a somewhat heady draught of general popularity. (P. 3)

Shannon warned that such popularity carried an element of danger: "If, for example, the human being acts in some situations like an ideal decoder, this is an experimental and not a mathematical fact, and as such must be tested under a wide variety of experimental situations."

So Shannon warned the scientific world against applying his information theory (which he saw as limited to engineering communication) more broadly to all types of human communication. Nevertheless, communication scholars have done so, without paying attention to Shannon's warning. Now we evaluate each of the three main components of Shannon's theory.

Information Theory and Cryptography

As with most intellectual breakthroughs, Shannon's information theory grew out of previous work by him and by other mathematicians and engineers. In his two 1948 *BSTJ* articles on information theory, Shannon cited earlier scholars of information like H. Nyquist, R. V. L. Hartley, and Norbert Wiener. The immediate source of inspiration for Claude Shannon's information theory was his work on cryptography at Bell Labs during World War II. Shannon's theory of communication grew, paradoxically, out of organized attempts to intentionally *prevent* effective communication from occurring (that is, his work on cryptography).

In an oral history interview with Robert Price, Shannon (28 July 1982) explained how information theory and cryptography developed symbiotically in his work: "I started with Hartley's paper and worked at least two or three years on the problems of information and communications. That would be around 1943 or 1944; and then I started thinking about cryptography and secrecy systems. There is a close connection; they are very similar things, in one case trying to conceal information, and in the other case trying to transmit it." So Shannon's cryptography work paralleled his information theory. He had largely worked out both in the five years previous to the 1945 Bell Labs secret report of his cryptographic research (Ellersick, 1984; Shannon, July 28, 1982). Shannon had actually developed much of his information theory at home, on nights and weekends, during the 1940–1945 period. Presumably, this explains the complete surprise of John Pierce, Shannon's colleague at Bell Labs, when Shannon published his 1948 *BSTJ* articles (as mentioned in note 5).

Cryptography is the study of transforming vocal and written messages into a coded form, so that enemy forces cannot understand them. During World War II, considerable cryptographic research was conducted by both the Allied and Axis powers. Bell Labs was heavily involved in the United States' wartime activities, as might be expected, given its reputation as America's leading R&D center in electronics. During World War II, Bell Labs carried out 2,000 research projects for the U.S. military services, ranging from developing radar, sonar, the bazooka, bombsights, antiaircraft gun control systems, and the acoustic torpedo, to the cryptographic work on message security in radio, teletypewriter, and telephone systems (Fagan, 1978, p. ix). About 2,000 of Bell Labs' 2,700 engineering staff were assigned to military projects from 1942–45.

Researchers in England had considerable success in breaking the German coding system, before Claude Shannon and his Bell Labs co-workers began their cryptographic research. The German system used encoding machines to scramble military messages transmitted by radio to submarines, ships, and other distant forces. Alan Turing, the brilliant Cambridge University mathematician, working at the Government Code and Cipher School (GC & CS) at Bletchley Park (outside of London), designed an Ultra machine that deciphered Enigma, the German military code. Turing's success was one of the most important turning points in World War II, aiding the British in protecting their Atlantic convoys from German submarines, helping the British know in advance about the actions of Field Marshal Erwin Rommel's Afrika Korps, and aiding greatly in the Normandy invasion. The British success in cracking the German code had to be kept secret during World War II, or else the Germans would switch to another coding system.

In early 1943, Alan Turing made a secret trip to the Bell Labs headquarters building at 463 West Street in New York City, where Claude Shannon was working on cryptography problems (Bell Labs moved from Manhattan to three locations in New Jersey in 1949). Turing spent two months at Bell Labs in collaborative research on the problem of safely encoding vocal messages. Almost every day at teatime in the Bell Labs cafeteria,[8] Turing and Shannon would meet to discuss their ideas about the human brain and computers (Hodges, 1983, p. 249).

However, they could not directly discuss the specific cryptographic projects they were working on, as such work was compartmented into separated partitions, to ensure security (Shannon, 28 July 1982). Shannon told Turing about the bit, as a measure of information, and Turing told Shannon about his concept of the "deciban," defined as the weight of evidence that made something ten times as definite (Hodges, 1983, p. 250).

Cryptographic problems fit well with information theory. Shannon saw that the encoding of military messages into secret codes theoretically amounted to adding deceptive noise to the original messages. By using the appropriate equipment at the receiver end, the disguised message could be decoded by removing the noise (that is, if one understood how the noise had been generated at the encoding end of the process). So the classified cryptography research that Claude Shannon conducted at Bell Labs was a specific application of his emerging information theory. Given that Shannon was developing his information theory at the same time that he worked on cryptography, it is not surprising that he utilized such terms as "encoding" and "noise," in his communication model.

During Shannon's 1939–1940 postdoctoral year at Princeton, the eminent mathematician, John von Neumann, told Shannon that he should use the concept of entropy in his emerging information theory, as no one else really understood what this concept meant (Horgah, 1990). But Shannon says that he did not get the concept of entropy from either von Neumann or Turing (Ellersick, 1984). Shannon derived his equation for the amount of information, and found that it was identical to the formula that physicists use to calculate the quantity known as entropy in thermodynamics (Bello, 1953). Shannon realized that the communication of information was a statistical problem. That realization was fundamental to his information theory.

It was somewhat of an accident of timing that Shannon worked on cryptographic problems when he joined Bell Labs, just as the U.S. entered World War II in 1941. Shannon says, "During World War II, Bell Labs was working on secrecy systems. I'd worked on communication systems and I was appointed to some of the committees studying cryptanalytic techniques. The work on both the mathematical theory of communications and cryptology went forward concurrently from about 1941. I worked on both of them together and I had some of the ideas on one while working on the other. I wouldn't say one came before the other—they were so close together you couldn't separate them" (Shannon, quoted in Kahn, 1967, p. 744). The work on both Shannon's "Communication Theory of Secrecy Systems," published in 1949, and his 1948 "A Mathematical Theory of Communication" articles was substantially completed by about 1944.[9] Shannon continued to polish his information theory, and then, in 1948, he submitted his pair of articles to the *Bell System Technical Journal* (Kahn, 1967).

Shannon's important contribution in his 1949 journal article on secrecy systems was to show that redundancy provides the grounds for cryptanalysis (Kahn, 1967). The basis of codebreaking is to assume that the most frequent letters in a secret message are cipher equivalents of "e," "a," etc., and then to proceed to the least frequent letters. As the degree of redundancy of a coded message decreases, codebreaking becomes more difficult. Alternatively, more text is needed to crack a code if a message has lower redundancy (Kahn, 1967).

Intellectual Influences on Shannon's Information Theory

Shannon's work on cryptography problems at Bell Labs brought him into contact with two scholars, R. V. L. Hartley and H. Nyquist, who were major consultants to the cryptography research (Fagan, 1978, p. 316). Nyquist (1924) had shown that a certain bandwidth was necessary in order to send telegraph signals at a definite rate. Hartley (1928) had attempted to develop a theory of the transmission of information. He defined the quantity of information as the logarithm of the number of possible messages built from a pool of symbols.

Claude Shannon was aware of Norbert Wiener's work on cybernetics (Shannon cited Wiener's book in his two 1948 articles on information theory). Although Wiener's book on this topic was not published until 1949, his cybernetic theory had been made available earlier, during wartime, as a classified document dealing with antiaircraft gun control known as the "yellow peril" (the cover was yellow).[10] Wiener had recognized that the communication of information was a problem in statistics. Shannon had taken a mathematics course from Norbert Wiener while he was studying at MIT. and Shannon had access to the "yellow peril" report while he worked on cryptographic research at Bell Labs from 1941–1945.[11] Some observers credit Wiener with being a co-discoverer of information theory.[12] For example, Bello (1953) says: "To MIT's eminent mathematician, Norbert Wiener, goes the major credit for discovering the new continent [of information theory] and grasping its dimensions; to Claude Shannon of Bell Laboratories goes the credit for mapping the new territory in detail and charting some breath-taking peaks."

In Shannon's 1945 Bell Labs secret memorandum, "A Mathematical Theory of Cryptography," he used the word "alternative" for his binary choice measure of information. As mentioned previously, the word "bit" was suggested by John W. Tukey, a professor of mathematics and statistics at Princeton University since 1939, who has also worked concurrently for Bell Labs since 1946. The story goes that several Bell Labs researchers, probably including Shannon, were meeting over lunch in the Bell Labs cafeteria in late 1946, bemoaning the awkwardness of the term "binary digit." John Tukey joined the table. "With a characteristic grin, and equally characteristic down-East inflection, he asked, 'Well, isn't the word obviously *bit?*' And it was" (Brockway McMillan, quoted in Troop, 1984). Claude Shannon extended Tukey's use of the term bit to count the number of independent choices required to identify a unique entity among a certain population; Tukey had used bit in a more restricted sense as "the generic name of a coefficient in the expansion of a number as a sum of powers of a base" (Macmillan, quoted in Troop, 1984). In his 1948 articles on information theory, Shannon credits Tukey with suggesting the word "bit." A chronology of significant events in the development of information theory is presented in table 2.1.

Impacts of Shannon's Information Theory

Shannon's information theory spread widely throughout academic communities in the physical and social sciences. Not only did information theory spread, but its influence has been quite persistent as measured by citations to it (Dahling, 1962). Shannon's concept of information (measured with the entropy formula) was the most important of his contributions in the information theory.[13] Perhaps that is why his theory is usually

TABLE 2.1
A Chronology of Significant Events in the Development of Information Theory

Date	Event
1924	H. Nyquist publishes "Certain Factors Affecting Telegraph Speed" in the *BSTJ*.
1928	R. V. L. Hartley publishes "Transmission of Information" in the *BSTJ*.
1936	Shannon graduates from the University of Michigan and arrives at MIT.
1938	Shannon's Masters' Thesis in electrical engineering is published.
1939	Shannon earns a Ph.D. degree in mathematics at MIT.
1939–1940	Shannon holds a post-doctoral fellowship at Princeton's Institute for Advanced Study.
1940–1945	Shannon works at Bell Labs on cryptography, and on anti-aircraft gun control accuracy.
1943–1944	Alan Turing visits Bell Labs, and holds frequent discussions with Shannon.
1948	Shannon publishes "A Mathematical Theory of Communication" in *BSTJ*.
1949	Shannon publishes *The Mathematical Theory of Communication*, the University of Illinois Press.
1949	Shannon publishes "Communication Theory of Secrecy Systems" in the *BSTJ*.
1963	Paperback edition of *The Mathematical Theory of Communication* is published by University of Illinois Press.
1964	32,000 copies of *The Mathematical Theory of Communication* have been sold.

called "*information* theory," rather than "*communication* theory," the terminology that Shannon mainly used for it.

On the basis of citations to Shannon's information theory, Dahling (1962) noted that it was applied in disciplines ranging widely from biology to brain research to psychology. Horgah (1990) says that Claude Shannon wrote "the Magna Carta of the information age." Similar enthusiastic notices about information theory come from many other sources. For example, in a review of the accomplishments of Bell Labs in communication science from 1925 to 1980, Millman (1984, p. 46) says: "Probably the most spectacular development in communications mathematics to take place at Bell Laboratories was the formulation in the 1940s of information theory by C. E. Shannon."

"By treating information in clearly defined but wholly abstract terms, Shannon was able to generalize it, establishing laws that hold good not for a few types of information, but for all kinds, everywhere" (Campbell, 1982, p.17). This author continues "The wider and more exciting implications of Shannon's work lay in the fact that he had been able to make the concept of information so logical and precise that it could be placed in a formal framework of ideas'' (Campbell, 1982, p. 17).

Information theory came as a complete shock when it was first published: "While of course Shannon was not working in a vacuum in the 1940s, his results were so breathtakingly original that even the communication specialists of the day were at a loss to understand their significance. Gradually, as Shannon's theorems were digested by the mathematical/engineering community, it became clear that he had created a brand-new science . . ." (McEliece, 1977, p. 13). Indeed, it is true that Shannon's colleagues at Bell labs were surprised when he published his two articles in the *BSTJ* in 1948 (for example, Pierce, August 17, 1990, and as mentioned previously in note 5).

Looking backward at the first forty years of Shannon's theory, Verdú (1990) stated, "The revolutionary nature of Shannon's paper [the 1948 articles in the Bell System Technical Journal] was quickly recognized as a result of its amazing density of new ideas and its persuasive, easy-to-read style." Indeed an active band of electrical engineers and mathematicians have been advancing the research front of information theory in the years since 1948, producing a large and growing literature of books and journal articles. Many communication scholars who only know of Shannon's 1948 articles or, more likely, of the 1949 Shannon and Weaver book, would be surprised to learn how information theory has progressed in the four decades since 1948. Shannon is not only universally acknowledged as the unique father of information theory on the basis of his two 1948 *BSTJ* articles, but he also is "the most important post-1948 contributor to the subject! Nearly every one of his papers since 'A Mathematical Theory of Communication' has proved to be a priceless source of research ideas for lesser mortals" (McEliece, 1977, p.13). For example, a 1974 collection of the *Key Papers in the Development of Information Theory* (Slepian, 1974) consisted of twelve papers by Shannon, while no other author was represented more than three times.

In 1956, Claude Shannon was appointed the Donner Professor of Science at MIT. He continued to make important contributions to advancing information theory, following up on his earlier leads, until the mid-1960s, when he gradually withdrew from academic activities in the MIT departments of electrical engineering and mathematics, taking emeritus status early (at about age fifty).

Shannon's Impact on Communication Research

Shannon's one-way model of the communication act (see figure 2.1) helped set off the academic field of communication theory and research

(Rogers and Kincaid, 1981, p.33). This model, with certain modifications, provided a single, understandable specification of the main components in the communication act: Source, message, channel, receiver (or "SMCR," as Berlo [1960] termed it). Thus, communication investigations of the communication act could identify source variables (like credibility), message variables (like the use of fear appeals), channel variables (like mass media versus interpersonal channels), and receiver variables (like persuasability). The dependent variables in these early communication researchers were usually either (1) knowledge change on the part of receivers; (2) attitude change, or persuasion; or (3) overt behavior change like voting for a candidate or purchasing a product.

Thus it seemed facile to translate the Shannon (1949) model of communication into a general classificatory scheme for the variables included in early communication research by social scientists. The Shannon model's seeming simplicity made it attractive to communication scholars. Notice, however, that the dependent variables became communication effects on the part of the receiver, a development which went beyond Shannon's original focus on channel capacity as the dependent variable in his model. Two further modifications were made in Shannon's communication model by later human communication scholars:

1. The one-way model of a communication act was extended somewhat by adding feedback about the communication effects on the part of the receiver, to the source. Although Shannon did not originally use the concept of "feedback," per se, he did present a model of source-transmitter-receiver with a "correcting device" (Shannon, 1949, p. 68). Communication scholars like Berlo (1960) added, and indeed stressed, the concept of feedback in their models of human communication, influenced by Norbert Wiener's (1948) cybernetics theory.

2. The one-way conception of human communication was later modified further in communication models of convergence based on information-exchange among two or more participants. Berlo's (1977) incorporation of feedback into the communication process was a step in this direction. Rogers & Kincaid (1981, pp. 37–75) depicted communication as a process in which individuals act as "transceivers," both transmitting and receiving information in order to reach common understanding. Increasingly, communication has been viewed in communication models as a *process*, rather than as an act. This movement toward communication-as-process was a movement away from Shannon's model of communication.

Shannon's Twenty-Three Propositions

The third element of Claude Shannon's information theory is a set of twenty-three propositions about channel capacity. As Ritchie (1986) pointed out, Shannon's twenty-three theorems constitute "a general theory of *signal transmission*," not "a *communication* theory as students of human communication understand the term." The essence of Shannon's (1949) twenty-three propositions state relationships among such concepts as (1) channels with, and without, noise; (2) the entropy of a source; (3) channel capacity; and (4) discrete versus continuous information.

While Shannon's conceptualization of information has been widely used by communication (and other) scholars, and his model of communication has, with modification, been given very wide attention, his twenty-three propositions have almost been ignored by social science scholars of communication. A basic reason is because human communication scholars are not much interested in channel capacity (in comparison to engineers of one-way communication systems like radio, television, and, in Shannon's conception of the communication act, one-way telephony). Shannon's main dependent variable of channel capacity did not fit with communication scholars' primary interest in communication effects. Further, the arcane but elegant mathematical expression of the twenty-three propositions may have turned off many communication scholars.

Impacts of Information Theory on Communication Research

The late Wilbur Schramm, an important founder of the field of communication research, popularized Shannon's work on information theory to communication scholars in the 1950s. Schramm (1) published the Shannon and Weaver (1949) book while he was editor of the University of Illinois Press, as mentioned previously, (2) authored an article in *Journalism Quarterly* (Schramm, 1955) utilizing the bit as an information measure in communication research, and (3) encouraged his students at the University of Illinois to apply information theory to communication research. One of his Ph.D.'s, David K. Berlo, popularized a version of Shannon's model in his influential 1960 book *The Process of Communication*. Another Schramm student at the University of Illinois, Wilson Taylor, developed an information-type measure of readability called the "cloze procedure" (Taylor, 1953; 1956).

The full integrating potential of the concept of information, and its measure, the bit, has not been realized (1) in the field of communication research because the new communication paradigm was adopted by already—existing university departments of journalism and speech, thus dividing the emerging field of communication research into the mass communication and interpersonal communication sub-disciplines (Reardon & Rogers, 1989), respectively; nor (2) more broadly in the social sciences, where information theory promised a means of intellectual integration (McCormack, 1986)

Shannon's twenty-three propositions about channel capacity have not been tested in communication research, in part because they were expressed in highly mathematical form by Shannon (1949), which most social science-trained communication scholars did not easily understand. Further, research on channel capacity did not fit well with communication scholars' main interest in studying communication effects, as mentioned previously.

The one-way, linear model of communication proposed by Shannon headed the field of communication research, especially mass communication, toward an overwhelming focus on communication effects. The study of communication effects was also encouraged by Harold Lasswell's famous series of questions (*Who* says *what* to *whom* via *what channels* with *what effects*?), and by Paul F. Lazarsfeld's close alliances with media organizations like CBS Radio and Time-Life Corporation, who were among the sponsors of his research at Columbia University's Bureau of Applied Social Research in the 1940s and 1950s. This focus on effects has been questioned, and alternative models of communication (like convergence) have been proposed (for example, by Rogers & Kincaid, 1981).

Conclusions

In their review of communication theories, Severin with Tankard (1988, p. 42) stated, "The mathematical theory of communication has been the most important single stimulus for the development of other models and theories in communication." Shannon's information theory provided the root-paradigm for the field of communication theory and research. It is no accident that the first communication research institutes and the first doctoral degree-granting programs in U.S. universities began very shortly after publication of Shannon's information theory. In fact, the single most important institutionalizer of communication schools in U.S. universities, and one of the founders of the field of communication, Wilbur Schramm, also managed the publication of Shannon's theory in book form, and was an enthusiast for Shannon's theory.[14]

The influence of Shannon's theory on the emerging field of communication was tremendous. As Krippendorff (1988) stated:

> Within a few years of its publication the theory [Shannon's] provided the scientific justification for academic programs in human communication (which sprang up largely at U.S. universities), expanded communication research to new media, created novel areas of inquiry as well as two new

journals, and stimulated the development of new communication technology for handling knowledge, including computers. The theory became a milestone in communication research and marked the transition from an industrial to an information society. (P. 59).

In short, *Shannon's information theory became the dominant paradigm for the field of communication research.*

The intellectual influence of information theory on the field of communication, while strong and lasting, has not been entirely a positive factor. The strength of the influence is indicated by the overwhelming dependence of contemporary communication scholars upon such engineering concepts as receiver, noise, and feedback, and upon such cryptographic terms as "encoding" and "decoding." Shannon's model of communication, after certain changes and additions were made by communication scholars (such as the addition of feedback), headed communication scholars toward a one-way conceptualization of communication behavior and a focus on determining communication effects. Shannon's twenty-three propositions about channel capacity have largely been ignored by human communication scholars. Shannon's concept of information has been of pervasive influence on communication scholars, and several scholars have utilized an entropic measure in their research.

Once a paradigm is accepted by scholars in an academic discipline, it provides useful guidelines for future generations of scholars, removing uncertainty about what topics to study, how to study them, and how to interpret the research findings (Rogers, 1986; Kuhn, 1962). A paradigm can also be an intellectual trap, enmeshing scientists who follow it in a web of assumptions that they may not fully recognize. David K. Berlo, on looking back at his Ph.D. training at the University of Illinois in the 1950s, stated, "Like many of my colleagues, I simply did not understand the underlying assumptions and theoretical consequences of what I believed, and had not grasped the limited fertility of the research tradition in which I had been trained. I did not recognize that the assumptions underlying linear causal determinism may account for the major proportion of communication events, but not account for the proportion that makes a significant difference in our lives" (Berlo, 1977, p. 12). Berlo's 1960 book, *The Process of Communication,* was an important means of popularizing Shannon's communication model to students of human communication.

Berlo later recognized that human communication is often unintentional and nonlinear (Berlo, 1977):

An information-communication relationship may be directional as we conceive it, or it may not. If we look at the 'source' as intentional and initiatory and the 'receiver' as passive and a receptive container—e.g., if the message is stimulus and the effect is response—the relationship is directional. On the other hand, if the relationship is one in which both users approach the engagement with expectations, plans, and anticipation, the uncertainty reduction attributable to the contact may better be understood in terms of how both parties use and approach a message-event than in terms of how one person uses the contact to direct the other. (P. 20).

Today there is need for reconceptualization of the Shannon model of communication so as to reflect a definition of communication as process, to recognize that communication may be nonlinear and unintentional, and to facilitate other important research topics than just communication effects.

Finally, communication scholars interested in information theory should review the work that is currently being conducted on information theory. Communication engineers and mathematicians are actively pushing forward the research front of information theory (Verdú, 1990). The advances in engineering and mathematical information theory may be applied to human communication research today.

The authors thank Dr. Robert Price of the Raytheon Corporation, Boston, for his considerable help with the history of information theory.

Notes

1. The term "bit" as a synonym for binary digit was suggested to Shannon by John W. Tukey, a mathematician at Princeton University and Bell Labs, in late 1946 during a luncheon in the Bell Labs cafeteria (Troop, 1948).
2. Shannon's model of communication has commonly been called "linear" by communication scholars (for example, Rogers and Kincaid, 1981, p. 33), meaning one-way, from left-to-right. But to engineers, "linear" means noninteractive.
3. However, Shannon seems to have been the first person to use the term "information theory," in a September 1945 classified Bell Labs memorandum (Troop, 1984).
4. As indicated in a 1939 letter from Claude Shannon to Vannever Bush, reproduced in Hagemeyer (1979, pp. 504–5).
5. Dr. John R. Pierce, a colleague of Claude Shannon's in the same department at Bell Labs in 1948, described Shannon as brilliant, but having to be encouraged by his supervisor, Dr. Hendrik Bode, and his colleagues to publish his work (Pierce, 1990). This view of Shannon's work habits is corroborated by Dr. Richard W. Hamming (1990) and by others who were at Bell Labs. Campbell (1982, p. 20) quotes Pierce as saying that Shannon's theory "came as a bomb, and something of a delayed action bomb."
6. Thus we follow the suggestion of Ritchie (1986), who argues that one source of confusion on the part of communication scholars is "the habit of citing 'Shannon and Weaver' when it is Weaver's speculations that are being quoted,

under the assumption that they are somehow supported by Shannon's mathematics."

7. The Shannon Weaver book must be one of the most widely selling academic books ever published by a university press. About 51,000 copies were sold from 1949–1990, and the rate of sales continued at more than 600 per year in the past decade (Stockanes, 1990). Further, Shannon is cited 1,472 times in the Institute for Scientific Information data-base of scientific journal citations over the eighteen-year period from 1972 (when the ISI system began) through 1989. Shannon continues to be cited at about the same rate recently, as in earlier years. Shannon's total citations rank favorably with such other communication theorists as Carl Hovland, 1,327; Harold Lasswell, 1,462; Paul F. Lazarsfeld, 1,766; Robert E. Park, 1,472; Wilbur Schramm, 1,013; and Norbert Wiener, 1,267. So we conclude that Claude Shannon's work continues to be regarded as important by contemporary scholars.

8. Alan Turing was regarded as an idiosyncratic, brilliant individual by his colleagues (Hodges, 1983). During one of his teatime discussions with Claude Shannon in the Bell Labs lunchroom, Turing cleaned his fountain pen on his own white socks (Price, 1990).

9. In fact, certain elements of Shannon's information theory, such as the entropy formula and a version of his linear model, are contained in his 1949 article on "Communication Theory of Secrecy Systems," which is an unclassified revision of Shannon's (1945) Bell Labs memorandum, "A Mathematical Theory of Crypotography," which was still classified.

10. The "yellow peril" report was declassified after World War II and published in book form by Wiener (1949) as *Extrapolation, Interpolation, and Smoothing of Stationary Time Series*.

11. As Claude Shannon confirmed in a personal interview with Robert Price (Shannon, 1982). In fact, with two Bell Labs colleagues, Shannon in 1948, published a report that built on the yellow peril report by sidestepping Wiener's formidable mathematical difficulties (Millman, 1948, p. 43).

12. Norbert Wiener does not seem to have fully understood Shannon's information theory, even though he wrote a book review of the Shannon-Weaver volume. In his autobiography, *I Am a Mathematician*, Wiener (1956, p. 263) claimed credit with Shannon, for information theory: "Shannon loves the discrete and eschews the continuum. He considered discrete messages as something like a sequence of yeses and noes distributed in time, and he regarded single decisions between yes and no as the element of information. In the continuous theory of filtering, I had been led to a very similar definition of the unit of information, from what was at the beginning a considerably different point of view. In introducing the Shannon-Wiener definition of quantity of information (for it belongs to the two of us equally), we made a radical departure from the existing state of the subject."

13. A number of communication scholars have utilized an entropy-type measure in their research: Krull, Watt, and Lichty (1977); Finn (1985); Chaffee and Wilson (1977); Darnell (1970, 1972, and 1976); Rogers and Kincaid (1981, pp. 281–285); Taylor (1953, 1956); Schramm (1955); Watt and Krull (1974).
The entropy measure deserves more attention from communication scientists than it has received (Finn & Roberts, 1984).

14. Wilbur Schramm (1971, p. 7), writing twenty-three years after publication of Shannon's information theory, stated: "We felt that Shannon's information

theory was a brilliant analogue which might illuminate many dark areas of our own field.''

References

Bello, F. (1953). The information theory. *Fortune, 48*(6): 136–58.

Berlo, D. K. (1960). *The process of communication.* New York: Holt, Rinehart and Winston.

Berlo, D. K. (1977). Communication as process: Review and commentary. In B. D. Ruben (Ed.), *Communication yearbook 1.* New Brunswick, NJ: Transaction.

Campbell, J. (1982). *Grammatical man: Information, entropy, language, and life.* New York: Simon and Schuster.

Chaffee, S. H., & Wilson, D. G. (1977). Media rich, media poor: Two studies of diversity in agenda-setting. *Journalism Quarterly, 54,* 466–76.

Dahling, R. L. (1962). Shannon's information theory: The spread of an idea. In W. Schramm (Ed.), *Studies of innovation and of communication to the public.* Stanford, CA: Stanford University, Institute for Communication Research.

Darnell, D. K. (1976). Information theory. In D. K. Darnell & W. Brockiziede (Eds.), *Persons communicating* (pp. 210–23). Englewood Cliffs, NJ: Prentice-Hall.

Darnell, D. K. (1972). Information theory: An approach to human communication. In R. W. Budd & B. D. Rubin (Eds.), *Approaches to human communication* (pp. 156–69). New York: Spartan Books.

Darnell, D. K. (1970). Clozentropy: A procedure for testing English language proficiency of foreign students. *Speech Monographs, 37,* 36–46.

Fagan, M. D. (Ed.) (1978). *A history of engineering and science in the Bell system: National service in war and peace (1929–1975).* Murray Hill, NJ: Bell Telephone Laboratories.

Finn, S. (1985). Information-theoretic measures of reader enjoyment. *Written communication, 2*(4), 358–76.

Finn, S. & Roberts, D. F. (1984). Source, destination, and entropy: Reassessing the role of information theory in communication research. *Communication Research, 11,* 453–76.

Hagemeyer, F. W. (1979). *Die Entstehung von Infromationskonzepten in der Nachrichtentechnik: Eine Fallstudie zur Theoriebildung in der Technik in Industrie—und Kriegsforschung,* Ph.D. Thesis, Berlin, Free University of Berlin.

Hamming, R. W. (4 September 1990). Personal correspondence with Everett M. Rogers.

Hartley, R. V. L. (1928). Transmission of information. *Bell System Technical Journal, 7,* 535–63.

Hodges, J. (June, 1990). Claude E. Shannon: Unicyclist, juggler, and father of information theory. *IEEE Information Theory Society Newsletter* (This profile also appeared in the January, 1990, issue of *Scientific American*).

Kahn, D. (1967). *The codebreakers: The story of secret writing.* New York: Macmillan.

Khintchin, A. I. (1956). On the fundamental theorems of information theory. *Uspekhi Matematicheskikh Nauk, 9,* 54–63.

Krippendorff, K. (1988). Claude Shannon (1916–). In E. Barnouw & others (Eds.) *International Encyclopedia of Communication* (pp. 59–61). New York: Oxford University Press.

Krull, R., Watt, J. H., Jr., & Lichty, L. W. (1977). Entropy and structure: Two measures of complexity in television programs. *Communication Research, 4*(1), 61–86.

Kuhn, T. S. (1962). *The structure of scientific revolutions.* Chicago: University of Chicago Press.

Lasswell, H. D. (1948). The structure and function of communication in society. In L. Bryson (Ed.) *The communication of ideas* (pp. 37–51). New York: Harper.

McCormack, T. (1986). Refections on the lost vision of communication theory. In S. J. Ball-Rokeach & M. G. Cantor (Eds.), *Media, audience, and social structure* (pp. 34–42). Newbury Park, CA: Sage.

McEliece, R. J. (1977). *The theory of information and coding: A mathematical framework for communication.* Reading, MA: Addison-Wesley.

Millman, S. (Ed.) (1984). *A history of engineering and science in the Bell system: Communication sciences (1925–1980).* AT&T Bell Laboratories.

Nyquist, H. (1924). Certain factors affecting telegraph speed. *Bell System Technical Journal, 3,* 324.

Peters, J. D. (1986). Institutional sources of intellectual poverty in communication research. *Communication Research, 13*(4), 527–559.

Pierce, J. R. (1973). The early days of information theory. *IEEE Transactions on Information Theory, IT-19,* 3–8.

Pierce, J. R. (17 August 1990). Personal interview with Everett M. Rogers at Stanford University.

Price. R. (8 October 1990). Personal correspondence with Everett M. Rogers.

Reardon, K. K., & Rogers, E. M. (1988). Interpersonal versus mass media communication: A false dichotomy? *Human Communication Research, 15*(2), 284–303.

Ritche, D. (1986). Shannon and Weaver: Unravelling the paradox of information. *Communication Research, 13,* 278–98.

Rogers, E. M. (in process), *History of communication theory and research in the United States.*

Rogers, E. M. (1986). *Communication technology: The new media in society.* New York: The Free Press.

Rogers, E. M., & Kincaid, D. L. (1981). *Communication networks: Toward a new paradigm for research.* New York: Free Press.

Schramm, W. (1955). Information theory and mass communication. *Journalism Quarterly, 32,* 131–46.

Schramm, W. (1971). The nature of communication between humans. In W. Schramm & D. F. Roberts (Eds.), *The process and effects of mass communication* (2nd ed.) (pp. 3–53). Urbana, IL: University of Illinois Press.

Severin, W. J., with Tankard, J. W., Jr. (1988). *Communication theories: Origins, methods, uses.* (2nd ed.). New York: Longman.

Shannon, C. E. (1 September 1945). A mathematical theory of cryptography, New York: Bell Laboratories, Classified Memorandum.

Shannon, C. E. (1948). A mathematical theory of communication. *Bell System Technical Journal, 27,* 379–423, 623–56.

Shannon, C. E. (1949). Communication theory of secrecy systems. *Bell System Technical Journal, 28*(4), 656–715.

Shannon, C. E. (1949). The mathematical theory of communication. In C. E. Shannon & W. Weaver (Eds.), *The mathematical theory of communication,* Urbana, IL: University of Illinois Press.

Shannon, C. E. (1956). The bandwagon. *IRE Transactions on Information Theory,*
    2(3), 3.
Shannon, C. E. (28 July 1982). Tape-recorded personal interview by Robert Price,
    Boston.
Shannon, C. E., & Weaver, W. (1949). *The mathematical theory of communication.*
    Urbana, IL: University of Illinois Press.
Slepian, D. (Ed.) (1974). Key papers in the development of information theory.
    IEEE Press. New York.
Stockanes, H. P. (17 October 1990). Personal Correspondence with Everett M.
    Rogers.
Taylor, W. L. (1953). 'Cloze procedure': A new tool for measuring readability.
    Journalism Quarterly, 30, 415–33.
Taylor, W. L. (1956). Recent developments in the use of cloze procedure. *Journal-
    ism Quarterly, 33,* 42–48.
Troop, H. S. (1984). Origin of the term *bit. Annals of the history of computers,*
    6(8), 152–55.
Verdú, S. (September 1990). The first forty years of the Shannon theory. *IEEE
    Information Theory Society Newsletter,* pp. 1, 4–10.
Watt, J. H., & Krull, R. (1974). An information theory measure for television
    programming. *Communication Research, 1,* 44–68.
Weaver, W. (1949a). The mathematics of communication. *Scientific American, 181,*
    11–15.
Weaver, W. (1949b). Recent contributions to the mathematical theory of communi-
    cation. In C. E. Shannon & W. Weaver (Eds.), *The Mathematical Theory of
    Communication.* Urbana, IL: University of Illinois Press.
Wiener, N. (1948). *Cybernetics, or control and communication in the animal and
    the machine.* New York: Wiley.
Wiener, N. (1949). *Extrapolation, interpolation, and smoothing of stationary time
    series.* New York: Wiley.
Wiener, N. (1956). *I am a mathematician: The later life of a prodigy.* Cambridge,
    MA: MIT Press.

3

The Impact of a Native Theory of Information on Two Privileged Accounts of Personhood

Hartmut B. Mokros

This paper discusses the nature of a native or everyday theory of information that views information as thinglike—objective and referential—and thereby discounts the inherently relational and socially constituted nature of information. It is argued that this theory implicitly and detrimentally influences privileged understandings of communication process and human agency. Empirical examples of the consequences of this implicit theory on privileged accounts of personhood are examined in two contexts: psychiatric evaluation and diagnosis and the interpretation of individual differences in the expression of nonverbal behavior.

For students of human communication, information has and continues to represent a central construct. This is readily apparent in several of the major theoretical distinctions introduced by studies of communication, such as between sender and receiver, encoding and decoding, signal and noise, all of which reference information for their understanding. It is not merely within the field of communication that information has achieved a privileged status. Indeed, information has become an increasingly central concept in the social sciences as well as in everyday discourse in the course of this century such that it may now be viewed as a central organizing metaphor for the understanding of a variety of disparate phenomena. For example, psychological explanation currently favors a conceptualization of the human mind as an "information processor." Simultaneously, macrosocial accounts have emphasized the significance of information for Western societies such that they may be said to have passed into an "information age." Within the information society, "information work" is said to define the activities of an ever-increasing social constituency with the ability to, knowledge of, and right to access information pivotal for understanding competent social agency and also the moral and ethical imperatives of what is increasingly identified as a new order.

It is then not coincidental that renewed scholarly interest has targeted an understanding of the role of information within communication as a focal theoretical concern (Ruben, 1992). The vigor of this interest was apparent at the 1991 International Communication Association Meeting in Chicago where an entire day was devoted to a session entitled "Information: A Root Concept for Communication" with some of the more prominent voices within the field of communication participating.

Several approaches to the conceptualization and study of the relationship between information and communication have been proposed. One approach has been to examine the interconnections between the fields of communication and information science by looking either at the overlap of citations in these fields (e.g., Rice, 1990) or the conceptual relationships between fields (e.g., Ruben, 1989; Schement, Botan, Ruben, & Lee, 1990). Because of its emphasis on the analysis of disciplinary integrity and interdependence this approach tends to sidetrack rather than focusing directly on issues of the relationship between information and communication. Communication and information are after all far from limited as phenomena of interest to the disciplines that claim them as their subjects. An alternative approach directly focuses on the interrelationship between communication and information within the context of human symbolic activity (e.g., Mokros & Ruben, 1991; Mokros & Lievrouw, 1991) without explicit concern with definitional and disciplinary issues. The aim of this paper is to contribute to this second orientation through a consideration of how research-based perceptions of persons are strongly shaped by a narrow and ideologically motivated conception of information.

Specifically, this paper argues that a "native" or everyday view or model of information in social interaction, which conceives of information as thinglike (e.g., Schement & Mokros, 1989) and thereby privileges objective, that is to say, referential information, leads to a discounting of the inherently relational, constructivist, socially based, or communicative nature of information. Empirical examples are considered to illustrate how the assumption of the thingness of information creates problematic understandings of human agency in two contexts; within the context of psychiatric evaluation and diagnosis and research of nonverbal and interpersonal communication.

Native Theory

Native models or theories refer to those conceptualizations of the universe implicit in the activities—in speech and action—of members of a cultural group. It is assumed that cultural agents have available to them understandings of all those phenomena that privileged systems such as physical sciences, social sciences, humanities, and the like claim as their phenomenological domain. This implies the existence of native psychological theories, native linguistic theories, native communication theories, native physics, and the like.

Discussions of native theory are of course not at all new. Anthropologists have traditionally, and more recently with the turn toward an emphasis on cognitivist accounts, studied native theories as for example in the work of D'Andrade (1976) on American beliefs about illness. Native awareness of such culturally grounded theories varies potentially along a continuum such that we may speak of implicit and explicit native theories. If native awareness of those theories that structure experience varies, it should then be possible to observe the native's scrutiny and evaluation of such theory as it approaches consciousness, and thus becomes explicit. One example of this is in recent years has been debate over the disenfranchising consequences of native gender theory in its structuring of social roles and expectations.

Privileged theories, particularly those associated with the positivist scientific tradition, have seen as their goal the replacement of native theories with more valid renderings of reality, assuming thereby a reality independent of social construction (Gergen, 1985). It is, however, possible that native theories pose questions and offer explanations that transcend the qualities of privileged theories. Such a perspective was recently offered by Jerome Bruner (1990) in his suggestion that "folk psychology" identifies issues of relevance to the understanding of human cognition that have been largely neglected by cognitive psychology. Nonetheless without critical examination of the consequences either poses for individuals and the social order by accepting the assumptions underlying such theories there is as much danger in romanticizing native theories as there is in assuming the greater veracity of privileged theories.

Although many scholars have argued that privileged theories are themselves constructed within native theoretical frameworks out of awareness of researchers (e.g., Bourdieu, 1977; Foucault, 1972; Semin & Gergen, 1990), concerns with the significance and consequences of this observation are largely repressed or denied by those researchers who view knowledge as a matter of discovery. It is precisely this issue, namely the impact that implicit native theory has on the development of privileged accounts of the nature of information about persons in social interaction that provides the focus of this paper.

Language and Native Theory

Scholars from a variety of perspectives have long argued that language systems themselves not only reveal but serve to implicitly structure native mental life (e.g., Lakoff & Johnson, 1980; Mead, 1934; Silverstein, 1979; Vygotsky, 1962; Wittgenstein, 1963; Whorf, 1956). This implies that no matter what the substantive nature of a native theory may be it is in some sense conditioned by the language employed by its culture. That is to say, constraints on the conceptualization and expression of activity reside within the possibilities provided by language, the most powerful semiotic system by which we analyze and construct experience. For example, as Hanson (1958) suggested there are classes of verbs that implicate causality. Thus, although a verb like "poison" identifies an action it also implicates consequences (or is "causally loaded" as Heise [1979] puts it) of that action, namely death or illness. Indeed one might think that linguistic propositional slots of agent, patient, and predication both condition and are conditioned by the possibilities of a native physics in that they presuppose the naturalness of linear causality. In this spirit, Whorf (1956) illustrated how dimensions of space and time built into grammatical systems are culturally specific. The implications of this are indeed profound since they suggest that physical concepts that we tend to perceive as primordial or panhuman, and basic to many privileged theories, are not "natural" at all. Instead they are cultural artifacts that achieve their primordial status for members of a culture by virtue of the linguistic grammars within which they are contained. These grammars, in use, continuously reference the physical categories that structure them, such as space, time, and causality, and thereby implicitly reinforce a taken for granted structure of reality that they project.

Lakoff and Johnson (1980) have explored the metaphoric qualities of everyday language use arguing that such metaphors express what is here called native theory. For example, orientational metaphors are reported to organize a variety of seemingly disparate concepts, such as emotions, consciousness, health, and status (Lakoff & Johnson, 1980, pp. 14–21). Thus, happy is up and sad is down (e.g., "I'm feeling up today" as opposed "I'm down in the dumps"); conscious is up and unconscious is down (e.g., "I woke up" as opposed to "I fell asleep"); health is up and illness is down (e.g., "I'm in top shape" as opposed to "I came down with a cold"); and, high status is up and low status down (e.g., "I climbed to the top of my profession" as opposed to "I fell from grace"). Such metaphoric consistencies reveal as well as condition the conceptual structuring of reality of everyday life.

A lack of native awareness of the complexity that language use entails may also be seen in attitudes toward the function of talk. Halliday (1973) suggests that we may think of at least seven different functions. Talk is instrumental, providing a means of satisfying wants and needs. Talk is regulatory, by which we control the actions of others and are ourselves controlled. Talk is interactional in the sense that it expresses relationship, a sense of self and other as products of and roles in social action. Talk has a personal function in that it expresses and creates self-identity. Talk is heuristic, a means by which we learn about and describe the world. Talk is imaginative that allows for both aesthetic possibilities as well as hypothetical constructions. Finally talk is representational, that is, done to inform others.

Yet it is representational or referential talk that is valued as talk—it is the native ideological standard of talk. We see this in a variety of ways. The emphasis on the dictionary as the standard for understanding language that achieves its acme in efforts toward the development of standard speech or a standard language as in the Esperanto movement is the most pronounced expression of this referential view of language. The impetus for such development holds a parsimonious, efficient, culture-free system of expression and exchange, devoid of ambiguity in use, as an ideal. Efforts toward the development of a thing-language of science in the project of an international unified science (Morris, 1938) posit as similar outlook. It is curious how positivistic science, which has traditionally been suspicious of everyday understandings of reality, holds a view of language that parallels native theory. For both, everything is ideally explicitly defined precisely because reality is assumed explicitly definable. To put it in the framework provided by the philosopher Charles Taylor (1991), language is here viewed as a tool toward the enframing of reality rather than as constitutive of reality.

Information as Thing

Native theories of language pose important consequences for both everyday and privileged accounts of information in human communication. Privileged accounts of social interaction, commonly view information as something that can be decoded and encoded, stored and recalled, received and transmitted, whereas communication is thought of as the act or process of transmission and reception, of exchange. Apparent in these accounts is the implicit assumption that information has substance, is thinglike. This assumption is reinforced by the nature of the view of communication as process (in a very simplistic sense), wherein process identifies a linear flow from sender to receiver, essentially the communication model proposed by Shannon and Weaver (1949). We might say that their model of the communication-information relationship is the formalization as scientific theory of the implicitly held native model of communication. It is a model driven by information, one that reduces communication process to a simple linear representational, referential process. It is a theory of communication that formalizes the conduit metaphor that is the heart of the native view of communication (Reddy, 1979). The conduit metaphor views language use or communication to involve the placement of ideas, viewed as objects, into words, viewed as containers for ideas that are then sent along a conduit to a hearer who then takes the objects (ideas) out of their containers (words). Reddy suggests that the majority of expressions of talk about the nature of talk he has analyzed are structured by the conduit metaphor. Although this is viewed as a native communication theory, it clearly privileges things over process—information over communication. Basic to the conduit metaphor is the notion that real, thinglike objects are exchanged in communication, objects which are increasingly referred to as information in both everyday and privileged use.

Schement (e.g., Schement & Mokros, 1989) has suggested that the evolution of the assumption of information as thing is traceable to the development of abstract writing systems, as a socially constructed product. However, to focus merely on the evolution of the thingness view of information to its powerful status in contemporary society ignores consideration of the consequences this assumption has had on the shaping of human experience. For one, the creation of writing systems, which in effect led to the freezing of language, made possible the emergence of a standard against which speech and future writing could be evaluated. Thus, writing systems make possible evaluation in a very new sense, and make possible debates over right and wrong ways to speak the language, and thereby introduce a standard for grading and evaluating individuals and social groups.

As has been suggested our native linguistic theory may most centrally be viewed as a dictionary-based or lexicon theory of language that holds that language production is the stringing together of words, words that are things that stand for things "out there." Lexicons describe material contents and their connections. The centrality of the dictionary for the native's understanding of his language is the most central manifestation of the thinglike view of language. As Silverstein (1979) puts it in his analysis of the relationship between language structure and linguistic ideology,

> Were I to begin by observing that 'Webster's dictionary defines ideology as . . . ,' you would have an example of a very common American linguistic ideology [i.e., native theory] in action. It would be the rhetorical appeal to the published dictionary as the codified authority on what words *really* mean. Even the whimsical force of such rhetoric rests on a large set of rationalizations about the nature of the dictionary's authority in such matters. Part of our educational establishment—and especially the publishers—encourage it as much as possible. (P. 193)

Specialized courses, recordings, and books designed to improve one's vocabulary along with those that offer remediative efforts to change one's style of pronunciation as a pathway to an upgrade in social status further illustrate how words are treated as possessions and regarded as the central elements of language. Heuristics learned as children for the translation of English speech into written form, as in "i before e except after c" are treated as authoritative accounts rather than as rationalizations that presuppose the written as a standard. Finally, the emphasis parents place on the utterance of a child's first words as a first index of linguistic competence further underscores the pervasiveness of the native theory.

This native theory with its emphasis on the word has, moreover, tended to develop grammars, as they have been made conscious in our schools and homes, that tend to emphasize the primacy of the referential, descriptive, and instrumental functions of language, at the expense of others (e.g., poetic, evocative, metalinguistic, social relational). Additionally slighted by native theory is that, as Whorf (1956) and Sapir before him argued, meaning is not to be found in words themselves but in the rapport established between words and the context of their use. As Whorf put it,

> 'common sense' is unaware that talking itself means using a complex cultural organization, just as it is unaware of cultural organizations in general. Sense or meaning does not result from words or morphemes but from patterned relations between words or morphemes. Isolations of a morpheme, like 'John!' or 'Come!' are themselves patterns or formulas of a highly specialized type, not bare units. . . . Apparent isolations of words in a vocabulary list also derive what meaning they have from the patterned 'potentials of linkage,' which ramify from them and connect them with complex patterns of linguistic formulation. (P. 67)

Vygotsky (1962) similarly pointed out that words are not mere labels for objects out there but are instead themselves conceptlike, only understandable in relation to other words, and always triggering much more than they at first appear to denote. The writings of Wittgenstein (1953), and his account of language as gamelike, and those of Austin (1962) and his emphasis on the performative basis of speech in use and Searle (1969) with his account of speech acts, may all be seen as reactions against a native theory of language that views the activity of speaking as describing reality rather than as constituting reality.

Thingness and Intentionality

An extension of the thingness assumption is an additional assumption that views communication as a motivated or intentional activity. Thus, students of communication (e.g., Lyons, 1977) and particularly some of the foremost students of nonverbal communication, a field within which conjecture as to the relationship between information and communication has occupied a notable theoretical niche (e.g., Burgoon, 1985; Ekman & Friesen, 1969; MacKay, 1972; Wiener, Devoe, Rubinow, & Geller, 1972), urge a distinction between communicative and informative actions where communicative actions are purposefully encoded with the intent of saying something to someone while informative acts are leakages of behavior that may be decoded by others as saying something about their source or sender but are not produced with an intent to inform. For Goffman (1953) this was a distinction between "the given" and "the given off." Thus, actions that are communicative ("the given") are distinct from mere information ("the given off") in that they incorporate motives. Given this assumption, communication is then viewed as sender based whereas information is viewed as receiver based. Yet to make necessary an intentionality valence if information is to be viewed as communicative reinforces the view of communication as primarily a referential activity. Thus, aside from a view of information as thinglike there is the corollary assumption that "true" communication involves the exchange of things valenced by an intent to be exchanged.

Whereas assumptions of thingness appear based in native linguistic theory the intentionality assumption suggests a link to native psychological theory. The contributions of Freud indicated that native psychological theory tends to deny the unconscious, or at the very least to view activities that are produced out of our awareness as expression of being out of control, as irrational. Likewise the non-Freudian sense of the unconscious, one based on systems of economy as discussed by Sapir (1949) is also largely outside of native awareness. "Communication" in the popular sense, where the qualifier "effective" is typically if not implicitly linked to the term, is viewed as a rational and conscious activity. Consider for example a common statement I see in papers from undergraduate communication students: "the [verbal] conflict between them was little more than a prolonged and continuous lack of communication." Intentionality and rationality are intimately equated. For the assumption that communication involves intentional and efficient message exchange is really but an extension of the basic thingness assumption of information in that it presupposes a view of communication in terms of a one-to-one correspondence between some reality and the symbolic representation of that reality in communicative messages.

It is also well worth considering how the power of this implicit privileging of a thingness view of information based in native linguistic theory is intimately related to other dimensions of native ideology, particularly gender ideology. It would be of interest to explore to what extent information is identified with attributes of maleness such as rationality, instrumentality, and autonomy, while communication is identified in terms of female relational attributes. It is after all of no small interest that male-female relationships are often ones that come to loggerheads over a "lack of communication," with females wanting more of it and males presented as incapable of adequately so doing (Tannen, 1990). As a consequence of this ideological linkage our very understandings of communication are skewed toward viewing communication in information terms that emphasize rationality, efficiency, and effectiveness, and define communication as a conduit that transports or a mechanism that gives rise to information. Just as social ideology surrounding gender has tended to devalue women, and reinforced the naturalness of male privilege, so also may we view the consequences of a native theory that has defined information as thing as leading to the denigration of communication and a highly skewed understanding of the relationship between communication and information. Given this line of analysis, it is possibly then not coincidence that the recent surge of interest in communication processes by information scholars within the context of their rethinking of the centrality of an objective view of information (e.g., Dervin, 1981; Neil, 1987) has occurred at the very same time that feminist scholars in particular have been challenging the "naturalness" of social structuring in terms of traditional gender ideology (Gilligan, 1982).

Information as Thing Assumption and Privileged Representations of Persons

The remainder of this paper examines the consequences of the native view of information as thing on privileged accounts of persons. To this end two examples of how in contexts of both everyday communication and research of communication the thingness assumption introduces the potential for the development of problematic conclusions about human beings when the aim is to make inferences about either the state or trait characteristics of persons. The first context is that of psychiatric diagnosis, with particular reference to child psychiatric diagnosis of depression. The second context is taken from the study of nonverbal behavior in get-acquainted encounters. Both of these contexts represent substantive areas of research interest for me. The examples are intended to be that: not formal presentations of results but examples to make the point.

Information as Thing in Psychiatric Diagnosis

Psychiatry is concerned with disorders of emotion and thought, and has traditionally relied on communication to identify such disorders as well to remediate them. That is, the primary methods of evaluation are through interview and observation of the communicative behavior of the patient, and although pharmacological intervention has become increasingly widespread, various forms of talk therapy still represent the primary mode of intervention for those who seek treatment from psychiatrists and allied mental health professionals. Moreover, several significant theories have made communicative dysfunction the nexus for understanding the etiology of such psychiatric disorders as schizophrenia (Bateson, Jackson, Haley, Weakland, 1956) and eating disorders (Minuchin, Rosman, & Baker, 1978). However, the reliance on communication has been a source of dissatisfaction for many psychiatrists, particularly those associated with what is now commonly referred to as the biological revolution in psychiatry.

Conventional social science methodology views concerns with validity and reliability as central. Indeed, the conceptualization of validity and reliability, of their measurement, and approaches to their maximization are among the most enduring developments of the social sciences to date. Psychiatry, as a discipline has over the past thirty years become exceedingly concerned with issues of reliability and validity. Thus, the emphasis on the development of standardized evaluation instruments and structured classification criteria since the early 1970s has been viewed as major advances in that these developments have led to a reduction of informant and criterion variance. This has made possible the identification of homogeneous subgroups of patient populations and thereby the development of disciplined research of diagnostic entities. Structured diagnostic criteria such as those contained in the DSM-III-R (American Psychiatric Association, 1987), invoke a common understanding of what is meant by a disorder like depression and thereby are felt to encourage scientific research and discourse because they establish a basis for consensual agreement as to what defines a case of disorder. Similarly, the use of standardized assessment instruments (interview based or self-report) which now include standardized elicitation procedures, criteria for evaluating symptom information, and delineation of the symptom domain that must necessarily be assessed in considering a diagnosis encourages consensual agreement.

However, the use of structured criteria and standardized instruments does not guarantee the quality of data generated in the process of diagnostic evaluation or therefore the validity of the diagnosis achieved. Indeed, a central assumption of the use of standardized approaches to diagnostic evaluation is the conviction that the patient or "informant" providing the physician with symptom information is able to provide information consistent with the physician's definition of what the disorder in question might be. This is an issue of establishing shared meaning. It is the physician's task in her interaction with the informant to attempt to establish a shared meaning system that is anchored to her theoretical model of disease. Thus, in order to identify that a patient is clinically depressed, for example, it is necessary to ascertain whether the patient's descriptions of malaise are consistent with the physicians working definition of depression.

Once shared meaning is assumed to have been established the psychiatrist then rates the information obtained from the informant as to whether it provides evidence of symptom presence. Table 3.1 provides the anchors and their definitions for presence of dysphoric or depressed mood, one of the symptoms defining clinical depression from two of the most prominently used instruments in research of childhood and adolescent depression. The first is taken from the Children's Depression Rating Scale-Revised (CDRS-R: Poznanski, Freeman, & Mokros, 1985) a semistructured

TABLE 3.1
Ratings of Dysphoric Mood
Contained in Two Depression Rating Scales

Children's Depression Rating Scale-Revised (CDRS-R)

1. Occasional feelings of unhappiness which quickly disappear.
2.
3. Describes sustained periods of unhappiness which appear excessive for events described.
4.
5. Feels unhappy most of the time without a major precipitating cause.
6.
7. Feels unhappy all the time. Accompanied by psychic pain (e.g., "I can't stand it").

Children's Depression Inventory (CDI)

0. I am sad once in a while.
1. I am sad many times.
2. I am sad all the time.

interview instrument that is clinician rated. The second, the Children's Depression Inventory (CDI: Kovacs, 1985), is a self-report instrument rated by the child or child's significant other. Both of these instruments define symptom severity in terms of the amount of time that the symptom defines the mood state of the patient. This then requires the patient or informant to not only clearly understand the theoretical model defining the symptom (particularly in the CDRS-R) but to also evaluate the persistence of this mood state within a defined time frame. Typically this time frame is defined as the prior two-week period. It should also be noted that in the case of the CDRS-R, the physician also needs to evaluate whether the symptom report is context dependent—triggered by an environmental stressor—or is context independent, as endogenously triggered. If the symptom report is found to be context independent, that is nonreactive to environmental conditions, then the physician views the quality of the depressed mood as clinically significant.

Recently Mokros and Merrick (Merrick, 1989; Merrick & Mokros, 1990; Mokros, 1991) conducted a study of the phenomenology of depression in adolescents using the Experience Sampling Method (Csikszentmihalyi & Larson, 1984). They studied three groups of adolescents: two clinical samples including currently and previously depressed youngsters and a "normal" control group of youngsters from the community. One of the questions addressed by this research concerned the relationship between single-time point ratings of depressive symptoms made during a diagnostic evaluation in a clinical setting and the continuous rating of these same symptoms made at random-time points over eight consecutive days in ecologically valid settings using the ESM procedure (Mokros, 1991). The ESM has subjects carry with them during the course of their waking hours an electronic pager and a questionnaire booklet known as the Random Activity Survey. During the course of the day subjects are randomly paged and at these times they are instructed to complete the questionnaire. Subjects were paged roughly eight times a day and at these times were to report the context in which they were paged (i.e., who they were with, what they were doing, and where they were) and to then rate a number of mood dimensions expressed as either semantic differential or likert scales.

Figure 3.1 provides the rating profile of two mood items provided by one subject in this study. The subject, a fourteen-year-old female, was diagnosed as suffering from a major depressive disorder for which she was currently hospitalized in a child psychiatric inpatient unit. The clinical evaluation of the severity of her depression showed it to be in the moderate to severe range based on the CDI and CDRS-R summary scores. Her summary CDI score was 26 and CDRS-S score was 62. A score of 19 on the CDI and 40 on the CDRS-R are routinely discussed cutoff scores for

FIGURE 3.1

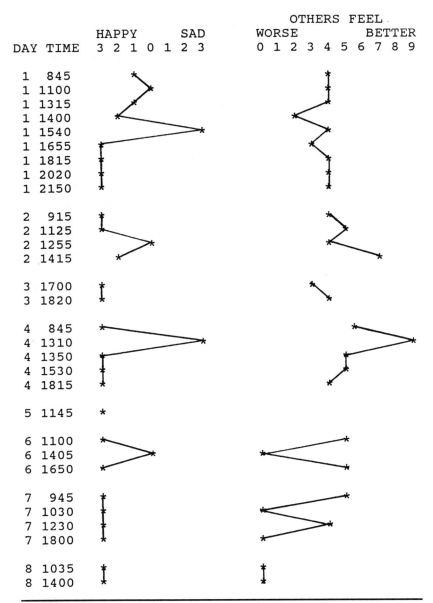

Dysphoric moods reported by a clinically depressed female adolescent during the course of one week.

identifying clinical depression. On the self-report dysphoric mood item of the CDI she described herself as "I am sad all the time" while the interviewing clinician rated her dysphoric mood as "feels unhappy most of the time without a major precipitating cause."

The items for which data are displayed in figure 3.1 provide two distinct perspectives of this youngster's dysphoric mood states. The first item asks the subject to rate themselves on a happy/sad continuum while the second asks them to evaluate whether they feel better or worse than others when beeped. Occasions when this child was beeped but failed to respond are omitted from the displayed data as the majority of these occasions were times when it was impossible for her to respond.

The subject's reported mood states, shown in figure 3.1, as obtained through the ESM procedure contrast sharply with the single-time point clinical ratings (i.e., CDI and CDRS-R). While the clinical ratings corresponded and suggested that this youngster persistently experienced sadness, that was nonreactive to environmental conditions, and that this characterized most of her waking state, the ESM data revealed quite the opposite. On only two occasions, day 1 at 1540 hours and day 4 at 1310 hours did she report experiencing sadness. Also only on two occasions did she report that others felt profoundly better than her, these being day 2 at 1415 hours and day 4 at 1310 hours. The discrepancy in the ratings obtained between these differing modes of assessment raises serious questions about the extent to which the psychiatrist and this child shared the same understanding as to what constituted sadness or dysphoria. Mokros (1991) has shown that this problem is not limited to this single symptom or to this particular case.

Psychiatrists have defined their structured criteria on the basis of clinical reports. In clinical contexts patients have reported persistence and lack of reactivity as characteristics of their sadness and these accounts have become central criteria in the definition of the symptom of dysphoria and the phenomenology of depressive disorders. Yet these reports reference experiences outside of the clinical context. Clearly the data in figure 3.1 illustrate that the persistence over time of dysphoria that a diagnosed depressed patient reported in a one-time clinical context was not consistent with reports of the same symptom made over many time periods in real world contexts. Moreover it is quite clear that the quality of the mood state is not "endogenously" determined, that is, lacks environmental reactivity, but is instead systematically related to the social environments in which the patient is situated when they evaluate themselves (Merrick, 1989; Merrick & Mokros, 1990). Thus, for example, happy/sad ratings made by clinically diagnosed depressed adolescents using the ESM procedure show considerable reactivity to the contexts within which they evaluated themselves.

Reports of happy/sad ratings of seven currently depressed adolescents were evaluated in three contexts: social locations, activity state, and social companionship. For each context, most notably the contexts of social location and social companionship, ratings of happy/sad varied by the nature of the context occupied at the time the rating was made. Thus happiest times were reported when adolescents were in public places, were socializing with others and were in the company of friends. Saddest times were reported when adolescents were at home, performing mainte-nance activities (e.g., eating, grooming, chores), and when alone. As Merrick (1989; Merrick & Mokros, 1990) has reported these data do not differ in their patterns from what is observed for normal adolescents. What is different though is that depressed adolescents report spending signifi-cantly more time alone and then most likely at home, and very rarely reported—relative to normals—spending time with friends. When in the company of friends, whether in public places (which includes a friend's house) or at home, their level of depressed mood was no different from that of normals. These data quite clearly illustrate that mood states for the subjects studied were highly reactive to context, and are thereby best characterized as relationally or interactively defined. Additionally, it is the tendency to socially isolate that seems to be the key phenomenological feature that distinguishes these youngsters from normals. Yet the psy-chiatrist's account, one which patients themselves seem to accept, is that their problems are internally based and nonreactive to the environment.

The faith psychiatry has placed in the use of standardized assessments and diagnostic criteria has resulted in a potential sense of overconfidence about the nature of the data or information obtained in the diagnostic situation. The claim being made here is that the problem is a product of the thingness assumption about information. This assumption has led to a view of the diagnostic situation as a linear information exchange system in which messages have one-to-one correspondence with the things to which they refer and that the more formalized and structured the situation the less likely is the degradation of these messages either in transmission or reception. Thus, I am suggesting that psychiatry has operated within an implicit native model of information that views communication as simple linear exchange of thinglike information, and thereby ignores how infor-mation is itself to be viewed as a relational entity, that is always commun-icationally constructed rather than prior to communication.

Indeed, the nature of structured criteria developed to date implicitly assume that psychiatric disorders are diseases that characterize the state of a person. Diseases are real things that are assumed to be located inside the person. Diseases, like depression, are indexed by a clustering of symptoms that are reported to covary through time. Symptoms then are treated as a type of information that represents a direct external manifestation of an internal disorder. Yet symptom data are relational accounts, intimately conditioned by the method through which they are obtained. That is, knowledge in psychiatry is built on data obtained through the use of specific methods. When symptom data are generated through an alternative method like the ESM procedure, the image of disease becomes quite different. In the ESM data there is a clear indication that the mood disturbance is not something that exists inside the person, but is best characterized as an interactive or relational process. Thus, symptom data are not only relational accounts but relational experiences. What I am suggesting is that in the case of psychiatric evaluation, the treatment of information from the patient as indexical of disorder in a context-independent sense, reinforces the very notion of diseases as entities and thereby negates the possibility of viewing disorder in terms of relational processes.

Information as Thing in Research of Nonverbal Communication

Much of the nonverbal communication literature has concerned itself with using nonverbal behaviors like gaze, smiling, gestures, voice qualities as indexical of enduring qualities of a person or as a reflection of a person's transient psychological states (Duncan, Kanki, Mokros, & Fiske, 1984). Discussion of gender differences in the expression of a variety of nonverbal behaviors represents a particularly noteworthy area of research in this tradition. Therein it has been suggested that differences in the expression of various nonverbal behaviors between males and females are indexical of stereotypic dominance and submission patterns in the social practices of the sexes (Henley, 1977) or alternatively as indexical of the greater desire for affiliation and social engagement of females than males (Burgoon, 1985).

As summarized by Burgoon (1985) in her overview of this literature women have been found, for example, to gaze more as both speakers and listeners in conversation. Depending on whether a researcher's orientation focuses on power or intimacy this observation has been interpreted as indexical of submissive or affiliative behavior respectively. Women have also been found to smile more than men in interaction as well as to be more expressive visually and vocally than males. As with gaze findings, these expressions have also been interpreted as indices of asymmetries in social power (as signs of appeasement) and desire for greater relational intimacy. By treating differences in the practice of nonverbal expressions as indices of a person's social attitudes or orientations, such behaviors are treated as properties of the person, as thinglike information about that person.

Methodologically, these types of claims have been based on data obtained from face-to-face interactions by counting the frequency of occurrence or the duration of display of a specific behavior like smiling. Measures of this type have been referred to as simple-rate variables, "one that is generated by counting or timing the occurence of an action during an interaction and dividing that number by some broader count or timing, representing the maximum frequency or total time that an action could have occurred" (Duncan et al., 1984, p. 1335). Thus, when a researcher studies smiling behavior in get-acquainted conversations, as will provide illustration below, and measures both the occurrence and frequency of smiles by males and females and discovers that females both initiate smiles more often and smile more of the time than do males it appears quite straightforward to interpret these data within a framework, for example, of differences in affiliative needs between the sexes. Yet the implicit assumption made in the process of deriving such an inference is that these simple rates for any given individual are indeed the product of that individual. While such an assumption would appear quite straightforward and unproblematic, this is apparently not the case. Essentially this assumption treats information as thing and fails to appreciate the relational properties of such simple-rate measures. For what is problematic with this assumption is that it fails to see that the measures that appear simply to refer to a person potentially reflect the influence of the social situation, particularly the actions of other interactants within that situation. Duncan et al. (1984) referred to the interpretive error that results from failing to consider the interactive properties of simple-rate variables as the "pseudounilaterality" assumption, namely "the false assumption that the variable is necessarily determined by the action of the participant" (p. 1336).

Mokros (1984; 1985) reported a study of interactional smiling behavior for sixteen get-acquainted conversations each roughly seven minutes in length. Eight females and eight males participated in this study. Each individual participated in two conversations, one with a same-sex and the other with an opposite-sex partner. In that study the moment-to-moment onset, continuation, and termination of all smiles was sequentially transcribed in relation to speech and other nonverbal behaviors. The sequential transcription approach made possible the analysis of the interactional coordination of smiling behavior by participants. Mokros found across the sixteen interactions studied that females smiled more frequently and smiled more of the time than did males. These types of simple-rate variable results assume that a person is the motivator of their smiling behavior. Consistent with tendencies in the nonverbal literature on gender differences these simple-rate variable results might well be interpreted as follows. Smiling may function either as an expression of deference or intimacy. The rate at which an individual smiles in interaction is indexical of that individual's perceived need for affiliation and/or perceived superior/subordinate status within an interaction. That females smile more frequently and smile more of the time than do males indicates that smiling practices in get-acquainted conversations are indexical of gender stereotypic orientations of what it means to be male and female in our society.

However, this line of interpretation based as it is on simple-rate variables ignores the contributions of the social situation and thereby runs the risk of misinterpretation precisely because of the failure to consider the pseudounilaterality assumption. Additional data and analyses of sequential variables, referred to as action-sequence variables, reported by Mokros (1984; 1985) illustrate this point.

Of specific interest are data reported on the contexts in which smiles occurred and the duration of smiles initiated in the context of a partner not smiling. Each smile was classified according to four contextual variables, the sex of the initiator of the smile, the sex of the partner, the interactional state of the initiator as either speaker or listener in the conversation, and whether the partner did or did not reciprocate an initiated smile during the course of its display with a smile of their own. Durations of smiling—referred to as smile runs—were measured according to the action-based units of analysis developed by Duncan and Fiske (1977) in their research of face-to-face interaction. Chronologically, a unit of analysis is roughly one second in length. Additionally, for those initiated smiles that were reciprocated, that is where mutual smiling occurred, the duration of smiling prior to mutual smiling, referred to as reciprocation latency, was also measured.

As noted already, Mokros (1984; 1985) found that females smiled more frequently than did males. This was true in terms of their tendency to initiate as well to reciprocate smiles. However, the likelihood of either reciprocating or initiating a smile was statistically unrelated to the sex of the smiler's partner. This finding might be viewed at odds with the interpretation of the simple-rate variable data discussed above since on the basis of that line of reasoning it might be predicted that females would both initiate and reciprocate smiles more often in the context of males than females. However, it is in the analysis of durational data, of smile runs, that the above interpretation that views smiling to be a unilateral product of a person and interpretable as an index of social and psychological dispositions is most directly challenged.

Figure 3.2 displays lengths in units of analysis of the three possible smile runs defined by Mokros. The distribution of smiles that were reciprocated

FIGURE 3.2
Distribution of Three Measures of Smile Duration

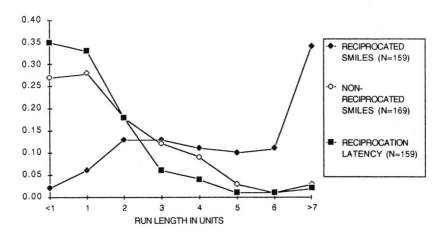

clearly differs from nonreciprocated smiles. That is, if a person smiled and their partner did not also begin smiling that smile was predictably brief. In contrast, smiles that were reciprocated, where the partner also began to smile accounted for the majority of time that a person smiled. The fact that the distribution of smile reciprocation latency did not differ from the distribution of nonreciprocated smiles indicates the operation of a conventional preference for how smiles were displayed in these get-acquainted conversations—that preference being mutual smiling. Putting these results together indicates that smiles initiated in a context of nonsmiling were durationally constrained by the actions of the partner, with gender having no bearing on this constraint.

Thus although significant gender differences in unilaterally represented smiling were identified, these unilateral tendencies fail to capture the interactional characteristics of smiling observable when contextual and sequential variables were included in the analysis. Clearly it is the action of the partner of a smile initiator, to smile or not smile in response, that is most significant for understanding whether an initiator will continue smiling or stop smiling at any given point in time. This suggests that summary measures of persistence or duration of smiling cannot be viewed as exclusively measures of a person, since they are not independent of the actions of their social partner. As suggested by the pseudounilaterality concept, interpretations of an individual's social or psychological dispositions based on either frequency or duration of smiling that do not consider the context in which those smiles occurred may include unwarranted attributions about the person precisely because of the reactivity of smiles to the actions of the partner.

It is common in social science literature that includes measures of nonverbal behavior to treat those measures as a product and thereby an index of the person producing the behavior. In essence this practice is to treat the measure of the behavior as a thinglike piece of information that represents a property of its agent. Yet it appears that the behavior produced by a person in the context of social interaction can never be exclusively regarded as information about them. The behavior of social agents is a relational or interactional product, not merely information about an individual agent.

Conclusions

I have tried to show how in two contexts where privileged accounts of persons were generated, assumptions made about the nature of information led to interpretations and characterizations of persons that have the potential of seeing persons in a reality that is not ongoingly socially constituted but given and unproblematic. In both contexts information was viewed as indexical of persons within a framework that views information as an unproblematic mapping of reality, that views information as a thing. It is a view of information that denigrates communication in that it treats it as a conduit. It should be an aim for students of communication to examine and challenge such assumptions underlying privileged interpretations of human activity for as Lakoff and Johnson (1980) point out,

> Communication theories based on the CONDUIT metaphor turn from the pathetic to the evil when they are applied indiscriminately on a large scale, say, in government surveillance or computerized files. There, what is most crucial for real understanding is almost never included, and it is assumed that the words in the file have meaning in themselves—disembodied, objective, understandable meaning. When a society lives by the CONDUIT metaphor on a large scale, misunderstanding, persecution, and much worse are the likely products. (P. 232)

The fact that practitioners who offer to remediate untoward conditions of human existence such as emotional distress as well as researchers interested in basic properties of human behavior seem to frame their understandings of personhood within an implicit communication framework that views information as thing is particularly distressing. For in the privileged accounts of personhood that they produce they create legitimacy for a set of labeling and stereotyping constructs by which individuals are defined while ignoring consideration of how personhood may be perceived as an ongoing process of social adaptation, conditioning and reactivity.

It is precisely the power of the semiotic, in its substance defined by our conditions, that allows us to transcend conditions and thereby to question what motivates our constructs of reality, our views of life, and our theories of personhood and its legitimate form. Thus I am suggesting that a focal aim of research is to unpack the assumptions we hold. The most important of these are implicit. They are the taken for granted assumptions. Before we may unpack them they must be stated and this in and of itself is no easy proposition as we intrinsically tend to fall back to referential accounts, to view the world as composed of information, of outcomes rather than to see it composed of interactive processes—as in fact always *in communication.*

References

Austin, J. L. (1962). *How to do things with words.* Cambridge, MA: Harvard University Press.

American Psychiatric Association. (1987). *Diagnostic and statistical manual of mental disorers (Third edition-Revised: DSM-III-R).* Washington, DC: American Psychiatric Association.

Bateson, G., Jackson, D., Haley, J., & Weaklund, J. (1956). Toward a theory of schizophrenia. *Behavioral Sciences, 1,* 251–64.

Bourdieu, P. (1977). *Outline of a theory of practice.* Cambridge: Cambridge University Press.

Bruner, J. (1990). *Acts of meaning.* Cambridge, MA: Harvard University Press.

Burgoon, J. K. (1985). Nonverbal signals. In M. L. Knapp & G. R. Miller (Eds), *Handbook of interpersonal communication,* (pp. 344–90). Berverly Hills, CA: Sage.

Csikszentmihalyi, M. & Larson R. (1984). *Being adolescent.* New York: Basic Books.

D'Andrade, R. G. (1976). A propositional analysis of U.S. American beliefs about illness. In K. H. Basso & H. A. Selby (Eds.), *Meaning in anthropology,* (pp. 155–80). Albuquerque, NM: University of New Mexico.

Dervin, B. (1981). Mass communicating: changing conceptions of the audience. In R. E. Rice & W. J. Paisley (Eds.), *Public communication campaigns,* (pp. 71–87). Beverly Hills, CA: Sage.

Duncan, S. & Fiske, D. W. (1977). *Face-to-face interaction: Research, methods, and theory.* Hillsdale, NJ: Lawrence Erlbaum.

Duncan, S., Kanki, B. G., Mokros, H., & Fiske, D. W. (1984). Pseudounilaterality, simple-rate variables and other ills to which interaction research is heir. *Journal of Personality and Social Psychology, 46,* 1335–48.

Ekman, P. & Friesen, W. V. (1969). The repertoire of nonverbal behavior: Categories, origins, usage, and coding. *Semiotica*, *1*, 49–98.

Foucault, M. (1972). *The archeology of knowledge*. New York: Pantheon.

Gergen, K. J. (1985). Social construction inquiry: Context and implications. In K. J. Gergen & K. E. Davis (Eds.), *The social construction of the person*, (pp. 3–18). New York: Springer-Verlag.

Gilligan, C. (1982). *In a different voice*. Cambridge, MA: Harvard University Press.

Goffman, E. *Communication conduct in an island community*. Unpublished doctoral dissertation. Chicago: University of Chicago.

Halliday, M. (1973). *Explorations in the functions of language*. London: Edward Arnold.

Hanson, N. (1958). *Patterns of discovery*. London: Cambridge University Press.

Heise, D. R. (1979). *Understanding events: Affect and the construction of social action*. Cambridge: Cambridge University Press.

Henley, N.M. (1977). *Body politics: Power, sex, and nonverbal communication*. Englewood Cliffs, NJ: Prentice-Hall.

Kovacs, M. (1985). CDI (The children's depression inventory). *Psychopharmacology Bulletin*, *21*, 995–98.

Lakoff, G. & Johnson, M. (1980). *Metaphors we live by*. Chicago: University of Chicago.

Lyons, J. (1977). *Semantics* (volume 1). Cambridge: Cambridge University Press.

MacKay, D. M. (1972). Formal analysis of communication processes. In R. A. Hinde (Ed.), *Non-verbal communication*, (pp. 3–26). Cambridge: Cambridge University Press.

Merrick, W. R. (1989). Dysphoric moods in normal and depressed adolescents: Toward a developmental psychopathological model of affective functioning. Unpublished doctoral dissertation. Chicago: University of Chicago.

Merrick, W. R. & Mokros, H. B. (1990, March). Ecological factors associated with the experience of dysphoria in adolescents. Paper presented at the meeting of the Society for Research on Adolescence. Atlanta, GA.

Minuchin, S., Rosman, B. L., & Baker, L. (1978). *Psychosomatic families: Anorexia nervosa in context*. Cambridge, MA: Harvard University Press.

Mokros, H. B. (1984). Patterns of persistence and change in the sequencing of nonverbal actions. Unpublished doctoral dissertation. Chicago: University of Chicago.

Mokros, H. B. (1985). Patterns of persistence and change in action sequences. In S. Duncan, D. W. Fiske, R. Denny, B. G. Kanki, & H. B. Mokros, *Interaction structure and strategy*, (pp. 175–232). Cambridge: Cambridge University Press.

Mokros, H. B. (1991). Communication process in psychiatric diagnosis: The impact of context on evaluations of depression in adolescence. *Health Communication* (under review).

Mokros, H. B. & Ruben, B. D. (1991). Understanding the communication-information relationship: Levels of information and contexts of availabilities. *Knowledge: Creation, Diffusion, Utilization*, *12*, 373–88.

Mokros, H. B. & Lievrouw, L. A. (1991). Communication-information relationship in self-representation: suicide notes and academic research narratives. *Knowledge: Creation, Diffusion, Utilization*, *12*, 389–405.

Morris, C. (1938). *Foundations of the theory of signs*. Chicago: University of Chicago Press.

Neil, S. D. (1987). The dilemma of the subjective in information organization and retrieval. *Journal of Documentation, 43*, 193–211.

Poznanski, E. O., Freeman, L. N., & Mokros, H. B. (1985). Children's depression rating scale-revised. *Psychopharmacology Bulletin, 21*, 979–89.

Reddy, M. (1979). The conduit metaphor. In A. Ortony (Ed.), *Metaphor and thought*, (pp.284–324). Cambridge: Cambridge University Press.

Rice. R. E. (1990). Hierarchies and clusters among communication and library and information science journals, 1977–1987. In C. Borgman (Ed.), *Scholarly Communication and Bibliometrics*, (pp. 138–53). Newbury Park, CA: Sage.

Ruben, B. D. (1989, November). The communication-information relationship in system-theoretic perspective. Paper presented at the annual meeting of the American Society for Information Science, Washington, DC.

Ruben, B. D. (1992). The communication-information relationship in system-theoretic perspective. *Journal of the American Society of Information Science 43*, 15–27.

Sapir, E. (1949). *Selected writings of Edward Sapir in language, culture, and personality*, edited by D. G. Mandelbaum. Berkeley, CA: University of California Press.

Schement, J. R., Botan, C., Ruben, B. D., & Lee, I. (1990, June). Common terms in scholarly definitions of communication and information: The ties that bind. Paper presented at the 40th annual conference of the International Communication Association, Dublin, Ireland.

Schement, J. R. & Mokros, H. B. (1989, November). The social and historical construction of the idea of information as thing. Paper presented at the annual meeting of the American Society for Information Science, Washington, DC.

Searle, J. (1969). *Speech acts: An essay in the philosohy of language*. Cambridge: Cambridge University Press.

Shannon, C. & Weaver, W. (1949). *The mathematical theory of communication*. Urbana, IL: University of Illinois Press.

Silverstein, M. (1979). Language structure and linguistic ideology. In P. R. Clyne (Ed.), *The elements: A parasession on linguistic units and levels*. Chicago: Chicago Linguistic Society.

Semin, G. R. & Gergen, K. J. (1990). *Everyday understanding: Social and scientific implications*. London: Sage.

Tannen, D. (1990). *You just don't understand: Women and men in conversation*. New York: Ballentine.

Taylor, C. (1991, April). Two theories of language and meaning. Mason Welch Gross Lectures, Rutgers University, New Brunswick, NJ.

Vygotsky, L. S. (1962). *Thought and Language*. Cambridge, MA: MIT Press.

Whorf, B. L. (1956). *Language, thought, and reality: Selected writings of Benjamin Lee Whorf*. J. B. Carroll (Ed.). Cambridge, MA: MIT Press.

Wiener, M., Devoe, S., Rubinow, S., & Geller, J. (1972). Nonverbal behavior and nonverbal communication. *Psychological Review, 79*, 185–214.

Wittgenstein, L. (1953). *Philosophical investigations*. New York: Macmillan.

4

Measurement of Information and Communication: A Set of Definitions

Robert M. Hayes

This paper presents, provides justification for, and discusses the implications of a set of measures of information. In presenting these definitions, the paper discusses their relationship to colloquial use of the two terms and of other relevant terms, to the historical development of measurement theories related to them, and to the problems that have to this point been unresolved in reconciling colloquial and theoretical uses of them. The paper concludes with a characterization of three contexts within which the communication meta-process may be considered: (1) that of the channel (with the source and the recipient taken as external); (2) that of a single source, a single channel, and a single recipient; and (3) that of multiplicity of sources, channels, and/or recipients. The effects of each context upon the measurement of information are discussed.

Information is defined as that property of data (i.e., recorded symbols) which represents (and measures) the effects of processing of those data.

Communication is a meta-process involving a source of information (i.e., of data and associated processing), a channel for data transfer, and a recipient of information (again, with associated data processing).

In the definition of information, *processing* of data plays a central role. Four levels of processing are considered in the paper: (1) data transfer;

(2) data selection; (3) data structuring; and (4) data reduction. For each, the paper defines an associated measure of the resulting amount of information and presents justification for it; each in the succession of measures generalizes from the earlier ones, involving the addition of variables that characterize the additional level of processing.

In the definition of communication, the term *metaprocessing* is used to differentiate between the level of processing involved in data transfer at the level of *data* (from which information is produced) and that involved in communication, in which the information is conveyed from source to recipient. Three levels of metaprocessing are considered in the paper: (1) mechanical communication (in which the level of information processing is limited to data transfer); (2) intelligent communication (in which one or more of the more complex levels of information processing are involved); and (3) interactive communication (in which the role of source and recipient repeatedly changes). Each of these levels is related to the measures presented for amount of information with focus on the effects of the metaprocessing involved in communication.

Summary of Measures

The following briefly summarizes the proposed measures for information at each of the four levels of processing, the variables for each of which will be defined in the later text:

1. Process: Data transfer
   Relevant Variables: x_i, $p(x_i)$
   The Associated Measure: $\log(1/p(x_i))$

2. Process: Data selection
   Relevant Variables: x_i, $p(x_i)$, $r(x_i)$
   The Associated Measure: $r_{(i)} * \log(1/p(x_i)) = \log(1/p(x_i))^{r_i}$

3. Process: Data structuring
   Relevant Variables: f_j, x_{ji} $p(x_{ji})$, $r(x_{ji})$
   The Associated Measures:
   Syntactic: $\log(\pi_j (1/p(x_{ji}))^{r_{ji}}) - \log(\Sigma_j (1/p(x_{ji})^{r_{ji}})$
   Semantic: $\log(\Sigma_j (1/p(x_{ji})^{r_{ji}})$

4. Process: Data Reduction
   Relevant variables: g_k, f_j, x_{ji}, $p(x_{ji})$, $r(x_{ji})$; M, F, G
   The Associated Measures:

Reductive:

$$\sum_{ij}^{MF} \log (1/p_{ji})^{r_{ji}} - \sum_{kj}^{GF} \log (1/p'_{kj})^{r_{kj}} - \sum_{ki}^{GM} \log (1/p''_{ki})^{r_{ki}}$$

Syntactic:

$$\sum_{kj}^{GF} \log (1/p'_{jk})^{r_{jk}} + \sum_{ki}^{GM} \log (1/p''_{ki})^{r_{ki}} - \sum_{k}^{G} \log \sum_{j}^{F} (1/p'_{jk})^{r_{jk}}$$

Semantic:

$$\sum_{k}^{G} \log \sum_{j}^{F} (1/p'_{jk})^{r_{jk}}$$

Existing Uses of Terms

Before considering the proposed measures of "information," it is important to discuss the colloquial uses of relevant terms. Unfortunately, while formal definitions may be acceptable in a mathematical context, the relevant terms carry a huge burden of colloquial use. Many of them colloquially are used in ambiguous, overlapping ways. Figure 4.1 reflects relationships among significant terms as they are used in this paper:

FIGURE 4.1

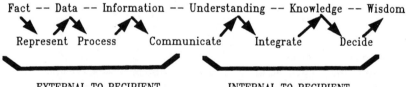

Fact -- Data -- Information -- Understanding -- Knowledge -- Wisdom

Represent Process   Communicate   Integrate   Decide

EXTERNAL TO RECIPIENT   INTERNAL TO RECIPIENT

That is, from the real world we observe aspects of phenomena (as Facts) and represent them (by Data); we process the Data to create Information; we communicate the Information to the recipient. Those are all aspects external to the recipient. Internal to the recipient, the communication presumably results in understanding by the recipient and provides a basis for integration into an accumulation of Knowledge; the recipient uses that knowledge as the basis, among other things, for making decision; and decisions that embody ethical principles result in Wisdom in that use.

Fact

Let's start with the term "fact." It is defined here to mean "a statement whose truth is testable" (what will be called a "verifiable truth") with reference to the real world. Thus, with this definition, when one says, "The facts are . . . ," one is making a statement about the real world and asserting a verifiable truth. Of course, even in this definition there are complications. Of special importance is the concept of "precision", reflecting the range of certainty and even perhaps of confidence one has in the fact. For example, it may be a fact that the population of the United States at this time is a specific number—say 256,123,456—though one should have no confidence that such was the case. On the other hand, one might have high confidence in the statement, "It is a fact that the population of the United States in July 1990 is between 250 million and 260 million." The difference, of course, is that the second statement incorporates a characterization of the precision.

A second problem is the implied need for a means for verification of a fact. Indeed, the statement that something is a fact by no means makes it a truth; all that it states is that its truth is verifiable. Furthermore, it is important to note that while facts may attempt to represent the real world, any representation must be partial and incomplete. That is, with this formulation any given fact is at most an extraction from the real world. It relates to only a limited aspect; even a massive accumulation of facts cannot in any way truly represent the full complexity of the real world. At best, a fact or an accumulation of them may provide a means for dealing with the real world in a specific context and for a specific purpose.

Data

We turn now to terms that are more central to the discussion. First is the term "data," defined to be "recorded symbols," which of course begs the question, what is a recorded symbol? For the moment at least, "recorded symbol" is taken as a "primitive," a term undefined here but taken to mean what it will in a specific situation. In passing, through, the forms of recorded symbols can be visualized as including: printed characters; bits in magnetic, punched, or optical form; spoken words; visual images; DNA and RNA protein molecules; financial accounts, as representation of capital; persons in positions of responsibility, as representations of groups. In other words, the specific meaning attached to a recorded symbol is almost unlimited.

Colloquially, the term "data" is frequently specialized to "numerical data," but it must be evident that it is not so limited in this paper. Sometimes, people will treat it as synonymous with "facts," but this paper does not do so and that is the reason that a formal distinction has been made between data, as the recorded symbol, and the "fact" that the data may purport to represent. To be more specific, data are not facts and treating them as such can produce innumerable perversions.

Indeed, it is fully possible for data, as defined here, to bear no relationship whatsoever to the real world or to facts. Mathematical proofs and computer programs are cognitive constructs and need not be derived from the real world at all; works of fiction are also products of the human mind even though recorded as words on paper; statements of "faith" may well be contrary to real world "facts"; propaganda, "disinformation," and lies are usually so. In other words, data as recorded symbols can well be a *ding an sich*, a "thing in itself," without any necessary real world referent.

Representation

In that context, though, a crucial point, as illustrated in the schematic shown above, lies in the use of data to *represent* facts for the purpose of recording them and, as we will see, deriving information. When we deal with data in that way we are at least two steps removed from reality: facts as representations extracted from the real world and data as representations of those facts. It is also in this sense that the issue of *precision* becomes operationally important. While in principle a fact might exactly represent an aspect of the real world, when the data representing it indeed are recorded there will almost certainly be a loss in precision because of the finite limitations of the means for recording.

Information

Now we turn to the core definitional problem—"information." This paper provides a formal definition that is intended to generalize from an existing one—the Shannon definition, which is tied to a specific measure. The two definitions are consistent, but clearly the one proposed here is more general and thus different from the Shannon definition, though including it.

Colloquially, though, the term is certainly much richer and more diffuse than the definition given in this paper. For example, we use the phrase "being informed," implying either a process of becoming informed or the state of being so. In either case, though, the term information (underlying the term informed) is intended to convey the state of a person's mind. The process of becoming informed is interpreted as that of receiving information, but nothing further is specific about either the process or the content; there is no clear definition of what "information" is or even of what the process of "becoming informed" is. We say "I have information," and perhaps that is synonymous with "being informed," though it appears to be less specific to the state of mind and more related to the process of becoming informed.

Paisley has formalized this colloquial use by identifying "information," in part, with a change in the structure of thinking. He says, "Information denotes an encoding of symbols into a message of any mode, communicated through any channel. Functionally, information denotes any stimulus that alters cognitive structure in the receiver. . . . Something that the receiver already knows (i.e., a stimulus that does not alter cognitive structure) is not information." With his definition, one is "informed" if such a change has occurred.

As will become evident later in this discussion, we identify cognitive structure with "knowledge"; the effect of information indeed may be a change in knowledge, though there is no reason for restricting the definition of information to requiring such a change. In this sense, then, we can identify a succession of stages—from receiving information, to having information, to becoming informed, to being informed—that reflects a progression of processes of internalization. One could suppose, for example, that one could receive information without being informed, except to the extent that colloquial use may make those two phrases synonymous (i.e., "he is being informed" meaning "he is being given information" meaning "he is receiving information"). But if the two phrases are distinguished, surely being informed is a comment about the internal state of the person.

Belkin provided a most comprehensive review of the range of concepts embodied in this term, so it is worthwhile briefly summarizing his analysis as a starting point for comment on both colloquial uses and more technical uses, either as amplifications of his discussion or as additions to it. He discussed a set of concerns with which any discussion of information must deal:

1. as part of human cognition;
2. as something produced by a generator;
3. as something that affects a user;
4. as something that is requested or desired;
6. as the basis for purposeful social communication;
7. as a commodity;
8. as a process;
9. as a state of knowing;
10. as semantic content.

He reviewed a number of specific definitions that to one extent or another embody those concepts of information:

1. Shannon: measurement based on *a priori* probability of signals;
2. Otten: a four-level model: physical, syntactic, . . . ;
3. Pratt: an event in a process of communication;
4. Wersig: an interaction between human and environment;
5. Yovits: a basis for decision-making;
6. Farradane: a surrogate for knowledge;
7. Thompson, Belkin: structure.

Moving into another arena, we have uses of the term information in forms such as "scientific and technical information" or "business information" in which the reference would appear to be to forms of data that have been organized for specific objectives. The implication is that something more than merely data are involved and that some level of processing, of organization, of interpretation, of distribution has produced something more, which we call "information." A related but different array of uses is represented by the phrase "information system" in which the focus is on the mechanisms for processing, producing, and distributing. This use has been generalized in such phrases as "national informtion system" and "national information policy" in which the emphasis shifts from the data and its organization to the political and societal issues related to the means for distribution. And, of course, we have the term "information science" with an array of multiple interpretations, including "science information," "library and information science," "computer and information science."

Process

In any event, with the definition presented and used in this paper, information depends centrally upon processing of data. At least four levels of data processing are identified: transfer, selection, analysis, and reduction. It is worthwhile amplifying on the interpretation and significance of them.

The simplest level of processing is *data transfer* or *data transmission.* If a sheet of paper containing data is given to someone, the process is that of data transfer; if those same data are copied to another medium or sent through a telephone line, the process is that of data transmission. In either event, the recipient has received some level of information as a result of that process even though nothing more may have been done.

The second level of processing, *data selection,* is best illustrated by the operation of a computer database search in which records "relevant to" a request are identified and retrieved from the database files. Note that this process is expected to include data transmission but it also includes much more. Data selection is also illustrated by the selection and acquisition of materials for storage in a library; the recipient in this case is the library itself. In each example, the recipient has received information as a result of the process of selection, but the amount of information clearly depends upon the degree to which the process of selection indeed identifies "relevant" materials (relevant to the request or to the library's collection development policies). At least for the moment in this discussion, we will not specify the meaning of the term "relevant" but will take it as a primitive, to be interpreted as may be appropriate to specific contexts.

The third level of processing, *data analysis,* as we will show later is best illustrated by placing data into a format or structure. As a result of that process, the recipient receives information not only as a result of the data transmitted or data selected but as a result of the relationships shown in the structure in which they are presented. The sentence "man bites dog" thus is meaningful both because of the data and of the "subject-verb-object" syntax of the sentence. In the context of an information retrieval system, data analysis might be illustrated by the sequencing of selected records according to some criterion (order of relevance, alphabetically by author, chronological by data, etc.). In a database system, data analysis is represented by the creation of matrices, tables, and relationships as the means for organization of the stored data.

The fourth level of processing, *data reduction,* is best illustrated by the replacement of large collections of data by equations. For example, linear regression analysis of a set of say 1000 two-dimensional data points replaces 2000 values by two values (the parameters of the linear regression line). The result is information derived both from the process of reduction and from the effective replacement of massive amounts of data by a few parameters.

Communicate

Colloquial use of the term "communication" is surely fully as ambiguous as that of "information". The OED says, "1. . . . the vehicles of information: *e.g.* of a letter, a paper to a society, an article to a magazine. . . . 2. The imparting, conveying, or exchange of ideas, knowledge, information, etc. (whether by speech, writing, or signs). . . . 3. That which is communicated, or in which facts are communicated; a piece of information; a written paper containing observations. . . . 4. Interchange of speech, conversation, conference. . . . 5. Converse, personal intercourse. . . . 6. Access or means of access between two or more persons or places; the action or faculty of passing from one place to another; passage (between two places, vessels, or spaces). . . . 7. Common participation.

Obs. . . . 8. Congruity, affinity, quality in common. rare. . . . 9. The Holy Communion; its observance. *rare . . .*

Some meanings are reflected in phrases and hyphenated expressions: "interpersonal communication," "mass communication," the "communications media," and "telecommunications." We see terms such as "communicable disease." Generally, the term is used to represent a process, but we have phrases such as "I received a communication," that makes reference to the content rather than the process, and "Have I communicated?" that makes reference to the effect on the recipient rather than the process.

The Recipient

To this point emphasis has been placed on *information* as something external to the user and indeed from the perspective of the creation of information by the processes upon data. However, there are important uses of the term information that are from the perspective of the user: Information User, Information Need, Information-Seeking Behavior. In this paper's frame of reference, this perspective is well-accommodated but doing so requires some discussion.

"Information user" is readily identifiable with the recipient of information especially in contexts in which the communication metaprocess has been initiated by that person, presumably with the intent to obtain information at some level of processing. The initiation of the communication metaprocess presumably would reflect a "need for information"; perhaps a decision must be made and there is a gap in the knowledge base (internal to the user) that could be filled by information. Information-seeking behavior is then the mechanisms by which the information user goes about initiating and establishing the communication meta-process.

Understanding

However the communication may have been initiated, though, the result for the recipient becomes meaningful only when it has been understood. Indeed, it is only then that "meaning" can really be ascribed to the data or to the information resulting from the processing and communication of data.

"Understanding" is a complex of things. At the primitive level, it involves recognition of the information, its structure and content. At the next level, it involves comparison of the content with appropriate dictionaries—determination of the meaning of the transmitted symbols that constitute the information by matching them with entries in the dictionaries and interpreting them. At the next level, it involves an understanding of the import of the information as an entity, as a thing in itself. At the next level, it involves integrating the information into the existing store of "knowledge," comparing, contrasting, organizing, evaluating, correcting, or otherwise changing.

For purposes of this paper, therefore, "understanding" is the result of an internal process of "table look-up" in which the data are matched against some form of list and interpreted for their significance. For example, the data transmitted might be simply the letter "A" but the internal code-book may say that "A" means "Alarm! Danger! Leave immediately!" If so, that message would then be so "understood."

It is possible, of course, that the transmitted data had been garbled to the point that it could not be understood, with no appropriate matching entry in the internal tables or list. Presumably, in such a case, the metaprocess of communication would have continued, with mutual interaction between source and recipient until there was understanding. It is important to note, though, that "understanding" includes the possibility of "misunderstanding". Nothing precludes a message from being understood but incorrectly so.

Knowledge

Turning to the next term, "knowledge," we again have an exceptionally diffuse array of uses. In a talk given by Daniel Boorstin at the White House Conference on Library and Information Services, he commented to the effect that we say "one can be informed" but we do not say "one can be knowledged." The implication is clear: Information is essentially external; it can be received. Knowledge is internal; it cannot be received but must be internally created.

The OED says, 1. Acknowledgment. . . . *Obs.* . . . 2. The fact of recognizing as something known. . . . *Obs.* . . . 3. Legal cognizance. . . . 4. Cognizance, notice only in phr. *to take knowledge of.* . . . 5. The fact of knowing a thing, state, etc. . . . 6. Personal acquaintance, friendship, intimacy. . . . 7. Sexual intimacy. . . . 8. Acquaintance with a fact; perception, or certain information of, a fact or matter; state of being aware or informed; consciousness (of anything). . . . 9. Intellectual acquaintance with, or perception of, fact or truth; clear and certain comprehension. . . . 10. Acquaintance with a branch of learning, a language, or the like. . . . 11. In general sense: The fact or condition of being instructed, or of having information acquired by study or research. . . . 12. Information; intelligence. . . . 13. The sum of what is known. . . . 14. A branch of learning. . . . 15. A sign or mark by which anything is known, recognized, or distinguished.

Nitecki discusses the efforts to bring formalization to the term and especially to the relationships between information and knowledge. He distinguishes three views of the two terms: (1) those views in which the two terms are identical or nearly so (information is knowledge of facts, knowledge is information processed with a point of view through representation); (2) those in which they are mutually exclusive (information as data and knowledge as inferred essence, information as outside and knowledge as created by human beings); and (3) those that regard both as the same when content oriented but as different when information is process oriented and knowledge is content oriented.

This paper chooses the second view, namely that the two terms are mutually exclusive. Thus, knowledge results from the understanding of information that has been communicated and integration of it with prior information. To an extent, it is a result of internalizing the information, but it is more than that, since it requires an active process, a restructuring of the cognitive structure as Paisley refers to it. Thus, what Paisley may be referring to as the "functional" characterization of information, is here referred to as knowledge. It is important to note that we should distinguish between two elements of a cognitive structure: the basic store of internalized information (with its structure) and "intelligence" as the means for internal processing of it. Both clearly are needed, but we will limit the meaning of knowledge to simply the basic store of information in the cognitive structure—the "knowledge base" as it is sometimes called.

Nitecki recognizes this progression in the concept of "continuity," representing a succession of levels of integration from (1) knowledge at its moment of origin, as a passive reflection of the given fact; to (2) interaction with other such passive reflections; to (3) combination of them into larger entities (much as frames in a film may constitute a scene). He also presents a Venn diagram (figure 4.2) that relates three aspects of knowledge—empirical, perceptive, explanatory—in a structure consistent with the schema used in this paper (distinguishing between facts, as derived from the real world, and knowledge, as the internal structure place upon received information) as follows:

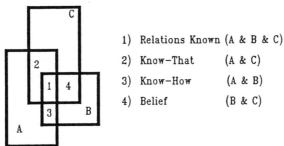

1) Relations Known (A & B & C)

2) Know-That   (A & C)

3) Know-How   (A & B)

4) Belief   (B & C)

It is important to note that knowledge may reside in a wide range of entities. It may reside in the individual, and thus is a component of the internal cognitive structure of the person; individual intelligence is then the means by which knowledge is used by the individual (to make decisions, for example). It may reside in societal memory, and thus is a component of society's cognitive structure; societal intelligence is then the means by which society uses its memory. It may reside in a library as a collection of records, and thus is a component of the library's cognitive structure; the library's intelligence is the body of knowledge, experience, and intelligence embodied in its professional and even non-professional staff. It may reside in an "expert system," in the computer sense, and thus is a component of the expert system's cognitive structure (usually called the "knowledge base"); the expert system's intelligence is then embodied in the decision tree by which it uses the knowledge base (plus data input to it from outside).

Wisdom

We conclude this set of conceptualizations by mentioning the term "wisdom" which is interpreted here as bringing ethical and moral considerations to bear. But it must be said that decisions may be controlled by paranoia or by insanity as well as by wisdom. While we may wish for wisdom, at the least we may hope for sanity in decisions by society as well as individuals.

Measures of the Amount of Information

In general the measurement of information is a complicated and as yet unresolved problem. However, this paper presents a series of measures of information, each a generalization of the prior one, based on the definition of "information" given above, which identifies it with "a property of data resulting from the processing of it." At least four levels of processing are identified:

1. data transfer (i.e., communication in a technical sense);
2. data selection (i.e., retrieval from a file);
3. data organization and analysis (i.e., sequencing and formatting);
4. data reduction (i.e., replacement of data by a surrogate).

For the first, there is a well established measure; for the other three successive generalizations are presented that reflect the increasing complexity of information provided.

The Shannon Measure for Communication (Data Transfer)

The only formally recognized measure is that provided by Shannon and used in "information theory" (for which read *communication* theory). It measures the amount of information (but not its value) by the statistical properties of the signals transmitted. That is, let $X = \{\times_1, \times_2, \ldots \times_M\}$ be a set of signals and let $p_i = p(\times_i)$ be the a priori probability that each of them will be transmitted; finally, let $n_i = \log(1/p_i)$. Then, the amount of information conveyed by signal x_i is given by

$$H(x_i) = -\log(p_i) = \log(1/p_i) = n_i$$

and the average amount of information conveyed by the entire set of signals is:

$$H(X) = -\sum_i^M p_i * \log(p_i) = \sum_i^M p_i * \log(1/p_i) = \sum_i^M p_i * n_i.$$

The following heuristic has been used to justify this measure. Consider two signals that are successively transmitted. Normally, one would want the measure of the amount of information provided by the two signals to be equal to the sum of the amount provided by each independently. That is,

$$H(x \text{ AND } y) = H(x) + H(y)$$

If information is to be a function of the probability of the signal, then the measure needs to recognize that the probability of the two independent signals x *and* y is the product of the two independent probabilities p(x) and p(y). The logarithm is one function that does so.

Typically, the amount of information conveyed by a signal is represented by the number of bits used in transmission of it (assuming appropriate encoding of it). As part of the basis for developing a heuristic justification for the generalizations of this measure that we will be presenting, it is valuable to examine a semantic interpretation of this measure. The recipient of a given signal needs to determine its "meaning " and, to do so, needs to perform some kind of "table look-up"; the amount of information provided by the signal is exactly the measure of the number of binary decisions that need to be made in that table look-up process (assuming a structure for the table that reflects the appropriate encoding of the signal). An underlying parameter is the size of the table (i.e., the number of entries in it), representing the size of the semantic vocabulary in the communication.

Simply to illustrate, consider the case where signals are all equally probable; then for all i, $1/p_i = M$, the size of the file of signals. The entropy measure for information is then simply $\log_2(M)$ and represents exactly the number of decisions in binary search of such a file.

Weighted Entropy (Data Selection)

The entropy measure has been exceptionally valuable in the context of communication theory where the only concern is with efficient transmission of signals. However, it has rarely if ever been successfully applied in contexts in which the value of the signal, measured in some way, is important.

As a result, a generalization of Shannon's measure, called "weighted entropy," has been developed that indeed seems to provide means for recognizing both the statistical issues involved in efficient transmission and the importance of the signal to the user or recipient of it. The measure assigns to each signal, x_i, in addition to the a priori probability, another function $r_i = r(x_i)$ which measures that importance. Such a measure of importance can be illustrated by the "relevancy" of the signal, in the sense in which that term is used in retrieval system evaluation. The resulting weighted entropy measure is then

$$S(x_i) = r_i * \log(1/p_i) = r_i * n_i$$

(which will be called the "significance" of the signal) and the average over the entire set of signals is:

$$S(X) = \sum_i^M r_i * p_i * \log(1/p_i) = \sum_i^M r_i * p_i * n_i$$

Note that if all signals are equally important (which is the necessary assumption for communication system design), the weighted entropy measure reduces to the Shannon measure; if all signals are equally probable, it reduces to what is called the *relevancy* measure in the field of information storage and retrieval. Thus, it is a suitable generalization.

To provide a heuristic justification for this as a measure of information, consider a file of items from which we wish to retrieve information. Let an item in the file consist of N bits, and let a request, Y, be matched against each item in the file in order to identify which of them matches the query on a specified set of n of the N bits. What is the amount of information provided by the file in response to such a query? As we have pointed out, Shannon's entropy measure considers only statistical probabilities, not measures of value (such as relevancy).

Let's define the concept of *the significance of a signal*, say x_i, as a function of two related quantities, $p(x_i)$, the a priori probability, and $r(i)$, the relevance: $S(x_i) = S(p(x_i), r(x_i))$. For simplicity in describing the heuristic, suppose each item consists of N bits, that each item is equally likely, and that $r(x_i)$ is measured by the proportion of the N bits on which x_i and the request y match. Then,

$$S(x_i) = S(1/2^N, (x_i \text{ AND } y)/N)$$

Consider now selecting a second item from the file. It is reasonable to expect that a measure of the amount of information from both should be treated as the sum of the amount from each, that is,

$$S(x_i, x_j) = S(x_i) + S(x_j)$$

One solution to this functional equation is the proposed measure:

$$S(x_i) = r(x_i) * \log(1/p(x_i))$$

Semantic vs. Syntactic Information (Data Analysis & Structure)

As a basis for development of a measure for the third level of processing—analysis and organization—we will examine the nature and effects of the structuring of data. The objective of structure is to establish "separability" of data into components, to reduce permutations to combinations, to reduce the number of decisions required to identify a symbol by increasing the number of dimensions embodied in its structure.

To illustrate, consider a set of symbols. If each of them is treated as independent, with no structure or organization imposed, the recipient of one of them must match it against the entire set of symbols in order to determine what it means. There is something we can do to improve the effectiveness by reducing the workload on the recipient.

Specifically, we can impose a *structure* on the symbols. For simplicity in exposition, we will characterize that as "subdividing the symbol into fields." Just to provide a simple illustration, consider a symbol set that is used to identify people. Each of sixteen persons could be uniquely identified by a four-bit array; one would need to have a table with sixteen entries in order to determine which person was represented by a given four-bit code.

But now, let's impose a structure on that code:

(Male/Female) (Young/Old) (Rich/Poor) (Urban/Rural)

Suddenly, instead of needing to recognize sixteen different things, we need recognize only eight different things, the *combination* of which gives us the full set of sixteen. Receiving a signal, say 0110, we can identify the category easily as "male, old, poor, urban"; we have looked at four tables of just two entries each, yet we have identified one from sixteen categories.

The imposition of a *matrix* upon a set of data accomplishes the same objective. One need deal only with $(N + M)$ things rather than $(N \times M)$ things (where N and M are the dimensions of the matrix).

Of course, there are two problems that must be recognized: symbols may not be uniquely characterized by the structure (e.g., there may be more than one person in a category); not all categories from the combination are necessarily represented. But while those effects may modify details of the illustration, they do not change the basic principles nor the significance of the reduction of effort provided by imposition of a structure.

Now, can we measure that effect? Let the source signal be N bits in length (so that we have 2^N symbols). Let's divide it into F fields of lengths $\{n_1, n_2, \ldots n_F\}$ bits, averaging N/F. Instead of looking among 2^N entries, we need look only among $\Sigma_i (2^{n_i})$. The original N bits of information is conveyed by $\log (\Sigma_i (2^{n_i}))$. We will call that "semantic information," since it is that part of the total symbol that involves table look-up (meaning) with the remainder being "syntactic information, " conveyed by the structure. Note that, as F increases, the amount of semantic information rapidly decreases, and the syntactic information increases.

To establish a measure for this division between syntactic and semantic information, consider a record of F fields. Let there be associated with each possible value in each field an a priori probability; thus for field j and value i, there is a probability p_{ji}. The probability of the particular combination, assuming independence, is then $\pi_j(p_{ji})$ and the amount of information conveyed by the symbol is $\log (\pi_j (1/p_{ji})) = \Sigma_j \log(1/P_{ji})$. That total amount of information, however, is divided between syntactic and semantic as follows:

Syntactic Information	Semantic Information
$\displaystyle\sum_{j}^{F} \log(1/p_{ji}) - \log(\sum_{j}^{F} 1/p_{ji})$	$\displaystyle\log(\sum_{j}^{F} 1/p_{ji})$

Substituting n_{ji} for $\log(1/p_{ji})$, we get:

$\displaystyle\sum_{j}^{F} n_{ji} - \log(\sum_{j}^{F} 2^n ji)$	$\displaystyle\log(\sum_{j}^{F} 2^n ji)$

This mesure identifies the process of analysis and organization with the decomposition (i.e., analysis) of the original symbol into component fields and the resulting structure (i.e., organization) with the syntactic result. The information produced by the process is then the syntactic information.

Note that if there is only one field (F = 1), the syntactic information is zero and the semantic information is simply the original entropy measure. This means that the proposed measure is a consistent generalization of the entropy measure.

We can very simply generalize from the process of selection of a signal as follows:

Syntactic Information: $\{\sum_{j}^{F} r(x_{ji})*\log(1/p_{ji}) - \log(\sum_{j}^{F} 2^{r(x_{ji})}*\log(1/p_{ji}))\}$

Semantic Information: $\log(\sum_{j}^{F} 2^{r(x_{ji})})*\log(1/p_{ji})$

or, substituting $n_{ji} = \log(1/p_{ji})$,

Syntactic Information: $\{\sum_{j}^{F} r_{ji}*n_{ji} - \log(\sum_{j}^{F} 2^{r_{ji}*n_{ji}})$

Semantic Information: $\log(\sum_{j}^{F} 2^{r_{ji}*n_{ji}})$

In this measure, the value of the signal (for example, relevance) affects both the syntactic and semantic content. Note that this formulation provides means for assigning differential value to the fields embodied in a signal. In other words, the response to a request might be given by providing only a selected set of fields from the items that are selected from the file.

The term for semantic information, expressed as the logarithm of a sum of powers, can be reformulated in a way that is more revealing of the meaning. For some value of j, say m(i), the product $r_{ji}*n_{ji}$ must be a maximum. Then,

$$\log(\sum_{j}^{F} 2^{r_{ji}*n_{ji}}) = \log\{(2^{r_{m(i)i}*n_{m(i)i}})*(\sum_{j}^{F} 2^{(r_{ji}*n_{ji})}/2^{(r_{m(i)i}*n_{m(i)i})})\}$$

$$= r_{m(i)i*n_{m(i)i}} + \log\{\sum_{j}^{F} 2^{(r_{ji}*n_{ji})}/2^{(r_{m(i)i}*n_{m(i)i})}\}$$

Since $r_{m(i)i1}*n_{m(i)i1}$ is the maximum, all terms in the sum are less than or equal to one. Hence:

$$\log(\sum_{j}^{F} 2^{r_{ji}*n_{ji}}) <= r_{m(i)i}*n_{m(i)i} + \log(F)$$

We will not, in this paper, discuss the means for creating structures or for analyzing data as the basis for doing so except to comment that the several parameters identified in the proposed measure—$r(x_i)$, $r(x_i, q)$, $r(x_i, y_i)$—potentially play roles in analysis and in data reduction. For example, we can use r as the basis for clustering. We can use linkages (such as embodied in a "hypertext" structure or a citation structure) as a basis for decomposition and reduction.

Data Reduction

We turn now to the final level of processing, data reduction. It can be exemplified by curve fitting, factor analysis, clustering, and similar means for reducing large amounts of data to a very limited set of parameters. In general these mathematical processes can be considered as transformations of the data, treated as a vector space, into alternative dimensional representations in which the original data have nearly zero values on a large number of transformed dimensions.

To illustrate, consider data representing a set of F test scores (represented by a total of N bits) for a number, M, of individuals (the classical example for factor analysis). Those can be considered as an (M × N) matrix. Methods such as factor analysis, eigen-vector analysis, and clustering are means by which an alternative "basis" (i.e., dimensional transformation) can be determined. The original data, treated as vectors, can now be represented by their "projections on the new basis. In virtually any realistic context, only a few of the new basis vectors contribute significantly to the representation of the original data.

The result is that much of the significant information from the original set of (M × N) data can be communicated by sending just the weightings on the new dominant basis vectors (F scores, or N bits, for say G dominant basis vectors); the full content can be conveyed by also sending the G values for the projections of each of each individual on them. Thus, the significant content of (M × F) items of data are communicated by (G * F) values; the full content by (G * (M + F)) values. Typically this might reduce data about 100 test scores for 1000 individuals to perhaps 5 factors; the substance of the original data could be transmitted by 5 values instead of 100 values.

How do we measure the amount of information conveyed by such a process of data reduction? As before, the total amount of information is represented by the original source data—F fields for each of M records. The semantic task for the recipient has been reduced to look-up in a table of G records. The distribution of information between the contribution from processing and that from syntactic structure and semantic look-up is thus:

Relevant Variables: g_k, f_j, $\times_{ji}$ $p(\times_{ji})$, $r(\times_{ji})$; M, F, G

The Associated Measures:

Reductive:

$$\sum_{ij}^{MF} \log (1/p_{ji})^{r_{ji}} - \sum_{kj}^{GF} \log (1/p'_{kj})^{r_{kj}} - \sum_{ki}^{GM} \log (1/p''_{ki})^{r_{ki}}$$

Syntactic:

$$\sum_{kj}^{GF} \log (1/p'_{jk})^{r_{jk}} + \sum_{ki}^{GF} \log (1/p''_{ki})^{r_{ki}} - \sum_{k}^{G} \log (\sum_{j}^{F} (1/p'_{jk})^{r_{jk}})$$

Semantic:

$$\sum_{k}^{G} \log (\sum_{j}^{F} (1/p'_{jk})^{r_{jk}})$$

As before, the semantic term can be bounded by

$$\sum_{k}^{G} \log (\sum_{j}^{F} (1/p'_{jk})^{r_{jk}}) <= \sum_{k}^{G} \{n_{m(k)k}*r_{m(k)k} + \log(F)\}$$

where $n_{m(k)k}*r_{m(k)k}$ is the maximum, over all j, of $n_{jk}*r_{jk}$.

Levels of Communication

We turn now to discussion of the relationships between information and communication, using the measures defined above as the context. Three levels of communication will be distinguished: (1) mechanical communication; (2) intelligent communication; and (3) interactive communication. The first is essentially identical with the process of data transfer; the information provided is therefore measured by the traditional entropy measure.

We will equate "intelligent communication" with the three more complex levels of information processes—selection, analysis, and reduction. In each case, the source of information has added some form of data processing to the simple process of data transfer. As a result, the recipient of the signal has received more information than would be implied by the mere number of bits transmitted.

What then is "interactive communication"? As defined here it, it is much more than merely successive reversals of the roles of source and recipient, but involves a much deeper effect. Specifically, if we consider the several levels of processing, each is characterized by specific parameters: $p(x_i)$, $r(x_i)$, F, and G—the a priori probabilities, relevancies, definitions of fields, and definitions of alternative bases for the data space. Real interaction occurs when the communication process results in changes to these parameters.

Thus, consider a succession of communications. The source (1) sends a signal, based on its established set of values for p, r, F, and G. The recipient (2) then becomes the source (2), sending signals that produce changes in those values for p, r, F, and G at recipient (1). Recipient (1) again becomes source (1), sending signals that incorporate the revised values, and the interactive process continues.

The need for interactive communication is a result of problems arising from mis-matches between the perceptions of the source and the recipient with respect to the characterizing parameters p, r, F, and G. In particular, noise in the channel for communication may cause errors in the data transmission and affect the data coding; in classical communication theory, the basic theorem is that exponential increases in the noise level can be dealt with by linear increases in the length of the signal. It is interactive communication in the identification of errors in transmission that would result in changes in the means for data encoding.

In the context of data selection, the counterpart to noise in the channel is "uncertainty" in the data to be transmitted. This is in part represented by diffusion in the assignment of indexing terms by even expert indexers and by the parallel diffusion in formulation of queries; it is in part represented by the difference between the source and the recipient in the assessment of the measure of value, $r(x_i)$, as illustrated by relevancy assessments. The method used in dealing with the problem of noise in the channel (i.e., redundancy by lengthening the signal) is clearly not appropriate, since the problems lie in the source data and the processing, not in the transmission.

How then do we deal with uncertainty? The answer is simple: we select and transmit a number of signals, so as to increase the probability of "recall" (i.e., selecting signals that are of value), though at the cost of decreasing the "precision." Improving the quality of the selection process obviously requires interactive communication so that the match between vocabularies and measures of value (of the source and the recipient) can be increased.

In the context of data structuring, the characterizing problem lies in the mismatch between syntactic structures. Again, improving the quality of the analysis requires interactive communication so that perceptions of structure by the source and the recipient can be brought into match. The problem in data reduction is a direct result of the processes by which the reduction is effected. If we attempt to represent a multidimensional data space by a reduced number of dimensions, there will be a loss of mathematical precision in representation of the source data; appropriate balance between precision and efficiency is determined through interactive communication.

Contexts

We conclude with some brief comments on three levels of context. The first is focused on the channel. The second considers all three components—source, channel, and recipient. The third considers a multiplicity of sources, channels, and recipients.

The most limited level of information processing, data transmission, is that which applies at the mechanical level of communication. The issues of importance, such as data coding, are all specific to the *channel,* having little if anything to do with the source or the recipient, and the classical entropy model for measurement of information provides the basis for decision. As a result, the channel is the important context for this level of communication.

When we consider the more complex levels of processing involved in intelligent communication and, especially, when we consider interactive communication, the source and the recipient become far more important than the channel. In fact, the critical issues involve the processing requirements at the source in selection, analysis, or reduction and at the recipient in interpreting the received data, in table look-up to determine its semantic significance, in assembling the received data into coherent structures, and in applying it to needs. As a result, the context must be broadened to include all three components.

For most of the technical problems in design of systems for communication of information, that second context is probably the appropriate one within which to work. However, the real world involves many sources, many channels for data transmission, many recipients of any one message. Certainly "the mass media" represent exactly this kind of large-scale context. The problems relate more to choices among alternatives than to the technical problems in design and evaluation. The publisher—representing a source—needs to determine who and what the market is, what that market requires in terms of information content, format, and level of processing, and what channel or medium is most appropriate for sale to that market. The buyer—representing a recipient—needs to choose among the almost bewildering array of sources and channels through which to acquire desired information. Any of the media—representing a channel—needs to determine what sources and recipients it will serve and to choose among the alternative means for matching the impedences among them.

The point, of course, is that this third, largest context involves complex interactions among many sources, many channels, many recipients. Each of them must make decisions not only about the processing and communication of data but about the possible choices and the effects of competition from other choices.

References

Bar-Hillel. Y. and Carnap, R. (1953). Semantic information. In Jackson of Burnley, Willis Jackson, Baron (Ed.), *Communication Theory* (pp. 503–12). London: Butterworths.

Belkin, N. J. (1978). Information concepts for information science. *Journal of Documentation, 34*(1), (March), 55–85.

Boorstin, D. J. (1979). *Gresham's law: Knowledge or information?* Remarks at the White House Conference on Library and Information Services, Washington, D.C., November 19.

Brillouin, L. (1962). *Science and information theory.* New York: Academic Press.

Brittain, J. M. (1970). *Information and its users.* New York: John Wiley.

Derr, R. L. (1985). The concept of information in ordinary discourse. *Information Processing and Management, 21*(6) 489–99.

Dretske, F. I. (1981). *Knowledge and the flow of information.* Cambridge, MA: MIT Press.

Ellis, D. (1984). Theory and explanation in information retrieval research. *Journal of Information Science, 8*(1), (February), 25–28.

Farradane, J. (1980). Knowledge, information, and information science. *Journal of Information Science, 2*(2), 75–80.

Guiasu, S. (1977). *Information theory with applications.* New York: McGraw-Hill.

Hayes, R. M. (1962, 1964). *The Organization of large files with self-organizing capabilities.* Final Report on NSF Contract C-280. Los Angeles: Advances Information Systems, Inc.

Hayes, R. M. (1967). A theory for file organization. In Walter Karplus (Ed.), *Online computing: Time-shared man-computer systems* (pp. 264–89). New York: McGraw-Hill.

Machlup, F., & Mansfield, U. (1983). *The study of information: Interdisciplinary messages.* New York: John Wiley.

MacKay, Donald M. (1950). The nomenclature of information theory. In *Proceedings of the First International Symposium on Information Theory.* London: American Institute of Radio Engineers.

MacKay, D. M. (1954). Operational aspects of some fundamental concepts of human communication. In *Synthese, 9,* 182–98.

MacKay, D. M. (1969). *Information, mechanism, and meaning.* Cambridge, Mass: MIT Press.

McHale, John. (1976). *The Changing Information Environment*. Boulder, CO: Westview Press.

Nitecki, J. Z. (1985). The concept of information-knowledge continuum. *Journal of Library History, 20*(4), (Fall), 387–407.

Osinga, M. (1979). Some fundamental aspects of information science. *International Forum on Information & Documentation, 4*(3), (July), 28–34.

Paisley, W. (1980). Information and work. In B. Dervin & M. J. Voigt (Eds.), *Progress in communication sciences,* vol 2. Norwood, N.J.: Ablex.

Otten, K., & Debons, A. (1970). Towards a metascience of information: informatology. *Journal of the American Society for Information Science, 21*(1), 89–94.

Von Foerster, H. (1982). To know and to let know: An applied theory of knowledge. *Canadian Library Journal, 39*(5), (October), 277–84.

5

Deconstructing Information

Lee Thayer

This chapter raises some "meta—" questions about the concept of "information" itself. Where "information" is presumed to be relevant to the workings of the human world, there is the question of the communicability of whatever is described as "information." This places what is presumed to be informative—whether natural or human-made—in a system which is itself nondecomposable. In a nondecomposable (human communication) system, what we call "information" cannot be described apart from that system—is a function of that system, and cannot be empirically independent of it. The "problematics" that this flaw in our concept of "information" leave in its wake include those of description, of order, of limits, of power, of meaning, and of "communication." While such systems may appear to be decomposable (reducible) to an observer (the "psychologist's" or "third-person fallacy"), there is no "information" which is infinitely transportable. Whether something can be "information" or not, and what kind of "information" it is construed to be, is a function of the irreducible system—the story— which the humans involved imagine themselves to be in. All "information" is therefore "deconstructed" information.

One problem with the notion of "information" is, of course, that the system in which it occurs is not decomposable.

That is, information is what it is only because it occurs in the system it occurs in. The "same" information, perceived as vital in one system, may be irrelevant in another—or even malignant.

We may speak about it in the abstract. But what we talk about when we talk about "information" is no part of the empirical world.

We could certainly say this about anything we talk about: The concept is not the same as the stuff we imagine we are talking about.

To speak of bulls, the Spanish proverb has it, is not the same as to be in the bullring.

Even so, there is something *especially* sticky about the notion of "information."

It seems unlikely that we would get much argument if we suggested that speaking of love is not the same as loving. To make the word "love" with voice or pen is not the same as making love.

We acknowledge the difference; it is not problematic.

But the difference between the "information" of which we might speak and the "information" which we posit to be "there" seems to evaporate. We assume an identity between them.

Conceptually, we have assumed that the system in which specific "information" obtains is decomposable. It is not.

The unit of analysis is the system. Information, thus, could never be an independent variable, transportable from system to system. Sherlock Holmes' great advantage was that he understood "information" to be system-specific.

Our disadvantage is that we don't.

To conceive of "information" as system-independent is to make it, and our mission, unnecessarily problematic.

Let us not be frugal. That's but *one* problem with the notion of "information." There are several others.

Let us feast upon them, for the time it takes to tell. And for the advantage that might lie in doing so. It won't do to mislead ourselves about what we imagine ourselves to be up to.

Describing

One might, indeed, imagine that there are two quite distinct paradigms. Two mind-sets or *mentalités*. If so, one might also imagine that this is where they come to clash.

You see the problem. (Or at least this way of "seeing" it.) If you have to stand in the common paradigm to address the uncommon one, you deny the uncommon one by how you talk about it. If you stand in the uncommon paradigm, what you say doesn't make much sense to those who are standing in (who *under*stand from within) the common one.

Which is to say that, no matter how adeqate or inadequate our descriptions may be, they do not so much lead us into the "truth" as into our future. What we say about things is always more consequential than referential.

But that, too, pretends to be descriptive. As someone once observed, it is difficult to get someone to understand something if his paycheck (or in this case, his paradigm) depends upon his not understanding it.

Are we (merely) *describing* what is? Or are we *constructing* what is and thus what will be? Is that question somewhere around the crux of the problematic? Or is that notion, being rather central to the common paradigm, the sort of notion that could only move us in the uncommon one?

Paradoxes abound. There is thus no informed way of getting from the common to the uncommon paradigm. Paradox is no part of "information."

Perhaps this is partly what Abraham Heschel [1965, p. 8] had in mind when he wrote, "Thus the truth of a theory about man is either creative or irrelevant, but never merely descriptive." If the theory—or even the "facts"—about us are not irrelevant, then they alter us. We become what we say about ourselves.

But so do our facts and theories about things alter us. What we conceive to be an aspect of the world beyond us is necessarily an aspect of that with which we conceive: mind. So it is impossible to describe the world without describing ourselves—if in no other way, invariably as those who do the describing.

To speak of "information" is to define ourselves as that creature capable of informing and being informed.

This does not say there is such a thing as "information." It creates us as purveyors of and believers in "information." We are who we are because "it" is what we say it is.

The question is not so much, "What is information?" It is more like "What are people to be, having made such a thing as 'information' an aspect of their lives?"

Order

Sense requires order. Or the two may be, perhaps, the same thing.

If you can't put something into some kind of order, it is not likely to make sense to you. Something as nonsensical as the ABCs makes sense to us because B follows A before C. Try it some other way.

Or, "Love and marriage (used to) go together like horse and carriage." The carriage, like marriage, follows. If the carriage gets before the horse, we may conclude that something is wrong—meaning that there is something that doesn't make sense to me (us).

It could well be, as the biologist D'Arcy Thompson once suggested, that things are the way they are because they got to be that way. But that won't do. The mind, which emerges in order, expects order. If it isn't there, or can't be readily assumed, then what we apprehend is either incomprehensible or we must fit it into *some* context, some order of things.

When Einstein said that the mystery of the universe is its comprehensibility, he was of course referring to the order that mind, which "knows" it, must be composed of, and which it must impose upon that universe, to exist.

Thus that about which we might inform ourselves depends upon the ways in which we—which is to say, our mindfulness of the world—has been in-formed.

What we get out of James's "booming, buzzing confusion" or Freud's chaos is an in-formed world. This is the world that correlates with nothing better than the ways in which our minds have been in-formed to take that world into account.

"Information," then, is the name we give to whatever happens to ratify the mind/world or extends it in some (for some particular set of minds) orderly way.

This is "creative," in Heschel's sense, because both the mind and the world it "knows" must be reconstructed on an hourly/daily basis.

We institutionalize the ordered world as best and as much as we can. We do so in order not to have to be forever testing "its" comprehensibility—any shortfall in which would be a threat to our way of minding the world.

A cosmology (universally it would seem the first of human attempts to order the world and thus give birth and trajectory to the mind [Snell, 1953; Radin, 1927]) is but one grand way of institutionalizing orderliness. Structuring everyday life (Braudel, 1979) and numbers and lists (Goody, 1977) are examples of how the institutionalization of orderliness has evolved.

What is institutionalized requires no thought, no uncertainty. We are so well in-formed with respect to the usual order of lights at an electric signal that even colorblind people can manage it: red, yellow, green.

The question is: what goes with what, what precedes or what follows what, what is the sequence of events, what "causes" what, what justifies what? These "orders" are so built into our minding of the world that we do not see them for what they are.

Something happens. A floor creaks. We consider the "cause." Since it has just turned much colder, that would "explain" the happening.

It may have been a burglar. But if we "explain" the happening otherwise, then there is, for all practical purposes, no burglar. If there were a burglar, we'd be doing something about the burglary going on. Bishop Berkeley explained all this.

So the "information" is more a function of the order we impose than it is of the event—which event would be, without such ordering as we may impose upon it, meaningless, because unapprehended, incomprehensible, unordered.

What is incomprehensible cannot be said to be very informative, one way or the other, about itself. It could still be very informative, perhaps, for making some orderly description of the mind(s) for whom it was incomprehensible. This is the anthropologists' dilemma: In Schopenhauer's words, "What Peter tells me about Paul tells me more about Peter than it does about Paul." But even this is the case only if it is easier to "read" Peter (the tenuousness of ethnography) than it is to "read" Paul.

"Information," then, must take the path of least resistance. That is, we do not typically avoid the easy explanation so as to pit ourselves against the difficult or even the impossible one.

Either our minds are some function of what is, or what is is some function of our minding of it. Or both.

"Information," then, is some function of the correlation. It can't be something else.

There is another angle on this matter of order.

Physicist David Bohm's notion of implicate order (1980) suggests, for those of us interested in such things as "information," that something is what it is because something else is what *it* is. Leaving aside the advantages this might have for problems connected with quantum physics, the heuristic it may provide for anything that may involve human "information" is that a mind is what it is because the world it comprehends is what it is.

This would make the knower and the known, as Dewey put it, two aspects of the same thing.

What informs us is whatever we are informable about. Or, "information" is therefore the link between what we know and what we know it with.

"Information" thus describes the "connection" between a mind or set of minds that "knows" something and the something which is known. It is what underwrites the claim to "knowing." Or to "seeing"—as in "I can see that."

Possible "information" is thus a measure of the system that is struck by a knower or set or knowers and a known.

Limits

"Information" could not have been, could not be, a problem for people of traditional societies.

Their truths were given. The task was to maintain them.

Our truths have to be "discovered," as the scientizers sometimes put it.

It is no coincidence that it is only in cultures that believe in an infinitely expanding universe that there could be such a thing as an "information explosion."

Parkinson may have suggested something more than suspected. "Information" expands to fill the reaches of a people's universe.

The "word" was at one time considered magical. What could be done with words was considered wondrous. At the same time, terrifying. Worlds could be made with words. But, once made, could not be stopped with mere words.

There was thus a sense that what ought not be done with words (or any other form of mental artifact) was as important as what could be done with words.

There were limits.

There was a certain pragmatism in those limits. The American Indian child was raised to understand talk/words/"information" as follows: Make sure, before you open your mouth to speak (or ready your word processor to print, presumably), that what you are going to say will add to the beauty that already exists in the world.

The idea was that "information" was not seen as the path to anything. Rather, what didn't fit the right path could not be spoken of.

Limits.

Our notion is that the more "information" we have, the closer we must be getting to the "truth" about this or that.

We pollute. We decimate the forests: 75,000 trees to make but one Sunday *New York Times*. We imagine the trade-off to be worthy—probably necessary, so that we may be "informed."

We pollute—the land, the air, hearts, minds—we can't be concerned. We are junkies, "information" addicts, and we have to have our fix.

We fill the world with "information," supposing, perhaps, that that is a reasonable substitute for what is destroyed to make "it."

"Information" is thus a kind of cancer, a reasonably useful tool run amok. We maximize, imagining the "answer" to be in the glut. We can no longer discern a benign from a malignant "bit."

A world of infinitely expanding "information" is a mindless world, held together only by "information."

Our "reach" exceeds our "grasp."

Our minds are "blown."

A limitless world is a world unsuitable for human habitation.

No matter. The engine of "progress" is "information."

What makes games fun is that they have limits: they end, somebody wins. This game is ceasing to be fun for most people.

We could ask them, but that would just generate more "information."

Power

Power could (usefully) be understood as the prerogative to explain things.

The gods had it. Kings and queens had it. Popes used to have it. As did teachers, preachers, even parents.

Now, perhaps, only muggers and terrorists and bosses—and the latter only if it's the only job one can get.

Locate the power and you have located the soul and the destiny of a civilization.

For us, power lies in "information." It is where "the answers" are. It is where we go to supplicate. It is our Mecca.

The Romans did us no favor by making something like "information" possible apart from the person who was its mother, apart from the person who brought it into existence and was therefore responsible for it.

It was appropriate that the messenger, before this gift of the Romans, was killed. The "information" died with the messenger.

"Information" thus dilutes power, shifts power from the one in power to the "information" itself. We would have killed it if we had known that this is where power would come to rest.

People no longer explain. There is no longer someone in charge. There is no longer a visionary, a leader. There is only "information."

What it "tells" us, we must do.

Economic "information" drives the economy. "Information" about the sentiments of the voters drives politics. We used to drive our own cars; now "information," better at it than we, intercedes.

If we are "hollow men," as Eliot said, it is because we no longer have power over ourselves, or the course of our lives. What can't be reduced to "information" doesn't exist.

Whatever exists, exists as "information." We are all "waiting for Godot." A birth announcement is as good as a birth. "We regret to inform you . . ." will call forth reactions that may have at one time been ours to give only to the "real" thing.

In a world where a description of a soda is the "real thing," we ourselves may be less than "real."

It is only where people know themselves to be impotent that they can fantasize that an "information" device like a lap-top can give them "power."

"Information" is power, we say. We should know. The more we depend upon "it," the less it returns the power to us. It raises our victimage to a sense of being empowered only by "information."

The problem with Paradise (at least our version of it) was that the two people involved were overdetermined.

Our appetite for "information," boundless, returns us to that state.

What we invented now invents us. To paraphrase Churchill, we shape our "information," then our "information" shapes us.

That's power. Yet here is no one to kill, no one to depose.

Meaning

Yet another "problem" with our modern concept of "information" is that it obscures a relatively important empirical phenomenon—which might otherwise constitute . . . what, "counter-information"?

What gets obscured is that the mind deals only in meanings. The mind does not deal in "information." It is not capable of dealing in "information."

The stuff of the mind is meaning. The world that it may therefore apprehend is also a world of meanings.

Meanings are *human* artifacts. They do not exist in nature. As von Foerster says [1981, p. 263], "The environment contains no information." It is what we can give to something that informs us, not what it can give us. Aquinas said, "Each receives according to his (or her) capacity."

It isn't "information" that capacitates us. We capacitate "information." But differentially.

People are not interchangeable with respect to "information." "Information" cannot be "conveyed" to someone who is not capable of informing that "information."

The dark side of "information" is that it fits only into a transitive world. Given an intransitive world—the world of the receiver, the human world—"information" becomes a byproduct of mind, rather than the other way around.

Do you find that meaningful? If not, there is something problematic about our concept of "information."

What is it, exactly, that makes a list of nonsense syllables meaningful to a particular person, a crisis of the environment not?

Collingwood says that something is meaningful to the extent that a person can ask the question to which that something can be taken as an answer.

What is the question, that "information" may constitute the answer?

Communication

Luhmann [1990, p. 10] says that "information" is "an internal change of state, a self-produced aspect of communicative events and not something that exists in the environment. . . ."

Well, yes. But what he's assuming is what constitutes the problematic for the great many who want to conceive of or concern themselves with "information." To take "information" out of *some* "communicative event" and conceptually thereby to render it into something *sui generis* contributes mightily to this problematic.

By "self-produced," Luhmann must intend to make "information" a function of the mind of the person who claims it, and not a function of the source.

It's all metaphor, as Nietzsche said. We can do useful things by pretending that the references of our representations are "objective." But this illusion works only if one is surrounded by others who take the world into account in a fundamentally similar way.

That's "objectification": two or more minds can deny their subjectivity by colluding in making that of which they speak (or think) "objective." This is the lesson of Wittgenstein's shoe box.

But to make the stuff with which we "objectify" the world an aspect *of* that world creates a cancerlike problematic that can only become more pervasive and thus more insoluble.

Not that we would want to "solve" it. In a culture where most of the growth comes from problematics, who is to deny employment dedicated to increasing them?

However *that* may be, what is conceptually challenging here is that "information" is an irreducible, nondecomposable product of a specific communication *system*. Not of a communication *event*, for that may make the "information" appear to be transportable.

But a *system*.

Systems

Even here the paradigms come to clash.

For the system at issue is not the "objective" one. It is the "subjective" one.

The "world" is the world in mind. And this, however we may manifest it or "objectify" it, remains "subjective." When it comes to "Show-and-Tell," as Wittgenstein averred, I can tell you what's "on" my mind. But I can't show "it" to you.

And "information" is mind-stuff. It is not a property of that about which we speak, of that which exists in our "minding" of "it."

So the system of which "it" is a property is a cognitive system undergoing change.

We can't extract the "information" because it is not a property of the material world. It is a property of a cognitive system.

That we can call something "information" is no more remarkable than the commonplace of calling a particular location of the sun with respect to the earth a "sunset." It is neither more remarkable nor more "scientific," whatever *that* metaphor may mean.

Nor is it special. It is a metaphor. We have simply forgotten that, like a sunset, that is what it is. And in our lust to be literal, we have abdicated the empirical fact that, in our minding of it, that is all it *can* be.

The mind deals only in metaphors—only in raising what may *be* to the level of what can be said of it. The proposition that "the limits of my world are the limits of my communcability" (Wittgenstein again) was not intended to exclude "information."

If we were to exclude "information" from such limits, we would thereby remove it from the world to which it belongs. With "information" as with everything else, when we apprehend "it," we transform it from what it "is" to what we may be capable of saying of it.

That transform is from no-story to story. The system of which all "information" is a property is ultimately a kind of "story." It is the story—or some part of a story—within which that "information" informs.

The story is the thing. All the rest is complicity. That "information" which is not complicit, in this sense, is nothing because it is no part of the story.

A story is the sort of thing where one thing is related by relating to another thing, which itself is related to another thing, and so on.

The "and so on" is a sign in a story. If it "informs," that is because the story is engaged.

So "information" is the next line in the script of the story which is being made up as we go along.

If it isn't that, "it" is irrelevant.

References

Bohm, D. (1980). *Wholeness and the Implicate Order*. London: Routledge & Kegan Paul.

Braudel, F. (1979). *The Structures of Everyday Life*. Trans. S. Reynolds. New York: Harper & Row.

Goody, J. (1977). *The Domestication of the Savage Mind*. Cambridge: Cambridge University Press.

Heschel, A. (1965). *Who Is Man?* Stanford, CA: Stanford University Press.

Luhmann, N. (1990). *Essays on Self-Reference*. New York: Columbia University Press.

Radin, P. (1927). *Primitive Man As Philosopher*. New York: Appleton.

Snell, B. (1953). *The Discovery of the Mind*. Trans. T. G. Rosenmeyer. Cambridge, MA: Harvard University Press.

von Foerster, H. (1981). *Observing Systems*. Seaside, CA: Intersystems.

6

A Foucauldian Perspective of the Relationship between Communication and Information

Gary P. Radford

Contemporary metatheoretical discussions in the disciplines associated with the terms "communication" and "information" have been dominated by the impact of intellectual diversity on their relative disciplinary identities. These discussions have characterized communication and information as fields which are intellectually fragmented and which have had considerable impact on the project to establish each as distinct and coherent scholarly fields. A recent addition to this metatheoretical discourse is the proposition that the fields of communication and information can be related in terms of their concepts, methodologies, techniques, and institutions to form new areas of scholarship and knowledge. The present essay takes as its focus the discourse *of the relationship and the conditions which make possible its appearance as a significant and legitimate theme in the metatheoretical discourse of communication and information. The analysis adopts the philosophical perspective developed by Michel Foucault and outlines the structure of a potential Foucauldian account of the communication-information relationship in which the relationship is described in terms of its status and role as an element in a prevailing discursive system.*

Contemporary metatheoretical discussions in the disciplines associated with the terms "communication" and "information" have been dominated by the impact of intellectual diversity on their respective disciplinary identities. These discussions have characterized communication and information as fields that are intellectually fragmented and which have had considerable impact on the project to establish each as distinct and coherent scholarly fields (e.g., Berger, 1991; Budd and Ruben, 1979; Dervin, Grossberg, O'Keefe, and Wartella, 1989a, 1989b; Dervin and Nilan, 1986; "Ferment in the Field," 1983; Littlejohn, 1989; Machlup, 1983; Machlup and Mansfield, 1983). A recent addition to this metatheoretical discourse is the proposition that the fields of communication and information can be related in terms of their concepts, methodologies, techniques, and institutions to form new areas of scholarship and knowledge (e.g., Borgman and Schement, 1990; Pemberton and Prentice, 1990; Ruben, 1985a, 1985b, 1988, 1990, 1992; Ruben and Lievrouw, 1990). This claim is represented by the following statement by Borgman and Schement (1990):

> [the] evidence indicates the possibility of a trend toward convergence of subject matter and institutional structures. If this trend proves accurate, convergent evolution [of communication and information studies] might reflect a paradigmatic overlap of the two fields. It might also mean that communication scholars and information scientists stand at a rare, but exciting, intersection between the two fields, posing an opportunity for realignment, cross-fertilization, and richer theory. (P. 43)

In this essay, it is proposed that the "communication-information relationship," and its place in this metatheoretical discourse, can be viewed in three ways. The first is the concept of the communication-information relationship from the perspective of the participants whose speech and texts comprise the metatheoretical discourse. This participant-perspective is explicitly concerned with the issues that the relationship entails, the nature of the disciplines that comprise the relationship, and the plans of practical action that can be built on its theoretical foundation. The communication-information relationship is deployed as a representation of the actuality or possibility of such ideas, theoretical linkages, or research programs.

A second perspective is to view the communication-information relationship as a product of particular practices and institutions and to address the nature of the practices through which the relationship can come to be expressed as a valid domain of scholarly inquiry. For example, the emergence of the communication-information relationship in the metatheoretical discourse of certain scholarly communities could be indicative of a transcending mechanism of a "paradigm shift" in which the understanding of communication of information may be changing relative to these communities. The emergence can be described and explained in terms of the convergence of two communities and their respective world views. Such a perspective is grounded in the philosophical consideration of science and social science, exemplified by the paradigm thesis of Kuhn (1962, 1970). The philosophy of science perspective is interested less in the products of scientific communities than in the processes by which such products are produced. In Kuhn's account, these processes can be located in the structure of the scientific communities themselves and how they come to constitute scientific knowledge through periods of normal and revolutionary science. Traditionally, the discourse of the participant and the discourse of the philosopher have been constituted as separate, each with its own domain of knowledge. The participant is engaged in the task of defining the theoretical nature of the relationship while the philosopher engages in the task of describing the practices in which the participant is engaged through which such knowledge is produced and accepted.

The third perspective is one that referred to in the present essay as the Foucauldian, following the "archaeological" studies of Michel Foucault (see Foucault, 1961/1988, 1963/1975, 1966/1973, 1969/1972a) and will form the focus of this paper. An archaeological analysis dissolves the discursive boundaries within which it *becomes possible* to speak about communication and information as intellectual disciplines and also about the idea of a relationship between the two disciplines. It also makes problematic the separation of the discourses of the participant and the philosopher. The general hypothesis that structures a Foucauldian archaeological account is that a scientific discourse, exemplified here by communication and information, follows rules and regularities that can be described, but the description of those rules does not give priority or privilege to any particular body of texts. These regularities are concerned with systems of possibility for statements of theories rather than that to which these theories refer. It proceeds on the assumption that *what counts* as a theory or evidence for a theory is always part of a system of discourse that is historically located and that *includes,* rather than demarcates, the co-presence of a philosophical discourse.

The heart of the archaeological account is the separation of knowledge from the discursive systems which constitute, or make possible, knowledge. Foucault (1969/1972a) describes this distinction through the deployment of two French words, *connaissance* and *savoir,* which both translate into the English term "knowledge." By *connaissance,* Foucault (1969/1972a) is referring to "a particular corpus of knowledge, a particular discipline—biology or economics, for example" (p. 15). *Connaissance* incorporates the perspective of the participants and the philosophers of science from which communication and information would be considered as an organized body with particular theories and concepts, including that of the communication-information relationship. *Savoir,* on the other hand, is used by Foucault (1969/1972a) to refer to "the conditions that are necessary in a particular period for this or that type of object to be given to *connaissance*" (p. 15). A discipline such as communication studies (an example of *connaissance*) is always linked with "that which must have been said—or must be said—if a discourse is to exist that complies, if necessary, with experimental or formal criteria of scientificity" (Foucault, 1969/1972a, p. 182). An archaeological account of the "communication-information relationship" would consider the discourse in which the claim to the relationship appears, how the discourse is structured, and why this discourse should be in force at this historical moment and not another. The archaeology makes no reference to that which this discourse refers to and has no explicit interest in whether the symbols or terms deployed are an accurate or inaccurate account of "the state of their field." Of importance is the fact that this discourse has appeared and that it is utilized.

The present essay explicates themes and parameters that an archaeological account of the communication-information relationship would take into consideration. Rather than carrying out a Foucauldian analysis, the objective of this essay is to outline a potential Foucauldian study and describe the insights such a study would provide for the understanding of the role of the communication-information relationship in a metatheoretical discourse of communication and information studies.

Discourse, Science, and the Constitution of Scientific Knowledge

This essay is grounded in the proposition that, ultimately, all scholarly activity is held together by systems of discourse, both informal and formal. Discourse is defined very broadly here to include all forms of speech and text that characterize a field, including journals, books, letters, journalism, jokes, first drafts, galley proofs, electronic correspondence, conference presentations, letters to journals, telephone conversations, and face to face conversation. The totality of this discourse constitutes the reality, shape, and substance of a discipline among the individuals who speak about it in this way. The archaeological analysis of the communication-information relationship proceeds on the claim that disciplines are "produced" and "reproduced" in this communicative activity, as are the identities of the "communication and information scholars." The relationship between a discipline and its discourse is ultimately circular; proponents of a discipline produce discourse, but the manner in which the discourse is structured produces the discipline and the conditions of possibility for the emergence of a proponent who can be recognized as such. In other words, from this perspective, there can be no objective or external reference point from which either proponents or discourses can be referred. Such reference points are always constituted *within* the discursive system.

The same analysis can be applied to scientific discourses and their proponents who produce knowledge claims concerning truths (or potential truths) about the nature of the individual, the world, and the universe. Scientific knowledge is constituted within the boundaries of its discourse and cannot step beyond these (see Rorty, 1989, 1991a, 1991b). Hesse (1981) describes this relationship between truth and discourse as follows:

> Science is ideally a linguistic system in which true propositions are in one-to-one relation to facts, including facts that are not directly observed because they involve hidden entities or properties, or past events or far distant events. (P. xi)

Similarly, Aronowitz (1988) describes the discourse of science as follows;

> Science is a type of discourse with special languages, rules of investigation, and forms of inquiry that determine the form of a result. Together, these constitute elements of an ideology that is accepted by the scientific community and, to the extent this ideology becomes hegemonic in the larger social context, that is accepted as 'truth.' (P. 148)

In order to be considered as scientific, the knowledge claims of communication and information must be located in the primacy of the knowable. They must be capable of producing knowledge that is a faithful representation of some objective aspect of an external world (see Churchland and Hooker, 1985; Fleck, 1935/1979; Longino, 1990; van Fraassen, 1980). According to this view:

> the picture which science gives us of the world is a true one, faithful in its details, and the entities postulated in science really exist: the advances of science are discoveries, not inventions. (Van Fraassen, 1980, pp. 6–7)

To be called a science, the discourse must satisfy at least two conditions (1) it must make possible the "discovery of truths" through the deployment of terms such as objectivity, validity, generalizability, and the claim to the "scientific method" (Rorty, 1991a, 1991b); and (2) it must mask the circular nature of scientific knowledge with respect to the discursive conditions of its possibility. In other words, scientific discourse must perpetrate a distinction between its knowledge and its language. To say that science *produces* knowledge through the deployment of its discourse would be to deny that science can *discover* objective truths. Therefore, the claim to knowledge production must be marginalized.

The equating of knowledge with discourse proposes that scientific knowledge is *constituted,* rather than discovered, and is contingent upon the intersubjective understanding of a *communication* community (see Apel, 1972). Within this framework, discourse operates to constitute knowledge of a world for that community through the ongoing accomplishment of human interaction. Discourse is no longer seen, to use Rorty's (1979) terminology, as a mirror of an autonomous reality. Instead "truth [is] made rather than found" (Rorty, 1989, p. 3). The concept of discourse, as opposed to the concept of method, is the primary mode of explanation in the constitution of scientific knowledge.

Scientific knowledge does not simply accompany or exist alongside the capacity to communicate, but resides *in* that capacity (Apel, 1972; Carey, 1977, 1982; Deetz, 1973, 1977). An understanding of the communication-information relationship, therefore, lies in the explication of the *practice of making knowledge claims.* This requires a description of the *conditions* in which a claim to knowledge is made, and the discursive forms that such claims take. There is no explicit concern with the aspect of reality that the knowledge claim refers *to.* Rather one seeks to describe the communication-information relationship as it is constituted in the communicative act of claiming it to be an object of knowledge, and the discursive conditions in which such an act of claiming takes place.

The emphasis on the role of discourse provides the framework for an important area of debate for communication scholars regarding the relationship of rhetoric and science and their place within the academic tradition of communication studies (see Condit, 1990; Craig, 1990; Cushman, 1990; Nelson, Megill, and McCloskey, 1987; Prelli, 1989, 1990). It offers a framework for raising questions of privilege and power with respect to forms of knowledge that are not easily stated within the received view of scientific knowledge (see Aronowitz, 1988; Deetz, 1982; Deetz and Kersten, 1983; Deetz and Mumby, 1990; Foucault, 1975/1979, 1976/1980; Habermas, 1968/1971; Mumby, 1987, 1988). For example, Levine (1987), in comparing the demarcation of communicative practices categorized as "literature" and "science," argues that "literature and science, whatever else they may be, are modes of discourse, neither of which is privileged except by the conventions of the cultures in which they are embedded" (p. 3). The object of an analysis grounded in the recognition of the primary nature of discursive practice is to account for the nature of these conventions by which the demarcation of the two discourses is carried out and the way in which such conventions become expressed *as* (as opposed to *in*) science and literature. Aronowitz (1988), Hayles (1984), Krippendorff (1990), Paulson (1988), Prelli (1989), and Radford (1989, 1990, 1991) have all adopted similar orientations in their treatment of science. Similarly,

Myers (1990) examined the discursive conditions under which "texts produce scientific knowledge and reproduce the cultural authority of that knowledge" (p. ix). Like Levine (1987), Myers is interested in such questions as the means by which those texts categorized as "scientific" come to take on more "cultural authority" than those texts categorized as "literary criticism," "art," or "philosophy."

The conceptualization of knowledge in terms of its constitution through discursive practice is a significant framework for the analysis of contemporary issues in communication, knowledge, and science, because it provides an intellectual structure and vocabulary to articulate issues beyond the limits of a received view of science. For example, this perspective is able to support the claim that the structure of scientific discourse operates to mask the conditions of its own constitution and to demarcate itself as an autonomous and independent realm of knowledge (see Foucault, 1971/1972b). With discourse made primary in the constitution of scientific knowledge, the examination of the discursive practices by which science is able to suppress this relationship are made available for description.

The Foucauldian account of scientific discourse is not just a different way of conceptualizing the role of discourse *in* science, but of the way in which a scientific discourse produces the role of its discourse. Scientific discourse is conceived as a particular organization of knowledge in which discourse is constituted in a particular way in order to substantiate the claim to discovery. The problematization of discourse in itself distinguishes the Foucauldian perspective from studies that conceptualize discourse about fragmentation and convergence as representative of something that is happening with respect to a real body of scholars. The philosophy of Kuhn (1962, 1970) and the sociological studies of Merton (1973), for example, claim to be descriptive of the work of real scholars and their relative intellectual relationships. Studies on the structures of invisible colleges (Crane, 1972; Granovetter, 1973, Ruben and Weimann, 1979) and the pattern among citations (Griffith, 1989; McCain, 1986; Small, 1986) represent empirical investigations of this "real" structure. The emergence of the "communication-information relationship" is claimed to be a manifestation of real changes in the literatures of these fields, the activities of its members, and the positioning of its groups.

From the Foucauldian perspective, these accounts become an *integral part* of the discursive system to be described. To make the claim that one can describe a paradigm, an invisible college, or a citation pattern, is to simultaneously validate the self-evidence that such structures "exist" to be described and to marginalize the claim that such structures are discursively produced. Similarly, to claim the possibility of a communication-information relationship reinforces the self-evidence of communication and information as being distinct fields. The discourse of the paradigm and the communication-information relationship constitute each other by virtue of their appearance in the same discursive field and stand in relation to one another; paradigms claim to "describe" the movement and progression of disciplines while disciplines utilize paradigms in the constitution of their identity as fields which can be related. This theme is taken up in the following section.

A Kuhnian Paradox and the Possibility of a Communication-Information Relationship

The major claim of the present essay is that the metaphors of fragmentation and convergence deployed in the discourse of the participant are structured by the co-presence of the discourse of the philosopher. To be able to talk about fields as "fragmented," "unified," or "converging" requires the intersubjective acceptance that something tangible exists that can be fragmented, unified, or converged. This entity is usually considered in terms of intellectual structures of knowledge and theory, or institutional structures of research practices and methodologies that are validated as a domain of knowledge by the appearance of the philosophical discourse on the nature of science. The appearance of a communication-information relationship is made possible by the co-presence of the philosophical discourse. Without it, there would be nothing to converge or relate. This theme is developed with respect to one particular manifestation of the philosophical discourse, the work of Thomas Kuhn.

The Kuhnian discourse of the paradigm (Kuhn, 1962, 1970) is an integral part of the metatheoretical discourse of communication and information and is actively deployed by them in the production and legitimation of knowledge claims. Kuhn's texts are themselves accounts, conceived within the boundaries of a discursive system in which the claim of the paradigm could come to make sense. Kuhn's account is one particular way of talking about the way in which sciences develop, progress, and transform themselves, and how such processes give rise to particular objects and problems at particular historical points. The key point here, however, is not whether Kuhn's account is an accurate representation of science as it exists as a institutionalized process, but the manner in which it has become part of the way communication and information scholars talk about their activities.

As one particular way of speaking about science, Kuhn's account has found a central place in the metatheoretical discourses of the social sciences. Holland (1990), for example, notes,

[Kuhn's] assertions as to the importance of revolutionary paradigm change in the natural sciences were taken up avidly by sociologists and psychologists, ever struggling to achieve scientific respectability while grappling with the elusive and changing subject matter of human behavior, experience, and interactions. (P. 23)

If the implicit acceptance of Kuhn's model of science as a *description* of the structure of the communication-information relationship is bracketed, then Kuhn's text can be considered in its status *as an account*; a set of knowledge claims made possible by a particular discursive practice. The paradigm thesis is one account that has appeared among others, such as the falsification model of Popper (1934/1959), the research program account of Lakatos (1970, 1978), or the pragmatic approach of Rorty (1979, 1989, 1987/1991a, 1988/1991b). The Kuhnian thesis cannot and does not make the claim to be the only account of science. In the present essay, the truth or accuracy of Kuhn's account is not in question. Of interest is the *role* that Kuhn's discourse has in the discourse of communication and information studies. How is the discourse of paradigm used? Why is it given privilege in the metatheoretical discourse of communication and information studies? What does it enable? How does it structure and make possible certain aspects of the metatheoretical discourse of communication and information scholars?

The key to understanding the deployment of the Kuhnian account is the concept of the paradigm. A paradigm is deployed as the heart of that which defines a scientific community, the acceptance of which allows the talk of its fragmentation and convergence. Kuhn (1970) claims that "a paradigm is what the members of a scientific community share, *and*, conversely, a scientific community consists of men who share a paradigm" (p. 176). Shared in this view is a common body of knowledge, ideas, theories, concepts, and vocabularies that are acquired through an individual member participating in various institutionalized activities. For Kuhn, the community structure of a science is defined in terms of the similar educations and professional initiations of its members and their absorption of the same literatures through these activities. In a very important sense, the boundaries of the standard literature of a discipline mark the limits of a scientific subject matter. They mark the limit of that which is shared by members of that community.

In the Kuhnian account, intellectual communities are conceptualized as existing at different levels. At the most global level is the recognition that an individual is part of the community of all natural or social scientists. Below this comes membership in more specialized communities of scientific practice, such as the study of physics, chemistry, and astronomy. Membership in communities at this level is marked by the individual's subject of highest degree, their membership in professional societies, and the journals they subscribe to and read. Within these communities, sub-communities can further be identified within general disciplines; groups of people who specialize in particular branches of the subject. Below this, groups can be identified that work on specific problems and are highly specialized. These groups form the fundamental units that Kuhn's (1970) account takes as the producers and validators of scientific knowledge. Kuhn claims that, typically, these communities consist of perhaps one hundred members, occasionally significantly fewer. The ablest scientists may belong to several of such groups. The claim that such core knowledge producing groups can be isolated through attendance at special confer-ences, the distribution of draft manuscripts or galley proofs, and formal and informal communication networks, such as those discovered in corre-spondence and in the linkages among citations, has provided the founda-tion of the claim that such groups can be discovered and their nature described (see Crane 1972; Small, 1986; Ruben and Weimann, 1979).

From the Kuhnian perspective, the nature of scientific knowledge claims can be understood only through reference to the groups that produce them, and thus is ultimately a sociological account. The activities of actual groups are crucial to describing the nature of the knowledge claims they make. Kuhn (1970) gives the following questions as the basis for a consid-eration of scientific progress:

> How does one elect and how is one elected to membership in a particular community, scientific or not? What is the process and what are the stages of socialization of a group? What does the group collectively see as its goals; what deviations, individual or collective, will it tolerate; and how does it control the impermissible abberration? A fuller understainding of science will depend on answers to other sorts of questions as well, but there is no area in which more work is so badly needed. Scientific knowledge, like language, is intrinsically the common property of a group or else nothing at all. To understand it we shall need to know special characteristics of the groups that create and use it. (Pp. 209–10).

The Kuhnian perspective of science is ultimately the description of socio-logical boundaries; of the way in which individuals join and operate within groups that produce scientific knowledge. Language and discourse play a central role in the establishment and identification of recognizable com-munities. Language is a key identiying characteristic of the community, along with its knowledge. As Kuhn (1977) claims,

> One thing that binds the members of any scientific community together and simultaneously differentiates them from members of other apparently similar groups is their possession of a common language or special dialect. . . . in

learning such a language, as they must to participate in their community's work, new members acquire a set of cognitive commitments that are not, in principle, fully analyzable within that language itself. (P. xxii)

From the Kuhnian perspective, to understand the language of communication and information, the question of "what community is being referred to?" becomes important. Since language is considered the property of the group, the understanding of the language requires the analysis of the norms and practices of the group which produces and uses it. From this perspective, it would be important to know who are the communication and information scholars who talk about communication and information. What are their names? What do they write about? What is their background? What is the nature of the knowledge base they draw upon? What are the educations, professional institutions, and communication networks, formal and informal, that define them? What do you have to know in order to be considered part of the community? What are the institutions in which this object makes sense? The list of concerns is long, but necessary if one is to analyze the knowledge claims of a particular group of scientists.

These questions are important from a Kuhnian perspective since the existence of different communities implies the existence of different languages. Since a different language is an important differentiating characteristic of one group, then the ideas and language of one group will be different from another. For example, Kuhn (1977) claims that

proponents of different theories (or different paradigms, in the broader sense of the term) speak diferent languages–languages expressing different cognitive commitments, suitable for different worlds. Their abilities to grasp each other's viewpoints are therefore inevitably limited by the imperfections of the processes of translation and of reference determination. (Pp. xxii–iii)

The understanding of the knowledge claims of communication and information from this perspective requires a hermeneutic operation. To understand the discourse of a particular scientific community requires that one understands the community, accepts the paradigms of that community, and thinks of a problem such as the communication-information relationship in a manner consistent with the language of that community. One cannot think about the problems of a particular scientific community using a frame of reference acquired from another community, even if this community were considered philosophers or historians. This is Kuhn's principle of incommensurability (Kuhn, 1970, p. 198). To understand the knowledge of a particular community involves using the same language and paradigms to get at what they "really meant" in their own terms.

Being able to identify the community and its boundaries is fundamental in understanding the way in which that community "thinks" about its objects of knowledge. The project is similar to the task of the anthropologist entering a new culture and attempting to make sense of it. Machlup and Mansfield (1983) explicitly adopt the culture metaphor in their discussion of the fragmentation of the information discipline:

> We go into areas whose inhabitants speak foreign tongues (with many words sounding like words in our own language but having very different meanings); we try to find some guides to help us learn the meanings of these strange sounds; and we try to make sense of what we see and hear, yet we probably misunderstand much and are bewildered by even much more. (P. 5)

In many respects a complete reading of Kuhn's thesis leads to the conclusion that the paradigm would not be an appropriate *description* or *representation* of the practices of scholars in communication and information. This is a claim that proponents of the communication-information relationship must either ignore or systematically suppress. For example, Kuhn's account explicitly deals with progress of the mature natural sciences, such as physics, chemistry, and astronomy. The same account makes explicit serious reservations about the ability of the paradigm concept to account for the nature of the social sciences, such as communication and information.

The Kuhnian account of scientific knowledge is dependent on the notion of crisis. A concept of crisis implies a prior unanimity of the intellectual community that experiences one. Anomalies, by definition, can only exist with respect to firmly established expectations. Experiments create crises when they repeatedly go wrong for a community for whom everything has been going right. In the mature physical sciences, things generally mostly go right. This is represented by the term "normal science" in which there is agreement on fundamental concepts, tools, and problems. Without such consensus, there is no basis for problem solving. Disagreement about fundamentals is reserved for situations of crisis. It is difficult to see if a consensus of anything like a similar strength exists for the social sciences, especially in communication and information (see Ruben, 1985b). Because there is no base that they can take for granted, communication and information are still characterized by fundamental disagreements about the definition of their fields, paradigm achievements, and problems. The nature of these definitions forms the core of the metatheoretical discourse that makes possible the emergence of the communication-information relationship. There are two poles to this discourse. The first is constituted by the discourse of those participants who consider that such a definition cannot be found. For example, Dance and Larson (1976) remark that the variety of events that have been termed communication is so complex and so broad, so lacking in unifying elements, that it causes a great deal of difficulty for anyone who is interested in defining the term 'communication' for the purpose of examination and explication. (P. 21)

Bochner (1985) contends that the presence of such diversity is choking the progress of the field of communication:

Interpersonal communication is a vague, fragmented, and loosely defined subject that intersects all the behavioral, social, and cultural sciences. There are no rigorous definitions that limit the scope of the field, no texts that comprehensively state its foundations, and little agreement among practitioners about which frameworks or methods offer the most promise for unifying the field. (P. 27)

Delia (1987) asserts that "a significant feature of communication research has been its fragmentation as a topical concern across virtually all the disciplines and fields of the social sciences and humanities" (p. 20). Thayer (1979) agrees that "there exists no single scientific discipline having an exhaustive interest in communication as a systematic body of knowledge" (p. 8).

The other pole is constituted through claims that metatheoretical discourse should be concerned with the construction of a unified paradigm— a grand metatheory under which the various subfields can be incorporated. A means to this end in both communication and information is the encouragement and development of a dialogue between disciplines which hold these terms in common. For example, Budd and Ruben (1979) assert that the interdisciplinary nature of communication is a property of its identity as a distinct field, arguing that subjects as diverse as the sociology of knowledge, symbolic interactionism, general semantics, neurophysiology, and general system theory are "essential ingredients for the development of a comprehensive theory of human communication" (p. 4). Gerbner (1983) similarly believes that "The ferment in the field, and the expression and response to it in this symposium, test to the vitality of the discipline and to its ability to tackle the critical tasks ahead" (p. 362).

With respect to the disciplines of information, Machlup and Mansfield (1983) enumerated almost forty fields in which "information" plays a strategic role" (p. 9) and note that "interdisciplinary conflict and controversy are rampant" (p. 14). As with the field of communication, the claim is made that an interdisciplinary dialogue is sorely needed. However, Machlup and Mansfield (1983) contend that few scholars know of the extent of its dissemination and the diversity of the usage of the term information. As such, the term can take on a range of different meanings to those who use it. As Machlup and Mansfield (1983) argue,

Information is not just one thing. It means different things to those who expound its characteristics, properties, elements, techniques, functions, dimensions, and connections. Evidently, there should be *something* that all the things called information have in common, but it surely is not easy to find out whether it is much more than the name. (Pp. 4–5)

These examples from the metatheoretical discourse suggest that there can be no paradigm of communication or information in the Kuhnian sense because the lack of any *fundamental* agreement creates a situation where "either there can be no crises or there can never be anything else" (Kuhn, 1977, p. 222). Thus Rosengren (1989) has claimed that "the social sciences and the humanities [including communication studies] . . . do not have any *paradigms* in the strong sense of the word" (p. 21) and Kuhn (1974) has lamented that

Monitoring conversations, particularly among the book's enthusiasts, I have sometimes found it hard to believe that all parties to the discussion had been engaged with the same volume. Part of the reason for its success is, I regretfully conclude, that it can be too nearly all things to all people. (P. 459)

This analysis reveals a paradox in the metatheoretical discourse of communication and information. The Kuhnian account is a discursive prerequisite to the metatheoretical discussions of communication and information and their claim that their disciplines are fragmented and, possibly, on the point of convergence. However, the Kuhnian thesis is also a poor model for describing the activity of metatheoretical discussion within communication and information. Communication and information simply do not display paradigms in the sense Kuhn deploys the term. There is an inherent contradiction here which foregrounds the claim made by the present essay that *the Kuhnian discourse is deployed in the metatheoretical discourse and is not an external description of it.* The discourse of the participant and the philosopher are not distinct. Their co-presence makes each discourse possible.

When one switches from the self-evidence of the claim that the paradigm is representative of scientific communities to the view that Kuhn's text is an account that is deployed in conjunction with other texts, a different understanding occurs. A Foucauldian analysis of the communication-information relationship would require a description of the *deployment* of Kuhn's text in a discourse that produces a particular kind of knowledge claim about its own identity. For example, the deployment of the Kuhnian paradigm allows talk of disciplines being *organized* along rational criteria according to the paradigm that describes it. Such an organizational scheme is the crux of Burrell and Morgan's (1979) account of research on organizations. Their analysis is based on the acceptance of the claim that the paradigm has "an underlying unity in terms of its basic and often 'taken for granted' assumptions, which separate a group of theorists in a very fundamental way from theorists located in other paradigms" (p. 23). They also claim that "Each set identifies a quite separate social-scientific reality. To be located in a particular paradigm is to view the world in a particular way" (p. 24). Finally, they claim, "For a theorist to switch paradigms calls for a change in metatheoretical assumptions, something which, although manifestly possible, is not often achieved in practice" (pp. 24–25). Paradigm is deployed as the most fundamental level at which objects of knowledge can be organized along metatheoretical criteria and organized into paradigmatic cells.

The splitting of knowledge into cells or groups also allows the conditions necessary to express conflict between those cells. Paradigms are not considered equal. At any particular time, some paradigms are considered dominant, and others suppressed. For example, Hall (1989) wishes to "reflect on the current state of relations between the dominant paradigm in communication theory and the critical alternatives that are being offered in opposition to it" (p. 40). In Hall's view, the dominant paradigm of communication research is represented by a positivistic social science tradition. Hall's work, based in critical approaches to communication, is perceived as being an alternative to the dominant paradigm, struggling for recognition. Becker (1989), however, has challenged Hall's assumption of a dominant paradigm based on the tenets of positivism. "I . . . find it interesting that one of those speaking of the 'dominant paradigm' is Stuart Hall, who may himself be the most dominant of influential figures in communication studies today" (p. 126). This particular discourse is a key device in the legitimation of new approaches, both in communication and information. The emergence of critical and interpretive approaches to communication is explicitly characterized as a response to a dominant paradigm based in positivism (Carey, 1977; Deetz, 1973, 1977, 1982; Hawes, 1977). Similarly, Belkin's (1978, 1980) work in information retrieval is a response to a dominant systems paradigm (Dervin and Nilan, 1986; Saracevic, 1975) The rights and wrongs of each position are not of concern here. Of importance is the debate itself, and the means by which it is expressed. The claims of "dominance" and "alternatives to domination" are clearly expressed in a Kuhnian vocabulary, and largely accepted. Holland (1990) makes the general point as follows:

for anybody wishing to challenge authorities and orthodoxies, Kuhn provides the opportunity to identify a ruling paradigm (resonant with radical ideas about a ruling class). They might then go on to declare a new paradigm, which of course would not be understood by their blinkered predecessors. (P. 23)

The Kuhnian discourse can also be deployed to stifle dialogue through the claim to incommensurability. Notturno (1984) makes this claim with respect to dialogue within the field of psychology:

> Today, psychologists of different schools proceed from such opposing perspectives and use methods and techniques that are so different that it often seems impossible for them to communicate with one another. In my view, this situation results less from an essential incommensurability of paradigms than from an almost smug unwillingness on the part of normal research workers to investigate the conceptual foundations of competing schools . . . Kuhn's description of science is sometimes appealed to as a justification for ignorance. (Pp. 288–89)

The communication-information relationship can be viewed as representing a further deployment of this theme with respect to a claim of convergence. Ruben and Schement (1990) explicitly make the claim that

> in recent years, researchers have begun to focus attention on the relationship between communication and information. Where formerly each was studied in isolation, now growing numbers of scholars are reformulating the research agenda to integrate both phenomena. (P. 1)

From the Foucauldian perspective, it becomes clear that a philosophy of science (such as Kuhn) does not stand above the discourse produced by communication and information scholars as a detached and objective account. Rather, the appearance and deployment of Kuhn *within* the metatheoretical discourse of communication and information makes possible the appearance of the communication-information relationship. Aronowitz (1988) argues that the Kuhnian account becomes "an adjunct to science's effort to consolidate its position as a discourse that can be distinguished by more than mere differences of its object knowledge" (p. 249). The same argument is employed here to demonstrate that Kuhn's thesis is *used* by the metatheoretical discourse to organize, justify, and demarcate claims to self-identity, conflict, domination, fragmentation, and convergence. The paradigm does not represent an external reference point against which the validity of the communication-information relationship can be described and evaluated. The relationship and the paradigm produce each other; they make sense with respect to each other, and the interplay between these systems of discourse makes possible the claim that the disciplines of communication and information can be related in a systematic manner.

References

Apel, K. O. (1972). The a priori of communication and the foundation of the humanities. *Man and World, 5,* 3–37.

Aronowitz, S. (1988). *Science as power: Discourse and ideology in modern society.* Minneapolis: University of Minnesota Press.

Becker, S. L. (1989). Communication studies: Visions of the future. In B. Dervin, L. Grossberg, B. J. O'Keefe, and E. Wartella (Eds.), *Rethinking communication. Volume one: Paradigm issues.* Newbury Park, CA: Sage.

Belkin, N. J. (1978). Information concepts for information science. *Journal of Documentation, 34*(1), 55–85.

Belkin, N. J. (1980). Anomalous states of knowledge as a basis for information retrieval. *Canadian Journal of Information Science, 5,* 133–43.

Berger, C. R. (1991). Communication theories and other curios. *Communication Monographs, 58*(1), 101–13.

Bochner, A. P. (1985). Perspectives on inquiry: Representation, conversation, and reflection. In M. L. Knapp and G. R. Miller (Eds.), *Handbook of interpersonal communication.* Beverly Hills, CA: Sage.

Borgman, C. L. and Schement, J. R. (1990). Information science and communication research. In J. M. Pemberton and A. E. Prentice (Eds.), *Information science: The interdisciplinary context.* New York: Neal-Schuman.

Budd, R. W. and Ruben, B. D. (Eds.), (1979). *Interdisciplinary approaches to human communication.* Rochelle Park, NJ: Hayden.

Burrell, G. and Morgan, G. (1979). *Sociological paradigms and organizational analysis.* London: Heinemann.

Carey, J. W. (1977). Mass communication research and cultural studies: An American view. In J. Curran, M. Gurevitch, and J. Woollacott (Eds.), *Mass communication and society.* London: Edward Arnold.

Carey, J. W. (1982). The mass media and critical theory: An American view. In M. Burgoon (Ed.), *Communication yearbook 6.* Beverly Hills, CA: Sage.

Churchland, P. M. and Hooker, C. A. (Eds.). (1985). *Images of Science: Essays on realism and empiricism.* Chicago: University of Chicago Press.

Condit, C. M. (1990). The birth of understanding: Chaste science and the harlot of the arts. *Communication Monographs, 57*(4), 323–27.

Craig, R. T. (1990). The speech tradition. *Communication Monographs, 57*(4), 309–14.

Crane, D. (1972). *Invisible colleges: Diffusion of knowledge in scientific communities.* Chicago: University of Chicago Press.

Cushman, D. P. (1990). A window of opportunity argument. *Communication Monographs, 57*(4), 328–32.

Dance, F. E. X. and Larson, C. E. (1976). *The functions of human communication.* New York: Holt Rinehart and Winston.

Deetz, S. A. (1973). An understanding of science and a hermeneutic science of understanding. *Journal of Communication, 23,* 139–59.

Deetz, S. A. (1977). Interpretive research in communication: A hermeneutic foundation. *Journal of Communication Inquiry, 3,* 53–69.

Deetz, S. A. (1982). Critical interpretive research in organizational communication. *Western Journal of Speech Communication, 46,* 131–49.

Deetz, S. A. and Kersten, A. (1983). Critical models of interpretive research. In

L. L. Putnam and M. E. Pacanowsky (Eds.), *Communication and organizations: An interpretive approach*. Beverly Hills, CA: Sage.

Deetz, S. A. and Mumby, D. K. (1990). Power, discourse, and the workplace: Reclaiming the critical tradition. In J. A. Anderson (Ed.), *Communication yearbook/13*. Newbury Park, CA: Sage.

Delia, J. G. (1987). Communication research: A history. In C. R. Berger and S. H. Chaffee (Eds.), *Handbook of communication science*. Beverly Hills, CA: Sage.

Dervin, B., Grossberg, L., O'Keefe, B. J., and Wartella, E. (Eds.). (1989a). *Rethinking Communication. Volume one: Paradigm issues*. Newbury Park, CA: Sage.

Dervin, B., Grossberg, L., O'Keefe, B. J., and Wartella, E. (Eds.). (1989b). *Rethinking Communication. Volume two: Paradigm exemplars*. Newbury Park, CA: Sage.

Dervin, B. and Nilan, M. (1986). Information needs and uses. In M. E. Williams (Ed.), *Annual review of information science and technology (ARIST)* (Vol. 21). New York: Knowledge Industry Publications.

Ferment in the Field. (1983). *Journal of Communication, 33*(3).

Fleck, L. (1979). *Genesis and development of a scientific fact* (F. Bradley and T. J. Trenn, Trans.). Chicago: University of Chicago Press. (Original work published 1935).

Foucault, M. (1972a). *The archaeology of knowledge* (A. M. Sheridan Smith, Trans.). New York: Pantheon. (Original work published 1969).

Foucault, M. (1972b). The discourse on language. In M. Foucault, *The archaeology of knowledge* (A. M. Sheridan Smith, Trans.). New York: Pantheon. (Original work published 1971).

Foucault, M. (1973). *The order of things: An archaeology of the human sciences*. New York: Vintage Books. (Original work published 1966).

Foucault, M. (1975). *The birth of the clinic: An archaeology of medical perception* (A. M. Sheridan Smith, Trans.). New York: Vintage Books. (Original work published 1963).

Foucault, M. (1979). *Discipline and punish: The birth of the prison* (A Sheridan, Trans.). New York: Vintage Books. (Original work published 1975).

Foucault, M. (1980). *The history of sexuality. Volume one: An introduction* (R. Hurley, Trans.). New York: Vintage Books. (Original work published 1976).

Foucault, M. (1988). *Madness and civilization: A history of insanity in the age of reason* (R. Howard, Trans.). New York: Vintage Books. (Original work published 1961).

Gerbner, G. (1983). The importance of being critical—In one's own fashion. *Journal of Communication, 33*(3), 355–62.

Granovetter, M. S. (1973). The strength of weak ties. *American Journal of Sociology, 78*(6), 1360–80.

Griffith, B. C. (1989). Understanding science: Studies of communication and information. *Communication Research, 16*(5), 600–14.

Habermas, J. (1971). *Knowledge and human interests* (J. J. Shapiro, Trans.). Boston: Beacon Press. (Original work published 1968).

Hall, S. (1989). Ideology and communication theory. In B. Dervin, L. Grossberg, B. J. O'Keefe, and E. Wartella (Eds.), *Rethinking communication. Volume one: Paradigm issues*. Newbury Park, CA: Sage.

Hawes, L. C. (1977). Toward a hermeneutic phenomenology of communication. *Communication Quarterly, 25*(3), 30–41.

Hayles, N. K. (1984). *The cosmic web: Scientific field models and literary strategies in the 20th century.* Ithaca, NY: Cornell University Press.

Hesse, M. (1981). *Revolutions and reconstructions in the philosophy of science.* Brighton, UK: Harvester Press.

Holland, R. (1990). The paradigm plague: Prevention, cure, and innoculation. *Human Relations, 43*(1), 23–48.

Krippendorff, K. (1990, June). The power of communication and the communication of power: Toward an emancipatory theory of communication. Paper presented at the 40th annual conference of the International Communication Association, Trinity College, Dublin, Ireland.

Kuhn, T. S. (1962). *The structure of scientific revolutions.* Chicago: University of Chicago Press.

Kuhn, T. S. (1970). *The structure of scientific revolutions* (2nd ed., Enlarged). Chicago: University of Chicago Press.

Kuhn, T. S. (1974). Second thoughts on paradigms. In F. Suppe (Ed.), *The structure of scientific theories.* Urbana: University of Illinois Press.

Kuhn, T. S. (1977). *The essential tension: Selected studies in scientific tradition and change.* Chicago: University of Chicago Press.

Lakatos, I. (1970). Falsification and the methodology of scientific research programs. In I. Lakatos and A. Musgrave (Eds.), *Criticism and the growth of knowledge.* Cambridge: Cambridge University Press.

Lakatos, I. (1978). *The methodology of scientific research programs.* Cambridge: Cambridge University Press.

Levine, G. (1987). One culture: Science and literature. In G. Levine (Ed.), *One culture: Essays in science and literature.* Madison: University of Wisconsin Press.

Littlejohn, S. W. (1989). *Theories of human communication* (3rd. ed.). Belmont, CA: Wadsworth.

Longino, H. E. (1990). *Science as social knowledge: Values and objectivity in scientific inquiry.* Princeton, NJ: Princeton University Press.

Machlup, F. (1983). Semantic quirks in studies of information. In F. Machlup and U. Mansfield (Eds.), *The study of information: Interdisciplinary messages.* New York: Wiley.

Machlup, F. and Mansfield, U. (1983). Cultural diversity in studies of information. In F. Machlup and U. Mansfield (Eds.), *The study of information: Interdisciplinary messages.* New York: Wiley.

McCain, K. W. (1986). Co-cited author mapping as a valid representation of intellectual structure. *Journal of the American Society for Information Science, 37*(3), 111–22.

Merton, R. K. (1973). *The sociology of science.* Chicago: University of Chicago Press.

Mumby, D. K. (1987). The political function of narrative in organizations. *Communication Monographs, 54,* 113–27.

Mumby, D. K. (1988). *Communication and power in organizations: Discourse, ideology, and domination.* Norwood, NJ: Ablex.

Myers, G. (1990). *Writing biology: Texts in the social construction of scientific knowledge.* Madison: University of Wisconsin Press.

Nelson, J. S., Megill, A., and McCloskey, D. N. (Eds.) (1987). *The rhetoric of the human sciences: Language and argument in scholarship and public affairs.* Madison: University of Wisconsin Press.

Notturno, M. A. (1984). The Popper/Kuhn debate: Truth and two faces of relativism. *Psychological Medicine, 14,* 273–89.

Paulson, W. R. (1988). *The noise of culture: Literary texts in a world of information.* Ithaca, NY: Cornell University Press.

Pemberton, J. M. and Prentice, A. E. (1990). *Information science: The interdisciplinary context.* New York: Neal-Schuman.

Popper, K. R. (1959). *The logic of scientific discovery.* New York: Basic Books. (Original work published 1934).

Prelli, L. J. (1989). *A rhetoric of science: Inventing scientific discourse.* Columbia: University of South Carolina Press.

Prelli, L. J. (1990). Rhetorical logic and the integration of rhetoric and science. *Communication Monographs, 57*(4), 315–22.

Radford, G. P. (1989, March). The subliminal discourse: A Foucauldian analysis of a controversy in psychology. Paper presented at the 10th Annual Conference on Discourse Analysis, Temple University, Philadelphia, PA.

Radford, G. P. (1990, June). Communication and the constitution of scientific knowledge: Dominance, privilege, and the politics of truth. Paper presented at the 40th annual conference of the International Communication Association, Trinity College, Dublin, Ireland.

Radford, G. P. (1991). Communication and the constitution of scientific knowledge: A Foucauldian examination of the discursive production of subliminal perception in psychology. Unpublished doctoral dissertation, Rutgers University, New Brunswick, NJ.

Rorty, R. (1979). *Philosophy and the mirror of nature.* Princeton, NJ: Princeton University Press.

Rorty, R. (1989). *Contingency, irony, and solidarity.* New York: Cambridge University Press.

Rorty, R. (1991a). Science as solidarity. In R. Rorty, *Objectivism, relativism, and truth: Philosophical papers* (Vol. 1). New York: Cambridge University Press. (Original work published 1987).

Rorty, R. (1991b). Is natural science a natural kind? In R. Rorty, *Objectivism, relativism, and truth: Philosophical papers* (Vol. 1). New York: Cambridge University Press. (Original work published 1988).

Rosengren, K. E. (1989). Paradigms lost and regained. In B. Dervin, L. Grossberg, B. J. O'Keefe, and E. Wartella (Eds.), *Rethinking communication. Volume one: Paradigm issues.* Newbury Park, CA: Sage.

Ruben, B. D. (1985a). The coming of the information age: Information, technology, and the study of behavior. In B. D. Ruben (Ed.), *Information and behavior* (Vol. 1). New Brunswick, NJ: Transaction.

Ruben, B. D. (Ed.) (1985b). *Information and behavior* (Vol. 1). New Brunswick, NJ: Transaction.

Ruben, B. D. (Ed.) (1988). *Information and behavior* (Vol. 2). New Brunswick, NJ: Transaction.

Ruben, B. D. (1990). Redefining the boundaries of graduate education. In J. M. Pemberton and A. E. Prentice (Eds.), *Information science: The interdisciplinary context.* New York: Neal-Schuman.

Ruben, B. D. (1992). The communication-information relationship in system theoretic perspective. *Journal of the American Society for Information Science, 43* (1), 15–27.

Ruben, B. D. and Leivrouw, L. A. (1990). *Mediation, information, and communi-cation—Information and Behavior* (Vol. 3). New Brunswick, NJ: Transaction.
Ruben, B. D. and Schement, J. R. (1990, April 4). Letter accompanying the Call for Papers for *Information and Behavior* (Vol. 4).
Ruben, B. D. and Weimann, J. M. (1979). The diffusion of scientific information in the communication discipline: Conceptualization and propositions. *Communication Quarterly, 27*(1), 47–53.
Saracevic, T. (1975). Relevance: A review and a framework for the thinking on the notion in information science. *Journal of the American Society for Information Science, 26*, 321–42.
Small, H. (1986). The synthesis of speciality narratives from cocitation clusters. *Journal of the American Society for Information Science, 37*(3), 97–110.
Thayer, L. (1979). Communication—*sine qua non* of the behavioral sciences. In R. W. Budd and B. D. Ruben (Eds.), *Interdisciplinary approaches to human communication*. Rochelle Park, NJ: Hayden.
van Fraassen, B. C. (1980). *The scientific image*. Oxford: Clarendon Press.

7

Information Theory and Telecommunications: A Review

Meheroo Jussawalla and Yale M. Braunstein

The implementation of dynamic changes in information technology (IT) has created a unique interdependence among nations, whether they are capitalist or communist, developed or underdeveloped. Adoption of new technologies for the creation, storage, and distribution of information has reduced the usefulness of the rigid hierarchical organization structures which were effective in the past. Greater informational efficiency makes for better utilization of scarce resources and minimization of effort duplication. If we are to reduce the hazards of a reckless application of information technology and to maximize the benefits from its use, then we need to fully understand the nature and characteristics of information and information technology. This paper will attempt to show the relationship between information theory and telecommunications and how the latter exercises a pervasive influence on several present day institutions.

How Economists Analyze Information

In 1970 Shackle identified the process of "continuous and endless search for knowledge" as a prime mover for production and exchange. Jacob Marschak (1974) described the modern economy as a process of inquiring, communicating, and decision making. Stocks and flows of information have been recognized as determinants of organizational change. However, conventional economic theory has been reluctant to view information as a commodity because it does not fit into the neoclassical framework of economic analysis. This framework is based on a set of "perfect information" assumptions and is a static equilibrium model that does not admit changing information flows.

Explicit models of the value of pricing information were an early area in which information, or the lack thereof, was explored. Stigler (1961) analyzed the market behavior of agents when information about prices is not known. Information search for prices was dealt with by Nelson (1970) and others. Akerlof (1970) dealt with market behavior in the presence of uncertainty about the quality of the products. Jonscher (1982) moved the analysis from market failure to an analysis of two aspects of the theory of information economics, namely the production and distribution of goods and services and the organization of these activities. The latter problem is one of handling and processing information, which the author claims consumes a very substantial proportion of a nation's resources.

The X-efficiency theory of the firm (Leibenstein, 1975) argues that environmental changes in which a firm finds itself will result in varying costs per unit of output rather than the minimal costs assumed by conventional microeconomic theory. This suggests the presence of structural elements within the organization of the firm that influence the flow of those signals (information) intended to spur effort and provide incentives. It may then be possible to consider this type of information either as an input for production or as a determinant of the worker's productivity.

Further studies have brought about a new dimension to the links between economics and information science (Lamberton 1984). One has to distinguish between the technology of distributing and transmitting information, which is changing and advancing rapidly, and the content of information that flows through these conduits. Spence (1974) pointed out that recent interest in computers and telecommunications overshadows the pervasive influence of information in markets and the impact of information sectors on the rest of the economy. Another distinction that has emerged is between the economics of uncertainty and the economics of information, the former being an analysis of how one adapts to uncertainty while the latter concerns how one overcomes it (Hirshleifer and Riley, 1979). Tying many of these areas together, Arrow (1974) introduced the importance of organizational change as a determinant in overcoming uncertainty.

The need to understand the processes of information dissemination has been a vital issue with economists. Hayek, in 1949, considered this problem as fundamental due to the fact that the way in which knowledge is communicated for people to plan their market activities is crucial to any theory explaining the economic process. But the concept of information dissemination needs to be seen in a broader context than the mere analysis of market signals, be they of price or quantity. Torr (1980) raised the issue of whether information should be introduced in a general equilibrium model as yet another commodity for which supply and demand curves can be derived. But information is an elusive concept. It is intangible, cannot be quantified, and defies inclusion in any complex of functional relationships. One of the virtues of general equilibrium models is that they suggest an optimal allocation of resources in a competitive market economy. Why then, if all the participants in the market are fully informed, should resources be devoted to the dissemination of information? The very existence of the commercial and consumer information services is sufficient evidence to challenge the neoclassical assumption.

Relaxation of the perfect-knowledge assumption has led to search models in which agents search for information until the marginal cost of acquiring it is equal to the expected marginal benefit (Newman, 1976). In departing from this assumption, Keynes stated that our knowledge of the future is both incalculable and subject to sudden changes. Lamberton (1971) interpreted this to mean that Keynes did not accept the assumption of perfect knowledge. This in turn implies that while the microeconomics of information is an outgrowth of the economics of uncertainty, it is actually changes in information that constitute the essence of Keynesian theory. In other words, the economics of information is active where the economics of uncertainty is passive, and gathering information for decision making is critical to the economics of information (Hirshleifer, 1973).

Technological uncertainty and market uncertainty are both considered relevant reasons for information search. Each individual wants to be certain about his own endowment and market opportunities; and obtaining this information is costly, not costless as implied by the previously assumed notions of perfect information. In this search for information, a distinction has been drawn between private and social value of information (Hirshleifer, 1971). Private information has no social value in the sense of redistribution and does not lead to any improvement in productive arrangements. Public information affects production decisions in a socially optimal sense. These gains are offset against the costs of acquisition and dissemination. Using this approach, informational efficiency becomes an important policy objective, and the method for achieving it is information resource management. Arrow (1962), in claiming that free enterprise does not result in an ideal allocation of resources to the production of knowledge, concluded that optimal allocation requires government financing of research and invention. Demsetz (1969), however, challenged Arrow's assumption that private enterprise does not invest sufficiently in invention and knowledge production because of aversion to risk. He argued that government institutions replacing the market may not bring about an efficient solution. However, technological dynamism has compelled current changes in regulatory policy (the removal of monopoly in the telecommunications sector) that have generated greater informational efficiency and organizational benefits that Arrow had pointed out in the 1960s.

Information is recognized both as a commodity and as a resource. Information as a commodity is sold at an equilibrium price set under the same competitive conditions as any other marketable item. For example, information providers use videotext gateways to market their commodity or service over databases like Prodigy, Nexis/Lexis, and Dialog. Likewise, the value of information varies depending on its utility and scarcity. The study of information as an economic commodity in its own right was recognized by Galbraith (1967). He emphasized "organized knowledge" as the basis for his postulated corporate technological imperatives. Galbraith's "technostructure" owed its existence to specialized scientific and technical knowledge; information, therefore, became the basic input in the process of decision making.

Goldsworthy (1979) claimed there is exponential growth in volume of information, and he characterized the information environment that resulted as having a greater interdependence of previously autonomous institutions and services. However, while information as a commodity has some characteristics in common with other goods and services, it has the special characteristic of being retained even after sale. Its availability is not affected by the number of persons using it and in this sense it can be treated as a resource. It is synergistic and grows on itself. It affects not only production and productivity but market integration and international trade as well.

The problem with considering information as a resource is that such an approach often creates a basic misunderstanding of its nature and value. It is unlike both natural and human resources. For example, information is usually transmitted through a channel or conduit, but its value may or may not be independent of the value of the medium. Furthermore, while we know we live in an information society, we do not fully understand the implications of such a society for economic development and cultural change, neither as it now exists nor as it is likely to develop in the future.

Arrow, in *Limits to Organization* (1974), affirmed that to the economist different bits of information will have different benefits and costs. But to the information theorist their value is equal. Communication then is not just information exchange, but a process in which participants create and share information with each other in order to reach mutual understanding. As a resource it is similar to capital and labor, but its uniqueness is accentuated by the fact that it is not depletable over time and forms an integral basis for service industries, for technology transfer, and for R&D. However, this uniqueness raises questions not only of how to handle information in an economic sense, but also of privacy, intellectual property rights, and freedom of information.

The economic concept of property rights and its impact on economic agents is difficult to apply to information either as a commodity or as a resource. The fact that information can be sold, exchanged, or given away and yet be retained by the transferor makes the enforcement of property rights ambiguous. To some extent information often has the characteristics of a "public good." The marginal cost of an additional copy is usually relatively low, and it is difficult to exclude nonpayers. There are multiple issues which have to be included in an economic theory that deals with the informational efficiency of economic systems, regulation of information flows, the economics of transborder information flows, and the economics of information transfer. Many of these will be discussed below.

The Theory of Information Economics

Against this backdrop of efforts made by economists to integrate information into economic theory, we will attempt to present the theorectical constructs in a consistent fashion, with no claims to this being the definitive treatment of an obviously wide and diverse literature. In the previous section, we noted that demand for information arises because of the presence of uncertainty. In fact, Arrow (1979) defined information as the reduction in uncertainty, stating that probability theory provides a useful way of characterizing learning or the modification of perceptions through the acquisition of information. Thus, in the process of decision making, a choice among alternative decisions will be a choice among probability distributions of consequences. The problem of information economics arises when the probability distribution of these consequences is a variable.

Information signals are a benefit to decision making because they enhance the utility of the decision made using that information over the utility of one made without the benefit of the information. The cost of information handling has declined over the last two decades and this has contributed to increases in productivity. Furthermore this decline in cost is independent of the scale on which it is used, such as in the case of Transborder Data Flows (TDF). Likewise, using computer access to information exhibits the economic property associated with the provision of "club goods." This involves an exchange of specialized of specific types of information available only to members of a closed user group. Therefore, it is the assumption of excludability which gives information so exchanged the characteristic of a club good or a quasi-public good (Jussawalla and Cheah, 1986). This type of specialized information flows has led to the concept that division of labor in information gathering is fundamental to any organization and results in higher gains in efficiency.

Lamberton (1984) emphasizes the value of the information content as the vital element of corporate growth and microeconomic productivity. According to this view, the extent of the exploitation of economic resources leads to informational efficiency, a more significant determinant of economic growth than per capita income or economic policies per se. Because asymmetric information resources result in differential rates of learning, Lamberton recommends that economics be reinforced with a theory of learning.

If we assume that there is continued presence of asymmetrical information, what will be its effect on market performance? Akerlof (1970) responded that high quality products will be withdrawn from the market if buyers cannot distinguish them from low quality ones. Thus, information signals should be symmetric for market forces to generate non-pathological outcomes. In their absence, sellers often devote valuable resources to acquire such signals. While this activity is rational from the individual seller's point of view, it represents a costly waste of resources on the part of society. When information is transmitted efficiently, either the market will come to equilibrium with full information and some spreading of risk or it will not equilibrate. However, if the cost of exogenous information is high, there is a likely welfare cost, in terms of Pareto optimal full information equilibrium.

Therefore, because the decision maker profits from the signals, the choice of signals becomes a variable in the decision-making process. But even apart from individual decision makers, organizational decisions must be based on information in order to minimize risk. However, as pointed out by Arrow (1979), organizations are not always quick to adapt to change, and, as a result, their structures may become rigid and unresponsive.

Any study of information economics is in reality the application of basic tools of economics such as demand functions, cost functions, production functions to problems of optimal pricing, and investment decisions. Hence the analytical emphasis is on the standard concept of resource allocation to satisfy certain marginality conditions of cost, benefits or productivity. If information economics adheres to the principles defined above, it suffers from the same conceptual restrictions as those of neoclassical economics in general. These restrictions stem from similar assumptions underlying both approaches, namely: (1) only consumers and firms within an economy consciously attempt to maximize utility or profit by economizing on scare resources; and (2) choices over available alternatives are made in the light of perfect information.

Economists have come to realize that models built within the traditional framework tend to overlook certain phenomena such as possibilities arising from the availability, use of, and access to information and the institutional changes that affect the incentive structure and thereby resource allocation.

These areas have been analyzed by many economists, who extend the concept of maximization in order to explain the behavior of politicians, governments, local authorities, and regulated industries. These themes are established within the economics of property rights, the theory of public choice, and the positive theory of economic regulation. The inclusion of an institutional framework helps to determine the ownership pattern of information resources, sets the limits of conflicts between economic agents (changes in rules of the game) and provides the basis for social decisions in information policies.

At the microeconomic level each firm sets its goals not merely according to market dictates, but by a desire to achieve strategic, long-term competitiveness. This is done through greater reliance on economics of scope, particularly in those industries affected by technical change (Lamborghini, 1989). Therefore, where information systems are used by corporations, be they large or small, to gain competitive advantage, they play an important role in cost reduction and operational efficiency.

Braunstein (1985) explicitly considered information as a factor of production using a variety of standard production functions. He found that the Cobb-Douglas production function does not adequately capture the manner by which information purchases are combined with other inputs in the production process. In assessing the value added of information by manufacturing firms he concluded that there was significant underutilization of information, and that the substitution of information for capital is less responsive to changes in relative prices than implied by the Cobb-Douglas assumptions. He attributed this underinvestment to in-house supply of information; however, the public goods nature of information may be another reason.

The shift in resources from the conventional production sectors of agricultural and industry to primarily information handling functions constitutes one of the most striking structural changes to have taken place in the economics of industrialized countries. Jonscher (1984) traced an intricate linkage between the information handling activities and the productivity of the economy. For example, he showed that growth in industrial output and efficiency can be the result of the utilization of information processing resources. Likewise, the information-handling sector itself has become sufficiently large, and its own internal productivity has a major effect on the overall output per worker. (See Nightingale [1988] for a critique of Jonscher's assumptions and approach.) This productivity can be attributed to technological changes that, according to Pulley and Bruanstein (1984), are scale and scope augmenting. Their results, drawn from the analysis of an information sector firm whose outputs are abstracts of articles in technical journals, indicate that technological change (a switch to computer processing) increased firm-specific returns-to-scale and scope while providing the potential for reduced future costs.

Information-intensive technologies have rendered economics of industrialized countries highly sensitive to the presence of information resources and to the need for efficiencies in their use. In addition, there is considerable research evidence to indicate the emergence of information-based economics. As a result of specialization in economic function, information acquisition and dissemination have become activities in which practitioners are rewarded by exchanges with other economic agents (Hirshleifer and Riley, 1979). The information component of advanced economic systems is seen to play more than just a cursory role in economic development, and this aspect has gained attention in works of Machlup (1962), Burck (1966), Drucker (1968), and Bell (1973).

Machlup's pioneering work indicated that, in the U.S., the knowledge industry accounted for 29 percent of GNP and employed 31 percent of the total work force in 1958. According to these estimates the knowledge industry grew at 10.6 percent per annum between 1947 and 1958. Machlup identified over fifty specific "information activities" within certain broad categories. He labelled these activities, in aggregate, to be the knowledge sector. It grew, during the decade under study, at a rate that was twice that of total GNP.

Porat's (1976) approach differed from Machlup's in that Porat relied on the accepted National Income and Products Accounts framework. He classified a group of industries as the "primary information sector;" this sector produced 25 percent of the 1967 GNP. He then identified the principal occupations in the primary information sector and found many workers with similar job titles in the other sectors (manufacturing, agriculture, etc.) of the economy. Using indirect approaches, Porat estimates that an additional 21 percent of GNP originated in this "secondary information on sector"; specifically, those "quasi-information-firms" engaged in information activities but contained within the noninformation sectors of the economy.

Based on this approach, the notion that 46 percent ("almost 50 percent") of a postindustrial economy such as the United States was devoted to the production and dissemination of information goods and services became current. (Rubin [1988] provides a cogent discussion of the problems involved in attempting to aggregate the primary and secondary information sectors.) Similarly, the information sectors in the OECD countries were measured using occupational classification data; the percentage of the workforce engaged in information work ranged from 27.5 (Finland in 1975) to 41.1 (U.S. in 1970). Similar studies were done for ten Pacific countries, including a rising trend of investment in the primary information sector (Jussawalla, Lamberton, Karunaratue, 1988). While these estimates are highly dependent on the classification scheme used to determined whether or not occupations were information-related, they show the emergence of new conceptual and measurement tools to analyze this important set of activities. They showed that, using Input-Output methodology and a derivation of backward and forward multipliers and linkages, it is possible to assess potential benefits that accrue from increased investment in the primary information sector either through derived demand for other goods and services produced in the economy or through lower input costs for other sectors of the economy.

What is of relevance to our discussion is the fact that information-related activities encompass certain features which are common to other economic activites. These are:

• the absorption of resources,
• claims on current production, and
• the function of being intermediaries to further production.

Information sector measurement is based on value added originating with the production and distribution of information goods and services. The factor incomes approach is used and interindustry relationships within an I-O framework are preserved. Economic structures vary across countries and, by implication, the information economy of a given country will be unique in its composition and inter-sectoral linkages. To facilitate inter-country comparisons, the derivation of an information sector must therefore proceed on the basis of a common theoretical principle, rather than on similarities of data bases. There appears to be a common pattern of structural transformation as the economic production system responds to changes in information technologies. With a better understanding of the array of processes by which new technologies are diffused, their opportunity costs become clearer; this allows decision makers to chose between alternative investment options.

The Role of Information and Information Technology

We now turn to the role of information services and information technology in international trade. Flows of data across international boundaries are contributing to the growth of international trade and creating problems of protectionism and intellectual property rights in information technology. These information flows have brought about the integration of global services markets. We use two specific cases—banking and financial services and telecommunications products and services—to examine the changes that have occurred in both industrialized and developing economies.

Information and International Trade

Both industrialized and developing countries are finding their markets integrated through the use of information and communication technologies such as improved interfaces between satellites and optical fiber, on one hand, and computers and computer networks, on the other. Although we cannot predict the final outcome of the changes taking place, we can identify some of the possibilities for international trade and anticipate the trends for future welfare.

Trade flows are not strictly comparable to information flows; for example, the latter influence and formulate changes in elasticity of demand for certain products and services in consumer markets and in international capital markets (Jussawalla and Cheah, 1984). The literature of economics has developed a powerful case against competitive markets as guarantors of Paretian resource allocation in developing countries (Helleiner, 1978). This is especially true of international markets because they are influenced by political and social systems, and political decisions often influence the scope of market operations.

Conventional theory based the terms of trade and patterns of exchange on factor abundance and factor intensity as determinants of specialization. It is assumed that free trade and specialization will bring about factor-price equalization, which is expected to eliminate differences in incomes paid to the factors of production. The identity of production functions and the nonreversibility of factor intensities was taken for granted. In such a static framework of comparative advantage there was no room for changes in the input of knowledge. As information technology becomes more pervasive, it becomes possible to introduce dynamic variables of technical change and the input of information into the production process (Braunstein, 1985).

The influence of technical change on trade is not confined to its direct effects on comparative cost ratios; instead, it may affect trade indirectly through its impact on economic growth. Changes in comparative cost may follow as an indirect response to price changes (Johnson, 1963). Every reduction in the cost of communication technology will have a trade increasing effect. On the other hand, protectionist barriers emerging from information technology will have the opposite effect. It is difficult, however, to separate trade caused by differences in technical knowledge from trade caused by differences in factor endowment. If there is a continued supply of new and innovative information as a result of R&D in any one country, then this rate of information processing and transmission will be closely linked to a higher rate of net investment. When information about science and technology is transferred to developing countries, they move up on the learning curve and this reduces the time lag for adaptation.

While transportation costs have generally been considered relevant in trade theory, information costs as part of the costs of transferring inputs and outputs have been generally ignored. The costs of information gathering to make trade possible are generally high and need to be considered explicitly. They vary across products and factors as do other production costs. The degree of risk and uncertainty prevailing in foreign markets adds to the cost of obtaining information to reduce the risks for trade in goods and services; hence, the higher the degree of risk, the greater will be the demand for information inputs.

With improvements in information technology, not only do input and output flows of information induce changes in trade patterns, but the very composition of trade flows is changed. Thus, the terms of trade are affected by the impact of information inputs on the marginal productivity of both labor and capital. The ratio of productivity to wages is higher in developed countries because information input leads to higher skill formation. This increases the technology gap and the wage differential gap between advanced and developing countries. Since free trade is unable to increase the relative information endowment of developing countries, conscious policy decisions have to be taken to direct information inputs to developing countries through aid, technical assistance, and preferential trade agreements.

In a real world situation, international trade theory and its explanation of the composition and terms of trade fails to operate either on the basis of factor abundance or on the basis of availability, due to the sphere of control of transnational corporations (TNCs) headquartered in affluent countries. As far back as 1976, Magdoff estimated that the internal capital accumulation of TNCs is generating output in host countries that exceeds the total volume of international trade. Today in the light of global mergers and agreements, such as those of Alcatel, IBM with Hitachi, and AT&T with Olivetti, subcontracting across continents often substitutes for trade. While large corporations are able to penetrate global markets, these corporations create barriers to entry by developing countries through their use of exclusive information networks and their international integration across different stages of production.

In the theory of international capital flows, a distinction is made between portfolio investment and direct foreign investment. The former is based on international differences in the rate of interest, the latter is related to industrial organization. Imperfect competition in international trade enables TNCs to control direct foreign investment and to coordinate production on an international scale. Jussawalla (1982) postulated that direct foreign investment is no longer just the export of surplus capital from the industrialized countries in quest of higher interest rates, but that the dynamics of expansion are in reality a part of the international organizational structure. TNC operations are tied to and dependent upon communication networks that in turn help to strengthen their oligopoly in the international economic system. Developing countries, on the other hand, do not have access to the same networks and must safeguard their balance of payments against adverse terms of trade, against problems of repatriating foreign capital, and against the transfer of profits and dividends to the headquarters of the TNCs.

Development economists have long contended that international trade theory based on the international division of labor is not mutually profitable to developing countries. In addition, there are important welfare implications of trade in information that have not been adequately dealt with by researchers or policymakers. Even if trade in telecommunications products and services makes a significant contribution to GNP, there is no guarantee that an equitable distribution of gains from trade will take place. Trade in information products and services has had a marked impact on the trade balances of developing countries. For example, trade processing zones have operated for the semiconductor industry in Southeast Asia, resulting in higher employment and more labor intensive output (see Jussawalla and Cheah, 1984).

In the microelectronics industry, the convergence of computers and telecommunications makes possible the availability of a coherent system of information processing and distribution. This trend alters comparative advantages, which according to Rada (1981), are now man-made and introduced through the mastery of science and technology. The share of developing countries in world trade in information goods (such as television and radio receivers, computers, telephone equipment, books, and journals) has been increasing. Their input into the production and export of other goods and services is also growing. The Newly Industrializing Countries (NICs) of Asia—Hong Kong, Singapore, Taiwan, and South Korea—are all stepping up their exports of electronic components for information and communication hardware. In general, international trade in its existing form has not generated adequate welfare effects for the developing world, but in the area of communication goods and services there are indications of a more equitable distribution of the gains from trade.

The international dimension of information technology radically altered the volume and pattern of trade relationships in the 1970s. While the flow of goods has been increasing, the movement of services and technology has grown much faster. This growth has become a challenge to the charter of the General Agreement on Tariff and Trade (GATT). At the insistence of the United States, the case of services trade was brought under an umbrella agreement considered by the GATT at its September 1986, meeting in Punta del Este. Many of the developing countries resisted including services issued in the Uruguay trade talks.

Even more impressive than the growth in information service trade itself has been the growth in volume and speed of international flows of capital. These flows have been made possible by the new electronic bridges that span continents and over which transborder data flows (TBDF) take effect. It is extremely difficult to estimate the value of intangible data flows that cross borders, but such knowledge-based services have acquired global importance in the application and use of information to economic activities.

There is a growing consensus in affluent countries that TBDF should be unrestricted, operating on a total laissez faire basis. Developing countries are reluctant to accept this policy on the grounds that until such time as they develop their own information processing and storage services, they are likely to become exporters of raw data and importers of processed information, resulting in a repetition of the colonial relationships in merchandise trade. "Electronic imperialism" is considered a threat to their cultural and social mores in particular. This, combined with economic aspects (monopoly ownership of data bases and control of transmission channels) and political aspects (pressure for nontariff barriers regarding data content and access), accounts for the reticence of LDCs in entering a multilateral framework of rules for TBDF.

Services are intangible and unable to be stored. Therefore, they have to be produced and consumed simultaneously. As a result trade in information services requires the "right of presence," which in the context of data services implies that a party in one country should be allowed to receive and transmit information to another party in another country via computer networks. Developing countries are affected by such trade in two ways. First, they are host countries to TNCs, and, second, their economies are penetrated by foreign direct investment (FDI) by TNCs, by international banks and financial institutions, and by providers of telecommunications hardware and software.

The economic effects of TBDF on the developing countries are linked to the distribution of costs and benefits associated with free trade in services. All countries want free trade, but at as low a cost to each as possible. One major impediment is the lack of trust. The GATT system has failed to evoke trust among its members, and LDCs are reluctant to commit themselves to an international regime that has the faintest semblance of mercantilist policies.

As telematics becomes widespread, TBDF is considered one of the causes for the dependence of low-income countries on the technologically advanced ones. This has led to much debate sponsored by the now defunct IBI (Intergovernmental Bureau of Informatics), the OECD, and the Council of Europe. Conceptually speaking, technological changes have made information an increasingly vital resource and a factor or production. Digits stored in computers are transferred around the world's financial systems, replacing paper currencies and paper transactions. Electronic delivery of information has become a saleable product. This convergence offers the greatest challenge and the greatest opportunity to both developed and developing countries for international trade. Deregulation and privatization of telecommunication networks further encourages the development of a global market by driving down the costs of the conduits that carry information with speed and accuracy. Technological and organizational changes cause the line of demarcation between providing network services and providing information over them to become invisible. As electronic markets develop, firms begin to adopt interfaces with them and trading becomes an increasingly important source of revenue.

With the prospect of ISDN and broad-band technology for all industrially advanced countries in the near future, issues of contention in TBDF will be further aggravated. This is because TBDF takes place in a complex mixture of mechanical and electronic processes, so that the demand for exports and imports of information grows as new technologies appear on the market. Information services are traded in response to intermediate rather than final demand and provide an essential link among economic agents for the interdependent functioning of the global market. In general, the theory of international trade has neglected the role of intermediate products. Conventional theory assumes that trade in intermediate products adds to the volume of trade but does not benefit the country that exports them. Gains from trade are considered to be lower than would result from the export of final goods. However in the exports of data, no such deterioration in terms of trade is observable. Data flows accompanying trade are also important because they provide information about markets, commercial policies, prices, product description and technical data. Efficiency of such slows is essential for the development of noninformation trade.

It is important to recognize that conventional theories of tariff and nontariff barriers to trade break down when applied to TBDF. For instance, it is difficult to locate the point of entry for information flowing through computers that talk to each other either via terrestrial, undersea, or satellite linkages. Information and data are intangibles, and the possibility of separating the conduit from the content is remote. In addition to the intrinsic nature of TBDF, there is the existence of foreign direct investment that is both caused by and is the effect of TBDF. TNCs operating in an imperfectly competitive international market are prepared to bear the extra costs of internalized networks in order to benefit from higher productivity of geographically dispersed units. When this advantage is threatened by barriers to trade, there is a demand for reciprocity.

Apart from threatening optimal utilization of tomorrow's technologies, there is a strong association between trade strategies and growth rates. Both developed and developing countries exhibit a varying mix of import restrictions and export promotion. While the individual effects of these policies can be measured in theory, the variety of ways they have been implemented often makes if quite difficult to unambiguously identify a preferred policy.

Trade economists have analyzed the relationship between the level of protection given to an industry and the economic characteristics of the sectors or business and political groups that influence the level of protection. The economic theory of protection is closely related to the theory of public choice, which is an application of economics to political decision making. Public choice theory is a way of justifying intervention on grounds of failure of market forces to achieve a Pareto-optimality in resource allocation (Baldwin, 1982). The theory of trade protection employs a hypothetical social welfare function. In analyzing import restrictions, this allows one to compare the gains from increased domestic production and employment with the losses from higher consumer prices. It is therefore possible that restricting imports will bring about an economic system that is better than one that would prevail under free trade.

Arrow (1962) made such a welfare function an explicit part of public choice theory by considering actions, such as trade protection, part of the social decision-making process. In this analysis, producers and groups demanding protection do so in order to maximize the present value of whatever additional income they can obtain by curtailing imports. Such a theory of public choice links the market for internationally traded goods with the market for political votes and show how protectionist policies need not always bring about the highest social welfare or Pareto-optimal distribution of benefits.

In international trade theory, the terms of trade between two countries for two or more commodities are determined by : (1) the production possibility curves for the traded goods in each country; and (2) the price elasticity of demand for them, assuming perfect competition and free trade. When we allow protection, we find the emphasis shifts to the consumption possibilities dependent on the offer curves of the trading partner. In theory, if there is a choice between a tariff policy that restricts consumption possibilities (as under import tariff barriers) and a free trade policy that enlarges consumption possibilities, the latter policy should be selected to make more persons better off. However, the selection of a free trade utility possibility frontier is not always based on such economic criteria. This positive theory of trade determinism has been applied to explain both why protectionism exists and why some industries are more protected than others.

In the framework of a theory of public choice, a tariff on imports and a nontariff barrier become public goods, inasmuch as no beneficiaries can be excluded from the benefits even though they do not contribute directly to the costs of providing and enforcing the tariff. Therefore a tariff gives rise to a free-rider benefit to domestic producers of the country that operates the tariff. The economic advantage to the domestic infant industry or protected industry will depend on how quickly and to what extent domestic producers take advantage of protection to enhance profits and strengthen their competitive base. However, a protective tariff is no guarantee that entrepreneurs will make greater investments in technology or revive depressed industries.

So far, in various theoretical solutions offered for protectionism, the rent-seeking activities of those producers affected by import penetration are based on the assumption of nonavailability of information. Therefore there is a need to explore solutions where rent-seeking activities take the form of informational expenditures, in which case protection may become unnecessary. Some of the information may be socially valuable from a cost-benefit point of view, even though it is specifically useful to a particular service industry. Levying a tax on the expenditure of an industry for obtaining information and using its proceeds to provide informtion to nonindustry users may promote greater Pareto-optimality than providing protection against imports of similar services. To capture even a second-best solution we need to assess the import penetration ratio of TBDF within firms and other businesses and individual flows. If the Coase theorem is applied to the tariff problem for TBDF, then within well-defined property rights, competitive rent-seeking by those who are for and against tariffs will lead to Pareto-optimality. This may not be proven in the case of TBDF where current trends show that low productivity jobs are often protected at the expense of high productivity jobs and where expenditures on innovative technology may be frozen.

Institutional parameters, other than the cost of providing communication channels can influence the prices set for transmitting data. Normally international information passes through leased lines whose prices are independent of the volume of use. This usage-insensitive pricing and other institutional arrangements create barriers to network access and influence the quantity, type, and quality of information transmitted.

A recent study by the U.S. Department of Commerce shows that the demand for information services is growing more rapidly than other parts of the economy (U.S. Industrial Outlook, 1989). All four information services sectors (data processing, computers, electronic databases, and videotext) show revenue increases that are higher than the rate of growth of GNP. The demand for data processing increased by 13 percent in 1988, and it is projected to grow to a $45 billion market by 1993. The bulk of this demand comes from Japan, West Germany, the U.K., and France; the biggest growth factors are electronic data interchange and transborder data flows. Two international organizations have been concerned about the issues arising from the impact of information technology on services trade. One is the International Telecommunications Union (ITU), and the other is the General Agreement on Tariff and Trade (GATT). Both these insititutions are attempting to reduce tensions arising from TBDF among their member countries. The late–1988 Montreal meeting of the GATT tentatively agreed that trade in services (including information services) should permit a balance of interests for all countries providing a broad coverage of sectors of interest. Progressive liberalization of trade in services has been agreed upon, but the rules are still indeterminate. The ITU on the other hand has issued what is called the Melbourne Package resulting from the December 1988, World Administrative Telephone and Telegraph Conference (WATTC) meeting. WATTC considered problems of compatibility, standardization of equipment, and connectivity. The result was a compromise calling for flexible international services that was reached between PTTs, nondeveloping countries wishing to continue regulation, and private systems operators from the developed countries.

Information services are playing a significant role in OECD economies and, as such, are greatly dependent on telecommunication networks. These services have important implications for the trade patterns that are evolving in information services markets. The telecommunications sector is closely intertwined with an array of information technologies. These include computers, software, and microelectronics. Telematics has a pervasive effect on the macroeconomy in that it tends to alter the modes of production and management. Convergence and overlap characterize the changes in international trade. The larger the availability of electronic highways, the greater the volume and value of international trade. Converging information technology widens the geographical limits of markets by reducing the cost of networks. The greatest impetus to trade in information will emerge from Integrated Services Digital Networks or ISDN. The ITU is setting standards of compatibility to make the use of broadband networks more profitable for users.

However there is still an existing gap between trade in computers and network-based services and corresponding policy adjustments. For example, there are insufficient international safeguards in the areas of computer-related crime and policy which brings to light the regulatory vacuum which constrains the free flow of information. The extent of free trade using telecommunications depends on the compatibility of networks and standards of interconnectivity. This is particularly true in the context of ISDN and OSI (Open Systems Interconnection) that are being increasingly accepted by users and manufacturers. The Consultative Committee on International Telephone and Telegraph (CCITT) of the ITU has been working for the achievement of worldwide standards for digital communications and this was discussed in detail at the Melbourne meeting of the World Administrative Telegraph and Telephone Conference (WATTC) in December 1988. All 113 member countries present accepted in principle the need for global interconnectivity to facilitate international trade in information, banking, financial, insurance and marketing services. The challenge is to forge a workable model of open interconnection that accommodates national differences. Lack of agreement will involve high economic and social costs to world trade.

The Importance of Information Technology to the Global Services Market

The next two sections examine the relationships between changes in information technology and the function of specific world markets. The two specific areas presented are banking and telecommunications services. This are chosen for two reasons: they are both large, archetypical service industries which have undergone significant changes in recent years and they both are major parts of the economic infrastructure of industrialized and developing nations alike.

Banking

The dynamic linkages between the world's savers and borrowers that now exist are performing a critical function, that is, the function of providing information, which is the primary input for financial markets. Because it influences decisions about the allocation of resources in various industries and economic activities, this information has to be provided cost-effectively, accurately, and speedily. Just as information is an input into the decision-making process, it is also an output of financial interme- diaries. In all free-market economies, financial intermediaries stand at the intersection of production and consumption. They are the conduits through which information about economic activities is exchanged both intra– and internationally.

The theoretical importance of information to financial markets indicates that technological advances in the ability to gather, process, store or exchange information would be quickly utilized by those trying to improve their profit-risk position, whether regionally or internationally. Informa- tion technology has made quantum leaps in the vast array of technologies like opto electronics (e.g., fibre optic submarine cables), teletex and videotext, digital telephone exchanges, integrated systems, cellular tele- phones, super-computers, satellites, and artificial intelligence. ATMs have taken the place of checking account and teller transcations, and EFTPOS transactions (Electronic Transfers at Point of Sale) have further integrated financial services worldwide.

Financial information exchange networks have seen the spread of tele- matics in the use of Fedwire, Bankwire, Euroclear, Reuters, and Telerate, all of which involve large risk-bearing investments. They provide access to financial information in order to minimize risks undertaken by insitu- tional investors such as pension funds and insurance companies. That is why Walter Wriston, former chairman of Citibank, stated that the most important financial change he has seen since the 1970s is that the United States became "a true common market bound together with telecommun- ications. But more than that, the United States became just one market in a global market" (*Wall Street Week*, 22 November, 1985). The increasing sophistication and capabilities of telematics are enhancing the ability to operate in unique ways in all financial markets, often beyond the reach of regulators.

The impact of information technology on financial markets has been a positive development in that it has provided financial institutions with the ability to be more responsive to customers and markets and to offer a broad range of financial services and products. On the other hand, it has reduced the efficacy of domestic monetary policies and made it easier to bypass legal and regulatory provisions and to blur the lines of distinction between banks and non-bank financial itermediaries. The impact of elec- tronic money in the retail market has resulted in specialized markets around the globe. Electronic banking involves high capital costs but low marginal costs for each transaction. Transactions done through EFT not only provide economies of scale but greater consumer sovereignty through the EFTPOS system. It is one technology that has changed the way banks and their non-bank competitors deliver financial services. But there is a battle over the owership and control of terminals and the question of who should pay for them. Furthermore, incompatibility of rival systems can have an adverse impact on consumers and users of networks.

Another important element in integrating financial markets is SWIFT (Society for Worldwide Interbank Financial Telecommunication) which was designed to provide an automated interbank funds transfer message system. Started in 1977 and headquarters in Brussels, SWIFT now has 2,700 institutions in more than fifty-six countries exchanging nearly one million messages a day. The system is an example of how information technology created a network to cater to the specialized communication needs of its members and simultaneously ensures authenticity and privacy for them. SWIFT assumes the financial liability for the banking instructions that pass through its networks. Its membership has now extended widely in the Asia-Pacific region with financial institutions there joining those in Europe and North America. The SWIFT network links its operations with automated clearing houses such as CHAPS (Clearing House for Automated Payments) based in London and CHATs (Clearing House for Automated Transfers) in Hong Kong. The use of information technology proves that information today is more than a commodity: it is a resource without which the global financial world would be paralyzed.

Bank profits today are less sensitive to interest rates, in so much as banks no longer rely primarily on interest rate margins for their profits. Instead, they collect fees from customized services, many dependent on new information technologies. Information technology costs, now a major component of the fixed costs of banking, are greatly determined by the pricing structure of network vendor, who in many instances may be a regulated monopolist. Both in banking and telecommunications there is neither a single product nor a single network. Both industries are experiencing technological change as well as changes in the underlying economies of scale and scope, and in both cases regulators have difficulty adjusting to new economic conditions. Furthermore, in the banking industry, central bankers have found it increasingly difficult to exercise control due to instantaneous movement of purchasing power across contintents.

Telecommunications

Only a dozen years ago there were no PCs, no CDs, no VCRs, and no genetically engineered vaccines. It is estimated that the next dozen years will bring progress that increases by a factor of ten. In corporate research centers, super computers that are 1000 times more powerful than today's will calculate interactions in molecules to create new materials. It appears that in contrast with earlier years of invention, homo sapiens now are moving into the Age of Insight in which the computer is being transformed into a machine for discovery and for future forecasting. Telecommunications are providing the electronic highways as they converge with computers. ISDN experiments in Japan, the United States and Europe are expected to result in savings of billions of dollars to corporations in terms of increased productivity and lower costs of communication. It is the speed with which these changes are being made that is impacting on changing market structures.

Convergence of computers and communications with broadcasting has ushered in a new era of disseminating information around the globe in real time. Multimedia technology and Virtual Reality promise to transform the transmission of information in a dramatic fashion. Based on digital technology, the three pillars of multimedia are compact discs, superchips, and fibre optic cables. Compression technology has introduced the tiniest microchips to carry incredible quantities of information. Such convergence may lead to a greater use of compression technology to squeeze video conferences and TV programs through narrow band channels.

These changes have forced suppliers into developing new strategies that will help them to adjust to the changing demands of a market-oriented environment. This has resulted in numerous large-scale mergers, joint ventures and acquisitions in the telecommunications industry. This initiative is being driven by coporate executives wanting to achieve a large share of the overseas market and, at the same time, achieve economies of scale by pooling their R&D resources. AT&T has successfully used joint ventures as a strategy for breaking into markets abroad with its rivals in Europe and Japan. It linked up with Philips of the Netherlands, Olivetti of Italy, Telefonica of Spain, and NTT and Toshiba of Japan. In France, CGE entered into a major partnership with ITT, creating Alcatel, the world's second largest telecommunications equipment manufacturer (AT&T is the largest). The venture has opened the way for European firms in the Pacific. For example, Alcatel has offices in Japan, Hong Kong, and Bangkok. Likewise, GTE has entered into joint ventures with its overseas rivals in two areas of its nonregulated business; its international transmission and equipment ventures were merged into a joint company with Siemens of Germany, and its terminal equipment subsidiary entered into a partnership with Fujitsu of Japan.

These changes in telecommunications have created such turmoil in the market that even the largest companies are having difficulty adjusting. The intensity of competition is causing:

* some major companies to experience declines in revenues;
* smaller companies to reorganize or go out of business;
* increased consolidation of both small and large companies;
* the creation of new carriers;
* mergers of and joint operations by former overseas rivals; and
* major plant consolidations and layoffs of employees.

Driven by the new technologies, new network concepts, equipment, and services, the PTTs, the equipment manufacturers, and computer firms are all positioning themselves toward the same markets, users, and revenues. Equipment and service boundaries are dissolving. Domestic markets are less protected from market influences than in the past. This has intensified competition within and among industries and between countries. Industries whose relationship in the past was remote, or even foreign, are challenging each other as direct competitors. Telecommunications monopolies are less able to rely on the argument of economies of scale to insure protection from new entrants. (It is not clear, however, whether the scale economies which they once enjoyed have eroded as compared to overall market size or whether they were never as great as alleged.)

Competitors are successfully operating against the PTTs, raising important policy concerns. Some of this competition is from foreign firms attempting to gain access to previously closed domestic markets. Economic arguments for restrictions on competition have been recast to rely on the importance of economies of scope and the continuing natural monopoly in basic exchange service and thin-route areas. Another trend is that existing telecommunications monopolies are gradually being allowed to freely compete in newly liberalized markets for equipment and services.

The Organization of Communication Industries:
Economic Regulation and Market Structure

This section deals with the development of new economic theory and concepts and the application of those concepts to communication industries.

Development of New Concepts

Public interest theory forms the fundamental basis for regulation in law and in economics. It assumes that the firm's conduct can be regulated effectively or that regulation can act as a substitute for market competition, in as much as it protects the consumer from the exercise of monopoly power by the supplier. However, sometimes the public interest is not fully protected because of administrative shortcomings. In 1971 George Stigler discarded the assumption that regulation is needed in those industries in which special technological problems prevent market competition. He posited the view that firms demand regulation to increase monopoly power by erecting barriers to entry and restricting competition from substitutable products. In such a case regulation becomes a means for redistributing income from consumers to producers. Another theoretical postulate is the protection of the status quo. According to this view, regulation is introduced to prevent firms from incurring sudden capital losses by preserving existing prices, and so both producers and consumers are protected.

Hirschman (1970), taking a different approach, argued that there is a dual element that characterizes regulation, namely "exit" and "voice." Exit refers to the market response of dissatisfied customers and voice refers to the response of politicians who want to change an unsatisfactory industry. Most organizations are controlled by a combination of the two, and regulation attempts to substitute voice for exit. Drawing on these two approaches, Brock (1981) stated that the essence of regulatory legislation is the establishment of property rights in the status quo for all parties.

The traditional assumption for industrial organization is that the structure of a particular market is perceived as fixed and this market structure determines performance. Michael Porter (1987) introduced a theory of mixed structural barriers to market entry and of created barriers which protect the investment activities of the firm. They maintain that it is the enforcement of antitrust laws, rather than the existence of market structures, that prohibits the growth of monpoly. However, the primary effect of regulation is to slow down change, and, therefore, it works best when there is technological stability. But with the kind of rapid technological progress characteristic of the modern telecommunications industry in both the United States and Europe, regulation is not as effective as a competitive weapon.

In the telecommunications industry, technological progress has changed industry boundaries. For example, new products and services have blurred the formerly clear distinction between computers and telecommunications (Brock, 1975). Firms in both industries have become competitors in providing the products and services for the transmission, storage, and manipulation of information.

In the United States, with the "open sky" decision of the FCC, any company was free to establish a satellite communication network. However, the incentive to do so was limited by significant economies of scale in satellite communication, by the cost of launches, the cost of the earth segment, and the traffic available to satellite competition. These economies of scale were much greater than in microwave communication. Even so, satellite transmission affected only the line-haul component of the communication system. The other components, such as switching, multiplexing, and terminal equipment were threatened by technological progress in the computer industry. As Roger Noll (1983) pointed out, the relatively homogeneous and simple structure of the telecommunications industry was lost with the innovations in technology. The definition of monopoly service became less clear, and the concept itself became more elastic.

Many argue that the main effect of telecommunication regulation in the United States was not to limit the monopoly profits telecommunications industry, as postulated in theory, but to protect it from competition. Deregulation of AT&T removed the incentives for the company to retain the parts of its organization for which it had no efficiency or cost-justifiable basis. Noll, in investigating the application of the dominant firm strategy in the new postdivestiture regime of AT&T, maintains that while AT&T retains a very large market share in telecommunications, it has no natural monopoly. He forsees that the principal competitor for AT&T in the 1990s to be the computer industry and IBM.

An opposing view is that of Shepherd (1984). He argues that the basic theory of competition is both sound and effective in guiding the main revisions which the U.S. telecommunications sector may need. First, technical scale economies have become less significant with the use of computer technology. Secondly, the ability of regulators to define and achieve efficient price structures and to identify predatory and other unfair pricing strategies has increased. The major sources of disagreement between Noll and Shepherd are their differences over the importance of potential entry and over the likelihood and effectiveness of informed regulatory action.

Starting in 1976, William Baumol and others have produced a series of papers on the sustainability of regulated utility firms facing new competition. They conclude that, even if regulated firms adopt optimal prices and outputs, new entrants may make those prices and outputs "unsustainable," and their entry can result in a welfare loss. Under natural monopoly conditions (e.g., the magnetic frequency spectrum for radio communications) and regulation, the firm offers products at "Ramsey" prices, which maximize consumer surplus.[1] In a multiproduct, multimarket industry, such as telecommunications, Ramsey prices are discriminatory (in the nonpejorative, economic sense) in that different groups of users may be charged different prices. The argument is then made that if entry is allowed in one or more of the markets some prices of the multiproduct firm will be forced so low that the original firm will exit from those markets, causing it and its customers to lose the advantages arising from economies of scale and scope. In other words, the original Ramsey prices, although welfare-maximizing, are not sustainable, and entry will reduce consumer surplus and welfare. On the other hand, Shepherd argues that this theory ignores the empirical evidence that regulated monpolies are often wasteful and that competition can improve their performance.

More recently the telecommunications industry has been analyzed according to the precepts of contestability theory. According to Baumol (1982) "the crucial feature of a contestable market is its vulnerability to hit-and-run entry." What does this concept mean for regulation? It implies that if a market is contestable, then just the threat of potential entrants will be sufficient to "discipline" incumbent suppliers. In other words, we do not need regulation. Industry studies may not be able to prove that IBM or AT&T have been vulnerable to "hit-and-run entry," or that such a threat has introduced "discipline" in their operations. What has, however, helped such giant corporations to contribute to consumer welfare has been the fact that technological innovation and the returns to investments in R&D have reduced costs over time. So far it has not been possible to separate empirically the benefits that may have arisen from contestability from those that are due to technological change or economies of scale and scope.

Application of the Concepts

The current movement toward deregulation started with the Carterfone decision in the U.S. in 1968 and has spread to many technologically advanced countries. In 1980 the Federal Communication Commission, in its Second Computer Inquiry, opened markets which were unregulated to entry by telephone companies. The next major structural change in the United States was the 1982 settlement of the long-running antitrust action against AT&T. This agreement required the parent firm to divest its local operating companies and led to the creation of the seven regional holding companies. Similar trends are underway elsewhere; for example, both Japan's NTT and British Telecommunications offered shares to the public in 1985 and now face domestic competitors. It is not easy for decision makers to strike a balance between permitting smaller competitors to flourish and not imposing too many constraints on the dominant suppliers so that their capacity to compete is hindered. The industrial structure on the supply side has to adjust to loss of captive markets due to deregulation, increasing costs of R&D for new products, and the rapidly increasing cycle of innovation. These factors are driving suppliers to seek new global markets, and competition is whittling away profit margins on many products. Europe has proven more vulnerable to these upheavals than the United States or Japan as its home markets have failed to provide the scale economies needed to absorb development costs. On a per capita basis Europe's investment in telecommunications equipment is a third of the U.S. level; European suppliers are trying to link up with international partners.

The distinction between the static setting (which abstracts from the passage of time) and the dynamic setting (which takes such passage into account) is a vital one in the analytical frameworks of economies, political science, and engineering. The following three examples illustrate the importance of this dichotomy in the economic investigation of information technology.

Consider first technological progress, which is an inherently dynamic concept. Economies of scale, by contrast, are a static phenomenon: within a given technology average cost declines as output increases. (This assumes that such costs can be measured unambiguously.) Dynamically, technological progress corresponds to an inward shift of the average cost curve itself, thereby reducing average cost for a given output level. Distinguishing economies of scale from technological progress statistically can be a challenging task.

The second instance of the static/dynamic dichotomy has to do with pricing policy in a public utility setting. In a static environment there are many convincing arguments for the use of some form of price discrimination (often referred to as value-of-service pricing or elasticity-based pricing) to achieve economic efficiency. When dynamic factors—in particular technological progress—are taken into account, however, cost-based pricing methods of obtaining welfare or efficiency goals become more appropriate and convincing.

Finally, the price elasticities of demand for different services and markets that must be known in order to implement any form of elasticity-based pricing are themselves sensitive to the passage of time, as are most other economic variables. Consumers are less able to react to price changes in the short run than they are in the long run. Thus, the absolute value of the price elasticity of demand is greater in a dynamic than in a static framework.

While it is obvious that technology can affect regulatory form, a subtler type of causality in the opposite direction can also be observed. For example, the evolution of cable television technology in the United States has clearly been influenced, at least in part, by regulatory developments at the state and federal levels. One can likewise maintain that both the nature and the extent of technological developments in areas such as private switchboards and value-added networks—domains which are by now extensively deregulated in many OECD countries—have been affected by deregulatory trends. A similar interdependence, one with which the history of science is replete, is exhibited between recent theoretical developments in economic science and the needs to which those developments have subsequently been applied. In many instances, theory has been driven by such needs rather than emerging in a vacuum. One example is afforded by the natural monopoly and contestability literature described in this section. It is not coincidental that much of this new theory was developed by economists at Bell Laboratories in the years prior to and during the judicial proceedings leading to the divestiture of AT&T in 1984. In addition, the statistical technology of multiproduct translog cost and production functions emerged at a juncture not unrelated to the need for better methods of cost determination and allocation in various information technologies, particularly telecommunications, that are inherently multiproduct.

Regulatory economics comprises a number of distinct traditions regarding both positive and normative aspects of the regulatory process. Those most relevant to information technologies will be briefly summarized here. They are the conventional or public interest theory, the capture school, the cooperative approach, and the political economy of deregulation.

Public interest regulation proceeds from the assumption of a monopolist producing a single output under economies of scale. Straightforward microeconomic theory suggest that this firm has an incentive to produce a smaller output and charge a higher price than would be the case under competition. Thus, the regulatory authorities preserve the monopoly in legal fact to prevent "needless duplication of facilities" but require the firm to reduce prices and increases output according to certain criteria (such as recovering a "fair" or market-oriented rate of return on its invested capital).

The capture theory, identified with the University of Chicago but sharing some insights with more radical viewpoints, suggests that various flaws in the regulatory mechanism—such as delays and asymmetries of information and differences in staff size and abilities between the regulated firms and the regulatory body—conspire to make regulators work in the interest of the regulated firms. They are in essence "captured" by the industries they are supposedly regulating in the public interest.

Cooperative approaches to regulation, tracing a line of intellectual ancestry to the English cooperative movement of the nineteenth century, are seldom found in practice. INTELSAT, the global intergovernmental commercial satellite consortium, is organized financially as a cooperative of owners and users. The French telecommunications authorities stress cooperation as an alternative to competition in obtaining goals of social welfare and economic efficiency. Finally, a German variant of cooperative theory, known as *Gemeinwirtschaft* (social economy), has been influential for decades in forming socialist arguments in the country for continued public ownership and operation of telecommunications and other public utilities.

The political economy of deregulation school, because of its more recent origin, has been applied more extensively to the regulation of information technology in industrialized countries. It stresses the role of the state, of interest groups, and of the institutional environment generally in affecting the outcome of policy debates. In particular, it addresses the following question: Why can the implementation of regulatory arrangements that are demonstrably superior to the status quo from a purely "technical" perspective (that of economics, law, or engineering, for example) be frustrated by interest group coalitions in the political process?

Most economic analysis relating to the regulating of information technology utilizes a neoclassical approach that involves the mathematical optimization of certain key variables subject to constraints imposed by institutional, technical, and political factors. Cost-benefit analysis is an example of this approach. Recent thought and investigation, however, has caused a number of researchers to qualify certain results obtained by neoclassical techniques. A summary of these reservations follows.

There are, first of all, a variety of what might be called technical difficulties. For example, the dependability of underlying cost and production data have been called into question. Communications carriers often have strategic incentives not to reveal costs and other data accurately to regulatory authorities. Another difficulty involves the presence of externalities, that is, those economic relationships not captured in the price mechanism. For example, improvements in the telecommunications infrastructure benefits not only individual consumers directly but aids in the overall macroeconomic development of a country as well, particularly if it is still underdeveloped. The latter effect, however, is still too diffuse to be captured fully by economic analysis. Finally, complex social and perhaps psychological phenomena impinge on changes in the economic structure and, given the current and probable future lack of a "unified field theory" in social science, cannot easily be detected or theoretically accommodated.

Political qualifications of neoclassical welfare analysis are also legion, but they show promise of being at least partially incorporated into the "political economy of deregulation" approach described above. At issue here is the ability of tightly organized groups of potential "losers" to frustrate any political transition to a regulatory and pricing regime that would demonstrably increase overall social welfare. Regulatory analysis of telecommunications is increasingly devoted to equity implications of new pricing regimes that emerge from deregulation.

Conclusions

In the course of this paper it has become very clear that several limitations have surfaced in the application of economic theory to information and telecommunications industries as they operate today. The growth of the service sector has focused policy decisions on telecommunications as a prime indicator of a nation's economic future. Staple and Mullins (1989), both economists at the International Institute of Communications, claim that minutes of telecommunications traffic (MITT) is a new economic indicator that can be used for tracking the business cycle. The major hypothesis underlying their work is that changes in technology and the importance of information flows have made telecommunications an integral part of economic activity, in general, and trade in services in particular. Business activity cannot be conducted effectively without telephones, fax machines, and computerized data bases. Telecommunication systems are used for market exchange, for negotiating deals, and for information search.

Current economic indicators are not relied upon because economic forecasts are not considered accurate predictors of future trends. The OECD is considering changes in its statistical categories to affect better policy coordination. Japan has urged the OECD to add statistics in the output ratios of the high-tech and service sectors, overseas investment and changes in national industry structures. Staple and Mullins have shown econometric models of outgoing international traffic data to be a reliable indicator of economic trends, and that with such models the probability of errors is low and the necessary data are relatively easy to compile. The real problem, however, is whether common carriers such as AT&T, British Telecommunications, Bundespost, and NTT are willing to divulge their statistics; and, if not, whether the regulatory authorities can compel them to do so. Competition in international value-added services may limit access to aggregate telecommunications traffic data, even if such access is required for macroeconomic planning.

Various institutional parameters, other than the cost of providing communication channels, influence the prices set for trading information. Normally international information passes through leased lines without price adjustments for the volume of use. Institutional limitations that raise concern at the level of international trade are access to the network, tariffs, and conditions relating to type and quality of information transmitted. This could result in arbitrary limitations on information flows across national borders.

The welfare aspects of trade in information also introduce constraints on policy. It is not always possible to extend the welfare hypothesis of conventional trade theory to information flows because external economies diverge between information-rich and information-poor countries. Not only do wage-price ratios differ, but social marginal rates of transformation also vary along with differences in available telecommunications infrastructures. In the ultimate analysis, the welfare effects will depend upon which industries, and which nations, are being strengthened by information technology and which are being weakened; and the volume and value of internationally traded information will become an agent for the equitable allocation of resources.

Currently, as international trade operates the objective of combining economic efficiency with distributive equity is difficult to achieve. The GATT deliberations continue to show that trade policy is moving away from the multilateralism contained in the GATT charter. Its ninety-three member countries (with ten more waiting to be admitted) claim to want an end to bilateral agreements. However, there is apprehension among GATT members that the world is moving toward managed trade—particularly, managed trade in services including telecommunications. Bhagwati (1989) challenges the belief that trade imbalances reflect the cultural and economic differences between trading countries. He argues against this fallacious reasoning on the grounds that while cultural differences between Japan and the United States have existed for over a century, Japan's surplus in trade balance has only emerged in the 1980s. So that the benefits of information trade might be extended to developing countries, services will have to be brought within the GATT charter, its Article XIX will have to be strengthened to improve enforcement of free trade, and a mutually acceptable evaluation of trade practices will have to be implemented.

This trend is being strengthened by the impact of telecommunications on the information economy (Snow, 1986). Deregulation of the telecommunications sector has been instrumental in the historic transformation of domestic structures in industrialized countries: the replacement of manufacturing by information activities as the primary output. It has introduced greater diversity and user responsiveness in telecommunications markets.

Note

1. Ramsey pricing refers to a situation where each price is set so that its percentage deviation from marginal cost is inversely proportional to the items' price elasticity of demand. Thus, the prices of items whose demands are relatively inelastic diverge from their marginal costs by relatively wider margins.

References

Akerlof, G. (1970). The market for lemons: Qualitative uncertainty and the market mechanism, *Quarterly Journal of Economics, 84* (3 August) 488–500.

Arrow, K. J. (1962). Economic welfare and the allocation of resources for invention. In *The rate and direction of inventive activity* National Bureau of Economic Research Conference Series, Princeton, 609–25.

Arrow, K. J. (1974). *The limits to organization.* New York: Norton.

Arrow, K. J. (1979). Economics of information. In M. L. Dertouzos & J. Moses (Eds.) *The computer age: A twenty-year view,* Cambridge, Mass.: MIT Press, 306–17.

Baldwin, R. E. (1982). The political economy of protectionism. In J. N. Bhagwati (ed.), *Import Competition and Response.* Chicago: University of Chicago Press, 263–92.

Baumol, W. J. (1982) Constestable markets: An uprising in the theory of industrial structure. *American Economic Review, 72* (1), 1–15.

Baumol, W. & Wolf, J. (1984) Feedback models: R&D, Information and productivity growth. In Jussawalla & Ebenfield (Eds.) Communication and information economics. Amsterdam: North Holland.

Beaird, R. C. (1989). Telecommunications as an engine of economic growth, U.S. Department of State, Bureau of Public Affairs, Washington D.C. Text of a speech delivered in Mexico City. February 16.

Bell, Daniel. (1973). *The coming of post industrial society.* New York, Basic Books.

Bhagwati, J. (1988). *Protectionism,* Cambridge, Mass.: MIT Press.

Bhagwati, J. (1989). Let GATT live. *Wall Street Journal,* July 28.

Braunstein, Y. (1985). Information as a factor of production: substitutability and productivity, *The information society, 3,* 261–73.

Brock, G. W. (1981). *The telecommunications industry: The dynamics of market structure.* Cambridge, Mass.: Harvard University Press.

Burck, G. (1966). Knowledge, the biggest growth industry of them all. *Fortune, 70,* (5) 128–31, 267–70.

Caves, R. E. & Porter, M. E. (1977). From entry barriers to mobility barriers: Conjectural decisions and contrived deterrance to new competition. *Quarterly Journal of Economics,* May 9:(2), 241–61.

Demsetz, H. (1969). Information and efficiency: Another viewpoint, *Journal of Law and Economics, 12* April, 1–21.

Drucker, P. (1968). *The age of discontinuity,* New York: Harper and Row.

Galbraith, J. K. (1967). *The new industrial state,* New York: Houghton Mifflin.

Goldsworthy, A. W. (1979). Information as a commodity in *Search, 10,* (6) 219–23.

Helleiner, G. (1978). World market imperfections and the developing countries. *Occasional Papers II.* Overseas Development Council, U.S. Government Printing Office, Washington, D.C.

Hirschman, A. O. (1970). *Exit, voice, and loyalty; responses to decline in firms, organizations, and states.* Cambridge, Mass.: Harvard University Press.

Hirshleifer, J. (1973). Where are we in the theory of information. *American Economic Review, 63,* (2) 31–39.

Hirshleifer, J. & Riley, J. G. (1979). The analytics of uncertainty and information—an expository survey. *Journal of Economic Literature, 17,* December 1375–1421.

Johnson, H. G. (1963). Effects of changes in comparative costs as influenced by technical change. In R. F. Harrod and D. C. Hague (eds.), *International Trade Theory in a Developing World*. London: Macmillan.

Jonscher, C. (1982). Notes on communication and economic theory. In Jussawalla and Lamberton (Eds.), *Communication economics and development* New York: Pergamon, 60–69.

Jonscher, C. (1984). Productivity and growth of the information economy. In Jussawalla and Ebenfield (Eds.), *Communication and information economics: New perspectives*, North Holland, 95–103.

Jussawalla, M. (1982). International trade theory and communications. In M. Jussawalla and Lamberton (Eds.), *Communication economics and development*, New York: Pergamon Press, 82–97.

Jussawalla, M. & Cheah, C. W. (1983). Emerging economic constraints on transborder data flows. *Telecommunications Policy*, December, 285–96.

Jussawalla, M. & Cheah, C. W. (1984). International trade and information: Same welfare implications. In M. Jussawalla and Ebenfield (Eds.), *Communication and information economics: New perspectives*. North Holland, 51–71.

Jussawalla, M. & Cheah, C. W. (1986). *Calculus of international communications: A study in the political economy of transborder data flows*. Boulder, Col.: Libraries Unlimited.

Jussawalla, M. & Cheah, C. W. (1987). Economic analysis of the legal and policy aspects of information privacy. In Jussawalla and Cheah (Eds.) *The Calculus of International Communications* (75–102). Littleton, Co.: Libraries Unlimited.

Jussawalla, M. (1988). Global impact of telecommunication deregulation in *Transborder data report*, March, 10–16.

Laffont, J. (1989). *The economics of uncertainty and information* (J. Bonin & M. Bonin, trans.) Cambridge, Mass.: MIT Press, 55–69.

Lamberton, D. M. (1971). *Economics of information and knowledge: selected Readings*. New York: Penguin Books, 11–12.

Lamberton, D. M. (1984). The emergence of information economics. In M. Jussawalla and Ebenfield (Eds.) *Communication and information economics: New perspectives*, 7–17.

Lamberton, D. M. (1984). The regional information economy: Its measurement and significance. In Punset and Sweeney (Eds.) *Information resources and corporate growth*. London: Pinter, 16–25.

Leibenstein, H. (1975). Aspects of the X-efficiency theory of the firm. *The Bell Journal of Economics, 6*, (2) Autumn, 580–606.

Machlup, F. (1962). *The Production and Distribution of Knowledge in the United States*. Princeton, N.J.: Princeton University Press.

Magdoff, M. (1976). Multinational corporations and social development. In Apte and Goodman (eds.), *Multinational Corporations and Social Change*, chap. 8. New York: Praeger.

Marschak, J. (1974). Economic information, decision and prediction. *Economics of Information and Organization, II*, (D). Boston: Reidel.

Newman, G. (1976). An institutional perspective on information. *International Social Science, Journal, 28*, 466–92.

Nightingale, J. (1988). Information and productivity: An attempted replication of an empirical exercise. *Information Economics and Policy, 3*, 55–68.

Noll, Roger C. (1983). The political foundations of regulatory policy. *Zeitschrift fue die gesamte Staatswissenschaft, 139*, 377–404.

Porat, M. (1976). *The information economy*, vols. I and II, Washington, D.C., Department of Commerce. U.S. Government Printing Office.

Pulley, L. B. & Braunstein, Y. (1984). Scope and scale augmenting technological change: An application in the information sector. In Jussawalla and Ebenfield (Eds.) *Communication and information economics: New perspectives*. North Holland, 105–17.

Rada, J. F. (1981). The micro-electronics revolution: Implications for the third world. *Development Dialogue, 2*, 41–67.

Rubin, M. R. (1988). The secondary information sector: Its meaning, measurement, and importance. In Jussawalla et al. (eds.), *The cost of thinking: Information economies of ten Pacific countries*. Norwood, NJ: Ablex.

Shepherd, William G. (1984). Contestibility versus competition. *American Economic Review*, 74, 572–87.

Snow, M. S. (1985). Regulation to deregulation: The telecommunications sector and industrialization," *Telecommunications Policy, 9*, (4) December 281–90.

Snow, M. S. (1986). Regulating telecommunications, information and the media: An agenda for future comparative research. In M. Snow (Ed.) *Marketplace for telecommunications: Regulation and deregulation in industrialized democracies* New York: Longman, 275–94.

Snow, M. & Jussawalla, M. (1986). Telecommunication economics and international regulatory policy an annotated bibliography. In M. Snow (Ed.) *Marketplace for telecommunications: Regulation and deregulation in industrialized democracies* New York: Longman, 141–54.

Spence, A. M. (1974). An economist's view of information. *Annual Review of Information & Science and Technology, 9*, American Society of Information Science, Washington, D.C.

Spence, A. M. (1976). Information aspects of market structure: An introduction. *The Quarterly Journal of Economics, 90*, (4) 591–97.

Staple, G. C. & Mullins, M. (1989). Telecom traffic statistics MITT matter. *Telecommunications Policy*, 105–27.

Stigler, G. J. (1961). The economics of information. *Journal of Political Economy, 69*, (3) June, 213–25.

Stigler, G. T. (1971). The theory of economic regulation. *Bell Journal of Economics*, 2(1), 3–21.

Sweeney, G. (1989). Introductory chapter. In E. Punset & G. Sweney (Eds.) *Information resources and corporate growth*. London: Pinter Publications, 1–16.

Torr, C. S. W. (1980). The role of information in economic analysis. *South African Journal of Economics, 48* (2) 115–31.

United States Department of Commerce Study on *The Indistrial Outlook 1989*. Government Bureau of Publications, Washington, D.C.

PART II

DISCIPLINARY CONNECTIONS

8

An Etymological Exploration of the Links between Information and Communication

Jorge Reina Schement

The purpose of this paper is to explore the etymological roots of the words "communication" and "information." In so doing, the paper demonstrates a connection between the two concepts and their evolution.

It seems reasonable to suggest that the tieing together of diverse cognitive phenomena via an organizing category, otherwise referred to as information, reflects a linguistic evolution carried out over thousands of years, and reaching its current meaning only recently; I suggest that the idea of information, that is, the social attitude which considers information an abstract essence and treats it as a thing, has historical antecedents which are quite old, although the actual tendency to treat information as if it were a physical object seems to have arisen in the eighteenth century. Moreover, there appears to be a close link between the entry and development of the concepts of information and communication in the English language, resultng in overlapping meanings and parallel variations. Since the idea of information emerged from historical and cultural processes, and since communication behavior is also a product of cultural history, the overlap between the two phenomena bears deeper exploration. However, the overlap has fallen into the blind-spot between the two fields which should exhibit the greatest interest; so that communication researchers have mostly focused on communication processes, while information scientists have mostly concerned themselves with information structures. Thus, if both com-

munication and information reflect cultural and historical processes, perhaps even the same processes, then convergence on a new research front offers significant potential, even so much as to suggest the possibility of a unified theory of information and communication.

Then one of the Twelve whose name was Judas Iscariot went off to the chief priests and said, "What are you willing to give me if I hand him over to you?" They paid him thirty pieces of silver. (Matthew 26: 14, 15)

His betrayer had arranged to give them a signal, saying, "The man I shall embrace is the one; take hold of him." (Matthew 26: 48, The New American Bible, 1983)[1]

What exactly did Judas sell for thirty pieces of silver? In Matthew's version of the gospel, it seems that the scribes and Pharisees did not know which apostle was Jesus. Therefore, Judas' offer contained great value. But since he did not have physical possession of Jesus, how exactly did Judas "hand over" Jesus? Matthew's choice of the phrase "hand over," as the crux of Judas' offer to the chief priests, presents a puzzle.

On the other hand, Mark, in his gospel, described Judas as "the betrayer," going on to describe the fatal embrace in the Garden of Gethsemane (Mark 14: 44). His choice of phrase established the interpretation that has come down to the present. Indeed, seen against Jesus' seizure by the chief priests and his subsequent crucifixion, Judas' presumed intentions have long reinforced the view of his action as a betrayal, especially in light of his suicide (Matthew 27: 5). But Mark's account also suggests something of a puzzle. How could Judas betray his master when Jesus did not wish to hide? There is no answer to the question, for Matthew and Mark's stories contain contradictions that will never be conclusively resolved. Did the city officials know the identity of Jesus? Who actually sought to arrest Jesus, the Jewish authorities or the Romans? What were Judas' motivations? There just isn't enough surviving information to piece together this part of Jesus's life. Nevertheless, seen through the experience of the information age, one point is clear.

Obviously, Judas sold Jesus' identity to his enemies, in one of history's most celebrated instances of the sale of information. Judas's question to the buyers, "What are you willing to give me if I hand him over to you?" establishes the economic nature of the transaction, while the thirty pieces of silver confirm the price and imply the value of his relevation (Matthew 26: 14, 15).[2] We are apprised of the identity of the parties, the price, and the conditions of the contract. The confusion stems from Matthew's (and

Mark's) inability to separate the item actually exchanged from the goal of the exchange. Neither apostle distinguished the act of identifying Jesus to the chief priests, from the act of seizing Jesus.

Two thousand years later, however, Matthew's ambiguous choice of words provides a clue to the emergence of the information society. Matthew wrote in Koiné Greek,[3] so when he quoted Judas offering to "hand over" Jesus, he used the word παραδω′σω, which could also mean to deliver, or to render up (Gingrich, 1983, p. 148). In addition, the same word is used to describe Judas later in the gospel as "the betrayer" (Matthew 26: 25, 46, 48). But if this part of the story of Jesus' betrayal is about the sale of information, then why didn't the gospel writers use the word λο′γοζ(logos), which generally meant "knowledge" and could also mean "word," "story," "name," "prayer," "teacher," or "sign," depending on the context in which it was used. In fact, to Koiné Greek speakers, λο′γοζ offered the word whose meaning might come closest to "information," Yet it would not have been used in the context of a sale of information regarding the whereabouts of Jesus. Its meaning would be closer to "The Word" (of Christ).[4]

Our confusion stems from the fact that neither Greek, nor Biblical Hebrew for that matter, contained a word for information to describe the particular exchange that occurred between Judas and the chief priests. Since the meaning of λο′γοζ and παραδω′σω depended on the context of the sentence, the intended meaning of the writers is clouded by the inherent ambiguity of the words.[5] Scholars have pondered the meaning of each word in the gospels for centuries, and will no doubt continue to do so. But in this one vignette, at least, it seems reasonable to infer that, without a word (or concept) for information, neither gospel writer recognized the offer of thirty pieces of silver as an exchange of information.

From Greek to English

At about the time that the idea of information failed to take hold in the Hellenistic cultures of the eastern Mediterranean, its taproot appeared in Rome. There the Romans conceived the ancestors of the words information and communication. The Latin *informare* meant to give form to, to shape (Klein, 1971, p. 377), perhaps to form an idea of, or even to describe (Onions, 1966, p. 473), so that the seed of the modern meaning can be discerned in the possible use of *informare* to mean the shaping of an idea in one's head, as in to inform. *Communico, communicare* conveyed the sense of making common (Barnhart, 1988, p. 195), but also of imparting, or sharing (Klein, 1971, p. 152). Writing more than a century prior to the recording of the gospels, Julius Caesar did not use *informare* in any of his commentaries, indicating that *informare* entered Latin at a later date. However, in his Gallic commentaries, *communico* appears with the following meanings: *communicato*, "he told," Book IV ¶ 13, line 4; *communicat*, "he proposed," V 36, 3; *communicare*, "were intriguing," VI 2, 3; *communicatur* (*neque honos ullus communicatur*), "excluded," VI 13, 7; *communicant*, "to match (a dowry), VI 19, 1; *communicet*, "if anyone hears," VI 20, 1; communicatur, "to share" (food), VI 23, 9; *communicato*, "to take part in," VI 33, 5; *communicandum*, "to pass on" (information) VII 36, 3; *communicat*, "shared" (money) VII 37, 2; *communicet*, "joint" [plan of attack], VII 63, 4. Yet the tendency to connect communication with information is present, for six of the eleven instances pertain to some application of the idea of information (Caesar, 50 B.C./1980; Caesaris, 50 B.C./1927; Meusel, 1893) (Sihler, 1891, p. 29). Thus, the modern use of communication to mean the transmission (i.e., sharing) of a disease comes closer to the Latin meaning. But here too, the kernel of the information related meaning can be traced to the potential use of communicare to mean the imparting of a message.

With the decline of the Roman Empire came the evolution of the Romance languages. In the case of the Gauls, the path to French lay in the seamless variegation of dialects cut off from the mother tongue. In Old French, *communicare* grew into *communis*, meaning common (Klein, 1971, p. 152), but also sprouted *communicacion* (Onions, 1966, p. 196; Hoad, 1986, p. 87; Klein, 1971, p. 152). Similarly, *informare* emerged as *enfo[u]rmer* with its original meaning largely intact (Onions, 1966, p. 473), and added *enformacion*, a learned borrowing from medieval Latin *informationem*, meaning outline, concept, or form of an idea (Barnhart, 1988, p. 527). But unlike the gradual evolution of *communicare* into *communicacion*, the entrance of French into English occurred more abruptly.

William's victory at Hastings caused a language clash that sent Anglo-Saxon English reeling into exile and imposed French as the tongue of the ruling class. In so doing, the Norman conquest precipitated an inflow of French words over the next 300 years. As part of this process, John Wycliffe introduced the first English use of the word communication in his Bible of 1382. As written in the following passage from Paul's second letter to the Corinthians, Wycliffe employed communication to convey a sense of imparting (Oxford English Dictionary, 1989, p. 944).[6]

Glorifyinge God . . . in simplenesse of comynycacioun into hem and into alle. (2 Cor. ix. 13)

At about the same time, the word information surfaced in Chaucer's "Tale of Melibee," with the denotation of an instruction.

Whanne Melibee hadde herd the grete skiles and
resons of Dame Prudence and hire wise
informaciouns and techynges
his herte gan enclyne to the wyl of his wyf
considerynge hir trewe entente. (Chaucer, 1940)

The "Tale of Melibee" was probably written sometime between 1372 and
1382 (Chaucer, 1400/1952), although the *Oxford English Dictionary* places
the tale at around 1386 (Oxford English Dictionary, 1989, p. 944). Thus,
given the rate of time necessary for words to evolve in usage, information,
and communication entered English within a very short span of time. In
the following decade, a third writer, John Trevisa, reinforced the arrival
when he used information to signify the word of God as a message in his
1938 translation of Bartholomæus Anglicus' *On the Properties of Things*.

therfore diuynyte vsith holy informacioun and poesies
that myistik and dirk vndirstondinge and figuratif
speches, . . . (Anglicus, 1398/1975, p. 41)

To be sure, the association of the date of a manuscript with the entrance
of a word into English represents an interpretation based on the inference
that writers choose words for the impact on the reader as well as for their
own delight. After all, written language can only be effective when oral
language has achieved common use, especially in a document with the
status of the bible. For this reason, writers are unlikely to choose a word
unfamiliar to their intended audience. Thus, by the end of the fourteenth
century when Wycliffe, Chaucer, and Trevisa, chose English for the
language of their writings, in all likelihood, words like *informacioun,* and
comynycacioun made sense to their readers.

Does the almost simultaneous entrance of information and communication, into English, bear significance—was there something special about
the 1380s? For the time being, this event remains a mystery. But given the
overlapping connotations of the two words, it is not surprising to find the
concepts of information and communication linked in time as well as in
meaning. Indeed, a parallel evolution toward the modern meanings of the
two words seems to have kept apace, so that by 1667, John Milton used
communication with a meaning that implies information,

Thou in thy secresie although alone,
Best with thy self accompanied, seek'st not
Social communication, . . . (Milton, 1667, Book VII, Lines 1064–1066)

Milton also used the verb communicate with the following meanings which
harken back to archaic usages: to partake (V. 72); to open from one to

another and to have continuity of passage (VII. 787); to share in or partake of (VIII. 755). He uses *communicable* in association with knowledge from God (VII. 124). In a further convolution of the etymological trail, the *Oxford English Dictionary* [OED] (1989) erroneously cites the above passage as occurring in Book VIII, on line 429. However, the OED relies on *The Poetical Works of John Milton,* (ed. H. C. Beeching, Clarendon Press, 1900), in which the preface states that *Paradise Lost* is taken from the 1667 edition. Instead, it seems likely that the lines in the OED are in accordance with changes made in 1674 (the second edition), when Book VII was divided into two at line 640 (according to a note in the 1900 *Works*).

Sixty-three years earlier, Shakespeare, in a foreshadowing of the modern idea of information as thing, had already pioneered the materialization of the symbolic. In *Othello* (1604), Iago protests,

> But he that filches from me my good name
> Robs me of that which not enriches him
> And makes me poor indeed. (Act III, Scene iii)

In *Gulliver's Travels* (1727), Jonathan Swift applied a meaning to the word information which sounds modern:

> It was necessary to give the reader this information. (Swift, 1727/1983, III. ii, p. 170)

While Swift's use of "information" is clearly modern, usages approaching this one appear as early as the mid-fifteenth century. (*Oxford English Dictionary,* 1989, p. 944, "information," 3. a.). Still, evidence that this meaning had gained wide acceptance by the beginning of the nineteenth century can be found in an 1804 letter, by Thomas Jefferson, to the economist Jean Baptiste Say, in which Jefferson also used information as an organizing category:[7]

> My occupations . . . deny me the time, if I had the information, to answer them. (Padover, 1946, p. 71)

As for communication, In *Voyage Round the World* (1725, 1840, p. 152), Daniel Defoe wrote,

> They had little knowledge or communication one with another.

with a meaning which we instantly recognize. In fact, by the middle of the following century, Tennyson's (1850) use of the verb communicate sounds similarly up-to-date.

> In dear words of human speech
> We two communicate no more.
> (Tennyson, 1862, LXXXV. xxi.)

That Defoe's use of communication in 1725 is completely compatible with Swift's use of information in 1727 underscores continued parallel formation, though in all fairness, Defoe's and Swift's connection might be purely random, as might Wycliffe's, Trevisa's, and Chaucer's. But the persistence with which the two words kept apace in their evolution toward modern meanings argues against simple coincidence. That Swift, Defoe, Jefferson, and Tennyson expressed themselves by choosing words and meanings that are completely familiar to us, further points to the current meanings of information and communication as part of the emergence of the modern era. Jefferson, especially, rings true because he wrote as though information were a material asset, thus applying the sense most commonly used today. Certainly, the perspective which equated information with a material thing had gained acceptance in literary circles by the middle of the eighteenth century, as witnessed by the following definitions excerpted from Samuel Johnson's 1755 dictionary (McAdam & Milne, 1963, pp. 103, 114, 212, 296):

bo'okful. Full of notions gleaned from books; crouded with undigested knowledge.

to ca'strate. [2] To take away the obscene parts of a writing.

hu'shmoney. A bribe to hinder information; pay to secure silence.

pla'giary. A thief in literature, one who steals the thought or writings of another.

In other words, today's meanings of information and communication arrived at a time when European culture was forming the world view which we now share (Ariés, 1962; Braudel, 1979; Burke, 1978; Cassirer, 1951/ 1979; Gay, 1966; Hampson, 1968). Clearly, then, the eighteenth and nineteenth centuries were a time when literate individuals, at least, were becoming aware of information as a distinct phenomenon and of communication as a determined act; so that, by the end of the nineteenth century, a writer like John Ruskin could choose language (and a theme) familiar to any reader of literature on the information society:

. . . the reward which rapidity of communication now ensures to discoveries that are profitable. (Ruskin, 1883, § 33)

Furthermore, by mid-twentieth century, scientists had adopted the idea of information in the form of a quantifiable variable; thereby, pushing the thinglike sense of information to a new level. Writing in the *Proceedings of the Cambridge Philosophical Society* (1925), R. A. Fisher chose a new meaning for information, and established the nomenclature of information science, by stating that,

What we have spoken of as the intrinsic accuracy of an error curve may equally be conceived as the amount of information in a single observation belonging to such a distribution. (XXII. 709)

While across the Atlantic, R. V. L. Hartley reinforced Fisher's British English with a comparable American meaning, when he wrote the following in the *Bell System Technical Journal* (1928):

What we have done then is to take as our practical measure of information the logarithm of the number of possible symbol sequences. (VII. 540 p. 944)

In turn, an unknown journalist seems to have solved the problem of communicating this difficult concept to the public at large in the November 1937 issue of *Discovery*, when he tentatively associated information with quantity, and, in so doing, opened the way for this particular meaning to move from the esoteric jargon of the laboratory into everyday common speech:

The whole difficulty resides in the amount of definition in the [television] picture, or, as the engineers put it, the amount of information to be transmitted in a given time. (Nov. 1937. 329/I)

Half a century later, English speakers are comfortable with the notion that information is a thing able to be quantified and with the notion that communication is a process for transmitting information. Taken together, they facilitate making sense of much that we identify with the information society. Yet the links between information and communication are also there because they represent two dimensions of one complex human behavior, and though English speakers bisect it into two words, both words retain an ambiguity by overlapping in meaning. Not surprisingly, the *Oxford English Dictionary* defines information in modern usage as:

[2] The action of informing . . . ; communication of the knowledge or 'news' of some fact or occurrence; the action of telling or fact of being told of something.

[3a.] Knowledge, communicated concerning some particular fact, subject, or event; that of which one is apprised or told; intelligence, news, . . .

and communication as:

[2] . . . The imparting, conveying, or exchange of ideas, knowledge, information, etc. [whether by speech, writing, or signs]. Hence [often *pl.*], the science or process of conveying information, esp. by means of electronic or mechanical techniques.

Hence, at the twilight of the twentieth century, English speakers still impute distinct meanings to information and communication. But increasingly, Information and communication are linked in meaning and in speech, so much so, that each concept depends on the other for its full explication.

The Idea of Information

As the twenty-first century approaches, we take it for granted that libraries, clocks, spying, and plagiarism, all have to do with information. We think in terms of information as an influence on our behavior, and we weigh the advantages of specific information in our competition with others. In fact, information is of such value to us that we buy it, sell it, and enact laws to punish its theft. We are so secure in our attitude that we expect others to share the same assumption. Furthermore, though information exists solely as the symbolic product of our brains, we easily translate it into the material world, so much so, that, for better or worse, we have reorganized our economy around the production and communication of information. But in order to do so, Americans have adopted a perspective in which information is conceived of as thinglike. As a result, messages are thought to contain more, or less, information; marketplaces exist for the buying and selling of information; devices are developed for the storage and retrieval of information; and devices exist for the purpose of communicating information. Moreover, and equally important, the thingness of information is coupled with an ethos that serves as a unifying concept thereby allowing individuals to see diverse experiences, such as a name, a poem, a table of numbers, a novel and a picture, as possessing a common essential feature termed information. Consequently, as people endow information with the characteristics of a thing (or think of it as embodying material characteristics) they facilitate its manipulation in the world of things (for example, in the marketplace). I call this complex association of meanings and connotations the idea of information; it includes our understanding of communication and is implicitly understood by most Americans, so much so, that its observable presence serves as an identifying badge of the information society as a culture. But it was not always so, as the exchange between Judas and the authorities of Jerusalem illustrates.

If this etymology of information and communication tells us something of the emergence of the information society, it does so by pointing to the ascendance of the idea of information. From what can be deduced etymologically, it seems reasonable to suggest that the tying together of diverse cognitive phenomena via an organizing category, otherwise referred to as information, reflects a linguistic evolution carried out over thousands of years, and reaching its current meaning only recently. Therefore, I suggest that the idea of information, that is, the social attitude which considers information an abstract essence and treats it as a thing, has historical antecedents which are quite old, although the actual tendency to treat information as if it were a physical object seems to have arisen in the 18th century. These developments further indicate that the idea of information is actually a social construction which evolved as part of the emergence of modernity.[8] Moreover, there appears to be a close link between the entry and development of the concepts of information and communication in the English language, resulting in overlapping meanings and parallel variations. In the twentieth century, information (along with communication) has been discovered in the physical sciences, the social sciences, and by the public, so that it currently operates as a key term for understanding change, so much so that it lends itself to the characterization of the times as an information age or information society (Artandi, 1973; Beniger, 1988; Borgman & Schement, 1990; Braman, 1989; Bruner, 1990; Campbell, 1982; Chamberlin & Singleton, 1987; Childers, 1975; Dawkins & Krebs, 1984; Farradane, 1976; Fox, 1983; Fredkin & Toffoli, 1982; Geertz, 1983; Halloran, 1985; Hirschleifer, 1973; Hixson, 1985; Kibirige, 1983; Lamberton, 1971; Machlup & Mansfield, 1983a; Mackay, 1952; Otten, 1975; Repo, 1989; Schiller, 1983; Sharrock, 1974; Thayer, 1988; Wiener, 1950).

That said, we know little of how the idea of information evolved and was acted out in daily life, or of the circumstances that caused words to be adapted for imposing a materialistic frame around ideas. Nor do we currently understand how the idea of information influenced interpersonal communication patterns among Europeans and Americans; and, surprisingly, we know little of how the idea of information became so visible to a widely dispersed group of scholars in the middle decades of the twentieth century that they too focused on information as a component in their theories.[9] Furthermore, while this paper presents an outline of the transformations that led to the current meanings of information and communication, we know next to nothing of the circumstances that led to those shifts in meaning.

Finally, since the idea of information emerged from historical and cultural processes, and since communication behavior is also a product of cultural history, the overlap between the two phenomena bears deeper exploration. But the overlap has fallen into the blindspot between the two fields which should exhibit the greatest interest; so that communication researchers have mostly focused on communication processes, while information scientists have mostly concerned themselves with information structures. Nevertheless, over the years, a few scholars have proposed a connection between information and communication (Bruner, 1973; Cherry, 1966; Krippendorff, 1977; Lawson, 1963; Machlup, 1962; Miller, 1965; Ruben, 1972; Ruben, 1979; Ruben & Kim, 1975; Ruesch & Bateson, 1951; Schroder, Driver, & Streufert, 1967; Shannon & Weaver, 1949; Thayer, 1968); while, more recently, a small literature has emerged with a primary focus on the convergence between studies of information and studies of communication, though as yet, there is not distinct pattern of findings (Beniger, 1988; Borgman & Schement, 1988; Braman, 1989; Campbell, 1982; Dervin & Voight, 1979–1989; Gumpert & Cathcart, 1982; Machlup & Mansfield, 1983b; Ruben, 1988; Ruben, Holtz, & Hanson, 1982; Schement & Lievrouw, 1988; Williams, 1982). Thus, if both communication and information reflect cultural and historical processes, perhaps even the same processes, then convergence on a new research front offers significant potential, even so much as to suggest the possibility of a unified theory of information and communication.

At the very least, the histories of words should remind us of the temporal limits of what we take for granted. Indeed, Judas made perfect sense two thousand years ago and still makes sense; yet he lacked the perspective to visualize his own offer of information, a perspective which we take for granted today. But even more importantly, the etymologies of information and communication testify to the power of ideas and the words associated with them. After all, the information society might not exist without the words to explain its meaning.

Notes

1. Translated from the original languages by the Catholic Biblical Association of America.
2. The price of thirty pieces of silver has significance beyond Matthew. It is also mentioned in Zechariah 11:12 as wages, and in Exocus 21:32 as thirty sheckles,

the reimbursement damages for a slave gored by an ox. (Brown, Fitzmeyer, & Murphy, 1968, p. 108).
3. Koiné Greek: the common speech of the whole Greek world, the lingua franca of the Hellenistic world at the time of Jesus. (Cary & Haarhoff, 1940, pp. 182–183).
4. English derivatives such as "logo" and "logarithm" reflect the Greek meaning of λο'γoζ. (Gingrich, 1983, p. 119).
5. I am indebted to Mahlon Smith of Rutgers University, and Irving Mandelbaum, formerly of The University of Texas at Austin, for clarifying this question.
6. Since oral culture has little permanence, it is written culture which records history. Consequently, it seems apparent that words enter oral circulation before they are written down, so that our ability to trace the presence of words depends on the survival of documents. Even so, many of the dates in this article constitute the best current approximations.
7. This is the same Jean Baptiste Say responsible for "Say's Law," the assertion that the total supply of goods must always equal the total demand for them. Money, in Say's Law, is merely a medium of exchange, or a kind of information, if you will. Thus, according to Say, any increase in production is also an increase in demand.
8. Nevertheless, I do not imply that humans conceive of information as a thing to the exclusion of other formulations—humans obviously process information cognitively, whether or not thinglike characteristics are ascribed.
9. Though beyond the focus of this book, looking upon information as a thing (that is stripped of its traditional and local discourse senses) would seem to be highly associated with a positivist view of the universe, a universe that is open to understanding through observation, and modeled through the identification of causal relationships. What is of interest, then, is that just as "information" has become visible to the mainstream of western thought, there has emerged an intellectual tension which reacts to this privileged status of information and positivism. Thus, contemporary reactions to positivism and the idea of information, as expressed in phenomenology and hermeneutics, reflect a dialect in thought made possible precisely because an unconscious organizing principle has been made conscious.

References

(1983). *The new american bible* (Translated from the original languages by the Catholic Biblical Association of America). New York: Thomas Nelson Publishers.
(1989). *Oxford english dictionary*. Oxford: Clarendon Press.
Anglicus, B. (1398/1975). *On the properties of things* (Trevisa, John, Trans.). Oxford: Clarendon Press.
Ariés, P. (1962). *Centuries of childhood: A social history of family life* (Baldick, R., Trans.). New York: Vintage.
Artandi, S. (1973). Information concepts and their utility. *Journal of the American Society for Information Science, 24*(4), 242–45.
Barnhart, R. K. (Ed.). (1988). *The barnhart dictionary of etymology*. New York: H. H. Wilson.
Beniger, J. R. (1988). Information and communication. *Communication Research, 15*(2), 198–218.

Borgman, C. L., & Schement, J. R. (1988). Communication research and information science: Models of convergence. *International Communication Association, New Orleans, LA.*

Borgman, C. L., & Schement, J. R. (1990). Information science and communication research. In J. M. Pemberton & A. E. Prentice (Eds.), *Information science: The interdisciplinary context* (pp. 42–59). New York: Neal-Schuman.

Braman, S. (1989). Defining information: An approach for policymakers. *Telecommunications Policy, 13*(3), 233–42.

Braudel, F. (1979). *Civilization and capitalism 15th–18th century: The wheels of commerce.* New York: Harper & Row.

Brown, R. E., [S.S.], Fitzmeyer, J. A., [S.J.], & Murphy, R. E., [O. Carm.] (Ed.). (1968). *The Jerome biblical commentary.* Englewood Cliffs, NJ: Prentice-Hall.

Bruner, J. (1990). *Acts of meaning.* Cambridge, MA: Harvard.

Bruner, J. S. (1973). *Beyond the information given: Studies in the psychology of knowing.* New York: Norton.

Burke, P. (1978). *Popular culture in early modern europe.* New York: New York University Press.

Caesar, J. (50 B.C./1980). *The battle for gaul* (Wiseman, Anne, and Wiseman, Peter, Trans.). Boston, MA: David R. Godine.

Caesaris, C. I. (50 B.C./1927). *Commentarii.* Lipsiae in Aedibus: B. G. Teubneri.

Campell, J. (1982). *Grammatical man.* New York: Touchstone.

Cary, M. J., & Haarhoff, T. J. (1940). *Life and thought in the Greek and Roman world.* London: Methuen.

Cassier, E. (1951/1979). *The philosophy of the englightenment* (Koellen, Fritz C. A. Pettegrove, James P., Trans.). Princeton, NJ: Princeton University Press.

Chamberlin, B. F., & Singleton, L. A. (1987). The law in an information society. In J. R. Schement & L. Lievrouw (Eds.), *Competing visions, complex realities: Social aspects of the information society* (pp. 121–139). Norwood, NJ: Ablex.

Chaucer, G. (1400/1952). *The Canterbury tales* (Coghill, Nevill, Trans.). Baltimore, MD: Penguin.

Chaucer, G. (1940). The tale of melibeus [Also known as the tale of melibee]. In J. M. Manly & E. Rickert (Eds.), *The text of the Canterbury tales: Studied on the basis of all known manuscripts* (pp. 213–214.). Chicago, IL: University of Chicago.

Cherry, C. (1966). *The communication of information* (2nd ed.). New York: Holt, Rinehart, and Winston.

Childers, T. (1975). *The information-poor in america.* Metuchen, NJ: The Scarecrow Press.

Dawkins, R., & Krebs, J. R. (1984). Animal signals: Information or manipulation? In J. R. Krebs & N. B. Davies (Eds.), *Behavioral Ecology: An evolutionary approach* Sunderland, MA: Sinauer.

Dervin, B., & Voight, M. (Ed.). (1979–1989). *Progress in communication sciences.* Norwood, NJ: Ablex.

Farradane, J. (1976). Towards a true information science. *Information Scientist, 10,* 91–101.

Fox, C. J. (1983). *Information and misinformation: An investigation of the notions of information, misinformation, informing, and misinforming.* Westport, CT: Greenwood Press.

Fredkin, E., & Toffoli, T. (1982). Conservative logic. *International Journal of Theoretical Physics, 21*(3/4).

Gay, P. (1966). *The enlightenment: An interpretation.* New York: Vintage Books.
Geertz, C. (1983). The way we think: Toward an ethnography of modern thought. In C. Geertz (Eds.), *Local knowledge* (pp. 147–163). New York: Basic Books.
Gingrich, F. W. (1983). *Shorter lexicon of the Greek new testament.* Chicago: University of Chicago.
Gumpert, G., & Cathcart, R. (1982). *Intermedia: Interpersonal communication in a media world.* New York: Oxford University Press.
Halloran, J. D. (1985). Information and communication: Information is the answer, but what is the question? In B. D. Ruben (Eds.), *Information and behavior* (pp. 27–39). New Brunswick, NJ: Transaction.
Hampson, N. (1968). *The enlightenment.* Harmondsworth, Middlesex: Penguin Books.
Hirshleifer, J. (1973). Economics of information: Where are we in the theory of information? *American Economic Association. 63*(2), 31–39.
Hixson, R. F. (1985). Whose life is it anyway? Information as property. In B. D. Ruben (Ed.), *Information and behavior: Volume 1* (pp. 76–92). New Brunswick, NJ: Transaction.
Hoad, T. F. (1986). *The concise Oxford Dictionary of English etymology.* Oxford: Carendon Press.
Kibirige, H. M. (1983). *The information dilemma: A critical analysis of information pricing and the fees controversy.* Westport, CN: Greenwood Press.
Klein, E. (Ed.). (1971). *A comprehensive etymological dictionary of the english language.* Amsterdam: Elsevier.
Krippendorff, K. (1977). Information systems theory and research. In B. D. Ruben (Eds.), *Communication Yearbook 1* (pp. 149–171). New Brunswick, NJ: Transaction-International Communication Association.
Lamberton, D. M. (Ed.). (1971). *Economics of information and knowledge.* Harmondsworth, UK: Penguin.
Lawson, C. A. (1963). Language, communication, and biological organization. In L. von Bertalanffy & A. Rapoport (Eds.), *General systems: Volume VIII.* Ann Arbor, MI: Society for General Systems Research.
Machlup, F. (1962). *The production and distribution of knowledge in the United States.* Princeton, NJ: Princeton University Press.
Machlup, F., & Mansfield, U. (1983a). Semantic quirks in studies of information. In F. Machlup & U. Mansfield (EDs.), *The study of information: Interdisciplinary messages* (pp. 3–59). New York: John Wiley & Sons.
Machlup, F., & Mansfield, U. (Ed.). (1983b). *The study of information: Interdisciplinary messages.* New York: John Wiley & Sons.
Mackay, D. M. (1952). The nomenclature of information theory. In H. Von Foerster (Ed.), *Cybernetics: Transactions of the Eighth Congress.* New York: Macy Foundation.
McAdam, E. L. J., & Milne, G. (1963). *Johnson's dictionary.* New York: Pantheon.
Meusel, H. (1893). *Lexicon caesarianum.* Berlin, Ger.: W. Weber.
Miller, J. G. (1965). Living systems. *10,* 193–237.
Milton, J. (1667). *Paradise lost: A poem written in ten books.* London, UK: Samuel Simmons.
Onions, C. T. (Ed.). (1966). *The Oxford dictionary of English etymology.* Oxford, UK: Clarendon Press.
Otten, K. W. (1975). Information and communication: A conceptual model as framework for the development of theories of information. In A. Debons & W.

Cameron (Eds.), *Perspectives in information science* (pp. 127–148). Leyden: Noordhof.

Padover, S. K. (Ed.). (1946). *Thomas Jefferson on democracy.* New York: New American Library.

Repo, A. J. (1989). The value of information: Approaches in economics, accounting, and management. *JASIS, 40*(2), pp. 68–85.

Ruben, B. D. (1972). General systems theory: An approach to human communication. In R. W. Budd & B. D. Ruben (Eds.), *Approaches to human communication* (pp. 120–144). New York: Spartan.

Ruben, B. D. (1979). General systems theory. In R. W. Budd & B. D. Ruben (Eds.), *Interdisciplinary Approaches to Human Communication* (pp. 95–118). Rochelle Park, NJ: Hayden.

Ruben. B. D. (1988). *Communication and human behavior* (2nd ed.). New York: Macmillan.

Ruben, B. D., Holtz, J. R., & Hanson, J. K. (1982). Communication systems, technology, and culture. In H. F. Didsbury Jr. (Eds.), *Communications and the Future: Prospects, Promises, and Problems* (pp. 255–66). Bethesda, MD: World Future Society.

Ruben, B. D., & Kim, J. Y. (Ed.). (1975). *General systems theory and human communication.* Rochelle Park, NJ: Hayden.

Ruesch, J., & Bateson, G. (1951). *Communication: The social matrix of psychology.* New York: Norton.

Ruskin, J. (1883). *The eagle's nest.* New York: John Wiley.

Schement, J. R., & Lievrouw, L. A. (1988). *Competing visions, complex realities: Social aspects of the information society.* Norwood, NJ: Ablex.

Schiller, H. I. (1983). Information for what kind of society? In J. L. Salvaggio (Eds.), *Telecommunications: Issues and choices for society* (pp. 24–33). New York: Longman.

Schroder, H. M., Driver, M. J., & Streufert, S. (1967). *Human information processing.* New York: Holt, Rinehart and Winston.

Shannon, C. E., & Weaver, W. (1949). *The mathematical theory of communication.* Urbana, IL: University of Illinois Press.

Sharrock, W. W. (1974). On owning knowledge. In R. Turner (Eds.), *Ethnomethodology: Selected readings* (pp. 45–53). New York: Penguin.

Sihler, E. G. (1891). *A complete lexicon of the Latinity of caesar's gallic war.* Boston, MA: Ginn.

Swift, J. (1727/1983). *Gulliver's travels into several remote nations of the world.* London, UK: Dent.

Tennyson, A. (1862). *In memoriam.* London, UK: Edward Moxon.

Thayer, L. (1968). *Communication and communication systems.* Homewood, IL: Irwin.

Thayer, L. (1988). How does information inform? In B. D. Ruben (Ed.), *Information and Behavior* (pp. 13–26). New Brunswick, NJ: Transaction.

Wiener, N. (1950). *The human use of human beings: Cybernetics and society.* New York: Avon Books.

Williams, F. (1982). *The communications revolution.* Beverly Hills, CA: Sage.

9

Context and Content of Citations between Communication and Library and Information Science Articles

Ronald E. Rice and Gregory A. Crawford

The present study considers the broad question, "Is there a conver-gence between information and communication?", by focusing nar-rowly on citation relations between the disciplines of communication and library & information science, but in depth by analyzing the articles' authors, dates, title words, nature, and citation context of the relations. The data consist of those articles in communication journals and library & information science journals that made cita-tions to or received citations from the other discipline from 1977 through 1987.

Most frequent article title words varied between citing/cited com-munication or LIS articles, with the most frequent including "infor-mation", "communication", "system", "research", "telecommu-nication", "organization", "computer-mediated", "policy", "library", etc. LIS articles not only cite Communication articles more frequently, but also do so a bit more quickly. Authors of cited communication articles were more numerous, with many multiple frequencies, than of citing communication articles, and belonged to distinct network positions representing domestic and international telecommunications policy, academic and bibliometric evaluation, theory and research about computer-mediated communication, use of print media, and network information services. In general, possi-ble areas of developing convergence between the two disciplines includes pragmatic issues of telecommunication policy, and social (not technical) research on computer-mediated communication, along with some uses of documents and archives, written about by a variety of authors who do not yet constitute a cross-disciplinary invisible college.

Problem Statement

In the past decade, increasing attention has been paid to possible areas of commonality between the concepts, subdisciplines, research methodologies, and researchers concerned with "information" and "communication." This attention has focused on two primary issues: what conceptual commonalities and relationships exist between these two concepts, and what behavioral evidence is there that individuals, institutions, and research activities are beginning to become aware of each other across formal disciplinary and conceptual boundaries?

In their monumental work, *The Study of Information*, Machlup & Machlup (1983) sought to define the boundaries of the concept of information. They identified more than thirty fields that focus in some way upon information. Among these fields, the following were considered to be tied closely to the field of communication: linguistics, phonetics, semantics, semiotics, lexicology, communication science, communication theory, and telecommunications research. The authors claimed, however, that the terms information and communication possess various meanings, often involving "strange uses for common words" (p. 49). The various uses of these terms have led scholars from the separate disciplines to attempt to "erect fences around their fields," instead of finding ways to collaborate in order to promote mutual understanding (p. 7). Their study of information was an attempt to encourage this mutual understanding and to seek a convergence between the disciplines which study information.

Paisley (1986) considered mass communication, interpersonal communication, and information science to be three subfields of a common discipline, partially because they are all "variable fields," ones that focus on a theoretical variable—communication and information, respectively—rather than "level fields," ones that focus on a level of analysis—the individual or group, as in most behavioral and social sciences (Paisley, 1984). He noted evidence of internal convergences, such as the formation of the International Communication Association, and the American Association for Information Science, and argued that "adequate models of the processes and effects of the new system require concepts from all three subfields" (1986, 124). The subfields share three sets of concerns or specialization: (1) social research approaches and methods; (2) issues of operations research, legal and regulatory issues, linguistics; and (3) training professionals. He analyzed various sources of data for evidence of convergence among the subdisciplines, and found that while several concepts have diffused among the disciplines (such as the knowledge gap, the information society, and the invisible college), there was little evidence of any convergence occurring among these subfields, or across communication and library and information science.

Beniger (1988) argued that there is, in general, an increasing convergence of the concepts of information and communication in social science and the humanities, if not across these two specific disciplines. Beniger claimed that

> the area of most general convergence involves theories of information, knowledge structures, communication, and the encoding and decoding of meaning, including broad topics in cognition, linguistics and language philosophy, hermeneutics and illocution, signs, subconscious and culture, and the social construction of knowledge. (P. 205)

However, Beniger argued that the field of communication, as represented by Berger & Chaffee's *Handbook of Communication Science* (1987), does not display this convergence of interest in theories of information and communication. Of the twenty-two authors who appeared on all three lists of the most cited authors in the disciplines of humanities, cognitive science, and semiotics, only ten were included among the 3,496 names indexed by the Handbook.

Crawford (1990) proposes that the concepts of information and communication are converging on the basis of three commonalities: (1) common language—"information" and "communication" are interrelated and frequently used terms in both science and everyday life, and communication and library and information science are concerned with how communicants and system users create meaning from information; (2) common technologies—both disciplines are, to some extent, interested in how media organize and provide access to information to allow communication over time, space, people and processes; and (3) common scholarly fields—both disciplines, to some extent, support research on processes involving information and communiucation as well as on the relationships of the terms themselves.

Others have analyzed such potential convergence between the specific disciplines of communication and library and information science (see editor's introduction and several chapters in Borgman 1990; Paisley, 1990; Pemberton & Prentice, 1990), considering, for example, concepts common

to communication and to library & information science, or cross-disciplinary citation patterns for a given year. Peritz (1981) found that 3 percent
of the citations from a select sample of information science journals during
the period 1950–1975 were made to psychology, sociology, or communication. So (1988) found that information science was not involved in
enough cross-disciplinary citations to include it in his study of cross-
disciplinary citing patterns among twelve disciplines from 1983–1985.
Barnett & Fink (1989) also found that information science received essentially no citations from other social science disciplines. And Paisley (1984),
found no cross-citation between communication and library and information science in 1980–1981, though he did find evidence that a few central
communication concepts had diffused into the information science literature.

Analyses of citation patterns among journals from 1977 through 1987
have shown that the discipline of communication consists of the two
subfields of mass communication and interpersonal communication
(Reeves & Borgman, 1983; Rice, Borgman & Reeves, 1988). Rice's (1990)
analysis of citations among journals of these two disciplines over the same
eleven-year time period shows these same two communication subdisciplines, and three information science subdisciplines of information science,
library science, and library practice. Over time, there was a general
progression toward clearer differences among the subdisciplines as well as
more internally structured citation relationships among journals in these
five subdisciplines. Borgman & Rice (1992) found a small but growing
trend toward cross-disciplinary citation, provided primarily by articles in
library and information science journals citing articles in communication
journals.

There is also anecdotal institutional evidence that these two disciplines
have begun to explore issues of common interest. Several library and
information science programs, such as Rutgers, Syracuse, and UCLA,
have hired faculty with doctorates in communication in recent years.

Thus most prior relevant studies either consider the question of convergence of information and communication from descriptive or normative
theoretical positions, or emphasize the citation relationships among subdisciplines without regard to the content of those relationships. The
present study attempts to contribute to the question, "Is there a convergence between information and communication?" by focusing narrowly
on citation relations between the disciplines of communication and library
and information science, but focusing in greater depth on the context and
content of those citation relations.

The present study asks the following research questions:

1. Who are the authors involved in cross-disciplinary citing?
   A. Who are the most frequently involved?
   B. Do these authors represent distinct structural positions?
   C. What research content do these structural positions represent?
2. Do the two disciplines differ in the lag time between citing and cited article?
3. What are the articles about?
   A. Which words appear in the most article titles?
   B. Do distinct sets of words appear in these titles?
4. What is the content context of cross-disciplinary citations?
   A. What is the nature of the citing article?
   B. What is the context of a cross-disciplinary citation?

Method

Data

As part of our ongoing research project (Borgman & Rice, 1992; Rice, 1990; Rice, Borgman, Bednarski, & Hart, 1989; and Rice, Borgman, & Reeves, 1988), we began with the citation data among the seventy-seven journals in the core lists entitled "communication" and "information and library science" obtained from the *Journal Citation Reports (JCR)* of the *Social Sciences Citation Index* (SSCI) for each of the eleven years from 1977 through 1987. The 1985 *JCR* list of journals was the basis for identifying which journals to use in the longitudinal analyses as it was the latest list at the time of the initial data collection. The dataset was extended by picking up aberrant forms of abbreviation, title changes, and citations made to journals listed in the 1985 core list that were not in the core list of that year, thus ameliorating some of the problems created by the changing journal coverage (see Rice et al., 1989, for details). In addition we also included cross-disciplinary citations not listed by the *JCR* as occurring between two specific journals in the *JCR* (as explained in Rice et al., 1989) but found during our detailed inspection process. Table 9.1 lists the specific journal titles involved in cross-disciplinary citation between 1977 and 1987, along with the number of citations involved.

The JCR and table 9.1 indicate only the citing and cited journal. Each citing journal was then inspected to identify (1) the full bibliographic reference of the article making a cross-disciplinary citation; and (2) the full bibliographic reference of the cited article, as listed in the citing article.

TABLE 9.1
Journals Involved in Cross-Disciplinary Citing, with Citation Direction and Strength,
1977–1987 (Source: Borgman & Rice, 1992)

Year	Library & Information Science	Citation Direction	Communication	Number of Citations
1977	American Archivist	cited by	Journ. Quarterly	1
	Library Journal	cited by	Journ. Quarterly	1
1978	Info. Proc. Management	cites	Journ. Communication	6
	Lib. Quarterly	cites	Journ. Broadcasting	2
	Lib. Quarterly	cites	Journ. Communication	3
	RQ	cited by	Journ. Quarterly	1
	Special Lib.	cited by	Journ. Quarterly	1
1979	Govt. Pubs. Review	cites	Col. Journ. Review	1
	Journ. Lib. Studies	cites	Ed. Comm. Tech. Journ.	5
	Wilson Lib. Bulletin	cited by	Ed. Comm. Tech. Journ.	1
1980	ARIST	cites	Journ. Broadcasting	1
	ARIST	cites	Journ. Communication	9
	ARIST	cites	Telecomm. Policy	22
	Information Age	cites	Telecomm. Policy	3
1981	ARIST	cites	Journ. Broadcasting	1
	ARIST	cites	Telecomm. Policy	2
	InfTeL	cited by	Journ. Quarterly	1
	Lib. Journal	cites	Col. Journ. Review	2
	Lib. Quarterly	cites	Public Opin. Quart.	1
1982	ARIST	cites	Journ. Communication	12
	ARIST	cites	Journ. Quarterly	1
	ARIST	cites	Telecomm. Policy	2
	Behav. Soc. Sci. Lib.	cites	Human Comm. Research	1
	Behav. Soc. Sci. Lib	cites	Cent. St. Speech Journ.	1
	Information Age	cites	Telecomm. Policy	5
	Journ. Info. Science	cites	Telecomm. Policy	3
1983	Info. Proc. Management	cites	Ed. Comm. Tech. Journ.	1
	IFLA	cites	Journ. Communication	5
	JASIS	cites	Journ. Communication	1
	JASIS	cited by	Journ. Communication	2
	JASIS	cites	Telecomm. Policy	7
1984	American Archivist	cites	Comm. Education	1
	Information Age	cited by	Media Culture Society	1
	Scientometrics	cites	Human Comm. Research	1
	Social Science Info.	cites	Telecomm. Policy	2
1985	College Research Lib.	cites	Comm. Education	3
	College Research Lib.	cites	Journ. Communication	1
	College Research Lib.	cites	Journ. Quarterly	2
	Libri	cites	Comm. Research	1
	Libri	cites	Journ. Communication	4

	Libri	cites	Public Opin. Quart.	1
	Nachrichten fur Dok.	cited by	Media Culture Society	1
	Proceedings ASIS	cites	Journ. Communication	3
	Proceedings ASIS	cites	Telecomm. Policy	2
1986	ARIST	cites	Comm. Research	1
	ARIST	cites	Journ. Broadcasting	1
	ARIST	cites	Journ. Communication	1
	ARIST	cites	Public Opin. Quart.	1
	ARIST	cites	Public Relations Rev.	1
	ARIST	cites	Telecomm. Policy	7
	Database	cites	Journ. Communication	4
	Govt. Pubs. Review	cites	Journ. Communication	1
	Govt. Pubs. Review	cites	Public Relations Rev.	1
	Govt. Pubs. Review	cites	Quart. Journ. Speech	7
	Govt. Pubs. Review	cites	Telecomm. Policy	3
	Journ. Lib. History	cited by	Comm. Research	1
	Lib. Quarterly	cited by	Human Comm. Research	1
	Proceedings ASIS	cites	Journ. Communication	2
	Proceedings ASIS	cites	Telecomm. Policy	5
	RQ	cites	Comm. Education	2
1987	ARIST	cited by	Comm. Research	6
	Info. Proc. Management	cited by	Comm. Research	1
	Info. Proc. Management	cites	Journ. Communication	13
	Info. Proc. Management	cites	Telecomm. Policy	2
	JASIS	cited by	Comm. Research	4
	Lib. Quarterly	cites	Comm. Education	1
	Lib. Quarterly	cited by	Journ. Quarterly	3

Based on the bibliographic reference information, several subsets of the full data, aggregated over the eleven years, were prepared for further analysis:

1. The authors' names of the articles in each of the four possible citation categories—Communication citing LIS, Communication cited by LIS, LIS citing Communication, and LIS cited by Communication.

2. The year of the citing article and the year of the article(s) in the other discipline that it cited.

3. The words in the titles of articles in each of the four possible citation categories.

4. Finally, each citing article was coded for the nature of the article and the context in which each citation was made.

Procedures Corresponding to Research Questions

Authors

A. Article authorship in each of the four categories of references was simply noted, and ordered by frequency.

B. Then network analysis was used to detect patterns of relationships among the authors based on their cross-disciplinary citations. First, to simplify the list of authors, all articles with the same first author were aggregated, and only the first author's name was used. Second, to remove the least involved authors in the data set, the authors making or receiving two or more cross-disciplinary citations, as well as other authors involved in cross-disciplinary citations with those authors, were identified and only their citation relations were represented in a asymmetric matrix. These authors represented 80 of the 153 unique first authors involved.

Third, a network analysis technique called CONCOR was used to identify authors' positions in the cross-disciplinary citing network (Breiger, Boorman & Arabie, 1975). A "position" is a set of nodes that has similar relations to all other nodes. That is, the authors in a position do not necessarily make citations to or receive citations from each other, but they do have similar patterns of making and receiving citations with the other authors. The concept of a "position" is grounded in sociological and anthropological theories that are concerned with one's role or position in a given social structure.

CONCOR converts the matrix of citation relations into a correlation matrix, which measures the similarity of citation activity between any two authors. In order to capture the influence of both making and receiving citations, both rows and columns of the initial raw matrix were used to create the first correlation matrix. The correlation procedure is repeated until the correlations converge toward 1.0 or 0.0. CONCOR then permutes the matrix to place together authors who are highly similar, and hierarchically separates them into various "positions" that are subsets of the initial positions.

C. The titles of the articles by each of the authors in each position were inspected to provide an informal content-based label for each of the positions.

Lag in Citation Years

The difference between the year of each cross-disciplinary citing article and the year of each of its respective cited articles was summarized and then tested for statistical significance.

Words in Articles Involved in Cross-Disciplinary Citation

Several standard text-management procedures were used to improve the consistency of the words in the article titles. First, the words were spell checked. Second, symbols such as quote marks or unnecessary apostrophes were removed. Third, variants such as US or U.S. were standardized. Fourth, plural forms for words were changed to singular forms (for example, "technologies" to "technology"). Finally, common stop words were removed (for example, "a" or "their").

A. After this preparation, each separate article title within each of the four citation categories was used as the basis for creating a word-frequency and wood-cooccurrence matrix (Woelfel, 1990). The word-frequency listing simply identifies the frequency with which each word was used in the entire set of article titles in each of the four categories. The word-cooccurrence matrix is created by keeping track of the number of times any two of these words appear in the same article title. That is, the article title is considered the unit of meaning, and the frequency of cooccurrence between any two words is an indicator of how related they are in meaning. There is considerable precedent for analyzing relations among words from reference structures such as article titles, reference descriptors, computer-monitored messages, responses to open-ended questions, focus group discussions, etc. (Braam, Moed, & van Raan, 1991; Callon, Courtial, Turner, & Bauin, 1983; Danowski, 1987).

B. Various outputs from this step were then transformed for input into the NEGOPY network analysis program (Richards & Rice, 1981; Rice & Richards, 1985). NEGOPY takes a list of "sending" nodes, "receiving" nodes, and the strength of their relationships as its input, and, based on a set of graph-theoretic criteria, identifies various network roles. Briefly, a *group* consists of (1) at least three nodes that (2) are more strongly related with each other than with other nodes; (3) have over 50% of their linkage within the group; and (4) no one of which can be removed without breaking apart the rest of the group. A *liaison* is a node that belongs to no particular group, but which is linked to two or more groups. A *dyad* is a pair of nodes linked only to each other. An *isolate* is unconnected, while a *type 2 isolate* is connected to just one other node which in turn may be connected to other nodes. A *tree node* is connected to isolates as well as to a group. For the present purposes, NEGOPY is useful in identifying how words in article titles in each of the four citation categories (citing or cited, for the two disciplines) are related, to get an indication of the kinds of topics emphasized by articles that make or receive citations across the two disciplines.

For the NEGOPY runs, the cooccurrence strength cutoff was set at two.

That is, the program ignored words that only cooccurred in one article. However, because there are so many LIS articles citing Communication articles, there were considerable linkages even with a cutoff of two. Therefore, we also used a cooccurrence cutoff of three, to identify greater distinctions among word goups and roles.

What is the content context of cross-disciplinary citations?

A. We content-coded and analyzed the general type of each article that made citations to an article in the other discipline to identify the general nature of the articles. The coding scheme was developed and tested on a small set of sample articles, revised, and then used separately by the two present authors. We simply coded for the categories shown in table 9.2, based on, in order, the abstract, the introduction, or the text of the article, until the article was categorized. The primary area of disagreement was whether certain social science reviews and studies should be categorized as theory/model/concepts. Intermediate percentage of agreement on all categories except these was 93 percent. We discussed the remaining citations, referring to the content codes, until agreement was reached.

B. The specific context of each cross-disciplinary citation was coded, as shown in table 9.2. As with the prior coding scheme, this was developed iteratively, and used on all citations separately by both authors. The context component concerns the process aspects and not about the content; the coding is within the context of the citation location within the citing article. Specific words used in the citing location were used to resolve ambiguity. For example, if a citation might seem to be both a results as well as a methodology context, but used the word "evidence", it was coded as a results context. The primary areas of disagreement centered around what constituted "prior results" as opposed to theory, methodology, problem, or review citations. Intermediate percentage of agreement on all categories except those involving the disputed "prior results" category was 88 percent. As above, we discussed these until agreement was reached.

Results

A Frequency of Authors

Table 9.3 (A-D) lists the authors of articles in both disciplines that cited, or were cited by, articles in the other discipline.

Only McKerns and Delahaye published more than one article that made citations from Communication to LIS, a 1977 original and a 1981 update

TABLE 9.2
Coding Scheme for Citing Article Type

1. Social Science: Review
   (of prior results in particular area, or of particular methods issues)
2. Social Science: Theory/Model/Concepts
   (code REVIEW here if the primary purpose of the review is as the basis for a theory or model or a meta-theoretical framework, as opposed to "what do we know so far")
3. Social Science or Policy: Study(s)
   (not including history, biography; include here what may have lengthy reviews if that is a background for a study(s); policy studies would include economic or market analyses that used financial or industry data, etc.)
4. Policy: Review
5. Policy: Theory/Model/Problem
6. Bibliography
   (essentially listing of references; however, if it is annotated and on a particular topic, then code as REVIEW)
7. History or biography

Coding Scheme for Context of Cited Article

1. Theory
   (including concepts, models, principles)
2. Results
   (including sources of facts or archival data)
3. Methodology
   (or operationalization/definition; this also includes simple descriptions of new media, such as videotex or computer-mediated communication, when that's not referenced as a conceptual or theoretical issue; also includes studies about particular data-collection or analysis method)
4. Problem claim
   (may be salient social issue, or non-social science theoretic position, such as a policy problem)
5. Review or Bibliographic list
   (for example, when one or several citations are lumped together as sources for review of or background on the topic, whether they include results or not; but code as RESULTS if specific results are referred to)
6. Not listed in text of citing article; only in reference section

about mass communication articles in U.S. and foreign journals, a sort of bibliometric study. Of the LIS authors making cross-disciplinary citations, Cawkell (information technology and communication, and privacy in the information society), Ford (library learning), Rice (communication technology studies and reviews, computer-monitored data collection), and Suprenant (information crisis in the library, international information and communication policies) provided at least two articles apiece that cite articles in communication journals.

There were numerous authors who had more than one Communication

TABLE 9.3
Authors of Articles in Communication Journals Citing Articles in Library & Information Science Journals

Baker, I.		Nitecki, D.
Becker, J.		Nord, D.
Fulk, J., Steinfield, C., Schmitz,		Rice, R. & Love, G.
J. & Power, J.		Rosengren, K.
Markus, M. L.		Showalter, S.
McKerns, J. & Delahaye, A.	(2)	Steinfield, C. & Fulk, J.
Myatt, B. & Carter, J.		
Nass, C.		

Authors of Articles in Library & Information Science Journals Citing Articles in Communication Journals

Adoni, H.		McClure, C.
Benadom, G. & Goehlert, R.		Milevski, S.
Bochnig, P.		Rice, R.
Bookstein, A. & Biggs, M.		Rice, R. & Borgman, C.
Brimmer, K.		Rice, R. & Torobin, J.
Cawkell, A.	(2)	Rice, R. & Shook, D.
Charlton, T.		Robinson, P.
Culnan, M. J. & Bair, J.		Rosenberg, V.
Dolansky, T.		Schement, J., Curtis, T. &
Ford, N.	(2)	Lievrouw, L.
Furuta, R.		Schubert, A.
Gavryck, J.		Springer, M.
Griffiths, J.		Steinfield, C.
Hart, P. & Rice, R.		Stevenson, G.
Hattendorf, L.		Surprenant, T.
Heim, K.		Surprenant, T. & Zande, J.
Kling, R.		Watson, P.
Love, G. & Rice, R.		Weiner, J.
MacAdam, B.		White, H.
		Zimmerman, E. & Brimmer, K.

Authors of Articles in Communication Journals Cited by Articles in Library & Information Science Journals

de Sola Pool, I.	(3)	Katzman, N.	
de Sola Pool, I. & Solomon, R.		Kernan, J. & Mojena, R.	
Adoni, H.		Kiesler, S. & Sproull, L.	
Anawalt, H.		King, J. & Kraemer, K.	(2)
Bamford, H.	(2)	Klemmer, E. & Synder, F.	
Becker, A.	(2)	Kling, R.	(5)
Beinstein, J.		Lamond, F.	
Berger, C. & Calabrese, R.		Langdale, J.	
Brezin, M.		Leduc, N.	(3)
Bryant, J., Comisky, P. &		Levin, H.	
Zillman, D.		Loory, S.	

Carey, J.
Clark, E.
Clark, R. & Snow, R.   (2)
Clippinger, J.
Codding, G.
Cole, R. & Bowers, T.   (2)
Cronholm, M. & Sandell, R.
Dance, F.   (2)
Danowski, J. & Edison-Swift, P.
Della Bitta, A., Johnson, E. &
    Loudon, D.
Dervin, B.
Dordick, H.
Dordick, H. & Goldman, R.
Dordick, H., Bradley, H.,
    Nanus, B. & Martin, T.
Dunn, D.   (2)
Edwards, G.   (3)
Edwards, J. & Baker, L.   (2)
Eisenstein, E.
Ellinghaus, W. & Forrester, L.
Garay, R.   (2)
Gardner, M.
Garramone, G., Harris, Allen C.
    & Anderson, R.
Gibb, J.
Glassman, M.
Gold, E.
Greenberg, A.
Greene, M.
Hamelink, C.   (3)
Hamlin, D. & Harkins, C.
Harkness, R.   (2)
Harris, A., Garramone, G.,
    Pizante, G. & Komiya, M.
Hays, E. & Mandel, J.
Helmreich, R. & Wimmer, K.
Hiebert, R. & Devine, C.
Hiltz, S.   (4)
Hiltz, S. & Turoff, M.   (2)
Hoban, C.
Holland, W.
Homet, R.
Honig, D.   (2)
Jacobson, R.   (2)
Johansen, R.   (2)

Marchand, D.   (3)
Marvin, C.
Masmoudi, M.   (2)
McCombs, E. & Eyal, H.
McEvoy, F. & Vincent, C.
McPherson, E.
Mendelsohn, H.
Meyer, N.
Morris, J.
Mosco, V.
Noll, A. M.
Owen, B.
Panko, R.   (3)
Parker, E.   (2)
Pfund, N. & Hofstadter, L.
Pipe, G.
Pye, R.   (3)
Raskin, A.
Read, W.
Reeves, B. & Borgman, C.
Rice, R. & Parker, E.
Rice, R. & Paisley, W.   (2)
Rice, R. E. & Case, D.   (4)
Roach, D. & Barker, L.
Robinson, P.   (2)
Saur, R.
Schement, J. & Lievrouw, L.
Segal, B.
Seitz, N.
Singh, K. & Gross, B.   (2)
Solely, L. & Reid, L.
Sreberny-Mohammad, A.
Starck, K.
Stevenson, R.
Thayer, L.
Trauth, E.
Tyler, M.   (2)
United States Library Congress
Vincent, R.
Weaver, D. & Wilhoit, G.
Wigand, R.
Williams, E.   (2)
Williams, F., Dordick, H. &
    Horstmann, F.
Wright, C.
Zeidner, M.

Authors of Articles in Library & Information Science Journals Cited by Articles in Communication Journals

Culnan, M. J.		Rice, R. & Borgman, C.	(2)
Culnan, M. J. & Bair, J.		Richard, O.	
Edelglass, E.		Robinson, S.	
Friedman, W.		Rubin, M. & Sapp, M.	
Harris, M.		Schmitz-Esser, W.	
Marshall, J.		Small, H.	
Nitecki, D.		Steinfield, C.	(3)
Rice, R.	(3)	Thomison, D.	
		White, H. & Griffith, B.	

Note: Figure in parentheses represents total number of *articles*, not total number of *citations*.

article cited by a LIS article. Those with at least three include de Sola Pool (international telecommunications policy, international computer communications and data flow), Edwards (all to the same article on impacts of office automation), Hamelink (all to the same article on the New World Information Order), Hiltz (computer conferencing, electronic funds transfer), Kling (social aspects of computing, electronic funds transfer), Leduc (all to the same article on a study of organizational computer communications), Marchand (all to the same article on privacy and computing), Panko (outlook, and standards for, electronic mail), Pye (monopoly or free market telecommunications services, information retrieval services), and Rice (electronic mail, videotex, communication satellites).

Selected article topics of those communication authors with two articles cited include computer conferencing, instructional media research, productivity of journalism faculty, the concept of communication, computer communication services and information policy, evaluation of doctoral programs in speech communication, telecommunications policy, office system policy, electronic funds transfer, the New World Information Order, implications of computers and telecommunication systems, teleconferencing research, reading habits, transborder data flow, and videotex.

Finally, the authors of LIS articles most frequently cited by Communication articles included Rice (review of impacts of computer-mediated communication, and, with Borgman, computer-monitored data), and Steinfield (review of impacts of computer-mediated communication).

Considering all four categories of citations, and using first author only, those authors either cited or being cited across the two disciplines more than once include: Rice (17 times), Hiltz (6), Kling (6), Steinfield (5), de Sola Pool (4), Culnan, Dordick, and Robinson (3 times each), and Adoni, Nitecki, Schement, Surprenant, White (2 times each). The articles by the four most frequently involved first authors were all concerned with research on and social aspects of computer-mediated communication or organizational computing.

B & C. Positions of Authors and Their Article Content

Table 9.4 provides the six authors' positions resulting from the CONCOR analyses. Along with the authors, it provides a summary of the major themes in the position's article titles. Most of the positions have quite consistent and clear "identities" based upon the article titles. The positions and their summary identities are: (1) domestic telecommunications policy; (2) international telecommunication policy; (3) diverse topics including academic evaluation (such as publication productivity and Ph.D. programs), educational media, privacy and censorship, archives and library learning; (4) research and theory on computer-mediated communication and information systems (especially reviews) and broad telecommunication policy issues; (5) use of print mass media; and (6) telecommunication, network, and computer communication services, especially computer conferencing and electronic funds transfer. Several more detailed hierarchical positions were possible, but these six were the most parsimonious and clear.

(2) Years Between Citing and Cited Articles

Communication articles making cross-discplinary citations were significantly older ($M = 1982.4$, s.d. = 3.6 versus $M = 1983.2$, s.d. = 2.8 for LIS articles making citations, $p < .05$), communication articles cited by LIS were significantly older ($M = 1977.5$, s.d. = 9.6 versus $M = 1979$, s.d. = 5.3 for LIS articles being cited, $p < .001$), and the lag time between citing and cited cross-disciplinary relation was significantly greater for communication articles ($M = -4.89$, s.d. = 8.25 versus $M = -4.18$, s.d. = 4.96 for LIS articles, $p < .001$). While the first two results are simply descriptive and may be attributed to a variety of causes, such as late updating for communication citations in the JCR, the last result, because it is based solely on the citation relation, seems more indicative. In general, communication authors seem to take a bit longer to become aware of and cite relevant LIS articles, or perhaps the review and publication cycle for communication journals takes longer. Thus LIS articles not only cite communication articles more frequently (absolutely and proportionally), but also do so a bit more quickly (about seven months faster).

TABLE 9.4
Structural Positions Among Authors Involved in Cross-Disciplinary Citations

Position 1 (Domestic Telecomm Policy)	Position 3 (Inst. Tech, Acad. Eval, Privacy, Archives, Comm. Theory & History)	Position 5 (Use of Print Mass Media, Subject Headings)
de Sola Pool, I.	Adoni, H.	Eisenstein, E.
Garay, R.	Becker, A.	McCombs, E.
Gold, E.	Bookstein, A.	McEvoy, F.
Greene, M.	Clark, R.	Robinson, P.
Harkness, R.	Cole, R.	Wright, C.
Noll, A. M.	Dolansky, T.	
Parker, E.	Edelglass, E.	**Position 6**
Pye, R.	Edwards, J.	(Computer Conferencing,
Tyler, M.	Ford, N.	Network Services, EFT)
	Glassman, M.	Bamford, H.
Position 2	Hoban, C.	Dordick, H.
(International Telecomm Policy & NWIO)	Marchand, D.	Dunn, D.
Anawalt, H.	McKerns	Edwards, G.
Clippinger, J.	Meyer, N.	Hiltz, S.
Codding, G.	Morris, J.	Johansen, R.
Danowski, J.	Rosengren, K.	King, J.
Ellinghaus, W.	Thomison, D.	Kling, R.
Gardner, M.	White, H.	Leduc, N.
Garramone, G.		Panko, R.
Greenberg, A.	**Position 4**	Williams, E.
Hamelink, C.	(Information Tech.,	
Honig, D.	Computer	
Jacobson, R.	Communication,	
Kiesler, S.	New Media Theories,	
Masmoudi, M.	Telecomm. Policy)	
Raskin, A.	Brimmer, K.	
Segal, B.	Cawkell, A.	
Singh, K.	Culnan, M. J.	
Stevenson, R.	Dance, F.	
Surprenant, T.	Fulk, J.	
U. S. Lib. Cong.	Furuta, R.	
Wigand, R.	Harris, M.	
	Hart, P.	
	Heim, K.	
	Helmreich, R.	
	Love, G.	
	Markus, M. L.	
	Marvin, C.	
	Rice, R. E.	
	Rosenberg, V.	
	Steinfield, C.	
	Zimmerman, E.	

Note: Based on those authors making or receiving two or more citations, as well as other authors involved in citations with those authors; thus 80 of the possible 153 authors were analyzed here.

(3) Words in Cross-Disciplinary Articles

A. Frequency of Words Occurring in Citing and Cited Article Titles

Simple frequency counts of words in article titles can provide some sense of the nature of citing and cited articles. Table 9.5 provides ordered word frequencies for each of the four categories of article citations.

For Communication articles citing LIS articles, the most frequent words are communication (4 times) and information (3), mass and foreign (3 times, relating to the bibliometric study of foreign published articles, and to transnational corporations), and a set of words relating to publications and to technology research and theory.

For LIS articles citing Communication articles, the most frequent word by far was information (14 articles), followed by communication (9), library, policy, and words relating to impacts of computer-mediated communication. Clearly the central concepts appear predominant in these articles' titles. Words occurring only twice included general terms about research, problems, science and trends.

For communication articles cited by LIS articles, the most frequent words were again information (25 times) and communication (23), followed by policy (18), and a set or words relating to computers/systems/telecommunications/technology/electronic, research, social/public/implication, and use/evaluation. These article titles also included a wide variety of words occurring 3 or 4 times, relating to international telecommunications policy, computer privacy, and the New World Information Order.

For titles of LIS articles cited by Communication articles, the most frequent word was communication (9 times), information or computer-mediated (6), and impact/organization/system (4 times). Bibliometric words such as book, co-citation, literature also occurred more than once. Several words about documents occurred once apiece, indicating a slight concern by communication researchers with traditional library topics.

It is clear that the hypothesized most central concerns between the two disciplines—information and communication—appear most frequently in cross-disciplinary citing or cited articles. Note also the rather clear affiliation of these two words with their disciplines; for the most part LIS articles that were either cited or citing had information as the most frequent word, while communication was the most frequent for communication articles that were either cited or citing.

B. Word Groups and Roles in Citing and Cited Articles

Although the word-frequencies provide a good sense of the nature of concerns of cross-disciplinary citations, they are in essence removed from

TABLE 9.5
(A) Words in Article Titles of Communication Journals Citing Articles in Library & Information Science Journals

4 Times: Communication
3 Times: Mass Foreign Information
2 Times: Article Journals Readers Research Technology Theory Organization Media
1 Time: Elizabeth Timothy America's First Woman Editor Sponsorship Nonmonetary Incentive Response Rate Sampling Picture Preferences Children Young Adults Four Activities Country New Effects Transnational Corporation Example Bertelsmann Working-class Family Community Reading Late Nineteenth-century America Electronic Emotion Guide Paradigm Socioemotional Content Role Toward Critical Universal Access Interdependence Diffusion Computer-mediated Network Interactive Social Processing Model Use Following Money Trail Years Measuring Economy

(B) Words in Article Titles of Library & Information Science Journals Citing Articles in Communication Journals

14 Times: Information
9 Times: Communication
5 Times: Library
4 Times: Policy
3 Times: Technology Impact System Analysis Computer-mediated Organization Electronic
2 Times: Review Public Learning Data Research Perspective National Computing Current Science Problems Production Media Social Trends

(C) Words in Article Titles of Communication Journals Cited by Articles in Library & Information Science Journals

25 Times: Information
23 Times: Communication
18 Times: Policy
17 Times: Computer
14 Times: System Research
12 Times: Telecommunication
11 Times: Electronic
10 Times: Social
9 Times: Technology
8 Times: EFT Service
7 Times: Media Office Public Implication Order World
6 Times: Use Evaluation Message
5 Times: Exchange Organization Data New University Alternative Instructional Productivity Description International
4 Times: WARC Agenda Teleconferencing Report Study Communicating Third Programs Article Computer-based Videotex Utility
3 Times: Concept Some Human Educational Findings Teletext Conference Automation Making Through Developing Privacy Confidentiality Analysis Emergence Standards Informatics Development Who National Foreign News Call Community Macbride Response Hidden Mass Speech

(D) Words in Article Titles of Library & Information Science Journals Cited by Articles in Communication Journals

9 Times: Communication
6 Times: Information Computer-mediated
4 Times: Impact Organization System
3 Times: Service Use Book Interpersonal
2 Times: Co-citation Literature Computer-monitored Science Research
1 Time: Writings Archives Historical Manuscripts Current First Librarian America Attitudes Toward Retrieval

their linguistic context. We are not conducting linguistic or structural analyses of the meaning of article titles, but analyzing the cooccurrences of words within each article title does retain some of the relationships and the meaning among the words. Here, word groups consist of words that appear in at least two articles (with the exception of the additional analysis with a cutoff of three articles). Table 9.6 portrays the network analysis results.

For communication articles citing LIS articles (9.6A), one word group resulted, derived from the bibliometric article on U.S. and foreign mass communication journals. Note that this group is a very specialized topic in just one article, indicating that the numerous frequent words noted in the prior section must occur throughout a variety of article titles. The only other set of frequently cooccurring words is information and organization, generally concerning impacts of information systems in organizational settings.

The word-network analysis of LIS articles citing communication articles (9.6B) shows a concern with impacts of computer-mediated communication systems. Other words that tend to cooccur as isolated links to this group involve policy, trends, review, technology, and electronic.

The much more frequent communication articles cited by LIS articles (9.6C) provide a rich word-network structure. The first group is quite large, involving a wide variety of topics such as communication, information, technology impacts, international communication, office automation, telecommunications policy, and bibliometric evaluations of publication productivity. The second group concerns standards about and evaluation of electronic mail. The third and fourth groups concern the New World Information Order. Related frequently cooccurring issues involve teleconferencing, development, and data. Teletext and videotex appear in article titles together more often than with other words. If we increase the cutoff threshold to 3 for these article titles (9.6D), the word groups become a bit more distinctive (these results are not portrayed in table 9.5). Group 1

TABLE 9.6

(A) Network Structure of Words in Titles of Communication Articles Citing Library & Information Science Articles, Cutoff Strength = 2

Group 1	Dyad Members
Article	Information
Mass	Organization
Communication	
Foreign	
Journals	

(B) Network Structure of Words in Titles of Articles in Library & Information Science Journals Citing Articles in Communication Journals, Cutoff Strength = 2

Group 1
Communication
Organization
Impact
Computer-mediated
Analysis

Isolate (T2)s	Dyad Members
Review	Library
Technology	Learning
Data	
Policy	
Research	**Tree Nodes**
Production	Information
Trends	Media
Electronic	

(C) Network Structure of Words in Titles of Communication Articles Cited by Library & Information Science Articles, Cutoff Strength = 2

Group 1	Group 2
Communicating	Use
Concept	Electronic
Communication	Standards
Information	Description
Research	Message
Human	University
Impact	Utility
Technology	
Media	**Group 3**
Alternative	Informatics
Instructional	Third
International	World
Computer	Call
EFT	New
Office	Order
System	

Agenda
Public
Policy
Service
Implication
Social
Telecommunication
Organization
Automation
Making
Through
Privacy
Confidentiality
Study
Emergence
Community
National
Evaluation
Article
Productivity
Programs
Speech

Group 4
Report
Macbride
Response

Isolate (T2)s
Some
Development
Teleconferencing
Developing
Data
Who
Foreign
Mass
Computer-based

Dyads
Teletext
Videotex

Liaisons
Exchange
Findings
Hidden

**(D) Network Structure of Words in Titles of Communication Articles Cited by
Library & Information Science Articles, Cutoff Strength = 3**

Group 1
Communicating
Information
Research
Technology
Computer
EFT
Public
Policy
Exchange
Findings
Implication
Through
Privacy
Confidentiality

Group 2
Use
System
Electronic
Description

Group 4
Impact
Office
Organization
Automation

Group 5
Communication
Programs
Speech

Isolate (T2)s
Instructional
Service
Teleconferencing
Making
Study
Article

Dyad Members
Teletext

Message   Videotex
University
Utility   **Tree Nodes**
                           Social
Group 3   Telecommunication
Informatics   Productivity
Third
World
Call
New
Order

**(E) Network Structure of Words in Titles of Library & Information Science Articles
Cited by Communication Articles, Cutoff Strength = 2**

Group 1	**Isolate (T2)s**
Information	Service
Use	Frontier
Impact	Extent
Organization	Nature
Interpersonal	Ownership
Computer-mediated	Southern
Communication	Indiana
Computer-monitored	1800–1850
Data	Dimensions
Science	Perceived
Research	Accessibility
System	Implication
	Delivery
Group 2	
Co-citation	**Tree Nodes**
Literature	Book
Measure	

concerns telecommunications and information policy; Group 2 is the set
of words from an empirical study of a university electronic mail system;
Group 3 is about the New World Information Order; Group 4 is clearly
about the impacts of office automation; and Group 5 is about the evaluation
of speech communication programs. Linking words include social, telecommunication, productivity, and teleconferencing.

The final word-network analysis concerns LIS articles cited by communication articles (9.6E). Two groups emerge: one concerning evaluation of
computer-mediated communication systems, as well as use of computer
monitored data for such studies, and one concerning bibliometric co-
citation.

(4) Content Context of Cross-disciplinary Citations.

Table 9.7 (A) shows that, overall, the three most frequent types of articles that made cross-disciplinary citations were social reviews, social science theory/method, and empirical studies, with about one/fifth of all citations made apiece. Policy reviews are next, with 15 percent, followed by policy theory/problems, bibliographies, and history/biographies. Communication articles making cross-disciplinary citations were primarily concerned with theory or empirical studies (approximately 29 percent each) and history/biography (21 percent), while LIS articles were primarily reviews (25 percent), followed by studies (23 percent) and policy reviews (15 percent).

Overall, the most frequent context for making a cross-disciplinary citation was as a reference to prior results (nearly 50 percent), as shown in table 9.7 (B). The next most frequent citation context was to a social or policy problem (17 percent). Approximately 7 percent of all cited cross-disciplinary articles were not in fact mentioned in the text of the citing articles! The primary context for cited communication articles was also for prior results, but the next most frequent context was as a problem (20 percent) or reviews (often a string of citations) (10 percent). The primary context for cited LIS articles was again for prior results (43 percent), followed by reviews (30 percent) and methodological issues (including descriptions or definitions) (17 percent).

Finally, what is the relationship between the nature of the citing article and the context of the citation made? Table 9.8 shows that the most frequent relationships all involved citations to prior results (including empirical studies, results, and archival sources of facts), from social reviews (17 percent), empirical studies (9.6 percent), policy reviews (8.5 percent), and social science theory/concept articles (7.3 percent). The only other frequent citation relationship was from policy reviews to articles concerned with social issues or some policy problem (9 percent).

Discussion

The variety of analytical methods used in this study provides a multidimensional perspective into the general question motivating this study: Are concepts, disciplines, and research involving information and communication converging? In spite of taking a narrow focus on this broad question by (1) considering only the content and context of the actual citations between the disciplines of communication and library and information science; (2) analyzing citations only during the period of 1977–1987; and (3) using one particular source for identifying the journals and citations to

TABLE 9.7
Cross-Tabulation of Disciplines of Citing Article and Context Category of Citing and
Cited Articles

Discipline of Citing Articles	Categories of Citing Articles							
Frequency Percent	Social Science		Either	Policy		Either		
Row Pct Col Pct	Review	Theory	Study	Review	Theory	Bibli.	History Biogr.	Total
Comm	1	4	4	0	0	2	3	14
	1.85	7.41	7.41	0.	0.	3.70	5.56	25.93
	7.14	28.57	28.57	0.	0.	14.29	21.43	
	9.09	40.	30.77	0.	0.	66.67	60.	
LIS	10	6	9	8	4	1	2	40
	18.52	11.11	16.67	14.81	7.41	1.85	3.70	74.07
	25.00	15.00	22.50	20.	10.	2.50	5.00	
	90.91	60.	69.23	100.	100.	33.33	40.	
Total	11	10	13	8	4	3	5	54
Percent	20.37	18.52	24.07	14.81	7.41	5.56	9.26	100.

Articles	Context Categories of Cited References						
Frequency Percent Row Pct Col Pct	Theory	Results	Method	Problem	Review	Unlisted	Total
Comm	11	76	10	30	16	11	154
	6.21	42.94	5.65	16.95	9.04	6.21	87.01
	7.14	49.35	6.49	19.48	10.39	7.14	
	91.67	88.37	71.43	100.	69.57	91.67	
LIS	1	10	4	0	7	1	23
	.56	5.65	2.26	0.	3.95	.56	12.99
	4.35	43.48	17.39	0.	30.43	4.35	
	8.33	11.63	28.57	0.	30.43	8.33	
Total	12	86	14	30	23	12	177
Percent	6.78	48.59	7.91	16.95	12.99	6.78	100.

Note: For Citing cross-tabulation, Chi-Square = 12.6, $p<.05$—however, 71% of cells have expected counts less than 5.
For Cited cross-tabulation, Chi-Square = 14.2, $p<.01$—however, 42% of cells have expected counts less than 5.

TABLE 9.8
Cross-Tabulation of Content Category of Citing Article and Context Category of Cited Article

Categories of Citing Articles	Context Categories of Cited References						
Frequency Percent Row Pct Col Pct	Theory	Results	Method	Problem	Review	Unlisted	Total
Social	3	30	6	6	4	4	53
Science:	1.69	16.95	3.39	3.39	2.26	2.26	29.94
Review	5.66	56.60	11.32	11.32	7.55	7.55	
	25.00	34.88	42.86	20.	17.39	33.33	
Social	8	13	3	2	6	0	32
Science:	4.52	7.34	1.69	1.13	3.39	0.	18.08
Theory	25.00	40.63	9.38	6.25	18.75	0.	
Concept	66.67	15.12	21.43	6.67	26.09	0.	
Social	1	17	3	1	8	0	30
Science	.56	9.60	1.69	.56	4.52	0.	16.95
or Policy	3.33	56.67	10.	3.33	26.67	0.	
Study	8.33	19.77	21.43	3.33	34.78	0.	
Policy:	0	15	2	16	0	7	40
Review	0.	8.47	1.13	9.04	0.	3.95	22.60
	0.	37.50	5.00	40.	0.	17.50	
	0.	17.44	14.29	53.33	0.	58.33	
Policy:	0	6	0	5	0	0	11
Theory/	0.	3.39	0.	2.82	0.	0.	6.21
Model/	0.	54.55	0.	45.45	0.	0.	
Problem	0.	6.98	0.	16.67	0.	0.	
Biblio-	0	0	0	0	5	0	5
graphy	0.	0.	0.	0.	2.82	0.	2.82
	0.	0.	0.	0.	100.	0.	
	0.	0.	0.	0.	21.74	0.	
History	0	5	0	0	0	1	6
or	0.	2.82	0.	0.	0.	.56	3.39
Biography	0.	83.33	0.	0.	0.	16.67	
	0.	5.81	0.	0.	0.	8.33	
Total	12	86	14	30	23	12	177
Percent	6.78	48.59	7.91	16.95	12.99	6.78	100.

Note: Chi-Square = 112.2, p<.001 however, 74% of cells have expected counts less than 5.

be analyzed (ISI's Journal citation Report), we can nevertheless begin to get an in-depth, empirical picture of one particular arena for possible convergence between information and communication.

What is the direction and pace of cross-disciplinary convergence in the form of citations? The bulk of the citations are from LIS articles to communication articles, and *to* a broader range of communication articles than *from* communication articles. Further, many communication authors are cited by two or more LIS articles. LIS articles also seem to cite Communication articles a bit more quickly.

*Who are the authors involved in cross-disciplinary citations?*Based upon the author analyses, the bases for convergence in communication and LIS include six distinct sets of authors concerned with domestic telecommunications policy, international telecommunication policy, privacy and academic evaluation, research and theory on computer-mediated communication and information systems, use of print mass media, and computer communication and information services.

What are the cross-disciplinary articles about, based on article titles? Overall, the most frequent words occurring in the titles of cross-disciplinary articles include (or are related to) information, communication, policy, and computer-mediated communication research and impacts, with a number of less frequent words such as co-citation. Word-network analyses identified meaning-units of the most frequently cooccurring words in article titles, such as telecommunications policy, international information policy issues, information and organization, and impacts and research on computer-mediated communication.

What are the cross-disciplinary articles about, based on the nature of the article? They are mostly concerned with empirical studies and reviews and theoretical discussions of social science topics. Communication articles are more concerned with theoretical issues and empirical studies, while LIS articles are more concerned with reviews and empirical studies.

What are the contexts of the cross-disciplinary citations? Articles are cited by the other discipline primary because of results that seem relevant to the purposes of the citing article. Other than this context, communication articles tend to cite LIS articles that provide reviews and methodological discussions (mostly about computer-monitored data), while LIS articles tend to cite communication articles that discuss social and policy problems and review topics of interest.

In summary, we can conclude that while there may be growing convergence between concepts, institutions, and disciplines interested in general and theoretical aspects of information and communication, there is a small amount of exchange of research on specific topics between the disciplines of communication and library and information science. The particular form of this exchange does not concern issues of linguistics, semiotics, social construction of knowledge, or language philosophy. Rather, the authors and articles that cross the formal boundaries of these two disciplines are concerned primarily (though not exclusively) with more pragmatic issues centered around telecommunication policy, research and theory on computer-mediated communication systems, and general bibliometric analyses of program and disciplinary evaluation. In most ways, the exchange is asymmetric, with LIS citing far more communication articles than vice versa, with citing communication articles being more theoretical in nature while citing LIS articles oriented more toward reviews, and, although both have equal frequent interest in prior studies, with citations to communication articles being in the context of social issues or problems and citations to LIS articles being in the context of reviews.

The data and analyses presented here seem to indicate that there is a need, and opportunity, for sharing and overlap between these two disciplines in these areas. As Crawford (1990) and Paisley (1984, 1986) proposed, both disciplines have interest in social aspects of communication and information systems, both are concerned with information policy issues, and both have some interest in ways of evaluating scientific communication. The initial forms of convergence between these fields are primarily social and behavioral, not cognitive or philosophical, and centered around the uses and implications (both organizational and social, for management and policy concerns) of new information/communication systems, rather than their design, performance, or technical characteristics. Institutions, curriculum developers, textbook authors, library collection decision-makers, Ph.D. admission committees, faculty search committees, and book editors, as well as others, may use such preliminary evidence to help guide them in fostering further convergence between the two disciplines perhaps most obviously interested in communication and information—communication science and library and information science.

The authors would like to thank the UCLA Senate (for funding some initial data collection under the guidance of Dr. Chris Borgman), Diane Bednarski (for design of the initial raw citation data collection and for gathering most of the citation counts), Eric Wade, Jian Ding, Yolanda Plute (UCLA students for additional data collection and compilation), George Barnett, William Richards, Douglas Shook, Ellen Sleeter, and Joe Woelfel (for providing and developing software programs). We especially thank Dr. Chris Borgman for her guidance and collaboration in other aspects of the larger bibliometric project.

References

Barnett, G. A., & Fink, E. L. (1989). Sciences based on citations. Buffalo: State University of New York at Buffalo.

Beniger, J. R. (1988). Information and communication: The new convergence. *Communication Research, 15,* 198–218.

Berger, C. R., & Chaffee, S. H. (Eds.). (1987). *Handbook of communication science.* Newbury Park, CA: Sage.

Borgman, C. L. (Ed.) (1990). *Scholarly communication and bibliometrics,* Newbury Park, CA: Sage.

Borgman, C. L. & Rice, R. E. (1992). The convergence of information science and communication: A bibliometric analysis. *Journal of the American Society for Information Science,* July.

Braam, R. R., Moed, H. F. & van Raan, A. F. J. (1991) Mapping of science by combined co-citation and word analysis. *Journal of the American Society for Information Science, 42* (4), 233–66.

Breiger, R., Boorman, S., & Arabie, P. (1975). An algorithm for clustering relational data, with applications to social network analysis and comparison with multidimensional scaling. *Journal of Mathematical Psychology, 12,* 328–83.

Callon, M., Courtial, J-P., Turner, W., & Bauin, S. (1983). From translations to problematic networks: An introduction to co-word analysis. *Social Science Information, 2* (2), 191–235.

Crawford, G. (1990). Information and communication: A reconciliation. Paper. New Brunswick, NJ: Rutgers University School of Communication, Information and Library Studies.

Danowski, J. (1987). Mapping organizational cultures via word-network analysis: Automated supra-communication auditing of electronic mail. In G. Goldhaber & G. Barnett (Eds.), *Handbook of organizational communication.* Norwood, NJ: Ablex.

Machlup, F., & Machlup, U. (1983). *The study of information: Interdisciplinary messages.* New York: Wiley.

Paisley, W. J. (1984). Communication in the communication sciences. In B. Dervin & M. Voigt (Eds.), *Progress in the communication sciences* (5, pp. 1–43). Norwood, NJ: Ablex.

Paisley, W. J. (1986). The convergence of communication and information science. In H. Edelman (Ed.), *Libraries and information science in the electronic age* (pp. 122–53). Philadelphia: ISI Press.

Paisley, W. J. (1990). Information science as a multi-discipline. In J. M. Pemberton, & A. Prentice (Eds.), *Information science: The interdisciplinary context.* NY: Neal-Schuman.

Peritz, B. C. (1981). Citation characteristics in library science: Some further results from a bibliometric survey. *Library Research, 3* (1), 47–65.

Reeves, B., & Borgman, C. L. (1983). A bibliometric evaluation of core journals in communication research. *Human Communication Research, 10* (1), 119–36.

Rice, R. E. (1990). Hierarchies and clusters in communication and library and information science journals, 1978–1987. In C. L. Borgman (Ed.), *Scholarly communication and bibliometrics* (pp. 138–53). Newbury Park, CA: Sage.

Rice, R. E., Borgman, C. L., Bednarski, D., & Hart, P. J. (1989). Journal-to-journal citation data: Issues of validity and reliability. *Scientometrics, 15* (3–4), 257–82.

Rice, R. E., Borgman, C. L., & Reeves, B. (1988). Citation networks of communication journals, 1977–1985: Cliques and positions, citations made and citations received. *Human Communication Research, 15,* 256–83.

Rice, R. E. & Richards, W. Jr. (1985). An overview of communication network analysis programs and methods. In B. Dervin & M. Voigt (Eds.), *Progress in communication sciences* (5, pp. 105–165.) Norwood, NJ: Ablex.

Richards, W. Jr., & Rice, R. E. (1981). NEGOPY network analysis program. *Social Networks, 3* (3), 215–23.

So, C. (1988). Citation patterns of core communication journals: An assessment of the development status of communication. *Human Communication Research, 15,* 236–55.

Woelfel, J. (1991). CatPac. (Software program for analyzing word cooccurences.) Buffalo, NY: New York State University Department of Communication.

10

Integrating Concepts for the Information Age: Communication, Information, Mediation, and Institutions

Brent D. Ruben

Developing integrated theories, curricula, or academic programs for the Information Age is a formidable challenge because the fundamental issues of concern are broader than any single discipline, the marketplace moves faster than the academic community, the "new" media/technology are new in some ways and not-so-new in others, and the most readily observed linkages are sometimes the least significant theoretically. Overcoming these barriers requires: (1) linking relevant disciplines and subdisciplines; (2) deciding which of the many manifestations of the Information Age are truly significant, of lasting important, and worthy of our study; (3) selecting an appropriate level of analysis for theoretical, curricular, and programmatic undertakings; and (4) identifying concepts that form the basis for a meaningful integrating framework. Four such concepts are presented: communication, information, mediation, *and* institutions. *Each is defined and discussed, and the implications and applications of the framework are explored.*

Developing integrated theories, curricula, or academic programs for what is variously referred to as the Information Age, the Communication Revolution, or the Information Society is a formidable challenge for several reasons:

1. *The fundamental issues of concern are broader than any single discipline.* Most theories and curricula are circumscribed within a single disciplines, yet the problems and prospects of the Information Age often transcend disciplinary boundaries. Issues of infrastructure, distribution, value, management, and regulation for instance, extend beyond the boundaries of communication and information studies to psychology, political science, sociology, engineering, computer science, economics, management, and perhaps other fields.

2. *The marketplace moves faster than the academic community.* Forces in the Information Age marketplace are advancing more rapidly than most academics are intellectually, programmatically, and sometimes personally prepared to move. The marketplace has created new labels, new technologies, and new concepts of communication and information. These terms and the underlying concepts are driven by production, marketing, regulatory, and technological considerations, and are not tied to nor necessarily guided by theoretical or substantive considerations of the type with which normally direct academic decision making.

3. *The "new" media/technology are new in some ways and not-so-new in others.* What the general public and marketing moguls mean by "new media" can be quite different from what thoughtful students and scholars want to mean by the phrase. Is a portable CD a new technology? Or FAX? Or on-line databases? Or cellular phones. One's answer depends, of course, on what one means by "new." "New" in *form?* "New" in *function?* "New" in *application?* "New" in *acceptance?* "New" in *accessibility?* Or, "New" in *consequence?* Some distinctions which are of great consequence in the newspeak of the Information Age, may be unimportant theoretically, and vice versa.

4. *The most easily observed linkages are sometimes the least significant theoretically.* In our efforts to understand and integrate the various facets of the Information Age, the most obvious bridges may be the least helpful. Computers, FAX, and cellular phones play an increasingly pervasive role in a broad range of personal, social, occupational, and geographical contexts. And the same can be said of databases, CD ROMS, video games and VCRs. These technologies and their applications, therefore, become obvious foci for efforts to develop integrated Information Age theories and curricula.

But are specific technologies such as these the most appropriate or profitable linkages or focal point for thinking about key issues of the Information Age? Not necessarily. History tells us that explanations that are tied too closely to particular technologies may be subject to limited generalizability and rapid obsolesce. Frameworks that offer more abstract explanations—frameworks, for instance, which emphasize individual uses and behavior, or social and cultural processes and outcomes—avoid this pitfall. More generic theories, however, may fail to give us much to say about the specific technologies with which the general public, the marketplace, and sources of research funding are often most concerned.

Considerations in the Development of Theories, Curricula, and Academic Programs

For those who seek to design integrative theories, curricula, or programs for the Information Age, the task essentially involves: (1) linking relevant disciplines and subdisciplines; (2) deciding which of the many manifestations of the Information Age are truly significant, of lasting importance, and worthy of our study; (3) selecting an appropriate level of analysis for theoretical, curricular, and programmatic undertakings; and (4) identifying concepts that form the basis for a meaningful integrating framework.

Interdisciplinary Considerations

As various authors have noted, a plethora of issues merit scholarly attention in the context of the Information Age (e.g., Hunt & Ruben, 1993; Ruben, 1985a, 1985b; Salvaggio, 1983; Schement & Lievrouw; 1987; Williams, 1991). Many of the important issues of the time transcend the boundaries of any one traditional discipline. These include:

- Impact of a growing emphasis on information as a commodity that can be bought and sold by individuals, private- and public-sector organizations, and societies.
- Personal, interpersonal, organizational, and societal impact of the increasing volume of available information, information sources, and information channels.
- Recognition of the need for broadened concepts of literacy that includes computer-based, and other information-handling capabilities along with reading, writing, and speaking.
- Personal, social, economic, and political infrastructure considerations for organizational, national, and international communication and information systems.
- Regulation and governance of communication and information technologies and applications by individuals, groups, organizations, and societies.
- Impact of communication and Information Age technology on ideologies and pragmatics of freedom and privacy.

- Influences of communication technology and transnational data flow on political, social, and economic development.

In addition to Communication and Information Studies in which these issues are of obvious concern, a number of other disciplines have a potential role to play in meaningfully addressing such matters, among them:

- Cognitive Science/Psychology: Emphasis on individual perception, interpretation, storage, and use of information.
- Economics: Emphasis on production and consumption of information as an economic resource.
- Political Science: Emphasis on information as a political and developmental resource.
- Computer Science and Electrical Engineering: Emphasis on mathematical properties, decision systems, and computer applications of information.
- Business and Management: Emphasis on information as a strategic resource and marketable commodity.

Communication and Information Studies, both of which are themselves largely interdisciplinary in origin and application, also suffer from some discipline-bound constraints that must be overcome to address many of the issues of the Information Age.

One school of communication theory and practice—that which grows out of speech communication—has traditionally emphasized verbal and nonverbal language, conversation, persuasion, and interpretative processes in interpersonal, group, organizational, and public communication contexts. A second subdisciplinary group within communication has focused more on media, mass communication, journalistic roles and institutions, and their individual and societal impact. Each orientation has an obvious contribution to make to the dialogue of our time, but connections between the two groups cannot be taken for granted.

Within information studies, scholars whose interests center around information organization, storage, and retrieval have much to contribute to the discussion of issues of the day. So do others more concerned with libraries and information institutions and their role in society. Here again, however, theoretical and research linkages between these two groups cannot be assumed.

Foci and Level of Analysis Considerations

Linkages among disciplines and subdisciplines can be significant only to the extent that an appropriate analytic foci and level of generality is selected. For instance, speech and media scholars have little in common if the former focuses solely on speeches, while the later examines media programs. However, if the focus is more generally placed on messages, sources, processes, audiences, and outcomes, a number of potentially valuable connections become possible. In the same sense, to the extent that scholars of library and information studies focus solely on libraries, and media studies scholars examine only mass media such as television, newspapers, and magazines, these groups have little to say to one another, though both play an acknowledged role in the developments that characterize the Age. If, on the other hand, students in each area shift to a somewhat more generic level of analysis, libraries and mass media can be viewed as institutions concerned with information organization, packaging, and dissemination, and in these respects have many things in common in terms of sources, message, processes, applications, technologies, outcomes, and economics.

Four Integrating Concepts

Taking account of considerations relative to interdisciplinarity, focus, and level of analysis, four useful integrating concepts are:

- Communication
- Information
- Mediation
- Institutions

Communication

There are, of course, any number of approaches to communication. For integrative purposes, one workable definition is: *Communication* is message-related behavior (Ruben, 1984, 1992a). Given this view, communication is seen as an inevitable activity involving the construction of messages and meaning, and responses to them. Consistent with this perspective is an understanding of communication as the process by which living systems interact with their environment and other systems through information processing (Miller, 1965; Thayer, 1968, 1986; Ruben, 1972, 1992a, 1992b).[1] Communication is seen necessary for the emergence and adaptation of living systems, and to the formation and maintenance of relationships among their component parts, between a system and its environment, and between systems. Thus, human communication is the process through which individuals in relationships, groups, organizations, and societies receive, create, and transmit messages to relate to their environment and one another (Ruben, 1992a).

The communication process involves messages and meanings which are constructed:

1. *intentionally* (e.g., a speech, a computer program, or a painting) or *unintentionally* (e.g., a regional accent, a programming error, or a blush of embarrassment);
2. in a *visual* (e.g., text or graphics), *auditory* (e.g., voice or music), *tactile* (e.g., tactile text or human touch), *olfactory,* or *gustatory* mode;
3. *to inform* (e.g., news or on-line catalogues), *to persuade* (e.g., advertising or promotion), *to entertain* (e.g., videogames or general appeal magazines), or *to deceive* (e.g., "misinformation" or "disinformation."

Biological and individual levels of analysis. At the most basic biological level, communication provides the primary means through which living systems function in and adapt to their physical and social environments. For animal, as well as human systems, communication plays an indispensable role in physiological self-regulation, navigation, territory establishment and maintenance, mating and reproduction, and parent-offspring relations, social and life-skill learning.

At the individual level, communication is also fundamental to higher-level perceptual, cognitive activity, and spiritual activity, and plays an essential role in personality development, self-expression, decision making, problem solving, self-reflexiveness, and self-monitoring, among other human activities.

Interpersonal, social, and cultural levels of analysis. At the level of social systems, it is through communication that relationships, groups, organizations, and societies are defined, relationships and networks among individuals formed, and joint task and social activities undertaken and coordinated. It is through these same mechanisms that social control is established and socialization achieved. By means of communication, culturally based messages and meanings are developed, intersubjectified, negotiated, and socially validated.

Information

As with communication, there are many perspectives on information. For present purposes, *information* can be defined as any coherent collection of messages or cues organized in a way that has meaning or utility for a system (Ruben, 1988). Such a view regards information as a phenomenon, or thinglike (cf. Buckland, 1991; Saracevic, 1991). It is important to note that such a perspective is more generic than some definitions. This view of information does not limit the use of the term based on *factuality* or *form*. Thus, "information" is used to refer to messages that are:

1. *factual* (e.g., scientific findings and news) or *fictional* (e.g., poetry or television drama); or
2. *environment-based* (heat from the sun or a flickering neon light in a classroom), *document-based* (e.g., books, journal articles, or government documents), or *interpersonally-based* (e.g., conversation and gestures) in form.

Three types of information. Information is often used to refer to a broad range of document/artifact/thinglike/representational entities, such as data in a computer, words in a book, utterances in a verbal exchange, concepts we think about, or the meaning of a red light at an intersection. While viewing any representation as information is convenient and even useful for some purposes, it can also be misleading and dysfunctional in other contexts.

For present purposes, at least, it is suggested that there is a need to distinguish among three rather distinct concepts of information-as-representation (Ruben, 1992b). The first order of information, which can be termed, $Information_e$ is environmental data, stimuli, messages, or cues—artifacts and representations—that exist in the external environment. This is the order of information that has *potential* significance for a living system, but that potential is not yet actualized. It is raw data, stimuli, messages, or cues yet to become attended to and utilized.

$Information_i$ refers to the second order of information—internalized, appropriations, and representations. This order of information is $Information_e$ which has been transformed and configured for use by an individual. $Information_i$ refers to: (1) the often transitory, internalized, idiosyncratic appropriations, representations, or constructions of $Information_e$; and (2) the long-term "artifactual" consequences of this process, variously re-

TABLE 10.1
Three Types of Information

- *Information_e*—(First Order Information): Environmental artifacts and representations; environmental data, stimuli, messages, or cues.

- *Information_i*—(Second Order Information): Individualized, internal appropriations and representations.

- *Information_s*—(Third Order Information): Socially constructed, negotiated, validated, sanctioned and/or privileged appropriations, representations, and artifacts.

ferred to as cognitive maps, cognitive scheme, semantic networks, personal constructs, images, rules, or mind (see table 10.1).

Information$_s$ refers to the third order of information-socially/culturally constructed, negotiated, validated, and sanctioned appropriations, representations, and artifacts. This is the order of information that comprises the shared information/knowledge base of societies and other social systems.

The Information$_e$-Information$_i$ distinction is a very fundamental one (Ruben, 1992b). It helps explain the multiple interpretations (Information$_i$) that exist for any message in the environment (Information$_e$). The representational or appropriate form (Information$_i$)—whether of a poem or a retrieved list of potential sources—is different than its environmental referent (Information$_e$). Moreover, the Information$_i$ that represents Information$_e$ is different for each individual, as it may well be for a particular individual over time.

The Information$_e$-Information$_i$ distinction helps to clarify why descriptions of a library, a concert, a speech, or the appearance of another person (at the Information$_e$ level), may bear little predictable relationship to their (Information$_i$ level) significance and meaning for particular audience members or users. For instance,

> For some a library (at the Information$_i$ level) is "an institution which plays a vital role in the life of a community or institution." For others it may be "a place to work," "a place to do research," "a place to do photocopying," "a place to go to be alone," "a place to go to make friends," even a "place to get change for the parking meter." (Ruben, 1992b)

The Communication-Information Relationship

Communication and information have long been regarded as interrelated topics by scholars and practitioners (e.g., Cherry, 1957, 1966; Cherry, 1971; Krippendorff, 1977; Lin, 1973; Otten, 1975; Ruben, 1972, 1975, 1979; Ruben & Kim, 1975; Shannon & Weaver, 1949; Thayer, 1961, 1968, 1979; Wiener, 1961.). And beyond a concern about the communication-information relationship in general theories, there has also been interest in connections between the two among researchers who have focused on specific contexts, including biological (e.g., Lawson, 1963, Miller, 1965), cognitive (Bruner, 1973; Lachman, R., Lachman, J. L., & Butterfield, 1979; Loftus & Loftus, 1976; Schroder, Driver, & Streufert, 1967), psychiatric (Ruesch & Bateson, 1951), information science (Belkin & Robertson, 1976; Greer, 1987; Pemberton & Prentice, 1989), library (Dervin, 1977; Penniman & Jacob, 1984), economic (Machlup, 1952, 1962), and cultural (Schiller, 1981; 1989, Smith, 1966).

In recent years, scholarly attention to the communication-information relationship has increased dramatically (Anderson, Belkin, Lederman & Saracevic, 1988; Beniger, 1986, 1988; Borgman, 1990; Borgman & Rice, 1990; Borgman & Schement, 1988; Budd & Ruben, 1988; Deetz & Mumby, 1985; Dervin & Voigt, 1979–90; Halloran, 1985; Machlup and Mansfield, 1983; Mirabito and Morgenstern, 1990; Mokros, 1989; Mokros & Ruben, 1990; Paisley, 1986, 1989, 1990a, 1990b; Pemberton & Prentice, 1990; Rice, 1990; Ruben, 1985b, 1987, 1990; Ruben and Lievrouw, 1989; Ruben, Anderson & Wang, 1990; Schement and Mokros, 1989; Wright, 1986).

In the integrative perspective being proposed here, the relationship between communication and information is seen as a very intimate one. Communication is a process—an interactive process involving the transformation of information. Information is an artifact, representation, of product (a text, vocalization, a document, an image). Information arises out of communication; it is the product of communication. Communication occurs with respect to information. Process and product are inseparable (Ruben, 1992b). Information is not, per se, transmitted between or retrieved by individuals when they interact. Rather, communication involves the ongoing creation of information I_e, I_i, and I_s—by interactants through a process that influences—and is influenced by—participation in relationships, groups, organizations, cultures, and societies.

Mediation

Mediation occurs when our natural individual abilities to create, transmit, receive, and process visual, auditory, olfactory, gustatory, or tactile messages are extended, expanded, or enhanced technologically by media, or interpersonally by human intermediaries. Mediation may occur with:

1. *formal information systems* (e.g., searching a computerized databases or watching cable television) or *informal information systems* (e.g., asking a friend a question over the telephone or giving lecture notes to a friend);
2. *"old media"* (e.g., pencils and paper), or *"new media"* (e.g., computers and cellular phones);
3. *media used for mass communication* (e.g., television or books), *media used for organizational communication* (e.g., intercoms or newsletters), *media used for scholarly/scientific communication* (e.g., journals or technical reports, or *media used for interpersonal communication* (e.g., telephones and answering machines); and
4. *technological interfaces* (e.g., keyboarding or a telephone answering machine) or *human interfaces* (e.g., a reference librarian or a newspaper editor).

Functions of Mediation

Mediation extends human communication and information processing relative to: (1) production and distribution; and (2) reception, storage, and retrieval. Production involves the creation of messages using communication media. Distribution has three components: (1) Transmission; (2) reproduction and amplification; and (3) display—making messages physically available once they arrive at their destination.

Mediation in production may involve messages that are auditory in form, such as spoken language or music produced by human performers or musical instruments, as well as those conveyed by telephones, letters, radio, or recordings. Visual mediation may involve text forms, illustrations and other symbols created, transmitted and displayed by means of hand and arm signals, signs, printing, or photographic equipment. Television, film, and satellites extend our auditory and visual capacities simultaneously; other tools such as pencils, pens, typewriters, and paints and brushes serve similar mediating functions. Such media also further our human capacity for transmitting and displaying these messages, as do computers, video games, and even hand-held calculators. Examples of media that duplicate or amplify messages include carbon paper, printing presses, duplicating and copying equipment. Radio and television receivers, and even magnifying glasses, radar, stethoscopes, and telescopes assist with the reception of visual information, while earphones and hearing aids expand capabilities for receiving auditory messages. Computers mediate storage and retrieval processes, as do all forms written and graphic documents.

"New," "Old," and Converging Uses of Media

Traditional distinctions between various communication media and their uses are rapidly eroding. The newspaper once was the primary means for providing society audience with the summary of events of the day. Television, radio, and film were primarily mass entertainment media, and telephones were traditionally used socially and in business contexts, generally as a substitute for short face-to-face conversation.

These traditional distinctions are rapidly becoming obsolete. Together, the computer, telephone, and television can become a newspaper, magazine, game, reference tool, catalog, index, and a variety of other things. When a printer is added, the telephone, television, and a computer become a typewriter and printing press, a group decision-making network, a card catalog and the stacks of books at a reference library in medicine or law. When connected to a video disc or video cassette, television is a movie screen. When the tapes played are recorded on a portable videotape unit, television is a a home movie—a family album. In combination, these tools are at once media for interpersonal, group, organizational, scholarly/ scientific, and mass communication.

Convergence and change are also apparnet in the patterns of ownership of various communication and information media. Particularly in the past twenty-five years, the pattern of single-medium specialization and owner-ship has given way to an increasing prevalence of cross-ownership of media.

Intermediaries

As mentioned earlier, and integrative concept of mediation refers not only to technological mediation, but also to human mediation and human intermediaries—journalists and editors in the context of journalism, acqui-sitions and reference librarians in the context of libraries, and curators and public information staff in the context of museums. Moreover, these gatekeepers have their counterparts in a great many other communication and information arenas including film, book publishing, public relations, advertising, theater, music, and politics.

Communication and Information Institutions

Communication and information institutions are organizations that cre-ate, organize, package, repackage, display, or distribute information prod-ucts and/or services to an audience (cf. Budd & Ruben, 1988, Hunt & Ruben, 1993; Ruben, 1992a; Schiller, 1989; Thayer, 1988; Turow, 1984, 1992).

Information products are collections of messages organized in a partic-ular way for a particular purpose or use by a particular audience (Hunt & Ruben, 1993). Corresponding to the broadened definition of information noted earlier, the phrase, information product includes not only news, but also entertainment, public relations and advertising, computerized data-bases, even museum exhibits or theatrical plays. Information services are activities associated with preparation, packaging, repackaging, distribu-tion, organization, storage, or retrieval of information. Information serv-ices include news or editorial research, abstracting and indexing, public relations consulting, and electronic information delivery.

The term *audience* refers to the group of individuals who have potential for being exposed to and using an information product or service. In the terminology of the Information Age, the audience is the *user group* (Hunt & Ruben, 1993; Ruben, 1992a).

Traditionally, "audience" was defined in terms of a large, diverse group of viewers or readers all being exposed to the same information products at more or less the same time, and all unknown to the information producers (Wright, 1986). However, mediating devices like VCR, CDs, portable cassette tape players, and personal computers suggest the value of broadening this concept. These media make it easier to direct messages to specific segments of a mass audience at varying times. Therefore, the view of audience presented here does not presume that the user group must be of a specific size, nor be particularly diverse, nor that all of its members must be exposed to the same information at a similar point in time, nor that members of the group must be unknown to the information producers. More basic is the requirement that the information product involved must have been purposefully produced, organized, and/or distributed by a communication or information institution for a particular constituency. A network television program fits this definition, as does a collection in a library, a videotape produced for a particular corporation, a church newsletter, or a museum exhibit.

Implications and Conclusions

In combination, the concepts of communication, information, mediation, and institutions provide a promising foundation for addressing many significant issues of the Information Age. As examples of the types of connections and questions suggested by the framework, consider the following:

- To what extent do similarities and differences exist between communications as it operates in mass, public, transnational, intercultural, organization, political, group, interpersonal, intrapersonal, and technological contexts? What processes, goals, and outcomes are comparable in varying contexts? What general principles and frameworks apply across these contexts—for instance, principles relative to sources, channels, functions, individual and cultural impact, and/or information reception, retention and use?
- How can a generic concept of information be useful for understanding the structure, organization, and use of messages not only in documents, but also in intrapersonal, interpersonal, group, organizational, and cultural domains?
- Can the distinction between varying types of information—in terms of whether it is environmental, personal, or sociocultural—be useful not only in information systems design and implementation, but also in other contexts?

- In what ways is technological mediation parallel to and/or distinct from human mediation? What are the functional similarities and differences among structurally diverse technological intermediaries, such as telephones, computers, television sets, VCRs, and answering machines?
- What commonalities in processes, goals, and outcomes exist across different classes of human intermediaries, such as newspaper editors, reference librarians, documentary film producers, social science researchers, college teachers, and textbook acquisitions editors?
- To what extent should computer-human interaction be viewed as a distinct class or context of interaction? How is computer-human interaction similar to and/or different from FAX-human interaction, movie-human interaction, telephone-human interaction, or face-to-face interaction? How are the communication processes, mediation dynamics, and information products involved similar and/or different? In what ways is the role of the audience member or user comparable? Considering sources, how is the role of the *computer* programmer different from that of the *movie* or *television* "programmer?" How can knowledge from individualized contexts and roles be productively applied in other mediated contexts or roles?
- To what extent do mass media institutions share common forms, functions, and roles with libraries, information services, software producers, and museums?
- How can theoretical, research, evaluative, economic, policy, and regulatory considerations that are pertinent for one institution be made more relevant and accessible for others? For instance, might not cultural studies, critical theory, and concepts of media uses and gratifications be applicable, in principle, to the study of libraries, museums, online information services, and "new" technology? To what extent are issues of library and information institution ownership/sponsorship, control, and regulation pertinent to concerns regarding the ownership/sponsorship, control, and regulation of mass media institutions?

Concepts of communication, information, mediation, and institutions— and the framework they collectively define—transcend disciplinary boundaries. Moreover, they suggest a focus and level of analysis which help to overcome limitations of overly specialized or overly abstract approaches, and provide the basis for a much-needed conversational linkage between scholars, practitioners, and the general public. These concepts are equally promising as cornerstones for the design and construction of integrative communication-information courses and programs.

Note

1. Presented here is an overview of basic concepts from General Systems Theory, sociology of knowledge, symbolic interaction, and animal communication. For background see Berger & Luckmann, 1966; Bertalanffy, 1956; 1968; Blumer, 1969; Boulding, 1956; Buckley, 1967; Duncan, 1962, 1968, 1969; Frings, 1967; Frisch, 1950; Goffman, 1974; Holzner, 1966, Kim, 1985; Laszlo, 1969; Lawson, 1963; Maruyama, 1968; Miller, 1965; Monge, 1977; Ruben, 1972, 1975, 1979, 1984, 1985a, 1985b, 1988, 1992a; Ruben, et al., 1982; Ruben et al, 1975; Ruesch & Bateson, 1961; Selye, 1956; Smith, 1966; Thayer, 1968, 1979; Tinbergen, 1965; Watzlawick, Beavin, & Jackson, 1967; Wiener, 1954, 1961; Wilson, 1975.

References

Anderson, J. D., Belkin, N. J., Lederman, L. C., & Saracevic, T. (1988). Information science at Rutgers: Establishing new interdisciplinary connections. *Journal of the American Society for Information Science. 39*(5), 327–30.

Belkin, N. J., & S. E. Robertson (1976). Information science and the phenomenon of information. *Journal of the American Society for Information Science, 27*(4), 197–204.

Beniger, J. R. (1986). *The control revolution.* Cambridge, MA: Harvard University Press.

Beniger, J. R. (1988). Information and communication: The new convergence. *Communication Research, 15*(2), 198–218.

Berger, P. L., & Luckmann, T. (1966). *The social construction of reality.* Garden City, NY: Doubleday.

Bertalanffy, L. von. (1968). *General system theory.* New York: Braziller

Bertalanffy, L. von (1956). General System Theory, *General Systems*, 1, Ann Arbor, MI: Society for the Advancement of General Systems Theory.

Blumer, H. (1969). *Symbolic interactionism.* Englewood Cliffs, NJ: Prentice Hall.

Borgman, C. L. (Ed.) (1990). *Scholarly communication and bibliometrics.* Newbury Park, CA: Sage.

Borgman, C. L. & Rice, R. E. (1990). *The convergence of information science and communication: A bibliometric analysis.* Unpublished manuscript.

Borgman, C. L. & Schement, J. R. (1988). Communication research and information science: Models of convergence. The social and historical construction of the idea of information-as-thing. Paper presented at the annual meetings of the International Communication Association, New Orleans.

Boulding, K. (1956). General system theory: The skeleton of science. *General Systems*, 1. Ann Arbor, MI: Society for the Advancement of General Systems Theory.

Boulding, K. (1956). *The image.* Ann Arbor, MI: University of Michigan Press.

Bruner, J. S. (1973). *Beyond the information given: Studies in the psychology of knowing.* New York: Norton.

Buckland, M. (1991). *Information and information systems.* New York: Praeger.

Buckley, W. (1967). *Sociology and modern systems theory.* Englewood Cliffs, NJ: Prentice Hall.

Budd, R. W., & Ruben, B. D. (1988). *Beyond media: New approaches to mass communication.* (2nd ed.). New Brunswick, NJ: Transaction.

Cherry, C. (1957). *On human communication.* (1st ed.). New York: Wiley.
Cherry C. (1966). *The communication of information.* New York: Holt, Rinehart, and Winston.
Cherry, C. (1971). *World communication.* New York: Wiley.
Deetz, S., & Mumby, D. K. (1985). Metaphor, information, and power. In B. D. Ruben (Ed.), *Information and behavior: Volume 1* (pp. 369–86). New Brunswick, NJ: Transaction.
Dervin, B. (1977). Useful theory for librarianship: Communication, not information. *Drexel Library Quarterly, 13*(3), 16–32.
Dervin, B., & Voigt, M. (Eds.) (1979–1989). *Progress in communication sciences.* Norwood, NJ: Ablex.
Duncan, H.D. (1962). *Communication and social order.* London: Oxford University Press.
Duncan, H. D. (1968). *Symbols in society.* London: Oxford University Press.
Duncan, H. D. (1969). *Symbols and social theory.* New York: Oxford University Press.
Frings, H. (1967). *Animal communicatin.* Washington, DC: Spartan Books.
Frisch, K. von (1950). *Bees: Their vision, chemical senses, and language.* Ithaca, NY: Cornell Univerisy Press.
Goffman, E. (1974). *Frame analysis: An essay on the organization of experience.* Cambridge, MA: Harvard University Press.
Greer, R. C. (1987). A model for the discipline of information science. In H. K. Achleitner (Ed.), *Intellectual foundations for information professionals* (pp. 3–25). Boulder, CO: Social Science Monographs.
Halloran, J. D. (1985). Information and communication: Information is the answer, but what is the question? In B. D. Ruben (ed.), *Information and behavior: Volume 1* (pp. 27–39). New Brunswick, NJ: Transaction.
Holzner, B. (1966). *Reality construction in society.* Cambridge, MA: Schenkman.
Hunt, T., & Ruben, B. D. (1993). *Mass communication: Producers and Consumers.* New York: HarperCollins.
Kim, Y. Y. (1985). Communication, information and adaptation. In B. D. Ruben (Ed.), *Information and behavior: Volume 1* (pp. 324–42). New Brunswick, NJ: Transaction.
Krippendorff, K. (1977). Information systems theory and research: An overview. In B. D. Ruben (Ed.), *Communication Yearbook 1* (pp. 149–71). New Brunswick, NJ: Transaction-International Communication Association.
Lachman, R., Lachman, J. L., & Butterfield, E. C. (1979). *Cognitive psychology and information processing: An introduction.* Hillsdale, NJ: Lawrence Erlbaum.
Laszlo, E. (1969). *System, structure, and experience: Towards a scientific theory or mind.* New York: Gordon and Breach.
Lawson, C. A. (1963). Language, communication, and biological organization. In L. von Bertalanffy & A. Rapoport (Ed.), *General systems: Volume VIII.* Ann Arbor, MI: Society for General Systems Research.
Lin, N. (1973). *The study of human communication.* Indianapolis, IN: Bobbs-Merill.
Loftus, G. R., & Loftus, E. F. (1976). *Human memory: The processing of information.* Hillsdale, NJ: Lawrence Erlbaum.
Machlup, F. (1962). *The production and distribution of knowledge in the United States.* Princeton, NJ: Princeton University Press.
Machlup, F. (1983). Semantic quirks in studies of information. In F. Machlup & U.

Mansfield (Eds.) *The study of information: Interdisciplinary messages* (pp. 641–72) New York: John Wiley & Sons.

Machlup, F., & Mansfield, U. (Eds.). (1983). *The study of information: Interdisciplinary messages*. New York: John Wiley.

Mackay, D. M. (1952). The nomenclature of information theory. In H. von Foerster (Ed.), *Cybernetics: Transactions of the Eighth Congress*. New York: Macy Foundation.

Maruyama, M. (1968). Mutual causality in general systems. In J. Milsum (Ed.), *Positive feedback: A general systems approach to positive/negative feedback and mutual causality*. New York: Pergamon.

Miller, J. G. (1965). Living systems. *Behavioral Science, 10*, 193–237.

Mirabito, M. M., and B. L. Morgenstern. (1990). *The new communications technologies*. Boston: Focal Press.

Mokros, H. B. (1989). Information and communication in social interaction. Paper presented at the annual meetings of the American Society for Information Science, Washington, DC.

Mokros, H. B., & Ruben, B. D. (1991). Understanding the Communication-information relationship: Levels of information and contexts of availabilities. *Knowledge, 12*(1), 373–88.

Monge, P. R. (1977). The systems perspective as a theoretical basis for the study of human communication. *Communication Quarterly, 25*, 19–29.

Otten, K. W. (1975). Information and communication: A conceptual model as framework for the development of theories of information. In A. A. Debons & W. Cameron (Eds.), *Perspectives in information science* (pp. 127–48). Leyden: Noordhof.

Paisley, W. (1986). The convergence of Communication and Information Science. In H. Edelman (Ed.), *Libraries and Information Science in the electronic age*. Philadelphia: ISI Press.

Paisley, W. (1989). Information Science as a multidiscipline: Twenty questions and a few answers. In J. M. Pemberton & A. Prentice (Eds.), *Information science in its interdisciplinary context*. New York: Neal-Schuman.

Paisley, W. (1990a). An oasis where many trails cross: The improbable cocitation networks of a multidiscipline. *Journal of the American Society for Information Science, 41*(6), 459–68.

Paisley, W. (1990b). *Communication science: The growth of a multidiscipline*. Norwood, NJ: Ablex.

Pemberton, J. M., & Prentice, A. (1989). *Information Science in its interdisciplinary context*. New York: Neal-Schuman.

Penniman, W. D., & Jacob, M. E. (1984). Libraries as communicators of information. In R. Rice et al. (Eds.), *The new media: Communication, research and technology* (pp. 251–268). Beverly Hills, CA: Sage.

Rice, R. E. (1988). Citation networks of communication journals, 1977–1985: Cliques and positions, citations made and citations received. *Human Communication Research, 15*(2), 256–83.

Rice, R. E. (1990). Hierarchies and clusters among communication and library and information science journals. In C. Borgman, (Ed.) *Scholarly communication and bibliometrics* (pp. 138–153). Newbury Park, CA: Sage.

Ruben, B. D. (1972). General system theory: An approach to human communication. In R. W. Budd & B. D. Ruben (Ed.), *Approaches to human communication* (pp. 120–44). New York: Spartan.

Ruben, B. D. (1975). Intrapersonal, interpersonal, and mass communication processes in individual and multi-personal systems. In B. D. Ruben & J. Y. Kim (Eds.), *General systems theory and human communication* (pp. 164–90). Rochelle Park, NJ: Hayden.

Ruben, B. D. (1979). General system theory. In R. W. Budd and B. D. Ruben (Eds.), *Interdisciplinary Approaches to Human Communication* (pp. 95–118). Rochelle Park, NJ: Hayden.

Ruben, B. D. (1984). *Communication and human behavior.* New York: Macmillan.

Ruben, B. D. (1985a). The coming of the information age: Information, technology and the study of human behavior. In B. D. Ruben (Ed.), *Information and behavior: Volume 1*, (pp. 3–26). New Brunswick, NJ: Transaction.

Ruben, B. D. (1985b). Introduction. In B. D. Ruben (Ed.), *Information and behavior: Volume 1*, (pp. xxi–xxiv). New Brunswick, NJ: Transaction.

Ruben, B. D. (1987). Redefining the boundaries of graduate education in Communication, Information and Library Studies: Theoretical and practical considerations. Paper presented at the annual conference of the Association for Library and Information Science Education. Chicago, IL.

Ruben, B. D. (1988). *Communication and human behavior.* (2nd ed.). New York: Macmillan.

Ruben, B. D. (1990). Redefining the boundaries of graduate education in communication, information and library studies: Theoretical and practical considerations. In J. M. Pemberton & A. Prentice (Eds.), *Information science in its interdisciplinary context.* New York: Neal-Schuman.

Ruben, B. D. (1992a). *Communication and human behavior.* (3rd ed.). Englewood Cliffs, NJ: Prentice-Hall.

Ruben, B. D. (1992b). The communication-information relationship: A system-theoretic perspective. *Journal of the American Society for Information Science,* 43(10), 15–27.

Ruben, B. D., Anderson, J. D., & Wang, Q. (1990). Disciplinary foundations for Ph.D. programs in library and information science. In P. Rolland-Thomas (Ed.), *Festschrift in memory of Laurent G. Denis.* Montreal, Quebec: ASTED.

Ruben, B. D., Holtz, J. R., & Hanson, J. K. (1982). Communication systems, technology, anc culture. In H. F. Didsbury Jr. (Ed.), *Communications and the Future: Prospects, Promises, and Problems* (pp. 255–66). Bethesda, MD: World Future Society.

Ruben, B. D., & Kim, J. Y. (1975). *General systems theory and human communication.* Rochelle Park, NJ: Hayden.

Ruben, B. D., & Lievrouw, L. A. (Eds.) (1989). *Information and Behavior? Volume 3. Mediation, Information and Communication.* New Brunswick, NJ: Transaction,

Ruesch, J. (1957). *Technology and social communication.* Springfield, IL: Charles C. Thomas.

Ruesch, J., & Bateson, G (1951). *Communication: The social matrix of psychology.* New York: Norton.

Salvaggio, J. L. (1983). *Telecommunications: Issues and choices for society.* New York: Longman.

Saracevic, T. (1993). *Information science revisited: Contemporary reflections on its origin, evolution, and relations.* New York: Academic Press.

Schement, J. R., & Lievrouw, L. (1987). *Competing visions, complex realities: Social aspects of the information age.* Norwood, NJ: Ablex.

Schement, J. R., and Mokros, H. B. (1989). The social and historical construction of the idea of information as thing. Paper presented at the annual meetings of the American Society for Information Science, Washington, DC.

Schiller, H. I. (1989). *Culture, Inc*. New York: Oxford University Press.

Schiller, H. I. (1981), *Who knows: Information in the age of the Fortune 500*. Norwood, NJ: Ablex.

Schroder, H. M., Driver, M. J., & Streufert, S. (1967). *Human information processing*. New York: Holt, Rinehart and Winston.

Selye, H. (1956). *The stress of life*. New York: McGraw-Hill.

Shannon, C., & Weaver, W. (1949). *The mathematical theory of communication*. Urbana: University of Illinois Press.

Smith, A. G. (1966). *Communication and culture*. New York: Holt,

Thayer, L. (1961). *Administrative communication*. Homewood, IL: Irwin.

Thayer, L. (1968). *Communication and communication systems*. Homewood, IL: Irwin.

Thayer, L. (1986). *Communication and communication systems*. 2nd. Ed. Lanham, MD: University Press of America.

Thayer, L. (1979). Communication: Sine qua non of the behavioral sciences. In R. W. Budd & B. D. Ruben (Eds.), *Interdisciplinary approaches to human communication* (pp. 7–31). Rochelle Park, NJ: Hayden.

Thayer, L. (1988). On the mass media and mass communication: Notes toward a theory. In R. W. Budd & B. D. Ruben, *Beyond media: New approaches to mass communication* (2nd. ed.) (pp. 52–83). New Brunswick, NJ: Transaction.

Tinbergen, N. (1965). *Social behavior in animals with special reference to vertebrates*. London: Methuen.

Turow, J. (1984). *Media industries: The production of news and entertainment*. New York: Longman.

Turow, J. (1992). *Mass media in society: Industries, strategies, and power*. New York: Longman.

Watzlawick, P., Beavin, J. H., & Jackson, D. D. (1967). *Pragmatics of human communication*. New York: Norton.

Wiener, N. (1954). *The human use of human beings*. Garden City, NY: Doubleday.

Wiener, N. (1961). *Cybernetics: On control and communication in the animal and the machine*. 2nd ed. Cambridge, MA: MIT Press.

Williams, F. (1991) *The new telecommunications: Infrastructure for the information age*. New York: Free Press.

Williams, F. (1991). The new telecommunications: Infrastructure for the information age. New York: Free Press.

Wilson, E. D. (1975). *Sociobiology*. Cambridge, MA: Belknap/Harvard University Press.

Wright, C. R. (1986). *Mass communication: A sociological perspective*. 3rd. Ed. New York: Random House.

PART III

INDIVIDUAL AND SOCIAL CONTEXT

11

Interrelationships between Information-Seeking Skills, Information-Seeking Behavior, and the Usage of Information Sources

Alison J. Head

This study, which is based on placement exam test scores and questionnaire responses from a sample of 314 incoming community college students, uses correlational analysis and factor analyses to show how the constructs of information-seeking behavior and information-seeking skills function in relation to one another and how the two constructs affect people's choices and uses of available information sources. Findings show that the behavior and skills are positively correlated with one another under certain circumstances but negatively correlated with one another in others. For example, skills levels are positively correlated with book readership but negatively correlated with television viewership. Results of these empirical findings lead to the conclusion that the more adept someone is at collecting information, the more active that person's information-seeking behavior is likely to be. And the opposite holds true—the worse someone is at collecting information, the less active that person's information-seeking behavior is likely to be, and it is more likely for them to engage in the use of "inferior" information sources, such as television.

Even though information and communication are often studied separately by researchers, an apparent though complex relationship exists between the two constructs. While information is commonly viewed as the object, the raw material, or even as "the strategic resource," communication is considered information's natural counterpart of exchange or the process of its dissemination.[1] In order to further understand the interrelationships between information and communication, this study applies an information science method of inquiry.

Within the field of information science, researchers who have explored the relationships between information and communication have, in many cases, turned their attention to the area of information-seeking behavior. The study of information-seeking behavior focuses on the traits, habits, and strategies that people exhibit in their search and use of information sources. Information scientists view information sources as the communication channels by which information is disseminated.

Information-seeking behavior research has largely focused upon how individuals search out and use information sources, but little research has explored how information-seeking behavior may be related to people's actual choices and uses of a particular information source or medium. The relationship between how individuals choose a certain medium for information and their ability to understand and accept the communicated information is integral to understanding the information/communication relationship because it describes how people interact with information within their daily lives, which in turn, affects the foundations of public knowledge.

The purpose of this study is, first, to further analyze and refine the construct of information-seeking behavior by making an explicit distinction between information-seeking behavior and information-seeking skills; second, to show how the constructs of information-seeking behavior and information-seeking skills function in relation to one another; and third, to describe how the two constructs affect people's choices and uses of available information sources.

Background

The study of information-seeking behavior has been defined as concerning itself with finding out "what kind of people seek what kinds of information through what channels" (Parker and Paisley, 1966). Researchers have often focused upon a particular group of people instead of on an information source to study that group's various information-gathering activities and habits.

The information-seeking behavior of scholars is one such example of this type of research. Scholars have been studied within the fields of humanities (Guest, 1987; Stone, 1982; Garfield, 1980), history (Stieg,

1981), the sciences (Garvey, 1979; Rowley and Turner, 1978), and the social sciences (Wilson, 1980). In general, the findings indicate that scholars, for the most part, do not use institutionalized sources for information, such as libraries, and instead prefer to use their own books or to rely on conversations with colleagues.

Researchers have also studied the information-seeking behavior of the poor. Much of the early research set about to prove that the poor rarely read magazines or newspapers; researchers have found that the poor instead prefer to watch great amounts of television and that they use it as their principle source of information because of their lack of print orientation (Parker and Paisley, 1966; Greenberg and Dervin, 1970; Childers, 1975; Comstock et al., 1978). Researchers have generally concluded that the poor don't use information sources that could help them because many of the poor do not recognize their needs as problems that are solvable by using helpful information in the first place (Dervin, 1984). And if the poor do, they lack the skills to find the information that might hold the problem's solution (Chatman, 1985).

Despite the different kinds of information-seeking behavior research that have been conducted, a key characteristic about information-seeking behavior has emerged from the research: The use of formal and informal information channels are a basis for determining information-seeking behavior. In his book, *The Information-Poor in America,* Childers (1975) identifies formal channels of information as consisting of the "media, social agencies and agents, and private enterprises—any commodity or activity in society, private or public, that is not related to individuals, personally known to the receiver of information" (p. 38). Informal channels consist of friends, neighbors, relatives—people whom the individual personally knows and consults for information (1975, p. 38).

The Present Study

This study examines incoming community college students' use of formal information channels and levels of skills to see in what ways the two factors work.[2] First, measures of information-seeking skills and information-seeking behavior are developed; second, the two different measures are compared to see how skills and behavior work together and independently of one another; and third, the way in which the two measures affect people's choice and use of information sources is described.

In the information science field, information-seeking behavior research is widely accepted as the means for describing the "information disposition" of particular groups. However, in most cases, the information-seeking behavior research has only examined a group's informational behavioral patterns instead of describing how both information-seeking behavior and information-seeking skills levels may be related to the choice of information sources. In this study, information-seeking skills level is assumed to be critically linked to the type and amount of information-seeking behavior and, therefore, skills level is separately measured. Consequently, the present study is significant because it measures *both* information-seeking skills and information-seeking behavior as a basis for determining the usage of particular kinds of information sources.

The Data

The data are from a 1989 survey and the entrance exam test results of incoming students at a community college located in Northern California. The students volunteered in two ways for this study. First, they completed a questionnaire that was used as a measure of their information-seeking behavior. Second, they released their standardized tests in reading, writing, and math which were used as measures of their information-seeking skills.

Measurement of Information-Seeking Behavior

The questionnaire was used to measure respondents' *type* and *amount* of information-seeking behavior. The questionnaire collected information on the use of formal information channels such as newspapers, television, books, and radio. Two measures of respondents' personal assessment of how knowledgeable they claim to be are also included. For the purposes of this study, the use of formal information channels and the personal assessment of information habits are used to represent the construct of information-seeking behavior. Survey items intended to measure information-seeking behavior appear in table 11.1.

TABLE 11.1
Measures of Information-Seeking Behavior

Use of formal channels
- frequency of newspaper readership
- frequency of magazine readership
- frequency of book readership
- frequency of television viewing

Respondents' personal assessment of their own information-seeking behavior
- personal assessment of amount of knowledge about world affairs
- personal assessment of habit of information collection for problem solving

Measurement of Information-Seeking Skills

Since they are necessary skills for the collection and use of information, the construct of information-seeking skills is assumed to include the ability to read and comprehend English, to write in a logical and clear manner, and to solve problems involving numbers and graphs. Information-seeking skills level was measured by respondents' Educational Testing Service scores in reading, writing, and math which were administered to incoming community college students.

Based upon their test scores, the class levels that the respondents were eventually placed in are used as a proxy measure of information-seeking skills level. Although the test scores were only *estimates* of a particular student's skills, test developers have argued quite forcefully that the test scores are valid proxies for students' abilities in communication and problem-solving (Herman, 1986).

Content validity is a common criterion of standardized test construction. Although content validity is a matter of judgement, the content validity established in this particular set of tests was considered by test developers. Tests were designed to meet the relevant background of students at community colleges. (*Comparative Guidance and Placement Program*, 1979).

The Study Population

A sample of 314 incoming students was used in this study. The overall response rate was 74 percent. Although the sample was not randomly determined because the participants were voluntary, the data, however, provide a certain representativeness of the student population at the college (Napa Valley College Census, 1989). First, the sex of the respondents is close to the college's actual population but has a slightly higher ratio among females to males (62.3 percent to 37.7 percent). Second, seven out of ten respondents were under twenty years old. The median age for a student at the community college is between thirty and thirty-four years and is higher than that of the sample. Third, the college has a high enrollment among whites and the racial composition of the sample (75 percent to 24 percent) is quite similar to that of the overall student body (75 percent to 19 percent), the remainder being nonrespondents.

Even though this sample is fairly representative of the college students, a limitation of the sample is that it is not necessarily representative of people in general. The results from the student population, however, are useful because they provide a description of skills level and information-seeking behavior patterns among a given population.

Findings

Correlational Analysis

In this study, information-seeking skills and information seeking behavior are considered separate constructs which may, under certain circumstances, behave independently of one another. In order to explore the relationships among the individual variables, the Pearson correlation coefficient was calculated by using pairwise comparisons for the variables measuring skills and behavior. Pearson's correlation coefficient is a common statistical method used to show the association between variables and to test for "strength." A correlational value can range from − 1 through 0 through + 1. The results of the pairwise comparison are in table 11.2.

Discussion. The findings in table 11.2 show that the variables used to measure skills and behavior are positively correlated with one another in some cases but negatively correlated with one another in others. For example, the writing score and math score (both skill variables in this study) are highly and positively correlated with book readership (a behavioral variable in this study). The two skills variables, however, share a negative correlation with television viewership. The reading score reaffirms these general findings, too. The reading score is highly and positively correlated with book readership but negatively correlated (at the .01 level) with television viewership. Overall, these findings suggest that those who performed well on the tests don't watch much television. This finding reaffirms what was suggested about information-seeking behavior of the poor: those with poor information-processing skills are often heavy users of television (Parker and Paisley, 1966; Greenberg and Dervin, 1970; Childers, 1975; Comstock et al., 1978). The results of these findings may also be applied in support of what Childers (1975) and others (Davie and Wright, 1988; Chatman, 1987) have argued about the information poor. Since the information poor, in general, often lack the skills to collect and use the information that they need, they do not conduct very active searches.

These findings can also be more broadly interpreted: the more adept someone is at collecting information, the more active that person's information-seeking behavior is likely to be. And the opposite also holds true— the worse someone is at collecting information, the less active that person's information-seeking behavior is likely to be. This finding further indicates that the lower someone's skills are the more likely it is for them to engage in the use of "inferior" information sources, such as television.

Another interesting finding exists among the two behavior variables that require respondents' self-assessment—self-assessment by respondents of

TABLE 11.2
Correlational matrix of skill factor variables and behavior factor variables

	Newspaper readership	Magazine readership	Book readership	TV viewership	Claims to be know-ledgeable	Claims to collect information	Reading score	Writing score
Magazine readership	.1988**							
Book readership	.0605	.3019**						
TV viewership	-.0582	.0106	.0151					
Claims to be knowledgeable about world	-.2859**	-.2845**	-.1883**	.0073				
Claims to collect info. for future use	-.1271*	-.1761	-.1424*	.0876	.3264**			
Reading score	.1601*	.2110**	.4022**	-.1845**	-.1351*	-.1217		
Writing score	.1032*	.0818	.2660**	-.1119*	-.0404	.0093	.4418**	
Math score	.0142	.1077*	.1984**	-.1395*	-.1491*	-.0325	.3422**	.3479**
NOTE:	*p≤.05	**p≤.01						

their knowledge about world affairs and self-assessment by respondents of their collection of information for future use. Table 11.2 shows that these two variables are the only ones that are significant and positively correlated with one another. Surprisingly, the variables are negatively correlated with newspaper, magazine, and book readership. What information sources are these people using to gain the knowledge they think they have? One reasonable explanation for this pattern of correlation is that those who *claim* to be knowledgeable about world affairs and those who *claim* to collect information to help them solve future problems are collecting their information from informal channels such as friends, relatives—or even teachers. Findings from other research about information-seeking behavior offer support for this explanation since informal channels have been found to provide receivers with information that is used for evaluation and decision making (Lazarfeld, et al.; 1948; Rogers & Shoemaker, 1971; Chatman, 1987).

Factor Analyses

Information-Seeking Skills. Factor analysis was used to further test the relationships between the groups of variables that make up the constructs of information-seeking skills and information-seeking behavior. In general, factor analysis shows how individual variables "load" on factors into groups represented by "likeness" among the variables. The statistical method was applied here because, unlike the correlational analysis that showed relationships among the separate variables, factor analysis allows for the statistical grouping of variables to occur and for underlying factor patterns to be revealed.

Descriptive statistics, including the means, standard deviations, and ranges for each of the variables used to make up information-seeking skills appear in table 11.3.

One common objective of factor analysis is to "represent a set of variables in terms of a smaller number of hypothetical variables" (Kim and Mueller, 1978, p. 9). These hypothetical variables account for the

TABLE 11.3
Descriptive Statistics for information-seeking skills variables

Variable	N	Mean	Std. Dev.	Range
Reading score	314	2.87	.90	3.0
Writing score	314	2.95	.77	3.0
Math score	314	24.32	9.15	46.0

Note: Scale from 1 (low) to 3 (high) in the first variables; to 46 (high) in the last variable

observed covariance. To determine the number of dimensions involved in the assessment of information-seeking skills, the eigenvalue criterion was used. The eigenvalue criterion defined one factor. Table 11.4 shows factor analysis results. Since there was only one factor in this analysis, it could not be rotated. The significance of all three variables loading on one factor is that one construct called "Information-seeking Skills" is made up of three highly correlated variables which represent a single underlying dimension of the test scores.

Unavoidably, factor names are somewhat subjective. However, they are used here because they provide a useful short-hand description of the set of variables used to construct the factor. The single factor extracted in this analysis, named "Test Scores," combines the three test scores in reading, writing, and math. The single factor explains 58.6 percent of the total variance in the skills variables as a whole. High communality values, such as exist in table 11.4, indicate large amounts of variance in the measures which are explained by the factor.

Information-Seeking Behavior. Although some of the variables used in this factor analysis were technically ordinal, the variables were considered interval for purposes of this particular analysis. Variables used to measure behavior included frequency of newspaper readership, frequency of magazine readership, frequency of book readership, frequency of television viewership, an assessment by respondents of their own level of knowledge about the world, and an assessment by the respondents of their own amount of information collection. Descriptive statistics, including the means, standard deviations, and ranges for the variables that make up information-seeking behavior appear in table 11.5

To determine the number of dimensions involved in the assessment of information-seeking behavior, the eigenvalue criterion was used. The eigenvalue criterion defined two factors. The two factors were then rotated using varimax rotation. A final rotated factor matrix was prepared from

TABLE 11.4
Information-seeking skills—Factor analysis

Items	Factor 1 "Test Scores"	Communality
Reading score	**.78584**	.61754
Writing score	**.78928**	.62296
Math placement	**.71837**	.51606
Eigenvalues	1.75656	
Percent of variance explained	58.6	
N = 314		

Note: Loadings are printed in bold and underlined which are ≥ than 0.3

TABLE 11.5
Descriptive statistics for information-seeking behavior variables

Variable	N	Mean	Std. dev.	Range
Newspaper reading	314	3.26	1.31	4.0
Magazine reading	314	2.69	1.03	4.0
Book reading	314	2.90	1.27	4.0
Television viewing	314	2.72	1.41	7.0
Claimed knowledge about world affairs	314	2.22	.67	3.0
Claimed amount of information collection	314	3.01	.95	4.0

Note: Scale from low (1) to high (4) in the first three variables; to high (7) in fourth variable; to high (3) in fifth variable, to high (4) in sixth variable

the computed results and factor loading values of less than 0.3 (in absolute terms) were considered meaningless (Kim and Mueller, 1978).

Again, factor names, although somewhat subjective, are useful for identifying particular factors. The first factor, named "Information Collection," combines a personal assessment of degree of knowledge about world affairs, a habit of collecting information for solving future problems, and a negative loading on newspaper which may be interpreted as a lack of newspaper readership. The first factor explains 31 percent of the total variance of the behavior variables.

The second factor, "Media Use," combines magazine readership, book readership, and television viewership. The second factor explains 17.7 percent of the total variance left unexplained by the first factor. Together, both factors explain 48.7 percent of the total variance in the behavior data as a whole. The results of the factor analysis appear in table 11.6.

The results of the factor analyses reported in table 11.6 indicate that the variables used to makeup the construct of information-seeking skills are more complexly interrelated than the variables that were used to make up information-seeking skills. But this is logical since in this study, information-seeking behavior was believed to be made up of different and complex groupings of variables.

Factor analysis was applied in this particular analysis because it proved to be an efficient method for showing predominant patterns among the groups of variables used to measure the constructs of skills and behavior. Factor analysis, however, is not a foolproof method of analysis, and it has important limitations which should be addressed. First, factor analysis always produces a solution in the form of factors, whether the data is logically related or not. Therefore, the generation of a factor must be

TABLE 11.6
Information-seeking behavior—Factor analysis

Items	Factor 1 "Information Collection"	Factor 2 "Media Use"	Communality
Newspaper readership	−.59292	.04991	.35404
Magazine readership	−.39408	.60578	.52228
Book readership	−.18759	.66570	.47835
Television viewership	.50189	.61069	.62483
Knowledgeable about world affairs	.65386	−.33050	.53676
Collects information for future problems	.63169	−.10077	.40918
Eigenvalues	1.86170	1.06374	
Percent of variance explained	31.0	17.7	
Cumulation percent of variance	31.0	48.7	
N = 314			

Note: Loadings are printed in bold and underlined which are ≥ than 0.3

carefully analyzed to insure that it actually has relevant meaning. Second, factors are generated without any substantive meaning: The researcher must interpret factor loadings to decide and determine what the factor actually represents.

Limits of the Study

This study has used an information science approach of describing information-seeking behavior to show how the construct can be further studied and applied to understanding how people choose and use information sources. Other approaches from different disciplines, such as cognitive psychology and the sociology of knowledge, are also necessary to fully describe how people choose and use information.

This study is limited in its generalizability by the nature of the sample. An examination of a broader general population, other than one made up of students, would offer a wider basis for studying information-seeking behavior. For example, a sample taken from a city population would allow for more of a heterogeneity among respondents in terms of age, education, employment, and income. Even though a general sample might provide more information, an operationalization of skills level, like the one that was used in this study, might prove to be very difficult to define for such a group. From the viewpoint of an information scientist, information-seeking skills are a basic component in understanding any kind of information-seeking behavior and, unfortunately, this complicates and affects choices made about research design and sample selection.

This study is also limited by the data available. Since the data were self-reported and based on voluntary participation, the results reported here may be biased, especially among the data from responses dealing with information-seeking behavior. For example, when the students were asked in the questionnaire if they themselves thought they were knowledgeable about world affairs, or if they, themselves, collected much information for future problem solving, a majority of them may have responded affirmatively. These respondents may have figured that they were in a college environment and should appear "knowledgeable," especially in a placement examination. These two particular questions also appeared at the end of the questionnaire, when respondents might have had a better idea about what type of information the questionnaire was actually seeking, and they may have wanted to appear a certain way. Since the question on newspaper readership appeared at the beginning of the questionnaire, respondents may have more candidly answered it because they were unaware of what the rest of the questionnaire would ask. Also, the newspaper question is slightly different than the other two questions because it asks about behavior instead of self-assessment.

Another limitation of the study is that the measures of information-seeking behavior are not designed to collect data on the use of informal channels of information, such as friends or relatives. This additional data would have proved more helpful in more fully describing information-seeking behavior. Furthermore, previous research has shown that informal channels are important sources of information (Parker and Paisley, 1966; Chatman, 1987).

Conclusions

This study has attempted to make a distinction between information-seeking behavior and information-seeking skills, to compare the two separate constructs to see how they work together and separately, and to see how, in turn, the constructs affect the choice and use of information sources. Since information sources are viewed as communication channels by information scientists, this study has attempted to offer further empirical evidence, from a disciplinary viewpoint, about the interrelationships between information and communication. We attempted this by exploring how people's choice and use of particular information sources is related to their information-seeking skills and information-seeking behaviors.

One significant result of the study is that information-seeking skills and information-seeking behavior are positively correlated with one another under certain circumstances, but negatively correlated with one another in others. For example, math, writing, and reading tests scores (skills variables in this study) are positively correlated with book readership (a behavioral variable in this study). However, the three variables all share a negative correlation with television viewership. These results from the correlational analysis and other similar ones suggest that the lower someone's skills are, the more likely it is for them to engage in the use of "inferior" information sources, such as television. Overall, these findings indicate that "inferior" information sources have the support of a strong following of those with low information-seeking skills.

Another result of the study involved respondents' self assessment of how knowledgeable they thought they were about world affairs and whether they ever collected information to use for solving future problems. Surprisingly, the more knowledgeable that individuals thought that they were and the more likely they thought they were to collect information, the less likely they were to read newspapers. At first this finding was puzzling. From what sources were these people obtaining their information? One explanation was offered for the results: these respondents may be using informal information sources, such as friends or relatives, to gain their knowledge.

In general, several ideas about how people choose and use information also emerged from the correlational analysis. The more adept someone is at collecting information, the more active that person's information-seeking behavior is likely to be. The less adept someone is at collecting information, the less active that person's information-seeking behavior is likely to be.

Further testing, using factor analysis, showed that the test score variables that comprised the information-seeking skills measure were highly correlated with one another and only represented one factor named "Tests Scores." The variables that made-up information-seeking behavior, however, were more complexly related with one another and two factors emerged from the analysis named "Information Collection" and "Media Use." This analysis suggests that information-seeking behavior, in general, is a complex construct with more than one central, underlying dimension.

Overall, the results of this study offer strong evidence that individuals choose and use particular information sources based on their information-seeking abilities (skills and behavior). One aspect of the information/

communication relationship that this research revealed is that information and communication are integrally tied to two other constructs—information-seeking behavior and information-seeking skills—and that the information/communication relationship is defined through how individuals choose and use information sources.

Although this study examined one aspect of the information/communication relationship, additional research needs to be carried out. Further research in this particular area might include the use of different measures of information-seeking behavior. The variables used to make up information-seeking behavior here are far too limited. Furthermore, a measure of information-seeking behavior should also include variables measuring the use informal information channels, too.

Notes

1. In the seminal work, *The Coming of Post-Industrial Society*, Daniel Bell (1973) argued that the major structural changes occurring in society are due to changes in the character of knowledge where in turn, information had become the "strategic resource."
2. For a recent example of research on the use of formal and informal information channels, see E. Chatman (1987) "The information world of low-skilled workers."

References

Bell, D. (1973). *The coming of post-industrial society: A venture in social forecasting*. New York: Basic Books.

Chatman, E. (1985). Information mass media use, and the working poor. *Library and Information Science Research, 7*, 97–113.

Chatman, E. (1987). The information world of low-skilled workers. *Library and Information Science Research, 9*, 265–283.

Childers, T. (1975). *The information-poor in America*. Metuchen, NJ: Scarecrow.

Comparative guidance and placement (CGP): Using and interpreting scores on the CGP self-scoring placement tests in english and mathematics. (1979). College Entrance Examination Board, Princeton, NJ: Education Testing Service.

Comstock, G. et al. (1978). *Television and human behavior*. New York: Columbia University Press.

Davie, J. F. and K. C. Wright. (1988). The information poor—disabled persons. In *Unequal access to information resources: Problems and needs of the world's information poor*. Proceedings of the Congress for Librarians, Ann Arbor, Michigan: Pierian Press.

Dervin, B. (1984). *Information needs of California—1984*. Davis, CA: Institute of Governmental Affairs.

Garfield, E. (1973). Is information retrieval in the arts and humanities inherently different from that in science? *Journal of Librarianship 5, 2*, 138–56.

Garvey, W. D. (1979). *Communication: The essence of science*. Oxford: Pergamon.

Greenberg, B. and B. Dervin. (1970). *Use of mass media by urban poor: Findings of three research projects*. New York: Praeger Publishers.

Guest, S. (1987). The use of bibliographic tools by humanities faculty at the State University of New York at Albany. *The Reference Librarian, 18,* 157–72.

Head, A. J. (1990). A survey analysis of supermarket tabloid readership. Unpublished doctoral dissertation, University of California at Berkeley.

Herman, J. (1986). What do the test scores really mean?: Critical issues in test design. Paper commissioned by The Study group on National Assessment of Student Achievement by the U.S. Department of Education.

Kim, J. and C. Mueller. (1978). *Factor analysis: Statistical methods and practical issues.* Sage University Paper #14, Beverly Hills, CA.

Lazarfeld, P.; B. Berelson, and H. Gaudet. (1944). *The people's choice.* New York: Columbia University Press.

Napa Valley College census data system. (1989). Selected Statistics, First Census, Office of Instruction.

Parker, E. and W. J. Paisley. (1966). *Patterns of adult information seeking.* Stanford, CA: Stanford University Press.

Rogers, E. M. and F. F. Shoemaker. (1971/3). *Communication of innovations: A cross cultural approach.* New York: Free Press.

Rowley, J. E. and C. M. D. Turner. (1978). *The dissemination of information.* Boulder, CO: Westview.

Stieg, M. F. (1981). The information needs of historians. *College and Research Libraries, 41,* 549–60.

Stone, S. (1982). Humanities scholars: Information needs and uses. *Journal of Documentation,* 292–313.

Wilson, Patrick, (1980). Limits to the growth of knowledge: The case of the social and behavioral sciences. In Don Swanson, (Ed.), *The role of libraries in the growth of knowledge,* Chicago: Chicago University Press.

12

Reducing Errors in Health-Related Memory: Progress and Prospects

Robert T. Croyle, Elizabeth F. Loftus, Mark R. Klinger,
and Kyle D. Smith

Research conducted by a diverse group of investigators has docu-
mented several kinds of error in health-related memory. These errors
pose significant problems for survey researchers, public health inves-
tigators, and health psychologists. Recent work suggests several
ways in which health-related errors in memory might be minimized.
Some of these efforts are described, and the practical limitations
surrounding attempts to improve memory performance are dis-
cussed. The development of techniques to improve the accuracy of
health-related self-reports that rely on memory is a goal that requires
ongoing collaboration between survey methodologists and experi-
mental psychologists.

Several months ago, an oncologist in Salt Lake City started using a new procedure that has revolutionized his practice. The procedure is extremely simple and it only costs a dollar. At the close of every important office visit, he hands the patient a cassette tape. The tape contains a complete recording of their conversation. According to this physician, the number of phone calls he later receives from these patients has been drastically reduced. More importantly, the incidence of misunderstandings with patients has been nearly eliminated. The explanation appears straightforward: his successful delivery of health care no longer depends on the vicissitudes of human memory.

Most problems caused by failures in health-related memory cannot be remedied so easily. When individuals are asked to recall their health history, for example, it is often impractical or impossible to verify their reports by examining medical records. Nevertheless, investigators and practitioners in a variety of disciplines must often rely on self-reports of health histories. This paper summarizes some recent psychological research concerning memory for health information and events. Our main purpose is not to provide an exhaustive review of research documenting memory failures. Rather, we wish to highlight recent attempts to improve memory performance in the health domain. Reflecting our own research interests, we pay special attention to the improvement of health event memory among survey respondents.

Health-Related Memory

Research on health-related memory has focused on three content areas: doctor-patient communication, dietary behavior, and health events. All three bodies of research have documented substantial problems in memory performance.

Physician Communications

The longest tradition of health memory research lies in the domain of physician-patient communication. Ley (1979) reviewed many of the studies of patients' memory for physician communications. He found that patients typically forget about half of the information presented by their physicians. Recent articles continue to document the widespread forgetting that occurs when patients are given information by physicians (DiMatteo, 1985). The consequences of these cognitive failures are significant. Patients who are uninformed often become dissatisfied and noncompliant (DiMatteo, 1991; Ley, 1986).

The doctor-patient communication literature also contains numerous examples of attempts to improve memory. Most of these have focused on the rehearsal and encoding stages of information processing. For example, Kupst, Dresser, Schulman, & Paul (1975) conducted a study of interactions between physicians and children. They tested the effect of repeating important information on patient recall. Their results indicated that memory performance was increased by 20 percent if either the clinician or child repeated the critical information. Categorizing and simplifying information has also been shown to improve communication. (See Ley, 1982, for a review of these studies.) The intervention strategies used in this research reflect what many investigators believe to be the major barrier to accurate memory performance in this context—the complexity of medical information.

Dietary Behavior

The assessment of dietary behavior has attracted a great deal of attention recently. One reason is that a rapidly growing field of public health research, nutritional epidemiology, relies heavily on self-report measures of dietary intake (Block, 1989). Some of the data concerning errors in diet-related recall are startling. For example, errors in recall occur even if the assessment is conducted immediately after a meal (Guthrie, 1984). Even though substantial errors can be observed after one week, many case control studies in epidemiology require respondents to recall diets that were consumed many years earlier. Memory errors among respondents in such studies can reduce significantly the power of a study to uncover important relationships. In the case of nutritional epidemiology research, this means that scientists may grossly underestimate the link between diet and disease (Hebert & Miller, 1988).

One reason why dietary recall is so difficult is that eating is such a frequent and habitual activity. Dwyer, Krall, & Coleman (1987) have argued that attention, an important determinant of encoding into long-term memory, is typically directed away from the food itself in most meal situations. Therefore, investigators who ask individuals to recall food intake may often be asking for information that was never encoded.

Attempts to improve memory performance in the diet and nutrition domain have met with mixed success. Most of these efforts have used study designs that do not include any verification of actual food intake. For example, Kristal and his colleagues tested the effectiveness of one memory aid during the development of a new, rapid food use checklist (Kristal, Abrahams, Thornquist et al., 1990). Respondents to a telephone survey were read a list of foods and asked which foods they had consumed the previous day. Half of the respondents were first asked a series of questions concerning the meals they had eaten (e.g., "Did you eat breakfast yesterday morning?"). The investigators expected that the preliminary questions about meals might improve the subsequent recall of specific foods eaten. The criterion measure was a comprehensive twenty-four-hour dietary assessment commonly used in epidemiological research. No difference was observed, however, between the two conditions.

Fisher and Quigley (1992) used an extensive cognitive interview procedure in an attempt to improve memory of specific foods eaten at a simulated party. Twenty-six subjects were allowed to select from thirty-four food items at the party. Four to fourteen days later, they were asked to recall the foods they had eaten and the foods they had not selected. Subjects assigned to the cognitive interview group were first asked to remember emotional and physical details of the party context. Extensive follow-up questions and a variety of other memory aids were used. The investigators found that the cognitive interview procedure improved memory performance substantially. Individuals given the cognitive interview recalled twice as many foods as individuals in the control group.

Inferring the Past from the Present

One factor that appears to contribute to systematic bias in dietary recall is the respondent's current diet. A number of studies have retested subjects who previously provided current dietary intake information. This test-retest method has been frequently used by epidemiologists to assess the validity of memory-based self-reports. Several of these studies have shown that recalled diets are more similar to current ones than to the original diet (e.g., Thompson, Lamphiear, Metzner, Hawthhorne, & Oh, 1987; Wu, Whittemore, & Jung, 1988). This is a fairly robust effect, for it has been observed across studies that employed different instruments and procedures (e.g., Byers, Rosenthal, Marshall et al., 1983).

Ross (1989) has proposed an explanation for the effect of current status on recall. He argues that individuals have implicit theories of stability and change concerning themselves that serve as guides when inferring past behavior. When individuals believe that they have consistently behaved in a certain manner, memory errors will tend to exaggerate the similarity between the present and the past. This is the type of effect so frequently observed in the dietary behavior studies discussed above. Ross's theory goes beyond this finding and predicts that memory can also overestimate the differences between the past and the present. When individuals believe they have changed, even when they have not, errors in recall will reflect this. This may explain why participants in pain treatment programs display errors of overestimation when recalling their level of disability before treatment (Linton & Melin, 1982). Together, these findings suggest that the effect of current diet on recall may be inversely related for weight-loss program participants.

If people infer the past from the present, an assessment of perceived change might be used to derive a more accurate measure of previous health behaviors. One group of investigators examined whether a measure of perceived change in diet could be used along with an assessment of current diet to predict previous diet. Byers, Marshall, Anthony et al. (1987) interviewed 323 persons who had been interviewed about their diet an average of six years earlier. In addition to the reassessment of current diet, subjects were asked whether their consumption of each food had increased, decreased, or stayed the same. When averaged across all subjects, perceived change was correctly related to actual change for all but two of the forty-seven food items. Nevertheless, subjects tended to overestimate their earlier consumption of foods, a finding that Ross's model would predict, given that perceived decreases in consumption were more common than perceived increases. Unfortunately, an estimate of past diet created by adjusting current diet for perceived change did not correlate more highly with the original diet than did the retrospective report. Future research might examine whether a more sensitive measure of perceived change can improve inferentially based measures of prior health behavior.

Memory for Health Events

There is now a large accumulation of published work documenting failures in memory for health events. A wide variety of health events have been studied. These include poisoning episodes, hospitalizations, illness episodes, and physician visits (Fowler, 1989). Generally, this research has shown that these kinds of health events are poorly remembered when recall is measured more than a month after the event. There are some exceptions, of course. For example, the accuracy of self-reports of cancer diagnoses is relatively high (e.g., Brambilla, Bifano, McKinlay & Clapp, 1989).

Although the error produced by failures in event memory is often assumed by public health investigators to be random, systematic biases have also been documented. Recent evidence has shown that the communication of health status information can affect memory for previous health activities. This type of labeling effect was examined by Croyle and Sande (1988). They tested subjects for a fictitious enzyme deficiency that the subjects were led to believe was a risk factor for pancreatic disorders. Half of the subjects were told they had the deficiency and half were told they did not have it. Subjects were then asked to recall the number of times they had performed several health behaviors during the previous month. Because subjects received randomly assigned test results, no actual differences in health behavior should have occurred. Nevertheless, subjects who had tested positive for the enzyme deficiency reported more health behaviors that supposedly contributed to the deficiency than did subjects who tested negative. Positive test subjects also tended to remember more symptoms associated with the deficiency.

Croyle and Uretsky (1987) examined the effect of current mood on the recall of health histories. They recruited subjects for a "film project" in which they were asked to rate clips of several popular movies. Subjects were randomly assigned to view either happy or sad film clips. After this phase of the experiment was finished, participants were asked by a second experimenter to participate in a health survey. After moving to another lab room, subjects completed a questionnaire that contained several questions about their health history. The results revealed a significant effect of the mood manipulation on memories of symptom episodes. Subjects who had viewed the sad film remembered substantially more physical symptoms during the previous month than did subjects who saw the happy film.

Verification Problems

Many studies of health-related memory do not include a verification of the accuracy of subjects' responses. There are two reasons for this. The first and most obvious reason is practical. It is often difficult or impossible to recover records or documents to verify autobiographical memories. Medical records can be incomplete or inaccurate, and most important health behaviors occur outside of the medical care context (Chrisman & Kleinman, 1983). Investigators have contrived a number of ingenious methods for obtaining verification in naturalistic settings. In one recent case, public health researchers resorted to videotaping cafeteria trays in order to verify twenty-four-hour dietary recalls of elderly women (Brown, Tharp, Dahlberg-Luby et al., 1990).

The second reason for not seeking verification is less obvious but important nonetheless. Many researchers are interested primarily in how memories are organized, and how, over time, they distort or change. These investigators are content to try to understand the structure and retrieval of autobiographical memories without worrying about how that structure relates to past reality. For example, a number of interesting theoretical questions can be tested simply by measuring the *relative* difference in performance produced by different recall strategies.

When we move to the health memory domain, however, it is clear that most of the consumers of this research are interested primarily in accuracy and how to improve it. A major challenge for health memory researchers is to combine the experimental control and theoretical rigor of the laboratory with the labor-intensive demands of the verification process. In this way, theoretical advances can be achieved in a manner that also contributes directly to the public health sciences.

Improving Memory for Health Events

Now that we know about the many problems of health-related memory, we can consider some possible solutions. Traditionally, solutions for memory errors in public health research have focused on sample size or statistical analyses. One reason why health surveys often recruit a large number of respondents is that a large sample size is assumed to minimize the effect of random error variance attributable to poor memory. This is a common strategy in nutritional epidemiology research, where reports of dietary behavior are plagued by inaccuracy (Dwyer, Krall, & Coleman, 1987).

Ideally, strategies for improving memory should be both theoretically sound and practically useful. These two criteria are not necessarily compatible. Means and Loftus (1991) tested the effectiveness of two techniques derived from research and theory in cognitive psychology. They conducted lengthy in-depth interviews with members of a health-maintenance organization, asking each to describe all of the occasions during the previous twelve months on which they had seen a staff member concerning their physical health. Reported incidents were then compared with medical records. These comparisons revealed relatively poor memory for events of a recurring nature. Two techniques, Time Line and Decomposition, were successful in enhancing memory for recurring events. The time-consuming nature of these techniques (about ninety minutes per subject), however, makes them impractical to use in most situations.

Time Frames

One type of error that has been the focus of several recent investigations is telescoping (Sudman & Bradburn, 1973). Telescoping occurs when an event is remembered as having occurred more recently than it actually did. For example, one study examined patients' reports of pap smear histories and compared these reports to medical records (Walter, Clarke, Hatcher, & Stitt, 1988). When the women were asked about the length of time that had passed since their last smear, they reported the smears as being more recent than the records indicated.

The use of time frames holds promise as a simple and effective means of reducing this type of memory error. Crespi and Swinehart (1982), for example, asked respondents which of several actions (had blood pressure checked, had physical exam, had eye exam, etc.) they had taken in the past two months. Other respondents were first asked whether they had engaged in each behavior during the past six months, and then asked the two month question. When the six-month question was asked first, affirmative responses to the two-month question averaged 12 percent less than when the two month question was asked alone. For example, when asked the six month question first, 11 percent claimed to have had an eye exam in the last two months, 32 percent claimed to have had their blood pressure checked, 20 percent claimed to have had a physical exam. However, if the two-month question was asked alone, these figures were higher: 23 percent, 48 percent, and 32 percent respectively. In short, the two-time frame questioning procedure produced quite different estimates of the extent to which respondents engaged in the various health-related activities.

While the two time-frame procedure reduced the number of affirmative responses, did it lead to more reporting? Crespi and Swinehart did not verify respondent's reports, but they had several reasons for believing that the lower reports were more accurate. Nonetheless, they appealed to future researchers to reinvestigate their method with personal memories that could be verified.

Recently, Loftus, Smith, Klinger & Fiedler (1992) conducted several experiments to test methods for enhancing memory for health events. The project was conducted in collaboration with Group Health Cooperative (GHC) of Puget Sound, the largest consumer-governed health maintenance organization in the United States. The Center for Health Studies at GHC conducts telephone surveys of Group Health clientele on a regular basis, using standardized questionnaires from which interviewers read. Loftus et al. used this survey as a vehicle for conducting their experiments. Most importantly, the accuracy of responses was examined through an audit of respondents' medical records.

One of the Loftus et al. studies followed up on the Crespi and Swinehart study (Loftus, Klinger, Smith, & Fiedler, 1990). Why do people report fewer activities within a two-month period if they are first asked about activities within six months? There are a number of hypotheses. First, it is possible that events from three and four months ago are "captured" by the six-month question and thus do not need to be reported in response to the two-month question. Forward telescoping due to response bias factors is prevented by the six-month question. Second, the need to demonstrate a socially desirable concern for health matters can be satisfied when respondents answer the six-month question; they may not need to demonstrate this concern again for the two-month question. Finally, it is possible that the two-time frame procedure conveys that the interviewer wants greater precision in dating than the single time frame question might imply.

These possible explanations were tested by comparing the effects of three time frame procedures. The critical measure was the number of activities reported for the previous two months. Some subjects were first asked about activities in the previous month. Others were first asked about the previous six months. In a third condition, respondents were first asked about the 2-month period and then were asked about the 6-month period.

Crespi and Swinehart showed that people reported fewer activities in the two month period when asked about a longer reference period first.

Would people also report fewer activities when asked about a shorter reference period first? If the percentage reporting an activity were reduced when a shorter period came first, what explanations could account for this result? The precision hypothesis would predict that respondents who were first asked about one month, and then about two months, might sense a greater demand for precision and respond more accurately to the two-month question. The telescoping explanation for the two-time frame effect would predict that asking about a shorter reference period first would not improve accuracy over a single time frame question.

The data revealed massive overreporting. Overreporting was highest, however, when patients were asked about the two-month period first. For example, overreporting for blood pressure checks was more than twice as high in the 2-month first condition than in the other two. Loftus et al. argue that the reason is that the preliminary question conveys that the interviewer desires greater accuracy in responding. Asking about the six-month period first reduced overreporting, but so did asking about one month first (see Abelson, Loftus, & Greenwald, 1992, for another test of the time frame procedure).

Retrieval Order

One approach to studying ways to improve memory is to first document the procedures that individuals use to recall certain material. Once these strategies have been identified, alternative strategies can be provided to subjects and tested against their typical or preferred strategy (Bradburn, Rips, & Shevell, 1987). This is the approach that has been used to study the role of retrieval order in event memory performance.

When an individual attemp₁s to retrieve multiple memories, there are different orders in which they can be retrieved. Some research shows a tendency to recall in a forward direction, starting with the most temporally distant memory and proceeding toward the more recent (e.g., Fathi, Schooler & Loftus, 1984; King & Pontious, 1969). Fathi et al. asked subjects to recall all the times in the preceding twelve months when they had visited a health care professional or facility. Subjects had to "think out loud" as they responded, and their comments were recorded. Analyses of the response protocols showed that for those who recalled more than one health event, recall tended to be in a forward direction: Subjects would typically start with the most distant instance and then report the next most distant, etc. The accuracy of their recall was not established.

A recent experiment examined the effects of different retrieval orders on the accuracy of health event memory (Loftus, Smith, Klinger, & Fiedler, 1992). The study also included a free recall group that were not directed to recall material in any particular order. As in the Fathi et al. experiment, respondents were asked to recall health events that had occurred during the previous year. The subjects were 329 members of the health maintenance organization described earlier. Responses of all of these subjects were compared to their medical records.

Subjects who had been randomly assigned to the forward condition were asked, "I'd like to ask you about the visits you have made to Group Health Cooperative for health care over the past 12 months. Starting with the first visit you made in the past 12 months, and then coming forward to the next one, and so on, will you tell me the month of each visit, and the provider you saw?" Other subjects were assigned to the backward condition and were asked to begin with the most recent visit. In the free recall condition, respondents were asked, "I'd like to ask you about the visits you have made to Group Health Cooperative for health care over the past 12 months. Will you tell me the month of each one, and the provider you saw?"

Regardless of version, when the subject had finished providing the list of specific visits, he or she was asked, "In all, how many visits did you make to Group Health Cooperative for health care during the past 12 months?" Thus it was possible for a subject to recall, say, two specific visits, but to estimate that in all there were more than two visits actually made.

The results showed that respondents specifically recalled an average 45 percent of their actual visits. Subjects in the forward retrieval condition recalled the fewest visits; those in the backward retrieval group recalled the most. However, these differences were not statistically significant. When subjects were asked to estimate the total number of visits for the year, the number increased to 87 percent of the actual number. There was also evidence of telescoping. About two-thirds of misdating errors reflected forward telescoping. Other common memory phenomena were replicated as well. As would be expected from a standard forgetting curve, for example, older visits were more likely to be forgotten.

The investigators conducted further analyses of these data that provide some additional insights into the retrieval process. In the free recall group, 44 percent of those with more than one visit used a forward order, while 22 percent of them used a backward order. Thus, there was a preference for forward order even though this strategy does not yield greater accuracy.

This study also examined the relationship between individual difference variables and accuracy scores. Contrary to folk wisdom, accuracy was unrelated to education, age, and subjective health status. An interesting but unexplained sex difference was observed as well. The recall of women was significantly more accurate than that of men.

Discussion

Research on health-related memory has focused on three content areas: doctor-patient communication, dietary behavior, and health events. Research in all three domains has documented important memory errors. Recently, investigators have shifted their focus toward the development of memory enhancement strategies. Interventions in each area have targeted different aspects of the memory process. Attempts to improve memory for physician communications have focused on rehearsal and encoding processes. Successful strategies have included categorization, simplification, and repetition of information. Attempts to improve memory for dietary intake have a shorter history, and the results so far have been mixed. Multiple strategies have shown some success, but less time-consuming interventions have not. Several studies have examined methods for improving health event memory, but only the most recent studies have included verifications of accuracy. Unfortunately, these three lines of work have been conducted largely in isolation from one another. One goal of health memory researchers should be the integration of findings and theory from these three lines of work.

This paper has focused on memory for health events. Several kinds of errors in health event memory have been described. Although health-related events are often assumed to be generally underreported, recent research has shown that this is not the case. Visits to medical facilities are underreported, but specific procedures are overreported (see also Walter, Clarke, Hatcher, & Stitt, 1988). When reporting health visits, respondents tend to report in a forward chronological order. However, when respondents are asked to recall these events in reverse order, the accuracy of their reports improves. Overreporting can be reduced by first asking people about a different reference period. This simple procedure improves the accuracy of reports for the critical period of interest.

Much of the recent work concerning cognitive aspects of health surveys was stimulated by a 1983 meeting conducted by the Committee on National Statistics. With support from the National Science Foundation, the meeting brought together survey specialists, cognitive scientists, and statisticians to discuss cognitive aspects of survey methodology (Jabine, Straf, Tanur, & Tourangeau, 1984). This conference encouraged the development of new collaborative research programs that were interdisciplinary in nature. This research is beginning to bear fruit, but a large number of questions remain to be answered (Croyle & Loftus, in press). Although the focus to date has been on the potential contributions of cognitive psychology to survey methodology, the survey context also provides a rich context within which to test theories of information processing, memory, and congitive function (Loftus, Fienberg, & Tanur, 1985). The study of health memory involves more than the application of basic theory and research on human memory. It also provides a complex and naturalistic context within which the realtionships between illness, communication, and memory can be uncovered.

The authors would like to acknowledge the support of grants HS 05521 from the National Center for Health Services Research and Health Care Technology Assessment and HS 06660 from the Agency for Health Care Policy and Research.

References

Abelson, R. P., Loftus, E. F., & Greenwald, A. G. (1992). Attempts to improve the accuracy of self-reports of voting. In J. Tanur (Ed.), *Questions about survey questions: Inquiries into the cognitive bases of surveys,* 138–53. New York: Russell Sage.

Block, G. (1989). Human dietary assessment: Methods and issues. *Preventive Medicine, 18,* 653–60.

Bradburn, N. M., Rips, L. J., & Shevell, S. K. (1987). Answering autobiographical questions: The impact of memory and inference on surveys. *Science, 236,* 157–61.

Brambilla, D. J., Bifano, N. L., McKinlay, S. M., & Clapp, R. W. (1989). Validity of self-reports of cancer incidence in a prospective study. In F. J. Fowler (Ed.), *Health survey research methods* (pp. 77–89). DHHS Publication No. (PHS) 89-3447.

Brown, J. E., Tharp, T. M., Dahlberg-Luby, E. M., Snowden, D. A., Ostwald, S. K., Buzzard, I. M., Rysavy, S. D. M., & Wieser, S. M. A. (1990). Videotape dietary assessment: Validity, reliability, and comparison of results with 24-hour dietary recalls from elderly women in a retirement home. *Journal of the American Dietetic Association, 90,* 1675–79.

Byers, T. E., Rosenthal, R. I., Marshall, J. R., Rzepka, T. F., Cummings, K. M. & Graham, S. (1983). Dietary history from the distant past: A methodological study. *Nutrition in Cancer, 5,* 69–77.

Byers, T., Marshall, J., Anthony, E., Fiedler, R., & Zielezny, M. (1987). The reliability of dietary history from the distant past. *American Journal of Epidemiology, 125,* 999–1011.

Chrisman, N. J. & Kleinman, A. (1983). Popular health care, social networks, and cultural meanings: The orientation of medical anthropology. In D. Mechanic (Ed.), *Handbook of Health, Health Care, and the Health Professions,* (pp. 569–590). New York: Free Press.

Crespi, I., & Swinehart, J. W. (1982). Some effects of sequenced questions using different time intervals on behavioral self-reports: A field experiment. Unpublished manuscript.

Croyle, R. T., & Loftus, E. F. (1992). Improving episodic memory performance of survey respondents. In J. Tanur (Ed.), *Questions about survey questions: Inquiries into the cognitive bases of surveys*, 95–101. New York: Russell Sage.

Croyle, R. T., & Sande, G. N. (1988). Denial and confirmatory search: Paradoxical consequences of medical diagnosis. *Journal of Applied Social Psychology, 18*, 473–90.

Croyle, R. T., & Uretsky, M. B. (1987). Effects of mood on self-appraisal of health status. *Health Psychology, 6*, 239–53.

DiMatteo, M. R. (1985). Physician-patient communication: Promoting a positive health care setting. In J. C. Rosen & L. J. Solomon (Eds.), *Prevention in health psychology* (pp. 328–65). Hanover, NH: University Press of New England.

DiMatteo, M. R. (1991). *The psychology of health, illness, and medical care: An individual perspective.* Pacific Grove, CA: Brooks/Cole.

Dwyer, J. T., Krall, E. A., & Coleman, K. A. (1987). The problem of memory in nutritional epidemiology research. *Journal of the American Dietetic Association, 87*, 1509–12.

Fathi, D. C., Schooler, J. W., & Loftus, E. F. (1984). Moving survey problems to the cognitive psychology laboratory. Paper presented at the Annual Meeting of the American Statistical Association.

Fisher, R. P., & Quigley, K. L. (1992). Applying cognitive theory in public health investigations: Enhancing food recall with the cognitive interview. In J. Tanur (Ed.), *Questions about survey questions: Inquiries into the cognitive bases of surveys*, 154–69. New York: Russell Sage.

Fowler, F. J. (ed.) (1989). *Health survey research methods.* DHHS Publication No. (PHS) 89-3447.

Guthrie, H. A. (1984). Selection and quantification of typical food portions by young adults. *Journal of the American Dietetic Association, 84*, 1440–44.

Hebert, J. R., & Miller, D. R. (1988). Methodologic considerations for investigating the diet-cancer link. *American Journal of Clinical Nutrition, 47*, 1068–77.

Jabine, T., Straf, M., Tanur, J. M., & Tourangeau, R. (1984). *Cognitive aspects of survey methodology: Building a bridge between disciplines.* Washington, DC: National Academy Press.

King, D. L., & Pontious, R. H. (1969). Time relations in the recall of events of the day. *Psychonomic Science, 17*, 339–40.

Kristal, A. R., Abrahams, B. F., Thornquist, M. D., Disogra, L., Croyle, R. T., Shattuck, A. L. & Henry, H. J. (1990). Development and validation of a food use checklist for evaluation of community nutrition interventions. *American Journal of Public Health, 80*, 1318–22.

Kupst, M. J., Dresser, K., Schulman, J. L., & Paul, M. H. (1975). Evaluation of methods to improve communication in the physician-patient relationship. *American Journal of Orthopsychiatry, 45*, 420–29.

Ley, P. (1979). Memory for medical information. *British Journal of Social and Clinical Psychology, 18*, 245–56.

Ley, P. (1982). Giving information to patients. In J. R. Eiser (Ed.), *Social psychology and behavioral medicine* (pp. 339–373). London: John Wiley & Sons Ltd.

Ley, P. (1986). Cognitive variables and noncompliance. *Journal of Compliance in Health Care, 1*, 171–88.

Linton, S. J., & Melin, L. (1982). The accuracy of remembering chronic pain. *Pain, 13*, 281–85.

Loftus, E. F., Fienberg, S. E., & Tanur, J. M. (1985). Cognitive psychology meets the national survey. *American Psychologist, 40*, 175–80.

Loftus, E. F., Klinger, M. R., Smith, K. D., & Fiedler, J. (1990). A tale of two questions: Benefits of asking more than one question. *Public Opinion Quarterly, 54,* 330–45.

Loftus, E. F., Smith, K. D., Klinger, M. R., & Fiedler, J. (1992). Memory and mismemory for health events. In J. Tanur (Ed.), *Questions about survey questions: Inquiries into the cognitive bases of surveys,* 102–37. New York: Russell Sage.

Means, B., & Loftus, E. F. (1991). When personal history repeats itself: Decomposing memories for recurring events. *Applied Cognitive Psychology, 5,* 297–318.

Ross, M. (1989). Relation of implicit theories to the construction of personal histories. *Psychological Review, 96,* 341–57.

Sudman, S., & Bradburn, N. M. (1973). Effects of time and memory factors on response in surveys. *Journal of the American Statistical Association, 68,* 805–15.

Thompson, F. E., Lamphiear, D. E., Metzner, H. L., Hawthorne, V. M., & Oh, M. S. (1987). Reproducibility of reports of frequency of food use in the Tecumseh Diet Methodology Study. *American Journal of Epidemiology, 125,* 658–71.

Walter, S. D., Clarke, E. A., Hatcher, J., & Stitt, L. W. (1988). A comparison of physician and patient reports of pap smear histories. *Journal of Clinical Epidemiology, 41,* 401–10.

Wu, M. L., Whittemore, A. S., & Jung, D. L. (1988). Errors in reported dietary intakes. *American Journal of Epidemiology, 128,* 1137–45.

13

Children's Interest in Computers: A Social Cognitive Perspective

Steven Pulos and Sarah Fisher

This chapter addresses tne role of computers in the lives of children and adolescents. Social scientists and educators have predicted that computers are inherently interesting and motivating to children. Consequently, they predict that computers will solve problems of academic motivation and social inequities. Four studies are reported in this chapter that suggest that most typical children and adolescents are indifferent to computers, regardless of gender and social economic status. They are not interested in them at the current time and do not appear to be interested in using them as adults. Experience with computers in school seems to lead to decreased interest, while contact with computer users outside of school seemed to lead to increased interest. Interest in computers appear to be related to social learning and the media's portrayal of computers and computer users, rather than to any intrinsic properties of computers.

Computers are entering the lives of children at an ever increasing rate. Many social scientists and educators claim that this will have a profound effect on the education and social development of children. They claim that children are so interested in computers that they will be motivated to: (a) learn in school, thereby increasing academic performance and reducing behavior problems (Greenfield, 1984; Donahoo, 1986; Levin, 1985); (b) learn about computers, thereby preparing them for life in a computerized society (Pantiel & Petersen, 1985; Turkle, 1984); and (c) interact with children they would not otherwise encounter, thus breaking down social barriers (Paisley, 1985). On the negative side others claim that children are so interested in computers that they may be seduced away from social interactions and become social isolates (Barnes & Hill, 1983; Ingber, 1981; Sigel & Markoff, 1985; Tittnich & Brown, 1982).

Important policy implications follow from these views. If the positive claims are valid, then we have a powerful tool for solving the problems of low academic motivation and social inequities. Such a tool is deserving of considerable support in time, effort and finance. If the negative claims are true, then we need to implement programs to alleviate the resulting social isolation.

Yet there is another possibility, computers may not be motivating to children. Consequently, expenditures based on the assumption that computers can solve problems of motivation and social inequities may be futile and can actually divert resources away from more fruitful endeavors.

Furthermore, if children are not interested in computers and we wish to prepare them for life in a computerized society, then we may wish to find ways of interesting them in computers. Otherwise computers may be just another boring aspect of school, that is soon forgotten by students.

In spite of the claims and policy implications, we know very little about children's interest in computers. Most studies on children and computers are concerned with cognitive consequences, and not with the social-affective aspects of the interaction. Two reviewers of computers and affect (Leeper, 1984; Lieberman, 1985) have made strong claims about the motivational and attitudinal effects of computers on children. Yet they cited few studies. The ones they did cite were based upon atypical computer experiences, such as university-run interventions, or investigations of gifted or learning delayed children. Few studies examined the impact of computers in typical settings with typical children.

The few studies that do exist appear to have serious methodological flaws that have plagued both research on computers (Clark, 1983, 1984) and interests (Rust, 1977). These problems include:

1. *A failure to control for the effect of "novelty" or the Hawthorne effect.* When a computer or a new computer curriculum is first introduced, children may show greater interest because of novelty, not because of the computer per se (Clark, 1983, 1984, Lipinski, Nade, Shade, & Watson, 1984).
2. *A confusion between interests and preference* (Getzel, 1966). A child faced with a choice of activities in school may prefer one to the other, but may not be interested in either.
3. *A failure to consider the contribution of historical time* (Schaie, 1965). It may be inappropriate to generalize from older studies to the current

generation. Children and society may be less interested in computers than they were a decade ago. There has been a decrease in home computer sales, and the decline of interest in computer related careers (Astin, 1986).

4. *A tendency to generalize from atypical samples.* Often, studies are conducted on upper middle class students in a university town. Yet it is widely known that differences in SES (Social-Economic-Status) are associated with qualitative differences in the way adolescents and children view knowledge, its use and the goals of schooling (Anyon, 1981; Bowles, S. & Gintis, H., 1976; Coleman, 1966; Ogbu, 1974). Further, early research with adults (Lee, 1966) has found SES to play a major role in people's attitudes toward computers.

5. *A reliance upon a single method of assessment.* Different modes of assessing interest can produce very different results (Rust, 1977). Generalizing from a single method can be misleading.

Accordingly, the existing research may lead us to faulty generalizations about children's interest in computers, and tell us little about the feelings of typical children in typical schools.

Those who claim that children are highly interested in computers tend to focus on the characteristics of computers that make them appealing to children (Condry & Keith, 1983, Lawton & Gerschner, 1982; Leeper, 1985; Leiberman, 1985), for example, their ability to respond with immediate and constant feedback. Some claim that children may be interested in computers because of transfer from positive experience with video games (e.g., Fisher, 1983). Yet interests are complex and determined by psychological factors as well as by the characteristics of the object (Eagle, 1983).

Social factors are a primary determinate of children's beliefs and behaviors. Interests are shaped by the beliefs and behavior of children's peers and parents (Baumrind, 1986, Youniss, 1980) and by children's perceptions of the role models they encounter (Bandura, 1986). From a social cognitive point of view, it is quite likely that children's interests in computers are determined by their social world, rather than by the characteristics of the computer per se.

To understand children's interest in computers we need to know how children view the computer user. Children's interests appear to be highly related to their perception of peers' interests and attitudes (Chi, 1966; Coleman, 1961, 1966; Gordon, 1971). For example, if children think their peers see computer users as asocial and unpopular, they may avoid computers because they don't want to be seen in an unfavorable light by their peers.

For the same reason it is important to examine children's contact with computer users. According to social cognitive theory such role models have a major impact on children's interests and behavior (Bandura, 1986).

Orientation to present research

The following questions were the starting point for this investigation: (a) how interested are typical children in computers; (b) how do they view their computer using peers; and (c) what are some of the factors related to an interest in computers. To reduce methodological bias and to attain increasing specificity, we conducted four studies that differed in methodology and focus. While the studies differed, they had a common focus. First, we looked at children in typical classes in middle- and lower middle-class schools (we avoided students in either remedial or accelerated classes). Second, we selected schools that had typical computer studies and avoided sites that had special support from a university or industry. Third, we selected sites that had an intact computer program for the academic year prior to the study. Fourth, we took a broad view of "interest in computers," rather than preference for computers. For example, rather than looking at a specific preference for a computer versus a workbook, we examined interest in computer usage versus other activities that children and adolescents chose to engage in.

Study I

Study I was designed to examine interest in computers among early adolescents. It was also concerned with whether interest varied as a function of SES, computer studies, and gender. Methodologically, Study I employed an unobtrusive interview. It focused on interests and activities, without explicitly mentioning computers. If adolescents were highly interested in computers, then they should have spontaneously mentioned them as an important part of their lives.

Method

The subjects were eighth-grade students from four schools that differed in SES and computer curriculum. Sixty students (thirty males and thirty females) were selected from typical classes in each school. Remedial or accelerated classes were not included.

School A was in a middle-class suburb and had an intensive computer curriculum. The ethnic makeup was predominantly white. The computer curriculum consisted of computer assisted instructions, games, simulations, computer literacy classes, experience with word processing, and programming in BASIC. Students had spent at least one hour a week working with the computer since the sixth grade.

School B was similar to School A in educational and socioeconomic level, but differed from it in ethnic composition and computer curriculum. It was predominantly black and Asian. The computer curriculum consisted of relatively extensive computer literacy classes with irregular usage of computers during the year. The computers were used primarily for computer assisted instructions and games.

School C was located in a lower middle-class urban area. The ethnic makeup of School C was similar to School B. Children in School C were told about computers in their class, and were exposed to them primarily through demonstrations.

School D was in a lower socioeconomic area of a city. The ethnic composition was predominantly black and Hispanic. There was no computer curriculum in School D.

After the children were interviewed, a subset of children in each school were asked if they had a computer in the home. The highest percentage of computers was reported in school A (29 percent) and the lowest was reported in School C (12 percent), Schools B and D reported 19 percent and 16 percent respectively. Except School A, the results were typical for the state (Law, 1982).

The students were individually interviewed by trained examiners representing each ethnic groups in the sample. Approximately half the students were tested by members of their ethnic group.

The students were asked about: (a) how they spent their time outside school; (b) what were the best and worst parts of their day in school; and (c) what were their most and least favorite classes in school. They were also asked about the reason for their choices.

Results

Computer use was rarely mentioned, either as an activity outside school or as a favorite or least favorite activity in school. Only two students, boys in School A, mentioned that they used computers during their free time after school. None of the students mentioned computer class as their most or least favorite class; but eight students mentioned computers with other courses as "favorites" (six in School A and two in School B). Upon specific query, these students mentioned liking computer classes because: (a) they could talk to friends; (b) they didn't get homework; (c) they thought computers were important; or (d) they thought it was fun. Fewer students in each school mentioned computer class as the favorite, than mentioned either math or science class. This is not a finding consistent with the view that children have a great interest in computers.

Discussion

These results suggest that computers are not a large part of the adolescent's lives in any of the four schools. Regardless of the socioeconomic class, computers were rarely mentioned. Despite the curriculum, computers were not a least or most favorite part of school for most students. It was surprising that students who attended a school with a rich computer environment and frequently had computers in their home, did not spontaneously mention computers much more than children with far more limited experience with computers.

Study II

Study II was designed to replicate the results of Study I employing a different methodology and to investigate possible reasons for children's low interest in computers. According to social cognitive theory, a child's interest is determined in large part by the interests and perceived views of his or her peer group. Accordingly, Study II was aimed at examining children's views of computers and computer users.

To understand something about the kind of activity children perceive computer usage to be, we examined the interests in noncomputer activities that were associated with an interest in computer usage. For example if children who like computers also like math games and children who do not like computers do not like math games, we may hypothesize that children see something similar about these two activities.

Method

A survey was developed to assess adolescent's interests in computers and other activities. These activities were selected from frequently reported interests in Study I. All activities reported by over 10 percent of the students in the middle-class schools were included in the survey with the addition of a computer item and items about their interest in mathematics and science. These two items were included due to their frequently assumed association with computers.

The interest survey consisted of fourteen nine-point Likert scale items. The adolescents were asked to rate how much they would like to do each activity. They were told that the questionnaire was a survey of teenager's interests. No emphasis was placed upon computers over the other items.

After completing the questionnaire the students were given a separate sheet of paper and were asked to describe "what kind of kids like computers?" This question was given after the survey because it was felt that it could influence the response to it.

The students completed the interest survey and open-ended question without identifying themselves. The responses were kept anonymous to facilitate truthful responding. This procedure had the disadvantage, however, of preventing the two parts of the questionnaire from being correlated.

The reliabilities for the items in the interest survey were estimated from their communality in a factor analysis of the fourteen items. Since communalities are the lower bounds for reliability, the actual reliability is equal to or higher than the communality (Harmon, 1976, p. 20). All items had acceptable reliabilities with communalities ranging from .61 to .82.

The questionnaire was given to 150 adolescents in grades six, seven, and eight at a middle-class junior high. All had been exposed to computers for the proceeding six months, with at least weekly visits to the computer lab. Most of them had also been exposed to computers in school since the fourth grade. The computer program at this school was one of the best in the area and served as an exemplary model for other schools. The sixth grade students had experience with computer assisted instructions and computer literacy, but by the eighth grade the students also had some experience with word processing and programming in BASIC.

Results

Interests in computers. Although all the adolescents in this study are routinely exposed to computers, most of them did not express great interest in computers (Mean 5.04, Standard Deviation 2.70, Mode 5). A grade-by-gender analysis of variance found no significant change in computer interest across the three grades, and no significant gender difference.

Compared to the other activities computer usage was placed rather low. Only homework, housework and mathematics were ranked lower than computers. In a series of Wilcoxon matched-pair tests, interest in computers was significantly lower (p < .001) than all other interests, except playing board games, doing puzzles, science, homework, housework and mathematics.

Patterns of interests associated with an interest in computers. As a first step toward examining the pattern of interests associated with an interest in computers, a principal component analysis (Harmon, 1976) was conducted on the interest survey. These principal components and other variables were then related to computer interest in a multiple regression.

The principal component analysis was conducted on all the interest items, except computers and video games. The resulting principal components represented general classes of interests. The computer and video games were not included because we were interested in them as specific variables. Video games have been hypothesized to have a unique facilitating effect on interest in computers (e.g., Fisher, 1983) and was kept as a specific variable. The results of the principal component analysis are summarized in table 13.1.

Three principal components were found. The components represent general interests and can be characterized as: (a) intellectual interest; (b) adult-approving interests for example, homework, housework; and (c) typical adolescent interest, for example, listening to music, watching television, being with friends. The second component, adult-approving interests, probably reflects a tolerance of these activities rather than an actual interest, since almost no adolescent gave them a high rating. Component scores were calculated for each principal component (Harmon, 1976).

To examine the relations between computer interests and the other variables a hierarchical-stepwise multiple regression (Cohen & Cohen, 1975) was conducted with the computer item as the dependent variable. The independent variables were entered in blocks in the following order: (a) general interests (Typical, Adult-Approving, and Intellectual); (b) an

TABLE 13.1
Principal Component Analysis of Interests Survey (Study II)

Items	PRINCIPAL COMPONENTS		
	I	II	III
Playing Board Games	.76	−.08	−.04
Doing Puzzles	.72	−.11	.10
Science	.61	.24	−.01
Reading	.54	.21	−.40
Doing Hobbies	.52	.11	.29
Homework	−.05	.82	−.11
Housework	−.01	.81	.01
Mathematics	.26	.70	−.09
Being with Friends	.12	.08	.75
Playing Sports	.10	.04	.58
Listen to Music	−.08	−.08	.47
Watching TV	−.01	−.23	.45
% Variance Extracted	20.3	15.9	11.7

Note: Component I = Intellectual Interests, Component II = Adult Approving Interests, Component III = Typical Interests.

interest in video games; (c) grade and gender; and (d) the interaction terms. Within each block the variables were allowed to enter in a stepwise manner. This order followed from our belief that general interests must be considered before specific interests, for example, video games. The results of the regression are summarized in table 13.2.

The results found that an interest in computers was only related to intellectual interests and video games. The interactions were not significant, suggesting that the effect of these variables is the same in all grades and for both genders. None of the other variables had a significant simple correlation with computer interest.

An interest in computers was primarily related to the principal component of intellectual interests. Twenty-three percent of the variance in computer interest was explained by intellectual interest, while only four percent of the variance was explained by an interest in video games. This suggests that those children with high intellectual interests are more likely to be interested in computers, and those with low intellectual interests are less likely to be interested in computers.

Stereotypes About Computer Users. One of the goals of this study was to examine adolescent's description of their peers who liked computers. The students' responses fell into three categories: intelligent (44.2 percent), ordinary (30.2 percent), and negative/miscellaneous comments—for example, "unpopular," "stupid" (25.6 percent). Few references to gender or racial stereotypes occurred (2.3 percent). Thus, about two-thirds of the students did not see computer users as typical.

Discussion

First, it appears that most adolescents who are exposed to computers in school are not highly interested in them. Thus, with different methods, Study II supports the main findings of Study I.

Second, children show little difference across grade, and computer experience, in their attitudes and interests. This recalls the lack of differences across sites in Study I, and suggests that mere exposure to computers may have little effect on interest.

TABLE 13.2
Significant Predictors of Interests in Computers (Study II)

Variable	Simple r	Beta
Intellectual Interests	.48***	.48***
Interest in Video Games	.21**	.20**

** = p < .01
*** = p < .001

Third, an interest in computers appears to be associated with intellectual interests by most adolescents. Almost half the adolescents considered those who like computers to be intelligent. This pervasive association of computers with intellectual activities and interests may lead adolescents to avoid computers. Many adolescents tend to view intellectually oriented students as unpopular and do not like to be seen as intellectually oriented (Baumrind, 1986; Coleman, 1966; Gordon, 1972). Children and adolescents seem to know that friendship requires shared interests (Youniss, 1980), and believe that if they have different interests from their popular peers they are not likely to be popular.

Fourth, there was a slight relation between and interest in computers and an interest in video games. Yet it is not known if an interest in video games predates, postdates or co-occur with an interest in computer. Nevertheless, it appears that video games may be an alternative path to interests in computer. One that is not associated with intellectual interests and is associated with typical interests.

Fifth, data on gender difference suggests that the degree of interest in computers might be equal, when both males and females have equal access to computers.

Study III

Study III was designed to examine the generalizeability of the findings from the Study II across different computer environments and SES. It was also designed to examine the relation between an interest in computers and attitudes toward computer users.

Method

Subjects and Settings. The subjects were 185 seventh grade students from two urban schools. Approximately half the students were boys (fifty-one in School A, and forty-four in School B) and half were girls (forty-two in School A, and forty-eight in School B). The subjects were selected randomly from all students except those in remedial or accelerated classes. The schools, designated A and B, were chosen for their academic and ethnic diversity.

School A was in a lower social economic area of an older sections of a large urban city. In ethnic composition, School A was 51 percent black, 35 percent Hispanic, 8 percent White, and 4 percent Asian. School A did not have computers for student use. A few of the math teachers reported that they occasionally talked about computers, but this was rare.

School B was in a middle-class suburb, close to the city in which School

A was located. In ethnic composition, the school was 58 percent white, 21 percent black, 14 percent Asian, and 7 percent Hispanic. All the students in the study at School B were exposed to computers for at least a year. The computer program consisted of weekly visits to the computer lab in which the students engaged in computer assisted instruction and computer literacy projects.

Interest Measures. The students were given a two-page questionnaire similar to the one employed in Study II. The first page contained sixteen nine-point Likert scale items that measured interest in computers and other activities. The second page contained open-ended questions about children who like computers and other questions that are not relevant to the current topic.

The interest items selected were based upon their frequency in the entire sample in Study I and not just in the middle-class sample as in Study II. The open-ended questions were on the back of the interest survey. Once the class finished the interest survey they were asked to turn the sheet over and answer the questions.

The reliabilities for the items in the interest survey were estimated from their communality in a factor analysis of all sixteen items. All items had communalities ranging from .49 to .74, suggesting acceptable reliabilities.

Results

To examine the effect of school and gender, an analysis of variance was conducted on the computer interest item. A significant main effect was found for school only (df 1, 182, F = 4.49, p < .05); neither gender nor the interaction (gender X school) was significant. An examination of the means suggests that children in School A, the lower SES school, were more interested in computers (5.56, SD = 2.54) than those in School B (4.58, SD = 2.27). These means also suggest, that these seventh grade students were only slightly interested in computers. The lack of interest in computers cannot be attributed to a general lack of interest, because they were interested in other activities. For example, the means for interest in video games in the two schools were 6.71 and 7.26 respectively.

Computers and Interests. All the items, except computers and video games, were subjected to a principal component analysis with a varimax rotation. Four principal components were found and are presented in table 13.3. The results are similar to the findings of Study II, except for an additional factor that contained interests in physical activities, for example, sports, working.

A hierarchical-stepwise multiple regression similar to the one in Study II was conducted with the computer item as the dependent variable. The variables were entered in the following four blocks: (a) general interests (Typical, Adult-Approving, Intellectual-Academic, and Physical); (b) an interest in video games; (c) school and gender; and (d) the interaction terms. Within the blocks the variables were entered in a stepwise manner. The results of the regression are summarized in table 13.4.

The simple correlations suggest that an interest in computers was related to intellectual interests, video games, and school attended. Interest in computers was negatively related to typical adolescent interests. Each of these variables remained a significant predictor, even when controlled for

TABLE 13.3
Principal Component Analysis of Interest Survey (Study III)

	PRINCIPAL COMPONENTS			
Items	I	II	III	IV
Listen to Music	.75	.03	−.06	−.04
Being with Friends	.71	−.04	−.08	.23
Watching Movies	.70	−.18	.11	.04
Watching TV	.54	.15	−.23	−.28
Dating	.45	−.35	.12	.18
Housework	−.20	.78	.02	.12
Homework	−.09	.77	.17	−.02
Cooking	.17	.65	.24	.11
Writing Stories	.00	.15	.80	.07
Reading	.01	.13	.72	−.23
Science	−.17	.09	.58	.33
Doing nothing	.11	.09	.02	−.73
Working for Money	.17	.26	.19	.52
Playing sports	.34	.14	−.12	.47
% Variance Extracted	16.5	13.9	12.3	9.9

Note: Component I = Typical Interests, Component II = Adult Approving Interests, Component III = Intellectual Interests, Component IV = Physical Interests

TABLE 13.4
Significant Predictors of Interests in Computers (Study III)

Variable	Simple r	Beta
Intellectual Interests	.25**	.31***
Typical Interests	−.09	−.17*
Interest in Video Games	.24**	.27***
School	.18*	.20**

* = $p < .05$
** = $p < .01$
*** = $p < .001$

the effect of the other independent variables. None of the interactions were significant, suggesting that the effects of these variables were the same in both schools and for both genders.

Stereotypes computer users. Another goal of the study was to examine adolescents' stereotypes about the "computer user." It was found that the adolescent's views could be classified into the same three categories as in Study II with 96 percent agreement between independent raters. The student's responses fell into three categories: ordinary, intelligent, and negative/miscellaneous (e.g., racial/sexual references). The results (table 13.5) are similar to the results of Study II. No significant difference in stereotypes views was found across schools (chi-square = .76, df=4) or gender (chi-square = 1.74, df=4). Adolescents tend to characterize the computer user as the "smart" or "brainy kid" despite gender or SES. There was no significant relation between interests in computers and stereotypes held about computer users (df 2,126, F=0.79, p < .46).

Discussion

Again the results suggest that computers are not a large part of the lives of adolescents. Though interest was not high in either school, the students from the lower SES school with less exposure to computers were more interested in them. Perhaps exposure to computers actually leads to a decreased interest in them.

As in Study II an interest in computers was associated with an interest in intellectual activities. An interest in computers was highly related to interests in intellectual activities and computer users were again most frequently seen as intelligent.

Unlike Study II interests in typical-adolescent activities were negatively related to an interest in computers. Perhaps the difference between studies is due to the somewhat greater computer exposure in Study II.

Surprisingly, there was no relationship between views of computer users and actual interest in computers. It may be that the views of computer users are related to a child's behavior but not to interests that are not

TABLE 13.5
Perception of Children Who like Computers (Study III)

Types of Children	SCHOOL		
	A	B	Total
Ordinary Children	41.8	30.0	38.2
Intelligent Children	50.5	62.5	54.2
Other	7.7	7.5	7.6

manifested in front of peers. Such a finding is consistent with the difference between learning and performance frequently found in social learning research (Rosenthal & Zimmerman, 1978).

Study IV

Study IV was designed to extend the scope of the previous studies by investigating the developmental trends in computer interest and to extend the examination of interest to include actual behavior and intentions to use computers as adults. In addition, we wanted to examine in greater detail how children's interest in computers is related to beliefs and experiences. Methodologically, Study IV differed from the other studies in the use of a semistandardized interview.

Method

Site. The study was set in a middle school and one of its feeder elementary schools. The schools were in a middle-class suburb. The schools' performance on standardized achievement tests was only slightly above the state average in mathematics and language. The ethnic composition of the school was mixed with about 60 percent of the students being white.

All the children and adolescents in the school had been exposed to computers since the fourth grade. The computer curriculum included weekly to biweekly visits to the computer lab. In the computer lab each child spent approximately twenty to thirty minutes with a computer. Those who were interested also could work with computers in their free time, during lunch, recess, or after school. The students have had experience with computer-assisted instruction, computer literacy, LOGO and rudimentary experience with word processing, and programming in BASIC. In general, the program is typical of elementary and middle school programs in this country in terms of activities, but slightly above average in computer usage (Becker, 1985).

Subjects. The subjects consisted of 140 children in the third through seventh grade, with twenty-eight students (fourteen boys and fourteen girls) at each grade level. The subjects were selected from typical classes in the school, and were chosen by the teachers to represent typical children in their class.

The interview. The students were interviewed by trained examiners using a semistructured interview. Each child was probed until the interviewer felt the child's answer was as explicit as the child could make it. Probing was necessary because many terms children used did not correspond to adults' usage of the same term, for example, many children used the word "programming" to refer to the act of putting a diskette into the disk drive.

Children were asked questions about their experience with computers and computer users. Specifically, children were asked: (a) where they used computers; (b) how often they have used them; (c) what did they do with them; (d) how did they plan to use computers as an adult; (e) who did they know that used computers; (f) how did these people use computers; (g) what kind of kids like to use computers; and (h) what kind of kids do not like to use computers. Children were also asked questions to assess their knowledge of computers (see Pulos & Fisher, 1985 & Pulos & Fisher, 1989 for details). The resulting scale was used in the current study to examine the relationship between knowledge of computers and interest and attitude.

Results

The description of the sample in terms of background variables is presented in table 13.6.

It is important to note that for many of these variables, e.g., having a sibling who uses a computer, the variability was very small. Thus the correlates of interest in computers will tend to be much lower in magnitude than if there was greater variability.

Interests in computers. Both current interest in and intention to use computers were investigated. Current interests were defined as the use of computers during free time at school. Intentions were assessed by asking the children about their plans for using computers as adults.

TABLE 13.6
Percent of Children with Computer Contacts Outside of School (Study IV)

Variable	Percent
Used a computer for games	70
Used a computer for programming	29
Computer in the home	28
Used educational software	19
Father uses a computer	14
Friend uses a computer	14
Mother uses a computer	09
Contact with another adult who uses a computer	09
Sibling uses a computer	06
Used a computer for drawing	05
Used a computer for word processing	01

Current Interests. The percent of children who reported using computers during their free time at school is presented in table 13.7. A breakdown
of how this time is spent is included. Children in the third grade did not
have the same access as students in the higher grades, so they were not
included in the table. Table 13.7 shows that after the fourth grade, interest
in computers decreased steadily for total usage and for programming
(including LOGO), while game playing decreased after the sixth grade. It
appears that with increased exposure to computers and increased age,
students became less interested in computers, particularly programming.

To discover whether the decrease in the use of computers for programming was due to a true decrease or to some unique aspect of the fourth
grade (i.e., a cohort effect) the percent of children who reported some
programming experience was examined. It was found that there was a
similar percentage of children in all grades, from the fourth to the seventh,
who reported programming experience (fourth grade, 40 percent; fifth
grade, 39 percent; sixth grade 22 percent; and seventh grade 39 percent).
Since many older children who had once engaged in programming during
their free time no longer did so, the drop in interest appears to be real.

In examining the correlates of current interest in computers, an ordinal
scale was used. It was based upon the frequency of reported computer
usage during free time at school in the current year. Using a computer
only for software was related to three factors: (a) saying that all kids liked
computers (tau = .20, p < .05); (b) saying that less intelligent children did
not like computers (tau = .19, p < .05); and (c) being a female (tau = .28,
p < .001). This finding suggests that interest in computers is associated
with the belief that typical children like computers.

Using a computer for programming and software had other correlates
including: (a) having a sibling who used a computer (tau = .19, p < .02);
(b) the total number of people they knew who used a computer (tau = .35,
p < .001); and (c) being a male (tau = .23, p < .01). The pattern of
correlations suggests that interests in computers usage, including program-
ing, is associated with the presence of role models.

Intentions. The percent of children who intended to use computers as

TABLE 13.7
Interest In Computers (Study IV), Percent of Children in Each Grade Using
Computers during Free Time at School

	GRADE			
Use	4	5	6	7
Programming & Software	29	17	04	14
Software Only	14	11	17	00

adults is presented in table 13.8. The respondents were classified into three categories: (a) planning not to use a computer as an adult; (b) having no plans for using a computer as an adult; and (c) planning to use a computer as an adult. Most children who plan to use a computer as an adult cited some work-related use, few mentioned recreational use. While the percent of children who planned to use computers as an adult increased with grade level, the same relative ranking of the three categories occurred within each grade. That is, most children didn't know if they will use a computer as adults. The next largest category of children planned not to use a computer as an adult, and the smallest category of children planned to use a computer as an adult. Although intention to use a computer was not related to grade level or with current interest in computers, it was related to the following variables: (a) understanding computers (tau = .31, p < .001); (b) having a mother who used computers (tau = .29, p < .001); (c) having friends who used computers outside school (tau = .19, p < .01); (d) having contact with an adult outside the immediate family who used a computer (tau = .16, p < .05); and (e) being female (tau = .14, p < .05).

Stereotypes of computer users. The following categories of children who like computers were identified: (a) Everybody (children are seen as liking computers, (b) Intelligent Children (users were identified as "brainy," "real smart," "do good in school," "like to do homework"); (c) Asocial Children (computers users were seen as children who don't like to play with other children or who likes to play alone); and (d) Negative/Miscellaneous (children said they don't know what kind of kids like computers or they said something like "I don't know anybody who likes a computer" or "I think it is silly to like machines").

It appears (table 13.9) that most of the children had negative views of computer users. If the "asocial," "intelligent," and "negative/miscellaneous" categories are combined, then most of the children (87 percent) had negative views of computer users.

The belief that everybody likes computers appeared to decrease after the third grade. This was the time that children were first exposed to

TABLE 13.8
Percent of Children Intending to Use a Computer as an Adult (Study IV)

Intention	GRADE					Total
	3	4	5	6	7	
Plans not to	29	18	26	29	32	27
Don't Know	61	78	59	54	40	58
Plans to	11	04	15	18	29	15

TABLE 13.9
Projected Attributes of Computer User and Nonusers (Study IV)

A. Projected Attributes of Computer Users (%)

Types	GRADE					Total
	3	4	5	6	7	
Everybody	29	15	8	11	4	13
Intelligent	21	46	56	39	50	43
Asocial	17	23	16	21	11	18
Misc.	33	15	20	29	36	27

B. Projected Attributes of Children who Don't Like Computers (%)

Types	GRADE					Total
	3	4	5	6	7	
Don't Know	64	42	36	40	40	44
Unintelligent	16	42	40	32	25	31
Social	20	15	24	18	14	18

computers. Apparently, this belief was affected by experience with computers.

Three categories of children who did not like computers were also identified (table 13.9): (a) Don't Know/Miscellaneous (children said they don't know what kinds of kids disliked computers or mentioned a specific type of child who did not like computers, e.g., "girls" or "boys."); (b) Unintelligent Children (children were identified as not liking computers, because they were "too dumb to use them"); and (c) Social Children (children didn't like computers, because they would rather be with friends or outside playing). Attributing intelligence to children who like computers, was not related to attributing unintelligence to children who did not like computers (tau = .08).

No significant difference was found between genders or across grades after the third grade. As previously noted, the only correlates between stereotypes and interest or intention was between using computers for software only and the belief that unintelligent children don't like computers and everybody does like them. Conversely, this correlation suggests that children who do not use computers in their free time see that children who like computers as atypical children.

Discussion

The results from Study IV are similar to the finding of the previous studies, though a different methodology was employed. The finding that most children at all ages were not interested in computers, as manifested by their behavior, is consistent with the findings in the previous three studies. Again it was found that most of the children did not view their computer using peers as typical. Instead the most frequent view of their computer using peer was an intelligent child.

Study IV, also presented new findings. Interest in computers, especially programming, was related to contact with people using computers (mother, friends, and siblings). Intention to use a computer as an adult was also related to contact with computer users and to conceptual understanding of computers. Therefore, children's contact with a computer user outside school had an impact on interest and intention, while direct contact in school did not, as suggested by the lack of correlation with grade level.

Unlike the previous study, a significant gender difference was found. While there was no gender difference in the proportion of children using computers during their free time, there was a significant difference in how they used computers. Girls tended to not to program and boys did. A similar finding has been reported by Miura (1985) with young adolescents and by Williams, Coulombe and Lievrouw (1983) with children. We also found that more girls than boys intended to use a computer as an adult. Nevertheless, the vast majority of boys and girls had similar interests and intentions, that is, the gender difference in usage is due to a small group of boys who like to program during their free time.

It was also found in Study IV that stereotypes were not only held by children who did not use computers, but also by those who did. Those children who used computers during their free time tended to see their peers who did not use computers as less intelligent. The failure to find this stereotype in the previous study may have been due to a failure to ask the question "what kinds of kids do not like computers."

General Discussion

The results of the four studies suggest that computers are not having a large impact on the social life of typical children and adolescents. Children do not appear to be very interested in using computers now or in the future. They see their peers who like computers as atypical, unusually bright or asocial. Clearly, the idea that computers are so interesting that childern are motivated to use them, plan to use them as adults, and look up to their computer-using peers is unwarranted. Moreover, computers are not so seductive that they disrupt social development of most children.

The results were very consistent across school, grade level, SES, mode of assessment, and computer experience. The only commonality in computer experience among these children was exposure to the media and its portrayal of computers. The media is filled with images of intelligent people using computers. It often focuses on college-bound children or successful upper middle-class professionals.

The media not only portrays the computer user as intelligent, but also as part of the white upper middle-class culture. For middle-and lower-class children, these images of computer users are far removed from their lives. They see computers associated with intelligent people, yet these children often do not want to be seen as more intellectual than their peers (Baumrind, 1986; Coleman, 1966; Gordon, 1972). They also see computers associated with professional businesspersons, when their parents and other adults they come into contact with are not professionals. This is important because parent's occupation has been found to serve as the major role model for children's own career choices (Bowles & Gintis, 1976). In Study IV we saw that the primary predictors of computer interests were the presence of role models who used computers.

Given these findings, we would expect computers to be more popular with upper middle-class children than with the children in the four studies reported here. Their parents are more like the professional seen in computer commercials and their intellectual striving is less discouraged by peers. Social inequities in computer education may exist, not because of a differential exposure in school, but because of an interaction of the media's portrayal of computers, subcultural values, and peer and family influences.

Interest in computers actually appear to decrease with increased exposure to computers in school. The phenomenon of decreasing interest may stem from the discrepancy between the computer as depicted by the media and the computer as experienced by children in school. The computers encountered in the school may be quite dull and disappointing compared to the ones they see in the movies and on television.

Another source of decreasing interest may stem from the dissociation between the computer classroom and the child's world. Some older students complained that they were taught about computers in school but could never use them to help with their homework. Typically, the computer is not used as a creative or useful tool, but is treated as a new form of obligatory "busy work." As a result, the students who have been exposed to computers have been disappointed. In contrast, the students who have not been exposed to computers have not yet been disappointed by sitting in front of a computer, and working through some educational software that has little meaning to them.

In summary, children's responses to computers are not based solely, upon the characteristics of the machine. The machine may have appealing characteristics like color graphics, instant feedback, and optimal level of difficulty; but the child's response to it is not based only upon these characteristics. Rather, the child's response is also determined by experience, beliefs, attitudes, peers, and family. We cannot assume that computers will be interesting to all children and we cannot rely upon them to solve the motivational problems seen in our schools. In considering the implication of these findings and the role of the computer in education, it is always important to consider the child's perspective and to recall the following quotation from David Dillon (1985):

> A further danger for us is that, as we ponder the educational issues about computers, pupils and literacy, we may settle for seeing through our own eyes, rather than through pupil's eyes, to try to understand these issues and reach conclusions about them. . . . We must discover what the experience is for pupls, not settle for adult-eye view, encapsulated explanations and theories that have been handed onto us and which we uncritically mouth.

References

Anyon, J. (1981). Social class and school knowledge. *Curriculum Inquiry*, *11*, 2–44.

Astin, A. (1986). Computer careers may be loosing appeal. *On Campus*, *5*(6), 6.

Bandura, A. (1986). *Social foundations of thought and action: A social cognitive theory*. Englewood Cliffs, NJ: Prentice-Hall.

Barnes, B. & Hill, S. (1983). Should young children work with computers -Logo before Lego? *The Computing Teacher*, *10*, 10–14.

Baumrind, D. (1986). A developmental perspective on adolescent risk-taking in contemporary America. Paper presented at the National Invitational Conference on Health Futures of Adolescents. Daytona Beach, Florida.

Becker, H. (1985). How schools use microcomputers: results from a national survey. In M.Chen & W. Paisley (Eds.) *Children and Microcomputer*. Beverly Hills, CA: Sage Publications.

Bowles, S. & Gintis, H. (1976). *Schooling in capitalist America: Education reform and contradictions of economic life*. New York: Basic Books.

Chi, L. (1966). A factorial study of academic motivation. Doctoral dissertation, Columbia University.

Clark, R. (1983). Reconsidering research on learning from media. *Review of Educational Research*, *53* (4), 445–59.

Clark, R. (1985). Confounding in educational computing research. *Journal of Educational Computing Research*, 1 (2), 137–48.

Coleman, J. (1966). *Equality of educational opportunity*. Washington, DC: U.S. Government Printing Office.

Coleman, J. (1961). *The adolescent society*. Chicago: University of Chicago Press.

Cohen, J. & Cohen, P. (1975). *Applied multiple regression/correlation analysis for the behavioral science*. Hillsdale, NJ: LEA.

Dillon, D. (1985). The dangers of computer in literacy education: Who's in charge here. In D. Chandler & S. Marcus (Eds.) *Computers and literacy*. Stony Stratford, England: Open University Press.

Donahoo, H. (1986). A school where computers make a difference. *Principal, 65* (3), 20–25.

Eagle, M. (1983). Interests as objects relations. In J. Masling (Ed.) *Empirical studies of psychoanalytical theories*, volume 1. Hillsdale, NJ: Lawrence Erlbaum Associates.

Fisher, S. (1983). Who's playing these games anyway? Paper presented at eighth annual West Coast Computer Fair, San Francisco.

Getzel, J. (1966). The problem of interests. In H. A. Robinson (Ed.) *Reading: Seventy-five years of progress. Education Monographs, 96.*

Gordon, C. (1972). *Looking ahead: Self-conceptions, race and family as determinants of adolescent orientation to achievement.* Washington, DC: American Sociological Association.

Greenfield, P. (1984). *Mind and media.* Cambridge, MA: Harvard University Press.

Harmon, H. (1976). *Modern factor analysis.* Chicago: University of Chicago Press.

Ingber, D. (1981). Computer addicts. *Science Digest, 114,* 88–91.

Law, A. (1982). *Student achievement in California schools.* Sacramento, CA: California State Department of Education.

Lawton, J. & Gerschner, V. (1982). A review of the literature on attitudes towards computers and computerized instruction. *Journal of Research and Development in Education, 16* (1), 50–55.

Lee, R. (1966). Social attitudes and the computer revolution. *Public Opinion Quarterly.*

Leeper, M. (1985). Microcomputers in education: Motivation and social issues. *American Psychologist, 40* (1), 1–18.

Levin, G. (1985). Computers and kids: The good news. *Psychology Today, 19* (8), 50–51.

Lieberman, D. (1985). Research on children and microcomputers: A review on utilization and effects studies. In M. Chen & W. Paisley (Eds.) *Children and Microcomputer.* Beverly Hills, CA: Sage Pub.

Lipinski, J., Nade, R., Shade, D., and Watson, J. (1984). Competence, gender and preschooler's free play choices when a microcomputer is present in the classroom. (ERIC Document No. ED 243 609).

Miura, I. (1985). Factors contributing to middle school computer interest and use. Paper presented at the 93rd annual meeting of the American Psychological Association, Los Angeles.

Ogbu, J. (1974). *The next generation: An enthnography of education in an urban neighborhood.* New York: Academic Press.

Paisley, W. (1985). Children, New Media and Microcomputers. In M. Chen & W. Paisley (Eds.), *Children and microcomputer.* Beverly Hills, CA: Sage Publications.

Pantiel, M. & Petersen, B. (1985). *The Junior High Computer Connection.* Englewood, Cliffs, NJ: Prentice Hall.

Pulos, S., & Fisher, S. (1985). Adolescents and computers. Paper presented at the annual meeting of the Western Psychological Association, San Jose.

Pulos, S., & Fisher, S. (1988). The child's understanding of computers. *Quarterly Newsletter of the Laboratory of Comparative Human Cognition, 10* (1), 17–21.

Rosenthal, T. & Zimmerman, B. (1978). *Social learning and cognition.* New York: Academic Press.

Rust, L. (1977). Interests. In S. Ball (Ed.), *Motivation in education.* New York: Academic Press.

Schaie, K. (1966). A general model for the study of developmental problems. *Psychological Bulletin, 64* 92–107.

Siegel, L. & Markoff, J. (1985). *The high cost of high tech.* New York: Harper and Row.

Tittnich, E. & Brown, M. (1982). Positive and negative uses of technology in human interactions. In M. Frank (Ed.). *Young Child in a computerized Environment.* New York: Haworth Press.

Turkle, S. (1984). *The second self.* New York: Basic Books.

Williams, F., Coulombe, J. & Lievrouw, L. (1983). Children's attitudes towards small computers. *Educational Communication and Technology Journal, 31* (1) 3–7.

Youniss, J. (1980). *Parents and peers in social development.* Chicago: University of Chicago Press.

14

Patient-Practitioner Information Exchange as an Asymmetrical Social Encounter: Do Patients Actually Know What Their Practitioners Think They Know?

Nurit Guttman

As patients are increasingly encouraged to partake in the manage-ment of their medical condition, information exchange between health-care practitioners and their patients becomes crucial. Yet, communication between practitioners and patients is often charac-terized as taking place in an asymmetrical relationship wherein practitioners dominate the interaction. Consequently, uninhibited information exchange may be an arduous task. On the one hand, practitioners expect their patients to understand their explanations and instructions and to diligently comply with the treatment regimen they recommend. On the other hand, research findings indicate that patients do not necessarily possess or understand the information their practitioners assume they do. Findings of a study which com-pared practitioners' assessments of the knowledge of their diabetic patients to their patients actual knowledge, support the notion that practitioners are not attuned to what their patients know. Since the practitioners tended to overestimate their patients' knowledge, they might be less likely to provide their patients with pertinent informa-tion regarding their health care. This has implications for the wide-spread phenomena of patient "noncompliance" with medical recom-mendations, and the need to enhance the health communication competence of the interactants.

Much recent research in the area of patient adherence to medical treatment suggests information exchange between health-care practitioners and their patients is crucial in promoting patient participation in health-care decision making and enhancing patient adherence to recommended medical regimens (Meichenbaum & Turk, 1987). Nonetheless, practitioner-patient information exchange is often encumbered by a variety of obstacles that inhibit competent information exchange between the patient and the health-care practitioner (Bochner, 1983; Meichenbaum & Turk, 1987; Waitzkin, 1984). This chapter explores some of the factors that contribute to an asymmetrical practitioner-patient interaction, that in turn may result in health-related behaviors that do not necessarily correspond with the recommendations of the medical practitioners.

Findings of a study by this author that compared health-care practitioners' assessment of their patients' knowledge and concerns regarding their medical condition—diabetes—and the actual knowledge and concerns, as reported by the patients, demonstrated that practitioners may not be attuned to what their patients actually know (or do not know); a discrepancy was found between what the practitioners thought their patients knew about their medical condition and its treatment, and what the patients actually knew. This implies that the information exchange in the medical encounter is amiss. Yet, as information exchange between practitioners and their patients and patient knowledge are increasingly seen as important factors in effective health-care promotion, it is important to identify and address the factors that inhibit information exchange, as well as conceptual and pragmatic frameworks to enhance the communication competency of the interactants.

The Growing Emphasis on Self-Care and Adherence

The notion that patients are becoming more active participants in their health care, and that they should be provided with increasing amounts of health-care information has gained momentum in the past two decades as a result of several factors. Medical care is becoming more concerned with the treatment and care of chronic, asymptomatic diseases, as well as with the prevention of illness. This requires acquisition of knowledge, skills, and motivation on the part of the lay person, that in turn may be highly dependent on the medical practitioner as a primary educational resource.

Another factor related to the growing emphasis on providing lay people with health information is the rise of the consumer movement, which has advocated the notions of consumer rights and demands for accountability of the service provider, the provision of more information and the participation of the lay person in decision making (Gartner & Reissman, 1974;

Rosengren & Lefton, 1975). In the early 1970s, with the growth of the consumer movement, the practices of different professions have come under close scrutiny, including the profession of medicine. Some authors believe that a fundamental change is occurring in the client-practitioner relationship as professional authority has been challenged by the consumer perspective (Haug & Lavin, 1983; Inlander et al., 1988). The aura of medicine and the authority of the physician have been seriously questioned as people are continually exposed to medical controversies, contradictions, and reversals (Gibbs, 1989; Meichenbaum & Turk, 1987). The rise of consumerism has promoted an image of the health-care client as a discriminating consumer, often "shopping" for medical services (Gibbs, 1989; Haug & Lavin, 1983), while the health-care professionals are cast as vulnerable providers of services in a competitive and litigious market (Altman & Rosenthal, 1990; Gibbs, 1989; Haug & Lavin, 1983).

Changing market conditions have contributed to the rise of the consumer trend in health-care services. Health care has become, on one hand progressively more expensive, demanding increasing specialization and sophisticated materials, equipment, and procedures, while on the other hand, it is a growing competitive business. Therefore, the concern for fostering consumer (i.e., patient) satifaction has become a major concern (Pascoe, 1983; Pendelton, 1983; Ruben, 1990; Speedling & Rose, 1985; Ware & Davis, 1983). Consistently, it has been found, that patient satisfaction is linked to communication and information exchange factors (Hall & Dorman, 1988; Hall, Roter & Katz, 1988; Ruben, 1990; Waitzkin, 1985). Also, medical professionals are legally required to obtain the "informed consent" of their patients for major as well as many minor medical procedures.

Consequently, the role of the lay person—the health care client—is increasingly seen as that of an active participant, rather than that of a passive recipient of medical care. This active participation requires considerable understanding, acquisition of knowledge or skills, as well as motivation to carry out the recommended health care regimen (Meichenbaum & Turk, 1987). Having patients follow the recommended health care regimen, has become one of the major challenges of modern health care (Pryor & Mengel, 1987; Peck & King, 1986).

Patient Adherence to Medical Recommendation

One of the medical professional's main goals in the practitioner-patient encounter is having their patient successfully follow the recommended medical regimen. It is generally agreed that not following medical recommendations may result in poor patient health, renewed rounds of diagnostic testing, and increased cost to both the patient and the health system (Peck & King, 1986; Meichenbaum & Turk, 1987; Pryor & Mengel, 1987). However, to the distress of many health-care practitioners, most studies confirm that at least one-third, and frequently up to 90 percent of patients fail to follow their practitioners' recommendations across various medical conditions (Byham & Vickery, 1988; Meichenbaum & Turk, 1987). The failure to follow a recommended medical regimen or health-promoting behavior is referred to by authors and practitioners as patient nonadherence, noncompliance, or lack of cooperation on the part of the patient. Although these different terms connote different perspectives regarding the practitioner-patient (or professional-lay) relationship, the main concern is the same: why is it that so many patients do not follow "the doctors' orders," and what can be done to improve this situation?

Several studies show that physicians tend to underestimate the rates of noncompliance in the general population as well as in their own patients. When confronted with occurrences of patient noncommplicance, researchers found that the physicians tended to attribute its cause to patients' characteristics or traits. Only a minority of practitioners believed that practitioners themselves might contribute to noncompliance (Gillum & Barskey, 1974). Empirical studies, however, have not found a "typical noncompliant personality," nor have studies located a typical set of patient personality traits or sociodemographic variables consistently associated with noncompliance. As Meichnbaum and Turk (1987) state, "Every patient is a potential defaulter" (p. 42).

A great deal of discussion and research has been devoted to this topic in the literature. Hundreds of articles have been published and reviewed in the literature. One review (Trostle, 1988) suggests that more than 4000 scholarly papers have been published in the past two decades. These publications demonstrate the growing recognition in scholarly literature that behavioral factors play an important role in health-care interactions, particularly communication and information exchange processes (Meichenbaum & Turk, 1987). While the quality of information exchange in medical encounters is dependent on the relationship or the communication between the interactants, the relationship between patients and health care practitioners is often characterized as problematic (e.g., Stone, 1979; President's Commission, 1983), particularly from an information exchange perspective.

Characteristics of the Practitioner-Patient Relationship

The medical practitioner-client relationship has undergone dramatic changes in the past several decades. Some characterize the health caregiver-client relationship as inherently paternalistic, where medical practitioners perform the role of the experts and authority, while the lay persons come to "consult" them in their "sick role" (Parsons, 1951). Other authors maintain that since patients are consumers, they should have greater control and autonomy over information and decision-making factors involved in the health care process (Childress & Siegler, 1984; President's Commission, 1983).

These different perspectives are reflected in the typology of Szasz and Hollander (1956) who present three basic types of doctor-patient relationships and the conditions of illness with which each type is likely to be associated: (1) The model of activity-passivity: the physician is active, the patient, passive; this model is appropriate for the treatment of emergencies, severe injuries or coma. (2) The model of guidance-cooperation: the patient seeks help and is willing to cooperate; the physician is more powerful and expects to be listened to. (3) The model of mutual participation: this model is predicated on the notions of equality. The assumptions underlying this model are that the participants have approximately equal power, are mutually interdependent, and engage in activity that in some ways satisfies both. This corresponds to the consumer-oriented approach that implies increasing input and demands by the health-care client (President's Commission, 1983). Alternative approaches view the ideal practitioner-lay person interaction as a process of negotiation (Brody, 1980) or mutual persuasion (Smith & Pettegrew, 1986).

In the first two models, the agreement between the physician and patient is taken for granted. In the third model, the physician does not profess to know exactly what is best for the patient. Rather, the determination of what is the best treatment regimen becomes the essence of the therapeutic interaction. The patients' own experiences furnish indispensable information for eventual agreement, as to what "health" might be for them. Open information exchange in this type of interaction, therefore, can be seen as an essential factor (Brody, 1980).

If we accept the latter model, particularly in the context of the management of chronic medical conditions (even Parsons, 1975, contends that patients assume a more active role in these situations), we need to address several issues: Are patients in actual practice equally active partners in the medical encounter? What communication and information exchange processes take place in this encounter? What are their effects on medical and sociopsychological outcomes? What are possible approaches to enhance information exchange and collaborative decision making between lay persons and professionals in the health care context? Substantial theoretical and empirical work point to factors that contribute to inhibited information exchange in the medical encounter.

Asymmetry in the Practitioner-Patient Relationship

Some authors believe that the problematic aspects of the relationship between the health-care client and the caregiver are embedded in asymmetric power relations and control in health-care encounters (Beisecker, 1990; Hardesty, 1988; Nelson & McGough, 1983; Stone, 1979). They point to structural factors which create an asymmetry in the practitioner-patient relationship that result in a practitioner-dominated interaction and inhibited patient-initiated exposition of their concerns and ideas (Hardesty, 1988; Waitzkin, 1985). Although asymmetry in a relationship is often a characteristic of professional-client relationships in general, the factors that contribute to the inhibition of information exchange in this relationship are particularly problematic in the health context (Antonovsky, 1979; Ruben, 1990), where decisions relate to sensitive matters that directly effect the welfare of the patient.

Friedson (1975, 1980) characterizes the medical profession as an occupation that has assumed a dominant position in the division of labor, since it has gained control over the determination of the substances of its own work. Medical professionals have been socialized into their professional role or have been working within a framework that provides them with power and dominance. Unlike most occupations, the medical profession is relatively autonomous or self-directing. It claims, and is legally empowered to be the most reliable authority on the nature of the reality it deals with; it changes the definition of and shapes the problems as they are experienced by the lay person; and it tries to manage the problems of its clients in its own fashion, within the confines of its own discipline, specifically, in the biomedical model (Engel, 1978; Stein, 1990).

Practitioners have more power than lay persons because of their professional knowledge and resources. By entering a medical encounter the lay person acknowledges that the medical professional has a particular technical expertise in dealing with certain kinds of problems, or has access to specific resources that the patient does not have. Thus the medical practitioner assumes a relatively superior position of power (Antonovsky, 1979). Also, the medical encounter usually takes place in an environment alien to the patient, such as clinics or hospitals (Cicourel, 1983; Pritchard, 1983; Ruben, 1990). Also disconcerting to the patient is the medical professionals' use of jargon or medical terminology (Barlund, 1976). Furthermore, the patient invariably perceives the situation as involving anxiety, uncertainly, and ambiguity (Antonovsky, 1979), and patients are often anxious or worried about their medical condition and well-being (Barlund, 1976).

The Illusion of Patient Autonomy?

Despite the rise of consumer orientation in health care, which has created according to Zola and Miller (1973) an erosion of medicine's license and mandate, medicine is spreading its influence even farther in terms of it becoming a major institution of social control. Thus, although new arrangements of service and the relationship between health-care providers and patients are emerging, medicine (as an institution) remains relatively in control. Moreover, practitioners, according to Hardesty (1988), are adopting strategies to overcome some of the tensions brought about by the consumer orientation.

An example of how, in a situation where the patients clearly identified with a consumer orientation, the physicians managed to maintain control over the actual decision making is provided in a study by Nelson and McGough (1983). The authors describe how the physicians managed to implement their own favored treatment option, despite the fact that their "consumer-oriented" patients specifically notified them that they were against particular options. The findings indicate that even when patients had high levels of information regarding childbirth, and had actively attempted to become informed, the physicians managed to gain these patients' compliance when they implemented procedures to which these patients previously had objected to. They did this, when the actual delivery time arrived, by presenting the situation to their patients as medically necessary. Interestingly, the patients of these practitioners did not view their physicians in a negative way, even though they actually went against their requests. This is because the physicians, suggest Nelson and Mc-Gough (1983), offered these patients what the authors call the "illusion of autonomy." Nelson and McGough (1983) propose that what occurs in such interactions is a process of negotiation: the client's assertions are legitimated by the physician by maintaining an illusion of autonomy, while actually maintaining the physician's control, and avoiding outright conflict between them. These authors predict that as consumer-oriented medical information becomes more available and more accessible to clients, the nature of the relationship between the client and the physician (or any professional) will change. Negotiations will become more overt, and the illusion of the client's autonomy may not continue to produce conflict-free outcomes.

Differences in Perspectives

In addition to factors relating to differential power in medical encounters, there is an inevitable built-in difference in the perspectives, which can be characterized as intercultural, of the patient and of the health practitioner (Antonovsky, 1979; Lazare et al., 1976; Ruben, 1990). Furthermore, the patient is mostly concerned with his or her self-interest, while the practitioner, in addition to being concerned with the patient's self-interest, has additional professional and societal normative commitments (Parsons, 1970).

Interaction-analysis studies have provided meticulous empirical data that support the theoretical frameworks regarding the asymmetry in the medical practitioner-patient relationship. Conversation analysts have noted that rules of discourse give differential rights to doctors and patients to pursue topics (Fisher, 1983; Frankel, 1983; Rost, Carter, & Inui, 1989) where patients are less likely to introduce topics in the discussion (Shuy, 1983). Doctors and patients utilize different conversational means. For example, physicians employ serial questioning sequences by which they maintain preeminence over the information exchanged during the visit, and patients rarely volunteer information or append comments on other topics (Rost, Carter, & Inui, 1989).

Medical consultation and advice are frequently given in circumstances in which discussion, feedback, and learning are inhibited (Ruben, 1990). It has been demonstrated that patients are interrupted disproportionately by physicians (Shuy, 1983; West, 1983), seldom ask questions (Waitzkin, 1985; West, 1983), and do not inform their doctors when they do not understand their instructions or explanations (Purtilo, 1978; Waitzkin, 1985; Putnam et al., 1985.) Thus, patients interpret what they have heard to the best of their understanding (Ley & Spelman, 1976; Matthews & Hingson, 1977). DiMatteo and DiNicola (1982) report that patients are often afraid to ask what specific terms mean for fear that the doctor will think they are uneducated or unintelligent.

A common consequence of asymmetrical communicative power, argues Cicourel (1983), is misunderstanding. The professional-bureaucratic setting creates informational constraints and resources for the doctor, but tends to weaken the patient's communicational capabilities. One result is that when people believe they are unable to express their views, or that their feelings and emotions are constrained by the organizational setting, they are likely to have doubts about what they are told, despite a desire to trust the doctor's communication. Cicourel (1983) also suggests that the professional-bureaucratic context can influence the preference for particular medical treatments by the way the problem is framed by the professional. Thus patients may not be aware, or may be discouraged to opt for health-care alternatives presented by the professional as the less desirable options. Yet the professional's criteria for recommending certain treatments may be influenced by their values or preconceptions, and they use persuasive strategies to convince their patients to follow what they believe is best for them or society (Fisher, 1983).

Structural elements of the practitioner-patient relationship, factors of power, dominance, and tension, as well as intercultural differences contribute to the problematic nature of information exchange in the practitioner-patient encounter. Practitioners tend to dominate the encounter implicitly or explicitly, and they typically follow a biomedical model of information seeking (categorizing symptoms), problem solving (reaching a scientific diagnosis), and prescription of treatment. Clients, however, may have various, often contradictory concerns that do not necessarily "fit" the scientifically oriented medical model (Engel, 1978; Stein, 1990). Since patients' major concerns may often not be presented to the practitioner as their "chief complaint" in the information exchange process, these concerns may be ignored or belittled by the medical practitioner (Frankel & Beckman, 1989; Shorter, 1985). In addition, since patients may feel inhibited in presenting their sensations, feelings, ideas, or suggestions, they are less likely to be involved in negotiating a true partnership with the practitioner. It could be argued that, as long as health practitioners are trained in and almost exclusively rely on an information-seeking model in the biomedical model (Shorter, 1985; Weston & Brown, 1989), information exchange and partnership building in the medical encounter will continue to be sadly impoverished.

Information Exchange in the Medical Encounter

Findings consistently indicate that regardless of their sociodemographic background, health-care clients are interested in knowing more about their health condition than is offered by their practitioners, and many are dissatisfied with the information provided to them (Blanchard et al., 1988; Covel et al., 1985; Ewles & Shipster, 1981; Korsch, Gozzi, & Francis, 1968; Waitzkin, 1985). Yet, despite their dissatisfaction, patients are reticent about asking questions because they believe physicians do not have the time to explain to them (Purtilo, 1978).

An example of research that focused on information exchange in patient-physician interactions is reported by Waitzkin (1985). Waitzkin and his colleagues analyzed 336 encounters recorded from several outpatient settings. The researchers coded measures such as the level of technicality of the doctor's explanations, the numerical count of doctors' explanations, and patients' requests for information. Their analysis reveals that doctors spent relatively little time informing their patients, overestimated the time they did spend, and underestimated their patients' desire for information.

Findings from several studies indicate that patients' social class or educational background were related to the information provided by their practitioners (Pendelton & Bochner, 1980; Waitzkin, 1985). Patients from corporate and upper middle-class backgrounds received more physician time, more explanations, more multilevel explanations than patients from lower middle- or working-class backgrounds. Also, reports of patient dissatisfaction with how physicians elicit information and ignore the patient's perspective are common in daily discussions by lay persons (Cicourel, 1983). In conclusion, clients are dissatisfied but nevertheless inhibited in their input in many medical encounters. In spite of this, health-care clients are increasingly expected by their health-care providers to actively participate (often effortlessly) in the management of their health care.

In order to carry out the medical regimen the patient must be sufficiently informed about how to carry out the recommendations. The conceptual framework of the Health Belief Model (Janz & Becker, 1984: King, 1983) implies that patients need to acquire an understanding of *why* the recommended regimen is needed, as well as knowledge and skills of *how* to carry it out. Unless lay persons turn to alternative information sources, they are most likely to depend on the information provided by their health practitioner (Gann, 1986). Thus health practitioners can be viewed as "gatekeepers" regarding important health information, and consequently the practitioner-patient interaction is particularly important as a source for the patients' health knowledge.

Patient Knowledge and Adherence

Knowledge and information enable lay persons to participate in their own health care (Gann, 1987). Some researchers propose that often the failure of patients to adhere to medical treatment can be attributed to patients' lack of appropriate information (Gann, 1986; Geller & Butler, 1981; Hulka, et al. 1975; Hulka et al., 1976) or a simple failure of comprehension (Ley & Spelman, 1967; Ley, 1983). Research findings demonstrate that individuals often lack knowledge regarding their medical regimen, the location of major organs, or causes of illness (Kreps et al., 1987; Ley, 1983).

Hulka and her associates (1976) suggest that patients often tend to adhere to the best of their knowledge but act on misinformation regarding their treatment regimen. They found that over half of the patients who made mistakes in their administration of medication assumed they understood their treatment, and only 5 percent asked their doctor for clarification (Gann, 1987). Stewart, Cluff, & Leighton (1972) lament that in our society individuals are provided with better instructions when purchasing a new camera or automobile than when they receive a life-saving drug.

Although there seems to be conflicting evidence regarding the relationship of information to adherence, a number of studies indicate that providing clear and accurate information is positively related to adherence as well as being cost effective (Gann, 1987; Slack, 1985). Hulka, Cassel, Kupper & Burdette (1976) found that communication of instructions and information was inversely associated with drug error rates: the better the communication, the lower the errors. Neither characteristics of patients nor the severity of the disease were associated with medication errors. Other studies indicate that better-informed patients were found to experience less stress and anxiety in the hospital setting or require fewer painkilling drugs and shorter hospital stays (Gann, 1987; Slack, 1985). Thus, the importance of competent information exchange in the medical encounter is a prominent concern in health care (Pendelton, 1983; Waitzkin, 1985). However, providing patients with information is not sufficient to influence health-related behavior. As much of the literature points out, having individuals attend, comprehend, and act upon information may greatly depend on the person's values, attitudes, or beliefs.

Health Care Beliefs

A growing body of literature suggests that patients' personal beliefs play an important part in adherence to medical recommendations. Western culture emphasizes the biomedical model of conceptualizing health conditions. Illness is explained in terms of pathophysiology, with practitioners focusing on the disease rather than the person. Yet the experience of illness is unique to each individual, and lay persons' perspectives often dramatically diverge from those of their practitioners' (Cassell, 1985; Cicourel, 1983; Bochner, 1983; Hamoson et al., 1990; Mishler, 1984; Weston & Brown, 1989).

Cicourel (1983) is particularly interested in the interpretive procedures and the ways people structure their knowledge or beliefs and points out that patients may hold beliefs contradictory to those of the practitioner. These will not be altered by formal explanations by the physician. Therefore, he suggests that "we need to understand the extent to which beliefs can resist new or contradictory information" (p. 236). This implies that both parties need to explore the assumptions and beliefs of the other and attempt to reach a mutual or a working definition of the health problem and how to address it (Weston & Brown, 1989). If there is a discrepancy in the beliefs of the interactants, if the interactants do not share the meaning of the terminology employed, and if there are inadequate efforts to bridge the gaps between the assumptions of the professionals and lay person, adherence to the medical advice and partnership building in the relationship is likely to be minimal. In other words, information exchange between the parties that does not involve a negotiation of shared meanings (Barlund, 1976; Brody, 1980; Mishler, 1984) may not result in health-promoting behavior.

The Health Belief Model formulated by Rosenstock and developed by Becker and his colleagues (Janz & Becker, 1984; Rosenstock, 1990) is the most frequently studied model of patients' health beliefs (King, 1983). It was originally developed to explain and predict preventive health actions but has since been employed to explain patient adherence as well. Becker and his colleagues suggest that whether or not individuals will undertake a recommended health action is dependent upon their perceptions of several factors: general health motivations; perceived susceptibility or vulnerability; perceived severity of the consequences of the health condition; perceived benefits and costs or barriers involved in taking the recommended health action; and the occurrence of cues which "trigger" the individual to action.

Although the Health Belief Model originally focused mainly on the patient, some suggest that the patient-practitioner interaction contributes to the health beliefs of the patient (Leventhal et al., 1983). For example, Inui and his colleagues (1976) developed a tutorial aimed at training practitioners in strategies for increasing hypertensive patients' adherence to the prescribed regimen. The results show that the patients of the tutored physicians were more aware of their own susceptibility and more compliant. Thus, enhanced communication between practitioners and their patients was related to enhanced outcomes.

However, communication of information between practitioners and their patients is limited, as reported in a study by this author (Guttman, 1990) that compared practitioners' assessment of the knowledge and attitudes of their patients with their actual responses. The findings of this research point to a gap between what practitioners think their patients know and what they actually know about their health care, which in turn may be related to the problematic factors associated with information exchange in medical encounters.

The Gap between Practitioners' Assessment of Their Patients' Knowledge and Patients' Actual Knowledge

Davis, Hall, & Boutaugh (1981) argue that it is important for health-care practitioners to have a careful and comprehensive assessment of patients' needs and their current knowledge base, limitations, and readiness to learn. They point out that practitioners' perceptions about the extent of patients' knowledge and self-management have been found to differ markedly from actual measures of these dimensions. Health professionals, like professionals in other fields, face the problem of transmitting technical information and advice to lay persons (Cicourel, 1983; Meichenbaum & Turk, 1987; Ruben, 1990) as well as the problem of not knowing what their clients want in this interaction (Davis et al., 1981; *Diabetes Forecast,* 1987; Innes, 1977; Wertz et al.', 1988). If indeed, patient knowledge is increasingly important in the health-care process and if the primary care health practitioner is often the major source of this information (Gann, 1986; Thompson, 1986), it is important to investigate whether what practitioners *assume* their patients know corresponds to what patients *actually* do know. If practitioners overestimate what their patients know they may not provide them with the necessary information needed to participate in decision making or in the implementation of the recommended health-care regimen.

Findings of this author's study that explored how well primary-care medical practitioners assessed their patients' knowledge and attitudes regarding the care of diabetes, indicate that practitioners overestimated the knowledge of their patients. The practitioners reported that they generally knew their patients fairly well. Thus, if practitioners are not well attuned to their patients' knowledge or feeling about their medical care, it may directly affect the management of the patient's medical condition. Diabetes, typically enlists a self-care regimen, and its successful management relies on considerable knowledge and skills on the part of the diabetics and their motivation to carry on with the prescribed regimen (Brown, 1988; Chandalia & Bagrodia, 1979; Etzwiller, 1984; Geller & Butler, 1981; Hulka et al., 1975; Romm & Hulka, 1979).

Clearly, if primary-care practitioners assume their patients are knowledgeable about the recommended diet for diabetics, they are less likely to inquire whether their patients actually know what they are or are not supposed to eat. Nor would the practitioners try to find out whether their patients know about the recommended daily allowances, or refer their patients to a dietician. Thus, one of the reasons patients may not be following a proper diet is their lack of knowledge.

A Study of Practitioners' Assessment of Their Patients' Knowledge

Two main research questions were formulated in this study: (1) Is there a gap between the practitioners' assessment of their patients' knowledge, and their patients' actual knowledge about diabetes care? (2) Is there a gap between what practitioners assess their patients feel about diabetes, and what these patients actually report they feel? The study focused on a specific domain of knowledge of diabetes care and utilized knowledge items that were identified as important for diabetics to know in order to control their medical condition. The practitioners were asked to assess how well their patients possess knowledge of diabetes care. The practitioners' assessments were then compared with the responses of the patients. This study, unlike most other studies that utilized general assessments of practitioners, asked the practitioners' to assess the knowledge of individual patients on specific items and compared their responses to the actual responses of the individual.

The study took place in three neighborhood clinics that are part of the largest health insurance organization in Israel. A sample of 102 diabetics, as diagnosed by their physicians, and their primary care practitioners were selected to be interviewed. The major criterion for the selection of the respondants, in addition to being diabetic, was that the practitioners said they knew these patients fairly well and had "good communication" with them. The medical practitioners in the study were either the primary-care physicians of the patient or their primary-care nurses.

A total of eighty-six completed sets of questionnaires, one per patient and one by the patient's practitioner, were obtained over the course of a three-month period. The questionnaire consisted of 166 items. The knowledge items were constructed to test the patient's knowledge in four areas of diabetes care: (1) the overall purpose of diabetes care; (2) nutrition or food exchanges; (3) hypoglycemia; and (4) skin care. In addition there were items addressing their feelings or emotions (affect) regarding diabetes and well-being in general, and sociodemographic data about the patient. While the patients' questionnaire was like a test, where the patients were given multiple choice answers on most of the items; the practitioners, on the "knowledge" items, were asked to reply as to whether the patient would know, or not know, the correct answer to the specific question.

Practitioners Assumed Their Patients Knew More Than They Actually Did

Analyses of the findings indicate that the practitioners in the study overestimated their patients' knowledge of nutrition or food exchanges, their knowledge of hypoglycemia and their knowledge of skin care. Interestingly, the patients themselves also overestimated their own level of knowledge of nutrition. However, the analysis of the items regarding affect (their feelings) indicated that the practitioners' assessments of the patients' responses to affect items were in accordance with the actual responses of the patients, with the exception of several items. For example, patients reported feeling more limited in their food because of their diabetes than assessed by their practitioner. Also practitioners overestimated the amount of concern their patients had with possible complications.

These findings are consistent with the conceptual and empirical work that characterizes the information exchange in the health practitioner-patient encounter as problematic. Specifically, in this study, patients knew less about the care for their medical condition than their practitioners assumed they did (in contrast to McKinlay, 1975). Whether this is a result of lack of comprehension on the part of the patient, poor instruction on the part of the practitioner, reticence on the part of the patient regarding asking questions, or other causes, should be investigated further.

The results of this study support results of a survey conducted by the American Diabetes Association (*Diabetes Forecast*, 1987) indicating that while 89 percent of the health-care professionals said that they trained their patients on how to use self-monitoring of blood glucose, only 54 percent of the patients responded that they were instructed in the method. In that survey, however, the diabetics surveyed were not the patients of the health-care professionals surveyed. The gap found in this author's study (Guttman 1990), between what the practitioners thought patients knew, and what patients actually knew, or rather, did not know, might have implications for patients' adherence to following a recommended medical regimen. If patients lack appropriate health-related knowledge, they are not likely to perform the recommended behaviors appropriately (Meichenbaum & Turk, 1987).

Mixed Prediction of Feelings or Affect

One of the interesting findings in the present study is that the practitioners predicted relatively well the responses on the affect items. Thus, they may be more attuned to their patients' concerns or feelings than is often attributed to them (Merkel, 1984). Nevertheless the analysis indicates that regarding complications of diabetes, the practitioners overestimated the concern their patients had, particularly those of insulin users. Thus, practitioners may believe their patients feel more susceptible (following the Health Belief Model) to detrimental complications of diabetes, when in fact they are not. This, according the Health Belief Model, may influence patients' motivation to adhere to the recommended regimen.

The analysis of the findings also indicates that the diabetics tended to feel more limited by their dietary restrictions than assessed by their practitioner. Perhaps this is related to the practitioners' overestimation of the patients' knowledge of nutrition. Increased patient knowledge regarding nutrition for diabetics might decrease their feeling of frustration regarding their diet, and in turn may increase patient adherence. Thus, mistaken assumptions that practitioners (and patients) have about what the patients know or believe may be both a result of, and contribute to the problematic patient-practitioner interaction, and consequently to problems in promoting the welfare of the particular patient and the health-care system as a whole. The literature portrays the medical encounter as often dominated by the medical practitioner, with little opportunity for feedback. The results of this study indicate that although what patients knew or did not know, was *not* communicated well to their practitioners, the patients managed to communicate effectively some of their general concerns to their doctor or nurse.

One possible explanation is that patients feel more comfortable expressing what *they* are "expert" in—their feelings and attitudes regarding their home, family, occupations, and general health. Yet, patients might be more reluctant to ask the practitioner questions that refer to medical knowledge and skills. Similarly, practitioners might be more likely to possess social skills that facilitate their finding out about what people feel. They appear to lack skills that would enable them to assess how well their patients understand or know technical or somatic matters. This view is supported by findings that physicians talked more openly to their patients when discussing psychosocial topics than somatic topics (Verhaak, 1988).

As the scholarly literature and everyday experiences suggest, patients may not possess the knowledge, skill, or motivation to effectively participate in promoting their health. Having interactants explore their health beliefs, knowledge, and assumptions are key elements in establishing a "common ground" on the definition of the health-care problems as well as optimal ways to address them. This goal however, is dependent on a complex process of negotiation that requires the active involvement of both the professionals and their clients.

Information Exchange as Involvement and Negotiation

Goffman (1963) describes involvement in an interaction as the capacity of individuals to give or withhold their concerted attention to some activity at hand. Involvement then is an admitted closeness between the individual and the object of involvement, in which a "working consensus" or a shared definition of the situation comes to prevail. The literature on the health practitioner-patient interaction implies that the involvement in the medical encounter is typically not symmetrical. The "working consensus" that generally is established in the medical encounter is characterized by a passive patient, and the situation is controlled by the practitioner. In light of the discussion above, an important question is whether this definition of the situation can undergo fundamental changes. For example, we may ask if it is possible to increase patient control of the information exchange in medical encounters.

The "mutual participation" (Brody, 1980; Stone, 1979; Szasz & Hollander, 1956) or "mutual persuasion" models (Smith & Pettegrew, 1986) recognize that an inherent conflict between patients' and their practitioners' perspectives is likely to exist, and therefore the process of negotiation between them is crucial. In the same vein, Rost, Carter, & Inui (1989) underscore the importance of reaching a mutual agreement on the definition of the (health) problem. These authors suggest that a necessary step in genuinely defining the patients' problem is the introduction of relevant information about the problem by both doctor and patient. These researchers investigated how doctors and patients negotiated what information is relevant in understanding the patient's problem, as it reflects both the patient's and physician's perspective and how it is was related to patient adherence. Their findings support the idea that the physician's willingness to allow patients to contribute input was related to patient adherence to physician recommendations. This, they suggest, might be due to increased partnership at arriving at treatment decisions that have meaning for both patient and physician. These findings support the notion that enhanced information exchange processes in medical encounters can promote positive health-related outcomes (Kaplan, Greenfield, & Ware, 1989).

Regardless of whether the changes in the doctor-patient relationship are undergoing fundamental revisions or merely adjusting to the marketplace conditions, there is evidence that the medical profession is undergoing changes in some of the elements of the therapeutic relationship with its clientele. This is manifested in the growing cautiousness of medical professionals in making sure they provide patients with certain information as they have entered the era of increased litigation. The medical literature and health practitioners are showing a growing interest in communication aspects of the medical relationship, particularly in communication skills or communicative competence (Leebov, Vergare, & Scoot, 1989; Meichenbaum & Turk, 1987).

Interaction Competence Skills: The Training of Health Practitioners, Patients and the Lay Public

There is a growing body of literature as well as training programs aimed at health-care professionals, urging them to enhance their communication skills (e.g., Burgoon et al., 1987; Campbell, et al., 1990; Cline, 1983; Kreps & Thornton, 1984; Leebov, Vergare, & Scott, 1989; Meichenbaum & Turk, 1987; Northouse & Northouse, 1985; Ruben, 1990; Thompson, 1986; Wakeford, 1983), and change their style from paternalistic (Taylor, Pickens, & Gedden, 1989) to empathetic (Squier, 1990; Suchman & Matthews, 1988) or partnership building (Ballard-Reisch, 1990). Increasingly, it becomes apparent that health-care communication interventions should include also the enhancement of patient communication competencies (Arntson, 1989; Ruben, 1990). Not only health practitioners, but lay persons should be provided with health-related negotiation skills (Hardesty, 1988).

Active participation of patients in medical encounters might be enhanced by encouraging patients to ask more questions (Roter, 1977); having them initiate topics or proffer their opinions and suggestions, and teaching them negotiation skills (Arntson, 1989; Argyle, 1983; Brody, 1980; Hardesty, 1988; Thompson, 1986). Patients can be encouraged to actively participate in the decision-making process by establishing mutual clarification of expectations each party has regarding their respective roles and responsibilities in the health-care process (Ballard-Reisch, 1990; Meichenbaum & Turk, 1987; Weston & Brown, 1989). In fact both the American Hospital Association's Patients' Bill of Rights and the American Civil Liberties Union Rights of Hospital Patients, underscore the role of active patient participation and collaborative negotiation in the treatment regimen (Meichenbaum and Turk, 1987).

Although the literature on enhancing health communication of patients is relatively sparse, there is growing empirical evidence that interventions to enhance patients' health communication are successful in increasing patients' input in medical encounters and may be related to long-term adherence or increased control of the medical condition. For example, Roter (1977), Robinson and Whitfield (1985), and Thompson and Nanni (1990) succeeded in increasing the number of questions asked by patients by aiding them to prepare questions ahead of time. In addition, in Robinson and Whitfield's study (1985), patients in the experimental group that received specific information about their condition and some training in interaction management, had better control of their medical condition. In Thompson and Nanni's (1990) study, it was found that "coached" patients were also more satisfied with the visit.

Greenfield, Kaplan, & Ware (1985) designed an intervention wherein patients in one group were helped to read their medical record and coached to ask questions and negotiate medical decisions with their physicians during a twenty-minute session before their scheduled visit. Patients in this group showed more active involvement in the interaction than those in the other group, and subsequently better control of their medical condition. Overall, the results of these studies suggest that increasing patient health communication skills can be beneficial to individual patients' well-being as well as to the health-care system (Kaplan, Greenfield, & Ware, 1989).

Although the findings of these studies indicate that the "trained" patients managed the information exchange relatively better than those who did not, these "improved" medical encounters are still a far cry from the "mutual participation model" (Szasz and Hollander, 1956), from real partnership building (Brody, 1980) or from the "mutual persuasion" model (Smith & Pettegrew, 1986). More so, the recommendations in the literature for enhancing the health communication competence of both practitioners and patients are often commonsensical (Rowland-Morin & Reuben, 1987; Sneider, 1986; Thompson, 1986). Although these efforts might indeed contribute to more effective communication skills of practitioners and clients, they do not address some of the more problematic aspects of the physician-patient interaction, as reviewed above.

Implications

Patient-practitioner information-exchange has been portrayed as problematic. Factors related to this problematic exchange have implications for dissatisfaction and frustration experienced by both parties, the inhibition of partnership building, and the phenomenon of minimal patient adherence to medical recommendations. These factors in turn, may adversely effect the welfare of the patient and health-care system as a whole. With growing dependence of lay persons on sophisticated health services, combined with escalating economic and social costs, scholars, lay advocates, and health-care professionals are increasingly concerned with both satisfying the public as well as with maintaining a viable health-care system that provides optimal care. Shared responsibility in decision making and participation in the implementation of health-care delivery may help address the contradictions, as well as the ethical and economic constraints lay persons, health-care professionals and administrators currently face.

It has been argued that lay persons need accurate and appropriate information to enable them to participate as partners in a negotiation process in medical encounters. This in turn has been related to outcomes that promote their health and well-being. Typically, the approach adopted to address the problematic aspects of information exchange in medical encounters has been to enhance practitioners' communication skills, with some initial attempts to enhance the communication skills of patients' in specific medical contexts.

However, communication skills training of individuals may not be sufficient to overcome the asymmetric nature of the professional-lay person relationship that takes place in a confined bureaucratic setting. For example, such training may not fully address some of the inherent problematic issues that are embedded in structural arrangements of the health care delivery system. In addition, it has been noted that characteristics such as gender (Verbrugge & Steiner, 1981), age (Waitzkin, 1985), physical attractiveness (Hadjistavropoulos, Ross, & Bayer, 1990), culture (Ellmer & Olbrisch, 1983), social class (Pendelton & Bochner, 1980), perceptions of personality or attributions (Fisher, 1983) have an impact on the information-exchange processes in medical encounters. Also, factors relating to intercultural differences, which stem from socialization of practitioners into medical professions (Bochner, 1983; Ruben, 1980; Stein, 1990), and the predominance of the biomedical model as the ultimate criteria for definitions of health and illness, can be seen as factors that will continue to perpetuate asymmetrical control of information exchange in medical encounters.

In conclusion, hopefully public discussion and educational programs will address the complexity of the factors that contribute to the problematic health-information exchange process in medical encounters. Clearly, this is only a fraction of the various facets constituting the problematic health-care context. Currently, health education programs tend to focus on how lay persons can participate in the management of specific medical conditions and design programs that aim to reduce people's behavioral and environmental risk factors. It is suggested here that the impoverished information exchange in medical conditions can also be recognized as a *risk factor* in optimal health-care delivery. Perhaps, if such recognition will take place it can help mobilize resources and encourage the development of new approaches in health-care delivery that will comprehensively address the structural, cultural, and communication barriers in health care partnership building. Consequently, more symmetrical information exchange in medical encounters, and perhaps a more satisfying and effective health care system will emerge.

References

Altman, L., & Rosenthal, E. (1990). Changes in medicine bring pain to healing profession. *The New York Times,* February 18, p. 1.

Antonovsky, A. (1979). *Health, stress and coping.* San Francisco: Jossey-Bass.

Argyle, M. (1983). Doctor-patient skills. In D. Pendelton & J. Hasler (Eds.), *Doctor-patient communication* (pp. 57–74). London: Academic Press.

Arntson, P. (1989). Improving citizens' health competencies. *Health Communication, 1*(1), 29–34.

Ballard-Reisch, S. S. (1990). A model of participative decision making for physician-patient interaction. *Health Communication, 2*(2), 91–104.

Barnlund, D. C. (1976). The mystification of meaning: Doctor-patient encounters. *Journal of medical education, 51,* 716–25.

Beisecker, A. E. (1990). Patient power in doctor-patient communication: What do we know? *Health Communication, 2*(2), 105–22.

Blanchard, C. G., Labrecque, M. S., Ruckdeschel, J. C., & Blanchard, E. B. (1988). Information and decision-making preferences of hospitalized adult cancer patients. *Social Science and Medicine, 27*(11), 1139–45.

Bochner, S. (1983). Doctors, patients and their cultures. In D. Pendelton, & J. Hasler (Eds.), *Doctor-patient communication* (pp. 127–138). London: Academic Press.

Brody, D. S. (1980). The patient's role in clinical decision-making. *Annals of Internal Medicine, 93*(5), 718–22.

Brown, S. (1988). Effects of Educational Interventions in Diabetes care: A meta-analysis of findings. *Nursing Research, 37*(4), 223–29.

Burgoon, J. K., Pfau, M., Parrott, R., Birk, T., Cocker, R., & Burgoon, M. (1987). Relational communication, satisfaction, compliance-gaining strategies, and compliance in communication between physicians and patients. *Communication Monographs, 54*(3), 307–24.

Byham, L. D., & Vickery, C. E. (1988). Compliance and health promotion. *Health Values, 12* (4), 5–12.

Campbell, J. D., Mauksch, H. O., Neikirik, H. J., & Hosokawa, M. C. (1990). Collaborative practice and provider styles of delivering health care. *Social Science and Medicine, 30*(12), 1359–1366.

Chandalia, H. B., & Bagrodia, J. (1979). Effects of Nutritional counseling on the blood glucose and nutritional knowledge of diabetic subjects. *Diabetes Care, 2*(4), 353–56.

Cassel, E. J. (1985). *Talking with patients: Volume 2, clinical technique.* Cambridge, MA: MIT Press.

Childress, J. & Siegler, M. (1984). Metaphors and models of doctor-patient relationships: Their implications for autonomy. *Theoretical Medicine, 5,* 17–30.

Cicourel, A. V. (1983). Hearing is not believing: Language and the structure of belief in medical communication. In S. Fisher & A. D. Todd (Eds.). *The Social Organization of Doctor-Patient Communication* (pp. 221–39). Washington, DC: Center for Applied Linguistics.

Cline, R. J. (1983). Interpersonal communication skills for enhancing physician-patient relationships. *Maryland State Medical Journal,* April, 272–78.

Covel, D. G., Uman, G. C., & Manning, P. R. (1985). Information needs in office practice: Are they being met? *Annals of Internal Medicine, 103,* 596–99.

Davis, W. K., Hull, A. L., & Boutaugh, M. L. (1981). Factors affecting the educational diagnosis of diabetic patients. *Diabetes Care, 4*(2), 275–78.

Diabetes Forecast. (1987). What you said about monitoring. February, 25–26.

DiMatteo, M. R. & DiNicola, D. D. (1982). *Achieving patient compliance: The psychology of the medical practitioner's role.* New York: Pergamon Press.

Ellmer, R., & Olbrisch, M. E. (1983). The contribution of a cultural perspective in understanding and evaluating client satisfaction. *Evaluation and Program Planning, 6,* 275–81.

Engel, G. L. (1978). The Biophyschosocial model and the education of health professionals. *Annals of the New York Academy of Sciences, 310,* 169–81.

Etzwiller, D. D. (1984). Diabetes education: The reason for its existence. *Diabetes Care, 7* (1), 15–18.

Ewles, L. & Shipster, P. (1981). *One to one: A handbook for the health educator.* Lewes, UK: East Sussex Area Health Authority.

Fisher, S. (1983). Doctor talk/patient talk: How treatment decisions are negotiated in doctor-patient communication. In S. Fisher & A. D. Todd (Eds.). *The Social*

314   Between Communication and Information

Frankel, R. M. & Beckman, H. B. (1989). Evaluating the patient's primary problem(s). In M. Stewart, and D. Roter (Eds.), *Communicating with medical patients* pp. 86–98). Newbury Park, CA: Sage.

Freidson, E. (1975). *Profession of medicine: A study in the sociology of applied knowledge.* New York: Dodd, Mead & Company.

Freidson, E. (1980). Dominant professions, bureaucracy, and client services. In W. R. Rosengren & M. Lefton (Eds.), *Organizations and clients: Essays in the sociology of service,* (pp. 71–92). Columbus, OH: Charles E. Merrill.

Gann, R. (1986). *The health information handbook: Resources for self care.* Hants, UK: Gower Publishing.

Gartner, A. & Reissman, F. (1974). *The service society and the consumer vanguard.* New York: Harper & Row.

Geller, J., & Butler, K. (1981). Study of educational deficits as the cause of hospital admission for diabetes mellitus in a community hospital. *Diabetes Care, 4*(4), 487–89.

Gibbs, Sick and Tired. *Time,* 31 July 1989, 48–53.

Gillum, R. F. & Barskey, A. J. (1974). Diagnosis and management of patient noncompliance. *Journal of the American Medical Association, 228,* 1563–67.

Goffman, E. (1963). *Behavior in public places: Notes on the social organization of gatherings.* Glencoe, IL: The Free Press.

Green, L. W. (1978). Health information and health education: There's a big difference between them. *Bulletin of the American Society of Information Science, 4*(40), 15–16.

Greenfield, S., Kaplan, S., Ware, Jr., J. (1985). Expanding patient involvement in care: effects on patient outcomes. *Annals of Internal Medicine, 102,* 520–28.

Guttman, N. (1990). Practitioners' assumed versus patients' actual knowledge and attitudes regarding diabetes care: Implications for practitioner-patient communication. Paper presented at the 40th International Communication Association Annual Conference, June 1990, Dublin.

Hadjistavropoulos, H. D., Ross, M. A., & Von Bayer, C. L. (1990). Are physicians' rating of pain affected by patients' physical attractiveness? *Social Science and Medicine, 31*(1), 69–72.

Hall, J., & Dorman, M. (1988). What patients like about their medical care and how often they are asked: A meta-analysis of the satisfaction literature. *Social Science and Medicine, 27*(9), 935–39.

Hall, J. A., Roter, D. L., & Katz, N. R. (1988). Meta-analysis of correlates of provider behavior in medical encounters. *Medical Care, 26,* 657–65.

Hamoson, S. E., Glasgow, R. E., & Toobert, D. J. (1990). Personal models of diabetes and their relations to self-care activities. *Health Psychology, 9*(5), 632–46.

Hardesty, M. J. (1988). Information tactics and the maintenance of asymmetry in physician-patient relationship. In D. R. Maines & C. J. Couch (Eds.), *Communication and Social Structure* (pp. 39–58). Springfield, IL: Charles C. Thomas.

Haug, M., & Lavin, B. (1983). *Consumarism in medicine: Challenging physician authority.* Beverly Hills, CA: Sage.

Hulka, B. S., Cassel, J. C., Kupper, L. L., & Burdette, J. A. (1976). Communication, compliance, and concordance between physicians and patients with prescribed medications. *American Journal of Public Health, 66*(9), 847–53.

Hulka, B. S., Kupper, L. L., Cassel, J. C., & Mayo, F. (1975). Doctor-patient communication and outcomes among diabetic patients. *Journal of Community Health, 1*(1), 15–27.

Inlander, C. B., Levin, L. S., & Weiner, E. (1988). *Medicine on Trial.* New York: Prentice Hall.

Innes, J. M. (1977). Does the professional know what the client wants? *Social Science and Medicine, 11,* 635–38.

Inui, T. S., Yourtee, E. L. & Williamson, J. W. (1976). Improved outcomes in hypertension after physician tutorials. *Annals of Internal Medicine, 84,* 646–51.

Janz, N. K., & Becker, M. H. (1984). The health belief model: A decade later. *Health Education Quarterly, 11*(1), 1–47.

Jaspars, J., King, J., & Pendelton, D. (1983). The consultation: A social psychological analysis. In D. Pendelton & J. Hasler (Eds.), *Doctor—Patient Communication* (pp. 139–57). London: Academic Press.

Joos, S. K., & Hickam, D. H. (1990). How health professionals influence health behavior: Patient provider interaction and health care outcomes. In K. Glans, F. M. Lewis, & B. K. Rimer, *Health Behavior and Health Education: Theory, Research and Practice* (pp. 216–241). San Francisco: Jossey-Bass.

Kaplan, S. H., Greenfield, S., & Ware, J. E. (1989). Assessing the effects of physician-patient interactions on the outcomes of chronic disease. *Medical Care, 27*(3), S110–27.

King, J. (1983). Health beliefs in consultation. In D. Pendelton & J. Hasler (Eds.), *Doctor-Patient Communication* (pp. 109–125). London: Academic Press.

Korsch, B. M., Gozzi, E. K., & Francis, V. (1968). Gaps in doctor-patient communication: I. Doctor-patient interaction and patient satisfaction. *Pediatrics, 42,* 855–71.

Kreps, G. L. (1987). The pervasive role of information in health and health care: Implications for health communication policy. *Communication Yearbook 11,* 238–76.

Kreps, G. L. & Thornton, B. C. (1984). *Health communication: Theory and practice.* New York: Longman.

Kreps, G. L., Ruben, B. D., Baker, M. W., Rosenthal, S. (1987). Survey of public knowledge about digestive health and diseases: Implications for health education. *Public Health Reports, 102*(3), 270–77.

Lazare, A., Eisenthal, S., Frank, A. Stoeckle, J. D. (1976). Studies on the negotiated approach to patienthood. In E. B. Gallangher (Ed.), *The doctor-patient relationship in the changing health scene* (DHEW Publication No. [NIH] 78–183) (pp. 119–39). Washington, DC: U.S. Government Printing Office.

Ley, P. (1983). Patients' understanding and recall in clinical communication failure. In D. Pendelton & J. Hasler (Eds.), *Doctor-patient communication* (pp. 89–107). London: Academic press.

Ley, P. & Spelman, M. S. (1967). *Communicating with the patient.* London: Staples Press.

Leventhal, H., Safer, M. A., & Panagis, D. M. (1983). The impact of communications on the self-regulation of health beliefs, decisions, and behavior. *Health Education Quarterly, 10*(1), 3–29.

Matthews, D., & Higson, R. (1977). Improving patient compliance: A guide for physicians. *Medical Clinics of North America, 61*(4), 879–89.

McKinlay, J. (1975). Who is really ignorant—physician or patient? *Journal of Health and Social Behavior, 16,* 3–11.

Meichenbaum D, Turk DC. (1987). *Facilitating treatment adherence: A practitioner's guidebook.* New York: Plenum Press.

Merkel, W. (1984). Physician perception of patient satisfaction: Do doctors know which patients are satisfied? *Medical Care, 22*(5), 453–59.

Mirowsky, J., & Ross, C. (1983). Patient satisfaction and visiting the doctor: A self-regulating system. *Social Science and Medicine, 17*(18), 1353–61.

Mishler, E. G. (1984). The Discourse of Medicine: Dialectics of Medical Interviews. Norwood, NJ: Ablex.

Nelson, M. K., & McGough, E. (1983). The informed client: A case study in the illusion of autonomy. *Symbolic Interaction, 6*(1), 35–50.

Northouse, P. G., & Northouse, L. L. (1985). *Health communication: A handbook for health professionals.* Englewood Cliffs, NJ: Prentice Hall.

O'Hair, D. (1989). Dimensions of relational communication and control during physician-patient interaction. *Health Communication, 1*(2), 97–115.

Parsons, T. (1951). *The social system.* New York: Free Press.

Parsons, T. (1970). How are clients integrated in service organizations? In W. R. Rosengren & M. Lefton (Eds.), *Organizations and clients: Essays in the sociology of service* (pp. 1–16). Columbis, OH: Charles E. Merrill.

Pascoe, G. C. (1983). Patient satisfaction in primary health care: A literature review and analysis. *Evaluation and Program Planning, 6*, 185–210.

Peck, C., & King, N. J. (1986). Medical compliance. In J. N. King & A. Remeny (Eds.). *Health care: A behavioral approach.* Orlando, FL: Harcourt, Brace Jovanovich,

Pendelton, D. A., & Bochner, S. (1980). The communication of medical information in general practice consultation as a function of patient's social class. *Social Science and Medicine, 14A,* 669–73.

Pendelton, D. (1983). Doctor-patient communication: a review. In D. Pendelton & J. Hasler (Eds.), *Doctor-patient communication* (pp. 5–53). London: Academic Press.

President's Commission for the study of Ethical Problems in Medicine and Biomedical and Behavioral Research. (1982). *Making health care decisions, Vol. 1.* Washington DC: U.S. Government Printing Office.

Pritchard, P. (1983). Patient participation. In D. Pendelton & J. Hasler (Eds.), *Doctor-patient communication* (pp. 206–23). London: Academic Press.

Pryor, B. & Mengel, M. (1987). Communication strategies for improving diabetics' self-care. *Journal of Communication, 37*(4), 24–35.

Purtilo, R. (1978). *Health Professional/Patient Interaction, Second edition.* Philadelphia: W. B. Saunders.

Putnam, S. M., Stiles, W. B., Jacob, M. C. (1985). Patient exposition and physician explanation in initial medical interviews and outcomes of clinic visits. *Medical Care, 23,* 74–83.

Robinson, E. J., & Whitfield, M. J. (1985). Improving the efficiency of patients' comprehension monitoring: A way of increasing patients' participation in general practice consultation. *Social Science and Medicine, 21,* 915–19.

Romm, F. J. & Hulka, B. S. (1979). Care process and patient outcome in diabetes mellitus. *Medical Care, 17*(7), 748–56.

Rosengren, W. R., & Lefton, M. (Eds.). (1970). *Organizations and Clients: Essays in the Sociology of Service.* Columbus, OH: Charles E. Merrill.

Rosenstock, I. M. (1990). The health belief model. Explaining health behavior through expectancies. In K. Glans, F. M. Lewis, & B. K. Rimer, Health

Behavior and Health Education: Theory, Research and Practice (pp. 39–62). San Francisco: Jossey-Bass.

Rost, K., Carter W., & Inui, T. (1989). Introduction of information during the initial medical visit: consequences for patient follow-through with physician recommendations for medication. *Social Science and Medicine.* 28(4), 315–21.

Roter, D. (1977). Patient participation in the patient-provider interaction: the effects of patient question asking on the quality of interaction, satisfaction and compliance. *Health Education Monographs, 5,* 281–315.

Rowland-Morin, P. A. & Reuben, D. B. (1987). Getting the most from your visit to the doctor: Make your office visit work for you. *Diabetes Forecast, 40*(10), 27–28.

Ruben, B. R., & Bowman, J. C. (1986). Patient satisfaction (Part I): Critical issues in the theory and design of patient relations training. *Journal of Healthcare Education and Training, 1*(1), 1–5.

Ruben, B. D. (1990). The health caregiver-patient relationship: pathology, etilogy, treatment. In E. B. Ray & L. Donohew (Eds.), *Communication in Health Care Contexts: A Systems Perspective.* Hillsdale, NJ: Lawrence Erlbaum Associates.

Shorter, E. (1985). *Bedside manners: The troubled history of doctors and patients.* New York: Simon & Schuster.

Shuy, R. W. (1983). Three types of interference to an effective exchange of information in the medical interview. In S. Fisher & A. D. Todd (Eds.), *The Social Organization of Doctor-Patient Communication* (pp. 189–202). Washington, DC: Center for Applied Linguistics.

Slack, P. (1988). Cost effective advice. *Nursing Times,* 81(14), 26.

Smith, D. H., & Pettegrew, L. S. (1986). Mutual persuasion as a model for doctor-patient communication. *Theoretical Medicine 7,* 127–46.

Sneider, I. (1986). *Patient power: How to have a say during your hospital stay.* White Hall, VA:Betterway Publications.

Stein, H. F. (1990). *American Medicine as Culture.* Boulder, CO: Westview Press.

Stewart, R. B., Cuff, L. E. & Leighton, E. D. (1972). Commentary: A review of medication errors and compliance in ambulatory patients. *Clinical Pharmacology Therapy, 13,* 463–86.

Stone, G. C. (1979). Patient compliance and the role of the expert. *Journal of Social Issues, 35,* 1 (34–59).

Suchman, A., & Matthews, D. A. (1988). What makes the patient-doctor relationship therapeutic? Exploring the connexional dimension of medical care. *Annals of Internal Medicine, 108,* 125–30.

Squier, R. W. (1990). A model of empathic understanding and adherence to treatment regiments in practitioner-patient relationships. *Social Science and Medicine, 30*(3), 325–39.

Szasz, T. S. & Hollender, M. C. (1956). The basic models of the doctor-patient relationship. *Archives in Internal Medicine, 97,* 585–92.

Taylor, S. G., Pickens, J. M., & Geden, E. A. (1989). Interactional styles of nurse practitioner and physicians regarding patient decision making. *Nursing Research, 38*(1), 50–55.

Thompson, S. C., Nanni, C., & Schwankovsky, L. (1990). Patient-oriented interventions to improve communication in a medical office visit. *Health Psychology,* 9(4), 390–404.

Thompson, T. L. (1986). *Communication for Health Professionals.* Lanham, MD:University Press of America.

Trostle, J. A. (1988). Medical compliance as an ideology. *Social Science and Medicine, 22*(12), 1299–1308.

Verbrugge, L. M. & Steiner, R. P. (1981). Physician treatment of men and women patients: sex bias or appropriate care? *Medical Care, 19*(6), 609–32.

Verhaak, P. (1988). Detection of psychologic complaints by general practitioners. *Medical Care, 26*(10), 1009–20.

Waitzkin, H. (1985). Information giving in medical care. *Journal of Health and Social Behavior, 26,* 81–101.

Wakeford, P. (1983). Communication skills training in United Kingdom Medical Schools. In D. Pendelton & J. Hasler (Eds.), *Doctor-Patient Communication* (pp. 233–47). London: Academic Press.

Wertz, D. C., J. R. Sorenson, & T. C. Heeren. (1988). Communication in health professional-lay encounters: How often does each party know what the other wants to discuss? In B. Ruben, (ed.). *Information and Behavior. Vol. 2.* (pp. 329–42). New Brunswick, N.J.: Transaction.

West, C. (1983). "Ask me no questions . . .": An analysis of queries and replies in physician-patient dialogues. In S. Fisher & A. D. Todd (Eds.), *The Social Organization of Doctor-Patient Communication* (pp. 75–106). Washington, DC:Center for applied Linguistics.

West, C. (1984). When the doctor is a "lady": Power, status and gender in physician-patient encounters. *Symbolic Interaction, 7*(1), 87–106.

Weston, W. W., & Brown, J. B. (1989). Importance of patients' beliefs. In M. Stewart, & D. Roter (Eds.). *Communicating with medical patients.* (pp. 77–85). Newbury Park, CA:Sage.

Zola, I. K. & Miller, S. (1973). The erosion of medicine from within. In E. Freidson (Ed.) *The professions and their prospects,* (pp. 153–72). Beverly Hills, CA:Sage.

15

Judgment Model Overlap and Decision-making Group Processes

Geoff Leatham

This research examines the effect of judgment model overlap on disagreement within decision-making groups. Judgment models were assessed for seventeen small groups using procedures drawn from Social Judgment Theory (SJT)-based research. Groups were formed where members had a high or low degree of congruency in factors they considered important in solving a personnel selection task. Analysis of variance indicated that groups with a high degree of judgment model congruency overtly disagree more often than groups with a low degree of judgment-model congruency. This counterintuitive finding is interpreted in the context of research on cognitive processing of conversation and tenets of the Socio-Egocentric Model (SEM) of group decision making.

Justification of a Judgment-based Approach to Small Group Process

Research into decision making in a small group setting has a history of looking to individual processes in decision making for insight and prescriptive advice. Currently, the functional approach advocated by Hirokawa and colleagues (see, for example, Gouran & Hirokawa, 1983; Hirokawa 1980, 1985) is based on the decision-making procedure outlined by John Dewey (1910) and has been among the most prolific research programs in small group research during the 1980s. Hirokawa used Dewey's five steps to predict the success of groups and at the same time, Dewey's prescriptions have been written up in undergraduate textbooks (e.g., Andrews and Baird, 1988) as an agenda for groups to follow in making decisions. The recent success of the functional approach encourages investigation of new developments in individual decision making. Perhaps the advances made since 1910 in understanding the decision-making processes of individuals can provide inspiration and guidance in exploring group decision-making processes. Research in human judgment processes has blossomed in the last twenty-five years. Examination of how people weigh evidence (Tversky & Kahneman, 1974), combine evidence (Anderson, 1979), and routinize judgments (Mandler, 1984) give a picture of how individuals *do* make decisions rather than how they should make decisions.

History alone does not suggest that our more sophisticated understanding of individual decision making should inform exploration of group decision-making processes. Judgment is a cognitive process that is central in decision making (Brehmer, 1984). In other arenas, cognitive processes and limitations have been shown to affect the production and interpretation of language (Glass & Holyoak, 1986; Berger, 1987). The effects range from encoding and decoding effects to strategy selection to construction and interpretation of relationships. If judgment is a cognitive process and judgment is important in making decisions, then assessing the cognitive state of individuals in the group may illuminate some of the communication processes that occur.

In an effort to create a more parsimonious model of small group processes, some group decision-making researchers have tried to "reduce" group processes to individual variables. The best-known and most successful effort has been the Social Decision Scheme approach of James Davis (1973). He and his collegues claim that group decision making can be best understood as a function of the preinteractional preferences of individuals and a rule governing how the group combines those preferences. Davis' approach and the approach of others who see communication as a neutral medium for social processes have been tested against an alternative formulation, that communication moderates the group decision-making process. In this view, communication plays a role beyond transmission of individual preferences and application of decision rules. For example, communication may allow for the correction of inferential errors (Gouran, 1986) or the exercise of positive influence over another (Seibold and Meyers, 1986). Susan Jarboe (1988), Burleson, Levine, & Samter (1984) and Hirokawa et al. (1990) have all set up tests comparing the utility of the mediating and moderating view of group processes. While the tests are still open to differing interpretations, it seems clear that individual variables can be useful in understanding decision quality as an outcome. Also, communication does seem to play more than a mediating role in at least some situations. Therefore, to get a complete picture of what is involved in making a high-quality decision, it is necessary to understand individual variables' effects on decision quality, processual effects on decision quality, and the relationship between individual variables and group process. The first two areas (also labelled "input-output" studies and "process-output" studies respectively) have been actively researched. This paper explores the nature of the input-process link, without necessarily generating a more comprehensive input-process-output model.

Also, assessing the judgment models of individuals also may help with a knotty methodological problem in group decision-making research. Small group researchers have no really good method of evaluating the decision quality of problems with no independently verifiable correct answer. To understand how judgment models can help deal with this problem, the nature of judgment models must be described.

A judgment model is represented as a regression equation. In making a complex decision, there are a number of factors (or attributes) that must be weighed. For example, in selecting which graduate students should be offered an assistantship, one may consider intelligence, drive, work ethic, interest, racial diversity, gender diversity, and/or other factors. These considerations, used in judging the suitability of a candidate for graduate school, are the factors of a judgment model. Each of these factors may differ in importance. And each factor will be measured on a different scale. Therefore, like a regression equation, each factor is weighted to eliminate scale difference and account for its importance in making a judgment. Finally, the factors must be combined in some way. Extending the analogy of the regression equation, linear regression uses an additive combinatory rule. There are alternative rules for combining weighted factors, including averaging (a variant of the additive rule) conjunctive (where all of the weighted factors are multiplied) and disjunctive (where all of the weighted factors are inverted, then multiplied). The effects of using different combinatory rules lies outside the scope of this paper. At this point, it is only important to understand what "factors" are, and that they are weighted and combined to form a judgment model. Alternatives that can be considered in solving a problem have "cues" associated with them. The GPA on the transcript may count as a cue indicating intelligence or scholastic aptitude, as will the strength of a letter of recommendation. Somehow, these cues must be scaled (if no more accurately than low/high) to be inserted into a judgment model to evaluate a choice.

In evaluating the output of small groups, an objective measure of decision quality is necessary (Brown, 1988). This has led to use of problem-solving tasks (McGrath, 1984) like the cannibals and missionaries (Shaw, 1932), the NASA moon problem (Hall and Watson, 1970) or the horse trader problem (Maier and Solem, 1952). All of these problems have an answer that is intuitively compelling, logically or mathematically demonstrable or provided by experts in the field. However, many tasks do not have an objectively correct answer. Policy decisions are often included in this group. Janis (1982) has used historical investigation to look at tasks with no objectively verifiable best answer. History does provide a measure of the quality of the decision that is actually made, but does not allow comparison with alternatives that were abandoned in making the choice as time only reveals the quality of actions that were actually performed. Therefore, Janis has been limited to evaluating "good" and "poor" decisions rather than the "best" decision. This limits the historical approach in looking at decision quality, in addition to the lack of controllability and intensive effort required by a historical approach.

Judgment models may give researchers a measure of the quality of a decision and its alternatives in a case where there is no objectively verifiable best answer. In order to be accurate, this method requires that two assumptions be met. First, the judgment models of the individuals in the group must be relatively stable. Finding out the factors that would go into making the best meal for a group will fluctuate from day to day depending on mood and will vary even more depending on time of day. So assessing the judgment models of individuals for food in the evening would be of limited use in assembling a breakfast for the group. Second, the evaluation of the quality of the decision will be valid only for those stakeholders who are represented in the group. In the task used for the present study, college students were asked to select a speaker for graduation ceremonies. Evaluating the decision of the group in the light of the factors considered important by these college students may not capture the preferences of relatives and university faculty and administration who may also be at graduation. In a case like this, evaluation of decision quality could only apply to the college students.

The quality of a solution to a decision-making task may be evaluated by combining the judgment models of the stakeholders into a staticized group-judgment model. To do this, individual judgment models are pared down from all of the factors that it is possible to consider to only those factors that contribute "significantly" to the judgment being made or to those factors that meet a given criterion like contributing a minimum amount of variance to the judgment model as evaluated. Then, if the factors are normalized to eliminate scaling differences, they can be weighted by adding 1 for each of the people that use a given factor in making their decision. Then, each alternative can be evaluated by assessing the strength of the cue associated with each factor in the group's model. A three-person group may have an equation that looks like this for the problem of selecting a graduation speaker:

$$\text{Evaluation of Candidate} = 3x(\text{Speaking Ability}) + 2x(\text{Achievements}) + 1x(\text{Humor})$$

A sample speech may indicate that a candidate has good command of the language (high cue strength on the factor "speaking ability") and that he cannot tell a good joke (low cue strength on the factor "humor"). Choosing this candidate would get a higher rating than choosing a candidate who could tell a joke but could not speak well. A good sense of humor and strong achievements may make up for some deficiencies of speaking ability. In this way, it is possible to specify which of the possible choices the group may consider is best *for that group*. The judgment of decision quality can be tailored to the group in question, providing an alternative method of measuring decision quality where holding all groups to the same standard of quality may be inappropriate.

While this method requires more work than simply declaring one choice as the best, it has already proven itself in real world applications. Decision analysis is big business. Academicians using Multi-Attribute Utility Technology (MAUT) have provided assistance to governmental and private groups faced with difficult decisions (see Edwards & Newman, 1982). MAUT essentially uses experts to evaluate the strength of cues associated with each outcome and uses the stakeholders of a decision to assess the weights associated with each factor.

The potential for further understanding of group process, the important role cognitive processes and limitations have played in other communication topics, the current interest in input versus process models of group communication, and potential methodological utility all encourage application of current decision-making research to the study of small group processes. I will be examining potential effects that having members with similar or different judgment models may have. In a decision-making group, the members may all think the same factors are important, or some people may think one set of factors is important, while others use a different set of factors. For complex decisions, it is not unreasonable to expect that everyone in a group will have different judgment models, in factor weighting if not in factor inclusion. This research project explores the effect of similarity of judgment models among members on the communication that occurs in the group. I call groups where members share essentially the same set of factors a *high overlap* group while groups where members have substantial differences in their set of factors are a *low overlap* group. An example of the factor models for high and low overlap groups are given in appendix 15.1. The significance of the R^2 will be discussed further in the methods section. This study only includes factors in the judgment model that account for at least 10 percent of the variance in a subject's response. As you can see from appendix 15.1, judgment models in high overlap groups are not identical. Also, people in low overlap groups may share some factors in common. But overall, there are more factors shared in high overlap groups than are shared in low overlap groups, as the sample groups in appendix 15.1 illustrate.

Overview of Judgment Research

Group processes have not been extensively investigated from a judgment model perspective. Brehmer's (1984) work in group conflict is based in Social Judgment Theory (Hammond et al., 1975) which is built around the concept of judgment models as presented here. However, Brehmer is primarily interested in how judgment models are affected by interaction. This paper examines the transverse of the topic: how is interaction affected by judgment models.

Brehmer and other judgment researchers have established a number of characteristics associated with judgment models (Arkes & Hammond, 1986):

1. Judgment models are not available for conscious inspection. People commonly report weighing more factors than they actually use. They also report combining factors with greater sophistication and complexity than they actually use.
2. People apply judgment models with some degree of inconsistency.
3. Including new/unfamiliar factors in a judgment model increases the inconsistency of application of the judgment model.
4. Conflicting judgments can arise from the application of different judgment models or inconsistent application of the same judgment model.
5. Exposure to the judgments of others will lead to a gradual inclusion of the factors they use in a person's judgment model.
6. Judgment models require more cognitive effort to apply when the factors are unfamiliar, when there are many factors, or when the combinatory rule is not linear.

Hypotheses

The research on judgment model adaptation (see 5 above) and cognitive conflict (see 4 above) leads to some speculation about how differences in judgment models may affect communication. As group members with a low degree of judgment model overlap interact over time, they will gradually include the factors that other members consider important. This process will be facilitated if groups must come up with some kind of consensus decision. People use new factors with less consistency than they use factors they are familiar with. Inconsistency in application of judgment models would seem to encourage confusion in the group and perhaps misunderstanding or miscomprehension. Because of difficulties in coordinating a low overlap group, it seems reasonable that it would take more time to come to a consensus decision. This is the first research question.

Hypothesis 1: Groups with low judgment model overlap take more time to make a decision than groups with high judgment model overlap.

Since this research uses groups that meet only once, to make a single decision, it is not clear how much adaptation of judgment models will occur in the hour allotted to discussion. Brehmer (1984) found that dyads did adapt their judgment models to their partner, but that was in an artificial case where there was one numerical cue for each person that was probablistically related to a judgment. Partners made judgments together and received immediate feedback after each judgment. The ambiguity of most nonexperimental judgments has been controlled out in this setting. Also, it took a number of trials before judgment models converged. In the case where a group meets to make a decision once, there may not be time for convergence to occur if there are major differences in judgment models. In a decision-making task like the one used in this experiment, there are opportunities for multiple judgments, but the cues are still ambiguous, there is no direct feedback on judgment accuracy and there are certainly not opportunities to make forty judgments as is common in judgment research. Therefore, groups with a low degree of overlap will have to find some way to reach a consensus without necessarily developing a single shared judgment model.

Ambiguous language may serve the purpose. As mentioned previously, the experimental task used here is to select a speaker for graduation. If person A thinks intelligence is the important characteristic in evaluating a candidate while B thinks that speaking ability is the most important characteristic, there may be an argument if A says, "I think we should select candidate 2 because she is the brightest of the bunch." Since B does not use intelligence as a discriminating criterion, he or she may not evaluate intelligence consistently and so may discount candidate 2's intelligence. On the other hand, A may say, "I think candidate 2 is a strong candidate." Then B is free to review candidate 2's qualifications and perhaps find a good reason to support the candidacy. Ambiguity allows people to reach agreement for different reasons. This generates the second research question.

Hypothesis 2: Groups with a low degree of overlap use ambiguous language more than groups with a high degree of overlap.

Conflict is the final area of inquiry in this research project. There are some reasons to believe that low overlap groups and high overlap groups may be characterized by more challenges of statements by group members. Members using different judgment models are likely to make different judgments about the quality of an alternative. This may give more opportunities for members to challenge each other's statements. And this is the intuitively compelling position. People that think about problems in different ways should argue with each other.

But there is some reason to believe that low overlap groups may not be characterized by a high degree of challenge. Hewes' (1986, 1990) Socio-Egocentric Model of small group communication maintains that when people in groups are thinking along different lines, they do not tend to overtly challenge the statements of others. Rather, they use a "vacuous acknowledgement" of the other's point to gain the floor and then launch into their own thoughts. Second, challenge requires a good degree of comprehension and critical thought to be successful. It has been established that working with judgments arising from different models requires more cognitive effort than working with another who has a similar model. Therefore, with the limited processing capacity of the brain, members may not be able to marshall their full critical abilities in low overlap groups because they are mentally working on keeping track of their own judgments and trying to figure out where others in the group are coming from. This leads to the final research question which is "two-tailed."

Hypothesis 3: Groups with a low degree of judgment model overlap will express a different amount of challenge than groups with a high degree of judgment model overlap.

Method

Task Development

In order to explore the research questions given above, a personnel selection task was developed. Subjects were to select an undergraduate speaker for commencement exercises. This subject was chosen because virtually all university students would have attended a graduation ceremony at some time. Also, evaluating other people is a common judgment task. Finally, a task like this made it easy for the subjects to see themselves as stakeholders in the outcome. Observation of the discussion and questioning during debriefing indicated that subjects had no particular trouble making sense of the task.

To find out which factors were likely to be relevant in making a decision of this nature, fifty-six students from an undergraduate communication class were surveyed. They were asked to list what attributes they considered most important in choosing a speaker for commencement. They were also instructed to circle the two to five most important factors. Finally, they were asked to indicate what kinds of materials they would find useful in selecting a commencement speaker. Responses included resumé information, transcripts, photos, recordings of speeches, letters of recommendations, and so on. People will commonly report more factors than they would actually use in making a decision, but they usually include among the list the factors they do use (Stewart, 1988). Therefore, this list is likely to include the relevant attributes and traits of a good graduation speaker. The list of characteristics is given in appendix 15.2.

Preassessment Instrument

The twelve most commonly cited attributes were used to generate a preassessment instrument to capture the judgment models of subjects. Thirty-six cases were developed where the levels of each of the twelve attributes were varied low, moderate, or high. Assignment of factor level was done randomly with the restriction that all factors had to have about equal numbers of low, moderate, or high conditions. The order of presentation of the attributes was randomized to control for any order effects. A sample case in given in appendix 15.3. Subjects were asked to evaluate thirty-two cases as though they were selecting a speaker for a 4th of July speech. The characteristics of a 4th of July speaker were deemed to be close enough to generate an accurate judgment model without prompting the students to begin thinking specifically about the commencement setting. The twelve factors at level low, moderate, or high were regressed using a stepwise procedure against the subjects' judgment of the candidate's suitability for the task on a 1–10 point Likert-type scale anchored by "Completely unsuitable for task" and "Ideal candidate for task". Those factors that accounted for 10 percent or more of the variance in the candidate's judgments were retained as factors in their judgment model.

After filling out the preassessment instrument, subjects were assigned to groups with others who had either a similar judgment model (high overlap) or a different judgment model (low overlap) and asked to come into the lab for a group discussion.

Candidate Profile Information

Eight candidate profiles were drawn up. Each profile included some resumé-type information, a partial transcript, a personal essay, and a letter of recommendation from a professor. Six factors were manipulated in creation of the profiles: intelligence, speaking ability, responsibility, achievements, sense of humor, and confidence. All candidates had some cues that could be associated with each of the six factors. All candidates were strong on three to five of the factors because they were supposedly the finalists from a larger pool of applicants. All materials were created and the subjects were informed that the information they were receiving was not based on actual people.

Subjects

Subjects were drawn from communication classes at a large midwestern university. All subjects received extra credit for their participation. Sixty-two students participated in the project. Subjects were divided into seventeen three- and four-person groups based on their judgment models and ability to meet at certain times.

Procedure

Groups were told to look over the candidate profiles and select a commencement speaker from among the eight candidates. They were instructed to reach a decision on a single candidate that all members could support. In addition, subjects were told to record their individual preferences every five minutes and place it in an envelope. Subjects were told that they could continue discussion until they had reached a consensus decision, but would only have an hour to complete their discussion. No discussion went longer than forty-five minutes. After discussion, subjects were allowed to ask questions of the experimenter and given a more complete picture of the purpose of the experiment.

Analysis

Group discussions were videotaped. Each time a candidate was mentioned, a factor was mentioned or a statement was challenged, it was coded along with its valence. For example, a candidate could be praised, as in the statement, "I think Conrad would be a good choice." This would be coded as a "C(+)" indicating that Conrad was evaluated positively. Or a statement could be made, "I think speaking skills are important." This would be coded as a 2(+), as speaking skill was designated as attribute #2. If a subject said, "I think Conrad is a poor speaker," it would be coded as "C2(-)". Finally, if an utterance challenged the utterance immediately before, they were circled to indicate that.

Measurement

These coded transcripts allowed the three research questions to be investigated. Time was measured in minutes of discussion. Ambiguity was measured as the number of utterances advocating a candiate without giving a specific reason for support (e.g., C(+), but not C2(+)) divided by the time of the discussion to control for unequal length of discussion. Challenge was operationalized as the number of challenges divided by the amount of time the discussion took.

Univariate analysis of variance was used to explore all three research questions. The independent variable was either low or high overlap.

Results

Research question 1 asked whether it would take more time for low overlap groups to reach consensus than high overlap groups. This experiment failed to reject the null hypothesis of no difference between discussion times for low and high overlap groups. ($F[1,15] = .67$, NS, Power[$\emptyset = .50$] = .41)

Research question 2 asked whether language would be more ambiguous in groups with low overlap of judgment models. The null hypothesis of no difference was retained for this question also. Low overlap groups did not use significantly more ambiguous language than high overlap groups. ($F[1,15] = .33$, NS, Power[$\emptyset = .50$] = .41)

Research question 3 asked whether low overlap groups would have a different number of challenges than high overlap groups. The null hypothesis was rejected ($F[1,15] = 5.45$, $R^2 = .266$) Groups with high overlap of judgment models contained more challenging statements than groups with low overlap of judgment models.

Discussion

The results of the analyses of variance indicate that overlap of judgment models probably does not exert the influence on small group communication that might be expected at first glance. Something other than underlying cognitive differences accounts for groups that make decisions quickly versus those that make them slowly. This is a surprising result and seems to imply that the speed of groups may be better explained by looking at communication or relational variables than looking at cognitive variables. Poole and Roth (1990) found that many groups began their discussion by immediately examining the solutions to the task facing them. This pattern was more common when the potential solutions were clear to the group members. Discussions in this experiments tended to follow that pattern. Group members would read the information provided for five to ten minutes. Then a member would say something like "well, why don't we go around and see who everybody liked." Only one of the seventeen groups had all members initially selecting the same candidate. Judgment model overlap did not discriminate between groups who had similar and dissimilar candidate preferences. Judgment models only measure one part of the decision-making process. Judges must also evaluate cues. This experiment used naturalistic cues like grade point average instead of an artificially constructed cue like indicating that a candidate has above average intelligence. Naturalistic cues are evaluated more inconsistently than cues that have been distilled to a single comparable number by the experimenter. Since high and low overlap groups had to reach consensus from equivalent levels of initial disagreement, overlap did not predict length of discussion.

The use of ambiguity does not seem to differentiate low or high groups either. If ambiguity is a technique for forging a consensus without necessarily getting complete agreement on all aspects of a decision, it may be equally useful for those groups with high overlap as well as those groups with low overlap. Since high overlap challenges more than groups with low overlap, ambiguity could be a way of dealing with potential conflict resulting from a challenge. Therefore, both low- and high-overlap groups may have use for retaining a degree of ambiguity in their discussions. In addition, a follow-up study (Leatham, 1991) indicated that high-overlap groups may attend to face maintenance concerns (Goffman, 1955/1976) than low-overlap groups. Ambiguity may be a viable strategy for maintaining the face of other group members. Therefore, low-overlap groups may use ambiguity to forge consensus while high-overlap groups may use ambiguity to attend to face maintenance. Analysis dependent on mean use of ambiguity will not be likely to detect a difference in this case.

The finding that high-overlap groups challenge statements more than low-overlap groups is intriguing. The vacuous acknowledgments of Hewes' Socio-Egocentric Model explains why we may not necessarily see more challenge from a low-overlap group than a high-overlap group. But it does not explain why a high-overlap group should challenge more often. A cognitive processing approach to group discussion may help explain this finding. If formulating a challenge to a statement and understanding a judgment from a model different from one's own are both cognitively difficult, factors that increase the prevalence of one should decrease the prevalence of the other assuming a fixed capacity for cognitive processing. Groups with low overlap have to spend more cognitive capacity processing judgments made from different judgment models than groups with high overlap. Therefore, groups with low overlap have fewer cognitive resources to critically examine the statements of others in the group.

If this is true, further examination of the language of low- and high-overlap groups may provide some support. If comprehension is relatively easy for high-overlap groups, the kinds of conflicts that occur in the group and its resolution should be different from the conflicts of low-overlap groups. High-overlap group conflicts should center around differences in evaluation of cues (like how well getting an A− in a public speaking class is evidence of a competent speaker) and should be resolved through conventional influence processes. Low-overlap group conflicts should center around misunderstanding and should be resolved through clarification or dropping the topic. A discourse processing approach looks like a promising avenue for further investigation.

Appendix 15.1

Examples of group composition with members indicating the use of factors in selecting an undergraduate speaker for Commencement exercises.

High Overlap Group

Member 1	*Member 2*
Intelligence R2 = 22%	Speaking Ability R2 = 55%
Speaking Ability R2 = 18%	
Member 3	*Member 4*
Speaking Ability R2 = 27%	Speaking Ability R2 = 31%
Intelligence R2 = 11%	Intelligence R2 = 16%
	Confidence R2 = 12%

Low Overlap Group

Member 1	*Member 2*
Intelligence R2 = 18%	Sincerity R2 = 19%
Speaking Ability R2 = 14%	Confidence R2 = 12%
Humor R2 = 10%	
Member 3	*Member 4*
Friendly R2 = 35%	Speaking Ability R2 = 42%
Outgoing R2 = 15%	Confidence R2 = 11%

Appendix 15.2

A list of the attributes that students in a large upper-division University of Iowa communications class would look for in selecting a speaker for graduation. If they felt the attribute was among the 2 to 5 most important, it received two votes.

Frequency	Attribute
93	Speaking skills
62	Intelligent
50	Friendly
42	Funny
40	Outgoing
36	Charismatic
34	Attractive
30	Motivated
29	Sincere
28	Confident
23	Positive attitude
20	Knowledgable of world affairs
18	Successful
14	Professional
13	Responsible
9	Creative
8	Sensitive
5	Talkative
4	Helpful
3	Fair
3	Leader
3	Mature
2	Experienced speaker
2	Insightful
2	Modest
2	Organized
1	Happy

Appendix 15.3

A Sample Case From the Judgment Model Assessment Instrument

1. very friendly, somewhat humorous, somewhat outgoing, not very charming, average intelligence, somewhat homely, not very hard-working, excellent public speaking ability, often sincere, often responsible, very confident, not very successful.

1	2	3	4	5	6	7	8	9	10

Completely
Unsuitable
for Task

Ideal
Candidate
for Task

References

Anderson, N. H. (1979). Algebraic rules in psychological measurement. *American Scientist, 67,* 555–63.

Andrews, P. H., & Baird, J. E., Jr. (1988). *Communication for business and the professions.* Dubuque, WI: W. C. Brown.

Arkes, H. R., & Hammond, K. R. (1986). *Judgment and decision making: An interdisciplinary reader.* Cambridge: Cambridge University Press.

Berger, C. R. (1988). Planning, affect and social action generation. In L. Donohew, H. E. Sypher, & E. T. Higgins (Eds.), *Communication, social cognition and affect* (pp. 93–115). Hillsdale, NJ: Lawrence Erlbaum.

Brehmer, B. (1984). The role of judgment in small-group conflict and decision making. In G. M. Stephenson & J. H. Davis (Eds.), *Progress in applied social psychology,* vol. 2, (pp. 163–83). New York: Wiley.

Brown, R. (1988). *Group Processes: Dynamics within and between groups.* London: Blackwell.

Burleson, B. R., Levine, B. J., & Samter, W. (1984). Decision-making procedure and decision quality. *Human Communication Research, 10,* 557–74.

Davis, J. H. (1973). Group decision and social interaction: A theory of social decision schemes. *Psychological Review, 80,* 97–125.

Dewey, J. (1910). *How we think.* Boston: D. C. Heath.

Edwards, W., & Newman, J. R. (1982). *Multiattribute evaluation.* Beverly Hills, CA: Sage.

Glass, A. L. & Holyoak, K. J. (1986). *Cognition.* New York: Random House.

Gouran, D. S. (1986). Interential errors, interaction, and group decision-making. In R. Y. Hirokawa & M. S. Poole (Eds.), *Communication and group decision-making* (pp. 93–111). Beverly Hills, CA: Sage.

Gouran, D. S., & Hirokawa, R. Y. (1983). The role of communication in decision-making groups: A functional perspective. In M. S. Mander (Ed.), *Communications in transition.* New York: Praeger.

Hall, J., & Watson, H. H. (1970). The effects of a normative intervention on group decision-making performance. *Human Relations, 23,* 299–317.

Hammond, K. R., Stewart, T. R., Brehmer, B. & Steinmann, D. O. (1975). Social judgment theory. In M. F. Kaplan & S. Schwatz (Eds.), *Human judgment and decision processes*. New York: Academic Press.

Hewes, D. E. (1986). A socio-egocentric model of group decision-making. In R. Y. Kirokawa & M. S. Poole (Eds.), *Communication and group decision-making* (pp. 261–91). Beverly Hills, CA: Sage.

Hewes, D. E. (1990). Challenging interactional influence on group decision-making processes: Extending the socio-egocentric model. Paper presented at the Speech Communication Association convention, Chicago.

Hirokawa, R. Y. (1980). A comparative analysis of communication pattern within effective and ineffective decision-making groups. *Communication Monographs, 47*, 312–21.

Hirokawa, R. Y. (1985). Discussion procedures and decision-making performance: A test of a functional perspective. *Human Communication Research, 12*, 203–24.

Hirokawa, R. Y., Salazar, A. J., Propp, K. M., Julian, K. M., & Leatham, G. B. (1990). In search of true causes: Examination of the effects of group potential and group interaction on decision performance. Paper presented at the Speech Communication Association convention, Chicago.

Janis, I. L. (1982). *Victims of groupthink*. Boston: Houghton Mifflin.

Jarboe, S. (1988). A comparison of input-output, process-output, and input-process-output models of small group problem-solving effectiveness. *Communication Monographs, 55*, 121–42.

Leatham, G. (1991). Explicit disagreements in groups with high and low judgment model overlap. Paper presented at the Alta conference on argumentation, Alta, Utah.

Maier, N. R. F. & Solem, A. R. (1952). The contribution of a discussion leader to the quality of group thinking. The effective use of minority opinions. *Human Relations, 5*, 85–115.

Mandler, J. (1984). *Stories, scripts, and scenes: Aspects of schema theory*. Hillsdale, NJ: Lawrence Erlbaum.

McGrath, J. E. (1984). *Groups: Interaction and Performance*. Englewood Cliffs, NJ: Prentice Hall.

Poole, M. S., & Roth, J. (1990). Decision Development in Small Groups V: Test of a Contingency Model. *Human Communication Research, 15*, 540–55.

Seibold, D. R., & Meyers, R. A. (1986). Communication and influence in group decision-making. In R. Y. Hirokawa & M. S. Poole (Eds.), *Communication and group decision-making*. Beverly Hills, CA: Sage.

Shaw, M. (1932). A comparison of individuals and small groups in the rational solution of complex problems. *American Journal of Psychology, 44*, 491–504.

Stewart, T. R. (1988). Judgment analysis: Procedures. In B. Brehmer & C. R. B. Joyce (Eds.), *Human Judgment: The SJT View* (pp. 41–74). Amsterdam: Elsevier Science Publishers B.V.

Tversky, A. & Kahneman, D. (1974). Judgment under uncertainty: Heuristics and biases. *Science, 185*, 1124–31.

16

Designing Groupware for Implementation

Raymond R. Panko

Groupware tools, including electronic message systems (EMSs) and computer conferencing systems, often suffer from implementation and ongoing use problems. Some of these problems include critical mass failures, stunted use, flaming, and junk mail. While these problems can be reduced through good attention to detail in implementation and by applying organizational pressure, many common problems can be reduced through the use of good product design. This paper discusses the use of good product design to create robust systems that can thrive even in the face of substantial implementation and use problems and that fit the varied needs of different kinds of users.

Introduction

Design and implementation are often viewed as separate processes. But several important implementation problems in groupware can be ameliorated by good design and exacerbated by bad design. This paper focuses on the design of groupware tools that can survive and bring good benefits even in the face of common implementation threats. We call such groupware tools *robust*.

During the 1960s and 1970s, implementation problems were a common focus of information systems research (cf. Robey 1979). Painful experience showed that many clerical systems were resisted and that managers often ignored their MIS reports. During the 1980s, resistance was temporarily forgotten as organizations struggled to keep abreast of the exploding demand for personal computers and other new end user computing tools.

Now, however, interest in implementation problems is reappearing as new tools take aim at the support of groups rather than individuals. In groupware—a term that we will use broadly to include all tools for groupwork support, from simple electronic message systems to complex tools for group project coordination—serious problems can occur during the implementation stage. These problems are important because many groupware products aim primarily at knowledge workers (managers and professionals), who account for 70 percent of the office workforce and who spend about 70 percent of their work time communicating (Panko 1990b). Now that many clerical and stand-alone knowledge worker needs have already been met, groupware promises to be the "wave of the 1990s"—unless its prospects are dimmed by implementation and ongoing use problems.

Critical Mass

The most dramatic implementation problem in groupware is the *critical mass* problem. It has long been known that if systems fail to attract a "critical mass" of users, they will fail entirely (Artle & Averous, 1983; Connolly & Thorn, 1990; Galleta, 1986; Grudin, 1988, 1989; Hammer, 1985; Hiltz & Turoff, 1978; Markus, 1987, 1990; Markus & Connolly, 1990; Oren & Smith, 1981; Panko, 1983, 1989, 1990a; Rice, 1990; Rogers, 1986, 1989; Rohlfs, 1974; Thorn & Connolly, 1987; Tucker, 1982; Uhlig, Farber, & Bair 1979; Williams, Rice, & Rogers, 1988). Markus (1987, 1990) has developed a comprehensive theory of critical mass effects, drawing from earlier work by Oliver, Marwell, & Teixeira (1987) on critical mass phenomena in social movements.

Tucker (1982) has illustrated critical mass failure with a specific example. In the early 1980s, a bank introduced an electronic message system. It had few terminals, however, so users had to walk to pick up their mail. Initially, there was low use, and users often got no mail. As a result, users checked the system for mail less often, so messages became less likely to be read promptly. In addition, there were many nonusers, so messages often failed to get through. These effects caused the system to be viewed as unreliable, so fewer messages were sent, causing people to pick up their mail even less frequently and prompting more users to drop out. This death spiral continued until a senior executive called an important meeting and only three people arrived. The rest had not read the message. The system was immediately discontinued.

While only a few cases of critical mass failure have been reported in the open literature (Galleta, 1986; Hammer, 1985; Tucker, 1982), this may be due primarily to a reluctance among organizations to report their failures. And although critical mass problems have been seen most often in electronic message systems (EMSs) and computer conferencing systems, this may be simply because these are the oldest and most established forms of groupware. Critical mass problems have also been seen in other forms of groupware (Connolly & Thorn, 1990; Grudin, 1988, 1989; Thorn & Connolly, 1987). Indeed, some newer and more advanced forms of groupware, such as group project management systems may need an even higher fraction of participation to achieve critical mass than EMS and computer conferencing.

Stunted Use

But what if the innovation gets beyond critical mass? Are its troubles over? The answer appears to be that infant mortality is only the first implementation danger to face groupware. The next hurdle to be faced is stunted use. A good number of groupware systems get beyond critical mass but then stagnate at low levels of use. While these stunted systems survive, they fall far short of their potential as an organizational communication medium, and organizations fail to reap their full benefits.

During the 1970s, for instance, the author interviewed managers of a dozen ARPANET electronic mail systems. He found that systems in which the average user sent much less than a message per day, EMS was not regarded as a form of rapid communication. While this result is rather obvious, if it is true, it means that studies of EMS must be examined very carefully. EMS surveys cover systems with wide ranges of use. Some cover systems in which the average person receives ten to thirty messages per day (e.g., Mackay, 1988; Sproull & Keisler, 1986), while others cover systems that are used to send only a few messages per month (e.g., Danowski and Edison-Swift, 1985; Rice, Hughes, & Love, 1989). If impacts are related to use, then comparing these studies must be done very carefully.

Perhaps the stunted use problem can be best explained by discussing its reverse phenomenon—the *takeoff* phenomenon, in which groupware systems do reach the level needed to make them mainline communication systems. During the 1970s, Texas Instruments built an internal electronic message system. It's use was significant initially, but when many sites were linked together, use spurted forward, and the EMS soon became the normal way for TI workers to communicate (White, 1979). On the ARPANET in the early 1970s, EMS also blossomed when network mail became available, giving people access to many people.

Other Problems

While skewed use and stunted use are dramatic, these implementation problems are often followed by ongoing use problems. In EMS, for instance, we have seen "flaming," in which people fire off heated messages, "junk mail," in which many irrelevant messages are sent via distribution lists, "information overload," in which heavy users become too swamped with groupware processing activities to handle their functional work, and the misinterpretation of humorous messages as hostile messages.

Robust Design

Some of these problems can be reduced by proper attention to detail in implementation, such as terminal availability, good training, proper promotion, and not charging for service. But even if many such actions are taken, serious implementation problems and use problems can still remain. Another option is to use direct *command* to require people to use groupware tools and to use them in specific ways. But as discussed below, knowledge workers have traditionally been given a great deal of discretion over how they do their work. As a result, few organizations are willing to mandate groupware use, and weaker mechanisms, such as boss or peer pressure, may still not be sufficient to avoid critical mass failures, stunted use, or other major groupware implementation problems.

In this paper, we will focus on another approach—*product design*—as a way to reduce or eliminate implementation difficulties. While the use of negative sanctions to force use is unlikely in most places and can have severe side effects, good design can simply avoid many problems—ameliorating many difficulties without creating more stresses and costs in the organization. While attention to detail and organizational pressure are important, good product design presents a relatively "free" way to reduce many difficulties; and for groupware tools that are especially prone to critical mass failures and stunted use disappointments, the use of robust product design may be critical to success.

Skewed Use

Before discussing specific problems and design approaches, we need to look at the importance of "skewed use" in groupware products. This phenomenon, long seen in consumer and industrial marketing, lies at the heart of critical mass, stunted use, and several other important implementation and use problems.

For nearly any consumer product, there are heavy users, light users, and nonusers. This pattern is known as *skewed use*. Table 16.1 shows that skewed use is ubiquitous for consumer products.

Research has shown that skewed use is also seen widely in information technology, products, including both stand alone products and groupware products (Collopy, 1988; Culnan, 1983; Fulk et al., 1987; Hiltz, 1984; Hiltz, 1988; Kerr & Hiltz, 1982; Lynch, 1980; Mayer, 1977; McLean, 1974; Panko, 1978; Panko & Panko, 1981; Reder & Schwab, 1989; Rice & Shook, 1990; Rice, Hughes, & Love, 1989; Rice & Manross, 1987; Rice & Shook, 1986; Rockart & Flannery, 1983; Rogers, 1982, 1986; Steinfield, 1985; Sumner, 1986). In fact, the author knows of no study that has looked at the distribution of use for an IT product and has failed to find skewed use.

Skewed use should not be confused with just the limited use that takes place early in a product's life cycle, when relatively few ultimate adopters have started to use it. While skewed use is certainly high in the early stages of a product's life cycle, skewed use typically remains high after a product has matured and has reached its ultimate level of penetration. (The data in table 16.1 are largely for mature consumer products, such as beer.) In addition, many of the IT studies cited in the preceding paragraph

TABLE 16.1
Skewed Use in Consumer Products

	Percentage of Nonusers	Percentage of Use from the Heavy Half
Beer	67	88
Dog Food	67	87
Bourbon	59	89
Hair Fixatives	54	88
Hair Tonic	52	87
Lemon-Lime Soda	42	91
Paper Towels	34	83
Frozen Orange Juice	28	89
Cake Mixes	27	85
Colas	22	90
Shampoo	18	81
Margarine	11	83
Bacon	6	82
Ready-to-Eat Cereal	4	87
Sausage	3	84
Soaps & Detergents	2	81
Toilet Paper	2	74

One-year diary survey

Source: Twedt (1964)

describe fairly mature implementations. *Skewed use, then, is not an artifact of the adoption cycle; it is a universal phenomenon occurring throughout a product's life cycle.*

Table 16.1 illustrates a simple way to represent skewed use. For this table, all consumers in the diary sample were rank ordered according to their frequency of purchasing in each of the product categories listed.

Nonusers recorded no purchase in the category during the time period, which was a full year. In measuring nonuse, it is important to specify a time period; because the shorter the time period, the higher the percentage of nonusers.

The table also divides users during the period into two strata: the *light half*, who make fewer than the median number of purchases, and the *heavy half*, who make more than the median number of purchases.

When very detailed information is available, it is useful to work with the entire distribution instead of aggregating it into three strata. Research has shown that the purchase distribution is approximated fairly accurately by the *negative binomial distribution* (Chatfield & Goodhardt, 1970; Ehrenberg, 1975).

For skewed use groupware, a number of subtleties tend to appear. Most obviously, there are often several candidate *dependent variables* for measuring degree of use, including frequency of use, total amount of use in some time period, and sophistication of use. While these three are likely to be correlated, the correlation may only be moderate (Panko, 1978; Panko & Panko, 1981). It may be useful to measure distributions for several light-heavy dimensions, because frequency of use may have different implications for controlling skewed use and judging the effectiveness of an innovation than either sophistication of use or the total amount of use within a given period. In electronic message system, for instance, how frequently a user checks his or her mail may be especially important for achieving critical mass, while sophistication of use may be important in avoiding crippled use.

There are other subtleties in skewed use for groupware, but rather than discussing them generally we will discuss them in the context of specific problems and the design actions that seem promising in meeting these problems.

Design Approaches to Problems Arising from Skewed Use

Having looked at skewed use in general, we will now turn to specific aspects of skewed use, the problems that they create, and the use of design to reduce these problems.

Nonuse and Lax Use

Nonuse. The most obvious implementation problems are nonuse and lax use. In nonuse, individuals do not use the system at all. There is ample evidence (e.g., Markus, 1987; 1990; Panko, 1978; Panko & Panko 1981; Steinfield, 1986) that the value of a communication medium depends heavily on the number of people it can reach. In fact, a goal of the telephone system from its earliest days has been Universal Access—the ability to reach everyone. Nonuse means that messages will have to be prepared twice, once for nonusers and once for users. It also means that there will be less incentive to use the system, since on many occasions the person one wants to communicate with is not on the system. A large percentage of nonusers can destroy a system, as in the Tucker (1982) example discussed earlier. A smaller number of nonusers can stunt the system.

Lax use. When a user fails to use the system frequently, he or she is called a *lax user*. If there are many lax users in an electronic message system, calendar management system, or other groupware system, people will stop using the system, because messages will not get through reliably in a short period of time, because calendars will not be updated with sufficient frequency, or because other needed maintenance activities will not be made sufficiently often. At best, a message system suffering from lax pickup will be used for primarily for communications that are not time-critical. In group project management systems and other groupware tools for which timely data input is critical, in turn, the system will fail to be used for real-time work.

Lax use is complicated by the fact that some users, after reading their incoming mail, do not respond promptly. One disappointed user, who had hoped that electronic message systems would reduce delays commented ruefully that people who fail to return their telephone calls also fail to return electronic messages. So even login frequency may not measure frequency of response to messages.

Designing for nonuse and lax use. The author (1982, 1985, 1989, 1990a) has previously suggested an approach to handling nonuse, lax use, and a third situation, namely *delegation,* in which the "user" delegates most or all terminal work to a secretary. Delegation is commonly seen in FMS (Crawford, 1982; Mackay, 1988; Panko, 1978; Panko & Panko, 1981) and information retrieval services (Culnan, 1983; Sieck 1984; Sullivan, Borgman, & Wippern, 1990). Although delegation may be on the wane as a result of broader computer knowledge and the proliferation of desktop equipment, delegation produces problems for secretaries who must log in successively to multiple EMS accounts or other groupware accounts instead of handling all work in one log in. The time wasted in successive log-ins caused secretaries to rate an EMS considerably lower than either direct users or delegators in one survey (Panko, 1978; Panko & Panko, 1981). In addition, delegation can be extremely complex, with different principals delegating different amounts and types of work to their responsible secretaries.

Figure 16.1 illustrates a possible design approach to reduce these problems (Panko, 1982, 1985, 1989, 1990a). First, as soon as the system is created, everyone can be assigned to one of three levels of use:

Direct users use the system in the traditional way, handling their own mail in most cases. Second, delegation is handled by responsible secretaries working for people who want to delegate all work and also for direct users who delegate some types of work (such as prescreening messages or typing long outgoing messages in the case of electronic message systems or inputting progress information in a group project management system)

FIGURE 16.1
Levels of Use and Bouncing

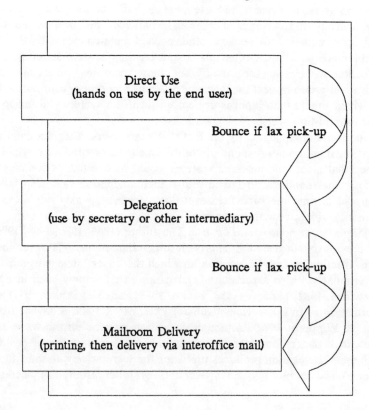

or who delegate all work occasionally, such as when they are on vacation or when they are on a business trip. The responsible secretary must be able to log in just once and handle work for all delegators without leaving that single account. Third, mail for pure nonusers is printed in the mailroom and delivered through interoffice mail.

With this approach, each message is prepared only once, and it always gets through. While delegators and nonusers get the mail later, they still get it. So messages need to be prepared only once, and the system will reach everyone with whom a user of the system needs to be in contact. In addition, because others receive corporate mail sooner than they do, they have an incentive for moving up ther service ladder to get their mail sooner.

The RANDmail system at the RAND Corporation, developed in 1983, uses the levels of service concept (Bikson, 1990; Eveland & Bikson, 1986). It allows direct use, mailroom delivery, and delegation. The delegation is somewhat limited, being aimed primarily at boss-private secretary dyads and working by giving the two a joint account and individual accounts instead of handling the broader complexities of delegation, but it fulfills Shaw's dictum: "Do not do unto others what you would have them do unto you; they probably want something else."

Even with universal service, there is still the problem of direct users and responsible secretaries being lax in picking up their mail. As shown in figure 16.1, however, lax use problems can be reduced if tasks are automatically *bounced* to a lower level if they are not completed in a timely way (Panko, 1982, 1985, 1989, 1990a). For instance, if a message to a direct user is not read in a certain period of time, say one day, it will be bounced to a responsible secretary for receipt. If a responsible secretary fails to read the message, it will be bounced to mailroom printing. In group project management systems, in turn, if data have not been updated in a timely manner by a direct user, the responsible secretary may be sent a message asking the secretary to enter the data.

There can even be communication generated by the system to reduce problems raised by lax use. For instance, in electronic message systems, messages can be sent asking for a reply by a certain date, and the system can automatically generate a reminder if no reply has been received by the required date. In addition, and EMS can inform the sender that a message has not been read by the receiver or has not been read in some period of time. In group project management and personal scheduling systems, in turn, the manager can be informed if data have not been updated recently by some group members. At the same time, it is somewhat dangerous to remove the traditional slack in organizations that allows people not to respond to mail or telephone calls in a timely manner; sometimes slow response or no response is a valid tactic in organizational life. A system with perfect memory that a response is due may force conflicts that could have been avoided by conditions merely "blowing over."

The Needs of Heavy and Light Users

While it is critical to design groupware systems for the needs of midrange users, it is also critical to consider the special needs of users at the light and heavy use extremes. If light users are not handled well, they are likely to drop out, weakening the usefulness of the system. Heavy users, in turn, may use the system an hour a day or more; if they are not provided with good tools, a great deal of valuable organizational time may be lost, and they may even quit the system in frustration.

Special support for light users. Light users of EMS appear to be like light users of 35 mm cameras and like most users of color television sets. They are casual users who like to keep things simple. If there are complex adjustments to be made in using a system, they will try to ignore them, and if this cannot be done or even if the system merely *looks* complex, they may not adopt it.

The special needs of light users are easy to overlook, because they are rarely vocal. Over time, in fact, the functionality of most systems tends to increase under pressure from heavy users. This may make the system more and more unpalatable to the light user, turning at least some into nonusers.

Consumer marketing has shown that many light users want use to be extremely automatic. The 35 mm camera market only exploded after highly automatic 35 mm cameras were introduced, allowing casual picture takers to snap better pictures than they could with 110 cameras without fussing with each picture. Even if some pictures were ruined by lack of precise control, casual photographers viewed this as more than acceptable.

One approach to making systems more automatic is to reduce the functionality available to light users. In Microsoft Word, for instance, some versions can be set to display only "short menus," that show only basic actions. In another approach, IBM has produced *training wheels* word processors with some functions deliberately crippled (Carroll & Carrithers, 1984). This kind of crippling can almost always be done with PC-based systems that use keystroke command entry by assigning keys to null strings through keyboard mapping utilities (Panko, 1988). In another paper, the author has suggested that there be several levels of functionality for users at different skill and demand levels (Panko, 1982, 1985). If functionality is reduced, however, there should be ways of adding it in gradually, so that users do not face a sudden rush of functionality when they move beyond the basic system.

But it is also important to understand that automaticity can be extremely difficult to create. For 35 mm cameras, to use the example again, it took several years of detailed study to understand how to make cameras very simple to use without losing large amounts of functionality. Designing for automaticity is an art, not just a matter of meat cleaving. Nor is it just a matter of KISS—keep it simple, stupid. Artificial intelligence may provide ways to add functionality gracefully and even to identify areas in which it would be valuable for a given user to pick up a new type of functionality.

Special support for heavy users. At the other extreme, heavy users also need special tools. As message volume or other tasks increase in magnitude, users begin to demand tools to cope with large volume efficiently. In electronic message systems, for instance, most use comes not in message composition but in message disposition—reading, deleting, forwarding, replying, filing, and retrieving (Panko, 1978; Panko & Panko, 1981). Heavy users may have to maintain extensive logs of incoming and outgoing messages by topics (Mackay, 1988), while heavy users of project management systems may need multiple ways of looking at schedules. In Mackay's sample of users of a system in which the average person received twenty-six messages a day (Mackay, 1988), many users reported being overwhelmed or nearly so, and several expressed worries over what such heavy use of the system was doing to their productivity.

In addition, heavy users may have extremely strong and complex needs for delegation. Having a secretary or administrative assistant prescreen mail each morning and prepare replies may save a half hour or more of valuable managerial or professional time. These needs may be rather different from the delegation needs of other users in intensity, in the types of work that will be delegated, and simply in the possible presence of a private secretary.

Heavy users might even be given "read boards" with printed copies of messages. Since reading if faster with paper than on a computer, the user could scan the messages, jot down replies and notes to the secretary, and hand them back for action. This would require the printing of one message on each page, for physical filing if needed and leaving space for notes and replies.

As noted above, one of the most pressing needs for very heavy use is message disposition, that is, the handling of messages after receipt. Most commands given in electronic message systems are message disposition commands (Panko & Panko, 1981). A very heavy user may spend a half hour to an hour a day in message disposition. Message filtering research is now underway to determine if significant amounts of message handling can be handled through preprocessing (Chang & Leung, 1987; Malone et al., 1987; Pollock, 1988).

Intermitten Use

Another complication in considering design approaches to reduce use problems is *intermittently use*. Everyone's use fluctuates to some degree over time. But some uneven patterns of use call for special attention.

Burst intermittent use. Most dramatically, some users may have bursts of intense use separated by long dormant periods. For instance, an outside consultant may need to use a message system during projects, or a group may have to engage in collaborative design exercises only every year or so. *Burst users* may need systems that are extremely easy to relearn, but at least some need to be able to relearn to use the system at a high degree of sophistication; design and help systems can reduce the problems of burst users considerably, especially if they take into account that relearning is a very different process than initial learning.

In addition to relearning support, sophistication intermittent users are likely to need human assistance. Their learning and support needs are very specific to their knowledge, and rigid computer-assisted instruction is not likely to fit their needs. Help desks with human assistants, the delegation of especially complex tasks, facilitators for the use of sophisticated electronic conferencing tools and other forms of human assistance are likely to be needed. If designers can anticipate these needs, they may be able to provide system functions to support them.

While serving sophisticated intermittent users will be important, it will also be important to give good service to light intermittent users. Because of the forgetting problem during dormant periods, many intermittent users try to use only a few functions of the program. Special relearning tools and novice menus might be provided to keep their lives as simple as possible.

Brief periods of intermittent use. A less extreme but more common type of intermittently use occurs on vacations and sometimes on business trips. In these cases, the user will not read his or her mail at all or may read it at dramatically lower frequencies than others have come to expect. Design innovations to reduce problems during these *away periods* may include sending out notices to anyone who sends a message to the mailbox and letting a secretary do delegation or more delegation. Even here, the situation is subtle. One EMS allows a person to specify a message when the person goes on vacation. When another user sends a message to the person, the message is sent to that user, so that immediate reply is not needed. But problems arose because the system always sends the message, even if the other user has already received one (or several) notification messages. This can clog inboxes with useless messages. In addition, many people forgot to turn off their message when they returned, so that senders still got the message saying that the person was still on travel or vacation.

Styles of Use

A final issue in skewed use is that different individuals and groups often adopt extremely different *styles of use,* not merely different levels of use. For instance, in studying a group of extremely strong EMS users, Mackay (1988) found that different people with similar heavy traffic loads often adopted very different approaches for managing their mail overload. In addition, EMS tends to be used for different types of work in different organizations and even differently among workgroups within organizations. It would be extremely dangerous to overlook such differences in systems design, as discussed later.

Design Approaches for Other Use Problems

Although we are concerned primarily with problems raised by skewed use in this paper, the idea of turning to design to help reduce what might be first viewed as implementation problems is a broader concern. We will mention just a few more of the possible areas in which design could reduce common implementation and ongoing use difficulties. In this section, we will focus on EMS, where there is especially rich history.

Interconnection

One of the most frequently voiced needs is for the interconnection of multiple EMSs. Many firms have multiple EMSs, and many users end up having to use an EMS in another firm or having to let an outsider use their corporate EMS. This requires users to learn multiple systems and often to prepare a message multiple times for users on different systems. Internationally, the X.400 standard, called MHS, promises to end interconnection difficulties. Among PC LANs, a different standard, unfortunately also called MHS, is becoming widely used. Third, in academic communities, the simple mail transfer protocol (SMTP) is used on many networks such as Bitnet and Internet. In the future these worlds will have to be interconnected. While the consensus in the industry today is that X.400 will dominate eventually, SMTP, the PC LAN MHS, and vendor-specific standards are much less complex, and this will make it difficult for X.400 to displace them.

Directory Assistance and Routing

Another common need expressed by EMS users is a directory assistance function. Many EMSs assign odd formal names to users. (The author's address is CBADRPA@UHCCVM.Bitnet) As a result, senders often waste a good deal of time looking up formal names for recipients. While personal lists of frequently used formal names are useful, systems might provide ways to look up formal names. In other groupware products, formal names are also given to rooms, projects, and other resources. Fortunately, the need for directory services is becoming widely understood. All of the major PC network operating systems now offer at least rudimentary naming service, and the CCITT X.500 standard for Directory Service standard promises to allow the interoperability of directory service in the future. At the application level, however, not all EMSs provide directory service, and many other LAN-based groupware tools also fail to provide directory service.

Another approach to specifying user names is used in the RANDmail system (Bikson, 1990). The user interface in this system allows the user to type a first name, last name, or part of a name. It then uses AI matching algorithms to identify the specific receiver. Several other systems, including the NLS Journal Mail system, developed in 1970, use a simpler approach, allowing the user to type a last name and then select from a list of people identified by full name and organizational affiliation. This addressing feature was interfaced with the Network Information Center on the ARPANET, so that the name list included people in many organizations.

In many cases, the sender may not even know to whom a message should be sent. They merely know that they have information on a topic of importance. One approach is to send information to a distribution list of people who have expressed interest in the topic or a related topic. In effect, this creates a computer conference. Distribution lists are extremely commonplace in EMS, and where distribution lists are used widely, it is difficult to distinguish an EMS from a conferencing system on the basis of traffic. In both cases, messages sent to individuals by name dominate the number of messages sent, but distribution list messages usually dominate the number of messages received. During the 1970s, the members of a geographically dispersed government directorate used a conferencing system, but only 5 percent of all messages were conference messages; the rest were private messages. For NLS Journal Mail, in turn, 58 percent of all messages were sent to named individuals, and these averaged 2.7 receivers per message; but the 42 percent of all messages sent to distribution lists averaged 26.2 receivers per message and completely dominated reception. A sample of 6350 messages from the HERMES system and of 9925 messages from a system at MIT both showed a pattern of many messages sent to a one or a few people by name and a small number of distribution list messages that substantially increased the number of receivers per message. Mackay's (1988) sample also appeared to have distribution lists dominate the number of messages received.

But the distribution list is an extremely blunt tool for dissemination to potentially interested parties. The Information Lens project at MIT uses a more sophisticated approach, using AI techniques to determine what general messages should go to what people (Malone et al., 1987). In general, the *selective dissemination of information* problem, which has been long discussed in the library sciences literature, needs much more attention in the future.

In some organizations, there are strong rules for the formal routing of certain types of messages to specific people or at least offices. This is especially true in the military. During the 1970s, the Military Message Experiment at CINCPAC headquarters in Hawaii demonstrated the ability of messages to be routed automatically to offices needing the material. Interestingly, the research for this project underscored the fact that routing tends to be very different in crises. A major crisis is given a specific name, and all messages related to the crisis are assigned this name designation. By singling out messages for important crises, this approach guarantees that crisis information is kept together yet avoids the need to assign topic categories to each incoming message.

Security and privacy

Although security and privacy are always concerns, most organizations have lived with relatively loose security and privacy in their mail and telephone systems. Even so, a number of security and privacy problems need to be considered in EMS and other forms of groupware.

Unauthorized access. First, while paper mail is often enclosed in envelopes and an unauthorized person usually has to be around a person's desk to violate paper mail security, computer mailboxes usually can be accessed from many places without a trace as to the reader's real identity or location. Extremely confidential mail cannot be sent on these systems unless there is very strong access control. Many groupware tools go beyond individual files, to include group databases, such as calendar systems (Connolly Thorn, 1990; Thorn & Connolly, 1987). For these systems, keeping confidential information requires exceptional access control at the group level. For safety against really determined attackers, even further lengths must be taken. As Oliver North discovered, for instance, deleted information may still have been captured on backup tapes.

For normal organizational use, however, it may be sufficient to brand mail and other information with access stamps, such as "company private," "client private," and "confidential." Normal reticence may then be sufficient to control access to most data. If more control is needed, messages or data with such labels may require an additional password. This will provide general protection as well as increased protection in cases where delegation allows another person to look at information in a mailbox or other private files.

Private information. Personal information is also private. Government agencies need to have special control over private material, and private organizations may also be liable if private information about individuals is accessed in an inappropriate manner. So group databases that contain personal information must be guarded carefully.

Employee privacy. One currently hot issue is whether companies should be able to read the electronic messages of employees and to look at other information that would normally be locked in drawers in the paper world. Some employees feel that they should have absolute privacy to say anything over EMS, while some companies take the other extreme position that company mail is property of the company. In scheduling systems, in turn, it can be demoralizing for bosses to have free access to the schedules of their subordinates. In general, whenever there are personally sensitive information collections, it is problematic to give superiors or other works free access.

There are currently lawsuits regarding companies reading the electronic mail of their employees. But regardless of what lawsuits eventually decide in the legal realm, clear corporate guidelines and expectations must be spelled out, so that employees know where they stand. A basic policy, for instance, might include maintaining personal privacy unless malfeasance is suspected, in which case something like a search warrant might be sought under prescribed rules. In addition, even if free access is the norm, employees should be notified of free access conditions; for instance, if the PROFS Calendar system is used, employees should be notified if the default is that anyone can read anyone else's calendar information. Design could assist in policy compliance, for instance by giving the user a password that can only be overridden centrally after proper sign-offs. And notifications of external access can be sent to employees.

Mail forwarding. Mail forwarding raises special security risks. Messages may go to unintended recipients and even people outside the company. Since many messages are quickly drafted, unauthorized redistribution can cause extreme problems. Again, clear guidelines and expectations need to be established. In addition, there might be system-enforced rules requiring the forwarding of messages marked "confidential" or given other security stamps.

Authentication. Good security also requires sender authentication, that is, proof that the person whose name is in the "From:" field really sent the message. During the 1970s, one message system designer, seeking to demonstrate authentication problems, sent a spurious message, ostensibly from a DARPA colonel, to many EMS users on the network. This was done simply by using a system text editor to edit the "From:" field.

While design may be useful in providing additional security for classified information, and handling such technical matters as authentication, it is also true that privacy and security are primarily organizational issues. Too much security can strangle a system or lead to counter-behavior, such as using obvious passwords that are easily guessed.

Data tampering. When databases are created to be shared, there is danger that someone will tamper with the data, either by "cooking the books" by supplying false data that hides problems or by changing data already entered in the system. Clear audit trails will help with the latter and somewhat with the former.

Inappropriate Messages

The issues mentioned so far and several others like them are fairly technical and have attracted the attention of both designers and standards agencies. But other issues are more behavioral and are often viewed by designers as implementation matters. We will turn to them now.

Regrettable messages. One of the most common problems in EMS is regrettable messages, that is, messages that the author sends and then wishes he or she had not sent. Regrettable messages happen not only in EMS but in spoken communication as well (Knapp, Stafford, & Daly, 1986).

One reason for regrettable messages is the fact that messages tend to be dashed off quickly, often in reply to an incoming message. The normal slack associated with typed memos disappears, and messages that would not be sent out in the paper world after reflection are delivered in EMS before problems are discovered. Another reason for regrettable messages is the lack of perceptual cues in typed messages. Something intended as a joke often comes across as serious. Yet another reason is the informality of EMS. It is common to dash off messages without editing for typos (or potential interpretation problems), and because this type of informality is widely tolerated, there are limited reasons for carefully deliberating over message content.

A controversial topic in regrettable communication is *flaming*. "Flaming" refers to the sending of emotion-laden negative messages, particularly early in the system's life. Flaming was first discussed on the ARPANET in the early 1970s. In fact, the term "flaming" was born on the ARPANET, and most other forms of socially and organizationally unsuitable messaging behavior was also seen within this highly permissive community. Keisler and her colleagues (Keisler et al., 1984, Siegel et al., 1986; Sproull & Kiesler, 1986) found instances of flaming among students and within a FORTUNE's 500 company. But Hiltz et al. (1985) found little or no flaming in computer conferences among adult professionals, and Robey, Saunders, & Vaverek (1989) also report little flaming in corporate systems. Given the existence of flaming in at least some systems, it may be a good idea to provide training in system etiquette, as was done in one ARPANET system (Brotz, 1983).

Message take-back. Research on spoken regrettable messages has shown that many regrettable spoken messages are regretted by senders shortly after they are transmitted (Knapp, Stafford, & Daly, 1986). Roughly three-quarters of all regretted spoken messages identified by respondents were regretted immediately. This suggests that EMS users should be able to "take back" messages after they are sent, at least until the recipient retrieves them. Few systems allow this, but the taking back of regrettable messages seems justified given the serious organizational problems it can raise.

Junk Mail

Finally, new design approaches might be able to reduce problems caused by "junk mail" in EMS (Denning, 1982). Because sending messages to mailing lists is easy to do, users often find themselves deluged by "junk mail" on topics of low interest. This can be an especially serious problem for users running at 1200 bps or 2400 bps, because scanning and getting rid of a message can often take half a mainute. Worse yet, if a message is sent to multiple mailing lists that overlap, some users will get two or more copies of each piece of junk mail. As noted above, Mackay (1988) found that many of the subjects in the group she studied found the handling of distribution list information to be very time consuming and daunting.

If mailing list filtering can be done to remove duplicates, and if users can easily have their names removed for certain types of messages, junk mail problems could be reduced by better design. And, as noted above, AI techniques may be used to enhance the selective dissemination of innovation.

At a more subtle level, some users become "transmission addicts," sending a long stream of messages to anyone and everyone. While this type of "glutting" behavior is often cured by peer sanctions, volume monitoring might be used to identify transmission addicts at the system level.

While it may be possible simply to forbid or greatly curtail distribution list transmissions, Sproull and Kiesler (1986) found that a larger percentage of all messages in their sample provided new information that would not have been provided otherwise. Hiltz and Turoff (1985) has argued that curtailing distribution list usage can cause very serious problems for organizations. So while design steps can be taken to curtail distribution lists, these steps must be considered very carefully.

Crank Mail

One of the banes of the telephone age is the "crank call," which may range from calling and hanging up to annoy the party called to outright obscenity. There are some indications that the same thing may be happening with facsimile. These cranks calls can include obscenity, threats, or practical jokes (Ball, 1968). In the telephone system (and in facsimile), sender anonymity has been a major contributing factor, allowing the perpetrator to send an unwanted message without fear of retribution (Ball, 1968; McLuhan, 1965).

In electronic message systems, anonymity is a rarity, and this may be the reason why there have been few reported instances of crank mail. But in other communication tools, anonymity may be supported. In computer conferencing and group decision support systems, for instance, the ability to send anonymous messages is fairly commonplace. On the positive side, this has allowed group members to "discipline" members behaving outside the norm. And while this may have led to an increase in emotion-laden messages (flaming and other aspects of emotionality are discussed above), the use on anonymity for prolonged harassment has not been reported. The potential, however, is there, and the ability to trace messages—under strongly prescribed and controlled circumstances—may be desirable as part of the authentication function of groupware systems.

Short Circuiting

A final behavioral concern is "short circuiting," in which formal lines of communication are bypassed by the ability of EMS to bypass formal lines of communication.

Upward short circuiting. In some situations, employees use EMS to send messages to their boss's boss and to other higher-level personnel to whom they would normally not have access, or at least not immediate access, without EMS. This can produce serious problems for the working relationships of all involved, especially if the communication reflects unfavorably on the sender's boss.

Downward short circuiting. Problems can also arise if a boss bypasses a direct subordinate to communicate with someone at lower levels in the organization without the subordinate's knowledge or approval. While this can be highly desirable at times, it can also be extremely demoralizing to the subordinate.

Horizontal short circuiting. Even horizontal communications can cause trouble. For instance, a staff member might send an electronic message to an operating unit in a crisis situation. Should this be taken as official staff guidance, despite lack of proper signoff?

In informal organizations, free flow is tolerable and often desirable, but this is not always the case in organizations across the spectrum. In particular, free access can greatly magnify information overload, in which people become overwhelmed by message traffic or other groupware handling work. More importantly, it can destroy working relationships. Design approaches to reducing vertical short circuiting might include mandatory sign-off for messages going above the sender's level in the organization or at least mandatory copying of upper communications to a person's boss, and having a formal message type for horizontal communication.

Issues in Robust Design

The purpose of this paper has been to discuss the broad importance of design approaches toward reducing implementation (and use) problems associated with groupware tools. Figure 16.2 lists a number of problems and design approaches discussed in this paper. This final section discusses a number of general issues to be faced as we consider design more closely as a way to avoid or reduce common implementation and use problems.

EMS Versus Other Groupware Tools

This discussion has focused on EMS because large-scale EMSs have been in use for more than twenty years, and their problems are well known. But other groupware tools are likely to have serious organizational problems. Grudin, as noted above, has noted that different people often receive the costs and benefits of a groupware tool (Grudin, 1988, 1989). Careful attention to the problems of different types of users is likely to be important in a wide range of groupware tools. And even within EMS, our discussion has focused only on a few implementation problems. For

FIGURE 16.2
Conditions, Implications, and Design Approaches

Condition	Implications	Design Approaches
Nonuse		
Some potential users do not use the system	Some communication partners will not be on the system Messages must be prepared twice Possible critical mass failure Possible stunted use	Universal service with three levels: Direct use; Delegation; and Mailroom Delivery (or some other low-level service)
Lax Use		
Some users do not do their work promptly	System will not be viewed as reliable Possible critical mass failure Possible stunted use	Bounce tasks to next lower level after a period of time Notification of affected parties
Delegation		
Some or all work is delegated to a secretary	Secretary may have to do a good deal of unnecessary work	Various special tools for total or partial delegation
Light Use		
Use well below the median	May not use or discontinue use if system is complicated to use	Special automatic interface for light users
Heavy Use		
Use well above the median	Overload Lost productivity	Sophisticated message disposition tools Delegation tools Read boards for offline reading Message screening

Intermittent Use

Bursts of use amid general nonuse Brief periods of nonuse (trips, vacations, etc.)	Intermittent burst users have special relearning needs and support needs Brief periods of nonuse harm expectation of rapid feedback	Learning and support services geared toward burst intermittent users Different learning and support tools for light, heavy intermittent burst users Notifications of trips, vacations to message senders Delegation during brief periods of nonuse

Styles of Use

Different users handle tasks in different ways	System may impose one way of handling such tasks, discouraging users with other styles	Tailorability to different styles of individuals and organizational units

Interconnection Needs

Users cannot communicate with colleagues on different systems	Users cannot contact needed colleagues Skewed user, stunted use	Standards for interconnection, translation services

Routing

Determining who should receive information	It may be hard to find someone's formal address Some people do not get needed messages	Tools to determine formal addresses from names, other information Selective dissemination of information (SDI) based on user profiles Mandatory routing rules

Security and Privacy

Unauthorized access	Loss of proprietary information	Various system-controlled restrictions on use
Private information	Lawsuit threats	
Employee privacy	Conflict with employees	Various system-controlled access to sensitive information
Forwarding messages, data to inappropriate third parties		
Authentication: proving that the sender sent the message		Audit trails for information entries, changes

Regrettable Messages

Emotion-laden messages sent at the spur of the moment	Organizational disharmony	Ability to "take back" a message immediately after it is sent
Humor mistaken for sarcasm, etc.		

Junk Mail

Heavy volume of broadcast mail through use of distribution lists	Increases overload on heavy users	Distribution list control
	Wastes organizational time	Removal of duplicates in mailings
		Right to be removed from distribution lists
		Identification of unusually heavy senders

Crank Mail

Use of anonymity to send offensive messages	Organizational disharmony	Sending party identification
	Sexual harassment law suits	Limits on use of anonymity

Shoryt Circuiting

Communication with normally inaccessible superiors Communicate with subordinates of subordinates Nonformal staff-line communication	Breakdown in normal chain of command Overload on senior management Lack of clarity of authority of staff message	Limits on access to superiors, peers of boss without boss' knowledge Requirements for formal communication between staff and line on sensitive matters

instance Rice (1987) lists a large number of media factors to be considered, and many of these involve implementation difficulties.

In addition, many groupware tools require fundamental redesign over time and even organization redesign to be useful. Even "simple" EMS will grow in complexity in response to the need to store group communications in a form more easily stored, retrieved, and managed by group members, not just by individuals. Computer conferencing and groupware message management tools such as Lotus Notes are already moving messaging in this direction, and even these tools have barely begun to tackle the thorny issues of how to manage message storage and retrieval in complex departments and workgroups. In tomorrow's world where the implementation of "organizationally invasive" groupware products may become increasingly common, careful attention will need to be paid to behavioral implementation difficulties.

Commanding Use

While using design to reduce implementation and use difficulties is desirable, it raises the issue of whether it is necessary. Perhaps the most obvious way to avoid both the critical mass and the stunted use problems would be to simply *command* use—use the corporation's line authority to require everyone to use the system at least daily. Markus (1987), for instance, has listed command as one of several ways to reduce critical mass problems. Grudin (1988, 1989) has also listed command as a possibility, and the earliest analyst of collective action, Olson (1965) lists "coercion" as one of the two key ways to achieve collective action, the other approach being incentives. The author knows of at least two organizations that have adopted command as a way to ensure adequate levels of use. One of these cases was discussed by Peter Keen at the 1988 International

Conference on Information Systems. Command could also be used to reduce other implementation and use difficulties.

Yet relatively few organizations use naked command apart from clearly unethical situations. To understand why, it is important to realize that groupware tools tend to be used by managers and professionals, and these "knowledge workers" have traditionally been accorded a great deal of discretion over what tools they use and how they use them.

This is not mere permissiveness. There are strong theoretical and practical reasons for according knowledge workers a high degree of discretion over their jobs. In management, many corporations have implemented or at least believe in *management by objectives,* or MBO. In MBO, the manager must be judged on the basis of results (Drucker, 1954; Ordione, 1965). As a corollary, managers must be given broad discretion over their work. If you force someone to do a job in a specific way, you cannot reasonably hold them responsible for results. While there may be constraints in critical areas, such as illegal behavior, constraints in general must be kept to a minimum.

In addition, a wide amount of discretion is seen in practice. Activity studies that have measured how managers spend their days indicate wide variations among the time use profiles of managers with similar jobs (Panko, 1990b). Figure 16.3 illustrates the range of discretion that managers and professionals appear to have. (This figure is similar to the model proposed by Stewart [1982].) The figure shows that each knowledge worker has *core requirements*—work that must be done. They also have *limits* over what they may do, providing outer limits on their discretion. In the middle is their *range of discretion.*

In the literature on professions, Benveniste (1987) has given a similar argument—one that is also useful in understanding managerial discretion. He has noted that if goals, methodology, and the application of the methodology are well understood, there is no need for using a professional. The task can be reduced to procedures and assigned to a clerical worker. Conversely, if the task cannot be reduced to procedures, this means that it must be given to someone with considerable discretion over goals, methodology, application of the methodology, or all three.

There is some evidence that the range of discretion given to managers and professionals may be increasing. During the 1980s, many organizations went through major "downsizing" exercises to reduce their office staffs. A key reason for doing so was to reduce staff department "interference" with line operations (Tomasko, 1987). Each staff department constantly bombards line management with suggested improvements, and each staff department has a deep belief that its own suggestions are extremely

FIGURE 16.3.
Range of Discretion for Managers and Professionals

Limits

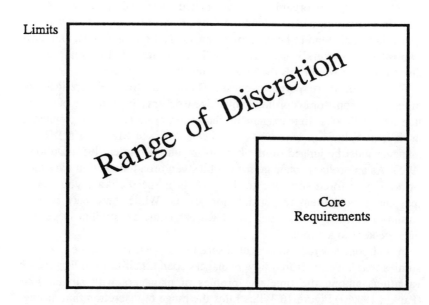

important. By reducing staff and guarding line discretion, the organization hopes to avoid "analysis paralysis."

When the information systems staff proposes groupware innovations, it often faces a great deal of resistance, because it too is only one of numerous staff groups proposing ways to make the organization work more effectively. Its chances of making use mandatory are very small under its own power. This is why top management support and other forms of line management "ownership" are critical.

But even with top management support, it is comparatively rare for upper management to be willing to mandate use and apply sanctions to nonusers. While jawboning from above and peer pressure from the side can put pressure on knowledge workers, there is still likely to be room for discretion, and even informal pressure is not likely to emerge unless quite a few stakeholders have a very strong interest in the innovation.

Sociologists studying collective action by groups also warn that negative sanctions can be very dangerous. For instance, Oliver (1980) warns that punishment can backfire in the long run. While it may give short-term benefits,'it also builds resentment and weakens organizational cohesion. Hostility is especially likely to result, Oliver argues, if unanimity was not required to implement the collective action; in some types of groupware, this is likely to be the case.

Since discretion is the root cause of skewed use and the problems it creates, it is important for IS researchers and professionals to understand reasons for the strong discretion normally accorded to knowledge users. It is also important to understand why line management is not likely to use command to enforce groupware use in most circumstances and to seek other mechanisms for coping with skewed use problems. While top-down pressure, peer pressure, and peer interpretation of what is desirable to do are important tools for the implementation of groupwork, command is not likely to be a viable option in most firms.

Dogmatism in Design

Another broad issue that must be considered in design is that while design innovations are likely to be important in addressing organizational problems, designs that tend to force certain patterns of work on organizations are potentially dangerous. For instance, The Coordinator™ (Winograd & Flores, 1986) is an EMS based on a particular linguistic approach for understanding organizational communication (Austin, 1962; Flores & Bell, 1984). Unfortunately, research has shown that real messages rarely fit neatly into the categories suggested by this theory (Bowers & Churcher, 1988). Yet early versions of The Coordinator forced adherence to the theory. Newer versions of the product allow the theory to be followed or not followed. Perhaps future products based on particular information management approaches will benefit from a similar focus on optionality, allowing the organization and subgroups to select the degree to which they will follow the model.

Sometimes there are strong reasons both for and against an aspect of design. As noted earlier, Steinfield (1986) notes a debate over whether to restrict traffic to prevent junk mail and level jumping in the hierarchy. While Denning (1982) argues for restrictions, Hiltz and Turoff (1985) argue that such restrictions could stunt the benefits from messaging. Again, optionality may be the answer. This will allow organizations, not designers, to determine what is proper in their particular circumstances.

Even at the individual level, care must be taken when removing traditional organizational slack. As noted above, some EMSs remember each message sent and allow senders to impose a deadline on responses. This removes the ability of receivers to avoid responding, which is useful in some contexts. By removing nonresponse as an option, these systems might force confrontations on organizations.

In general, there is a danger that a particular work paradigm favored by designers will be forced on users against their will. This raises serious ethical questions about the proper role of designers in systems that have strong potentials for changing the way that workgroups and larger units do their work.

System Blame and a Reverence for Diversity

In his analysis of the diffusion of innovation literature, Rogers notes (1983) that many early studies tended to blame individuals if an innovation failed. More recently, however, there has been growing interest in "system blame," which looks at problems within the implementation system when things go wrong. For instance, Ryan (1971) noted that when children died or were injured by eating lead-based paint, a promotional campaign aimed at individuals had little effect, and the ultimate solution was simply to stop buying lead paint.

This paper, by focusing on design rather than individual decision making, falls strongly into the "system blame" category. While there may be individual negligence in such problems as critical mass and sending regrettable messages, any system must be designed in a way that reflects the reliability of its subsystems or cosystems. To design a human-used system that does not fit and compensate as much as possible for the foibles of humans is simply unprofessional.

The real key to the design of robust systems seems to be simply working hard to develop a *complex* view of the user "market," effectively seeing it as highly segmented, with different segments having very different needs and wants. The vision of a stereotyped user must be replaced by a vision of diversity among users. Or if idea seems overly abstract, there is the case of the Greek bandit Procrustes. He placed his victims on a bed. Those too tall had their feet cut off. Those too short were stretched on a rack. "One size fits all" rarely works in life, and we cannot expect it to work in groupware.

References

Artle, R., & Averous, C. (1983). The telephone system as a public good: Static and dynamic aspects. *The Bell Journal of Economics and Management Science, 4*, 1 (Spring), 89–100.
Austin, J. L. (1962). *How to do things with words.* Cambridge, MA: Harvard University Press.
Ball, D. F. (1968). Towards a sociology of telephones and telephoners. In Marcello Truzzi, *Sociology and everyday life.* Englewood cliffs, NJ: Prentice-Hall, 59–75.
Benveniste, G. (1987). *Professionalizing the organization: Reducing bureaucracy to enhance effectiveness.* San Francisco: Josey-Bass, Publishers.

Bikson, Tora K. (1990). RAND Corporation, personal communication, September.

Bowers, J. & Churcher, J. (1988). Local and global structuring of computer mediated communication: Developing linguistic perspectives on CSCW in COSMOS. *Proceedings of the Conference on Computer-Supported Cooperative Work.* Portland, OR, September 26–28.

Brotz, D. K. (1983). Message system mores: Etiquette in Laurel. *ACM Transactions of Office Information Systems,* 1, 3 (April), 179–92.

Carroll, J. M., & Carrithers, C. (1984). Training wheels in a user interface. *Communications of the ACM,* August, 800–5.

Chang, S., & Leung, L. (1987). A knowledge-based message management system. *ACM Transactions on Office Information Systems,* 5, 3 (July), 213–36.

Chatfield, C., & Goodhardt, G. J. (1970). The beta-binomial model for consumer purchasing behvaior. *Applied Statistics,* 19, 3, 240–48.

Collopy, F. L. (1988). White-collar computing: A field study using automated logging. *Proceedings of the 21st Hawaii International Conference on System Sciences.* IEEE, January, 236–44.

Connolly, T., & Thorn, B. K. (1990). Discretionary databases: Theory, data and implications. In J. Fulk, & C. W. Steinfield, *Perspectives in organizations and new information technology.* Newbury Park, CA: Sage Publications.

Crawford, A. B., Jr. (1982). Corporate electronic mail—A communication-intensive application of information technology. *MIS Quarterly,* 6, 3 (September), 1–13.

Culnan, M. J. (1983). Chauffeured verses end user access to commercial databases: The effects of task and individual differences. *MIS Quarterly,* March, 55–67.

Danowski, J. A., & Edison-Swift, P. (1985). Crisis effects on interorganizational computer-based communication. *Communication Research,* 12, 2 (April), 251–70.

Denning, P. J. (1982). Electronic Junk. *Communications of the ACM,* 25, 3 (March), 163–65.

Drucker, P. F. (1954). *The practice of management.* New York: Harper Brothers.

Ehrenberg, A. S. C. (1975). *Data reduction.* London: John Wiley & Sons.

Eveland, J. D., & Bikson, T. K. (1987). Evolving electronic communication networks: An empirical assessment. *Proceedings of the Conference on Computer-Supported Cooperative Work.* Austin, TX, 1986, pp. 91–101, cited in Markus, M. L., Toward a "critical mass" theory of interactive media: Universal access, interdependence, and diffusion. *Communication Research,* 14, 5 (October), 491–511.

Flores, F., & Bell, C. (1984). A new understanding of managerial work improves system design. *Computer Technology Review,* Fall.

Fulk, J., Steinfield, C. W., Schmitz, J., & Power, J. G. (1987). A social information processing model of media use in organizations. *Communication Research,* 14, 5 (October), 529–52.

Galleta, D. F. (1986). A longitudinal view of an office system failure. *SIGOA Bulletin,* 7, 1 (Spring), 7–11.

Grudin, J. (1989). Why Groupware Tools Fail: Problems in Design and Evaluation. *Office Technology and People,* 4, 3, 245–64.

Grudin, J. (1988). Why groupware tools fail: Problems in design and evaluation of organizational interfaces. *Proceedings of the Conference on Computer-Supported Cooperative Work.* Portland, Oregon, pp. 85–93.

Hammer, M. (1987). *Intra-company electronic mail: Its impacts on managers' work methods.* Technical report, NYU Graduate School of Business Administra-

364   Between Communication and Information

tion, 1985, cited in Markus, M. L., Toward a "critical mass" theory of interactive media: Universal access, interdependence, and diffusion, *Communication Research*, 14, 5 (October), 491–511.

Hiltz, S. R. (1988). Productivity enhancement from computer-mediated communication: A systems contingency approach. *Communications of the ACM*, 31, 12 (December), 1438–54.

Hiltz, S. R., & Turoff, M. (1985). Structuring computer-mediated communication systems to avoid overload. *Communications of the ACM*, 28, 7 (July), 680–89.

Hiltz, S. R., Turoff, M., & Johnson, K. (1985). Disinhibition, deindividualization, and group processes in computerized conferences: A field experiment concerning pen name and real name conferences. Paper presented at the 35th Annual Conference of the International Communication Association, Honolulu, Hawaii, May 23–27.

Hiltz, S. R. (1984). *Online communities: A case study of the office of the future*. Norwood, NJ: Ablex Publishing.

Hiltz, S. R., & Turoff, M. (1978). *The network nation: Human communication via computers*. Reading, MA: Addison-Wesley.

Keisler, S., Siegel, J., & McGuire, T. W. (1984). Social psychological aspects of computer-mediated communication. *American Psychologist*, 39, 19 (October), 1123–34.

Kerr, E. B., & Hiltz, S. R. (1982). *Computer-mediated communication systems*. New York: Academic Press.

Knapp, M. L. Stafford, L., & Day, J. (1986). Regrettable messages: Things people wish they hadn't said. *Journal of Communication*, August, 40–58.

Lynch, C. A. (1980). Practical electronic mail through a centralized computing facility: Communicating information. *Proceedings of the American Society for Information Science (ASIS) 43d Annual Meeting*. Anaheim, CA, October 5–10, pp. 34–37.

Mackay, W. E. (1988). Diversity in the use of electronic mail: A preliminary inquiry. *ACM Transactions on Office Information Systems*, 6, 4 (October), 380–97.

Malone, T. W., Grant, K. R., Lai, K-Y., Rao, R., & Rosenblitt, D. (1987). Semistructured messages are surprisingly useful for computer-supported coordination. *ACM transactions on office information systems*, 5, 2 (April), 115–31.

Markus, M. L. (1990a). Toward a "critical mass" theory of interactive media. In J. Fulk & C. W. Steinfield (Eds.), *Perspectives on Organizations and New Information Technology*. Newbury Park, CA: Sage Publications.

Markus, M. L. (1987). Toward a "critical mass" theory of interactive media: Universal access, interdependence, and diffusion. *Communication Research*, 14, 5 (October), 491–511.

Markus, M. L., & Connoly, T. (1990). Why CSCW applications fail: Problems in the adoption of interdependent work tools. To be published in the *Proceedings of the Conference on Computer-Supported Cooperative Work*. Los Angeles, CA, October.

Mayer, M. (1987). The telephone and the uses of time. In Ithiel de Sola Pool (Ed.), *The social impact of the telephone*. MIT Press, 1980, cited in Fielding, G. & Hartley, P., The telephone: A neglected medium. In A. Cashdan & M. Jordin, *Studies in communication* (pp. 110–24). London: Basil Blackwell.

McLean, E. R. (1983). End users as application developers. *Proceedings of the Guide/Share Application Development Symposium*. October 1974, cited in

Rockart, J. F. and Flannely, L. S., The management of end user computing, *Communications of the ACM,* 26, 10 (October), 776–84.

McLuhan, Marshall. (1965). *Understanding Media: The Extensions of Man.* New York: McGraw-Hill.

Oliver, P., Marwell, G., & Teixeira, R. (1985). A theory of the critical mass I. Interdependence, group heterogeneity, and the production of collective action. *American Journal of Sociology,* 91, 3 (November), 522–56.

Oliver, P. (1980). Rewards and punishments as selective incentives for collective action: Theoretical investigations. *American Journal of Sociology,* 85, 6, 1356–75.

Olson, M., Jr. (1965). *The logic of collective action: Public goods and the theory of goods.* Cambridge, MA: Harvard University Press.

Ordione, G. S. (1965). *Management by objecties.* Pitman.

Oren, S. S., & Smith, S. A. (1981). Critical mass and tarriff structure in electronic communication markets. *Bell Journal of Economics,* 12, 468–86.

Panko, R. R. (1990b). The office workforce: Dimensions, needs, and research congruence. PRIISM Working Paper 90–001, January 1990.

Panko, R. R. (1990a). Discretion and skewed use in computer-supported cooperative work. In K. M. Kaiser & H. J. Oppelland, (Eds.), *Desktop information technology: Organizational worklife in the 1990s.* Amsterdam: Elseiver/North Holland.

Panko, R. R. (1989). Discretion and skewed use in computer-supported cooperative work. *Proceedings of the International Federation of Information Processing Working Group 8.2 Working Conference on Desktop Information Technology.* Thiaca, NY, June 2–4.

Panko, R. R. (1988). *End user computing: Management, applications, and technology.* New York: John Wiley & Sons.

Panko, R. R. (1985). Electronic mail. In *Advance in office automation,* vol. 1. New York: Wiley Heyden Ltd.

Panko, R. R. (1983). Directions in electronic mail. *Office Systems Research Journal,* 2, 1 (Fall), 19–28.

Panko, R. R. (1982). Electronic message and document delivery. *Conference Digest, 1982 Office Automation Conference.* American Federation of Information Processing Societies, San Francisco, April.

Panko, R. R. (1978). *Final report: A cost/benefits analysis of electronic message systems for the U.S. Army Materiel Development and Readiness Command.* Menlo Park, CA: SRI International.

Panko, R. R., & Panko, R. U. (1981). A Survey of EMS users at DARCOM. *Computer Networks.* March, 19–23.

Pollock, S. (1988). A Rule-Based Message Filtering System. *ACM Transactions on Office Information Systems,* 6, 3 (July), 232–54.

Reder, S., & Schwab, R. G. (1989). The communicative economy of the workgroup: Multi-channel genres of communication. *Office: Technology and People.* Elsevier Science Publishers, Ltd., 4, 3, 177–95.

Rice, R. E. (1990). Computer-mediated communication system network data: Theoretical concerns and empirical examples. To appear in *International Journal of Man-Machine Studies.*

Rice, R. E., & Shook, D. E. (1990). Voice messaging, coordination, and communication. In J. Galegher, R. Kraut, & C. Egido (Eds.), *Intellectual Teamwork:*

Social and Technological Foundations of Cooperative Work (pp. 327–50). Hillsdale, NJ: Lawrence Erlbaum.

Rice, R. E., Grant, A., Schmitz, J., & Torobin, J. (No year). Critical mass and social influence: A network approach to predicting adoption, use, and outcomes in electronic messaging.

Rice, R. E. (1987). Computer-mediated communication and organizational innovation. *Journal of Communication*, 37, 4 (Autumn), 65–94.

Rice, R. E., & Manross, G. (1987). The case of the intelligent telephone: The relationship of job category to the adoption of organizational communication technology. In M. McLaughlin (Ed.), *Communication Yearbook 10* (727–42). Beverly Hills, CA: Sage.

Rice, R. E., & Shook, D. (1986). End-user computing: Access, usage, and benefits. In J. Hurd (Ed.), *Proceedings of the 49th Meeting of the American Society for Information Science*, 23 (271–76). Medford, NJ: Learned Information.

Robey, D., Saunders, C., & Vaverek, K. (1990). Social Structure and Electronic Communication. Unpublished paper, Florida International University, Department of Decision Sciences, 1989, cited in Rice, R. E., Computer-mediated communication system network data: Theoretical concerns and empirical examples, to appear in *International Journal of Man-Machine Studies*.

Robey, D. (1979). User attitudes and management information systems use. *Academy of Management Journal*, 22, 3 (September), 527–38.

Rickart, J. F., & Flannery, L. S. (1983). The Management of End User Computing. *Communications of the ACM*, 26, 10 (October), 776–84.

Rogers, E. M. (1989). The "critical mass" in the diffusion of interactive technologies in organizations, to be published in the *Proceedings of the Workshop on Survey Research in MIS*. Irvine, CA, February 10–11.

Rogers, E. M. (1986). *Communications technology: The new media in society*. New York: Free Press.

Rogers, E. M. (1986). *The diffusion of innovations* (3rd ed.). New York: Free Press.

Rogers, E. M. (1986). The diffusion of home computers. Stanford University, Institute for Communication Research, 1982, cited in Rogers, E. M., *Communications technology: The new media in society*. New York: Free Press.

Rohlfs, J. (1974). A theory of interdependent demand for a communications service. *Bell Journal of Economics, Management, and Service*, 5, 16–37.

Ryan, W. (1983). *Blaming the Victim*. New York: Pantheon, cited in Rogers, E. M. *The diffusion of innovations* (3rd ed.), New York: Free Press.

Sieck, S. K. (1984). Business Information Systems and Databases. In *Annual Review of Information Science and Technology* (pp. 311–27). Knowledge Industry Publications.

Siegel, J., Dubrovsky, V., Keisler, J. & McGuire, W. (1986). Group processes in computer-mediated communications. *Organizational Behavior and Human Decision Processes*, 37, 2 (April), 157–87.

Sproull, L., & Kielser, S. (1986). Reducing social context cues: Electronic mail in an organizational setting. *Management Science*, 32, 11 (November), 1492–1512.

Steinfield, C. W. (1987). Computer-mediated communications systems. In M. Williams (Ed.), *The Annual Review of Information Science and Technology*, 21, White Plains, NY: Knowledge Industry Publications, 1986, cited in Markus, M. L., Toward a "critical mass" theory of interactive media: Universal access, interdependence, and diffusion. *Communication Research*, 14, 5 (October), 491–511.

Steinfield, C. W. (1985). Explaining task-related and socio-emotional uses of computer-mediated communication in an organizational setting. Presented at the Human Communications Technology Interest Group at the annual meeting of the International Communication Association, Honolulu, HI.

Stewart, R. (1982). A Model for understanding managerial jobs and behavior. *Academy of Management Review, 7*, 1, 7–14.

Sullivan, M. D., Borgman, C. L., & Wippern, D. (1990). End-users, mediated searches, and front-end assistance programs on dialog: A comparison of learning, performance, and satisfaction. *Journal of the American Society for Information Science, 41*, 1, 27–42.

Sumner, M. (1986). User-developed applications: What are they doing? *Journal of Information Systems Management, 3*, 4 (Fall), 37–46.

Thorn, B. K., & Connolly, T. (1987). Discretionary data bases: A theory and some empirical findings. *Communication Research, 14*, 5, 512–28.

Tomasko, R. M. (1987). *Downsizing.* New York: AMACOM

Tucker, J. H. (1982). Implementing office automation: Principles and an electronic mail example. *Proceedings of the SIGOA Conference on Office Information Systems.* Association for Computing Machinery, June 21–23, pp. 93–100.

Twedt, D. W. (1964). How important to marketing strategy is the "Heavy User"? *Journal of Marketing, 28* (January), 71–72.

Uhlig, R., Farber, D. & Bair, J. (1979). *The office of the future: Communication and computers.* Amsterdam: North-Holland Publishing Co.

White, J., VP. (1979). Texas Instruments, personal communication with the author.

Williams, F., Rice, R. E., & Rogers, E. M. (1988). *Research methods and the new media.* New York: The Free Press.

Winograd, T., & Flores, F. (1986).*Understanding computers and cognition.* Reading, MA, Addison-Wesley.

17

News Story Generation with Hard Copy and Magnetic Media Information Sources: The Impact of Information Technology

Kenneth M. Nagelberg and Donald H. Kraft

While previous research on computerized writing laboratories has concentrated on the computer as a writing tool, this study centers on the computer as an information source. Changes occurring at Louisiana State University news writing laboratories from hard copy databases and simple Associated Press (AP) wire capture systems to a computerized newsroom in which information sources are available for retrieval provides an opportunity to compare the news generation process by students as their news gathering technology changes.

This research focuses on two aspects of the use of computerized retrieval systems: first, how news stories are selected, and, second, the degree to which stories are rewritten by the student journalists. It is hypothesized that news story selection in the hard copy setting, will be directed primarily by the pragmatics of physical access. Whereas it is hypothesized that journalistic considerations, such as proximity, timeliness, and impact, will play a greater role in news selection where students have complete access to all copy in a computerized setting. In addition, it is hypothesized that technical considerations, such as ease of use of a computerized system or knowledge of good search procedures, will affect use of computerized retrieval systems for news story selection.

It is also hypothesized that students will rewrite news stories to a

*greater degree when the wire copy source stories are retrieved from
the computer than when they are in hard copy form.*

*The initial phase of this study was carried out by interviewing
student journalists who had access to hard copy news sources and
indexes, wire capture and search software, and online (computerized) retrieval systems.*

It is clear that information technology is being used more and more in
this modern, so-called information age. Books such as *Future Shock* and
Megatrends 2000 tell of the important influence information is, and will
be, having on much, if not all, of society. It is clear that one important
area of impact is the use of information technology for the news media.
Clearly, access to more information is important in terms of generating
news stories. As a case in point, Trautman (1990) cites a 1988 research
report from International Data Corp. that says that full-text retrieval
shipments will go from $83.9 million in 1987 to about $680 million in 1992
(a 52.3% per year growth rate).

Moreover, it is clear that while there are more and more data available,
perhaps even too much data to be useful, there is often a dearth of useful
information. Thus, the ability to search properly to wade through the
mountains of available data to get the pertinent information is important
for the news media. Hunter (1989) reports that "although database searching will never replace the traditional library, sources describe it as a
powerful research tool that has revolutionized the quality, quantity and
accessibility of information." Hunter quotes Brad Schepp, associate editor
of the *Datapro Directory of On-liner Services,* as saying that "once you
start searching in databases you never want to go back. . . . Somebody at
Dialog [a major database vendor] says a minute spent searching [data-
bases] is equivalent to an hour spent in a library. I think he's being a little
conservative."

The use of computers to help gather, store, process, and disseminate
information is not new. However, the incorporation of computers to do
these tasks for news media personnel is somewhat new and is an ongoing
process. Thus, it is imperative that this use be studied to understand how
journalism is being affected and how technology can best be put to proper
use.

For example, the Sphinx system has been developed in the former West
Germany by the television station Zweites Deutsches Fernsehen (ZDF) in
Mainz and the Software AG company (Trautman, 1990): "The freedom
Sphinx gives the user in searching for information is the system's best

feature, because it allows the user to research in a creative way. . . . The journalist is a kind of detective when he uses Sphinx. Ultimately, the database positively affects the depth and quality of the journalist's work. Moreover, journalists and editors appreciate the chance to form complex queries and search databases without having to be IS experts.'' Trautman reports that the system is up to the minute and that journalists work better when they do their own searches rather than having a clippings librarian do it for them. On the other hand, Hunter (1989) states that news reporters often use ''information brokers,'' since reporters are not overly familiar with computerized systems and often waste time and money on searches. Brokers develop ''presearch strategy'' to select key words and specific databases.

Walker (1990) notes that before database journalism, reporters were ''stenographers.'' Today, however, journalists are allowed to move from ''event coverage'' to understanding how institutions function or fail to achieve their stated goals. Newspapers are beginning to build their own databases from the records of state agencies, such as the Department of Motor Vehicles or a state housing agency. For example, Walker cites three episodes of children killed by school buses in Rhode Island that were supposedly parked. A reporter used database searches to find that some drivers had ten to twenty traffic violations, while others had drug violations.

Examples of database use in journalism include stories that would have been impossible to write without computerized information retrieval. In 1987, the *San Francisco Chronicle* did a story on who belonged to the Bohemian Club by searching the *Who's Who* database for club membership (Hunter, 1989). Hunter also notes that for a biography of Geraldine Ferraro, journalist Ted Miller used a database to locate former law schoolmates by searching combinations of the term ''Fordham University'' and the graduation year ''1961.'' Miller then called those schoolmates for interviews, and one of the things he found was that Ferraro always sat in front of the class. Several studies of potential bias in political coverage have been done by counting mentions of specific political candidates in newspaper databases.

Information retrieval systems have been in existence for eons, if one considers libraries as examples of such systems. However, in terms of computerized retrieval, these systems have been around for just about a quarter of a century. Printed indexes of the literatures of various fields, such as physics, biology, chemistry, medicine, and psychology, had been in existence for some time. Then, it was felt that the computer could be used to help in the generation of those manual indexes. Early retrieval systems thus started out as batch systems to use these machine-readable bibliographic representations of printed texts as databases that could be searched in response to queries. Eventually, this led to online retrieval systems that have been refined to incorporate modern storage and search capabilities. An example of this is the automation of *Index Medicus,* from the printed index to Medlars (the batch system) to AIMtwx (the experimental online system using an abridged version of *Index Medicus*), to Medline (the online version of Medlars). In fact, now there are user-friendly, intelligent front-ends, such as Grateful Med for Medline users, to assist users in using online retrieval systems. Moreover, the use of CD-ROM and hypertext and hypermedia are just beginning to come into their own in terms of influencing use of retrieval technology.

It is clear that journalists are beginning to notice information retrieval systems. Wendling (1989) describes the principles of searching, including an introduction to Boolean operators. He notes that understanding these operators is 90 percent of searching. He also compares online and CD-ROM databases, which are all indexed rather than full-text.

However, computerized databases have not won universal approval from journalists. Walker (1990) quotes Burnham as saying that "Overwhelmingly, though, the biggest difficulty for newspapers wanting to pursue database journalism is 'cultural': reporters tend to be word people. If they have to deal with numbers, they want someone else to interpret them."

Gerhard (1990) notes that 14 percent of journalism schools now subscribe to an online database, and that the percentage is higher in larger programs. Ninety-two percent of journalism school administrators think that students should be provided with information about online database searching, and 80 percent of those administrators think that undergraduate courses should provide "hands-on" experience with database searching. The only obstacle seems to be money, as 62 percent of the administrators think online databases are too expensive. Only 40 percent of the journalism schools actually allow students to do their own searching. Newspapers and news wires were cited as the most beneficial sources in online searching.

In Gerhard's study, 43 percent of the administrators said that online searching improved journalism instruction, although more than half were not sure. More than a third of the administrators said that the quality of the students' work had improved as a result of searching, but 60 percent of them were not so sure of this.

It may be surprising to some, but it is only in the last few years that online retrieval systems have become objects of study in their own right. Scholars have begun to wonder how users actually use such systems, how the performance of such systems affects users, and how such systems can be refined to do even better at their assigned tasks. Moreover, the literature seems bereft of studies of use of information technology by news media personnel. Thus, we seek to blaze new trails in investigating the role of computerized information retrieval systems for student journalists. We hope that this study can identify some of the parameters for a framework in which to investigate the role of information technology in helping the media provide society with the news and information it needs and deserves.

Background

The Louisiana State University (LSU) Manship School of Journalism currently has two database systems available with search capabilities available for journalism students' use. The first is the WireReady system for capturing Associated Press (AP) wire copy. The system is presently part of a Novell network of IBM-compatible microcomputers (PCs) in the newsroom of the campus newspaper, the *Daily Reveille*. This newspaper is student staffed at LSU. Moreover, the WireReady system was installed in the late spring and summer of 1990, and became fully operational during the fall 1990 semester.

Staff members of the *Daily Reveille* have access to the WireReady system when they log on to the network workstations. The system includes a communications server that receives the AP "slow wire" and saves the stories in a one-megabyte "capture file" on the system. All other workstations in the network can access this file through the software package.

On initial use of WireReady during each session, a list of stories appear on the screen, last story first. The stories are identified by American Newspaper Publisher's Association (ANPA) categories (e.g., national, sports, weather), story "slug" (abbreviated headline), and date and time received. Students can page through the listings and browse the full text of stories that are of interest to them.

The WireReady program also has capabilities for editing the AP copy in one of three ways. First, the story can be saved on a "notepad" and rewritten using WireReady's built-in editor. Second, WireReady has a split-screen facility whereby students can view the AP copy on half of the screen and write their own version of the story on the other half. Third, students can save the AP copy to a file in their own DOS subdirectory on the network hard disk, and then use the WordPerfect word processor on the system to edit the story. After editing, stories are sent to a common subdirectory area for any additional editing by the staff and eventual publication in the newspaper.

The WireReady program also provides limited search capabilities within the captured file. Users can search through all data fields: (1) ANPA story category; (2) story slug; (3) story text; and (4) time received. WireReady also allows for keyword/phrase searches within story slugs and story texts.

The search capabilities of WireReady are, however, quite limited when compared with most online and CD-ROM information retrieval systems. First, the capture file is quite small. The system at the *Daily Reveille*, for example, has a capture file that is big enough for only two or three days' worth of AP copy. As new stories enter the system, the oldest stories are erased to make room. There are currently no means for archiving these purged stories. The capture file can be expanded up to three megabytes, but this would slow down the initialization process considerably and would still only allow for about a week's worth of stored news.

The second limitation of WireReady search capabilities is that the system is limited to only three keyword/phrase sets and only two Boolean operators, "and" and "or." The Boolean operators cannot be mixed, that is, no combined and/or searches; and it often takes several minutes to run through the 500–800 news stories in the capture file.

In point of fact, the WireReady system was not the first AP wire capture program to be used in the student newspaper newsroom. Prior to the 1990–91 academic year, the newsroom staff used a dedicated terminal link that incorporated wire capture software and hardware. The difference is that the earlier system had no search capabilities and a very limited editing capability. Moreover, this earlier system could only store about fifty stories.

The second information retrieval system available to journalism students is Mead Data Central's Lexis system, which actually includes three subsystems: (1) Lexis, a legal and governmental information database, with court cases, corporate filings, and other legal/corporate documents and reports; (2) Nexis, a news database; and (3) Medis, a medical information database.

The primary subsystem of interest to student journalists is Nexis. The Nexis database is broken down into a number of "files." These files are groups of sources, such as newspaper, magazines, and wire copy, or groupings of data in topic areas, such as people, trade, computer/communications, and advertising/public relations. Nexis also allows for more focused searches using individual news source files, such as the *New York Times,* ABC Television News, and UPI News. Nexis has over 350 full-text databases as of now, and Mead Data Central has been involved in this business since 1973. Gerhard (1990) notes that Nexis was one of the most frequently used databases for journalism schools, second only to Dialog.

LSU currently subscribes to Nexis through an educational package that provides unlimited use for up to three users simultaneously for a flat monthly fee. Initial installation of a single terminal was achieved in

November 1990. A temporary installation was set up in January 1991 in a converted classroom using three IBM-compatible microcomputers (PCs) with 2400 baud modems and individual dot-matrix printers. The system is presently being converted to tie those PC's into the Manship School of Journalism's Novell network. This will allow stories to be directly saved on the network's hard disk for retrieval from other workstations or for printing at a later time.

The Nexis system is currently being used by the Public Affairs Reporting and the News Reporting courses at LSU. Both courses are geared for students with career interests in newspaper reporting, and many of the students enrolled also write for the *Daily Reveille*. But, word of the system has spread, and students in other journalism classes have begun to learn how to log on and to conduct searches. For example, several students in the graduate media law class have discovered that computer searches take a fraction of the time that case searches in the LSU Law Library take. Thus, these students have begun to make use of Lexis for such searches.

Nexis is a much more complete service than the WireReady system discussed above. It allows for complex combinations of Boolean operators and also allows for limiters, such as proximity and story author. The Nexis database also goes back much further, as far as twelve years for some newspapers, although many other data files are only accessible for stories from the last year or two. The only limitation in information availability is that the database lags at least twenty-four hours behind publication, so that the most timely stories are often not in the system. Obviously, for a newspaper, this can be an important limitation.

Nexis is also a much more difficult system to use, with combinations of function ("F") and Shift/Alt keys needed to perform display and print functions. Users must consult a keyboard template and user's manual unless they have memorized all of the system functions. In contrast, the WireReady software uses only single-key functions employing the "F" keys. All functions are displayed on the bottom of the screen, so no template or manual is needed.

The Nexis software is also not conducive to manipulation of the copy of retrieved stories. There is no on-screen editor, nor is there any way of easily saving retrieved stories. Stories must either be printed or downloaded to a disk, although there is a screen save capability. The saved ASCII files could then be massaged using a word processor.

Methodology

In order to ascertain the effects of this new information retrieval technology on the perceptions and attitudes of student journalists, a series of interviews were conducted with these students. Over a period of two weeks, students working in the *Daily Reveille* newsroom and using the computerized retrieval systems described above were interviewed. This was a nonrandom sample of use to get a preliminary idea of who used these systems, how they were used, for what purposes they were used, and what capabilities were not being used to their fullest, if at all. In all, ten staff members, including reporters (staff writers) and editors, the faculty advisor (a professor of journalism at LSU) for the student newspaper, and a faculty member who teaches related courses, were interviewed.

Results

The faculty advisor noted that the limited storage and search capabilities of the first AP capture program, the one acquired prior to the WireReady system, combined to drastically limit the utility of the AP wire service. He noted that many stories and features were missed because students were not able to check the database frequently enough. For example, he said most features came across the wire during the weekend, but were gone by Monday afternoon when students checked the computer files. He also noted that the limited editing capabilities meant that most stories were printed "as is" from the AP copy. The most frequent form of editing was achieved by printing out the wire stories as galleys and physically cutting the printed output to fit the space budgeted. This also meant that *The Daily Reveille* was a slave to the writing style of the AP news story writer. If the story was not written in "inverted pyramid" style, important facts were cut out.

Despite the many advantages of the WireReady program, as compared to the older computer system, many students make only partial use of WireReady's capabilities. Many of the students using the WireReady program are not making use of the search potential or were using it in a minor capacity. Most of the students say that they are simply paging through the screens of stories and browsing through those that have interesting slugs or fit certain criteria. Such searches are time consuming, since a full capture file can require paging down thirty or forty times to scan all of the stories.

One of the primary uses of the WireReady system is to assemble news briefs and/or select significant noncampus stories for the paper. The page-by-page scanning used by many of the staff members results in only a limited scan of the stories available. An impatient copy editor, who is likely to try to find useful stories in just the first few pages, will quit before seeing all the stories that are available, which means that improper use of the technology can lead to poor journalistic practices.

One of the editors says she is disappointed with the system and in many respects prefers the older computers it had replaced. She says the previous system was able to preselect out certain categories of stories that the newspaper did not use, for example, the livestock reports. However, the faculty advisor notes that the earlier system did *not* select out such stories; instead, the system flushed them from its memory due to its limited storage facilities. By late afternoon when the editor viewed the system's contents, the livestock reports had been deleted. Thus, the student's perception of improved performance was actually a drawback due to limited storage. More importantly, the student is unaware of the fact that she can use WireReady to deselect categories, such as agriculture, in order to avoid cluttering her screen with unwanted material.

Other staff members say they do some limited searching, primarily by using the ANPA category scan. This was particularly useful, according to one copy editor, during the Persian Gulf war in January and February of 1991, when the newspaper included a "Gulf roundup" column of AP news briefs. The student said he used the search feature to find Gulf War stories without having to wade through sports, weather, and other unrelated news.

The editor-in-chief and managing editor do a fair amount of "grazing," that is, paging down through the capture file in order to find stories that might interest other editors and staff writers. One advantage of the WireReady system is the ability of any of the staff to put stories in any other staffer's private subdirectory areas. One example cited is that of a staff writer working on an in-depth story on AIDS. The managing editor selected any stories that she noticed on the subject and saved them in the writer's subdirectory.

Other anticipatory uses of the capture program occurred when the managing editor saved a story on the Oscar nominations for the entertainment editor, and when the editor-in-chief saved a list of the top popular songs of the week as a possible entertainment filler. However, these examples also point out the weakness in having a relatively small capture file. A larger archival storage capability would allow the entertainment editor to search back and select relevant stories, instead of relying on someone else to catch them before the system purges them.

Almost none of the *Daily Reveille* staff are using the keyword search capabilities of WireReady. Moreover, of those doing keyword searches, there is some confusion as to how to correctly search for phrases. One student, for example, could not understand why she kept getting more stories, even though she kept adding qualifying terms to her search. It turns out that this student was unknowingly using the "or" conditional, rather than the "and," and thus expanding her set of selected stories, rather than reducing it. Another student says that she uses keyword search extensively, but does not know how to do ANPA category searches. Thus, the ability to conduct searches is highly individualized and idiosyncratic.

Some staffers indicate that they are using the wire capture program to find background information for local stories that they are writing. One student was writing a story on the legality of releasing campus crime reports at LSU and used WireReady to find a national story on a similar case in Missouri. On another story, this student said that she scanned page-by-page for story slugs related to transportation. Not only is such a search agonizingly long, but there is also a significant chance of missing a relevant story due to the brevity of the slug.

Another student says that she finds AP copy to be useful in determining the "history" behind a story. She says that this information is often near the end of AP stories and often doesn't show up in the newspaper articles based on the AP copy. All of the staff writers who were interviewed say that they use the AP copy to check quotes against their own notes from news conferences or speeches. However, one of the staff writers says that she often finds that the AP quotes are inaccurate when compared to her own tape recordings. Thus, she uses the AP copy to direct her toward newsworthy comments, but transcribes her tapes for the exact wording.

The writers and editors who were interviewed all use the word processing software to edit stories, but in different ways. Most of them edit copy on the screen, directly changing the AP copy that they save in their subdirectories. There is almost no use of the split-screen edit capabilities of Word Perfect. Some students say that they are unaware of this feature, although one of them says that it is "too confusing" to jump back and forth between windows.

Two of the students have created their own system for editing copy by saving the desired AP copy and then writing their own story above it. When they need portions of the AP copy, they mark blocks at the bottom and move them into their stories. Apparently, this practice started with one of the students, then the other started to imitate this editing methodology.

Most of the copy is edited without the use of hard copy printouts. This is due in part to a preference for on-screen editing and may reflect the fact that this is the first significant daily writing experience for many of the students. Moreover, these students are learning to write via a computer, rather than transferring writing skills learned using other technologies (e.g., pen and paper, typewriters).

A few of the students say that they prefer using hard copy, especially for longer stories. A printer has just been installed to allow for increased ease in printing stories, so that it will be interesting to see if hard copy editing increases in the future as a result.

The faculty advisor suggested that one area for significant expansion of the WireReady system is in the archiving of stories. While we noted earlier that there is no automatic archiving software in the WireReady system, individual reporters can create their own "notebooks," in effect creating their own miniature databases. One of the student writers goes even further, suggesting that software be purchased to allow for individual database creation using AP copy, interview transcripts, and other resources. Students could then use search phrases to find desired quotations or other data on major story products.

The Nexis system has been used less extensively due to its more recent introduction at LSU and to the limited number of workstations available to the students. However, a few students have made heavy use of the Nexis databases for background information. One student says that she could "spend hours" using Nexis and that it saves her a great deal of time when compared to printed library indexes. Another student says that she first used the InfoTrac CD-ROM system in the university library to research a story on the Persian Gulf war. However, she became unhappy when she found that the latest entries were out of date, being at least two months old. Clearly, the use of Nexis would have given her more up-to-date data. Moreover, by using both the Nexis databases and the Wire-Ready AP copy, students would have both up to the minute and archival information access in a readily available form.

One student has been using Nexis for background information on a story on battered women. She says that she quickly discovered just how much had been written on this subject and that she could quickly become a "parrot expert" on facts and figures relating to this subject. Thus, she can repeat a large set of numbers and statistics that sound impressive but do not provide the reader with analysis and perspective, which are needed for useful information. She says that she realizes that she needed to build her story around interviews with local women, rather than to just summarize facts published in other stories. The *Daily Reveille* faculty advisor also says that he is wary of students becoming "bibliophiles" who merely gather facts but don't do the primary research needed for good reporting.

Others on the newspaper staff have shied away from using the Nexis system, possibly because it is more complex than the WireReady system. They must use the WireReady system regularly to assemble the daily newspaper. On the other hand, the use of Nexis is more or less optional. Some students admit to having merely looked "over the shoulder" while other students or faculty use the Nexis system, but they say that they have not personally carried out any searches on this system.

At least one student says that she doesn't use Nexis because it is "national" in scope and doesn't include Louisiana stories. However, Nexis does indeed include a number of state stories from the UPI Regional news wire database and could provide a useful extension beyond the two or three day limits of the WireReady capture file. Thus, this student is wrong and could clearly benefit by knowing the facts. This student says that she ended up using the information retrieval system at the local Baton Rouge newspaper, the *Morning Advocate,* for her story. The use of that system again points up the need for archival storage of news past the two-to-three day limitations of the WireReady system.

Students report that the Nexis system is inconvenient to use, because the terminals with which to access the system are in a separate building from the one that houses the student newspaper. We hasten to add that the WireReady and Nexis systems are not networked together in any manner. Therefore, students cannot go to one central system for their retrieval needs.

The students do not seem to be inconvenienced by the inability to edit Nexis stories, a capability that is readily available on the WireReady system. This suggests that they may be using the Nexis information retrieval system in a different manner than that of WireReady. Perhaps Nexis is used to provide background rather than to give a more direct source of news copy. However, further research is needed to determine if it is just the students' adaptation to these computerized retrieval systems or characteristics inherent in the systems themselves that is the cause of this observed phenomena. Moreover, further investigation is needed to see if students will begin to edit Nexis stories more often when the system is soon upgraded to allow for easier disk storage of retrieved stories or portions of stories and for direct word processing of those files without an intermediary hard copy.

Conclusions

The interviews conducted for this study suggest some preliminary conclusions regarding the use of computer-based information retrieval and search systems for news reporting and editing in a university environment. First, the expanded storage capabilities and the ability to save files to DOS subdirectories with the WireReady program, compared to the earlier AP wire capture system at the *Daily Reveille,* allow for enhanced abilities in story selection.

The WireReady system provides a significantly larger number of stories from which to select. Moreover, those stories date back farther, thus providing a greater degree of selectivity and making it less likely for students to miss material that came across the wire more than a couple of hours before the students were able to scan the capture file. In addition, the WireReady system allows editors and other newspaper staffers to select stories for staff writers and department editors (e.g., sports and entertainment) and save them in the writers' or editors' subdirectories for later editing.

Second, the system has proven to be useful for at least three specific newsgathering purposes: finding story ideas, providing background information for locally generated stories, and checking on quotations from speeches and news conferences attended by the student newspaper's staff writers. Each of these three uses of the WireReady system is identified as a new use of the AP wire source that was either impossible or impractical using the earlier computer system, and each use is consistent with what are generally considered to be good journalistic practices [Meyer, 1973].

Third, most editing of the AP wire copy (saved on DOS files) is accomplished through on-screen edit facilities using WordPerfect word processing capabilities. Students rarely use hard copy as an intermediary in the editing/writing process, perhaps due to the limited printout capabilities of the system. Students also are reluctant or unable to use the split-screen editing facility of the system, but some have shown the ability to create individualized systems for combining their own copy with AP copy on the screen.

Fourth, one of the most significant advantages of the WireReady system, its ability to search through headlines, story text, and story categories, is either not being used or is being misused by the staff of the *Daily Reveille*. Many staffers are manually searching the headlines of all stories, a laborious task given the larger capture file compared to the earlier system. Others are able to search using ANPA story categories, but are unaware of how to do keyword searches through the story text or headlines. Still others are able to do keyword searches, but do not seem well versed in the relatively simple system of Boolean connectors used by WireReady.

With regard to the Nexis system, some preliminary conclusions are also in order. First, the system is recognized as being a powerful tool for gathering background data for stories and is seen as being far faster than conventional print indexes and far more up to date than CD-ROM sources. Students use Nexis to provide statistical data from national or international sources for stories they are writing for local audiences.

Both the students and the faculty advisor to *The Daily Reveille* recognize the danger of overloading their reporting with facts gathered from secondary research. They seem to be aware of the difference between information retrieval and reporting, and of the need to supplement the large quantity of data gathered from Nexis with primary research, mainly through interviews with local subjects.

Some of the students appear to be reluctant to use the Nexis system, although that could be partially due to the limited access to the terminals at the time the study was conducted. Some have expressed the sentiment that the Nexis system is too complicated to operate, with the potential of a split between those student journalists who are computer literate and have access to computerized retrieval systems and those who are not computer literate and are therefore denied such access.

Finally, the students using Nexis do not appear to be overly concerned with their inability to save and edit stories, somthing they are able to do with WireReady. This lack of concern could be due to a difference in the way the system is used, or it could be due to their adaptation to the limitations of the system.

In addition to the aforementioned observations about the use and misuse of the WireReady and Nexis information retrieval systems, the interviews also provided information about useful additions to the database resources for Louisiana State University journalism students. First, the *Daily Reveille* users could benefit greatly from an extended archiving system to allow for searches farther back than two or three days. While the WireReady system has eliminated the loss of desired stories due to the small capture file on the previous system, writers and editors must still be vigilant to avoid missing relevant stories and features. One can surmise that numerous significant stories do not end up in the subdirectories of those who need them. Furthermore, a more advanced search system could be beneficial to many student journalists as they develop more skills (particularly through their exposure to more complex search systems such as the one used in the Nexis system).

Moreover, a tie-in with between the Nexis terminals and the *Daily Reveille* computer network would be beneficial both for the newspaper's staff writers and for students in journalism classes. The WireReady capture file and the Nexis database form an excellent complement to each other, with the former providing up-to-the-minute news coverage and recent news and features while the latter provides background information from several years back up to the previous day.

Finally, an enhanced save and edit capability is needed for the Nexis system. Some elements of this will be available when the Nexis terminals are connected into the School of Journalism's computer news lab network, so that hard copy will not be required. However, more advanced ways of saving stories in machine-readable format would enhance students' ability to combine previously published sources with their own writing, much as they currently do with WireReady.

The projected increase in the number of users of both the WireReady and Nexis information retrieval systems in the LSU Manship School of Journalism offers the potential for quantitative research, building on the preliminary findings of this study. This research will proceed in one of two directions.

First, surveys of the users of the WireReady and Nexis systems will be conducted to compare their perceptions of journalistic research with online information retrieval as opposed to hard copy indexes and CD-ROM databases. Specifically, such surveys will compare the relative speed of such searches, the thoroughness of the searches in terms of sources cited, the ability to use Boolean operators and the utility of searches using Boolean operators, and the students' ability to master the technical aspects of the systems.

We initially hypothesized that news story selection in the hard copy setting, not using computerized retrieval systems, would be directed primarily by the pragmatics of physical access. We also hypothesized that journalistic considerations, such as proximity, timeliness, and impact, would play a greater role in news selection in this environment, since students have complete access to all copy in a computerized setting. These hypotheses have not yet been fully tested and deserve further consideration.

A second line of inquiry to follow in future research will use experimental methodology to compare users of the online database with those using hard copy and/or CD-ROM databases. Experimental and control groups will be set up and given journalistic assignments. Then, the student journalists' work will be evaluated on such criteria as the number of citations to previously published data, the time it takes to retrieve background information, the number and quality of story ideas generated with different information retrieval resources, and the quality of writing generated by the students.

The bottom line is that it has become clear that the profession of journalism has begun to be influenced by the influx of information technology. It is also clear that this influence is growing by leaps and bounds, but that only with education and study will this influence be guaranteed to be a positive one.

References

Gerhard, M. E. (1990). Administrators say funding inhibits use of databases. *Journalism Educator* 44, 4, (Winter), 39–42.

Harter, S. P. (1986). *Online information retrieval: Concepts, principles, and techniques*. Orlando, FL: Academic Press.

384   Between Communication and Information

Hunter, M. (1989). Writers score with databases. *Folio: The Magazine for Magazine Management*, 18, 5 (May), 128.

Meyer, P. (1973). *Precision journalism: A reporter's introduction to social science methods*. Bloomington, IN: Indiana University Press.

Nasibitt, J., & Aburdene, P. (1990). *Megatrends 2000: Ten New Directions for the 1990's*. New York, NY: Morrow.

Salton, G. (1989). *Automatic text processing: The transformation, analysis, and retrieval of information by computer*. Reading, MA: Addison-Wesley.

Salton, G. & McGill, M. J. (1983). *Introduction to modern information retrieval*. New York, NY: McGraw-Hill.

Toffler, A. (1971). *Future shock*. New York: Bantam Books.

Trautman, P. (1990). Integrating text for tv databases: Sphinx for broadcast journalists. *Datamation*, 36, 10 (May) 15, 102.

Walker, R. (1990). Computer databases can be valuable sources. *Christian Science Monitor*. September 25, 14.

Wendling, D. (1989). Database searching for the service journalist: Some theories and mechanics: An Introduction. Technical Report, Columbia, MO: University of Missouri, Columbia Library.
Between Communication and Information

18

Communication, Information, and Surveillance: Separation and Control in Organizations

Carl Botan and Maureen McCreadie

This article uses the workplace setting to inform the relationship between communication and information, concluding that, although the potential exists for information technology to contribute to empowerment in the workplace, the dominant philosophy of workplace organizations often leads to the limiting of communication. First, because current definitions of information work often obscure the distinction between communication and information, a definition of information work is constructed which facilitates understanding the relationship. Second, this definition is used to identify the organization of information work as a specific instance of more general work organization. How established and emerging information technologies are used as monitoring devices to extend traditional organizational schema into information work is discussed, and how such use of these technologies makes them upwardly mobile and may contribute to stress is considered. Finally, indications of a possibly antagonistic relationship between information technology, when it is employed in the service of traditional policies, and the communication process, are identified.

The purpose of this article is to contribute to an understanding of the relationship between communication and information by examining surveillance in the information workplace and its impact on communication. Our conclusion, that workplace surveillance and communication have a generally antagonistic relationship, would be, we suspect, no surprise to many information workers. Our purpose, however, is to explain why this relationship exists. In doing so we also assert that, despite some good research pointing to the *possibly* empowering role of information technology in the workplace (Zuboff, 1988) the dominant philosophy of workplace organization means that, in many cases, such technology actually diminishes communication.

First, we argue a definition of information work that helps in understanding the relationship being investigated. Second, we identify the organization of information work as a specific instance of more general work organization, and discuss how established and emerging information technologies are used as monitoring devices to extend traditional organizational schema into information work. We also consider how such use of these technologies makes them upwardly mobile and may contribute to stress. Finally, we identify indications of a possibly antagonistic relationship between information technology, when it is employed in the service of traditional workplace policies, and the communication process.

Information Work

The information society of Beniger (1986), Dordick (1987, 1989), Machlup (1962), and Machlup & Mansfield (1983) is characterized by a preponderance of the labor force's being engaged in information work (Schement, 1989). The nature of information work is therefore a key question in the information society. Central to the nature of information work are the social relationships, manifested in both information policy and communication practice, that define the information workplace.

Paisley (1980) defined information work as "the production, distribution, transformation, storage, retrieval, or use of information" (p. 118). By including the production and use functions in the definition of information work Paisley may have obscured distinctions which are relevant in the workplace. If the term information work subsumes the whole communication process by which information is produced and used, the distinctions, and therefore the relationship between the two, become obscured. One cannot speak of a relationship between two things if they are merely two labels for the same thing.

We distinguish the terms "information work" and "communication" by labelling the production and exchange of meaning as communication, and the transmission, storage, and retrieval of meanings created and used by others as information work. Communication is best understood not as transmission, but rather as a process of meaning creation, a process enacted through dialogue (Dervin, 1989, p. 72). If information workers transmit information, delivering letters or operating a mainframe computer that transmits E-mail, for example, without creating any meanings out of that information, they are making a contribution to the process of communication but are themselves not engaged in meaningful communication.

The term "information worker" connotes someone who engages in the handling or transmission of information as a commodity (from the perspective of the information handler). Such handling implies discrete units of information that, in addition to being transmitted, might be stored, as by a file clerk, accumulated, as by a database manager, or stored and archived, as by a librarian. We distinguish the handling of information as a commodity, or information work, from communication, which also requires the handling of information, in part by virtue of the former's separating the act of handling from the process of creating and exchanging meaning. Therefore, whether one functions as an information worker or as a communicator is, in part, a matter of whether the individual involved perceives meaning in the information handled and whether, through interaction, he or she creates new meaning.

Identification of information workers is not entirely, or even principally, a subjective endeavor however. For example, an information worker can be such by virtue of language, law, or the like. An instance of the former is an information worker's handling of information in a language she or he does not know, in which case there is little question of sharing or creating meaning with it. An instance of the latter is a postal worker's passing on of information while being prohibited from sharing in its meaning.

The distinction between information work and communication is not absolute. First, all information workers are also communicators because, among other things, they communicate about the information work in which they are engaged. Second, it is probably not possible to transmit meaning without some interaction with the workers' own meanings. Therefore, information workers and communicators might better be represented on a continuum with an information worker defined by his or her proximity to the commodified, nonmeaning centered end, and a communicator defined by proximity to the processual, meaning-centered end. An information worker is, therefore, one whose principal endeavor is the handling or transmission of information regardless of its meaning. Division of labor in modern information work partitions information to the degree that any one worker may not have enough pieces of the mosaic at any one time to detect a pattern and make sense of it.

Organization of Information Work

New information technology, employed in the service of organizational philosophy and policy, has increased the likelihood of separating communication (meaning) and information work. Both established and emerging technologies can contribute to this policy of separation, and their application is expanding upwards in the organizational structure, with one common effect being an increase in stress.

General Organizational Philosophy and Policy

In steel, rubber, auto, and other industries, the philosophy that guides organizations is centered around functional supervising, called functional foremanship by Frederick Taylor. The central policy is that those who execute—labor—do not make decisions about the work they do and do not have to understand it while those who conceptualize and plan—management—do not execute. In the industrial workplace functional supervision marked the separation of the mind and its conceptual functions from the conduct of physical labor by the hands.

Scientific management, also called Taylorism, is built upon "separation of conception from execution" (Braverman, 1974, p. 114). The first and greatest tool for dividing conceptualization from execution was the task idea, of which Taylor (1911) said,

> The work of every workman [sic] is fully planned out by the management at least one day in advance, and each man receives in most cases complete written instructions, describing in detail the tasks which he is to accomplish, as well as the means for doing the work . . . this task specifies not only what is to be done but how it is to be done and the exact time allowed for doing it. (P. 39)

Today, time and motion study, coupled with modern industrial engineering, is used to plan and coordinate the work of thousands of employees in large factories.

Greater and greater subdivision of the job has made possible tighter and tighter control, and correspondingly, less and less freedom of action on the part of the worker. Salutary effects of this division of work include greater productivity, consistency of product, and a resulting high ability to control quality and balance it with production. For these reasons, as the economy grew and changed, the method of division and control of the workplace developed in the manufacturing setting was transported into the service sector. For example, Garson (1988) found that

By combining twentieth-century computer technology with nineteenth-century time-and-motion studies, the McDonald's corporation has broken the jobs of griddleman [sic], waitress [sic], cashier and even manager down into small, simple steps. Historically these have been service jobs involving a lot of flexibility and personal flare. But the corporation has systematically extracted the decision-making elements from filling french fry boxes or scheduling staff. They've siphoned the know how from the employees into the programs. They relentlessly weed out all variables that might make it necessary to make a decision at the store level, whether on pickles or on cleaning procedures. (P. 37)

Organizational Philosophy of Information Work

Lessons learned in the industrial setting and refined in the service setting are now being applied in the information setting. Just as in manufacturing and service, subdivision of information work has changed the nature of the job and the role of the people doing the job. As the assembly-line worker who tightens the same nine bolts little resembles a skilled carriage maker, and the McDonald's food preparer little resembles a chef, so the information worker/processor may bear little resemblance to a communicator.

Division of labor in the modern information workplace has allowed the separation of mind from hands in information work, making it possible for workers to be excluded from meaningful communication processes while at the same time vastly increasing their efficiency in handling information. Such a division is based on the notion of information as a commodity which can be transmitted, stored, accumulated, even archived in isolation from the human process of communication—the creation and exchange of meaning. As a result, information workers are now part of an "invisible electronic assembly line" (Shaiken, 1987).

The same policies that lead to division and control of the commodity of information also lead to division and control of the work flow of each employee. The very technology that makes advanced information work possible also provides the means for monitoring an employee's every movement in the course of a workday. The information resulting from monitoring is also a commodity, and can be transmitted, stored, accumulated, and archived. So, new information technologies, in the service of established policies are transforming the American work environment in part by blurring the distinction between the information being handled and information about the handling of information.

Established Technologies

In the late 1980s five to seven million clerical, professional, technical, and retail sales workers were continuously subject to monitoring in the electronic workplace (U.S. Congress, 1987). In one study, 98 percent of data processing, word processing, and customer service operations in 110 work sites were using computers to track the movements of workers (Bureau of National Affairs [BNA], 1987). An estimated 350,000 Communications Workers of America (CWA) operators were working daily at monitored video data terminals (VDTs), and nearly 400,000 CWA members were potential targets of monitoring through their workplace telephones (Newsom, 1987).

In 1985, 20,000 telephone station message detail recording (SMDR) devices were sold in the United States (Marx & Sherizen, 1986). Designed to gather statistics for analysis of use patterns, the data generated includes the time, duration, called number, and number from which the call was placed. In 1987 there were an estimated 130 firms producing hardware, software, or services related to SMDR, with a projected market growth of 50 percent per year. Congress's Office of Technological Assessment (OTA) reported that "call-accounting equipment and software represent the fastest growing segment of the telecommunication industry in the past few years" (U.S. Congress, 1987, p. 12). Along the same vein, New Jersey Bell supervisors are reported to listen to roughly thirty of an operator's monthly 20,000 directory assistance transactions (Kramer, 1988).

VDT operators are often monitored according to the number of keystrokes entered. At Northwest Orient Airlines in Minneapolis, the data entry pace is set by the three fastest operators. The keystroke output of other operators is expected to come within at least 75 percent of this pace. At another company, an older woman, now a word processor, complained that, "The worst thing is when work comes by me with wrong spelling, wrong information. Sometimes I think I should correct it. I did at first. But that's not how they judge me" (Garson, 1988, p. 174). She voiced her frustration at a management policy that stipulated she be evaluated solely on the number of keystrokes she entered in relation to the amount of time she spent on a document. According to a study by the National Association of Working Women (1984), programs such as "The Messenger" provide a VDT operator with calming images on the monitor accompanied by subliminal messages. Other programs allow management to send subliminal messages to the operator without the employee's being aware they are present.

Monitoring is not limited to VDTs and telephone systems, however. Electronic mail is easily monitored and, in some instances, video cameras record an employee's activities. Nor is monitoring limited to traditional office environments. Retail sales workers and grocery clerks can be monitored through the cash registers they operate, and the time a nurse spends with each patient can be tracked through portable computers

(Amend, 1990). Truckers, long thought to be independent and freewheeling, now frequently travel in the company of Tripmaster, a black box that records average speeds, the number and length of stops, mileage, and even shifting patterns. Newer technologies, such as digital branch exchanges (PBXs), local area networks (LANs), and digitally switched telephone networks have also made it easier to monitor workers.

Those most likely to be monitored right now are directory assistance and long distance operators, health insurance company employees, Internal Revenue Service employees, airline and hotel reservation clerks, and VDT operators (BNA, 1987). The majority of workers holding such positions are women. The Office of Technological Assessment (U.S. Congress, 1987) concluded, "since clerical work is increasingly being done on computer terminals, women are disproportionally affected by the microelectronic technology in the office environment" (p. 7).

Emerging Technologies

The future offers a variety of technological possibilities for increased workplace monitoring, two of the most startling of which are genetic testing and brainwave monitoring. Hunt (1986) reported that

genetic techniques are either now available or may soon become available that can help screen applicants for employment, and employee and managerial candidates for promotion. (P. 519)

Marx and Sherizen (1986) were addressing the compilation of general databases when they warned that monitoring may help create a class of permanently unemployed and underemployed people. The databases generated through genetic testing may pose similar risks as a portion of otherwise intellectually and educationally qualified workers could be genetically designated for exclusion from certain kinds of (higher paying?) employment and tracked into work which may end up being less well paid, less dependable, or less central to the line function of the organization and therefore less likely to earn promotion.

An additional concern arises when we consider that genetic testing carries with it the potential for corporations to avoid having to eliminate or modify the use of toxic substances in the workplace. Corporations can sidestep liability for such substances by hiring only those who are not susceptible to the toxins.

Given that "the panorama of diseases [about 3,000] with some hereditary etiology affects at least half the population" (Rowe, Russell-Einhorn,

& Weinstein, 1987, p. 520), large masses of this information may be accumulated into databases. In 1983, for example, while only twenty-five of 366 firms reported having conducted genetic screening, another fifty-nine of the 366 had plans to do so in the future (U.S. Congress, 1987).

The nature of this information technology dictates that if a substantial minority of employers start using it, other employers may "become by default a haven, and therefore an insurer, for those who are more likely to develop expensive genetic diseases" (Hunt, 1986, p. 519). This may force nonusers into adopting these techniques. What would be relatively benign information in the hands of a patient and his or her physician may become a weapon, in the face of which women, minorities, and others less able to protect themselves would be particulary vulnerable because "genetic susceptibilities are unequally distributed among different races or ethnic groups" (U.S. Congress, 1987).

An even newer information technology is brain wave testing. Brain wave analysis

> could lead to usable technologies with possible application in the workplace. If developed as practical systems, they could be used to gather extensive information about a subject's psychological state, genetic propensities, or honesty; they might be useful in new means of measuring or pacing work. (U.S. Congress, 1987, p. 138)

Research at the University of Illinois indicates that some brain waves directly reflect cognitive processes such as memory, language, and learning (U.S. Congress, 1987). Such brain wave signals are called event-related brain potentials (ERPs) when measured electrically, but they can also be measured magnetically using a superconducting quantum interference device or SQUID. Future systems are envisioned that would

> monitor the operator's ability to cope with information flows and to make decisions. On the basis of the information about his [sic] performance, the system could either adjust the rate of information flow to the operator or automatically take on some of the operator's tasks to optimize his performance. Some future applications could include pilots, air traffic controllers, and other computer-based work. (U.S. Congress, 1987, p. 138)

The Office of Technological Assessment of the U.S. Congress concluded, "such technology might actually give the ability to 'read the mind,' removing all possibility of a person's keeping information private" (U.S. Congress, 1987, p. 138). In fact, through monitoring the P300 brainwave, the level of attention and cognitive processing can be detected. This has led one Westinghouse researcher to predict that by the mid-1990s Westinghouse may be able to market "a complete system capable of monitoring the mental processing efforts of employees as they worked" (Schrage, 1983, p. C1).

Many of these newer information technologies are not functional today, but they do serve to illustrate the importance of establishing clear policy.

Upward Mobility

If the separation of conceptualization and execution is a major outcome of information technology, it should follow the technology as it expands upward in organizational hierarchy. Barnard (1938) said that "The first executive function is to develop and maintain a system of communication. This involves both a scheme of organization and an executive personnel" (p. 271). The upward mobility of computer monitoring may reduce the functions of some of those called executives. Even the freedom of executives to make judgments is being altered by new information technology as "more and more middle managers who use computers [are] monitored on how many appointments they have and how many hours they spend on various activities" (BNA, 1987, p. 1). The same source warned that "monitoring can do away with some of the layers of middle management" (p. 2). This capability may be appealing to the "89 of the 100 largest firms [which] have established programs to reduce the number of management levels" (Neubecker, 1985, p. 34).

Some executives may be deskilled to high-status information workers because the essence of the executive function, skilled communication, can be broken down into distinct parts as with other information work. One Wall Street broker interviewed by Garson (1988) described the process as he saw it:

> With computers the company can calculate not only how much business you're doing, but exactly how much money they'll make on each piece of business. . . . So now the pressure on the broker is not only to do more business but to do it exactly "our way." (P. 147)

In practice, the result, through the increased centralization of decision making, is an increase in the number of clerks and a decrease in the number of professionals (BNA, 1987; Garson, 1988).

Stress

Finally, if increased separation and control—through information technology—are required by existing organizational philosophy, they would be employed to the greatest extent possible in each particular context. An increase in workplace stress could be one indicator that this is so because, although not firmly established, one of the effects frequently attributed to employee monitoring is an increase in stress levels and in stress-related illnesses among employees. Included among the symptoms suffered due to stress are headaches, gastrointestinal pain, anxiety, chest pain, and musculoskeletal discomfort. In a study conducted by the National Association of Working Women (1984), stress was found to cost employers between $50 and $75 billion annually. Among unmonitored workers, one-fifth missed work due to stress. By comparison, one-third of monitored workers missed work because of stress or stress related symptoms. For example, one fifty-four-year-old TWA worker believes her chronic fatigue syndrome was brought on by severe stress at work from having been continuously subject to surveillance through the telephone headset she wears to perform her job (Amend, 1990).

Stress related to monitoring can lead to another cost as well, a decline in the quality of service. Telephone operators and reservations clerks who are evaluated according to the time spent on a transaction have been known to disconnect or give incorrect information to a caller with a complex request (Garson, 1988; Marx & Sherizen, 1986; Shaiken, 1987). Word processors rated according to number of keystrokes entered can hold down one key to improve their rate (Marx & Sherizen, 1986) or pass along mistakes to maintain a rate that would be lowered by taking the time to correct errors (Garson, 1988).

Summary of Information Technologies

As a whole, information technologies have the potential to increase the gathering and handling of information, but it is an organization's philosophy and resulting policies that determine how they are used. How productivity is measured reflects this philosophy and policy. Work with new information technologies, when organized from a traditional perspective, is likely to be measured in traditional ways that may not be appropriate to the new kind of work. It has been argued, for example, that measurement of productivity in information work requires a different approach than in the production of goods (Hall, 1981; Rice & Bair, 1984; Williams, Rice, & Rogers, 1988), that more attention must be given to qualitative measures than has traditionally been the practice, and that the impact of the technology on the employee must also be considered in the evaluation process.

Relationship of Information to Communication in the Workplace

The preceding analysis of the information workplace illustrates that the relationship between communication and information in the workplace is a complex one. Communication and information may, in workplace practice, have a relationship analogous to a teeter-totter. As one goes up the other may have to decline, but only as a result of information policy. New information technologies are as capable of being employed to expand the communication role of individuals and enrich their communicative experience (Zuboff, 1988) as they are to being applied to bring about greater division and control of information work.

As subdivision and control of information work increase, information workers become increasingly further removed from the meaning-centered end of the work continuum. Possessed only of sometimes fragmentary commodity units of information, and with quantity and time controlled, sometimes to the point of stress-related illness, these workers have little opportunity to share in the creation of meaning. The more purely their labor is information work, the less it is communication, a trend that appears to be upwardly mobile in the hierarchy of labor.

The future holds promise of increases in the role of information technology in the workplace. Corresponding to this increased role for technology will be a continually evolving role for information policy. Information technology and policy may evolve toward the greater and greater separation of hands and minds. Should this happen it is reasonable to assume that greater and greater numbers of information workers will become alienated from their workplace experiences, viewing new information technologies negatively. An industry largely unorganized by labor unions may well evolve into fertile organizing ground as the same kinds of social and economic relations which marked the industrial workplace in the first half of this century become more and more characteristic of the information workplace of the second half of this century. Information as a commodity may lead to the same employee responses as have cars, coal, and tires as commodities.

References

Amend, P. (1990, March 4). High tech surveillance: The boss may be watching. *USA Today*, 11B.

Barnard, C. I. (1938/89). The executive functions. Reprinted in J. S. Ott (Ed.), *Classical readings in organizational behavior* (pp. 265–75). Pacific Grove, CA: Brooks/Cole.

Beniger, J. R. (1986). *The control revolution: Technological and economic origins of the Information Society*. Cambridge, MA: Harvard University Press.

Braverman, H. (1974). *Labor and monopoly capital. The degradation of work in the twentieth century.* New York: Monthly Review Press.

Bureau of National Affairs (1987 March 24). Technological monitoring of employees said increasingly, Not always productive. *Daily Labor Report,* No. 55.

Dervin, B. (1989). Audience as listener and learner, teacher and confidante: The sense-making approach. In R. E. Rice & C. K. Atkin (Eds.), *Public communication campaigns* (2nd ed.) (pp. 67–86). Newbury Park, CA: Sage.

Dordick, H. S. (1987). The emerging information societies. In J. R. Schement & L. A. Lievrouw (Eds.), *Competing visions, complex realities: Social aspects of the Information Society* (pp. 13–22). Norwood, NJ: Ablex.

Dordick, H. S. (1989). Telecommunications in an information society. In S. S. King (Ed.), *Human communication as a field of study: Selected contemporary views* (pp. 203–9). Albany: State University of New York Press.

Garson, B. (1988). *The electronic sweatshop: How computers are transforming the office of the future into the factory of the past.* New York: Simon and Schuster.

Hall, K. (1981). The economic nature of information. *The Information society, 1*(2), 143–66.

Hunt, H. A. (1986). Technological change and employment: Fears and reality. In *IRRA 39th Annual Proceedings.*

Kramer, L. (1988, January 31). Call-monitoring under fire: Operators, official debate telephone procedure. *Home News,* I23.

Machlup, F. (1962). *The production and distribution of knowledge in the United States.* Princeton, NJ: Princeton Unversity Press.

Machlup, F., & Mansfield, U. (1983). *The study of information: Interdisciplinary messages.* New York: Wiley.

Marx, G. T., & Sherizen, S. (1986, November/December). Monitoring on the Job: How to protect privacy as well as property. *Technology Review, 89,* 62–72.

National Association of Working Women (9 to 5). (1984). The 9 to 5 national survey on women and stress: Office automation.

Neubecker, R. (1985, September 16). Middle managers are still sitting ducks. *Business Week,* 34.

Newsom, C. (1987, November). Report on employee monitoring draws mixed comments. *Presstime,* 62.

Paisley, W. (1980). Information and work. In B. Dervin & M. Voigt (Eds.), *Progress in Communication Sciences,* vol. 2 (pp. 113–66). Norwood, NJ: Ablex.

Picht, R. (1988, September 6). Phone-call monitors help. *Home News,* C8.

Rice, R. E., & Bair, J. H. (1984). New organizational media and productivity. In R. E. Rice (Ed.), *The New Media: Communication, Research, and Technology* (pp. 185–216). Beverly Hills, CA: Sage.

Rowe, M. P., Russell-Einhorn, M. L., & Weinstein, J. N. (1987). New issues in testing the work force: Genetic diseases. Proceedings of the 1987 Spring Meeting of the Industrial Relations Research Association.

Schement, J. R. (1989). The origins of the Information Society in the United States: Competing visions. In J. Salvaggio (Ed.), *The Information Society* (pp. 29–50). Hillsdale, NJ: Lawrence Erlbaum.

Schrage, M. (1984, June 3). Technology could let bosses read minds. *Washington Post,* C1.

Shaiken, H. (1987). When the computer runs the office. *New York Times,* sec. 3, p. C3.

Taylor, F. W. (1911/67). *Principles of scientific management.* New York: Norton.

U. S. Congress, Office of Technology Assessment. (1987). *The electronic supervisor: New technology, new tensions*. (OTA Publication No. OTA-CIT-333). Washington, DC: U. S. Government Printing Office.

Williams, F., Rice, R. E., & Rogers, E. M. (1988). *Research methods and the new media*. New York: Free Press.

Zuboff, S. (1988). *In the age of the smart machine: The future of work and power*. New York: Basic Books.

PART IV
SOCIETAL CONTEXTS

19

On the Prospects for Redefining Universal Service: From Connectivity to Content

Frederick Williams and Susan Hadden

The prospect of redefining "universal service" in U.S. telephone policy provides an occasion to reexamine the relationships between communication and information. Heretofore, the essence of universal service was simply access to connectivity. Although the term, per se, is not defined in the Communications Act, universal service has served as a general concept indicating access to voice service at an affordable rate. However, the new capabilities of the "intelligent network" suggest that the definition of basic service may need to be revised to include access to information, the specific designation of which we call "content." The United States has built up a considerable tradition of government guarantee of public access to information to serve the needs of citizenship, to improve the operation of the market, and to ensure safety—a tradition which could form the basis for developing a right to certain kinds of information over the electronic network. The Toxic Release Inventory, the first federally mandated public access electronic database, provides an example of the kinds of information that might be made available and illustrates possible problems with mandated information access. Adoption of expanded universal service as a goal is inextricably linked to the present system for regulating telecommunications, and especially to any ban on telephone company entry into information services. Establishing a right to certain content provides a policy goal that could guide decisions about such regulatory problems.

The Relevance of Information to Universal Service

The prospect of redefining "universal service" in U.S. telephone policy provides an occasion to reexamine the relationships between communication and information. For years, regulators, industry, and consumer groups have agreed that universal service meant widely available, affordable, and intelligible voice telephone service. Universal service was considered important because of the central role played by the telephone in calling for help, doing business, or keeping in touch with friends and family. However, the essence of universal service was simply access to connectivity, or, as they say in the business, "dial tone."

As common carriers, telephone companies were not concerned about the kinds of calls subscribers made, about the content of those calls, or about content generally.[1] Taken together, the concepts of common carrier and universal service illustrate traditional telecommunications policy regarded basic communication as connectivity, albeit with implications for content such as access to directory assistance. Now, however, the content component may be moving to center stage as the network becomes capable of delivering a much enhanced variety of services. The relationship of growing "intelligent network" capabilities to new social and economic concerns has raised the possibility that telephone companies might provide universal access to certain services—telemetry, data, and perhaps video—beyond voice dial tone. As this prospect is debated, we may well see attempts to define various "levels" of content thought to be important for everyday life in the information age.

At present, universal service is typically mentioned in conjunction with financial issues in telephony. The two subjects are so closely tied due to the regulatory structure that in turn has given rise to the complex cross-subsidies that have characterized the telephone business. Traditionally, long-distance revenues were used to subsidize residential services—that is, to keep residential costs low in the name of universal service. Many rural service providers draw from "high cost" pools so their customers do not have to pay rates they cannot afford (costs of a rural line can be up to ten times that of an urban one). Businesses pay higher rates and, in effect, subsidize residential access, again in the name of universal service. Indeed, one of the motives for the divestiture of the Bell System was to separate services and reduce cross-subsidies to improve efficiency. In rate cases, consumerists may argue that a rate hike will drive the poor (elderly, minority, handicapped, rural) off of the network, threatening the universality of service. The remedy is a mix of federal and state "teleassistance" plans that provide reduced cost options to those who cannot pay full rates for the purpose of keeping them on the network.

The connection between universal service and rates is also reflected in the difference between basic connectivity and "enhanced" telephone services. Such special services as "speed dialing," "call waiting," "call forwarding," or "three party calling," entail an extra charge. Individual subscribers pay for "900" calls, including charges for the particular information, and they can pay to have home security systems connected to the telephone network. In contrast, the provision of "equal access" to different long distance providers has become a new basic service, included in everyone's telephone bill without a choice. Similarly, each subscriber must contribute to the cost of "911" emergency services to which all have access. Thus, as conditions or network capabilities change, the lowest-rate "basic" telephone package may expand to include additional services (or contract as services are unbundled).

If telephone companies start to provide information services, the definition of basic service will have to be reconsidered. Should "data dial tone" be an enhanced service, or should certain information or information services be a part of basic service? Are some of these services critical to the well-being of the modern citizen? Or, put another way, what information services should be a basic entitlement, a part of the basic price of public telephone service? Beyond these, what information services fall more in the realm of "enhanced" options and should involve an extra price to the user? These challenging questions may be overshadowed if video services come to the public switched network. Would we consider "video dial tone" to be a universal service or would we want to include certain video information?

In short, the availability of new technologies and likely services forces us to consider *content,* an element not included in the traditional connectivity definition of universal service for voice telephone. Connectivity is a prerequisite of communication, and heretofore policy focused simply on enabling people to communicate. The new technologies not only blur the distinction between connectivity and information by automatically carrying such information as the originating telephone number along with the substantive message, but they also enable us to provide easily certain sustantive content. In this respect, we consider "content" to be the designation or description of the specific meaning of the information. Thus, certain enhanced services could include content of different types, such as news headlines, government services, or personal mail. In broad perspective, then, we see "connectivity" as having an enabling function for the transfer of information, and, again, the description of the meaning of that information as "content."

Our goal in this chapter is to examine this potentially new kind of universal service, especially as it relates to technology development, regulatory change, and considerations of citizens' rights to information. At the same time, by pondering the incorporation of information services into a redefined universal service, we can contribute to the communication/ information theme of this volume, namely, the growing levels of information that may be seen as an extension of basic communications connectivity.

The Coming Intelligent Network

Major advances in telecommunications and computing technologies, along with the coalescence of the two, have greatly increased the capability of the public telecommunications network over the past thirty years. These advances have made it possible to increase services beyond basic voice and to develop the so-called "intelligent network" (Williams, 1990) through which expanded services are delivered. In order to understand the questions surrounding expanded definitions of universal service, it is helpful to review these technological advances.

Telecommunications is traditionally defined in terms of transmission and switching technologies. Transmission technologies have evolved from the traditional "twisted pair" of copper wires capable of carrying an intelligible (but not high fidelity) voice conversation. Today, service providers can combine ("multiplex") many conversations in the same wired circuit that now integrates cable, microwave, fiber, and satellite components. Given computers equipped with modems (modulator-demodulators), it has been possible to transform digital computer codes into an analog form for transmission over this traditional network. Users of electronic mail or of the "on-line" services like CompuServe or Prodigy have already availed themselves of this technology. The new network is increasingly able to carry not only an abundance of voice circuits, but also data, a variety of other information services, and where capacity allows, video.

Switching, or managing the flow of messages within the network, is where "intelligence" enters into the system. Over the years, switching technology has evolved from hand placing of jacks to electromechanical, all electronic, and now to all "digital" switches. Digital switches are special purpose computers that can convert voice traffic into computer readable rather than analog message form. These networks are capable of a high degree of self-management (e.g., call routing, toll calculations, trouble shooting) and are as amenable to transmitting data as voice. The network itself generates signaling information as a part of its management operations. It is this level of network sophistication that allows for caller identification and other enhanced services.

As standards for digitizing the public network enhance its compatibility with computers, an all-digital mode of computer-to-computer communication becomes possible. This all-digital mode is typical of many present-day "local area networks" (LANs). Additional capability will be achieved in implementing the international standard for the "Integrated Systems Digital Network" (ISDN) that can combine two voice or data channels and one signaling channel over the same circuit connection. This allows a user to exchange computer screen data or images, voice, or FAX simultaneously in the same "call." With the proper interface for ISDN services, a modem will not be necessary, another step toward ease of acquiring data and information services over the public network. Experimentation now indicates that a reasonable quality "compressed video" moving image can be carried over the two major channels of a basic ISDN link. This may mean an interim move to home video services over the network even before it is upgraded by use of fiber optics. These advances in transmission and switching have allowed development of the "intelligent network," one in which information and data services (content) may become as ubiquitous as voice traffic. A network with these capabilities can deliver a wide variety of home-oriented services, many of which are listed in table 19.1. Similar advantages will accrue to businesses. Note how many of these services go beyond basic connectivity to include information; network growth seems to go hand in hand with information services. Are these services a preview of the coming redefinition of universal service? The universal service implicit in the list still reflects connectivity, but expanded to data and video as well as voice.

In short, the move towards digitization of all communications, regardless of initial format, combined with advances in switching, have created the potential for a qualitative shift in telecommunications. Demonstration

TABLE 19.1
New Home Services

- Dial-up Television Services
- Integrated Emergency Alarms (Fire, Police, Medical)
- Personal, "Transportable" Telephone Numbers
- Simultaneous Voice, Data, or FAX Calls
- Dial-up Educational Services
- Personal Communications Networks (PCNs)
- Practical Videophone
- Direct Computer Links (no modem)
- Other Multimedia Communications Services
- Customized Newspaper or Videotext
- Improved Home Shopping and Banking
- Multimedia Catalogs for Shopping
- Wireless FAX and Personal Computer Links

Source: Adapted from Williams (1990)

projects have confirmed the utility of the new technologies in areas as diverse as education, medicine, and home security. As in so many other areas, unfortunately, social institutions lag behind technological developments. A review of the concept of universal service up until now illustrates this point clearly.

Regulatory Dimensions

The rapid advances in the intelligent network are placing serious strains on the regulatory framework. In an era of converging technologies, regulation still differs for different modes of transmission (broadcast, telephone, cable). The digitalization of the telephone network means that certain information, such as the identification of the call originator, is part and parcel of transmission capability. Yet telephone regulation still focuses on rates and access, issues at the heart of the traditional view of universal service.

Universal service was first referred to by Theodore Vail, president of AT&T, in the company's 1910 annual report, where he wrote,

> The position of the Bell system is well known. . . . The telephone system should be universal, interdependent and intercommunicating, affording opportunity for any subscriber of any exchange to communicate with any other subscriber of any other exchange . . . annihilating time or distance by use of electrical transmission.[2]

Vail was referring primarily to connectivity, specifically to linking the many currently existing but isolated networks. He proposed to the federal government that only a monopoly could ensure maximum benefits from the telephone by providing an efficient, nationwide network to which all could have access. In return for remaining a monopoly, AT&T would work with regulators to see that rates for using the telephone would remain low enough that there would be "universal" service. Because everyone could be reached through the network, its value to each other user would rise.

The goal of universal service became public policy, albeit indirectly, in two ways: the Supreme Court's *Smith* decision and the Communications Act of 1934. In *Smith v. Illinois,* the court held that some of the costs of providing local service should be allocated to long-distance rates, since the same equipment was needed for both services. This decision resulted in a structural readjustment in telephone rate-setting, in which pooling and nationwide rate averaging reduced basic telephone tariffs to the point at which they were affordable for most Americans.

The idea of universal service was also embodied in the preamble of the 1934 Communications Act, which requires regulation to

make available, so far as possible, to all people of the United States, a rapid, efficient, nationwide, and worldwide wire and radio communication service with adequate facilities at reasonable charges.[3]

In short, the goal—and near achievement—of universal service grew out of a system in which a monopoly, with acquiescence from regulators, subsidized rates with profits from other services. Rates were low enough that almost everyone could afford basic telephone service; they tended toward uniformity despite the different costs of providing service in remote or rough terrain.

Even though AT&T's monopoly was increasingly circumscribed by the FCC in the years after World War II, the goal of universal service remained unexamined and unchanged. The opening of competition in telephony culminated in the divestiture of AT&T, which was announced in 1982 as a "Modified Final Judgment" (MFJ) of an earlier antitrust agreement and implemented on 1 January 1984. One of the key premises underlying the dismantling of AT&T was that it would be possible to separate the monopoly components from the competitive components of the telephone business, a premise with important effects on the kinds of rate pooling that supported universal service.

The MFJ awarded AT&T the increasingly competitive long-distance business and added computer sales, an area in which the company had long been interested, at least in part because of its unregulated status. The divested Bell companies, which were assigned monopoly positions in "Local Access and Transport Areas" (LATAs), remained regulated and, presumably, focused on their basic line of business, the provision of local telephone service.

In the MFJ, Judge Greene specifically barred the Bell companies from providing long-distance service, manufacturing equipment, or offering information services. After issuing the MFJ, but before its implementation, Judge Greene also barred AT&T from entering the information services business for a period of seven years.[4]

Although universal service has been widely used and accepted as a goal, it is important to note that the term per se, does not appear in the Communications Act, nor is a specific definition found elsewhere in the law. Instead, universal service is a general concept indicating access to voice service at an affordable rate. In state rate cases, it may refer to a particular package of basic services at an agreed upon price. Although its essence is connectivity, there have always been implications of content.

As services have evolved, information in the form of "directory assistance," 976 services, and network management have crept into the picture. Because the intelligent network is well adapted to the delivery of information services, and telcos are pushing to provide them, it may be that the first expansion in the definition of universal service will add information services to basic connectivity.

Expanding Universal Service

Calls for Redefinition

Some observers reject the idea that universal service has been accomplished; they believe that it is a relative term whose meaning changes as technology advances. Because information plays such a paramount role in our society today, people adhering to this view feel that the original goals of universal service are no longer sufficient. According to this view, regulators not only need to assure continued low rates, but also to adopt policies to ensure that our society does not become one of information haves and have-nots. This view is becoming more widespread, with proponents in government, industry, and the consumer sectors. Some typical statements follow:

• The Intelligent Network Task Force of California (Pacific Bell, 1988) recommended in its 1987 report that universal service should include "access to the Intelligent Network and to a specific set of essential applications services."
• The National Telecommunications and Information Administration, the president's telecommunications policy advisory body, in its *Telecom 2000* report states,

> in light of the possibilities for new service offerings by the 21st century, as well as the growing importance of telecommunications and information services to U.S. economic and social development, limiting our concept of universal service to the narrow provisions of basic voice telephone service no longer serves the public interest. Added to universal basic telephone service should be the broader concept of universal opportunity to access these new technologies and applications. (NTIA, 1988, p. x)

• The Rural Telephone Coalition, consisting of the National Telephone Cooperative Association (NTCA), the National Rural Telecom Association (NRTA), and the Organization for the Protection and Advancement of Small Telephone Companies (OPASTCO), recommended that Congress establish universal information service and a nationwide intelligent network as national goals. They also recommended that Congress make use of the federal-state joint board process to evaluate universal service needs. The United States Telephone Association (USTA) has made similar recommendations.

Unfortunately, widespread agreement about the need to redefine universal service is undermined by disagreement about the correct way to achieve expanded public access to advanced services. We can identify three positions concerning methods to promote expanded universal service.

1. *Maintain the monopoly.* Increased competition undermines the goals of universal service and competition should emerge only gradually. Adherents of this position believe that the old monopoly system was the best model to achieve reasonably priced basic service. A related view has been advanced by Michael Brunner (1986) executive vice president of the NTCA, who argues that federal regulators and Congress have, for the most part, fulfilled their "obligation" to protect and preserve universal service. The real threat to universal service, he believes, lies in the states' willingness to dispose of the mechanisms that have thus far preserved universal service. For example, the New Mexico Public Utility Commission recently adopted a plan that is, in effect, toll-rate deaveraging, which puts rural residents at a great disadvantage. Nebraska has almost completely deregulated.

2. Competition will eventually bring better technology and services to local subscribers. Adherents of this position believe in increased competition and deregulation but maintain greater state control of regulation. Many of the state regulatory incentive plans that allow telephone companies to retain extra earnings in return for investing them in upgrading the network exemplify regulatory flexibility. Such investments may make the public telephone company more competitive.

3. Competition should be allowed even at the local level to "eliminate the perverse incentives of regulated monopoly" (Noll, 1988, p. 6). This is the position of the NTIA, for example, which believes that less, rather than more regulation in the industry will remove the barriers to expanded access. Chief among the barriers is the bypass syndrome: large users are prevented from obtaining the advanced services they require because of regulated limits on the public network, while bypassing the public network contributes further to the network's inability to compete. Legal obstacles such as the line-of-business restrictions in the MFJ of AT&T also impede investment in the public network. Finally, according to NTIA, mechanisms such as cross-subsidies that keep rates down artificially also impede investment, trading short-term benefits for long-run inability to compete globally in the information age.

What is striking about the reports cited is their juxtaposition of far-sighted views of universal service and public information access with more tradtional views about regulation. By merging the two issues—universal service and regulatory method—the stakeholders limit the scope of the debate to what can be achieved through existing regulatory structures. The Congressional Office of Technology Assessment (OTA), is its recent publication *Critical Connections* (1990), offers several strategies and options Congress could pursue to implement universal service that cut across these more traditional regulatory approaches. These include restructuring the prices at which communication services are offered, providing direct government support for users to access information and communication paths, and assuming a more proactive role in assuring lively debate on issues related to expanded universal service.

We would like to suggest yet a different approach to considering the relationship between universal service and regulatory policy. Figure 19.1 illustrates the idea. In the early years of the public network, and even in the post-World War II years, as telephone penetration passed 90 percent, basic connectivity was a positive policy concept. But in postdivestiture times, universal service has seemed to conflict with the move toward competition and has therefore acquired negative connotations. Instead of serving as a positive planning goal, universal service has become a sort of "warning signal"—something to be achieved through teleassistance plans when the imperfections of the regulated environment become intolerable. We believe that this view misses the important point. Competition is indeed an important means to stimulate development of the network, but it cannot be an end unto itself. It is only a means to a goal. It is now time to recommit to a goal of universal service—a redefined version that takes into account the new capabilities of the network. With such a goal, we have a benchmark against which to assess the value of particular regulatory approaches, such a rate caps, deregulation, toll rate deaveraging, or

FIGURE 19.1
Redefinition and Repositioning Universal Service as a Policy Goal

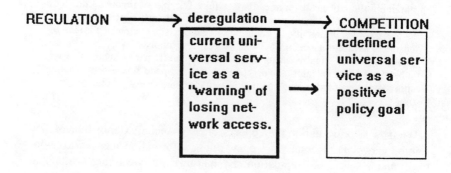

even a shift of regulatory responsibility from the federal to the state level. As our discussion above showed, moreover, this goal is already being widely considered and, often, adopted. Let us first debate the nature of universal service, only then turning to a discussion of the appropriate regulatory methods for achieving it. The following section contributes to this debate by raising issues associated with expanding universal service to include content as well as conectivity.

Universal Content?

Background

The possibility of expanded universal service raises a host of questions, including what kinds of information should be universally accessible, whether it should be accessible in the home or central information nodes similar to libraries, and whether users should be charged for access time.

Although the intelligent network and, therefore, the delivery mechanism is new, existing public policies provide some guidance about the kinds of information to which the public needs access. Probably the most important guideline comes from the discussions and writings of the Founding Fathers, who believed that access to information is an essential feature of a democracy because only informed citizens can participate usefully in public decision making. The Constitutional provision requiring Congress to report to citizens is echoed in twentieth-century laws giving the public access to records to ensure that government is not exceeding its rightful power.

Other areas of information provision in which government gradually came to have an accepted role included consumer products, since competition would be harmed by manufacturers who misrepresented their goods. This power was gradually expanded to include providing the public with a wide range of information about product risks and ways to avoid them. An expanding notion of individual rights also led to government activity concerning information about people. On the one hand, the Privacy Act limited government and outside access to information about an individual; on the other, individuals have obtained increasing access to publicly and privately held records about themselves, ranging from consumer credit to arrest records. (Flaherty, 1989).

Although citizenship, hazards, market operation, and personal data constitute a broad range of areas in which government has intervened to ensure public information access, there are limits to this activity. Then new technologies constitute a special source of difficulty. No longer can information simply be added to product labels or provided in printed pamphlets. Instead, full access to information requires that people be able to obtain digital information, especially now that some information is available only in electronic formats.

The experience of the Montgomery County, Maryland public library is instructive. The staff defined four categories of library services, of which "basic services"—those that no other government or private agency provides, or for which fees would negatively affect particularly needy groups—must be provided without fees (NCLIS, 1988). However, the latter criterion turned out to be relatively ineffective in discriminating among types of data services because any fee-based service could be said to affect lower income people adversely. As on-line reference or literature searches became more widely available, for example, libraries began to provide them if users paid the commercial fee. Yet, to the extent that such electronic databases constitute the most effective or only available way to conduct a literature search, they become a basic or minimum service and charging for them discriminates against those who have little money. Fortunately, in this case technological advances may come to the aid of library patrons, because CD-ROM technology can increasingly substitute for on-line searches.

The growing capacity of the telephone network and the increasing number of electronic databases challenge the incremental nature of government information access policies. Until now, new concerns such as product risks or consumer rights have been accommodated in existing policies by adding to the list of providers who must make sure that their customers have certain information. We now face the possiblity that virtually all information could be made available over the electronic network, apparently at low cost. How can we select among the available information to determine which should be available to all and which should be available only for a fee? Will our new capability seduce us into trying to provide more information than people want or will use, wasting network capacity and public monies? Is there information that should be available whether or not the public uses it?

Toxic Release Inventory: Example of an Information Mandate

Some insights into these questions can be gained from our experience with the first statutorily mandated public access electronic database (Hadden, 1989). In 1986, Congress responded to growing public concern about hazardous chemicals in the environment by requiring manufacturing facilities to submit annual reports about their emissions of some 300 hazardous chemicals. Recognizing that the data would be most useful in aggregated form, Congress also required, for the first time, that the reports be made available to the public in the form of an electronic database. Implementing the database provision proved difficult precisely because the government had no experience in building an electronic database intended for widespread public use.

The very novelty of the exercise discouraged private information providers, who asked the government to guarantee minimum income or use to overcome the high degree of uncertainty about demand for a database whose information was primarily of benefit to the community rather than individuals. As a result, the database (called the Toxics Release Inventory or TRI) is operated by a public agency. The implementing agencies also had to consider the structure of the database and user interface. Representatives of public interest groups, reflecting their constituents' general lack of experience with computers and large databases, demanded very user-friendly interfaces. They also asked for alternative means for obtaining the data because of the difficulty they felt the public would have in working with an on-line database.

Although the chemical and other affected industries anticipated widespread public reaction to the release of the emissions data, relatively few members of the public have exercised their right to know by accessing the TRI. There are many possible explanations for the public's relative indifference to this potentially explosive data. First, despite the best efforts of the agencies, the data remain difficult for novices to acquire and use. Access to the electronic database is cheap but requires learning the procedure for obtaining an account, while a diskette version is expensive and available only from a relatively obscure federal agency. The database itself is far from user friendly, and even its menus are awkward and fail to anticipate many of the questions citizens are likely to ask. Equally important, the data available through the TRI are limited—they are truly data rather than ''information.'' In order to understand their significance, the data need to be placed in a larger context. Unfortunately, Congress did not require the implementing agencies to perform this service. Since placing data in context is likely to highlight its political implications, the agencies chose not to provide the contextual information that would make the data useful to the public.

The "Right to Content"

The experience with provision of toxic emissions data suggest additional criteria we may want to use in selecting a minimum level of public data access. Some information may have to be provided by government precisely because demand for it is so small or uncertain. That is, regardless of profitability, there may be some information that people simply have a right to know. Other information services might be cost-beneficial to provide on a societal basis; for example, in-home monitoring of the chronically ill could reduce the growing national burden of long-term health care. Some information may be so complex that it must be provided with backup or complementary information that allows the user to understand it. People's difficulties in using the TRI suggest that software interfaces will have to be very friendly indeed. Who should design the interfaces or whether there should be standards to ensure software compatibility are issues that will help determine the success of any universal electronic information system.

The almost unimaginable capacity for delivering new information services to homes or neighborhood information nodes challenges earlier policies that provided information to the public through libraries and product labels to achieve goals of citizenship education or market protection. Public provision of almost every information service could be justified by combined reference to income disparities and the growing importance of information to full participation in the economy. More discriminating and realistic criteria might limit universal information services to those of benefit to society as a whole, including health and nutrition information, basic education services, Yellow Page marketing services, and directories of other users. The important point here is not to develop specific criteria, however, but to suggest the need for a more careful consideration of the policy implications of an expanded universal service.

Regulating Information Services

Again, the expansive vision of the preceding sections is constrained by the present regulatory regime, especially the inability of the Bell operating companies to provide their own information services. Frustrated by the limits that this restriction places on their growth, the companies sought and gained permission from Judge Greene to experiment with "gateway" services in the information area. They could thus transmit services offered by other companies, provide the connection in the home, and carry out billing and collections. Despite their pleas, however, Judge Greene would not alow them to own the content of the information services provided. Other stakeholders, including publishers, broadcasters, cable-television operators, and AT&T, argue that allowig the Bells to own the content they provide would create a conflict of interest with their status as "common carriers" who must transmit the messages of all subscribers at reasonable fees and without regard to content.

In our interpretation, there are three major reasons that the Bells continue to seek ownership of content, despite this powerful opposition.

First, they believe that they are already involved with content. This involvement arises in two ways. As we have seen, operation of the intelligent network entails transmission of certain kinds of content, especially relating to billing and call origin. It is this capability that allows operation of the 911 services, in which the operator can identify the calling number and retrieve the address from a database without assistance from the caller. In addition, the telephone companies are being criticized for the content of certain calls, especially sex and pornography available through 976 toll calls. They believe that if the public expects them to control this kind of content, in violation of their common carrier status, in return they should also be allowed to provide more appropriate kinds of information.

The second reason that the Bell companies would like to control content is that many company executives feel that their profit margins would be better if they bought and resold services or orginated same, rather than collecting royalties from the content providers. There is more money in the payment for content than in collecting a fee for its transmission.

The third reason reflects the understanding that customers need some kind of lure ("trigger") before they will adopt on-line information services. French Minitel, for example, stopped printing telephone books, forcing customers to turn to their terminals for direcory assistance. Similarly in this country, on-line directory and Yellow Pages hold particular promise as "triggers" for a successful information service. The information services business seems a logical next step for companies already in the telecommunications business with a gigantic current customer base and with network and billing systems already in place. Since the Bell companies already own crucial individual and business directory information that could lure customers into the world of electronic services, they would have a natural advantage in the marketplace—it they were allowed into it (Williams, 1991b).

This discussion does not lead to a clearcut answer to whether the Bell companies should be permitted to deliver information content. It does show, however, that discussions about the expanded goal of universal service are difficult to separate from the present regulatory context. Again, we argue that the higher level debate about the content of universal service should precede and be separated from debates about particulars of regulation. For example, it seems entirely possible, if present regulatory incentives concerning enhanced services remain in place, that voice will continue to constitute the basic inexpensive and universally available service, while all supplementary services will fall into the expensive, unregulated, enhanced category. This could lead to a two-tiered network, in which that part of the population most in need of the new services, especially education, emergency, and information, will be the least able to afford them. If, however, we first determine which services will be socially beneficial when provided to all citizens, we can then decide whether the constraints on telco information provision help or hurt our chances of achieving that goal.

The View Ahead: From Connectivity to Content

We have suggested that the technological advances associated with the intelligent network have created both the ability to expand universal service beyond the mere voice dial tone and the pressure to do so. Until now, universal service has entailed access to interactive speech capability, with the information content of the transmission left entirely to the senders. However, the new technologies make it likely and possible that people will expect access to certain kinds of content along with the simple ability to communicate over long distances. The issues and problems created by the convergence of connectivity and content—of transmission and the content transmitted—become particularly clear when we are considering universal service.

As we indicated above, one area strongly affected by the blurring distinction between communication and information is the regulatory area. Historically, telephone regulation focused on communication; in the case of universal service, it focused on ways of keeping rates reasonable enough to maximize public access to telephone lines. However, perhaps without intending to, telephone companies have already gone beyond transmission because the basic operation of the network entails transmitting certain kinds of information, such as routing, billing, and originating telephone number. Expansion of 800 and 900 services has further enhanced the importance of content to telephone users and providers. New services, especially caller ID and call forwarding, entail information transmission. As presently constituted, the regulatory system has difficulty taking these developments into account, even though divestiture and deregulation have clearly hastened their arrival.

In contrast to telephone regulation, and despite the strictures of the First Amendment, content regulation has been part and parcel of broadcast regulation from the outset. The trend toward deregulation has brought about reduced requirements for "equal access" by competing political viewpoints, but content for vulnerable groups, especially children, continues to be regulated.[5] At the same time, the distinctive characteristics of broadcasting, particularly spectrum scarcity, are disappearing, especially in the area of cable distribution. The resulting merger of concerns in the regulatory arena is clearly shown by Congress's nearly successful attempt to limit costs of cable in order to ensure universal accessibility of a certain basic level of channels, including public access channels and weather as well as the major networks (Andrews, 1990).

Nevertheless, it is clear that the present regulatory system is unprepared to consider deep issues relating to the kinds of information that should be widely available. If we do expand universal service to include provision of information on-line, moreover, we must consider carefully not only the specific types of information to which everyone should have ready access, but also the format and ownership of such information. The Bell companies' interest in providing information rather than merely transmitting it takes on additional importance in this context, since they could create a user interface to which other providers would have to conform, even to be able to use the telephone network. If this interface is proprietary so that users must pay royalties to the Bell companies, the potential for complete control of the information system is high.

A related issue, nowhere addressed in the regulatory system, is quality of information. For example, many companies searched their own data submission on-line in the TRI, only to find serious transcription errors. With interactive on-line data services, they might have been able to correct these errors on the spot, but this might create opportunities for competitors or ill-wishers to alter the data as well. At the same time, there was no way for citizen users to know that the data were of uncertain quality. If information access is truly universal, clever providers could mislead users with data of questionable quality.

Similarly, recent experiences in communicating about chemical and other environmental risks have revealed that citizens place high value on the perceived trustworthiness of an information source and on the willingness of experts to listen to their side of an issue. These lessons cannot be ignored simply because an electronic service is likely to become the primary information source. Trustworthiness may have to be established by careful documentation of sources of on-line information along with information about those sources. Alternatively, certain information companies may come to be regarded as especially trustworthy—a sort of information age brand of loyalty. Desire for the information purveyor to be a "good listener" is a little harder to operationalize for electronic information; interactivity and consumer control over the rate, form, and nature of information received may go a long way toward meeting this requirement.

With a discussion of the quality and format of information, we have moved away from traditional regulatory concerns towards issues that clearly illustrate how the intelligent network and information products mark a qualitative as well as a quantitative transformation in information access. The electronic context for information provision has yet another important consequence: it transfers at least some of the burden for "communicating" from the source to the receiver. Imagine a public meeting in which chemical company representatives are describing the possible health effects of exposure to their pollutants. Anyone attending will be provided with all the information the public relations and technical staff feel is relevant; in addition, by asking questions attendees can acquire still other information. An electronic source, however, requires much more active participation by the user. To help ensure that people use the available capacity of the system to the fullest, we will have to provide appropriate education, including practical use of telecommunications information systems in the schools. The additional burdens that will fall on the educational system include teaching students to formulate problems, identify the kinds of information appropriate to resolving the problem, locate that information, and bring it to bear. Designers of software or telecommunications interfaces who can help make one or more of these tasks easier will be very powerful; indeed, they will be in a position to control at least some of the information that users acquire. Only adequate education can counteract this power, perhaps assisted by governmental regulation.

The primary importance of the blurring of the distinction between communication and information, therefore, is that it seems to presage a shift in power within society. Providing communications access through universal telephone service links people to the wider society and gives them a safety net for emergencies. Providing information itself can affect people's most basic ideas about society and determine the ways in which they participate. Yet the very essentiality of information provision also suggests the need for it to be a universal service. Thus, from a policy standpoint, the blurring of the distinction between connectivity and information forces us to reexamine many of our institutions, from telecommunications regulation to education and beyond.

Notes

1. Minor exceptions to this would be their obligation to provide operator assistance, including telephone numbers (remember people referring to this service as "calling information?"). Also, crank or obscene calls, a type of content or information, was occasionally a matter for company intervention.
2. As cited in U.S. Congress, Office of Technology Assessment, *Critical Connections: Communication for the Future*, OTA-CIT-407 (Washington, D.C.: U.S. Government Printing Office, January, 1990.)
3. The language of Title 1 is dissected phrase by phrase in Pressler and Schieffer, 1988.
4. This was after pressure from the American Newspaper Publishers Association,

which feared that AT&T's entry into the electronic publishing business would threaten their own forays into it, and might also draw away advertisers. Shortly before the end of the seven year prohibition, at AT&T's request, Judge Green indicated that he would not further bar the company from entry into electronic test services (National Commission on Libraries and Information Science, 1988).
5. A new law reducing the amount of commercials on children's television programs was approved by Congress in September, 1990 and signed by the president. The law requires broadcasters to offer more educational programming for children (Nash, 1990).

References

Andrews, E. (1990). Senators block bill to regulate cable tv prices. *New York Times* (National Edition). September 29, A1.

Brunner, M. E. (1986). Regulation and rural telephony. *Telephony*. September 8.

Flaherty, D. H. (1989). *Protecting privacy in surveillance societies*. Chapel Hill: The University of North Carolina Press.

Hadden, S. G. (1989). *A citizen's rights to know: Risk communication and public policy*. Boulder, CO: Westview Press.

Nash, N. (1990). White house gets bill to cut ads on children's tv shows. *New York Times* (National Edition). October 2, A1.

National Commission on Libraries and Information Science (NCLIS). (1988). *The role of fees in supporting library and information services in public and academic libraries*. Collection Building 8:1, 3–16.

Noll, R. (1988). *Telecommunications regulation in the 1990s*. Publication No. 140, Stanford, CA: Center for Economic Policy Research, August.

NTIA. (1988). *Telecom 2000*. NTIA Special Publication 88-21, Washington, DC.

Office of Technology Assessment. (1990). *Critical connections: Communication for the future*. Washington DC: Congress of the United States, Office of Technology Assessment (Publication OTA-CIT-407).

Pacific Bell. (1988). *Pacific Bell's response to the intelligent network task force*. Sacramento, CA: Pacific Bell.

Pressler, L., & Schieffer, K. V. (1988). A proposal for universal telecommunications service. *Federal Communications Law Journal*, 40, 3 (May).

Smith v. Illinois Bell Telephone Company. (1930). 282 U.S. 133.

Williams, F. (1990). The coming intelligent network: New options for the individual and community. In *The annual review of communications and society*, vol. 2, Washington, DC: Institute for Information Studies, The Aspen Institute.

Williams, F. (1991a). *The New Telecommunications: Infrastructure for the Information Age*. New York: The Free Press.

Williams, F. (1991b). The intelligent network: A new beginning for information services on the public network? In F. Phillips (Ed.), *Thinkwork: Working, Learning and Managing in a Computer-Interactive Society*. New York: Praeger.

20

Transaction-Generated Information (TGI): Signaling, Sorting, and the Communication of Self

Oscar H. Gandy, Jr.

Gidden's emphasis on the importance of routines, roles and re-
sources in the reproduction, or structuration of social systems is the
perspective reflected in this essay. This essay suggests that the battle
to control personal information is just beginning. The author believes
that we are likely to see a massive "educational" effort, coordinated
by leaders of the direct marketing industry, which will attempt to
overcome the influence of direct experience, media distributed re-
ports of individual cases and the occasional campaigns by privacy
activist such as that which brought about the defeat of Lotus
Marketplace, and slowed the growth of "Caller-ID."

In his recent book, Christopher Dandeker (1990) explores the theoretical space between the major contending perspectives on the nature of power in modern capitalist societies. In his effort to forge a middle ground between Marxist critiques of capitalism, neo-Weberian critiques of indus-trial society, and the totalizing systems of power described by Michel Foucault (1979), Dandeker draws heavily upon the insights of Anthony Giddens (1984, 1985). It is Giddens' emphasis on the importance of routines, roles, and resources in the reproduction, or structuration of social systems that carries the most analytical weight in this task, and that perspective will be reflected in this essay as well.

Dandeker identifies surveillance as a means of administrative power that is linked intimately with the bureaucratic form of social organization that characterizes the modern industrial, and postindustrial economies. For Dandeker, the growth and spread of surveillance that increases the relative power of bureaucratic organizations, is paradoxically a response to a growing demand for equality between citizens within modern democracies (1990, p. 17). The demand for social services, including planning and coordination by the state, increases the importance of information for the rationalization of a large-scale government bureaucracy. David Flaherty (1989) offers a similar analysis that finds that the ultimate welfare state, that which has developed in Sweden, has also resulted in that nation's dubious distinction as the most complete of surveillance societies (pp. 93–103). Indeed it is argued that in Sweden, "there is virtually no information irrelevant to the evaluation of tax duty" (Simitis, 1987, p. 717). Dandeker (1900) asks a critical question however, about the relationship between the power associated with this surveillance, and the systems of accountability that may or may not be in place to insure that these bureaucracies operate in the long-term interests of the citizenry. Systems of accountability appropriate to government actions rarely have been developed for the private, corporate sector, even though in an era of privitization and deregulation, the influence of corporate policy and practice is at least as important as that of the state.

Thus, contemporary studies of surveillance seek to include the modern corporation alongside the state bureaucracy (Gandy, 1989). The managerial surveillance of labor is seen to be linked to the disciplinary surveillance of the consumer, where production and consumption activities are coordinated through marketing. James Beniger's (1986) study of the emergence of an information society in the West identifies the "revolution in control of mass consumption" (pp. 344–89) as the bureaucratic control of demand through advertising enhanced by the development of "market feedback technology." The return of sales information to the production system helps to complete the loop of bureaucratic rationalization and control made possible by modern surveillance.

An expansion of the surveillance described by Dandeker would conceivably result in a catastrophic information bottleneck if it were not for the development of an associated technology of rationalization that Beniger describes as preprocessing. This preprocessing involves the "destruction or ignoring of information in order to facilitate its processing" (1986, p. 15). Preprocessing is commonly recognized as an enhanced form of classification, and the representation of groups or classes by categories on standard forms moves the technology toward automation.

Imagine how much more processing would be required . . . if each new case were recorded in an unstructured way, including every nuance and in full detail, rather than by checking boxes, filling blanks, or in some other way reducing the burdens of the bureaucratic system to only the limited range of formal, objective, and impersonal information required by standard forms. (Beniger, 1986, p. 16)

Spiros Simitis (1987), then serving as the data protection commissioner in the German state of Hesse, suggested that this management of options, including those faced by consumers, is implicated in the creation of an illusion of enhanced individuality and freedom of choice, when in fact, individuals are being guided more efficiently into predetermined, prese-lected, standardized responses. Surveillance helps bureaucratic organiza-tions to assign individuals to groups whose members' past responses to structured options suggest that they share more interests, resources, and orientations among themselves than they do with members of other analyt-ical (as opposed to naturally occurring) groups. The resultant assignment of individuals to groups on the basis of the personal information derived from the record of choices made is at the heart of the emergent "micro-physics of power" (Foucault, 1979) we refer to as the "panoptic sort."

Triage: The Panoptic Sort

Webster's *New Collegiate Dictionary* (1984) offers only a single defini-tion of triage: "The sorting and allocation of treatment to patients and especially battle and disaster victims according to a system of priorities designed to maximize the number of survivors." However, while the instrumental, rationalist function of the process is clear in this definition, Webster's *Third New International Dictionary* (1976) adds a bit more to our understanding by extending the definition to inlcude "the grading of marketable produce," and more pointedly still, a reference to "the lowest grade of coffee berries, consisting of broken material." In the familiar medical sense, the wounded were sorted into three groups: (1) those who would survive without any further assistance; (2) those whose lives might be saved through prompt intervention; and (3) those who are beyond hope, and where any further intervention, perhaps beyond some humanitarian effort to reduce the experience of pain, was unjustified as wasteful. A similar efficiency rationale can be seen to apply to the marketing triage. People are sorted on the basis of estimates of their expected value as consumers.

Expected value estimates include the costs of realizing each sale, including the cost of advertising and promotional discounts. In some businesses, the top 20 percent of a firm's customers will account for 52 percent of sales, and as much as 77 percent of the profits (Kestnbaum, 1989). Some customers represent an actual, or potential net loss in terms of what they might actually cost before they are transformed into a sale. This triage, or sorting of consumers is described as panoptic because as the costs of gathering, storing, and processing of information declines, more and more information comes to be treated as being potentially relevant to the sort.

While the response of privacy advocates forestalled the introduction of a CD-ROM database of some 80 million U.S. households by Lotus/Equifax (Lewis, 1991), an ever-increasing number of commercial firms are finding new ways of combining disparate bits of personal information to facilitate the classification of consumers for targeted marketing appeals (Novek, Sinha, & Gandy, 1990). List vendors serving the direct marketing industry provide a host of services related to the identification of individuals on the basis of some characteristic indicative of their potential market value. Data flows into these organizations' databases through a variety of means, some straightforward, some increasingly sophisticated and devious.

One firm recently introduced a new data coding system that would imprint coupons that could then be mailed to individuals. The "softstrip" barcoding, visible, or hidden by a color overlay, might identify the consumer by name, occupation, household income, number of children under eighteen, and other information about past market behavior. When the consumer submitted the coupon to their local store, perhaps in response to a special offer or contest, the encoded data could then be immediately enhanced with information about the date, place and associated purchases made at that time (Paulin, 1989).

The computer-based consumer videotex service offered by Sears and IBM (Prodigy) takes information gathering to an entirely new level. The service provides information about a dizzying variety of consumer goods and services in addition to general information about movies, access to an electronic encyclopedia, and generous use of bulletin board and messaging services. Each use of these services generates information of potential value to Sears, IBM, and other service providers. Recently, a new wrinkle emerged. The software necessary to interconnect with the Prodigy system is stored in the user's computer, but it can be modified remotely by Prodigy each time the service is used. One such use is the generation of "paths" and "pathlists" that describe the usual services and offerings the identified individual scans each time they log into the service. This information increases the efficiency of the telecommunications link but also generates potentially sensitive information about each user. A recent story (Miller, 1991) warned of problems in the software that caused some confidential material from other files within users' hard disks to "migrate" into the Prodigy files.

A review of the kinds of databases that are offered each week to the direct marketing industry (Novek, Sinha, & Gandy, 1990) suggests that no information is without potential value as a component of a consumer profile. Purchases, inquiries, responses, and even failures to respond to uninvited communications, especially when accomplished through the telecommunications network, generate data that can be stored, shared, and combined with other data to facilitate identification, and then classification of a consumer (McManus, 1990). This telephone transaction generated information (TTGI) includes the highly personal and potentially sensitive information that is generated through calls to premium services ("900") of the sort which deal in sexual content (Gumpert, 1987, pp. 128–131), or a community service such as an "AIDS Information Hotline." Telecommunications devices that will forward an identification of the calling party may be linked to a variety of ancillary services that will add information to the simple numeric identifier forwarded by the telephone company (Gandy, 1990; Shultz, 1990). On the basis of such identifiers (e.g., Caller-ID), callers may be classified and then sorted into queues reflecting their presumed value in addition to generating information about calls they have initiated.

Individuals may soon discover that the level of service they receive may vary as a function of the neighborhood or telephone exchange from which they place their calls. This "electronic redlining" suggests that not only individuals, but entire neighborhoods are subject to being classified and then sorted into market-relevant categories. Michael Weiss's (1988) recent book describes the elaboration of forty different neighborhood or community types. These classifications have been applied to each of the nation's 36,000 ZIP code areas by a commercial vendor, Claritas Corporation. While the social and economic data might have been used to create any number of different clusters, with the clusters ordered along any number of underlying dimensions, the dominant marketing triage reflects a particular economic rationalism. The first cluster (ZQ1), labelled "Blue Blood Estates," describes the neighborhoods of America's elite upper crust. These neighborhoods are described as the "super-rich" suburbs, where 72 percent voted for Reagan and were more likely than most to read the *New York Times,* the *Wall Street Journal,* and *Gourmet* magazine, and most unlikely to read *Ebony.* In sharp contrast, at the bottom of the list (ZQ40), we find the "Public Assistance" neighborhoods. The median household income was pegged at $11,000, in communities where "predominantly black singles and one-parent families" lived in multi-unit housing, and voted overwhelmingly for Mondale in 1984 (Weiss, 1988, pp. 269–392).

While some metaphors speak for themselves, we should be clear that for this chapter, the privileged reading of *triage* is one that emphasizes the means through which surveillance is used to facilitate the sorting of individuals and groups into graded categories reflecting their presumed market value or trustworthiness. Such a reading does not shrink from the implication that those at the bottom of the sort are people who are subject to being treated as damaged goods, discarded, or sold at bargain basement prices.

This use of the metaphor reflects a perspective on power that resists the mainstream notion of consumer sovereignty. Choices are constrained by a variety of social, economic, and structural factors, including the influence of differential social learning that structures the development of tastes and preferences. For example, while television viewers may be said to choose television programs in accordance with their preferences, it should also be clear that they are choosing only from among the programs that the advertiser-supported industry is willing to present. The alternative is exit from the audience pool (Bowles and Gintis, 1987, pp. 127–30). Similar constraints face individuals in every encounter with a market-based sorting mechanism. The dominance of exit over voice provides an illusory sovereignty at best.

This sovereignty is weakened still further by the recognition that consumers are dependent upon advertising and promotion for information about the costs and consequences of particular choices in the marketplace. A kind of a deviation amplifying loop, or a self-fulfilling prophesy may come to operate where the surveillance and sorting system determines that some individual or group is unlikely to be interested in some class of information product, thereby reproducing their ignorance of its qualities. This is increasingly likely in the context of a segmented and isolated marketplace where individuals no longer engage in an active search of the array of available goods, but each responds to the limited range of options that have been presented to them following some remote determination of their likely responsiveness.

This restriction on choice is almost inevitable because the predictive models which guide the panoptic sort are necessarily conservative, based, as they are on information about past choices, many of which are based on circumstance, rather than informed selection. To use another television example to illustrate this point, we note along with Barwise and Ehrenberg (1988) that our apparent "revealed preference" for television programs is largely accidental consequence of our being available to view a program at one time rather than another. Program preference models have such limited predictive utility because they are unable to include those exogenous forces which influence a person's availability to view. Yet, the tendency toward the preprocessing of consumers into narrow interest segments forecloses the possibility of a serendipitous discovery of a "taste" for some previously unknown genre. This tendency toward "trait-taking" rather than "trait-making" serves to reify whatever content preferences the influence of caste, class, and circumstance might have generated in the past.

Structuration and Transformation

If we are not to join Weber, and take this increasingly restrictive process of bureaucratic rationalization and depersonalization as inevitable (Brubaker, 1984, pp. 40–42), we have to look toward Giddens' "stratification model of the agent" (1984, pp. 5–16) for the suggestion that the unintended consequences of actions (pp. 293–97) by goal-directed agents, both individuals and "corporate persons," may introduce contradictory forces, perhaps even generating active resistance to the panoptic sort. Individuals, driven by their complex, and often contradictory motivations, guided by their rational understanding of the circumstances and consequences of their actions (which they monitor as best they can), act in ways that produce intended and unintended consequences for those individuals, and those with whom they are most closely connected through interaction. Structuration, that is, reproduction as well as change in social systems takes place as a function of the routine, day-to-day complex of interactions between individuals. The fact that computers and telecommunications systems increase the surveillance or monitoring capacity of the bureaucratic entities with which individuals must interact will come to play a more significant role in the rationalization of individual action as those individuals learn more about the consequences that flow from this surveillance. If individuals come to believe that purchases, responses to surveys, even inquiries generate information that may be used to restrict their attainment of what they perceive as legitimate goals, their interaction with those systems is bound to be changed (Simitis, 1987). Of course, it is also possible that individuals will become desensitized, will come to accept the loss of autonomy as inevitable, or at least they may perceive that because they are "contract takers", the alternatives (such as giving up their credit cards) are too costly (Jussawalla & Cheah, 1987).

Our best estimates about how individuals will respond to a changed awareness about the consequences of bureaucratic use of transaction generated information (TGI) are derived from surveys of the population. We recognize, of course, that the attempt to generalize to the day-to-day experiences of specific individuals on the basis of aggregations of a sample's responses to fixed interview questions, leaves us a long way from the ideal circumstances that would allow us to assess the nature of structuration in this area. We note Giddens' own identification of the differences between practical and discursive consciousness, and the difficulties such a distinction implies for the pursuit of social science knowledge (1984, p. 7). People may be competent, goal-directed actors, but, likely as not, they will not be able to articulate the reasons or the logic behind their actions.

While much has been written about privacy, relatively little has been published about public opinion regarding perceived threats to privacy, and even less has focused on questions of individual control over TGI (Equifax, 1990; Harris & Westin, 1979; Katz & Tassone, 1990). Very little of the work on attitudes toward privacy has been sufficiently analytical to contribute to our understanding of the social origins of the similarities and differences in perspective (Burgoon, 1982). One important exception is the report of a field experiment by Stone, Gueutal, Gardner, & McClure (1983). Structured interviews gathered data that could be combined into an index of "information-privacy values" reflecting respondent's desire to retain control over personal information. This index value could be estimated as an organization-specific measure reflecting differential concern about the uses to which particular organizations would put personal information, and the potentially harmful consequences which might flow from that use. Individual responses were seen to vary with their past experience with the aversive consequences of organizational use of personal information. Although the authors did not include Giddens' perspective on structuration in their theoretical discussion, the experiential basis for privacy orientations is a common assumption of their research design.

Several results are worth mentioning: the more respondents valued information privacy, the less control they actually believed they had. However, the information experience index measure, composed of eight items reflecting experience or awareness of negative consequences was the least reliable index in the analysis. Perhaps this unreliability explains the fact that this measure was less strongly correlated with the other measures of values, beliefs, attitudes, or policy orientations.

The difficulty of associating particular experiences with sets of attitudes, values, and policy preferences is not easily overcome. In an attempt to explore the influence of surveillance in the workplace, an analysis of data gathered through a telephone survey of adults in 1989 (Kristel & Gandy, 1990) utilized a hierarchical ranking of occupational titles in the 1977 issue of the *Dictionary of Occupational Titles* (DOT). Jobs of respondents were rated according to the likelihood of surveillance pressure that workers would experience in nine categories of work. A five-point surveillance pressure scale was constructed, and housewives, not included in the DOT, were assumed to experience a "low-medium" level of surveillance pressure. When compared with the influence of gender, education, and measures of political ideology, workplace experience was a relatively insignificant factor in explaining perspectives on privacy.

Schooling is commonly conceived as a site for social learning, a key mechanism for the production and reproduction of social capital (Bourdieu & Passeron, 1990). Thus, the correlations of attitudes toward the control of personal information and measures of educational attainment may be argued to be reflections of a process of structuration. Of course, such a conclusion requires the rather untenable assumption that all schooling is equivalent in terms of the social learning that it produces in most of those who experience it.

When education is measured in terms of levels of training accomplished, including particular markers such as high school and college graduation, education is a powerful explanatory factor. An examination of data generated by a national telephone sample[1] suggests that educational attainment leads people to have more confidence in their ability to exercise control over their personal information, although the more highly educated are still more likely to agree that concern about privacy is legitimate. At the same time, we find that education is associated with a stronger belief in the validity of predictions based on past behavior. That is, those with more education are more likely to agree with the statement that "how a person behaved in the past is a good indicator of how they'll act in the future." Yet, the more highly educated seem less willing to allow businesses unlimited freedom to gather personal information to use in their decisions about potential clients or employees. Of course, we have less reason to believe that this mistrust of business is derived from experiences in school than from the later experiences as consumers that might be correlated with levels of educational attainment. Unfortunately, those experiences have not been captured very well by any of the survey questions in this, or in other published studies.

Political activism emerges as a factor with as much or more explanatory power than educational attainment, although it is easier to conceive of such activism as a consequence, rather than a source of structuration. Activism was measured as an additive index based on participation in recent political activities that included marches and demonstrations, signing petitions, letter writing, making financial contributions, and seeking information about particular issues or candidates. The greater one's level of activism, the more likely one was to see concern about privacy as legitimate, and the more likely one is to want to restrict corporate information gathering. In a multivariate regression equation exploring factors that might explain differences in estimates of the legitimacy of concerns about privacy,[2] political involvement was the most important predictor.

In bivariate analyses, age was also a consistent correlate of particular privacy orientations. We noted an important change in the relationship between age and privacy orientation over time. In the 1979 Harris study, older respondents were relatively less concerned about privacy invasions than they appeared to be when surveyed in 1989. Although we have no direct evidence of common aversive experience upon which to base our interpretation, it seems likely that between 1979 and 1989, older Americans have been targeted most heavily by the direct marketing industry, and as a result, they have become more angry and resentful about such invasions of their privacy. In a multivariate regression assessing the predictors of respondent orientation toward more restrictive legislation controlling the collection and use of information by organizations, age was an important factor, second only to a measure of attention paid to politics and public affairs in the newspapers. Some support for this interpretation is found in an analysis of the relationship between age and direct marketing. The older the cohort, the greater the proportion of that cohort that agrees strongly that "there should be a way to keep your name off a mailing list." Although the relationship is not linear throughout the range, as the ages of cohorts increases beyond fifty years, greater proportions of those cohorts agree strongly that they would like to have a device "which would let them know who is calling before they answered the phone." The same pattern of increase, but with a higher proportion agreeing overall, these older cohorts also agreed that there should be a device "which would automatically screen out calls from people trying to sell you things."

Stalling the Panoptic Sort

These data are highly suggestive that resentment and resistance are emerging out of our daily experience as targets of segmented marketing campaigns. It is not at all clear however, that the public is making a connection between the information they provide about themselves as they go about their lives as employee, citizen, and consumer, and the telephone calls that disturb their privacy, or the direct mail solicitations that crowd their mailbox each day. There is some evidence that the public is increasingly unwilling to participate in public opinion surveys, in part because they believe such surveys to serve marketing rather than political ends (Schleifer, 1986). Thus, while it is likely that the growing willingness to restrict direct marketing is a reflection of its status as an annoyance, and the willingness to limit data gathering by insurers, employers, and other service providers may be based on the desire to avoid denial of service, we have not yet arrived at the point of crisis suggested by Simitis (1987) that will occur when people come to recognize that virtually *all* of their activities generate data that can be used by organizations to influence the quality of their lives.

We are likely to see a massive "educational" effort coordinated by leaders of the direct marketing industry and other businesses dependent upon unhindered access to personal information. This public relations campaign will attempt to overcome the influence of direct experience, media distributed reports of individual cases, and the occasional campaigns by privacy activists such as that which brought about the defeat of Lotus Marketplace, and slowed the growth of "Caller-ID." The battle to control personal information is just beginning to take shape. It will provide scholars of communication a unique opportunity to examine the relationships between concrete daily experience, mediated interaction across time and space and between individuals and relatively abstract entities and devices, and the resultant variations in social consciousness and public policy.

Notes

1. A random sample of telephone households served as the basis for a study of 1,250 adults between January and February 1989. Structured interviews averaging 15.7 minutes gathered data about respondents knowledge, attitudes, behavior, and policy preferences regarding information privacy. The study was funded by a grant from AT&T through the Center for Communication and Information Science and Policy at the University of Pennsylvania.
2. The criterion measure was a five-point Likert-type item which asked respondents to agree or disagree with the statement that "The only people concerned about their privacy are those with something to hide."

References

Barwise, P., & Ehrenberg, A. (1988). *Television and its audience*. London: Sage.

Beniger, R. (1986). *The control revolution: Technological and economic origins of the information society*. Cambridge, MA: Harvard University Press.

Bowles, S. Gintis, H. (1987). *Democracy and capitalism*. New York: Basic Books.

Bourdieu, P., & Passeron, J. (1990). *Reproduction in education, society and culture*, 2nd Edition. London: Sage.

Brubaker, R. (1984). *The limits of rationality: An essay on the social and moral thought of Max Weber*. London: George Allen & Unwin.

Burgoon, K. (1982). *Privacy and communication. In M. Burgoon (Ed.). Communication yearbook* (pp. 206–49). Beverly Hills, CA: Sage.

Dandeker, (1990). *Surveillance, power and modernity, bureaucracy and discipline from 1700 to the present day*. New York: St. Martin's Press.

Equifax, Inc. (1990). *The Equifax report on consumers in the information age.* Atlanta: Equifax, Inc.

Flaherty, D. H. (1989). *Protecting privacy in surveillance societies.* Chapel Hill: University of North Carolina Press.

Foucault, M. (1979). *Discipline and punishment.* New York: Vintage Books.

Gandy, O. H. (1989). The surveillance society: Information technology and bureaucratic social control. *Journal of Communication, 39* (Summer), 61–76.

Gandy, O. H. (1990). Caller identification: The two-edged sword. In D. Wesemeyer & M. Lofstrom (Eds.) *Pacific telecommunications: Weaving the technological and social fabric* (pp. 207–14). Honolulu: Pacific Telecommunications Council.

Giddens, A. (1984). *The constitution of society: Outline of a theory of structuration.* Cambridge: Polity Press.

Giddens, A. (1985). *The nation state and violence.* Berkeley: University of California Press.

Gumpert, G. (1987). *Talking tombstones & other tales of the media age.* New York: Oxford University Press.

Harris and Associates, L. (1979). *The Dimensions of the Privacy. Stevens Point WI: Sentry Insurance.*

Jussawalla, M., & Cheah, C. W. (1987). Economic analysis of the legal and policy aspects of information privacy. In M. Jussawalla & C. W. Cheah. *The calculus of international communications.* (pp. 75–102). Littleton, CO: Libraries Unlimited.

Katz, J. & Tassone, A. (1990). Public opinion trends: Privacy and information technology. *Public Opinion Quarterly, 54,* 125–43.

Kestnbaum, R. D. (1989). Database Marketing: Friend or Foe. Conference paper, International Newspaper Marketing Association, June.

Kristel, T. & Gandy, O. H. (1990). Conditioning consent: In search of the social locations of all privacy orientations. Conference paper. International Association for Mass Communication Research, Bled, Yugoslavia, August.

Lewis, H. (1991). Why the privacy issue will never go away. *New York Times,* April 7, p. 4.

McManus, T. E. (1990). *Telephone transaction-generated information: Rights and restrictions.* Report P-90-5, Center for Information Policy Research. Cambridge, MA: Harvard University.

Miller, M. W. (1991). Prodigy headquarters offered peeks into users' private files. *Wall Street Journal.* May 1, p. B1.

Novek, E., Sinha, N. & Gandy, O. H. (1990). The value of your name. *Media, Culture and Society, 12,* 525–43.

Pualin, David. (1989). Supermarket uses data strip to build customer profile. *Direct,* February 20, p. 1.

Schleifer, S. (1986). Trends in attitudes toward and participation in survey research. *Public Opinion Quarterly, 50,* 17–26.

Schultz, P. (1990). *Caller ID, ANI & privacy: A review of the major issues affecting automatic number identification.* Report Series no. 4 Washington, DC: Telecommunications Reports, Inc.

Simitis, S. (1987). Reviewing privacy in an information society. *The University of Pennsylvania Law Review, 135,* 707–920.

Stone, F., Guetal, H., Gardner, D., & McClure, S. (1983). A field experiment comparing information-privacy values, beliefs, and attitudes across several types of organizations. *Journal of Applied Psychology, 68,* 459–68.

Weiss, J. (1988). *The clustering of America.* New York: Harper and Row.

21

Media Development and Public Space: The Legislating of Social Interaction

Gary Gumpert and Susan J. Drucker

Interaction in a public place and the need and form of the most basic type of communication—face to face interpersonal communication—has been altered by innovations of media technology. Public places remain media of communication coexisting and interacting with other media and social functions. Land-use laws, zoning chief among them, both directly and indirectly regulate communication and interaction in public places. This essay examines the nexus of urbanization, zoning laws, and the development of media technology. It discusses whether the effect of zoning is to promote, hinder, or redirect interaction in public places.

All interaction requires context and circumstance. Information and emotion is conveyed (1) in the interaction between two or more human beings located in the same time and place; or (2) in the interaction between two or more persons located in a different time and/or space in which case such communication is mediated. Both always include the interaction between objects in the environment and the individual. In all cases individual and venue link and the reverberating ambience alters and shapes the nature of the communicative experience. It is the extraordinary impact of media technology upon face-to-face social interaction and venue that has altered and influenced each person to such an extent, that the very essence of social interaction has traumatically transformed both interpersonal communication and the environment in which such communication takes place.

In the case of interpersonal communication, the omnipresence of communciation technology has transmitted the functions of the communicative act. The telephone is, in that sense, not simply an alternative to face-to-face communication, but is, for some, a preferable mode of communication. Whereas, at some point in the past, social interaction occurred in the face-to-face realm, today, an increasing proportion of each person's work and play is mediated. The amount of time allocated to electronic communication will reciprocally decrease the finite time available for face-to-face social interaction. While in many cases electronic communication may be more efficient and convenient than face-to-face communication, mediated communication is qualitatively different than face-to-face interaction. Any mediated communication alternative engages fewer senses than face-to-face interaction and occurs inside controlled private space. Thus the mediated relationship is always a surrogate experience and the inherent danger is that its proxy nature is not recognized.

As mediated communication accelerates the significance of privacy, as that value increasingly permeates American life, that aspect of living that has been public, that has been there to be shared with others, is deemphasized and discouraged. A complex consequence of the assent of mediated communication is the ascension of privacy. The link between privacy and access to information has been articulated by Graham Murdock and Peter Golding when they point out in their essay "Information Poverty and Political Inequality: Citizenship in the Age of Privatized Communications:"

> First, people must have access to the information, advice, and analysis that will enable them to know what their rights are in other spheres and allow them to pursue these rights effectively. Second, they must have access to the broadest possible range of information, interpretation, and debate on areas that involve political choices, and they must be able to use communications facilities in order to register criticism, mobilize opposition, and propose alternative courses of action. And third, they must be able to recognize themselves and their aspirations in the range of representations offered within the central communications sectors and be able to contribute to developing those representations.

Interaction occurs in those places that are perceived to be safe, controllable, and private. The dominance of mediated communication has produced an aspatial communication environment. Conversation, sociability, and information are maintained and facilitated through the media of communication.

It is particularly in the public venue that social interaction has undergone startling transformation. The public venue or public place refers to those public and private places in which individuals come to meet and watch others. It includes streets, plazas, promenades, malls, cafés, pubs, taverns, and so on—any place open to all with few restrictions. This chapter is concerned with *public space as a social environment which facilitates the transfer of information.*

Generally we think of communication as occurring between two or more individuals. Some communication scholars have examined the use that individuals make of objects to communicate about themselves (Burgoon, Buller, & Woodall, 1989; Cathcart & Gumpert, 1983; Goffman, 1961). But few communication scholars have examined the environment and its artifacts in terms of either setting the ambience of communication or setting the communication agenda. Environmental Psychologist Albert Mehrabian has said,

> Put bluntly, it is assumed that people's feelings or emotions are what ultimately determine what they do and how they do it. It is also assumed that environments can cause in us feelings of anger, fear, boredom, pleasure, or whatever, and do so regardless of how we think we should feel in such environments; and furthermore, that these feelings will cause us to behave in certain ways, regardless of how we should behave. This is not to say that we cannot exercise fairly substantial control over our public behavior. (Mehrabian, 1976, p. 8)

But while individuals may control their public behavior, such control however does not rest solely in their own hands since those regulatory policies and laws that govern urban and surburban land use and planning influence public social interaction. This chapter examines the nexus of urbanization, zoning laws, and the development of media technology. It discusses whether the effect of zoning is to promote, hinder or redirect interaction in public places.[1]

Public and Electronic Space

For a number of complex reasons, the *good street* evolved from a place of *interaction* to a locale of *safety*. Although interaction has been emancipated from place, public places still function as sites of face-to-face interaction. While the form and function of interaction has been altered, public places remain a medium of communication necessary for the public welfare of a society.[2] At one time community was a geographic concept in which the major functions of social activities took place. Major social activities involved commerce, production, and residence. These three activities resulted in two primary affects: (1) the creation of a sphere of privacy; and (2) the creation of a sphere of interaction. With urbanization, automobiles, and advances in electronic media came changes in social activity and communication patterns. Workers and employers who had lived and worked in close physical proximity to where goods were manufactured or services supplied were freed from the need for such physical presence. Each activity elevated the importance of either privacy *or* interaction. Interaction became paramount in commerce while privacy became all important in residential areas. Spheres of privacy and interaction were in turn altered by media.

Communication while influenced and shaped by the context of where it occurs is no longer restricted by the limitations of place. The electronics of telegraphy, telephony, radio, television, facsimile, computers, and satellites transcend the walls of home and work. We have shifted from an industrial society to one in which value is produced by information processing activities.

Paradoxically, while the innovations of media technology facilitate communication, they also alter the immediate need and form of the most basic type of communication—face to face interpersonal communication. Joshua Meyrowitz in *No Sense of Place* explores how electronic media have affected social behavior through the reorganization of social settings and the alteration of the relationship between physical place and social place." He notes that media theorists suggest that changes in the means of communication patterns are one very important and often overlooked contributant to social changes (Meyrowitz, 1985).

As the work, residence, and commerce configuration changed, also altered was the opportunity, but perhaps not the need, for accidental and incidental interaction with others. Absent was the possibility for unplanned interludes of people watching and potential relationships. Planners and those creating land use regulations have joined media theorists by failing to integrate the impact of media on face-to-face interaction in urban and suburban environments.

Land-Use Regulations and Communication

Land-use laws have manifest and latent functions. Government intervention (i.e., public control) of private land use has been seen as a means of resolving conflicts in the use of land and bringing order and beauty to cities (Mandelker & Cunningham, 1985). Courts repeatedly assert that property rights are always held subject to the police power of the state (Powell & Rohan, 1968).[3] The scope of governmental control over land use has increased steadily in this century. The early American concept of the owner's right to use his or her own land as he or she chose has given way to an increasing recognition of the necessity for community action to handle the problems of modern life (Mandelker & Cunningham, 1985). There has been some difficulty in defining the legitimate social purposes that justify governmental action. Social purposes have included efficiency (Michelman, 1967), protection of natural resources (Hines, 1977), conservation of property values, aesthetics, and the general welfare (Anderson, 1973). Interpersonal interaction has not been enunciated as a legitimate social purpose justifying land use regulation, however, the concept of general welfare is broad enough to encompass this.

There are several regulatory approaches towards the control of land: nuisance laws, restrictive convenants, and zoning laws (Mandelker & Cunningham, 1985). Aside from zoning, which is the primary form of regulation to be examined in this essay, nuisance laws provide an alternative means of regulating land use and thereby interaction. Before the beginning of this century common-law nuisance was a principle means of regulating use of real property. Private nuisance provides a tort action (civil liability) upon which to litigate, focusing upon the reasonableness of conduct while enjoying one's property as compared to the inconvenience and harm inflicted upon others for activities such as excessive noise (Prosser, 1977). Private nuisance applies to the interest of a possessor of land in freedom from any unreasonable, nontrespassory interference with use and enjoyment of land. The blaring stereo or raucous outdoor gathering that disturbs the neighbors constitutes a private nuisance.

Another approach to land-use regulation comes from rights that one may have in the land of another that may bear upon communication opportunities. Specific communication activities may either be limited or encouraged based upon enforceable promises (i.e., covenants and easements) between two parties. Covenants are provisions in a deed limiting the use of property and prohibiting certain uses that may further serve to limit interaction by prohibiting certain activities on premises (Black's Law Dictionary, 1979). When a covenant is said to "run with the land" this means it is actually a contract between parties that, by virtue of meeting certain requirements, is binding and enforceable on those who later buy the land. Easements, privileges to use the land of another, provide an alternative source of restrictions on land use. An affirmative easement entitles its holder to do a physical act on the land while a negative easement enables its holder to prevent the owner of land from using land for particular purposes. Through creation and enforcement of rights created under covenants or easements use of land for gatherings, restaurants, pubs, meeting halls, and other businesses that are open to the general public may be prohibited or the hours property is open to the public could be limited thus affecting the opportunity for public interaction.

The History of Zoning and Urban Communication

The most important form of governmental control of land use in urban areas has been zoning, which involves a legislatively created tool placing limitations upon the "use" of property (Manelker & Cunningham, 1985). Zoning laws regulate communication in four ways; they may restrict or stimulate communicative activity, either explicitly or implicitly. Regulations imposed on the "use" of property guide social behavior in that environment.

Public controls of private use of land have been with us to some degree almost from the beginnings of civilization (Bassett, 1936). Early Roman laws and regulations recognized the need for zoning of certain areas, protection of streets against specific encroachments, and building height regulations (Yokley, 1978). The earliest code of Roman Law, the Twelve Tables (drafted in 451–445 B.C.) provided:

> Whoever sets a hedge around his land shall not exceed the boundary; in the case of a wall, he shall leave one foot; in the case of a house, two feet. If a grave or pit, the required depth. If a well, a path, an olive or fig tree, nine feet. Finally, whoever plants other trees shall leave a space of five feet between [his] property and his neighbor's. If there is litigation about boundaries, five feet. (Bescher, Wright, & Gitelman, 1976, p. 2)

Concern for health and safety led to laws creating use districts within a city. This approach to land-use regulation dates back to 1581 in an act which limited making of iron metal in iron mills within the compass and precinct of two and twenty miles from the city of London or its suburbs.[4] Authorities differ as to the origins of modern zoning. A German authority, Baumeister, published a treatise in 1876 reviewing the early history of zoning. He records "use" zoning as having been founded by the decree of Bonaparte-Napoleon I in 1810 with the protection of certain districts from the invasion of injurious uses (Metzenbaum, 1955).[5] In England land use restriction in the modern era came through the official action of the "Town Planning Act" of 1909.

In the United States urban planning was brought by the first settlers who conceived of planning as laying out streets, locating public buildings and implementing systems for the distribution of land.[6] In 1692 an act prevented the common nuisances arising from slaughterhouses, stillhouses, tallow chandlers, and curriers in the Province of Massachusetts Bay. Many cities established fire zones which may be traced back to as early as those passed in 1692 in Boston (Metzenbaum, 1955, p. 4).

Regulations and community planning reflected concern for health and social conditions. Population density was regulated through "tenement house codes." Building codes, sanitary codes, height ordinances, and nuisance ordinances followed as cities came to perceive a need to protect the public welfare (Metzenbaum, 1955 p. 7). These restrictions were often recognized as within the inherent police powers of municipalities (Bassett, 1936). The United States Supreme Court upheld a Massachusetts "fire control" passed in a 1904–5 measure that fixed height limits in certain residential areas in the city of Boston (Welch v. Swasey, 1909). In 1909 the City of Los Angeles passed an ordinance dividing the city into industrial and residential districts prohibiting certain buildings and uses such as laundries (*Ex parte* Quong Wo, 1911).

New York City is often credited with the first modern zoning law in the United States which was significant as the first complete and comprehensive system of building control.[7] It established districts and restrictions throughout the five boroughs as to uses permitted for property within the city, height regulations, and the proportion of area which might be built upon (Bescher, Wright, & Gitelman, 1976).

The New York zoning resolution adopted provided for three separate classes of use districts: (1) residence districts; (2) business districts; and (3) unrestricted districts. Residence districts prohibited all trade and industry while business districts only excluded specified "nuisance" types of businesses such as manufacturing of ammonia and paint (Bescher, Wright, & Gitelman, p. 502). The New York City ordinance was attacked but the courts upheld the validity of comprehensive zoning as a proper exercise of the police power (*Lincoln Trust Company v. Williams Building Corp.*, 1920). The court stated that the conduct of an individual and the use of his property may be regulated.

Regulations similar to those adopted in New York City were enacted almost immediately by hundreds of municipalities.[8] During the early 1920's the United States Department of Commerce encouraged the spread of comprehensive zoning by publishing a model state enabling act, and by 1926, the Supreme Court of the United States, upheld the constitutionality of zoning by districts or divisions of the community.[9] Under such a system land uses are allowed on an as-of-right basis, meaning that zoning regulation would be largely "self-executing" (Manelker & Cunningham, 1985). After the formulation of the ordinance text and map by a local zoning commission and its adoption by the local governing body, most administrations would require only the services of a building official who would determine whether proposed construction complied with the requirements.

Great discretion developed within the administration of zoning ordinances as a result of post-World War II urban sprawl which compelled planners to find methods to improve the *quality* of urban life. They were asked to enact land-use controls that would create and preserve a healthy, aesthetically attractive community with proper regard for the finite quality of resources and the historical patrimony of the community. This led to more flexibility with the issuance of variances permitting a parcel of land to be used differently than prescribed by zoning ordinances.

Zoning, Expression, and Public Interaction

The objectives of zoning include protection of property values, preservation of the character of neighborhood insurance of adequate governmental services, minimization of traffic congestion, aesthetics and historic preservation. Zoning divides the municipality into districts and prescribes requirements within each district dealing with use (i.e., industrial, commercial, residential), density (i.e., number of units per acre) and siting of development on each parcel (e.g., setback or landscaping requirements). Zoning regulations may influence communication by controlling *communication activities* or by controlling *communication contexts*. No law operates in isolation, particularly zoning laws. Behind each zoning law can be found an interactional consequence.

Zoning and the regulation of communication activities

Zoning has excluded certain communication activities from some districts and limited where they might be permitted. Such laws determine the lawful location of theaters, the clustering or dispersing of adult bookstores, or limit the placement of billboards. The Supreme Court has upheld the constitutionality of Anti-Skid Row Ordinances (for example, in Detroit) that required that adult theaters be more than 1,000 feet from adult bookstores, cabarets, and bars. In the case of Detroit, the government's interest was to prevent a concentration of adult theaters that might lower property values, attract transients, and encourage flight of legitimate business. The court upheld the use of zoning in this case as a tool to promote legitimate interest in "planning and regulating the use of property for commercial purposes." (*City of Renton v. Playtime Theatres, Inc.,* 1986; *Young v. American Mini Theatres, Inc.,* 1976). The Court has not permitted the use of zoning to prohibit nonobscene materials and sexual expression and struck down a New Jersey law banning all commercial live entertainment, including nude dancing (*Schad v. Borough of Mount Ephraim, 1981*) as well as a Florida ordinance forbidding drive-in movie theaters from showing films with nudity, if the screen was visible from streets and sidewalks (*Erznoznik v. City of Jacksonville*, 1975).

Direct regulation of communication activities occurs when zoning laws place limitations upon the types of signs (Kelly & Raso, 1989) and billboards permitted in an area thus affecting commercial expression in an effort to prevent traffic hazards and promote aesthetic concerns (*Metromedia v. San Diego*, 1981). In obscenity and billboard cases governmental authorities attempt to regulate in the name of public welfare, but are aware of the impact their actions may have upon communicative activity.

Zoning and the regulation of communication contexts

The less obvious approach to zoning and the regulation of public communication contexts pertains to unintended communication ramifications. Examples from New York City and its environs serve to illustrate some of the implications.

The Setback: Buffer from Interaction. The restrictions of New York City and its suburbs illustrate the social implications of zoning. Most zoning ordinances specify that new buildings be constructed within a *setback line* (distance from the street) for the purposes of protecting commerical vistas and providing space for front yards in residential districts (i.e., aesthetic objectives).[10] The size of the setback and width of a sidewalk either encourages or discourages interaction.

In New York City residential setbacks range from twenty feet to fifteen feet with required side yards on all detached residences ranging from a minimum of five feet on each side to fifteen feet. In suburban areas the size of setbacks is stressed even more and reflects or sets the agenda of a community which prizes privacy over connection: "In a B-A residence district, no building shall have a depth of front yard of less than fifty feet" (Town of Oyster Bay Building Zone Ordinance, 1989, Section 217). In the Village of Great Neck residential districts the minimum front yard depth shall be thirty feet or twenty feet (Village of Great Neck Zoning, 1987, Section 210-11; 210-50 and 210-63). The Village of Great Neck Plaza proscribes front yards of not less than twenty-five feet with side yards of not less than fifteen feet, to minimum front yards of twenty feet with side yards of not less than five feet (Local Zoning Law Amendments, Village of Great Neck Plaza, Article III). A residential structure set at these distances from the front line and side line of the building to the front line and side line of the street or next building may be placed behind a landscaped buffer strip. This helps reduce traffic noise and creates a private environment deemphasizing the presence of neighbors. The setbacks offer a vantage point for the "safe" observation of the activities of the street. The depth of setback establishes a communication context or social agenda which can either deter or facilitate communication with others.

The windows and balconies of high-rise apartment buildings are the urban equivalents of suburban setbacks. They provide inhabitants the luxury or an aesthetically distanced and sometimes voyeuristic relationship with the outside world. Similarly, the automobile has become an extended living room transporting its inhabitants through threatening streets in detached safety. Darkened one-way automobile windows permit observation without interaction in the same way that setbacks operate in the home.

Currently, some architects assert that the closer one lives to the street, the more one is likely to participate in street life. The distance of a home from the street becomes a border which is not conducive to social interaction (Moore & Sullivan, 1988). However, it is more likely that the distance is a variable that can either facilitate or deter interaction. According to Jane Jacobs (1961),

> A good city street neighborhood achieves a marvel of balance between its people's determination to have essential privacy and their simultaneous wishes for differing degrees of contact, enjoyment or help from the people around. (P. 59)

Setbacks allow control of privacy, permitting visual interaction shielded from social isolation. In *The Fall of Public Man* Richard Sennett asserted "human beings need to have some distance from intimate observation by others in order to feel sociable" (Sennett, 1974, p. 15). If this is so, setbacks may actually encourage social interaction—if coupled with complementary design structure and site of potential interaction. The amount of setback that might encourage interaction is determined, in part, by the psychological and social attitudes generated by proximity to the street. Does the street offer visually inviting, entertaining, nonthreatening activity? If so, then a suitable setback would be that distance from structure to street which offers a clear view while offering a sense of detachment.

The Café: a Cup of Coffee and A Conversation? Cafés worldwide serve a variety of social functions. In the café business is conducted, news is exchanged, reaction to events shared. The café provides a meeting place, a place in which to be entertained (i.e., chess, backgammon, cards, etc.), a place to avoid loneliness, to watch television or listen to radio with others, a place to read newspapers. The café is a place to write, a place to belong and be identified with, a place to which one can escape.

In the residential areas of Paris the sidewalk café functions as a meeting place, a site of interaction, a perch from which to leisurely observe ones neighbors (the French café is designed for display and observation). However, in New York City there are specific streets, neighborhoods, small areas and portions of streets in which sidewalk cafés are not permitted.

Chapter 4 of the Zoning Resolution of the Department of Planning of New York City addresses the regulation of sidewalk cafés. It established that the general purpose is "to establish city-wide regulations designed to encourage sidewalk cafés in locations where they are appropriate and discourage them in locations where they are inappropriate and to promote and protect public health, safety, general welfare and amenity. . . . Sidewalk cafés may be established only at the discretion of the City of New York pursuant to Section 14-02." The regulations governing sidewalk cafés specify area eligibility, sidewalk locational, and physical criteria for both enclosed and unenclosed cafés. No sidewalk café shall be permitted in residential districts (Zoning Resolution, 1988, Section 14-04). Many of the potential social functions of the local café been "zoned out" by New York City regulations.

"Sidewalk cafés shall be permitted in street malls" and "may be permitted in Historic Districts or in designated Landmark Buildings" (Section 14-04). As a result an institution intended for authentic everyday interaction has been relegated to "pseudo" streets; to becoming an artificial oasis without a permanent constituency. No sidewalk cafés are permitted on major thoroughfares.[11] These establishments are regulated for the stated purposes of ensuring adequate space for pedestrians on the adjacent sidewalks; the preservation, enhancement of the character of neighborhoods; and promotion of the most desirable use of land and conservation of the value of land and building and thereby protect the city's tax revenues. (Zoning Resolution, 1988). Such restrictions shape not only the physical but the psychological maps of areas. They regulate movement on the streets while they keep pedestrian traffic moving without fostering the social intercourse which is one of the factors defining community and neighborhood.

Suburban cafés are regulated as restaurants. Any shop or store that makes available food or beverages for consumption on the premises outside a building, open-front shops and stores are all prohibited in the Village of Great Neck (Zoning Code Section 210-102 (C); Section 210-93A). In some central business districts services are permitted on an adjacent terrace (Town of Oyster Bay Building Zone Ordinance, 1989, p. 1424). Permitted occupancy of restaurants are specifically defined based on size, type of seating, and activities.

So-called "unnecessary noise" regulations prohibit the use of "musical instruments or sound reproduction devices" within a sidewalk café for any purpose (Zoning Resolution, 1988, Section 14-26). The sound environment is an integral part of the character and social function of the café with television, radio, recorded music, videos being part of the café's sound environment. The choice within that environment sets tone, perhaps even establishes a sense of decorum. The "regulation of a café boundary" mandates that "no portion of sidewalk cafés, such as doors, windows, walls or any objects within the café may swing or project beyond a designated exterior perimeter" (Zoning Resolution, 1988, Section 14-21). The interior acoustical environment is therefore regulated because it potentially affects the exterior activity of the street.

Use Districts: Segregating interaction. Yet another way in which the regulation of communication context is regulated may be seen in the restrictions placed upon the *uses of buildings within a district.* Zoning laws implement functionalism; planning that separated residential and work area based upon uses (Gehl, 1987). Residential use districts articulate the types and uses of dwellings and may restrict an area of single-family dwellings or multiple residences. Not only is density of population controlled, but also housing availability and costs. The de facto result of such restrictions may very well affect the economic and ethnic makeup of a community's population. Permitted uses in residential districts may not include restaurants, schools, or places of worship (typical locations of interaction) which require special permits (Zoning Resolution, 3, section 8.17). These residential districts have been criticized for creating an artificial separation of houses and work that in turn leads to intolerable rifts in people's inner lives (Alexander et al. 1977). Even in a commercial area zoning ordinances may delineate the permissible type of businesses and prohibit conducting business outside of a building as a reasonable aesthetics regulation (*People v. Clover Dairy Corp.,* 1959).

Zoning Bonus Plazas: Creating Space for Social Interaction. Existing zoning ordinances in New York have encouraged private property owners to provide *open spaces and urban plazas.* The regulation of floor area, density, and the spacing of buildings establish minimum open space ratios (i.e., the number of square feet of open space required on a zoning lot expressed as a percentage of the floor area on that zoning lot). Such open space includes courtyards and community facility buildings attached to the building (Zoning Resolution, 1988, Section 81-24)—uses which provide enhanced opportunity for interaction. Plazas (open areas accessible to the public at all times) have been simultaneously encouraged and regulated. Private property owners have been persuaded to provide plazas for the public through the use of incentive zoning.[12] The builders could build beyond zoning limits *if* they provided a public plaza, an arcade, or a comparable amenity. Incentive zoning was introduced in New York City in the 1960s and over the next ten years it was to prompt the creation of more new open space in the center city and other cities in the country followed. This marked a move to more negotiation and case by case dealing with developers. Property owners could get a "plaza bonus" by which a developer could add up to 20 percent more floor space to a building if a plaza was provided. The results of such incentives include the Seagram Building plaza and the plaza in front of the One Chase Manhattan Plaza, the Citicorp Center, the IBM and AT&T headquarters—all in Manhattan, International Place in Boston, and Fountain Square in Cincinnati. These plazas are regulated as to size, curb level, seating, railings, awnings, steps statuary and ornamental fountains (Whyte, 1988).

Between 1961 and 1973 some 1.1 million square feet of new open space was created through the use of incentive zoning (Whyte, 1988). New kinds of spaces were invented for bonuses: galleries, atria, garden courts, through-block circulation areas, covered pedestrian areas, roof gardens.[13] While such bonuses have spurred the building of plazas that theoretically would increase the opportunity for public interaction, many have failed to accomplish the desired effect. Once the plazas were provided the property owners were required to maintain and improve these areas, however, there appears to have been little governmental supervision to insure that the plazas were actually fulfilling the intended functions. William Whyte set up the Street Life Project to observe how people used city spaces such as plazas and arcades knowing that no government body had been established to do this. He found that while many places were excellent many places were sterile, empty spaces only used for transit (Whyte, 1988).

Conclusions

The trend in zoning today is to focus upon protection and promotion of the undefined "general welfare" rather than on historical concerns of public health and safety. As society moves from industrial- to information-related technologies the distinctions grounded in an industrial vision become outmoded. Zoning laws were designed to protect the public welfare, not to discourage social interaction. It is somewhat ironic, that such laws have become relics protecting a past that no longer exists. While some forms and aspects of zoning remain essential, their social impact has become socially dysfunctional since public interaction is discouraged in the name of efficiency and safety. At the same time, as the original necessity for such laws changed, a concomitant dependency upon mediated communication stimulated by the extraordinary acceleration of media technology increased the individual's dependency upon face-to-face social interaction. Community planners evaluating land-use regulations must recognize the changes in patterns of interaction. The zoning paradigm of separating social activities must begin to accommodate an age where in the technology of communications has altered our sense of space. Zoning and communication technology united to transform the nature of social interaction and their combined impact suggest related and interdependent solutions to a rapidly deteriorating public life. These solutions call for (1) a reexamination of the contemporary concept of zoning along with the revision of many antiquated zoning regulations which deter interaction; (2) the reevaluation of the medium of communication offered by public places and the potential integration of electronic media into the public sector. The infra- and social structure have abandoned the public place for the chic and the private. Media technology is one of the major forces responsible for the shift. The challenge is to choreograph our media and public performances.

Notes

1. The scope of this chapter is zoning although other land use regulations such as nuisance laws and restrictive covenants also have an impact upon public interaction.
2. In this context we regard public places as media of communication. Streets and public spaces are essential carriers of communication (Rykewert, 1978). Cities have the capability of providing for an easily accessible web of contacts (Czarnowski, 1978).
3. See also *People v. Reeves* (1955); *Elopoulous v. City of Chicago* (1954).
4. This was enacted by the Act on touching Iron-Mills near unto the City of London and the River of Thames 23 Eliz.c.5 (1581) (Bescher, Wright, & Gitelman, 1976, p. 5.)
5. Thirty five years later the Prussian Code provided a more comprehensive development of the zoning concept which was developed by laws of the German Empire. These restrictions upon the use of land gained popularity and were adopted in principal cities such as Frankfurt, Berlin and Coblenz. According to Harold M. Lewis in *City Planning*, others trace zoning as beginning in Germany in 1884 (Metzenbaum, 1955).
6. Planning in the United States reflected the European orientation of planning. Settlements in the southwest were based upon traditional Spanish planning of a gridiron with a central plaza while Louisiana was patterned after French design of string villages divided into long lots perpendicular to the Mississippi River (Anderson, 1986, p. 10).
7. The terms zoning and planning are not synonymous. Zoning is a separation of the municipality into districts, and the regulation of buildings and structures in the districts in accordance with the nature of their use. It pertains to use as well as the structural and architectural design of buildings. Planning may be defined as a broader term connotating a systematic development designed to promote the common interest of a community such as streets, parks, industrial

and commercial undertakings, civic beauty and other matters within the police power (Yokley, 1978).
8. By 1922 it was reported that twenty state zoning enabling acts and fifty municipal zoning ordinances were in force or in process of formulation (Manelker & Cunningham, 1985).
9. By 1926 zoning was commonplace in large cities, and not uncommon in smaller communities (Euclid v. Ambler Realty Co., 1926). This type of zoning became known as Euclidean Zoning.
10. Zoning Resolution, Department of City Planning, New York City, 1988, 3, section 7.10.
11. In areas such as Manhattan's 86th Street from the East River to 5th Ave., 34th Street and 23rd Street from the East River to 8th Ave., 14th Street from 2nd Ave. to 8th Ave., and the entire length of Lexington Ave (Zoning Resolution, 1988, appendix A). No enclosed sidewalk cafés are permitted in areas such as Central Park South from 5th to 8th Ave., and Park Ave. South from 31 Street to 38th Street (Zoning Resolution, 1988, appendix B). In New York City sidewalk cafés may be permitted in all commercial districts and all manufacturing districts with certain blocks exempted. In Manhattan the theater district, Lincoln Square district, United Nations area, Fifth Ave., and Madison Ave. are just a few of the commercial or manufacaturing areas which are specially zoned areas prohibiting cafés.
12. New York courts have recently endorsed the use of incentive zoning to promote certain amenities as a trade off (rather than an exaction) from developers. Developers providing amenities such as low income housing are being encouraged via incentive zoning (*Asian Americans for Equality v. Koch*, 1988).
13. In 1982 the New York City planning commission came through with a sweeping revision of midtown zoning. Incentive zoning bonuses were dropped except for the creation of *plazas* and *urban parks*. The bonus for a plaza was reduced. The planning commission got tougher about amenities. Instead of giving bonuses for them, it mandated them (Whyte, 1988).

References

Alexander, C. et al. (1977). *A pattern language: Towns, buildings, construction.* New York: Oxford University Press.
Anderson, R. M. (1986). *American law of zoning*, third edition. Rochester, New York: The Lawyers Co-Operative Publishing Co.
Anderson, R. M. (1973). *New York zoning law and practice*, second edition. Rochester, NY: The Lawyers Co-Operative Publishing Co.
Asian Americans for Equality v. Koch, 72 N.Y.2d. 121. (1988).
Bassett, E. (1936). *Zoning: The laws, administration, and court decisions during the first twenty five years.* New York: Russell Sage Foundation.
Bescher, J., Wright, R., & Gitelman, M. (1976). *Cases and materials on land use*, second edition. St. Paul, MN: West Publishing.
Black, H. C. (1979). *Black's law dictionary*, fifth edition. St. Paul, MN: West Publishing Co.
Burgoon, J., Buller, D., & Woodall, W. G. (1989). *Nonverbal communication: The unspoken dialogue.* New York: Harper & Row.
Cathcart, R., & Gumpert, G. (1983). Mediated interpersonal communication: Toward a new typology. *The Quarterly Journal of Speech, 69*, 267–77.

450   Between Communication and Information

City of Renton v. Playtime Theatres, Inc. 475 U.S. 41 (1986).

Czarnowski, T. V. (1978). The street as a communications artifact. In S. Anderson (Ed.), *On Streets* (pp. 207–212). Cambridge, MA: MIT Press.

Elliott, D. (1983). Open space legislation: Innovative concepts create public amenities. *Urban Open Spaces*, Cooper Hewitt Museum.

Elopoulous v. City of Chicago, 120 N.E. 2d 555. (1954).

Erznoznik v. City of Jacksonville, 422 U.S. 205. (1975).

Euclid v. Ambler Realty Co., 272 U.S. 365. (1926).

Ex parte Quong Wo, 118 P. 714. (1911).

Gehl, J. (1987). *Life between buildings: Using public space*. New York: Van Nostrand Reinhold Co.

Goffman, E. (1963). *Behavior in public places: Notes on the social organization of gatherings*. New York: Free Press.

Goffman, E. (1961). *Asylums: Essays on the social situation of mental patients and other inmates*. Garden City, NY: Anchor Books/Doubleday.

Gumpert, G. (1987). *Talking tombstones and other tales of the media age*. New York: Oxford University Press.

Hall, E. T. (1966). *The Hidden dimension*. Garden City, NY: Doubleday.

Hines, W. (1977). A decade of nondegradation policy in Congress and the courts: The erratic pursuit of clean air and clean water. *Iowa Law Review, 62*, 643.

Jacobs, J. (1961). *The death and life of great American cities*. New York: Vintage Press.

Kelly, E. D., & Raso, G. J. (1989). *Sign Regulation for Small and Midsize Communities* (no. 419). Planning Advisory Service Report.

Lincoln Trust Company v. Williams Building Corp., 229 N.Y. 313. (1920).

Local Zoning Law Amenments, Village of Great Neck Plaza, Article III.

Manelker, D., & Cunningham, R. (1985). *Planning and control of land Development*. Charlottesville, VA: The Michie Company.

Manelker, D. R. (1971). *The zoning dilemma: A legal strategy for Urban Change*. Indianapolis: Bobbs Merrill.

Mehrabian, A. (1976). *Public places and private spaces*. New York: Basic Books Inc.

Metromedia v. San Diego, 453 U.S. 490. (1981).

Metzenbaum, J. (1955). *The Law of zoning*. Cleveland: Baker, Voorhis, and Co. Inc.

Meyrowitz, J. (1985). *No sense of place*. New York: Oxford University Press.

Michelman, F. I. (1967). Property, utility, and fairness: Comments on the ethical foundations of "just compensation" law. *Harvard Law Review, 80*, 1165–83.

Moore, A., & Sullivan, J. P. (1988, June 26). Putting the old neighborhood in the new. The *New York Times*, p. 30.

Murdock, G., & Golding, P. (1989). Information poverty and political inequality: Citizenship in the age of privatized communications. *Journal of Communication 39* (3) (Summer), 180–95.

People v. Clover Dairy Corp. 199 N.Y.S. 2d 554. (1959).

People v. Reeves, 287 P.2s 544. (1955).

Powell, R. R., & Rohan, P. J. (1968). *Powell on real property*. New York: Matthew Bender.

Prosser, W. L. (1971). *Law of Torts*. St. Paul, MN: West Publishing Co.

Rykewert, J. (1978). The Street: The use of its history. In S. Anderson (Ed.), *On Streets* (pp. 15–28). Cambridge, MA: MIT Press.

Schad v. Borough of Mount Ephraim, 452 U.S. 61. (1981).

Sennett, R. (1974). *The fall of public man: On the social psychology of capitalism.* New York: Vintage Books.

Sharp, W. (1989). Special permits and site plan approval. In *Basics of Zoning and Land Use Control* (pp. 53–68). Albany: New York State Bar Association.

Sweet, J. (1987). *Legal aspects of architecture, engineering and the construction process.* St. Paul, MN: West Publishing.

Town of Oyster Bay, 1989 at Section 217.

Village of Great Neck Zoning. (1987).

Webber, M. M. (1964). *The Urban Place and the Nonplace Urban Realm, Explorations Into Urban Structure.* Philadelphia: University of Pennsylvania Press.

Welch v. Swasey, 214 U.S. 91. (1909).

Willis, H. (1989). Zoning board of appeals appellate jurisdiction. In *Basics of Zoning and Land Use Control.* (pp. 45–50). Albany: New York State Bar Association.

Whyte, W. H. (1988). *City: Rediscovering the center.* New York: Doubleday.

Yokley, E. C. (1978). *Zoning law and practice 4th Edition.* Charlottesville, VA: The Michie Co.

Young v. American Mini Theatres, Inc. 427 U.S. 50 (1976).

Zoning, The Village of Great Neck, Section 210–11; Section 210–50 and 210–63.

Zoning Resolution, Department of City Planning, New York City (1988), 3, section 7.10; Chapter 4, Section 1400.

22

The Politics of Information: A Study of the French Minitel System

Richard Kramer

This paper describes the development of the French Minitel videotex system and its impact upon communications and information access by the French elite and public. The first part discusses the politics of technology development. The second part notes the climate of industrial policy and state intervention in which Minitel was nurtured. The third part focusses on the efforts to publicize and implement Minitel. The fourth part surveys the patterns of user behavior which emerged from the marketing of Minitel and the international significance of its symbolic success. The conclusion argues that considerations of the political and symbolic needs of the state in deploying communications technologies must precede discussions of the social use of those technologies, and in turn, any speculation on the indistinct relations between information and communications.

Information and communications are widely accepted as the foundation of modern economies and societies. However, the relationship between communications and the acquisition and transfer of information remains poorly understood. This is often due to a lack of concern for the broad range of other factors that affect such a relation, notably, the technologies that facilitate communication and the politics that shape their development. Scholars are still seeking conceptual models to explain human interaction with such widely diffused technologies as telephones, television and computers. This paper approaches a relatively new technology,

454   Between Communication and Information

videotex, that incorporates elements of these three core technologies to shed light on the factors affecting the nexus of communications and information. It presents a largely political model of a new communications technology and the circumstances which surrounded its birth and growth.

The first part discusses the politics of technology development and the institutional forms that define the potential for users to communicate and access data. The second part notes the French climate of industrial policy and state intervention in which Minitel was nurtured, and offers a functionalist model of its growth. The third part focuses on the need to manage dissent and arouse publicity for the Minitel system, and the efforts which typified that struggle. The fourth part continues with a discussion of the usage patterns and user behavior that emerged from the marketing of Minitel and the international significance of its symbolic success.

The Politics of Technology

Information technology reshaped and reconstituted institutions across social boundaries by altering their common modus operandi: its adoption by one actor rapidly ups the ante for others. The personal computer, for example, has revolutionized a enormous range of institutions and practices in the past decade. Technology also bleeds into the political sphere, as a powerful symbol of progress and economic force in the increasing transformation to a technology-based "information age."

The incorporation of technological goals and symbols in political institutions typically involves a deterministic drive towards innovation, under the pressure of an ongoing external threat. A complex technocratic society places the onus upon institutions and political actors to adopt new technologies. Displays of technical competence confer important benefits; industrialists make money, politicians reach voters, consumers gain prestige. Whilst all-encompassing technologies (such as the computer or television) defy reductionism, they nevertheless encourage utopian descriptions: men convince themselves, as Ellul notes, that they are constantly on the brink of techno-paradise. When this goal appears (or remains) elusive, a scapegoat may be sought, summoning a malevolent other to account for difficulties.

These views see technology as responsive to social needs, which legitimates the institutional contexts upon which technology depends. In turn, members of technological societies grow increasingly reliant upon their innovations: individuals know less and less about core structures and processes sustaining them, and the gap between realities and the pictures individuals have of the world widens.[1] Ignorance of and bedazzlement with technology allows the promotion of technological symbols to the exclusion of concerns over costs or benefits, underscoring the imbalance of power between individuals and technically proficient institutions.

Accordingly modern states, and in turn their citizens and institutions succumb to the seductive symbol of technology and elevate it to near-religious status. Technology acts as a talisman,[2] invoked as a restorative tonic for national ills. Academic critiques of technological progress have focused on narrow effects, foregoing wider claims about technology's architectonic influence on social structures. Even broader works such as those by Ellul and Mumford ascribe quasireligious powers to technology. Modern man is presented as infinitely malleable, subsumed under the state-driven tidal wave of progress: "Roughly speaking, the problem here is to modify human needs in accordance with the requirements of planning" (Ellul, 1964, p. 225).

This limited perspective was seen in the French government's Manichean framing of Luddite and techno-optimist arguments in 1978: "Are we headed toward a society that will use this new technology to reinforce the mechanisms of rigidity, authority and domination? Or on the other hand, will we know how to enhance adaptability, freedom and communication in such a way that every citizen and every group can be responsible for itself?" The state offers its own, unsurprisingly favorable conclusion: "in fact no technology, however innovative it may be, has long-term fatal consequences" (Nora & Minc, 1978, p. 10–11). Although nuclear weapons for one spring to mind, such a benign view of technology is a central rhetorical strategy used to promise a version of Ellul's techno-paradise. Through this rhetoric technology is introduced into political and institutional discourse, calling forth a powerful symbolic grammar; the following debate is framed by those who claim technical expertise and fluency in technological language.

The notion of autonomous, benign technology contrasts with the instrumental employment of technologies to control markets relevant to its operation. Galbraith notes the market control strategies employed by France in economic reconstruction: vertical integration, market control that "reduces or eliminates the independence of those with whom the planning unit deals" and market suspension through contract, where market power is established for extended periods (1968, p. 39).

Technological systems control or strongly influence the political processes that ostensibly regulate them. Numerous expositions of "capture theory" in the U.S. (Stigler, 1971) attain heightened meaning for the French: regulations are promulgated by political fiat and agencies are staffed by political loyalists. The resulting technological politics invokes the rhetoric of a "mission" to match its capabilities, propagating and manipulating the needs it purports to serve. Unlike the fabled Alexander, institutions do not weep for new worlds to conquer; they create them in the form of technological imperatives. States may suggest new missions, projects, or imperatives, placing influence behind an effort to convince persons in the political sphere of this new need. The institution proclaims the importance of its project, discovering or creating a crisis to justify expansion. Under threat, "the system finds an external and usually nebulous enemy whose existence demands the utmost in technological preparation" (Winner, 1977, p. 249).

Technological decisions are cloaked as imperatives: refusal to support growth can bring disaster. Despite this faith, technology cannot be removed from economic and political forces calling it forth. Technology may thus be seen as a protean subinstitution, a symbolic construct reshaped to suit its makers' needs. Its impact upon communications and the sharing of information within the social technologies is determined more by the clash of competing interests than by inherent characteristics of the technology itself. Such a politicized developmental model was clearly followed in the case of the French Minitel system.

The French Minitel System

The French Minitel videotex system offers an example of technological politics; it carried its own set of symbolic referents and was constituted toward specific ends. Its mission filled no endogenous need, but responded to the threat of a generalized other while remaining under centralized control. Minitel has in many ways altered French society. Its rapid rise since 1978, its politicization and implementation, provides a case study of the introduction of technological symbols. The Minitel system enables users to communicate efficiently, much as the telephone does, providing remote access to databases that provide information, games, services such as shopping or banking, and movie listings. Minitel remains a unique example of videotex introduction; no other system in the world has even 10 percent of its subscriber base.

Minitel is also unique as an example of politicized technology policy, an elite tool largely symbolic in importance, deployed ostensibly to confront threats to national sovereignty and support the institutions that nurtured it. Its potential to undermine institutions is mitigated by systemic technical limitations, reliance upon state support, and the economic logic of technology distribution. These in turn allowed only a specific form of communications to occur, limited in the quantity and speed of information transmission. Minitel also draws together concerns over impending technological developments in a neat and painless package to emphasize

France's technical competence in the face of challenges to the nation's character.

Minitel provides an example of a technology pursued, developed, and introduced as much on highly symbolic political ground as it was on technical or marketing turf. It was conceptualized foremost as a tool of communications—one which conveyed the technological prowess of the French nation, and its position in the global migration to information-based economies. The microprocessors, screens, and keyboards, as well as the databases that constitute Minitel are of secondary importance to the political rhetoric and images offered in defense of its existence (and later, success). The communications of its users were most valuable as a unified population, sending a message to other nations of an information savvy vanguard of French society. This vanguard was in keeping with the venerated French tradition of elitism and centralized political power.

Centralization and Elites in French Society

One issue conflated with Minitel, and its information and communications functions is the role of centralized elite groups and actors in creating and fostering the deployment of technological symbols. Elite groups are the most fluent in symbolic discourse, accustomed to crafting symbols, investing them with meaning, and deriving meanings from complex symbolic actions.

At its base, the French national plan to manage telecommunications, information, and computing resources was highly elite-driven, a product of France's rhetorical establishment. This reflects the character of French society: highly centralized power is guarded within state institutions with a high degree of influence over private enterprise. The rewards of adopting elite symbols are all but guaranteed: "there is a tacit understanding between big business and the state in France that the state will initiate and define economic objectives, and to the extent that private enterprise collaborates it will be compensated" (Sulieman, 1978, p. 273). The French predilection for economic planning extends to the symbols that represent it in the global context of the *defi americain* challenge, met with Japanese-style technological imperatives. The French ambition as the "the third electronic nation" was premised on what Mitterrand has described as "reconquering the internal market." Robins & Webster write,

> what is particularly striking about the French is the self-conscious and articulate character of the state's role . . . rather than being socialist, the French strategy should be seen as corporatist, an example of state involve-

ment of a directive kind determined to achieve success within the framework
of an international market economy. (1986, p. 266)

Programs such as Minitel were nested within a broad *filière electronique,*
an French model of industrial economics geared towards the exploitation
of economies of interrelated goods from primary to intermediate and final
sectors. The *filière* also sought to introduce basic computer terminals into
society, offering data central held in mainframe computers through transmission over the newly deployed digital networks (Dang-Ngyuen & Arnold, 1986).

The presence of such a program reaffirms the secondary nature of the
actual uses of Minitel. Information and communications technologies were
deployed instrumentally to further political control of technological innovation in society. The movement of Minitel from a political weapon to a
technological reality reveals the lack of attention paid to its actual, rather
than symbolic use.

Minitel's Founding Document

Constitutions, charters, declarations, and religious tracts all play a role
as both seed and midwife of infant social structures. Such methods
typically implicate symbolic and rhetorical grammars: the founding document of French videotex, the Nora-Minc Report, introduced the term
"telematics" and infused it with a reasonance uniting French society in a
battle against a foreign threat. It offered a blueprint for the political and
rhetorical battles to be waged for the introduction of technology.

Three years after the Council of Ministers requested a report on computer applications, Inspecteur General des Finances Simon Nora[3] and
deputy Alain Minc completed an "exploratory mission aimed at stimulat-
ing thinking on how the computerization of society should be carried out"
and submitted *L'informatisation de la societe,* (The Computerization of
Society) to President Valery Giscard D'Estaing (Nora & Minc, 1978, p.
xviii). As this implies, the goal of computerizing had been accepted by the
French elites; the task at hand was to delineate the implementation
program.

Hyperbolic public promotion aided in this endeavor: for the first time in
the history of the government printing house, Documentation Française, a
matter-of-fact report became a best-seller. As Marchand notes (reversing
the logic of generation of these ideas from elites to the general public):
"conditions were therefore favorable; political decision-makers could not
resist the goundswell of modernism reflected in the report"[4] (1988, p. 33).
Moreover, telematics won approval as an answer to the ficticious threat of

IBM's expansionism. Bell notes how the coinage of the neologism "telematique" crystallized the popularity of bold, futuristic prose calling for a national policy for new technologies.

Rhetorical and Public Needs

One key function of Nora-Minc was to elaborate the agenda for public debate over new technologies. It began with an attack on France's *societe bloquee*, its bureaucracy-choked, politically rigid centralized authorities. Calling forth an alternative set of symbols, Nora-Minc likened the interconnection of information technologies to "an alteration in the entire nervous system of social organization," as mass computerization became "as indispensable to society as electricity" (1978, p. 3). This image reveals the contradictory forces of technology deployment: Minitel allegedly offers a more efficient conduit than bureaucratic channels, yet a significant state role is retained in constituting social structures (beyond pedagogical responsibilities). Thus, information (and the technologies of its access) are only available as a function of state largesse.

Though appeals to flexible systems of bypass were frequent, the metaphor was inconsistent with the centralized organization of computing: "Telematics" they state, "offers varied solutions which can be adapted to all forms of control and regulation." It "finds itself at the heart of the power game through the movement it generates in information networks. It allows the autonomy of basic units, and facilitates decentralization by providing peripheral or isolated units with data from which heretofore only huge central entities could benefit. It influences certain professions by modifying their social status." This said, they add the caveat that it would "be unrealistic to expect computerization to overturn the social structure and the hierarchy of power which governs it" (Nora & Minc, 1978, p. 5). Thus, telematics was not introduced as a revolutionary tool; far from it: it was intended to facilitate extant power.

Elitism is obscured in Nora-Minc's utopian vision of communications evolution, which all but erases the role of the state. The rhetoric also posits telematics as an inevitable development: "once the initial connections are made, the network will spread by osmosis. Users will connect to each other directly; files will accumulate in one place when reason or profit so dictate; the transparency of networks will gradually increase. The computer network will come to resemble the electrical network" (Nora & Minc, 1978, p. 28). Nora-Minc also sought to counteract fears of the reshaping of professional life. As service sector capacity to absorb displaced industrial workers was reached and productivity gains from information technology were expected to displace even more workers, fear of automation exacerbating unemployment problems of the 1970s were soothed by arguments for increased productivity from computerization, in turn bolstering the French economy. Nora-Minc is full of contradictory logic on this point: it recognizes the bureaucratic tendency of French society but rejects strict Japanese planning models by appealing to the French character: "French individualism is an obstacle to the plasticity the (Japanese) project assumes" (1978, p. 50).

The Political Response to Technology Challenges

Through references to Japan and the United States, Nora and Minc express the centrality and global significance of telematics introduction in the move towards a competitive information economy. In calling for deliberate movement towards computerization, they describe the need for vigilance against foreign menace: "the state cannot be the only entity to promote such a policy, however and cannot be allowed to adopt an all-or-nothing position." They discuss the need to "establish a dialogue with IBM," and call upon the state to "perceive and correct the imbalances that computerization can aggravate, and the restrictions and constraints it may generate, and realize the necessary changes without setting off the inflexibility/explosion sequence familiar to our country" (1978, p. 9). Nora and Minc write in response to the symbolic threat of a generalized other, bluntly stating the imperative to shore up French competitiveness:

> Governments have always tended to turn communications into a field of sovereign prerogatives. In the past, the stakes in the computer game were limited—they were commercial, industrial, or military. Now it is drawing society as a whole into its net. To decide on a policy of computerization for society it to prepare for the future. To do so, the challenges of the present must be met in all haste (1978, p. 29, 31).

Thus, telematics leapt from dictionary entry to a map for the battleground of global politics; to cede advantage in technological mastery would seal a nation's fate.[5] The report thus adopts an alarmist tone, arguing for rapid deployment of information technology to secure the edge of computerization for the French economy.

Nora-Minc paints a grim portrait of IBM, AT&T, and other network controllers extending beyond the industrial sphere to participate in global governance. "In effect, it (IBM) has everything it needs to become one of the world's great regulatory systems" (1978, p. 71). The need for coordinated resistance to such firms offers a rationale for state control: "It is not a simple reflex of authority, a state using telematics to shore up its prerogatives. Without control, the state will not overcome the effects of network domination or preserve sufficient freedom for each of the participants'' (1978, p. 73). The image of invading multinational firms sees the presence of network providers in national markets as a loss of communications sovereignty.

While overstating the threat of global competitors, Nora-Minc touted telematics as an omnipotent technological fix. It was not initially seen as a new medium, but as a boost for the electronics industry. Nora-Minc was much criticized for its submission to a crude technological determinism and technocratic approach. Still, in setting the boundaries of discourse, articulating the threat to French sovereignty, and providing a sense of mission for public and industry alike, the report was highly effective rhetoric. It delineated a set of symbols over which the political battles were to be waged: foreign threat, French innovation and the promise of enabling, pluralist technology.

Symbolic Action and Industrial Policy

The Nora-Minc report and subsequent telematics program reveal the politicized nature of European technological deployment. From its birth as a minor element of Nora-Minc, telematics, in the form of Minitel, developed as a high-visibility, high-tech project also providing revenues for the DGT. These were not market-driven, demand-led services. The provision of communications conduits and the information that flowed over them was not a natural development, but a forced industrial policy program. The French commitment to new technologies was based on perceived economic and industrial needs. The resulting *filière electronique* was a politically motivated attempt to give France the veneer of a information society, though the reality would be different for years to come. Ths political reality colors any subsequent interpretations of Minitel user behavior regarding access to information and communications tools.

French telecommunications was accorded lowest priority after World War II and remained poor until the 1980s. A standing joke plaguing the DGT was that half of the country was waiting for a telephone, and the other half was waiting for a dial tone.[6] The subsequent *crise du telephone* was sharply at odds with the society de Gaulle publicly envisioned. France was simply unable to respond to challenges of modern technology and thus exercise a global role. De Gaulle's influence in setting a symbolic stage cannot be underestimated.[7] One of his persistent legacies was an impatient desire for French world eminence through innovation, a quasi-religious crusade seized upon by the Socialists, pushing Minitel as one of the "new cathedrals." The welding of polar opposites in de Gaulle's rhetoric was replicated in the Minitel debate, where enthusiasts and technophobes agreed on a common set of distinctively French goals.

The events of 1968 dramatically highlighted the need to adapt the social infrastructure to a rapidly changing economy (Hoffman, 1974, p. 209). Starting with the VIth Plan in 1971, the visibility of telecommunications increased, and network modernization became a Priority Action Programme in the VIIth Plan of 1974. From 1967 to 1978, the PTT gradually won financial and political commitments and administrative reforms which increased its powers. Investments increased rapidly and a coherent structure emerged in French telecommunications through industrial policy plans for nationalized firms such as Thomson, CIT-Alcatel, and ITT.

Once the French network showed signs of improvement, the Socialists adopted high-technology as imperative; telematics was incorporated into the Socialist *vision* of a high-tech France (Epstein, 1986, p. 48). After France established the information distribution channels it desperately needed, it faced the need to generate traffic on its modern network. Moreover, basic telephony neared a saturation point in the early 1980s. Thus new services were needed to offset the massive cost of network upgrades. Minitel fit this bill. It first provided a source of traffic (and revenues) on the expanding telecommunications network. Also, network growth worsened problems with the atrocious directory service and out-of-date paper directories. The cost of electronic updates proved far cheaper than repeated printings of paper directories. Minitel thus had a stable platform of services on which to operate. Since France built from the ground up and had little outmoded plant to be integrated in its network, the French PTT deployed advanced digital technology in its modernization program.

Moreover, Minitel had been in the works before it was elevated to symbolic status in the service of politics. During the 1970s, the French telecommunications administration, the Direction Générale des Télécommunications (DGT) and its research labs, the Centre Nationale des Etudes Télécommunications (CNET) investigated the use of television sets for data and text services. After the 1976 call for the Nora-Minc report and prodding by British videotex advances, the DGT adopted a coordinated videotex initiative. Videotex development therefore must not be seen in a vacuum; Minitel (first dubbed Antiope) was (1) a direct reaction to the United Kingdom's Prestel (and sought to block Prestel from becoming the de facto world standard); and (2) aimed at boosting French equipment firms to the forefront of global markets.

PTT Minister Gerard Théry was well aware of his dominant role in the marketplace: the lesson of the French experience is that the very nature of the PTT monopoly distorts signals from the market which guide oligopolistic or competitive actors. Théry's PTT dominated the *filière electronique*, vertically integrating its activities into software, hardware, and distribution channels. As inventors of videotex hard- and software, the French pursuit of domestic and foreign markets followed a path regardless of the communication or information needs of the public.

The Need for Dissent

The institutional midwifery that delivered Minitel also brought a need to create and manage dissent, to present the illusion of public participation in technology deployment. The publicity surrounding Nora-Minc stressed egalitarian principles, requiring that the public be informed of policies. A week of seminars about computers and society drew large audiences (Durand, 1983, p. 151). Meanwhile, the tonal urgency of the international threat justified the program's existence and provided a foundation for its symbols. This was a rhetoric that proved highly effective: for example, academic discourse on Minitel has rarely been critical[8] while the press has focused on the need for Minitel services to offset foreign and domestic threats. The latter threat invoked Orwellian fears of technology, a spectre raised in Nora-Minc: "the computer and the card file have assumed a symbolical value that crystallizes allergic reactions to modern life" (1978, p. 65). While Nora-Minc demands that the public be made aware of the risks involved, "public authorities must avoid responding to fears concerning civil liberties by blocking efficiency" (1978, p. 64). Minitel overcomes these fears by serving as a modern alternative conduit for communications; the French PTT publicized the use of Minitel bulletin boards as an organizational tool in the French student protests of 1986.

In outlining telematics policy goals, Nora-Minc weighed heavily on the side of the citizen, obscuring the political realm of control: "The pressure in the direction of structured, centralizing networks is so strong that it is necessary to counteract it. Some people claim that the government engages in a discriminatory policy by favoring decentralized small scale computerization. Yet it is the only way of maintaining some degree of autonomy and responsibility for the weakest actors on the social stage" (1978, p. 67). The dangers of providing society with computing power were judged minimal, indeed necessary: "If society is sufficiently democratic to allow the emergence of counterforces, if it is sufficiently mobile to organize the fight against the 'new delinquency' that may come into being as a result of computer techniques, the risk is not one of openness" (1978, p. 66). This outward openness was trumpeted as protecting the liberty of all versus the threat of concealed elite power. In reality, it provides little more than slightly enhanced communications capabilities to would-be revolutionaries.

In support of these ostensible state attempts to establish "an acceptable balance" among economic and social rivalries, Nora-Minc links telematics to other powerful symbolic forces: "Some organizations are the bearers of an eschatology that ceaselessly tries to rearrange its operative machinery, for example the Catholic Church or the Communist International. Today each is experiencing the difficulties of this constant hubbub" (Nora & Minc, 1978, p. 72). This provides further rationale for state mediation of technology development, equating computerization with political (and religious) symbolic imperatives.

Managing the Press

Following the 1981 Socialist victory, new DGT Minister Jacques Dondoux was confronted with broad resistance to the videotex policy. The press, for example, was reeling from the arrival of satellites, increased television outlets and tax code revisions. Minitel was viewed as another threat around which a "radical defiance" movement was formed, uniting leading newspapers across France in opposition. Their expressed fears (as opposed to the unspoken issue of lost advertising revenues) centered on a popular theme, as noted in the journal *Telequal:* "Whoever controls the telephone is powerful. Whoever controls the telephone and the TV is very powerful. Whoever should one day control the telephone, TV, and computer would be as powerful as God the Father" (Suffert, 1979, p. 12). Big Brother was thus called forth to protect newspapers; eventually the press won guarantees of privileged status on the system. The switch of the electronic directory service to a voluntary and the early deployment of an exclusive system to politicians were similarly attempts to defuse opposition to the DGT's technocratic moves. This opposition was subsequently incorporated in a large trial in Vélizy, a Paris suburb. The DGT subsidized press applications to encourage development of the Teletel videotex service, and set rates through an advantageous "Kiosk" system. The DGT also situated its goals within a broader rhetoric, heralding each numerical milestone (a million terminals, 1000 service providers, etc.) as the ultimate determinant of French success.

Epstein unwittingly alludes to the state's management of dissent (and ultimately consent) over videotex in the internalization of the popular belief in its profitability; "With the medium's financial potential well established, the newspapers are now among its staunchest supporters. Says Manuel Lucbert, a reporter for *Le Monde:* "We don't write much about Minitel anymore. It is now a secure thing. It is not news anymore.

Videotex has become very fashionable for us" (Epstein, 1986, p. 49). Moreover, with direct economic competition to classified advertising revenues removed, it was difficult for the press to remain critical of Minitel, since the reasons for implementing the French videotex system were either intangible (i.e., largely symbolic) or long-range in nature (e.g., increasing the computer literacy of the French population and creating an export industry). Such ambiguity sealed Minitel's symbolic success and complicated evaluations of the initiative. Evaluation was, (and remains) further compounded by the fact that "the data by which any such assessment would be made are controlled by the promoters of the system"[9] (Mayer, 1988, p. 63).

Early Trials and Technophobias

The Vélizy trial was rich with political overtones; on one front, the French were desperate not to cede the world videotex market to the rapidly developing Prestel system. This was also the world's first large-scale trial, requiring the "commitment and voluteerism" of local entrepreneurs. Moreover, there were numerous technical hurdles: commands, service design, terminal ergonomics and production and instruction in service use. Of the trial, Marchand writes "a premium was placed on educating consumers . . . five years earlier those who had used a microcomputer were few and far between" (Marchand, 1988, p. 69). This statement again buries the fact of the French failure in generating a domestic personal computer industry.

The task of developing usage of Minitel as a communications and information access tool were clearly on the minds of political officials. PTT Minister Louis Mexandeau stated at Vélizy that "a first-class technological success should be matched by its successful insertion into society." Throughout the trials, the service was emphasized as merely evolutionary, not revolutionary. An example of this emphasis noted: "Banking with Teletel Videotex is *"a natural extension of a bank's existing computerized environment."* Fundamental communications skills were touted as the system's building blocks: "Anybody who understands French and has ever pecked at a typewriter or an adding machine can use it [Minitel]" (Intelmatique, 1983, p. 3). Marchand describes this marketing effort, "from something forced on people, Minitel became an object of desire" (Marchand, 1988, p. 77).

The 1982 Group of Seven summit at Versailles offered Mitterrand a unique public relations opportunity to showcase French prowess. Technology was a main theme of talks among the nations; all had public or private videotex projects in the planning stages, but none as advanced as France's.

The juxtaposition of *ancien* French splendor and modern French technology was presented as proof that France had shed its low-tech image. The press, its concessions as privileged information providers secure, chimed in with headlines such as "Magic Slates for the Princes" and "Electronic Orgy at the Palace."

Still, Minitel's elevation to an object of desire required changes in user behavior as well as extensive public relations efforts. Ultimately, human operators were employed to entice new users and guide them through the system (Kramer, 1991). The 1983 Grenoble trials offered *telematique de relais* of mediated videotex ("Minitel with a human face"), combining database access with operators for state administrative contacts. Human interaction went further than was expected as the discovery of hackers and software piracy by entrepreneur Michael Landaret led to the "Gretel" bulletin-board, the first *"messagerie."* While utilitarian behavior among users was discovered at Vélizy, the trial was called "suffocating" compared with the enthusiasm sparked by conversation service" (Charon, 1988, p. 313).

This enthusiasm must not be inflated beyond its significance. Communication is typically a simpler process than accessing information. Such was certainly the case with Minitel, where interpersonal communications required only knowledge of two commands in addition to typing skills. Access to the information in remote databases, such as financial data, weather reports or news was often more complicated (not to mention more costly, which dissuaded users from trying the services), and greatly limited in the depth of available information. No database held the equivalent content as a daily version of *Le Monde* or *Le Figaro,* and the time for accessing information was far greater over Minitel than through user-friendly media such as newspapers. Successful applications of videotex consistently revolve around the user-friendliness of interfaces, as seen with the use of touch-screens in malls, hotel and supermarkets; automated teller machines and the success of the elegant Apple computer interfaces.

Marketing Minitel

Télétel Director Jean-Paul Maury writes that from 1983 to 1985 (in classic "let a thousand terminals bloom" rhetoric): "a technological innovation flowered into an established means of communications" (Maury, 1986, p. 1). Still, the French felt a compelling need to convince others that Minitel had "acquired a life of its own" (Intermedia, 1985). The first president of Intelmatique, a U.S. sales outlet for Minitel terminals and services, cautiously recalibrates the terms of success to vindicate the

French: "Many things have been said or written about videotex. However, very few people have managed to stand aloof from old concepts and definitions, whether in the technical or marketing fields" (Nahon, 1985, p. 10).

To foster its use, the rhetoric surrounding Minitel went from elite (oriented towards information) to public (stressing the enabling power of communications). France celebrated media-savvy videotex entrepreneurs such as Daniel Populus, who assembled the user-driven Claire system, Maurice Jeanneau, who sought to demystify the aggravating French bureaucracy by placing state records on the Telem system in Nantes, and Landaret's messaging services. What prompted the subsequent fascination with *messagerie*, especially given the state's reticence to promote them? Minitel publicist Marchand reveals a key focus in the relation between information and communications in arguing that it was "nothing more than the opportunity to communicate. But communication of a third kind: anonymous, instantaneous, fleeting. . . . Trifles to be sure. Nothing earthshaking, as "earnest" people pointed out. Identity games, asserted sociologists." (Marchand, 1988, p. 90). The system was driven by much the same forces as drove the introduction of the telephone, basic access to timely information and communications capacity at distance insensitive tariffs.[10] The process was further aided by the lack of computerization, both in business and within the telephone network. While U.S. suppliers require customers to interconnect with its computers or use its audiotex system to order goods, the French had only the Minitel system to rely upon. Nevertheless, of these pioneers, Marchand gushes: "What gusto! The energy, vitality, grit, and entrepreneurial capacity of the pioneers of consumer videotex are truly awe-inspiring" (1988, p. 101).

One reason (glossed over by Marchand) for the unique ability of the French to pursue Minitel was that the initial project, with the compulsory Minitel terminal, presented almost a caricature of the public monopoly, able to enforce a particular mode of behavior on the citizen. System centralization by virtue of the DGT monopoly also allowed the French to impose standards in technical and most importantly behavioral terms. The DGT established the "look and feel" of electronic directory services, and in turn, for all equipment, screen design, and commands, as well as the parameters of service operation. Moreover, the staggering cost of the Minitel program could not have been borne by entrepreneurs like Landaret, and costs remained "hidden" in telephone subscriber's bills: the Kiosk billing system did not separate Teletel services from regular phone usage on the monthly bill. Even in 1990, "one never knows exactly how much the actual Teletel bill is" (Minitel USA, 1990, communication).[11]

Towards Mass Market Status

Although Minitel was launched amidst great fanfare, the service faced a tentative consumer base. The political imperative thus turned from technological—the introduction of the service—to social and economic—its spread through French culture and establishment as a viable institution. When initial demand was under a half-hour monthly, the DGT encouraged usage by generous subsidized rates, no subscription costs, free terminals, and incentives to service providers. The net of symbols was woven larger, as cultural promotion was added to the technical state propaganda; for example, a January 1985 one-hour television show on the main state-run channel entitled *"Minitel mon amour"* publicized the erotic nature of messagerie services on Gretel. Services such as Sextel, Ludotel and Jane soon followed.

The Economist points out the ironic popular image of Minitel as an erotic service, as well as the facts: "Minitel would not be the first French business that lived off sex. In fact, it does not: agreed, the sex services helped get Minitel free publicity, but more humdrum household usage is growing at the expense of games and videosex"[12] (1989, 74). Charon argues that market forces now dictate videotex content: information providers must cut prices to win over and keep telematics public, offer basic services that are cheap to operate and attract a jaded public's attention (1987, 328). While the operator of the "Fantasm" messagerie defends his livelihood as a struggle against the anomie of big-city life, Charon claims that Minitel "only modestly enriches the palette of communications." Still, many accept hype for reality. One consulting firm argues "chatlines are the product that drive all other services. The basic premise holds that consumers use the Minitel as a screen-based telephone, to communicate with other people, not retrieve information" (Jupiter, 1989, 1).

Patterns of Minitel Use

Given the elitist character of the system and the political nature of its growth, what sort of user behavior did the Minitel system elicit? Well, by and large, it elicited little behavior at all. While Minitel use for information gathering and access is greater than for communications, both of these (overlapping) services must be placed in the context of the systems limited reach and impact. The primary fact of Minitel usage is its under-use. As table 22.1 shows, over half of France's 5.5 million terminals are essentially unused. Recent cost reports are less than optimistic about reliance of Minitel services upon consumers; of all individuals with Minitels, 50 percent are classified by France Télécom as non-users; another 20 percent

TABLE 22.1
Frequency and Typology of Minitel Usage

No Use	20.0%
Little (< 3x/month)	30.5
Moderate (1-5x/week)	27.0
Intensive (> 1x/day)	22.5
Young Urban Executives	17 %
Youngsters	14
Working Women from the Upper Middle Class	11
Business Users	10
Retired Users	9

Source: France Télécom, 1990; Arnal, 1990

use them only for accessing the electronic directory service (EDS). Among users, only 34 percent accessed more than one service, and 15 percent (under 1 million users) had used three or more services (Arnal, 1990).

The institutional history of Minitel however, appears determined to present the system as the opposite of an elite tool, user surveys to the contrary: "Callers need not identify themselves, need not present any credentials. Everything is within Everyman's grasp in the loosely defined realm of videotex, where the clever or the curious may discover the latest unexpected service" (Marchand, 1988, p. 10). Ths egalitarian image of Minitel use is contradicted by the typology of residential Minitel users; a strong class-structural logic underpins the distribution and use of terminals (see table 21.1). Blue-collar workers accounted for only 5 percent of home use, while white-collar workers, middle managers and top executives comprised 58 percent. (Teletel Newsletter, 1988) Business use was similarly concentrated among executives (41 percent and middle managers (24 percent). By 1989, only 10 percent of blue-collar workers had access to a Minitel, compared with 45 percent of senior executives. France Télécom identified the average user as under forty, professional, married with children (Dupagne, 1990). Among business users, functionalism defined behavior: a 1989 France Télécom survey identified lower costs (19 percent) and faster transmission rates (15 percent) as the most desired improvements (France Télécom, 1989a).

Elitism is also reflected in the target audience for new technologies, driven by advertisers' and marketers' desires for new outlets. In a study of innovative French consumers, Perin (1989) notes disparities between leading edge, elite ("precursor") populations, and average consumers. In 1987, only 19 percent of the French had phones, televisions, stereos and another appliance, as opposed to 60 percent of precursors. Leading edge consumers, already more likely to be elites, were further privileged with early access to the videotex technologies they devised and fostered, and for whom the symbol of potential access to information was most resonant.

In 1990, France Télécom admitted that "in-depth integration of videotex still seems in the hands of a group of precursors" and even more startling that "many services are not relevant to a large part of the population." Not surprisingly, Minitel users were spatially concentrated as well. In 1989 the greatest penetration of terminals was in the Ile de France district containing Paris, where 21.6 percent of telephone subscribers had access to a Minitel. Twenty-five percent of Minitel terminals were located in the Paris district, while penetration (a fact of state distribution programs as well as consumer demand) in rural areas was negligible (Teletel Newsletter, 1989, p. 4).

Many reasons may explain this bias. One is that the elites have the disposable income to spend on Minitel services, or information in general. They also have a greater demand for travel, financial and product information, as well as news. They are also more likely to be habitual users of technology in the workplace (a key determinant of home use) as well as in the home. Moreover, they are likely to have the background to rapidly adopt new modes of communications, especially those that have been vested with a status advantage over traditional media, such as cellular telephony, paging services, and electronic mail. Variants of these forms of communications, such as specialized databases or newsletters also carry a range of information not available to the non-elite populations.

It took two foreigners, Meier & Bonfadelli, to suggest that new information technologies such as Minitel often "sharpen social inequalities," and point to the government "back-up" research that ensures the role of "the government and state apparatuses [which] expect to strengthen their power and prestige" (1987, 77). In reviewing pilot studies in other nations, they found a fundamental inability to formulate questions regarding demand or realistic services, and the denial of weak social science data by self-interested political and industrial actors (1987, p. 83).

The division of Minitel audiences has other consequences. Guillame argues that Minitel is "creating a "Spectral society" where the individual, protected by the screen and relieved of responsibility by anonymity, can communicate without revealing his or her identity." (Marchand, 1988, p. 141). Minitel also came with its own simple vocabulary: *envoi, messagerie, minitelisier,* etc. (Peterson, 1986, p. 85).

Socialization into this new world came through the innocuous directory services, which Mayer writes "initiates the user, provides immediate positive reinforcement (in most cases), and demonstrates the power of using a computerized database" (Mayer, 1988, p. 61). To this end, France Télécom offered users three minutes of free directory service each month. This reinforcement was needed to overcome user reluctance: French consumers often preferred using paper directories (Dupagne, 1990), which are still requested by 60 percent of Minitel users. The bait-and-switch policy used by the DGT to inculcate users into the Minitel system is reflected in the fact that in user surveys, 92 percent claim to use the directory while no other service earns more than 36 percent. This also confirms the dubious, fragmented nature of demand for Minitel services, either of an information or a communications nature. However, in a nation of little personal computing, Minitel familiarized the French with machine-based interactions and communications.

Ease of use was also emphasized as an egalitarian feature of the system: the Minitel 12 offered in 1989 was advertised as "the perfect communicator" that requires "a single gesture to be on-line" (France Télécom, 1989c).[13] This attribute allows a nonthreatening personal side in simple "grass-roots" technology. For example, Marchand promotes the glossy, high-tech image of Minitel, but calls attention to the necessary human dimension of on-line hosts, system monitors who channel and mediate traffic.

> A phalanx of new professionals has penetrated to the heart of the communications network and information systems. They aim to make communications less intangible, less artificial, but also to facilitate it and mesh it with the desires and needs of those who call in. . . . Enter the on-line network hosts, who are there to see that callers find what they are looking for: pleasure, assistance adventure, company or a simple piece of information. (1988, p. 170)

What Marchand neglects to mention is the central economic role of the hosts; by keeping system users engaged in on-line conversation, they generate revenues for service providers. Moreover, the hosts underscore the fundamental need to manage the communications portion of the service so as to generate usage of the limited group of information services.

Perhaps even the French psyche was ripe for colonization: the managing director of France's largest Teletel service claimed that messaging was "breaking the solitude of the cities, replacing the psychologist and the confessor" (Ricklefs, 1986, p. 31d). Such colonization is nothing if not a boon to the French populace: Marchand's "authorized biography of Minitel" gushes the following paragraph about the electronic directory service:

> There we go again: "a world's first." France was back at it, showing that it could outdo the rest of the world; that come hell or high water it could come up with the boldest technological strategy, that France can go it alone, with no international help; that its engineers are the best, and can accomplish any project, so long as it seems impossible—the more impossible the better. Precisely therein lies their glory—and indeed there was glory to go around, because no one would have bet the farm on the electronic directory. (1988, p. 73)

Her prose reveals the terms of success for judging Minitel as the fulfillment of domestic political goals,

> Once the electronic directory was extended throughout France, outside observers would be lavish with praise. The American press devoted considerable space to this French success story. But the system was not to be sold abroad, good press notwithstanding. After all, have the French ever been interested in the challenge of selling? Had it ever occurred to them that to sell, technological excellence has to be played down, not paraded like the flag? Do they not have a nasty habit of thinking because their products are the best they will be bought? (1988, p. 74)

Although Marchand is hardly an objective student of Minitel,[14] two aspects of her prose underscore deeply embedded political claims. One concerns the need for heroes or figureheads; objects of mass affections and gratitude who offer the citizenry a chance to participate in a Pareto-optimal game. Another is the reflexivity of Marchand's world view, satisfying the nationalistic goals of the Nora-Minc report, which enabled the French state to tap the legacy of independence and Gaullism while submerging the actual failure in exporting Minitel technology, and the program's limited impact upon the French economy.

Symbolic Triumph in Failure

The transformation of the Minitel network failures into successes is most plausible when explained in terms of the public reaction to complex technical discourse. One event is particularly symbolic of this public relations effort: In July of 1985, the DGT announced limitations on videotex traffic due to the crash of the Transpac packet-switched network handling Minitel traffic. This event was trumpeted as an accomplishment;

Minitel "was experiencing a crisis of growth." The network was reopened two weeks later, as "the victim of its own success." This incident paradoxically gave "gratuitous publicity to the program" (Dang-Ngyuen & Arnold, 1986, p. 159).

The Transpac crash also revealed patterns of Minitel use; buildup of traffic at pressure points and erratic connection patterns were unknown before software was developed. The crash provoked Malthusian reforms; services and terminal distribution were slowed, since the cost of adding computers to the Transpac network was great, and the DGT was already committed to the project, the authority adopted a more long-term investment and amortization strategy, aimed at accomplishing slow but steady growth in traffic volume and tariffs.

Most observers overlooked the economics and focused on the crash as a symbol of Minitel's success. "Much of the national videotex framework went down because of overloading. This in turn was caused by genuine attempts to create a user friendly technology capable of being used by a grand mere" (Intermedia, 1985). Perhaps the grossest overstatement (or acceptance of Minitel's ephemeral importance), posits that "much of France's commercial life ground to a halt." Vedel argues that "this incident marked the real take-off of telematics: demand exceeded the network as well as expectations" (1987, p. 18). It is instructive to note the *type* of demand that led to the Transpac failure: sheer volume did not cause it, Minitel calls account for 40 percent of Transpac traffic and only 25 percent of the data transmitted. What failed was the switching capacity, as Minitel users, with a growing awareness of the connection charges and a desire to check several messaging and information services in a single brief session, rapidly shifted from service to service. The failure was actually in the network switching software, which was designed for constant connections between large data banks. A "snowball" effect rippled through the Transpac network, deluging the rerouting system. Ever the propagandist, Marchand calls the crash "a blessing in disguise," and "an extraordinary stroke of luck," which "was so good that it was transformed into a publicity stunt!" (Marchand, 1988, p. 131).

Monopolies and User Behavior

As mentioned above, the centralization of Minitel allowed the DGT to impose operating parameters for the system and to reach specific elite subscriber groups. It also helped the French limited negative discourse about Minitel. Charon, a rare French critic of Minitel, claims "it is a much more disputable a success than many think or others would like us to believe. It is a result of a very voluntarist strategy which is beginning to feel the limits of the model with an artificial and fragile market and speculative profits'' (Markham, 1988, p. D1). Charon alone suggests Minitel is "a failure disguised by the scale of penetration," expressing shock at the lack of critical observations: "it is astonishing how the DGT's partners are unable to evaluate the phenomenon of which they are a part. The only indicators available are quantitative and descriptive. Uncertain of the general public's take-up, the medium's proponents and opponents have been content to base their judgment of its success (or failure) on a *perceived* rate of penetrations and level of use" (Charon, 1987, p. 304).

In addition to forestalling academic criticism, the centralization of the Minitel system can sharply affect service providers.[15] Isolated messaging services are highly dependent upon France Télécom's good graces and required by law to have an operator, who participates in conversations to keep patrons on-line (and paying the fee). Operators cannot risk allowing racy chat: France Télécom proudly notes that services are frequently ousted from the system; the threat of lost access is imminent. Information providers cannot exercise control over business policies and are subject to rulings on tariffs and hardware. Such a dependency exacerbates tensions between service providers and their desire to counter the medium's professional, utilitarian self-image. Services are licensed by the government, which is not legally obligated to permit their existence and takes over half of the revenues they generate. Given this, the potential for subversive, low-cost, or "rogue" services is slim. Nevertheless, the democratizing simplicity of Minitel is continually emphasized as a symbolic of its egalitarian promise. In 1989, France Télécom offered its new Minitel 12 model advertised as "the perfect communicator" requiring only "a single gesture to be on-line" (1989c, p. 2).

In contrast to the progressive mission of computerizing France versus economic foes, an internal Minitel USA document states that Minitel was pressed to combat backwardness:

> Minitel was viewed as an opportunity for technological development. This objective has been achieved through the creation of thousands of PC-based businesses and a videotex (hardware, software, services) industry that sponsors thousands of jobs and entrepreneurial ventures. The government is very pleased with the results achieved by Minitel in terms of economic development, industry jobs and the personal skills development. (Ribb, 1989, p. 3)

Despite these sentiments, Minitel remains a poor substitute for France's weak computer industry, which has been heavily subsidized by the state. Per capita sales of PCs in France are less than half that of the United States; from 1982 to 1989, only 2.5 million computers were sold in a nation of 55 million (< 5 %), while in the same period the U.S. purchased nearly

40 million PCs (> 15%). In this respect, Minitel is simply another part of the French effort to aid its computer industry. Numbers of terminals, at each successive plateau, remain prime indicators of Minitel's success. France Télécom celebrated its 1990 "milestone" by writing that 5 million terminals "reflects the simple success of a phenomenon of society. Today, everyone can see the maturity of the telematics market" (France Télécom, 1990, p. 2).

Technological Dreams, Financial Realities

In the face of sluggish demand, extensive marketing campaigns sought to increase Minitel usage, but to little avail. Even with a yearly subsidy of $800 million from France Télécom, the state accounting watchdog agency, the Cour des Comptes (tr. the Court of Accounts) reported in 1989 that the Minitel system lost $742 million in 1988, projected yearly losses to be down to $574 million in 1995. (However, the analysis did not include Transpac revenues.[16]). At that point, the report suggested overall Minitel deficits would be $1.3bn (Dixon, 1989). "The government auditors say that Minitel is making too flimsy of a return on the FF 8.3bn invested in it up to the end of 1987" (Roussel, 1989b).

The report met with tremendous political resistance: In response to criticism of Minitel's losses, PTT Minister Paul Quiles was quick to reveal the fundamental purpose of the Minitel program: "Teletel is beneficial for other than financial reasons." The Treasury Administration should be "capable of looking beyond the numbers to the benefits the Minitel program brought to the French economy and to the image of French telecoms in the world" (Roussel, 1989a). Quiles' remarks reveal the primarily symbolic nature of Minitel; the state's investment of effort and capital in such high profile programs is not easily relinquished. Viewed as costly public relations, Minitel must explain losses which are double its gross income, a paltry $660 million in 1989.

Supporters insist that "a capital investment project of this scale is commonly profitable in this time period, achieving high profits thereafter" (Ribb, 1989, p. 3). This view assumes accurate France Télécom data for terminal cost recovery by 1995. Of actual and planned Minitel investments of FFr 17 bn from 1984 to 1995, 54 percent goes towards to Minitel, 18 percent to Transpac, 15 percent for additional lines, and 13 percent for the DGT network. Annual investment costs are FFr 1.5 bn ($240 million). At the present use and revenue rates given above, annual system investments per subscriber are FFr 750 ($150), while revenues are only 550 FFr ($90) (Noam, 1991). At that rate, a terminal which cost FFr 2000, would not be repaid in ten, not five years as France Télécom promised.

Certainly counterinstitutional movements are rarely heavily subsidized by the state, as was noted by the Cour des Comptes. Such is the price of fostering a limited amount of social interaction among select households and providing an equally limited information access service to small businesses which cannot afford computerization. If anything, the cost of Minitel has served the state's explicit policy goals as described in the Nora-Minc report, to foster the "informatization" of society and to boost France's image as a competitor in global high-technology markets. A plan to charge for terminals drew sharp protests and cries of imminent demise for the system not from the users, but from the Association Française de Télématique, a trade association composed of software vendors and service providers.

In response to financial critics, France Télécom found a new threat in public opinion: "The savings opportunity (of electronic directory services) was successfully underway when a Socialist government was voted into power. The new government asked that the savings opportunity be forfeited and the hardcopy telephone books remain in print. By choice, the savings opportunity was no longer pursued (Ribb, 1989, p. 2). Such caveats aside, the publicity surrounding the cost of Minitel makes it increasingly difficult for France Télécom to appeal to principles of public service while offering a medium for heavy telephone users. The medium "is based on tariffs that provide for renumeration of the publisher/information provider, included in which is the amortization of a specialized network, which benefits above all business" (Charon, 1987, p. 329). Thus, the revelation of the service's elite character and largely symbolic effect upon French society as a whole has undermined its stated goals, although for long enough to alleviate fears of lost economic sovereignty.

Unintended Consequences in Ancillary Markets

Part of the symbolic challenge of Minitel was ensuring that its users, in a cyclical pattern of social reproduction (de Certeau, 1984) would accept and adopt its high-tech veneer. This image was tarnished by the *messagerie* services. Moreover, the Cour des Comptes raised specific legal concerns over Minitel, stating that "the administration should be careful that it does not find itself in a situation of furnishing the means for activities which might be declared illegal by a criminal judge, for which the Minitel network forms the base." They warned that the Minitel network of erotic and other message services makes the government an unwitting accomplice in criminal acts from which it profits (Tempest, 1989).

Such complaints received additional publicity in a best-seller (Perier, 1989) which described the brutal murder of Paris call girl Anne Trinh, set up through Minitel. (The system was also used to solve the case.) The book led to public outcry and lawsuits from the Federation of French Families (FFF) and the National Federation of Catholic Family Associations (CNAFC) arguing that the potential audience (of children), and government-enforced anonymity make Minitel a safe and effective criminal tool. The plaintiffs claimed to have twenty cases of serious crimes linked to Minitel, stating that "this new technology of communications can be used under the protection of anonymity for pederasts, sadomasochists, prostitutes and why not drug dealers? . . . we just wish the state were not so active in this pursuit, not so directly linked in this activity" (Tempest, 1989).

Fears of censorship allowed the Minitel network to avoid the touchy problem of state-enforce morality, and in turn, avoid revenue loss without the erotic messagerie services. Messaging usage, however, has declined as a percentage of Minitel use since 1988, after passage of a law known as the *code d'onotologie*, under which messaging operators *(animateurs)* were required to warn users "to be polite" after the first lewd sentence and disconnect them after the second. Related legislation placed a 33 percent tax on erotic *messagerie* (Dupagne, 1990, p. 13). Even with the decline (as a percent of total system use), messaging attracted 14–15 million hours per year from 1986–89. In response to the lawsuits France Télécom established a monitoring board which cuts five to ten services per month. "Overt" advertising of pornographic services was banned in a 1989 ruling invoking a centuries-old statute barring "literature that incites the corruption of morals" (Ribb, 1989, p. 3). The main publisher of Minitel magazines, François de Valence, has since refused advertisements from erotic services: "The whole electronic communication world was being corrupted by them; they had developed into a plague." The paradox of that plague is its immense profitability.

Minitel continues to reap its highest yield from "messaging" which accounts for 8 percent of calls and 22 percent of revenues, for use of 19 percent of total Minitel time. (France Télécom, 1989b). The electronic directory is a clear loss-leader, providing just 18 percent of revenue from 33 percent of the calls. (Thomas, 1988) Since, as the Cour des Comptes report notes, the anticipated savings from not having to print paper telephone directories was far less than expected, less than 10 percent of the cost of terminals, the DGT has grown increasing reliant on *messagerie* for generating income. This reliance has not been easily accepted by system planners hoping for more traditional uses: "The vision of a user indulging in play, committed to entertainment, developing social exchange via erotic 'chat,' often provokes discomfort and a violent reaction to these 'ingrates' who 'pervert' and 'dirty' a sophisticated technology by using it this way" (Charon, 1987, p. 313). Charon further describes the "sense of hurt experienced by some engineers" from these "sick sex maniacs. To reassure themselves they suggest that the economics of the medium preclude this state of affairs lasting very long." Public opposition crystallized around this issue: reduced tariffs would make Minitel more available, but price cuts were fought out of a refusal to subsidize "morons whose minds are obsessed with thoughts of how, thanks to Minitel, they will get lucky and score" (Charon, 1987, p. 314).

Symbolic Tourism: Exporting Minitel's Image

Despite Marchand's assertion above that the French are not interested in salesmanship, Minitel has involved a host of international appeals based upon the desire to export French technology. Fostering a successful image of Minitel abroad was crucial to the project's continuation, solidifying agreement with the system's core principles. Minitel had willing proselytizers beyond French borders: one Englishman wrote "Minitel is beginning to look like the prototype of the basic working tool of that much discussed, long expected beast, the information society" (Malik, 1988, p. 26). As early as 1985, Americans had dubbed Minitel "a smashing success" (Page, 1986, p. 45). Minitel was invested abroad with a favored status, beyond reproach; cost data was controlled by the DGT, leaving the main concern in international circles, after accepting the need for such a system, the reason for its absence. Many, such as Epstein, fawned over Minitel's potential: "far more than a consumer toy or a way to meet new lovers, the sophisticated videotex network is a profitable enterprise with virtually unlimited growth potential" (1986, p. 46).

In addition to co-opting the press, the DGT won converts in academia; Professor Daniel Resnick called Minitel "an enormous success, the most promising public experiment using telephone lines around the world" (Epstein, 1986, p. 49). Resnick was also the head of the Centre Mondial, a French-sponsored agency promoting computing around the world, which had close ties to Resnick's university. A French political scientists at the state Centre Nationale de Recherche Scientifique writes that "the French telematics program quickly achieved an astonishing and unique degree of success" (Vedel, 1987, p. 10). Vedel's defense of Minitel downplays the role of the state in implementation: "it would be a mistake to believe that the French videotex plan succeeded because of government subsidization. The DGT acted as a public developer, concerned about getting its investment back and making profits" (1987, p. 2). Vedel calls the DGT's strategy judicious, calling the FFr 2000 cost of terminals marginal compared with the FFr 10000 cost per subscriber for telephone service.

A British journalist was equally sanguine about Minitel: "information services on offer today are as wide as human ingenuity can make them. They include all expected shopping services, public information and time-tabling services, transfers into electronic form from existing media" (Malik, 1988, p. 28). Malik expressed astonishment at the scope of an electronic real estate listing: "it allows the concept of place to be country and no longer simply the town or district covered by the particular advertising medium" (1988, p. 29). To Malik, the French seem to have just discovered national advertising, which indicates that "Minitel is changing the face of France, and will also change that of much of the rest of Europe" (Malik, 1988, p. 29).

The lack of critical distance in academia is seen most strongly in Hart's fawning 1987 review,[17] which begins "The Teletel/Minitel system has been very successful from the start." Hart accepts the DGT's role in compelling usage. "Home consumers were given a further *incentive* to accept the terminal when the DGT announced it would no longer publish a hard-copy version of its telephone directories. Thus, anyone wishing to access the new EDS would have to use a Minitel terminal, either at home or at the nearest post office" (1987, p. 22). These sentences epitomize DGT thinking that "incentives" connote compulsory behavior. This statement includes a glaring logical fallacy: how else could one access the EDS other than through a Minitel?[18] Hart replicates Marchand's effusive optimism: "perhaps the most important success has been in winning over the French public to the idea of using advanced telecommunications technology, reducing the barriers for information technology in French society" (Hart, 1987, p. 25).

Added to the desire for favorable international publicity was the need for additional revenues. Not surprisingly, given French pride in the project, one trade publication writes "the French view the failure [of videotex in other nations] as opportunities to export the Minitel system," (Lynch, 1989). Accordingly, Minitel USA changed its marketing slogan from "Access to Success" (since success was a foregone conclusion) to "Profit from our Experience," stressing the benefits of the system's technology.

The 1989 internationalization of Minitel services over Minitelnet was heavily promoted: "the results obtained by Minitelnet present a promising perspective for the creation of a worldwide videotex network" (Teletel Newsletter, 1989). Reaching many European nations and Japan, Minitelnet generated 30,000 hours of traffic in 1989 (45 percent from Belgian users, 20 percent from the United States and Canada), but this was a paltry .00038 percent of the system total, which itself was a fraction of the world's online database market revenues. The largest service accessed by foreigners was *messagerie* (34 percent) followed by the EDS (24 percent).

The U.S. Minitel Services Company has made French services available over BellSouth, US West, and Southwestern Bell gateways, all of which failed to gain even a handful of subscribers (the total for all RBOC trials was under 20,000 subscribers). The lack of success casts further doubt on France Télécom's hope of exporting French technical prowess, as one journalist writes, "Most countries are resigned to the fact that such a mass market is prohibitively expensive" (Woollacott, 1989).

The U.S. still has its share of optimists (Kramer, 1991). One early convert, *Direct Marketing* publisher Pete Hoke, saw the DGT's disaster as a boon, and in turn reveals the limited skepticism:

> Young people are spending a fortune just to meet and talk with one another regardless of their location in France. Subjects vary from politics, personal problems, or sex and communication often leads to a date for dinner. Certainly we don't need much more evidence that business and the consumer would welcome such a system. So let's get to it (1986, p. 148).

In the following issue, Nahon & Pointeau contradict Hoke's optimism: messaging services are not mentioned once! Clearly reluctant to call greater attention to the embarrassing erotic *messagerie,* they instead focus on infant commercial applications: gleaning market data, retail sales, and the placement of a terminal "somewhere between the VCR and microwave oven." They also inflate official DGT statistics for the U.S. audience, stating that EDS receives 50 percent of Minitel calls, while the DGT places that figure at 33 percent (Nahon & Pointeau, 1987, p. 125; Teletel Newsletter, 1987, p. 11).

The Politics of Information

As economic and social life is increasingly defined through information and communications technologies, it is not surprising that institutions should adopt the rhetoric and symbols of these technologies. In the modern idiom, technological symbols help display competence and command over the exploding global economy. This is consistent with the institutional need for symbol-making that predates the electronic age, solidifying and obfuscating the conditions of empowerment. This process is well documented with respect to technology, from Marxist models of hegemony and false consciousness to Ellul's technique, de Bord's society of the spectacle, Beniger's control revolution and even Bloom's complaints of a befuddled narcissistic citizenry, besieged by technological choice.

The French Minitel project offered a direct avenue for state involvement in the creation and manipulation of a symbol, as well as a new communications technology. It relied upon the threat of a generalized other, and garnered support for a new technology by invoking its democratizing, pluralist bent, the fostering of public empowerment. In reality, deployment was closely controlled by technically competent institutions and elites, despite the vaunted user-friendliness of new technologies. On that note, it is also important to understand that technologies and the symbols they produce are already the products of a narrow elite, consecrated into status by displays of competence at creating and manipulating symbols. This is perhaps best represented by Marxist models of overdetermination that attempt to flesh out the reticulated institutional forms prevading social relations. Another approach is that of cultural anthropologists (and the rare communications scholar) who present the shimmering and contradictory forms of state, capital, and public as they trade the common currency of information (Garnham, 1979; Rose, 1989).

The usage patterns of the Minitel system reveals a manner by which the media of information access and those of communications coexist and enhance one another. Given the limited amount of overal usage that the Minitel system has fostered, it has little value in isolating distinct forms of technology use. However, it is important to recognize the range of forces that constrain and control information through the deployment of access technologies. The political forces that introduced and nurtured the Minitel system into "a phenomenon on society" did so largely in a technological vaccuum. Little consideration was given to the potential users of the system, which may explain its limited impact. The above discussion has therefore stressed that understanding the political and symbolic needs of the state (or corporate actors) in deploying communications technologies must precede discussions of the social use of those technologies, and in turn, any speculation on the indistinct relations between information and communications.

Notes

1. One expression of this technological atomization is offered Andre Gorz: "we may speak of the schizophrenic character of our culture: the more we learn, the more we become helpless, estranged from ourselves and the surrounding world. The knowledge we are fed is so broken up as to keep us in check and under control rather than to enable us to exercise control" (1976, p.64). A further discussion of the dislocative effects of high technology (i.e., the postmodern condition) is seen in Lyotard (1983) and Rose (1989).
2. Webster's defines a talisman as "an object bearing a sign of character . . . (which is) held to act as a charm to avert evil and bring good fortune; something producing magical or miraculous effect."
3. The choice of Simon Nora fit the elite character of French governance. Ten years earlier, Nora prepared a similar report proposing that national industries

play a more integral role in they dynamic economy (Nora, 1967). In 1978 Nora held the top post at the Ministry of Finance after serving as an advisor to Prime Minister Chaban-Damais and as CEO of Hachette, the largest French media firm. He was also a graduate of ENA (as was Minc) a required credential for public service in higher office.

4. Moreover they asked for it. The document's creation followed a similar elite path as its principal authors; the duo "established commissions of experts in which the DGT was very well represented by its engineers. Without a doubt, this presence of the DGT contributed to one of the crucial conclusions of the report: namely, the necessity for the public authorities to take a new interest in the telecommunications sector" (Vedel, 1987, p. 13).

5. These battles were by no means temporary. Thirteen years after Nora-Minc, French Prime Minister Edith Cresson spoke of her nation as being "at war" with Japan and the United States and invoked French sovereignty over its economic future as a defense for state subsidies to its ailing high-tech firms Groupe Bull and Thomson Consumer Electronics. Bull and Thomson had each lost $1 billion in 1990 in markets dominated by Japanese and U.S. firms.

6. One of DGT Director General Gerard Théry's prime obstacles was encouraging the use of the newly deployed network; "he had been seared by the humiliation inflicted on generations of Telecom people by the ever-popular Asnières 22 comedy routine," in which comedian Fernand Raynaud found it was easier to make a call from Paris to the suburb of Asnières by calling through New York City via AT&T long-distance circuits (Marchand, 1988, p.27).

7. De Gaulle's impeccable standards (as France's self-appointed spokesman) allowed him to seize the mantle of leadership; what French citizen could have opposed his grandeur, integrity, and independence? This "cycle of identifications" was further facilitated by de Gaulle's charisma, arrogance, and ability to speak from a position of historical privilege. His "arbitration" principle allowed little argument, and his appeals for growth, religious faith in technological prowess, and missionary zeal on behalf of France were hard to deny, especially given his personal detachment from immediate rewards. Minitel grew out of a fundamentally Gaullist predilection for stagecraft that allowed him to draw from a rich cultural font in crafting exaggerated dramas in starkly contrasting colors. The Minitel project may be defined in rhetorical terms as the deconsecration of content in the face of context in de Gaulle's cultural milieu.

   The importance of de Gaulle to Minitel is twofold: one, a leader such as he could tap into an almost limitless stream of appeals to discover what symbols best support technological and institutional goals. His success stemmed from total immersion in classical French culture from birth. The second vital notion is the ironic dualism of French propensities towards bureaucracy and innovative entrepreneurialism. DeGaulle himself remarked it was impossible to rule a nation with 500 cheeses, yet he managed to do so. Perhaps French society (or all societies) require such self-orchestrated struggles to maintain stability. De Gaulle codified a symbol structure of tremendous resonance within the French policy: his lifelong predilection for stagecraft indirectly infused Minitel with its most dramatic dimensions (Hoffman and Hoffman, 1968).

8. An exensive bibliography (available from the author) gleaned from articles on videotex in Communications Abstracts and from other sources revealed a

veritable paucity of work; only two articles in 1988 and 1989 dealt explicitly with the system, both were fawning, uncritical reviews of its success.

9. Mayer points out how the Department of Programs and Financial Affairs within the DGT consistently forecasts a positive rate of return of state investments, and Intelmatique, the international marketing arm for Minitel offers exaggerated data beyond the domestic claims of the DGT (1988, p.79).

10. There was also a distinct similarity in institutional forces which promoted the technologies of telephony and videotex. Both were introduced under a monopolistic market structure with close ties to the political needs of their home countries.

11. Recently, France Telecom (FT) began to show Minitel charges on their bi-monthly phone bills; although there is a FF10 fee for this service, and usage is only shown by Kiosk level (3615,3616, etc.), not by the individual services which are accessed.

12. The irony of the *Economist* statement is that another prominent technology, the telephone, was also driven early on by sexual uses. Prostitutes in the red-light Bois de Boulogne district in Paris were among the first to make extensive use of the telephone (Pool, 1977).

13. This user-friendliness has also backfired on the DGT, as was the case with the July 1985 Transpac network crash, not from sheer volume (Minitel calls account for 40 percent of Transpac traffic and 25 percent of data transmitted) but from switching failures, as Minitel users were rapidly left one service for another. The software which controlled this switching function was designed for constant connections between large data banks. This example serves to underscore the complexity of developing a mass, rather than targeted computing system, although it may be argued that computational power is most advanced in the United States.

14. Marchand's writes under the aegis of France Télécom. After seven years there, she left to start Telemarket, an on-line grocery shoppig service, stating in her breathless style "when you have written books and papers saying that money can be made on Minitel, you just want to see if you can do it" (Booker, 1988, p. 32).

15. This issue of separation of content and conduit under monopolies is at the heart of an intense legal and regulatory battle in U.S. telecommunications. For a review of the application of Minitel as a model for U.S. information services see Kramer, 1991; copy available upon request.

16. Transpac is another example of technology by government fiat. The world's largest public packet switched network, it is completely isolated by DGT policies from private competitors, who are forced to interconnect their networks with the French public network.

17. Hart's work is crafted from four citations, an obsequious *New York Times* article, two press releases and one French newspaper article, and includes a footnote stating that his data came from an Alcatel sales meeting.

18. Emulation software was first provided only as his article was going to press. Such software has since been a source of great consternation to France Télécom, as it allows user to speed up their access to information through faster presentation graphics, thus reducing online time and system revenues.

References

Arnal, N. (1990). The Residential Users of Teletel in France. International Communications Association Conference, Dublin.

Booker, E. (1990). Vive Le Minitel. *Telephony*. August 8.

Charon, J. -M., (1987). Videotex: From Interaction to Communication. *Media, Culture and Society*, 9 pp. 301-332.

Dang-Ngyuen, G. & Arnold, E. (1986). Videotex: Much ado about nothing. In Margret Sharp (Ed.), *Europe and the new technologies*. Ithaca, NY: Cornell University Press.

de Certeau, M. (1984). *The Practice of Everyday Life*. Berkely, CA: University of California Press.

Dixon, H. (1989). France Hooked on Minitel. *The Financial Times*, December 13.

Dupagne, M. (1990). French and US Videotex: Prospects on the Electronic Directory Service. *Telecommunications Policy*. Dec.

Durand, P. (1983). The Public Service Potential of Videotex and Teletext. *Telecommunications Policy*. June.

The Economist. (1989). High-wired society. August 19.

D'Utilisateurs De Télétel. (1989b). Télétel: French Videotex, Paris: DAII.

D'Utilisateurs De Télétel. (1989c). Minitel 12: Le Parfait Communicateur.

D'Utilisateurs De Télétel. (1990). 5,000,000 de Minitel: La Maturite de Marche de la elematique. Service de Presse.

Ellul, J. (1964). *Technological Society*. New York: Knopf.

Epstein, N. (1986). Et Voila, Le Minitel. *The New York Times*, March 9.

France Télécom. (1989a). 5eme vague D'Enquette Du Panle.

Galbraith, J. K. (1967). *The New Industrial State*. New York: New American Library.

Garnham, N. (1986). Towards a Political Economy of Mass Communications. In R. Collins, et al (Eds.), *Media, Culture and Society*. Beverly Hills, CA: Sage.

Gorz, A. (1976). On the Class Character of Science and Scientists. In S. Rose (Ed.), *The Political Economy of Science*. London: Macmillian.

Hart, J. (1988). The Télétel/Minitel System in France. *Telematics and Informatics*, 5(1).

Hoffman, S. & Hoffman, I. (1968). The Will to Grandeur: de Gaulle as Political Artists. *Daedelus*.

Hoffman, S. (1974). La Drame Derriere le Psychodrame. In *Essais sur la France*. Paris: Sevil.

Hoke, P. (1986). Editorial. *Direct Marketing*. December. Intelmatique. (1983). Bank on Télétel Videotex User's Guide/Promotional Brochure, October.

Intermedia. (1985). Videotex: Take-Off at Last? *Intermedia*, *13*, 6.

Jupiter Communications. (1989). Revenue Streams of Mass Market Videotex, Jan.

Kramer, R. (1991). Misapplying the Model: The French Minitel and U.S. Videotex. Columbia University Institute for Tele-Information, Working Paper #461.

L'Expansion. (1985). La Compagne de France du Micro-ordinateur, Jan.

Lynch, K. (1989). France's Minitel Success Shows up U.S. Videotex Failures. *Communications Week*, December 10.

Lyotard, J. -F. (1984). *The Postmodern Condition: A Report on Knowledge*. Minneapolis: University of Minnesota Press.

Malik, R. (1988). Videotex: France and the Sinews of the Future. *Intermedia*, 16(3).

Marchand, M. (1988). *The Minitel Saga: A French Success Story*. Paris: Librairie Larousse.

Markham, J. (1988). France's Minitel Seeks a Niche. *New York Times*, November 8.

Maury, J. -P. (1986). *Videotex in France*. 1986 Facts and Figures. France Télécom.

Mayer, R. (1988). The growth of the French Videotex system and its implications for consumers. *Journal of Consumer Policy*, *11*(3).

Meier, W. & H. Bonafadelli. (1987). Comparative analysis of Videotex pilot projects in three European countries. *Telematics and Informatics*, *4*(1).

Nahon, G. (1985). The growth of Videotex in France beyond the forecasts. *Videotex International*. Printer, UK: Online Publications.

Nahon, G., & E. Pointeau. (1987). Minitel Videotex in France: What We Have Learned. *Direct Marketing*, January.

Noam, E. (1992). *Telecommunication In Europe*. New York: Oxford University Press.

Nora, S. & Minc, A. (1978). L'infomatisation de la societe. Paris: Documentation Française.

Page, B. (1986). Vive Le Mintel. *CO*, Sept.

Perier, D. (1989). The black file on the Pink Minitel. Paris: J. -C. Lattes.

Perin, P. (1989). Global approach to forecasting demand for new home market. Paper prepared for the International Telecommunications Society Conference.

Peterson, T. (1986). Why the French are in love with Videotex. *Business Week*, January 20.

Ribb, T. (1989). Internal memorandum. Minitel Service Company, October 25.

Ricklefs, R. (1986). French connections. *The Wall Street Journal*, February 24.

Robins, J. & Webster, K. (1986). *Information technology: A luddite analysis*. Norwood, NJ: Ablex.

Rose D. (1989). *Patterns of american culture*. Philadelphia: University of Pennsylvana Press.

Pool, I. (ed.). (1977). *The social impact of the telephone*. Norwood, NJ: Ablex.

Roussel, A. -M. (1989a). French may move to charge for Minitel. *Communications Week International*. January 13.

Roussel, A. -M. (1989b). Woe is Télétel. *Communications Week*, August 10.

Stigler, G. (1971). The Theory of Economic Regulation. *Bell Journal of Economics and Management Science*,*2*(1), 3–21.

Stuffert, G.(tr.).(1979). The match of the century: Teletex vs. paper. *Telequal*, October.

Suleiman, E. (1979). *Elites in French society*. Princeton, NJ: Princeton University Press.

Télétel Newsletter. (1987, Fall). 1987 Minitel statistics: January to June. Paris: France Télécom.

Télétel Newsletter. (1988). Minitel: 1987 Facts and Figures. Paris: France. Télécom. Special Issue No. 10.

Télétel Newsletter. (1989). Minitel: 1989 Facts and Figures. Paris: France Telecom. Special Issue No. 5.

Tempest, R. (1989). Minitel: Miracle or monster? *Los Angeles Times*, October 24.

Thomas, H. (1988). Minitel USA. November.

Vedel, T. (1987). New media politics and policies in France from 1981 to 1986:

What's left? New York: Columbia University Institute for Tele-Information, Working Paper #223.

Woollacott, E. (1990). Small Screen Services. *Communications International*, *February*.

23

Information, Information Society, and Some Marxian Propositions

Klaus Krippendorff

The following is an attempt to place information theory into the larger context of society, particularly into the context of a society that has been called postcapitalist *(Dahrendorf, 1957) and* postindustrial *(Bell, 1973) and is now increasingly referred to by the term* information society. *The idea of identifying current global structural changes, particularly in the United States and Japan, with a shift in the predominant mode of production has not been very popular in the West. Yet it seems to promise to bring into focus, to an extent still unclear, some of the ongoing information-technological developments.*

The idea of explaining structural changes in terms of changes in the mode of production goes back to Karl Marx, of course, who developed this analytical perspective a century ago and from experiences with what he knew best, a society at the beginning of industrialization. Having taken a path not predicted by Marx, the West thought his system to be dead, full of ideology and void of social reality. Surprisingly, the new information technologies, enriched by advanced knowledge of computation, communication theory, systems theory and above all cybernetics, force us back to reconsider Marx's level of analysis and its sociopolitical implications.

The scope of this paper is large compared with the space available here. This favors a style of presentation that is schematic, definitional, and propositional leaving many details undeveloped. Perhaps further discussion and subsequent work will bridge the gap that will remain open.

I will start with a notion of information that has the dynamic qualities required for understanding structural changes, define it, place it into alternative paradigms, and elaborate some of its properties. The notion of information society will be sketched in terms of employment, in terms of the development of information technology and in terms of modern corporate forms of organization. In this analysis, information turns out to be a meta-economic currency. This leads to several propositions that I believe extend Marxian ideas so that they may be applicable to the social dynamics presumably underlying the emergent information society.

Information

Definition

Elsewhere, I identified information with the organizational work a message enables its receiver to perform.

By organizational work I mean arranging things, imposing a particular pattern on a situation or constructing something new from otherwise organized parts. Information connotes the dual meaning of "bringing something into form" and of "forming something from within." Both are intended in our definition. Both imply a process. In Shannon and Weaver's (1949) original formulation, information is seen as the difference between two states of uncertainty, the uncertainty before or without knowledge of a message and the uncertainty after receipt or with knowledge of that message. The reduction of uncertainty is but a simple kind of "organizational work" that takes place in the mind of a receiver. Their theory turns out to be not powerful enough to explain the kind of information processes ongoing in society, even so, "making a difference" is the minimal evidence for organizational work.

Accordingly, a computer program informs a general purpose computer by "wiring" it to perform a desired task. A blueprint informs a group of diverse construction workers to get organized such that a building is assembled from available materials. A command informs a military unit by directing its deployment. And genetic material informs the embryonic form of an organism by specifying that organism's growth.

These examples show that the term receiver must be understood quite generally. It applies not only to a single human being but also to a machine, a social group, or a biological organism. Similarly, the term, "message" is intended to denote any arrangement of physical markers in a medium, whether these are holes punched into a Hollerith card, characters printed on paper, waves of sound or chemical compositions of DNA. To perform organizational work a message must be put into a context (a receiver) consisting of rearrangeable parts or building blocks and the arrangement that emerges must not be explainable without reference to the pattern (message) initiating the process. It is also important that the energy required to perform the organizational work is not supplied with the physical markers initiating the process. Reading a message neither "empties its content" nor destroys its "container" and this container metaphor is not only inappropriate but also distracts from the generality of the notion of information.

Defined in terms of organizational work, information displays some analogy to energy which is the classical measure of work in physics. In both cases, we must distinguish between its *potential* and its *actual use*. A gallon of gasoline has potential energy that is consumed in the mechanical work of driving a car. A book has potential information that may become empirically manifest when it yields practical results (from changing someone's mind to restructuring a portion of social reality). A library is a storehouse of potential information. Both concepts are also defined in context. The measure of potential energy is expressed relative to a level of entropy in the surroundings of the object measured. As this level increases, potential energy erodes. Similarly does information become powerless as the organizational work it specifies is already performed. Ignoring psychology, saying something twice is simply redundant. In the absence of the material entities that a certain message could help rearranging or transforming, the potential information cannot be utilized.

The important difference between information and energy lies in their level of description. Information is *a property of pattern,* arrangement, structure, and so on, *not of matter*. The possibility of coding information, for example, from my voice to the electrical impulses generated in a microphone to the mechanical movements of a stylus in the grooves of a record, makes different media carry the same kind of information. Although information unquestionably requires some material form to be transmitted, stored, or used, this *materiality is irrelevant* to the organizational work it is capable of. Energy, on the other hand, is *a property of matter*. The modulations of the flow of energy, the arrangement of physical markers carried by a medium, all of which have the potential of carrying information, do not enter the measure of energy but may enter the measure of information. When we say that a tank of hot water has the same potential energy as a wax candle, we compare two material forms. When we say that one message can carry the same information as another message, we compare two patterns regardless of their material forms. *The organizational work information is capable of is one level removed from the mechanical work energy is capable of.*

There are several common confusions I wish to prevent here. First is the confusion of information with *data*. Data, a collection of facts, recorded observations for instance, may or may not convey information depending on whether they are or are not capable of reorganizing the context in which they are placed. Many data never pass the stage of a check mark on a piece of paper. It is only when they start to support a theory, change a course of action, or lead to policy recommendations that they can be said to convey information. Otherwise they are just collections of markers manifesting patterns, perhaps, but without organizational consequences.

Second is the confusion of information with *knowledge*. Knowledge is partly derived from interpreting observational data and partly created in the mind of an observer or by communicating within a community of observers. All three parts make knowledge indigenous to and a construction by an observing system. Knowledge can become information if it is communicated, written down, expressed. The library stores only potential information and makes it available to a community of interested readers. It will become used information only when it does something, when it is applied at least to a reader's mind but more particularly when it organizes something outside that reader, when an idea is put to work whether it helps designing a machine, changing a practice, organizing a group or making better management decisions. The kind of knowledge that is purely appreciative, self-satisfying, a value in itself—which has been part of Western liberal ideology since the period of the Enlightment, however important it may be individually—this kind of knowledge does not support any work and is not to be equated with information. The closest characterization of information in terms of knowledge is that it is *"know-how"* not "know-what," not "know-why" and not "know-what-for."

Third is the confusion of information with *neg-entropy*. Neg-entropy makes reference to the second law of thermodynamics according to which entropy always increases, patterns found in nature generally degrade and orderliness necessarily diminishes in the world. In contrast, the whole evolutionary history on earth depicts living organisms as increasing their own complexity, creating pattern in their environment where there were none before and thus increasing orderliness in the world. The increasing sophistication in agriculture, technology, and government is cited as evidence of man's counterentropic intelligence. This observational fact has lead a good many thinkers to jump to the biocentric conclusion that life contradicts the entropy law with information being the agent that reverses the natural trend toward increasing entropy. Since Prigorgine (1980) we know that all of these supposedly counterentropic tendencies are natural and not in violation of the entropy laws. Since Maturana (1970) and von Foerster (1981) we know the increasing orderliness to be a property of the cognition by an observer or by a community of observers who impose their construction of the world onto their environment including onto themselves. Information measures this organizational effort but is not necessarily directed against nature. To take a complex system into parts may take as much organizational skills as assembling it. Both rearrange something and use information.

Fourth is the confusion of information with *symbolism*. To be sure, anything placed in a context may acquire meaning by interacting with it, and defining the context for a given message delineates how this message is to be interpreted, what it means. Information could be said to bestow a particular meaning to a message that focuses attention not on a static and socially constructed relationship between signs and their referents but on its dynamic consequences, on the behavior it sets in motion. Symbols may convey information because of this vicarious and largely conventional relationship but their information value is contextually bound. The information conveyed by symbols wears out by repetition (satiation), becomes redundant after they have done their "work" or remains mere potential when the surrounding conditions are insufficient to support the organizational work possible. The information content of symbols is different from the semantic relationship that gave rise to it.

Finally, there is the somewhat less problematic confusion between information and communication. (Note Shannon and Weaver's now-called "information theory" was published in 1949 as *The Mathematical Theory of Communication!*) Processes that involve a mere one-to-one relationship between signals sent and signals received, telephone communication and Xerographic duplication, for example, reproduce an original pattern at a distant location and thus retain the potential information in the original. The channel accomplishing this is actually immune to, unaffected by and ignorant of the sequentially coded and transformed patterns and might be said to transmit signals. The full power of the idea of communication as transmission of information becomes apparant when organizational work (yielding patterns, structure) in one system causes or influences the organizational work done in another system. Such a "channel" may have to "understand" some of the information involved and may require human beings or intelligent mechanisms of vastly different complexity than displayed by a telephone line.

Although I will say more about information, the fact that the concept is not tied to a particular materiality does not make it subjective, idealistic, or void of reality. As a measure of organizational work, it describes an important intellectual activity in the real world which, I contend, has considerable social implications.

Diverging Paradigms for Information

Information has not always been defined so generally. For example, by emphasizing "facts," "news value," and "social responsibility," journalism links information to some concept of truth and to a professional ethic about which consensus must exist, at least in that profession. What is not always recognized is that this consensus is not an isolated phenomenon. It is regulated by stable institutional configurations and supported by a much larger paradigm that prescribes a particular ontology (what exists), a logic (an appropriate pattern of reasoning), a notion of causality, and so on, all of which are tied to the concept of a particular society and to the role of the individual within it. Information is just one part of it and it is useful to sketch some of the basic paradigms to see what information does within them.

Maruyama (1974) describes four alternative paradigms, each of which subsumes and distinguishes among a good many approaches to theory and practice. Paradigms of this kind serve to highlight conceptual differences and to accentuate what goes together. The reality we live in might not make such sharp distinctions. In table 23.1, I am using Maruyama's terms rather liberally, primarily to compare different notions of information with. For lack of space, I will "read" and comment only on the left column and the last row hoping that the remainder of the table is self-explanatory.

Accordingly, the journalistic conception of information might belong to his *hierarchical* type which has its roots, as the name suggests, in hierarchical forms of organizations whose overriding purpose is superior to or outside the reach of its members. In the extreme, this paradigm incorporates notions of a linear causality that is ultimately traceable to a prime mover, a god, an unquestioned authority, or a universal principle to which everyone is subjected to. In this paradigm, the dominant philosophy is absolutism, universalism, holism, organicism, or various forms thereof. It favors deductive axiomatic and theological patterns of reasoning, deriving true statements from axioms or particular purposes from general goals or from universal principles. Truth must be sought. Information is *absolute* and works unidirectionally to narrow the gap between ignorance and (a typically single) truth. The extreme form of such an organization is found in the Catholic church but it is also present in most rational forms of

TABLE 23.1
Four Paradigms for Information

	Hierarchical	Isolationistic	Homeostatic	Morphogenetic
Ontology of organization	Parts are subordinate to the whole. Stable hierarchical organization of categories.	Whole is fictional or subordinate to its parts. Aggregation.	Existing parts interact. Behavior converges towards an equilibrium and a stable pattern of relationships.	Parts interactively define their own organization, co-produce other parts including those producing them.
Causality	Linear causality ultimately traceable to a prime mover.	Non-causal. Synchronicity.	Circular causality. Negative feedback = deviation counteracting and converging. (Positive feedback is destructive and undesirable).	Self-referential (circular) dependencies and interactions creative of new forms (positive feedback) but also of closed realities.
Logic Pattern of reasoning	Deductive, axiomatic, theological.	Distributive, statistical.	Teleological, operational	Circular, computational.
Philosophy	Absolutism, holism.	Pluralism	Equilibrial Systems	Constructivist epistemology
Individual values	Fulfilling overall objectives, duty.	Achieving individuality, self-realization, independence.	Achieving equilibrium, balance, harmony in interaction with others.	Maintaining local autonomy while creatively participating through interaction in other autonomous organizations.
Primary stimulus of social development	Deviations from principles. Obstacles to reaching goal. Problems.	Similarity or uniformity of individuals. Social entropy.	Inequalities in power, preferences and access to material resources. Social differences.	Multi-lectical (including di-alectical) contradictions, conflicts, paradoxes.
Information = ability to perform intellectual-organizational work	Narrows the gap between ignorance and the (single) truth. Solves problems. Is absolute.	Achieves individuality, distinction, differentiation. Is subjective.	Reduces uncertainty, exhausts uncommitted variety, achieves (mutual) control and stability. Is contextual.	Increases organizational diversity while synthesising higher forms of organizational closure. Is in-formative.

organization; for example, advertising agencies, which measure information by the degree to which it yields desired results.

In an *isolationist* paradigm, information is *subjective*. Individuals interpret messages in their own way and as there is complete tolerance for individual differences, a communication problem hardly arises. Such individuals use information to achieve individuality, self-realization, distinction, and individual differentiation.

Within a *homeostatic* paradigm, whose dominant feature is the interaction among existing components, information is at once contextual and constraining. It is *contextual* in the sense that messages are interpreted in the context of other messages and in the context of communicative exchanges and it is *constraining* in the sense that the receipt of such messages has the effect of reducing uncertainty (e.g., in the mind of a receiver), eliminating alternatives (e.g., in decision-making situations), exhausting uncommitted variety (e.g., in a social group that is instructed to perform a certain task), control (e.g., making someone do something he would not otherwise do) and coordinates (e.g., correlating otherwise uncorrelated or independent parts of a system). Shannon and Weaver's (1949) information theory formalizes this interpretation. Naturally, the theory is unable to consider what is alien to this paradigm: (a) the production of new components, the creation of new information, the invention of more powerful alternatives, the synthesis of dialectical opposites; and (b) the unequal significance associated with information (in Shannon's sense). It measures the extent to which a message enables its receiver to achieve an equilibirum, balance, or harmony, sometimes even if he does not desire it.

Although circular causality is common to the homeostatic and to the *morphogenetic* paradigm, the morphogenetic paradigm is able to see positive or deviation-amplifying feedback as a creative process that accounts for increasing organizational diversity. It is able to account for the interaction among components that produce other components (allopoiesis) and that enter the process that produced them (autopoiesis) (Varela, 1979). It is able to account for the resolution or synthesis of paradoxes, of contradictions and of higher-order conflicts (in the sense of involving many parties) which I call multilectical processes of transcending higher-order interactions. The paradigm moreover places the observer into the context of his own observations and accounts for the emergence of cognitive constructions of reality. In this paradigm, information emerges largely *from within* and may therefore be called *in-formation* (Varela, 1979). Positive feedback increases organizational variety, negative feedback achieves organizational closure, both are organization-formative processes.

In proposing these four kinds of paradigms, Maruyama also suggests a historical development, the hierarchical being the oldest of the four, the morphogenetic the most recent one. The homeostatic paradigm relies heavily on an ontology provided by systems theory, game theory, information theory (of the Shannon type) and control theory, all of which are subsumed by the cybernetics of observed systems (first-order cybernetics) whereas the morphogenetic paradigm has largely transcended the homeostatic one and heavily relies on an epistemology of systems that includes their observers as constituent parts. It particularly recognizes the important role of self-referential constructions that the largely Western philosophy has exorcised (Krippendorff, 1982). This paradigm is being developed in the name of a cybernetics of observing systems (second-order cybernetics) (von Foerster, 1974).

Properties of Information

Probably the most outstanding failure of economics is that it has been nearly unable to account for information and, because contemporary society has become increasingly involved in processing information within itself, economic predictions have increasingly been failures. The reason lies squarely and simply in certain properties of information that distinguishe it from those traditionally accounted for by economic analysis.

Much of economic analysis rests on the invariance of value. Marx's observation that capitalists become fewer and richer as they buy each other out and extract more and more profit from the working poor is an example of this reasoning. Another is the notion of a commodity as something that is exchanged for its value. However, this invariance is rooted in the properties of matter and energy to which economic values ultimately refer. Odum & Odum (1976) have shown that the flow of matter and energy in society is correlated with the flow of money. It proceeds along the same paths but in the opposite direction and regulates them in the social domain. Similar to capital, according to the first law of thermodynamics, matter and energy can be transformed and redistributed but neither created nor destroyed. This law makes material processes easily accountable, and economics thrives on the invariance underlying it.

In contrast, information can be *created* like artistic productions, technological inventions, and the development of plans for socioeconomic institutions. Information *can be mass-produced* at very little cost by sequentially repetitive processes, such as in printing, copying, or by disseminating numerous replicas of one original, as is done by radio and television. Information *can also be destroyed* as is true for much of human history that may never become known to the full level desirable. Destruction of information was attempted but failed (owing to its wide distribution) in the Watergate case. Quantities of information are thus not subject to the same laws governing quantities of energy and the related economic quantities of value.

Many economists in the West have responded to the unquestionable economic importance of information in terms of number of jobs available, level of investment, and volume of transactions, by regarding information as a commodity, parallelling such traditional categories as steel, chemicals, automobiles, social services, and so on. This seems entirely inadequate. A commodity is a product of humans or of nature that is exchanged for the value either of its consumption like food, clothes, automobiles, or of its use in the production of other commodities, as with tools, machines or production facilities that are subject to slower wear and decay. Because information is cheaply reproducable and may not loose its value when used repeatedly, *information does not have the property of a commodity* and cannot be accounted as such without total disregard for its organizational role. That part of information processing that consumes raw material and energy, that is, the production of the physical carriers of information and the maintenance of the media of communication, all of which are accountable economically, is relatively insignificant if not irrelevant to the structural changes these media are able to cause by the information they provide.

Information may be purchased either in the form of *access rights* or the *privilege of use*. In both cases, institutional structures mediate between the economic transactions and the information flows within a society, moving information outside the traditional realm of economics. For example, in buying a newspaper, what changes hands is not information alone but also several pages of newsprint. Reading the newspaper neither destroys its material form nor consumes its content. It does not even prevent others from reading it later. Not knowing exactly what the newspaper contains, the first reader pays for having physical access to a known category of content. After reading what he wants, the newspaper has lost its value for him but not necessarily for secondary readers to whom he can pass it on without appreciable loss to himself. This can surely not be said for consumer goods and for the means of production. The subscription to a newspaper, the acquisition of a television set, the registration for a course of study at the university, and so on, purchases *access rights to a category of information*. Industrial espionage aims at acquiring a category of information without paying for the access rights. On the other hand, when one commissions research on the optimal reorganization of a plant, when one acquires instructions to produce a pharmaceutical product or when one buys a plan to assemble a microcomputer, the purchaser knows quite specifically what the information will do when he has obtained it. And the implication of the economic transaction is that he will have *the privilege to use the information* obtained by him. The money paid may compensate the seller for his physical effort but it is the privilege of use that the buyer acquires. Granting or depriving someone of this privilege of use is independent of the possession of the information. For example, the knowledge of a plan to rob a bank does not imply the privilege of its use.

Relative to the production, exchange, and consumption of commodities, information assumes a *superordinate position* and an economic analysis of the information processes involved ought to take this extraordinary position into account. In the input-output table for an economy in which exchanges between and transformations within industries (categories of industries, sectors of an economy, or geographical regions) are entered, information participates in the process by changing the table. It may change the transition function within one cell (e.g., when information is geared toward a more efficient organization of the process), it may change the interaction between cells otherwise considered independent (e.g., when industries, etc., become more informed about each other and coordinate their production and consumption) or it may add new cells, rows, or columns. (e.g., when information introduces new technologies, communication technology for example, that cause structural changes in the economy). In such an analysis information is seen to be about or superordinate to the economy. It guides, controls, and rearranges the economic activities and has, hence, the characteristic of a *meta-economic quantity* that cannot easily be built into a system of analysis that is essentially flat and provides no opportunity for self-reference.

Information Society

In this section I will sketch what might be the three most important indicators of the transition to a form of society in which information seems to be the predominant feature. These are the changing patterns of employment, the widespread adoption of a new technology and the emergence of modern corporate structures.

Changes in Employment Pattern

Probably the first serious recognition of the role of information in society came with Price's (1961) work showing how the development of science, as an institution and measured in terms of number of scientists, correlated with, and in fact predicted, economic development. At the same time Machlup (1962) collected a wealth of data on *The Production and Distri-*

bution of Knowledge in the United States and came to the startling conclusion that in 1958 about 29 percent of the existing GNP was spent for knowledge. The figure was rightly criticized as too broad. It included under education, for example, not only schools and universities but also education at home, on the job, in church. It also counted entertainment, the mass media in particular, as a knowledge industry.

Subsequently, Porat (1977) analysed some 440 occupational categories and 201 industries. He separated those concerned with information from those related to the production of goods and found that in the year 1967, 25.1 percent of the U.S. GNP was due to that part of the economy which creates, processes, and distributes information. Included in this category are education, advertising, accounting, the mass media, printing, telecommunications, and computer manufacturing, as well as parts of the finance and insurance business. He called this the *primary information sector* and proceeded to estimate the contribution made by information-related jobs *within* industries that are not part of the primary information sector and found an additional 21.1 percent of the GNP coming from information activities in this so-called *secondary information sector* or 46 percent in total and 53 percent of all income earned. This increase in economic activity devoted entirely to information processing is further demonstrated in a recent study at MIT which found that of the 19 million new jobs created in the United States in the 1970s, only 5 percent were in manufacturing, 6 percent in services, both in the goods producing sector, and 89 percent were outside the goods producing sector.

There is no doubt that information is necessary in the functioning of any society. Formal education has been with us for several centuries and if one includes socialization—the slow integration of individuals into the working of society—intergenerational transmission of information is a functional prerequisite. There is also no doubt that farmers, craftsmen, and industrial workers always required considerable amounts of information to be productive. But what is different here is that there are now many more jobs and many more employment categories, not just teachers, that specialize in the creation, production, and dissemination of information without using it themselves. Information processing, which had before been the unalienable domain of the human mind, is now becomming professionalized and has entered the public and corporate domain, involing human beings as mere mediators of an unfolding process of societal organization.

One can quibble over the validity of the occupational categories or demand a finer differentiation between kinds of information produced by them, but all these figures support the staggering growth in the economic significance of information in contemporary society. Following the above discussion on the properties of information, I suggest that these figures might be indicative more of the *production of the material vehicles* for information processes to take place than of the amount of information that is potentially available or actually used. The latter would be manifest in an acceleration of structural changes about which we may not have objective measures but sufficient anecdotal evidence.

Information Technology

One mark of the coming information society is the above shift in the pattern of employment. Another is the widespread use of electronic computers, a new technology that may underlie this shift and the likely cause of social changes of a magnitude not yet fully imaginable. I will sketch the development of this technology, not so much because of its obvious importance but because its history sheds light on how technology might develop generally and what role information plays in a society in transition. This sketch could also be considered a demonstration of what a morphogenetic theory of information might entail and serve as a general scheme for accounting for the kind of large-scale societal changes of ultimate interest.

I am suggesting that all technological developments, and by generalization, all interactively growing social features, go through four stages: embryonic, opportunistic, self-assertive growth, and systemic maturity or institutionalization.

Embryonic. Information enters a context of material entities it is capable of organizing into a new form. In the 1940s mechanical calculators were common. The telephone with its elaborate switching technology was in place. Radio communication, which relied on the mass production of receivers including relays then in the form of vacuum tubes, was available. Owing to the large scale planning effort at the beginning of World War II, the 1940s were also marred by logistical problems, making financial resources readily available to find practical solutions. The idea of a robot, a human-made replica of humans that would do what it is told to do was an idea well-established in literary fantasies. In this environment, which provided all the parts needed to build electronic computers (and, for that matter, a lot of other things too) the idea of a computing machine was realized at the University of Pennsylvania where two professors worked for years to wire a room full of vacuum tubes and switches into a functioning whole. It was a change from a collection of independently available components to an organized whole, a change from quantity to quality, guided by the information then available to the inventors. To be sure this information was available elsewhere too (Ledger, 1955) and could have been applied at other places with similar results but it did not come to fruition there, the question of why being a separate issue. The embryonic stage of a technology, which might last for a long time, terminates with the social recognition that something new has been found, invented, realized, named and thereby considered organizationally-structurally distinct from what was known before.

Opportunistic. The new technology is narrowly categorized, cast into traditional terms and applied where it causes the least changes in the adopting institutions, primarily substituting for existing functions. It is noteworthy that the machines of this new technology were called "electronic calculators," signifying that they were seen as calculating devices that used numbers as inputs and outputs and served the function previously performed by applied mathematicians. The first applications, say between 1945 and 1970, were largely for national-scale projects such as national defense, space exploration and in support of scientific research involving a great deal of computation such as in physics and statistical work. The computers of this period were largely sequential machines that centralized computational work into a single unit. Concurrent to the growth of big computers three embryonic developments must be mentioned: (1) the use of computers in toys and games, now a major industry, which again posed no threat; (2) the application of computers in business and the accompanying recognition that computers actually process information not just numerical data; and (3) the continuing research at American universities, developing theories of computation, of programming languages and of systems design, creating new academic disciplines, computer sciences, artificial intelligence, computational linguistics, for example, and producing a considerable number of highly trained and motivated computer buffs who could realize their dreams in niches not yet explored and work outside traditional domains of institutional controls, starting corporations of their own. This development largely took place beneath the surface of conventional applications.

Self-assertive growth. The technology now expands and finds unanticipated applications that no longer replace older forms but create new needs and new variates to satisfy them. These tend to challenge existing institutional structures. Self-assertive growth characterizes today's use of computers in the United States and in Japan. One technological innovation making this expansion possible is the development of microcomputers, that is, computers that are nearly as capable as the larger ones of ten years ago but portable and comparatively inexpensive. A second is the combination of microcomputers with telephone networks, rendering centralized information processing obsolete and introducing a kind of parallel processing on a large scale. The third is the shift in emphasis in development from hardware to software, which is the kind of information that organises computation. This shift enormously increases the adaptability of computers to emergent situations. In the course of this growth, computers are making inroads into education, not replacing teachers as had been feared, but creating individualized learning experiences, making more information faster available to students than teachers could provide and producing a generation of people familiar with and capable of handling information processing tasks. Under the name of "word processors" computers are replacing typewriters, a variety of financial accounting tasks, and modifying office communication by offering electronic mail services, computer conferencing, networks for accessing data banks stored elsewhere and also making optium management decisions. Computers are scheduling a great many complex activities from civilian air travel to inventory control which the ordinary person barely experiences when buying a ticket or paying at the cash register of a supermarket. Computers are naturally taking over banking and one speaks of electronic money that no longer exists in the form of coins but in the memory of a computer to which owners have limited access. Programmable robots are solidly in place in industry, replacing workers in mass production from automobiles to computers themselves. Software is created for a great many applications for running hospitals and for crime control. The knowledge of experts such as in medical diagnosis and in geology has reached the state of computerization at which it can be marketed through and accessed by telephone lines (Feigenbaum & McCorduck, 1983). Japan has adopted a national policy of computerization (Masuda, 1981). The United States lets these self-stimulating developments grow within the context of the market place. A challenge of traditions is inevitable in either case.

Systemic maturity or institutionalization. Having superseded all obstacles in its way to become dominant within a given ecological niche, the technology develops stable relations with other technologies and supports the institutional arrangements it helped in part to create, it has become a "cultural complex" no longer a "dynamic technology". We cannot be certain at this point what computers will ultimately do and which institutions they will favor in a mature information society. Since we have no experiences with such a society we can only speculate. We know the automobile is in this phase, having surrounded itself by an automobile industry, an oil industry, a system of roads and car services, legislation, safety control, even folklore, not to speak of the population of drivers who consider this complex most "natural." The industrial mode of production had reached a similar state of maturity when it was successfully challenged by the emergence of bureaucratic practices and now by the advent of information technology. Information technology is not likely to replace any of the older existing technologically motivated cultural complexes but it may overcome their dominance and leaving enough room for initially unnoticed innovations to emerge that may become dominant in the future.

I am convinced though that information technology is of a kind qualitatively different from older technologies, whose institutionalization we have seen, for it does not primarily process matter and energy but organizational work in the social domain that is so much more connected with man's intellect than any other technology in the path of history.

Modern Corporate Structures

The church and the army are classical forms of large-scale organizations. Industrialization added the enterprise and later the state to the repertoire. But the twentieth century created the corporation.

A corporation is a self-governing entity whose life span is independent of that of its members. Members enter a corporation by contractual agreements that stipulate functional responsibilities, obligations, and benefits and such agreements may be terminated by mutual consent. This voluntary membership gives a corporation considerable flexibility in responding to emergent opportunities. Corporations have generally fewer levels of organization and grant its components a greater independence. Interaction among corporate components is regulated by something like an "internal market" and a corporate policy, both of which are overseen by a board of directors. Corporations also have assets, but the ownership of these assets is typically functionally distributed and rarely in the hands of specific people. For this reason corporations have sometimes been called "legal fictions." Although the functional rationality of corporations may make them transparent internally, their self-government makes it often difficult to penetrate them from the outside or to apply effective governmental control. This may be one reason for their recent growth in numbers as well as in political power.

Big business corporations like AT&T, General Motors, Standard Oil, and IBM date all back to the 1920s and were created by skillful organizers, neither by managers nor by owners, who had the wisdom to economize by decentralizing corporate decisions and by making the "internal market" to define the link between corporate components. This internal market is similar to but more efficient than the external market in which corporations compete, thus thriving on this difference with a minimum of expense for governance. For example, at General Motors, the producer of batteries sells his products to the car manufacturing unit at a certain percentage above production costs. Efficiency is further enhanced by the sharing of information and the internal compensation of profits and losses. Because there is otherwise no systemic difference between the internal manufacture of a product and its purchase from the outside, the corporation remains competitive as a whole as well as in each of its parts.

Corporate forms of organization have been widely applied even to nonprofit organizations, such as American universities. At the University of Pennsylvania, for example, each school functions to some extent as an independent company with a separate accounting mechanism. Through a complete breakdown of the costs and services provided, the university administration can check on the efficiency of each school and make appropriate decisions on the allocation of resources. The financial assets of the university are formally owned by its board of trustees, which oversees the operation of the university as a whole. Faculty, students, and administration probably are the university's most important assets, but they are not ownable except through the mechanism of loyalty and are nearly exclusively informational. Faculty, students, and administration also participate in the university's self-government through such organs as the faculty senate, the student assembly, and the president of the university. Thus the informational assets check on, if not dominate, decisions regarding the allocation of the formally owned financial assets. With the increased role of information, it seems that modern corporations are becoming more university-like.

The use of information technology certainly made traditional forms of organization, the military, the state bureaucracy and the industrial enterprise, more efficient. But it has significantly elaborated the structure of corporations. The first and most noticeable impact on corporate structures is probably due to telecommunications, telephone, teletype and data transmission. Its effects are two-fold. First, it allows organizationally decentralized corporate components to disperse geographically and geographically separate companies to become newly recruited parts of existing corporations. Second, it allows for a more efficient balancing of budgets and instant accounting for larger numbers of corporate components. The result is the emergence of increasingly powerful "invisible empires," invisible in the sense that it is difficult to locate corporate entities. The traditionally "solid" organizations that represented themselves by moving into a complex of adjacent buildings, including the production facilities, is being dissolved into a communication network of interacting components. Space is no longer a delimiter of growth, multinational corporations being the most outstanding examples.

A corollary of the efficient use of telecommunications is superior access to information about changes in labor markets, costs of raw material, local tax structures, political stabilities, and so on. Coupled with the inherent corporate flexibility, this leads to the relocation of production facilities into more cost-effective areas, often into developing countries that are eager for industrial development. Fearing widespread unemployment, labor unions in the United States have tried to prevent such relocations and are now forced to make concessions on wages and benefits and to participate in economizing production. They become thus absorbed into corporate processes rather than fight them. The large-scale effect is that a significant portion of U.S. industrial production becomes either fully automated or is slowly moving to foreign countries, yielding increasingly significant corporate earnings from abroad. The term "de-industrialization" quite appropriately characterizes what increasingly happens to the United States.

Probably the most significant impact on modern corporate structures results from the use of information technologies, electronic computers and computer networks in particular, for data processing and for corporate decision making. Owing to the need to coordinate the increasingly many loosely connected corporate units, corporations pioneered the business use of computers before traditional forms of organizations caught up with them and they used this technology not to automate subordinate processes of production (industrial robots and automated offices) but to process, correlate, and condense vast quantities of data about their internal and external corporate environments and to thereby prepare decisions that are better informed than those made without the availability of this technology. Generally, better-informed decisions made at corporate headquarters and at negligible costs can generate or save much more capital than can be obtained by painstaking improvements in production at the periphery of a corporation. The increasing truth of this condition clearly favors investments in the information processing facilities of a corporation over investments into its means of production. Consequently many modern corporations divest themselves of their production facilities (provided that separate operation and ownership poses no threat to the corporation), become increasingly involved in information processing, create information jobs, and invest in such information resources as experts, data banks and computer networks to connect them. By not recognizing that ownership of means of production means little when the production facilities exist primarily in conjunction with the policies of larger corporations, the current tendency of foreign governments to restrict U.S. ownership of foreign factories only speeds up the process of the increasing alliance of corporate structures with information processing technology. American know-how, advanced communication technology and information processors might not be appreciated in some corners of the world, but they become increasingly indispensable in making production and society work everywhere.

In the emerging information society, corporations are amassing so much capacity to display intelligence (in the sense of their ability to make informed decisions concerning the very societal organization of which they are a part), that the social use of this capacity increasingly dominates older forms of organization including those traditionally charged with the responsibility of government. The volume of information corporations can produce to further their interests can easily exceed a government's capacity to process it (see the volume of documents AT&T produced in its divestment case that required an army of lawyers to read them). Corporations employ the most well-informed lobby in the U.S. congress. Members of corporations occupy top level positions in the U.S. government. Although the new technology has produced a large number of very small corporations that can respond faster than large corporations can, their markets often exist as the result of larger corporations' decisions and they easily accept their model and guidance.

Although corporations are clearly kept alive by employing real people, it is the information that is processed in corporate structures, not people, that govern the contemporary economy. The corporate use of information processing technology has made corporations the "social brain" of the emerging information society.

Some Marxian Propositions

In turning the idealist Hegel "upside down," the materialist Marx had a thorough disrespect for mental constructs, ideas, and knowledge. He might have even included the modern conception of information in this list of "epiphenomena." I believe this proved fatal for his theories but not necessarily for his constructions in which I find several modern ideas. Let me elaborate some of them from a morphogenetic perspective.

System Change: Succession vs. Supercession

Marx saw social history as a history of class struggles, creating a *succession* of social systems. So the ancient slave system was replaced by the feudal system, the feudal system was replaced by the capitalist system which Marx believed would cease with the emergence of socialism. Having built his conception of society on an economic base, including the prevailing material conditions, the physical means of processing these, and the workers required in production, Marx saw the way this economic base was operated, the relations of production, ownership in particular, as coming into necessary conflict with the forces of production and thereby nourishing the seed of its own destruction. With the help of revolutionary forces that come into being as the result of such necessary conflicts, a new social system emerges from "the ashes of the old."

However, history does not support the contention that social systems are mutually exclusive, antagonistic, or in necessary opposition to each other and that they succeed each other in a chainlike progression. The ancient slaves did not erect the feudal state nor did the journeymen and servants of the feudal landlords engineer the capitalist system. Capitalism was not preceded by a class struggle between the serfs and nobles or between the journeymen and their exploiting guild masters. The capitalist economy and the society of the bourgeoisie responsible for it grew up as an independent structure within feudalism. In fact the patriarchical organization of the guild and the freewheeling merchant associations probably constituted an embryonic state of capitalism while the feudal system flourished with their help. Although there were drastic cases in which functionally superfluous feudal lords were forcefully evicted from power, this was merely symbolic because the capitalist system already in force had made the old ruling elite dispensable. It did not simply eradicate the old organizational forms and values but absorbed them into their own. Emerging systems were all structurally more powerful, could exist on a higher level of organization, and were particularly capable of resolving conflicts the older systems could not master within their own powers.

Socialism, which according to Marx should have come about in highly industrialized societies, England, France, Germany and the United States, for example, succeeded primarily in industrially less advanced countries, Russia and China, for example, largely in the aftermath of a war and because the revolutionary leadership was convinced of Marx's ideas. This speaks against the strict economic determinism Marx advocated and in favor of the role of information in social development. Marx's theories demonstrated their potential of doing organizational work.

History speaks forcefully in favor of the contention that social systems do not succeed by replacing each other. They may coexist, often for a long time and without a struggle. New systems tend to emerge in ecologically insignificant niches where the controls by the prevailing system are marginal or ineffective. One system may *supersede* another if the latter proves to be structurally more capable of coping with problems the other is unable to master.

In the true spirit of Marx's dialectic, the new system often represents a synthesis that need not be "built on the ashes of the old" but may well integrate the old system into a more complex, adaptively more successful, and, as far as its ability to control society and its material environment is concerned, more powerful organizational form. We have ample evidence for supercession (not succession) in the social development of the industrialized countries.

Currencies: Capital → Authority → Information

Marx saw capital as the principal currency of social development within the capitalist system of production. Curiously, his definition very much conforms to the underlying structure of the definition of energy on the one side, information on the other side, and authority in between. For Marx, capital is neither money nor property owned but putting both *to work*. The distinction is crucial and applies also to the distinction between potential energy (the energy in a tank of gasoline) and the energy consumed by performing a mechanical task (driving a car from one place to another), between potential information (a plan for a factory) and actual information (organizational work expended when building the factory). Authority too has this duality. It need not be exercised in the form of rewards and punishments but is effective by perceiving the potential of their enactment.

I would say that capital, authority, and information are three currencies among several minor ones operating simultaneously in interacting parts of a social system. The materialist Marx had no conception of information as a measure of intellectual work about which we have become aware only recently and he underplayed the significance of authority by favoring a one-dimensional framework of analysis that permits only a single all-penetrating currency: the capital. His differentiation of people into two classes, the capitalist class, which controls the capital by owning means of production and by letting it work for them, and the working class, which does not possess any capital to control, nearly exhausted the distinctions he saw as important. He observed near the end of his life the emergence of the banking system that mediated among capitalists, and he was very much concerned with the role of the state in the capitalist system which assumed a somewhat similar mediating role, he grouped the people employed in these institutions, next to two other groups to be mentioned later, into a third category, so-called *"dritte personen"* of whom those who "command in the name of capitalism" include merchants, middlemen, speculators, commercial laborers (white-collar employees), managers, foremen, and so on.

It was the category of people who "command in the name of capitalism" that developed bureaucratic administrations whose dominant currency was not ownership but authority. Authority developed within such administrations as a semiautonomous currency. Authority could not be purchased. For example, the emerging concept of "corruption" indicated the bureaucratic effort to control its own currency against the intrusion of money.

Apparently without developing a class consciousness by itself, this group introduced legislation and enacted practices that institutionalized the conflicts arising between the owners of the means of production and their workers (Dahrendorf, 1959), making ownership more of a responsibility than a way of getting rich. The banking system, insurance companies, the stock market, the labor unions, and democratic governments all cooperated, albeit implicitly, in the wider distribution of economic benefits without eliminating the capitalist class and without destroying the capitalist mode of production by absorbing both into a new and more encompassing system of bureaucratic control. (Interestingly, bureaucratic systems have also taken over the management of noncapitalist countries, such as the Soviet Union, creating there what some writers have called a "New Class" (Djilas, 1958). This transition occurred without revolution.

In the emerging information society, the ancient wisdom that knowledge can erode authority seems to have been put into large scale social practice. Interestingly, Marx's second category of *dritte personen*—by his definition those who live in the capitalist system but do not participate in it, priests, lawyers, professors, artists, teachers, physicians—having existed in an embryonic phase for a very long time now appears to come into the forefront of this lastest social development. These are the creators and communicators of information. These are the experts consulting government and industry on how to do what they cannot do within their own limitations. These are the inventors and early users of computer systems and communication networks which process and distribute data at quantities never before known in history. These are also the designers of algorithms for automatic control of production processes and for the monitoring of the environment, from the weather to military movements, for making administrative and managerial decisions, for accounting for the flow of money, merchandise and people, and for governing parts of the economy without human interference, often without an understanding by those affected by these semiautomated systems.

Even so nobody doubts that information is one of the most significant currencies in the technologically advanced countries of the West, traditional methods of controlling its flow, of tracing its organizational consequences and of directing its morphogenesis have largely been failures. As already mentioned, entering information into an economic input-output table accounts only for the material characteristics of information, not for the organizational work it does. Legislation concerning copyrights of computer software, concerning the control of flexible and geographically dispersed corporate structures which are fundamentally based on information technology, concerning privacy of information, etc., are far behind and largely ineffective in the face of the speed of actual developments.

Morphogenetic theories of information are in their infancy. It is therefore no surprise that the information technology has grown exponentially and increasingly becomes a force that dominates authority, capital and other currencies and directs socioeconomic development.

Dynamics: Dialectical → Hierarchial → Multi-lectical

The original ideal of a dialectical process is very much rooted in the use of language, the Greek *dialektikos* denoting a method of intellectual investigation by dialogue. Reasoning in these terms seems to be trapped in the linguistic preference for binary opposites. One cannot easily imagine a negation, an opposite or a distance between more than two things. Although dialectical processes involve three entities, it is the pairwise interaction between thesis and antithesis (the first binary relation) that the synthesis of the two is to overcome (the second binary relation). Accordingly, Marx forced nearly all his observations into the binary scheme of a conflict between oppressors and oppressed. I already mentioned this so-called *dritte personen* who did not fit into the scheme and were considered inessential by him. Similarly, agricultural production which was initially noncapitalist in organization was not considered a third part to the conflict but a mode of production that would eventually end up being capitalist and therefore required no specialized conception. Marx made many other binary distinctions, such as the distinction between an economic base and the superstructure of a society, the distinction between forces of production and relations of production, or the distinction between use value and exchange value; all are binary.

The first blow to this binary way of thinking came, I believe, with the emergence of mediating institutions, the already mentioned banking system and state government, both of which had to simultaneously juggle with various parts of the capitalist economy. Marx was aware of the role of the state but quickly characterized it as an instrument of the ruling class, the capitalists, and thus managed to maintain the basic distinction between two antagonistic forces.

However, the increasing numbers of industrial managers not only mediated between the capitalists and the workers (if this was the primary conflict in the society Marx experienced) but they also developed independent bureaucratic forms of organization that institutionalized these conflicts. Being based on a currency that had little to do with the ownership of capital, as elaborated above, the bureaucracies had some autonomy in themselves. Authority can either arise with the emergence of individuals who are noticeably outstanding in commonly agreed upon characteristics, for example, experts, geniuses, leaders, or be assigned by virtue of the office held, the position maintained, the work done, for example, foremen, priests, presidents, policemen. It is the latter kind of authority that brought about and was in turn instituted by the bureaucractic forms of administration that overcame ruthless capitalism. The use of this kind of authority within bureacracies made them clearly *hierarchical* forms of organization in which each level was on the one hand responsible to and on the other hand obtained its authority from the next higher level. The top of this hierarchy was, for whatever reasons, not occupied by the owners of the means of production but by those who either rose through the ranks of the bureaucracy, were elected to the office, or were legitimized by formal procedures.

The crucial point to be made here is that hierarchical forms of organization are fundamentally different from a free market of products, money, and services and require a logic of description more powerful than the one capable of describing social change in terms of conflicts, contradictions, or oppositions between just two, or primarily two, entities. I believe the laws of bureacracy escape Marx's original categories and the dynamics of the information society is even further removed from these categories.

I would argue, both with and against Marx, that if the idea of a dialectic has some reality beyond its ability to account for the social dynamics of early capitalism, then it should be applicable to itself and be generalized or transcended to account for the failures of earlier accounts. I am suggesting that Marx's dialectical thesis encountered its first major antithesis in the no-longer binary antagonism motivating the reality of hierarchically organized bureaucracies. The logic appropriate to account for this new reality is as much a synthesis of initially incompatible forms as the system it describes is more powerful in the sense of encompasing initially conflicting elements.

Just as in Marx's conceptions, all organizational hierarchies are based on a simple unidirectional causality, but unlike in Marx, it is a top-down causality, not necessarily directed forward in time. This top-down determinism, from a position of higher authority to a position of lower authority, coordinates individual activities and assumes that overall purposes are served on each level of the hierarchy. Each such level is constituted by (in the sense of defined within itself and in terms of) an organizational synthesis of cooperating and competing elements, whether these are holders of offices or departments (having hierarchies of their own), that are forced to interact with each other and jointly report to the level above. Each level is a synthesis of a higher ordinality than the elements contained in it. Thus a hierarchical bureaucratic system may be described as the coexistence of several levels of synthesis, each referring to or including elements that are syntheses of elements subordinate to them. Koestler (1967) created the term "holon" to denote an entity that both consists of an arrangement of parts and participates in (higher-order) arrangements of parts. Thus a bureacratic system is both a natural synthesis of the tension within a marketlike system, such as in early capitalism, and a natural co-growth of authority, a new currency that is largely unaffected by money flows. The synthesis arising out of binary oppositions is just a specialized (two-level, two-part) case of a hierarchy (multilevel, many-part system). There are also numerous laws of bureaucratic organizations, the most popular being Parkinson's Law and The Peter Principle, the former explaining the growth of hierarchical control, the latter the movement of individuals up the hierarchy—but I am not concerned with these here.

This hierarchical thesis is in direct conflict with the realities of an information society and it appears that the synthesis between the two is now emerging within cybernetics, the discipline most closely associated with the morphogenetic properties of systems. These morphogenetic properties are particularly prevalent in the emerging information society. This synthesis offered by cybernetics (a) recognizes and advances systems for describing the *interaction* among many entities, people, corporate units, or machines. Interaction among many entities clearly generalizes the "interaction" (conflict, opposition, contradiction) between two. It (b) recognizes and is increasingly capable of describing *unities* as formed on the basis of the interaction among parts. This explanation of the emergence of unities is wholly consistent with the intentions of Marx's dialectic but a generalization of the notion of level in a hierarchy which is there static and nominal, whereas in cybernetics it is dynamic and self-defining. Finally, and probably the most important contribution of cybernetics is the ability to describe the process as embodied in (c) a *circular form of organization,* forming unities from parts with the unities possibly becoming parts of themselves, that is, being self-referential. This overcomes the paradigmatic unidirectional causality implicit in hierarchical forms of organization and in Marx's historical determinism. It removes the ultimate authority from the top of a hierarchy, the prime mover as the unexplicable initiator of a process and the final destination, by entering the top of the hierarchy into its own bottom or by closing the circle of causality, this circle being its own best explanation. It also overcomes the binary logic implicit in Marx's class struggle, etc., which has little to say about the complex reality of contemporary society. It retains Marx's process-toward-higher-order-complexity notions. I have called this circular and multivariate process of systems development: *multilectical.*

Feedback and Closure

Marx clearly recognized how capital was put to work and, using time, extrapolated how this closed system would disequilibriate and eventually break up: the factory owner derives profit from selling his products above production costs. A portion of this profit is reinvested in production facilities which thereby continue to grow bringing him higher profits in return. The factory worker who has to ultimately pay for the ever-increasing profit becomes poorer the more he participates in trying to improve his own lot within the system of capitalist production. Finally, workers will recognize their own functional indispensability on the one side and comparative misery on the other and destroy the system of which they were a part.

Marx here described what is now known as feedback, more specifically positive feedback, which is a circular causal process that continuously amplifies an original inequality as the process goes around and around this cycle (Maruyama, 1963). In the capitalist system of production the result can be stated in a nutshell: "the rich become richer and the poor become poorer," the ideal of uniform equality being an unstable equilibrium. The fact that the system did not collapse in the industrialized West and grew instead is the result of counteracting forces or what is known as deviation-reducing, or negative feedback, which limited the apparent determinism before reaching a point of breakup. These forces were mobilized from outside the positive feedback cycle Marx described as closed.

It has been a thesis in this paper that the "counteracting forces" (a terminology derived from the homeostatic paradigm) are in fact created by the synthesis of more powerful systems, transcending those unstable forms and developing new "currencies of control." However, I would maintain that positive feedback is a feature in any societal growth, regardless of the system involved. In bureaucracies it is easily observed that people in positions of authority become more powerful by the very fact that they have easier access to the means of exerting power and amass authority at the expense of those who have little to begin with. The emergence of dictators and the growth of government bureaucracies are examples that suffice here. The same positive feedback can be observed in an information society, now checking the otherwise unlimited inequality regarding authority and capital.

To begin with, most of the traditional applications of information are rather unproblematic and have for this reason not been considered an important problem. A worker at an assembly line must have sufficient amount of information (through education, training, and experience) to do his job of putting things together. Even a manager who is to perform leadership functions and to make responsible decisions must have acquired the appropriate skills to organize his environment optimally. Although feedback about the results of informed actions may increase success the next time around, the process is unproblematic in this context because the information involved is essentially located within the actor, not communicated to and applied by others, and the process is ultimately converging toward a stable equilibrium, defined by the optimum utilization of organizational skills and the limits of success. This feedback is negative.

Information is subject to *positive feedback* if the *information that is produced and communicated to others at least in part reenters and improves on the process that produced it*. This is probably the most outstanding procedural feature underlying the emergence of an information society. On the level of the individual, this process has been described by Bateson (1972) as deutero-learning or learning how to learn. On the level of society this process increases its ability to organize its own organization. Let me give a few examples of this positive feedback involving information rather than authority or capital with which we are familiar.

One obvious example is the use of computers in the computer industry. The design of computers requires a good many decisions regarding the most advantageous arrangement of components, the optimization of such interdependent variables as speed, storage capacity, and physical size, and the development of suitable software, not to speak of marketing considerations. Such decisions are quite common in the design of complex systems, but they are also usually made by highly trained engineers. Naturally, computer manufacturers had early access to computer technology, understood its capability better than others did and used it to make their own decisions. Current electronic computers are very good at enumerating and exploring vast numbers of alternatives, some hardly imaginable by human designers, and they can easily search for an optimum path provided algorithms are general enough to be applicable to a given situation and can be stated iteratively. What a computer can do best is very much related to its own makeup and design and the application of computers to its own design has greatly increased the speed of development towards increasingly capable, increasingly flexible, increasingly portable, and increasingly interfacable computers. The Hollerith cards I punched ten years ago are now uncommon and difficult to enter in a computer. Ten years ago only a fews social science students had done something with a computer, now children are introduced to this technology in toy stores. With a history of at best forty years, Feigenbaum and McCorduck (1983) now speak of a fifth generation of computers. As it is, each generation of computers is designed with the help of the computers of the previous generation. For those able to compute computation, computational ability increases exponentially relative to those merely able to compute other things. This positive feedback has magnified the discrepancy between the speed of development of computers relative to the speed of development of a technology that can not be applied onto itself, regardless of how socially important it may be.

Katzman (1974) explored the social use of communication and similarly finds, that, whenever a new medium of communication, a new kind of programming, or a new technology for accessing information is introduced, those individuals that are already rich informationally become informationally richer. This applies, for example, to educational television programs, such as Sesame Street, designed to improve learning skills and interest in basic education among children, especially among the poor and intellectually deprived part of the population. In developing countries it is also used to promote literacy. While the program is indeed successful in the sense of improving motivation and knowledge in the aggregate, however, those children who come from educationally higher levels of the population benefit more from it than those who do not start with the same level of information. The improvement in the aggregate does not narrow the informational differences in the population, rather it magnifies them. In developing countries, literary programs tend to be of greater benefits to those who already have a better chance to become literate to begin with. The same amplification of informational differences is observable in the individual use of communication technology. Those who know how to use it first become literate with it earlier and obtain more information about a lot of other things faster than those whose level of information does not prepare them as well for such involvement. Information breeds itself in the fertile ground of a population that provides the positive feedback for this process to take place.

I already mentioned the propensity of corporate structures to absorb information technology faster than other structures. Here too positive feedback loops magnify the differences initially existing among organizations. Those early adopters and heavy users of information processors become increasingly more brainlike vis-à-vis their environment, tend to produce more information than material products and move into positions of control commensurate with the role their information production plays in the social processes of which they are a part.

As repeatedly mentioned, Marx observed this deviation amplifying circular casuality only in how capital was put to work. Presumably owing to the extremely slow growth of information processing capacity in Marx's time, which was then nearly entirely confined to the human brain, Marx neither recognized the generality of his proposition, nor did he consider the circular causality he did observe to be open to constraints arising side-by-side with the increasing economic differences. The examples show positive feedback to be present in the work that information does well. In Marx's extrapolation, the continuous amplification of existing economic differences spells doom to the system that contains this circular causality. Experiences in the industrialized West show such differences to reach limits much before the complete breakdown of the system sustaining them. It is the knowledge of such feedback loops (including the capability of recognizing the system) that ultimately invalidated Marx's deterministic extrapolations. Information of this kind was at least important if not decisive in opening up and curbing the process Marx described as a closed and deterministic one.

Determinism → Creation of Potential

There is an inherent paradox in trying to predict the inevitable outcome of a process that involves people who have information about that process and about their involvement in it.

Marx saw the wheel of history rolling perhaps with variable speed but in a predetermined direction. In charting the inevitable progression from one system to the next, he had to assume as he did that people had no information about their system in the sense that they had nothing that would enable them to reorganize their own situation and thereby change history. Neither the capitalists nor the workers could escape their individual destinies. He considered ideas as epiphenomena of the basic (material-economic and hence deterministic) mechanism. Enlightened people could speed up this progression but neither reverse it nor deviate from it. Prediction must always assume an observer-independent determinism which excludes information about and within the system so described thus rendering the above stated effort untenable.

By definition, individuals who possess information about something can at least in principle engage in organizational work directed towards changing this something. There may be good reasons why people might not use the information they have access to. They may not wish as a matter of preference to realize what they could do. They may not have the resources to apply all they could. They may experience psychical, social, or moral constraints restricting the use of information available to them. It may also be the case that the material circumstances (the resources to which available information refers or that are required to engage in the organizational work specified, for example, time, financial resources, and material conditions) are insufficient, rendering available information inapplicable or irrelevant. Whatever the case may be, the possession of relevant information characterises the ability to change and the possibility to exert one's will, thereby making the process affected by it to that extent unpredictable. Thus, when people do have information about a process involving them, the process can no longer be described in deterministic terms and is to some extent unpredictable. This renders the above stated effort unacceptable for reasons complementary to those preferred by Marx.

The paradox lies in the apparent impossibility of a system to be both predictable and in possession of information about itself. Only one or the other seems possible. The resolution of this paradox involves a change in the role of the observer from an outsider (a role Marx claimed for himself) to one that is part of the system he wishes to predict (or create, actually), that is, one that allows him to communicate with other observers in and of the system including with himself. This resolution is being developed under the name of second-order cybernetics (von Foerster 1974; Krippendorff, 1982). But it is also possible to remove oneself from the paradox without relinquishing the role of an outside observer. This means abandoning the predictability criterion of validity and describing a system with information about itself in terms of constraints on its potential. The criterion of validity implied here is a negative one in that a theory about such a system can not say what will happen but what cannot happen. Such a theory is valid if the observations fall within the range of those considered possible by the theory. Bateson (1972) considered this negative form of reasoning a characteristic of cybernetic explanations. I will briefly comment on how this pertains to understanding the role of information in society.

There is little doubt that all societies require some information to cope with environmental threats and to insure the continuance of the group. The organizational work required in primitive societies may have been more reactive than is now the case but even in modern society much of the information sought is intended to solve emerging problems. But there is also little doubt that modern problems are more human-made than natural, and that the technology creating these problems is to a large extent premediated, that is, guided by information in the form of creative ideas, inventions, and improvements. It is the availability of information that provides options for alternative paths of behavior. The emergence of an information society is therefore also the emergence of a new kind of determinism that provides more options than constraints.

Elsewhere (Krippendorff & Steier, 1979) we suggested that social systems, actually any kind of system including machines, may have three kinds of input: energy or matter, organization, and information. Organization refers to how the parts of the system interact and co-produce material entities or information. The form of this interaction may have historical, individual, or informational explanations with which we dealt briefly in the foregoing. Together with energy and material input in the form of food, fuel, material resources, and so on, from an environment, they form the *ecosphere* of the system, which consists of the interaction among several populations of different species. Contemporary society particularly includes machines and social institutions that are species in their own right. As I said above, complete knowledge of the laws of interaction operating within the ecosphere would make the ecosphere predictable save for the occurrance of genuinely random events.

The information available within a system constitutes what Boulding (1978) calls the *noosphere*. It is constituted by the collection of plans, of representations, of procedures, of ideas for the construction of objects or of instructions to realize certain interaction patterns, including "the totality of the cognitive content (and) values, of all human nervous systems, plus the prosthetic devices by which this system is extended and integrated in the form of libraries, computers, telephones, post offices and so on" (Boulding, 1978, p. 122). The noosphere contains all the options available that members of a social system can draw from. To the extent courses of actions are chosen, the noosphere also contains all possible futures of that system. It is in the absence of a noosphere that the behavior of a system is deterministic in the sense that it is doomed to follow just one "plan." To describe a system's noosphere is to describe the system's *potential* to behave and to develop, that system's possible futures.

In previous societies, the noosphere was more limited than it is today, not just by the properties of the inquiring mind and by its capacity to premeditate, to invent and to create new ideas, but particularly by the availability of storage facilities to preserve, and of communication media to transmit, the collectively created potential. It is this potential that information technology now transforms in ways unprecedented in human history. Information technology, which operates in the ecosphere as all technology does, draws from elements in the noosphere and feeds its products back into it, making the noosphere expand both in volume of options available as well as in the length of time governed by it. It is fair to say that an *information society essentially creates its own possible futures and is limited primarily by the futures it can compute* and only secondarily by its material history.

Boulding observes several processes that account in part for the unprecedented growth of the noosphere. There is the already mentioned *replication,* duplication or reproduction of information such as in printing, broadcasting and telecommunications. The power of replication gives a great deal of stability and coherence to a system in which information can decay or be selectively eliminated from circulation.

There is *recombination* or the organization of numerous existing pieces of information into a new unit. This multilectical process is probably the one that is most unique to the noosphere. Unlike in biology where genes are combined bisexually, recombination in the noosphere is multisexual in the sense that a great many diverse things can be synthesized into a new form. For example the car was invented from knowledge of a four-wheeled carriage, of steering devices, of the need for a (mechanical) power source, and so on. A factory integrates many workers, production facilities, material and energy resources into a functional unit. The bisexual metaphor like the dialectical metaphor breaks down when it comes to recombination processes in the noosphere. Whereas bisexual recombination has great combinatorial advantages over monosexual replication, *multilectical processes are unimaginably more powerful than dialectical ones.*

There is *mutation,* the modification of existing pattern in the course of transmission, the adaptation of information to particular circumstances. Societies differ in the rate of mutation they permit and in which area of the noosphere they allow mutation to occur. When it is high, information is distorted, imitated, and elaborated. When it is low, efforts must usually be expended to counteract biases and decay.

There is *communication,* the reproduction of information at different geographical locations in society, and its complement, the *selective elimination* of information no longer "fit to survive" the competition for validity, relevance and purpose.

There is *realization* and *production,* the conversion of potential to actual organizational work, for example, the assembly of a piece of equipment, the scheduling of events or the execution of a plan. Just like the DNA is ultimately responsible for growing a particular organism, so may information bring complex processes into being. A particularly powerful form of realization, and one that operates on the noosphere itself, is the realization of information to organize other information, for example, the assemblage of computer programs into larger packages and in turn into larger systems of compatible packages, etc.

There is *description,* the complement of realization and the codification of actual organizational work into storable form, perhaps for subsequent analysis or replication of the process giving rise to it.

There is also *pollution,* the overloading of the noosphere by irrelevant information that occurs in the absence of criteria to determine its usability. The ability of computers to generate voluminous outputs from small numbers of insignificant data is a case in point. Unable to separate the wheat from the chaff, libraries are often overloaded with never-read books that nevertheless may contain some important information in the future.

There is also *cancerous growth,* the autonomous growth of a category of information at the expense of destroying information in another category. Cancerous growth ranges from the domination of the noosphere by fads to large-scale destruction of information for the sake of an ideology or to support a social system unable to cope with the deviant information available, for example, Nazism and many modern authoritarian regimes restrict access to information that would challenge its roots.

In the emerging information society, the tremendous increase in the capacity for information storage, the phenomenal speed with which such information can be accessed, processed, and fed back into storage, the extraordinary density of communications from the telephone to the mass media which is now linked to computer processing and large data banks through powerful institutions like corporate structures, the growth of science in universities and associated with governments, all these increases in the ability to handle information, have expanded the noosphere of contemporary society to an extent still unimaginable. They also redirect social attention from tradition, from how things were done in the past and what was good about them, to the future, to what is conceivable or can be done. They also force us to reconsider the categories of sociopolitical analysis. The idea of historical determinism can certainly no longer be left unquestioned. The *creation of a society's potential* that comes with the development of a powerful noosphere including its sometimes self-generated properties will have to occupy our foremost attention.

Conclusion

We know that any system that produces, processes, and disseminates information and uses this information to continually realize and improve on this production magnifies its own systemic (specifically technological) biases, becomes organizationally closed, confining, and autonomous. We already know that the emerging information society is magnifying informational inequalities that could conceivably force another form of organization to overcome what we see happening now. While the notion of information as a form of work is, as I have tried to show, quite different from energy, capital, and authority, it is closer to the inquiring intellect and therefore of a radically different kind. What we do not yet know is whether the emerging information society with its tremendous increase in the human-societal potential to determine its future and its promise of liberation from the constraints of the past is indeed an expansion of the human mind, its ultimate trap or a mere transitional form. This paper merely suggests a framework for raising the question.

This paper was written in November 1983.

References

Bateson, G. (1972). *Steps toward an ecology of mind*. New York: Ballantine.

Bell, D. (1973). *The coming of post-industrial society*. New York: Basic Books.

Boulding, K. E. (1978). *Ecodynamics: A new theory of societal evolution*. Beverly Hills, CA: Sage.

Dahrendorf, R. (1959). *Class and class conflict in industrial society*. Stanford, CA: Stanford University Press.

Djilas, M. (1958). *Die neue Klasse; Eine Analyse des kommunistichen Systems*. Munich: Kindler.

Feingenbaum, E. A., & McCorduck, P. (1983). *The fifth generation artificial intelligence and Japan's computer challenge to the world*. Reading, MA: Addison-Wesley.

Koestler, A. (1967). *The ghost in the machine*. New York: Macmillian.

Katzman, N. (1974). The impact of communication technology: Promises and prospects. *Journal of Communications, 24* (4), 47–58.

Krippendorff, K., & Steier, F. (1979). Cybernetics properties of helping: The organizational level. In Richard F. Ericson (Ed.), *Improving the human condition: Quality and stability in social systems* (pp. 89–94). Louisville, KY: Society for General Systems Research August.

Krippendorff, K. (1984). An epistemological foundation for communication. *Journal of Communication 34* (3): 21–36.

Krippendorff, K. (1987). Paradigms for communication and development. In D. Lawrence Kincaid (Ed.), *Communication theory: Eastern and western perspectives*. New York: Academic Press.

Ledger, M. (1981). The case of the E.N.I.A.C. *Pennsylvania Gazette, 81* (October), 30–35. The E.N.I.A.C.'s Muddled History. *Pennsylvania Gazette 81:* 29–33, September.

Machlup, F. (1962). *The Production and Distribution of Knowledge in the United States*. Princeton, NJ: Princeton University Press.

Maruyama, M. (1963). The second cybernetics: Deviation-amplifying mutual causal processes. *American Scientists 51,* 164–79, 250–56.

Maruyama, M. (1974). Paradigmatology and its Application to Cross-Disciplinary, Cross-professional and Cross-cultural Communication. *Cybernetica, 17,* 136–56, 237–81.

Marx, K. (1932). *Capital,* Max Eastman (Ed.), New York: Modern Library.

Masuda, Y. (1981). *The information society as post-industrial society*. Washington, DC: World Future Society.

Maturna, H. R. (1970). *Biology of Cognition*. Urbana: Biological Computer Laboratory, University of Illinois.

Odum, H. T., & Odum, E. C. (1976). *Energy basis for man and nature*. New York: McGraw Hill.

Porat, M. U. (1977). *The information economy*. Washington, DC: Office of Telecommunications, U.S. Government Printing Office.

Prince, D. (1961). *Science since Babylon*. New Haven, CT: Yale University Press.

Prigorgine, I. (1980). *From being to becoming. Time and complexity in the physical sciences*. San Francisco: Freeman.

Shannon, C. E., & Weaver, W. (1947). *The mathematical theory of communications*. Urbana: University of Illinois Press.

Varela, F. G. (1979). *Principles of biological autonomy*. New York: Norman Holland.

Von Foerster, H. (1974). *Cybernetics of cybernetics or the control of control and the communication of communication*. Urbana: Biological Computer Laboratory, University of Illinois.

Von Foerster, H. (1981). *Observing Systems*. Seaside, CA: Intersystems.

Contributors

CARL BOTAN is associate professor in the Department of Communication at Purdue University.

YALE M. BRAUNSTEIN is associate professor at the School of Library and Information Studies of the University of California at Berkeley. He has published articles on the economics of information and communications including "Setting Technical Compatibility Standards; An Economic Analysis" (*Antitrust Bulletin, 30* (Summer 1985) 337–55) and "Economics of Intellectual Property Rights in the International Arena" (*Journal of the American Society for Information Science, 40* (January 1989), 12–16). His current research interests include economic models of the production and use of information, market structure in information and communications industries, and the economics of intellectual property rights.

GREGORY A. CRAWFORD is currently a doctoral candidate in the School of Communication, Information and Library Studies, at Rutgers University. He was formerly reference and public services librarian at Reeves Library of Moravian College in addition to serving as the director of automation for the library. He also served as technical services librarian at Lafayette College. He received his MS.L.S. from University of North Carolina at Chapel Hill and his A.B. in Latin from Davidson College.

ROBERT T. CROYLE is an associate professor of psychology at the University of Utah. He received his Ph.D. from Princeton University. His research examines the cognitive and social psychological aspects of health and illness behavior. Most recently, he has conducted experimental studies of psychological reactions to risk factor testing. He is co-editor of *Mental Representation in Health and Illness* (Springer-Verlag, 1991).

SUSAN J. DRUCKER is assistant professor of speech arts and sciences at Hofstra University. Her scholarly publications dealing with legal issues relating to communication have appeared in both communication and law journals. Current research focuses upon land use, environmental design, and social interaction.

SARAH FISHER received her Ph.D. from the University of California, Berkeley, in interdisciplinary studies in mathematics, science, and technology education. Currently, she is pursuing postdoctoral education in the School of Optometry at the University of California. Her interest have included informal education, computers in education and cognitive rehabilitation, and the effects of video games on social development.

GARY GUMPERT is professor emeritus, Department of Communication Arts and Sciences, Queens College of the City University of New York. He is co-editor of *Inter/Media: Interpersonal Communication in a Media World* (Oxford University Press, 1986), *Talking Tombstones and Other Tales of the Media Age* (Oxford University Press, 1987), and is co-editor of *Talking to Strangers: Mediated Therapeutic Communication* (Ablex Publishers, 1990).

NURIT GUTTMAN is a Ph.D. candidate at the School of Communication, Information, and Library Studies at Rutgers University. She has worked as a Health Education Coordinator and has been doing research and consulting in practioner-patient communication and organizational communication.

SUSAN G. HADDEN received her B.A. from Harvard College and Ph.D. in political science from the University of Chicago. She is a professor in the Lyndon B. Johnson School of Public Affairs, University of Texas in Austin. She is the author of two books on citizen access to and use of technical information: *Read the Label: Providing Information to Reduce Risk* and *A Citizen's Right to Know: Risk Communication and Public Policy*. She has also published more than sixty articles on citizen participation, risk communication, science and technology policy, and policies intended to reduce risks to human health or the environment. Her recent work has focused on government information policy, especially on the use of computers and expert systems to assist agencies in fulfilling their mandates and in providing information to the public. She is presently at work on a book about a public broadband network and associated information policies entitled *Informing Ourselves: Social Equity and Global Competitiveness in the 21st Century*.

ROBERT M. HAYES is a professor at Graduate School of Library and Information Science at UCLA. He has published widely, including co-authorship, with Joseph Becker, of two basic texts: *Information Storage and Retrieval: Tools, Elements, Theories* and *Handbook of Data Processing for Libraries*. His teaching, research, publications, and professional work are focused on analysis of information systems, ranging in scope from libraries to national.

ALISON J. HEAD recently earned her Ph.D. in the School of Library and Information Studies at the University of California at Berkeley. In her doctoral dissertation, "A Survey Analysis of Supermarket Tabloid Readership" (1990), she developed a model of tabloid readership and determined a basis for quantitatively measuring information poverty. She currently teaches within the School of Library and Information Science at San Jose State University.

MARK R. KLINGER is an assistant professor of psychology at the University of Arkansas. He received his Ph.D. from the University of Washington. His research interests include social cognition, unconscious information processing, and human memory.

DONALD H. KRAFT received his Ph.D. from the department of industrial engineering at Purdue University. He is currently professor and chairman of computer science, and adjunct professor of library and information science at Louisiana State University. His present research interests include information retrieval, fuzzy statistic theory, and operations research. He is the co-author of *Operations Research for Libraries and Information Agencies: Techniques for the Evaluation of Managements Decision Alternatives*, (Academic Press, 1991), and author or co-author of several articles in his research areas. He is the editor of the *Journal of American Society for Information Science* (JASIS) and the database and retrieval systems area editor for the Operations Research Society of America (ORSA) *Journal on Computing* (JoC).

RICHARD KRAMER is an independent consultant in New York City. He is affiliated with the Columbia University Institute for Tele-Information (CTI), which he served as assistant director and has worked for the U.S. Federal Communications Commission, He holds an M.A. from the Annenberg School for Communication, University of Pennsylvania and an A.B. from Columbia University, His research interests lie in the fields of international telecommunications economics and policy, the social impact of new technology, and ethnography and communication.

KLAUS KRIPPENDORFF is professor at the University of Pennsylvania's Annenberg School of Communication. He is author of *Information Theory, Structural Models for Qualitative Data* (1986); *Content Analysis, An Introduction to its Methodology* (1980); editor of *Communication and*

526   Between Communication and Information

Control in Society (1979); Co-editor of *The Analysis of Communication Content, Developments in Scientific Theories and Computer Techniques* (1967) and numerous publications on communication theory, statistical techniques and methodologies in social research, cybernetics and systems theory, and product semantics. His current work centers on cybernetic epistemology for human communication.

GEOFF LEATHAM is a doctoral candidate in the Department of Communication Research, University of Iowa. The author acknowledges the assistance of Ann Wahlig in coding interaction and Abran Salazar, Irwin Levin, and Randy Hirokawa for their comments on an earlier draft of this paper.

ELIZABETH F. LOFTUS is professor of psychology at the University of Washington. She received her Ph.D. from Stanford University. Her research interests include human cognition and memory, and psychological aspects of trial law. Dr. Loftus has served as president of the Western Psychological Association, the American Psychology-Law Society, and the Experimental Psychology Division of the American Psychological Association. She is the author or co-author of sixteen books, including *Eyewitness Testimony* (Harvard University Press, 1979) and *Witness for the Defense* (St. Martins Press, 1991).

MAUREEN MCCREADIE is a Ph.D. candidate in the School of Communication, Information and Library Studies at Rutgers University, and is senior associate professor at Bucks County Community College in Pennsylvania.

HARMUT B. MOKROS received his Ph.D. from the University of Chicago. He is assistant professor of communication in the School of Communication, Information, and Library Studies at Rutgers University. He is co-author of *Interaction structure and strategy* (Cambridge University Press, 1985). His published research focuses on human communicative and interactive processes and affective disorders in youth.

KENNETH M. NAGELBERG received his Ph.D. from the Department of Speech Communication at Penn State University. He is currently assistant professor of broadcast journalism in the Manship School for Journalism at Louisiana State University. He is also responsible for overseeing of the computerized news writing and journalism research laboratories at LSU. His research interests focus on qualitative analysis of electronic media with special interests in television news and music video.

RAYMOND R. PANKO is a professor of decision sciences in the College of Business Administration at the University of Hawaii. Before coming to the university, he was an analyst at SRI International. He received his Ph.D. from Stanford University. His research specialty is the management of managerial and professional work groups, including their use of technology.

STEVEN PULOS is an assistant professor of educational psychology at the University of Northern Colorado. He received his Ph.D. in psychology at York University and postdoctoral education at the University of California, Berkeley. His research interests include the effects of technology and cultural change on psychological development across the life span.

GARY P. RADFORD received his Ph.D. from Rutgers. He is an assistant professor in the Department of Communication at the William Paterson College of New Jersey. His research interests include applying the work of Michel Foucault to the analysis of contemporary systems of discourse which constitute the disciplines of communication, information, and modern psychology.

RONALD RICE received his Ph.D. from Stanford University in 1982. He is associate professor, School of Communication, Information and Library Studies, Rutgers University. He is co-editor or co-author of *Public Communication Campaigns* (1981, 1989, Sage), *The New Media: Communication Research, and Technology* (1984, Sage), *Managing Organizational Innovation* (1987, Columbia University Press) and *Research Methods and New Media* (1988, Free Press). He has published widely in the areas of diffusion of innovation, network analysis, and organizational computer-mediated communication systems.

EVERETT M. ROGERS is Walter H. Annenbrg Professor in the Annenberg School for Communication, University of Southern California. He is presently writing a book about the history of communication theories focusing on the rise of the academic field of communication.

BRENT D. RUBEN is professor II (distinguished professor) of Communication, and director of the Ph.D. program in Communication, Information and Library Studies at Rutgers University, New Brunswick, New Jersey. His scholarly writings address issues of communication theory, systems, and processes in medical, educational, mass, and intercultural contexts. His works include *Communication and Human Behavior, Mass Communication: Producers and Consumers* (with Todd Hunt), *General Systems*

Theory and Human Communication (with John Kim), and *Interdisciplinary Approaches to Human Communication* (with Richard Budd). Dr. Ruben was founding editor of the International Communication Association's *Communication Yearbook,* and is editor of the *Information and Behavior* series.

JORGE REINA SCHEMENT is associate professor in the School of Communication, Information, and Library Studies at Rutgers University. He received his Ph.D. from the Institute for Communication Research at Stanford University. He is co-editor or co-author of *Spanish-Language Radio in the Southwestern United States* (Texas, 1979), *Telecommunication's Policy Handbook* (Praeger, 1982), *The International Flow of Television Programs* (Sage, 1984), and *Competing Visions, Complex Realities: Social Aspects of Information-Oriented Society* (Ablex, 1989). His research interests include theories of the information society, information policy, international communications, minorities and communication issues.

KYLE D. SMITH is a visiting assistant professor of psychology at the University of Washington, Bothell Campus. He received his Ph.D. from the University of Washington. His research interests include the role of affect in judgement and memory, altruistic behavior, and survey methodology.

LEE THAYER is professor and past chair of the Department of Communication and past founding director of the honors program at the University of Wisconsin, Parkside. He was for several years the editor of the international journal *Communication,* and presently serves on the editorial boards for four communication journals worldwide. He is the author or editor of fourteen books in this and related fields, including *On Communication: Essays in Understanding,* and of more than a hundred articles and essays. His next two books to appear will be *Communication and the Life of the Mind,* and *Communication/Information Ethical/Moral Issues.* His research interests include organizational transformation, and communication, cognition, and competence.

THOMAS VALENTE is a doctoral candidate in the Annenberg School for Communication, University of Southern California. Valente's main research interests are mathematical models of communication and the diffusion of innovations.

FREDERICK WILLIAMS occupies the Mary Gibbs Jones Centennial Chair in the College of Communications at The University of Texas at Austin, where he directs the Center for Research on Communication Technology and Society. He is a visiting professor at the LBJ School of Public Policy and W. W. Heath Research Fellow in the IC2 Institute, also at The University of Texas. He is currently a senior fellow at the Gannett Foundation Media Communications at the University of Southern California, and he is the author of thirty-six books on communications and other topics as well as of some 75 articles. His more recent books include *The New Telecommunications* and *Technology Transfer: A Communication Perspective.*

Index of Names

Subject Index